High-Powered Investing
All-in-One For Dummies®

Cheat

Key Financial Ratios

Following are some common ratios that investors use to help make se... financial reports. For more on ratios, see Book VII, Chapter 3.

Ratio	Formula	Use
Liquidity Ratios		
Current ratio	Total current assets ÷ total current liabilities	Gives some indication whether a company has enough financial cushion to meet its near-term obligations.
Quick ratio	(Current assets less inventory) ÷ current liabilities	Same as current ratio, without including inventory in the calculation. Provides another sign of a company's strength or weakness.
Operating Ratios		
Return on equity (ROE)	Net earnings ÷ owners' equity	Measures how well the company is managing its resources.
Return on assets (ROA)	Net earnings ÷ total assets	Reflects the relationship between a company's profit and the assets used to generate it.
Solvency Ratios		
Debt to equity	Total debt ÷ owners' equity	Indicates how dependent a company is on debt.
Debt to assets (or "debt ratio")	Total debt ÷ total assets	The higher the ratio, the more financial risk the company has assumed.
Valuation Ratios		
Price-to-earnings (P/E)	Stock price per share ÷ net earnings per share	Clues you in to how much you are paying for the company's earnings.
Price-to-book (P/B)	Stock price (total market cap) ÷ book value	Compares the company's market value to its accounting (or book) value.

Essential Economic Reports

To be a serious investor, you have to do some serious research. Following are just some of the economic reports you should peruse regularly. For all the details, see Book V, Chapter 4.

- ✔ The monthly non-farm payroll report (NFP), which assesses the overall labor market
- ✔ The consumer price index (CPI), which measures the cost of goods and services at the retail level
- ✔ The producer price index (PPI), which measures prices at the wholesale level
- ✔ The Institute for Supply Management (ISM) and regional purchasing manager's reports, which indicate current business conditions and future outlooks
- ✔ The Beige Book from the Federal Reserve, which compiles regional economic assessments from the Fed's 12 district banks
- ✔ Existing-home sales and housing starts
- ✔ The index of leading economic indicators (LEI), which is considered a gauge of the economy's direction over the next six to nine months
- ✔ Gross domestic product, which measures total economic activity

The Modern Greeks

Mathematical explanations for the world mark modern finance, and wherever math is, you're bound to see symbols and variables. You don't need to know all the equations that shape financial theory, but you'll have a leg up if you know the Greek letters used to describe different sources of risk and return:

- **Alpha** (Α, α): Investment return that's different than you'd expect, given an investment's beta, which is its exposure to market risk and return. Alpha (which can be positive or negative) describes an intangible value that accounts for the extra return generated (or lost) for the amount of risk taken. Some researchers aren't sure that alpha exists at all.

- **Beta** (Β, β): The market beta is 1, so an investment with a beta of more than 1 is more volatile than the market as a whole. You'd expect the investment to return more than the market in an up year and less than the market in a down year.

- **Delta** (Δ, δ): The percentage change in an investment. Delta often describes how much an option changes in price when its underlying security changes in price.

- **Gamma** (Γ, γ): The rate of change in delta. Gamma is exposure to any change in price, positive or negative.

- **Sigma** (Σ, σ): Standard deviation, or the likelihood that any one number in a series — like a series of investment returns — will be different from the return that you expect. The higher the standard deviation, the greater the investment risk.

For Your "Favorites" List

`http://finance.yahoo.com`: Navigate your heart away . . . tons of information on financial markets.

`www.bankrate.com`: Compare rates on all sorts of fixed-income investments.

`www.bloomberg.com`: Rather hardcore financial data.

`www.cnnfn.com`: Get your daily fix of everything money related.

`www.dinkytown.com`: Calculators of all sorts.

`www.moneychimp.com`: For the more advanced investor.

`www.morningstar.com`: Exclusive ratings of funds, and more.

`www.riskgrades.com`: A novel way of looking at investment risk and return.

`www.sensible-investor.com`: A huge gateway to other financial Web sites.

High-Powered Investing

ALL-IN-ONE

FOR DUMMIES®

By Amine Bouchentouf; Brian Dolan; Dr. Joe Duarte;
Mark Galant; Ann C. Logue, MBA; Paul Mladjenovic;
Kerry Pechter; Barbara Rockefeller; Peter J. Sander, MBA;
and Russell Wild, MBA

Wiley Publishing, Inc.

High-Powered Investing All-in-One For Dummies®
Published by
Wiley Publishing, Inc.
111 River St.
Hoboken, NJ 07030-5774
www.wiley.com

WILEY

About the Authors

Amine Bouchentouf *(Commodities For Dummies)* is President and Chief Executive Officer of Renaissance Investment Advisors LLC. Renaissance is an international financial advisory firm headquartered in New York City, which provides long-term strategic advice to individuals and institutions. He is also the author of *Arabic For Dummies*.

Brian Dolan *(Currency Trading For Dummies)* has 15 years of experience in the foreign exchange markets, including trading and analyst roles at top-tier financial institutions. In addition to overseeing fundamental and technical research at FOREX.com, Mr. Dolan publishes a daily technical analysis report and weekly macro research report for the exclusive use of FOREX.com clients. He has also published numerous articles on currency trading strategies and risk management. Mr. Dolan is a graduate of Dartmouth College.

Dr. Joe Duarte *(Futures & Options For Dummies, Futures Trading For Dummies)* analyzes intelligence and global geopolitical events and their effects on the financial markets. He reaches thousands of investors daily through his own Web site (www.joe-duarte.com) and FinancialWire, where he is a featured syndicated columnist. Dr. Duarte is frequently quoted in the major media, including CNBC, *The Wall Street Journal,* the Associated Press, Marketwatch.com, and CNN.com. He is the author of *Successful Energy Sector Investing* and *Successful Biotech Investing,* and the coauthor of *After-Hours Trading Made Easy.* One of CNBC's original Market Mavens, Dr. Duarte has been writing about the financial markets since 1990.

Mark Galant *(Currency Trading For Dummies)* has enjoyed a 25-year career in and around Wall Street, first as a trader and market maker and from 1994 to 1999 as Vice Chairman of FNX Ltd, the trading technology firm. Mr. Galant's last trading position was global head of FX options at Credit Suisse; he has also been a money manager for famed hedge fund manager Paul Tudor Jones. Mr. Galant founded GAIN Capital in October 1999; today, the firm's proprietary trading platform is used by clients from 140 countries and supports a monthly trading volume in excess of $100 billion. Mr. Galant holds a BS in finance from the University of Virginia and an MBA from Harvard Business School.

Ann C. Logue, MBA *(Hedge Funds For Dummies)* has 12 years of working experience in financial services and has taught finance at the University of Illinois at Chicago. She is a finance writer who has written numerous articles on investment and hedge funds, and she has edited publications on equity trading and risk management.

Paul Mladjenovic *(Stock Investing For Dummies,* 2nd Edition*)* is a well-known certified financial planner and investing consultant with over 19 years of experience writing and teaching about common stocks and related investments. He owns PM Financial Services.

Kerry Pechter *(Annuities For Dummies)* is a finance writer whose work has appeared in *The New York Times, The Wall Street Journal, Men's Health,* and many other national publications. He is currently the senior editor for *Annuity Market News,* a monthly newsletter published by SourceMedia, Inc.

Barbara Rockefeller *(Technical Analysis For Dummies)* is an international economist and forecaster specializing in foreign exchange. She was a pioneer in technical analysis and also in combining technical analysis with fundamental analysis. She publishes two reports daily using both techniques (www.rts-forex.com) for professional fund managers, corporate hedgers, and individual traders. The trading advice newsletter has an average annual hypothetical return over 50 percent since 1994 and has never posted a losing year. She is the author of three other books and contributes a regular column to *Currency Trader* magazine.

Peter J. Sander, **MBA** *(Value Investing For Dummies)* is a professional author, researcher, and investor. His 15 titles include *The 250 Personal Finance Questions Everybody Should Ask, Everything Personal Finance,* and the *Cities Ranked & Rated* series. He has also developed over 150 columns for MarketWatch and TheStreet.com. He has completed Certified Financial Planner (CFP) education and testing requirements and has invested actively for over 40 years.

Russell Wild, MBA *(Bond Investing For Dummies, Exchange-Traded Funds For Dummies)* is the author or coauthor of nearly two dozen nonfiction books, including *The Unofficial Guide to Getting a Divorce* (Wiley) with attorney Susan Ellis Wild (his ex-wife). Wild is also a NAPFA-registered, fee-only financial advisor based in Allentown, Pennsylvania.

Publisher's Acknowledgments

We're proud of this book; please send us your comments through our Dummies online registration form located at www.dummies.com/register/.

Some of the people who helped bring this book to market include the following:

Acquisitions, Editorial, and Media Development

Compilation Editor: Tracy L. Barr

Project Editor: Joan Friedman

Acquisitions Editor: Tracy Boggier

Technical Editor: Noel M. Jameson

Technical Consultant: Russell Wild, MBA

Senior Editorial Manager: Jennifer Ehrlich

Editorial Supervisor: Carmen Krikorian

Editorial Assistants: Erin Calligan Mooney, Joe Niesen, Leeann Harney, David Lutton

Cartoons: Rich Tennant (www.the5thwave.com)

Composition Services

Project Coordinator: Katie Key, Erin M. Smith

Layout and Graphics: Carl Byers, Alissa D. Ellet, Melissa K. Jester, Shane Johnson, Christine Williams

Proofreaders: C. M. Jones, Caitie Kelly

Indexer: Broccoli Information Management

Publishing and Editorial for Consumer Dummies

Diane Graves Steele, Vice President and Publisher, Consumer Dummies

Joyce Pepple, Acquisitions Director, Consumer Dummies

Kristin A. Cocks, Product Development Director, Consumer Dummies

Michael Spring, Vice President and Publisher, Travel

Kelly Regan, Editorial Director, Travel

Publishing for Technology Dummies

Andy Cummings, Vice President and Publisher, Dummies Technology/General User

Composition Services

Gerry Fahey, Vice President of Production Services

Debbie Stailey, Director of Composition Services

Contents at a Glance

Table of Contents

Introduction

Many investors are perfectly satisfied with the more traditional investing opportunities: They build solid portfolios containing individual stocks and bonds, mutual and exchange-traded funds, and so forth, and are generally content to let investment counselors manage their accounts. Other investors, however, prefer to take a more active role: Perhaps they want to manage their accounts themselves or broaden their investment horizons (and increase their potential returns) by delving into more volatile markets.

As an investor, you can be as aggressive as your personality and bank account allow. To be successful, however, you need more than the right attitude or a boatload of cash. You need information, and that's what we've tried to give you in this book. *High-Powered Investing All-in-One For Dummies* is a book written specifically for experienced investors who want to pursue and manage more aggressive investment vehicles.

About This Book

The key to successfully expanding your investment opportunities is, of course, information. This book introduces you to high-powered investing techniques and options you can pursue as you expand your portfolio — all in plain English.

Whether you're just beginning to explore more advanced investing or have been dabbling in it for a while but need strategies to increase your success, this book can give you the information you want. For example, you can find

- **What your high-powered investing or trading options are:** There are a whole series of investment opportunities beyond the traditional stocks and bonds. You can trade commodities, foreign currencies, and futures and options, all of which require a more hands-on approach. If you're well-heeled, you may decide that hedge funds — private investment partnerships — are the way to go. You can find information on all these vehicles in the books that follow.

- **Keys to being a successful trader:** There's a big difference between investing and trading. With the former, you buy and hold with the expectation your returns will increase over time as the value of the security goes up. With the latter, your success depends on how accurately you're able to read the market and how quickly you can react to fluctuations. Nearly all the higher-end investment options covered in this book — currencies, commodities, futures and options — rely to a greater or lesser extent on these trading skills.

✔ **How to value a business or spot pricing trends:** One key to being a successful investor is knowing how to get the information you need to make good — and timely — decisions. When the value of the underlying security is important, you need to know how to evaluate it. When being able to recognize market trends is the key to success, you have to know how to forecast them.

High-Powered Investing All-in-One For Dummies gives you the information and answers you need to incorporate these investing strategies and options into your own personal investing style. And even if you don't adopt most of the principles and techniques described in this book, your awareness of them will make you a better investor.

Conventions Used in This Book

To help you navigate the text as easily as possible, this book uses the following conventions:

✔ Whenever a new term is introduced, such as, say, *callability* or *discount rate,* it appears in *italics.* Rest assured that a definition or explanation is right around the corner.

✔ All Web addresses appear in `monofont` so they're easy to pick out if you need to go back and find them.

What You're Not to Read

Unless you're going to become a professional trader (rather than simply an empowered personal investor), you probably don't need to know everything in this book. To help, we've made it easy for you to identify what is and isn't vital information:

✔ **Technical Stuff icon:** Some people love the details: the esoteric ratios and percentages or the background info that only an economics professor would appreciate. We've included such information precisely for those who get off on this stuff. For those of you who prefer the straight scoop, we highlight this information with a Technical Stuff icon.

✔ **Sidebars:** If a dizzingly technical explanation goes on for more than a paragraph (and don't they usually?), we've put it in a shaded box. These boxes also contain non-technical information that's related to the topic at hand but not vital to your understanding.

Foolish Assumptions

Aggressive or high-end investing options aren't an ideal fit (or a good option) for everyone, and *High-Powered Investing All-in-One For Dummies* was written with a particular reader in mind. Here's what we assume about you:

- You're fairly familiar with basic investments and have some experience in the world of investing. You know what the markets are, for example, and have already bought and sold some securities.

- You want to expand your investment options to include more than the traditional stocks and bonds.

- You want to become a more active trader and make money more consistently by letting your profits run and cutting your losses short.

- You have enough investment capital that you can safely invest in more volatile markets or participate in a hedge fund.

- You understand basic market forecasting strategies but want to know more about how to use technical analysis to anticipate and react to trends.

How This Book Is Organized

Like all *For Dummies* books, *High-Powered Investing All-in-One For Dummies* is a reference, and as such, each topic is relegated to its own book. Within that book are individual chapters relating specifically to that topic.

Book 1: Investment Basics

As an investor, you need to know certain things — about investment vehicles, about risk, about exchanges and indexes, and so forth — that pertain to investing in general. The topics in this part comprise this knowledge. All are applicable, to a greater or lesser extent, to the advanced investing topics covered elsewhere in the book. If you're already an experienced investor, you can consider this part primarily review of information you no doubt already know. If you're relatively new to investing or are just thinking about expanding your portfolio, this is a good place to begin.

Book II: Basic Investments: Stocks, Bonds, Mutual Funds, and More

Most investors are familiar with the vehicles in this part. Considered traditional investments because they rely on investing principles rather than speculation strategies, stocks, bonds, mutual funds, and the relatively new exchange-traded funds are vehicles that beginners and casual investors can participate in with minimum involvement. That doesn't mean, however, that they don't play an integral role in advanced portfolios. The chapters in this book give you the details.

Book III: Futures and Options

Futures and options markets are resurging and are likely to be hot for several decades, given the political landscape. Changing world demographics and the emergence of China and India as economic powers and consumers, coupled with changing politics in the Middle East, are likely to fuel the continued prominence of these markets. As a futures and options trader, you have to be a stock trader, a geopolitical analyst, a money manager, and an expert in the relevant markets. Book III gets you started on that path.

Book IV: Commodities

Commodities, as an asset class, are going through a transformational period, moving from the fringes to the mainstream. Why? Good performance. This book offers you a comprehensive guide to the commodities markets and shows you a number of investment strategies to help you profit. In addition, because commodities markets are global, so are the investment opportunities. This book also helps you uncover these global opportunities.

Book V: Foreign Currency Trading

If you're an active trader looking for alternatives to trading stocks or futures, the forex market is hard to beat. Online trading innovations over the past decade have made it accessible, both technologically and financially. But as an individual trader, gaining access to the forex market is only the beginning. You need to know how the market works and how to use a few key tactics and strategies. This book gives you the no-nonsense information you need, with the perspective, experience, and insight of forex market veterans.

Book VI: Hedge Funds

Hedge funds, private investment partnerships, are the crème-de-la-crème of high-end investing. They're so high-end, in fact, that only the wealthiest investors need (or can) participate. This book offers straightforward explanations of how hedge funds are structured, the different investment styles that hedge fund managers use, how you can check out a fund before you invest, and what to expect after you've joined a fund.

Book VII: Value Investing

Value investing is a strategy that focuses on determining a company's real worth in order to identify companies that are undervalued and, hence, underpriced. Why? Because the greatest potential for significant returns involves buying for relatively little an asset that is worth much more. To be a value investor, you need to know what data to focus on to get a true picture of a business's worth and how to apply that knowledge in making sound investing decisions. This book has the details.

Book VIII: Technical Analysis

Whether you aspire to become a self-supporting trader, need to sharpen your trading skills, or just want to get out ahead of another crash, you may decide that technical analysis is the tool to help you. As this book explains, technical analysis is a way of studying how securities prices move so that you can use the information to maximize your returns and minimize your losses. Essentially, it's a way of identifying pricing trends. Get good enough at identifying these market fluctuations — up, down, or sideways — and you can improve the timing of your investment decisions.

Icons Used in This Book

You'll see four icons scattered around the margins of the text. Here's the function of each:

This icon notes something you should keep in mind about the topic at hand. It may refer to something covered elsewhere in the book, or it may highlight something you need to know for future investing decisions.

Tip information tells you how to invest a little better, a little smarter, a little more efficiently. The information can help you ask better questions or make smarter moves with your money.

Plenty of things in the world of investing can cause you to make expensive mistakes. These points help you avoid big problems.

Here's where you'll find interesting but non-essential information. Whether this icon highlights background info, investment theories, or trivia, it's all skippable. Read it or pass it up as you like.

Where to Go from Here

Where you go from here depends entirely on you. If you're a start-at-the-beginning-and-read-through-to-the-end type of person, by all means, feel free. But you may find that picking and choosing a topic of interest is more suited to your style. Fortunately, there are a number of ways to find what you're looking for. You can use the Table of Contents to find general discussions or the index to find specific topics. Or if you prefer, you can simply thumb through the pages and alight on whatever topic catches your eye. The bottom line? Use this book however you need to. If you're just beginning your foray into more advanced investing, however, you may want to begin with Books I and II, which contain basic information.

Book I
Investment Basics

The 5th Wave — By Rich Tennant

"We were told to put our money into something that got more interest, so we started sticking it into this mason jar that's got some dang thing in it we bought from a traveling freak show."

In this book . . .

Most topics run the gamut from very basic information to very advanced information, and most people need to start at one end (usually the first) and work their way to the other (usually the last). Books III through VIII are devoted to the advanced investing information. Book II shares info on traditional investment options that even high-end investors can (and often do) take advantage of. This part? It covers the very basic information: the fundamental principles of investing and investing options, and basic information about the role of indexes and exchanges.

If you're a high-end investor, you probably already know quite a bit of this stuff. But if you're a beginner or still trying to get a handle on how to approach your portfolio or what the difference is between an index and an exchange, this is a great place to start.

Chapter 1

What Every Investor Should Know

For anyone who's inclined to invest in the markets or engage in trading, there are a few fundamental things to know, like the different types of investments and investment strategies, what the SEC does (and why you should care), and who brokers are and what they do. (The next chapter outlines the indexes and exchanges, another basic but important bit of information.)

If you're an experienced investor already, these things will be familiar. But if you're just beginning to branch out from more traditional investments to more aggressive ones, spend some time with this chapter to get up to speed.

Seeing Your Investment Options at a Glance

As an investor, you have a variety of options to choose from. Which you choose depends on your financial goals, your investment preferences, and your tolerance for risk. Some are suitable for all investors; others are geared more toward the experienced investor.

Traditional investment vehicles

The investment vehicles mentioned in this section are those that, by and large, any investor — big or small, novice or experienced — can take advantage of. You may have some of these in your portfolio already.

These options represent traditional investments: You put your money down and hold on. Although you want to make changes as necessary to protect your investment, these types of investments can add ballast to more aggressive investment strategies (like trading and hedging).

Stocks

When you buy stock, you're buying ownership in a corporation (or company). The benefit of owning stock in a corporation is that whenever the corporation profits, you profit as well. Typically, investors buy stocks and hold them for a long time, making decisions along the way about reallocating investment capital as financial needs change, selling underperformers, and so on.

As an investor, you want to make sure that your stock portfolio is carefully balanced among the different types of stocks (growth, value, domestic, international, and so on) and your other investments. A well-balanced traditional portfolio (which includes stocks and long-, short-, and intermediate-term bonds) generally offers a steady return of between 5 and 12 percent, depending on the specific investments and the amount of risk you're willing to assume. For more on investing in stocks, see the first chapter in Book II.

Bonds

To raise money, governments, government agencies, municipalities, and corporations can sell bonds. When you buy a bond, you're essentially lending money to this entity for the promise of repayment in addition to a specified annual return. In that sense, a bond is really nothing more than an IOU with a serial number. People in suits, to sound impressive, sometimes call bonds *debt securities* or *fixed-income securities.*

Although some entities are more reliable than others (the federal government isn't as likely as a company that's facing hard financial times to go bankrupt and renege on its obligations), bonds generally offer stability and predictability well beyond that of most other investments. Because you are, in most cases, receiving a steady stream of income (the annual returns, for example), and because you expect to get your principal back in one piece (at the end of the bond's life), bonds tend to be more conservative investments than stocks, commodities, or collectibles. To find out more about bonds, go to Book II, Chapter 2.

Mutual funds

Simply put, a mutual fund is an investment company. Investors put money into that company, and an investment manager buy securities on behalf of all the investors. Those securities may include various types of stocks, various types of bonds, or both. If you invest in mutual funds, you have thousands of options to choose from, each representing a different mixture of securities.

Because so many shareholders pool their money into each mutual fund, an investment manager can buy a diverse portfolio of securities — much more diverse than most individuals can manage to buy on their own.

Mutual funds are extremely popular investment vehicles. More than 23 percent of household financial assets were invested in mutual funds as of the end of 2006. For all the details on mutual funds, see Chapter 3 of Book II.

Exchange-traded funds

Exchange-traded funds (ETFs) are something of a cross between an index mutual fund and a stock. Although relatively new, they've grown exponentially in the past few years — nearly 50 percent in 2005 — and they will surely continue to grow and gain influence.

Among the characteristics that make ETFs so compelling is the fact that they're cheap. Many ETFs carry total management expenses under 0.20 percent a year. Some of the larger ETFs carry management fees as low as 0.07 percent a year. The average mutual fund, in contrast, charges 1.67 percent a year. ETFs are also tax-smart. Because of the way they're structured, the taxes you pay on any growth are minimal. Chapter 4 of Book II gives an overview of ETFs.

Annuities

Annuities are investments with money-back guarantees: You invest a certain amount of money for a promise that you'll get your money back, with interest, after (or over) a certain time period. That's all that annuities really are — along with enough exceptions, disclaimers, and contingencies to fill a medium-sized law library. Bottom line? The exact nature of the guarantee varies with the type of annuity. In fixed annuity contracts, for instance, your rate of return is guaranteed for a certain number of years. In the latest variable annuity contracts, you can lock in a guaranteed rate of return. With an immediate annuity, you get guaranteed income.

Although guarantees always sound good, annuities aren't for everyone. To find out more about them and decide whether your investment portfolio should include one, read Chapter 5 from Book II.

High-end investment or speculation vehicles

In some ways, higher-end investments aren't much different than traditional investments: You invest your money in stocks or bonds or mutual funds or ETFs and make all the same decisions that an average investor does. The difference is the amount of capital in play (typically a lot) or the risk exposure (typically high).

In other ways, high-end investing is an almost completely different beast. It's not so much investing (buying and holding on) as it is *trading* or *speculating* — assuming a business risk with the hope of profiting from market fluctuations.

Successful speculating requires analyzing situations, predicting outcomes, and putting your money on one side of a trade based on those predictions. Speculating also involves an appreciation of the fact that you can be wrong 70 percent of the time and still be successful if you apply the correct techniques for analyzing trades, managing your money, and protecting your account. Basically, high-end investing means you have to chuck all your preconceptions about buy-and-hold investing and asset allocation, and essentially all the strategies that stock brokerages put out for public consumption. The following sections outline the high-end investment vehicles you can find out about in this book.

Futures and options

Futures and options, by their very nature, are complex financial instruments. It's not like investing in a mutual fund, where you mail your check and wait for quarterly statements and dividends. If you invest in futures and options contracts, you need to monitor your positions on a daily basis, often even on an hourly basis. You have to keep track of the expiration date, the premium paid, the strike price, margin requirements, and a number of other shifting variables.

That said, understanding futures and options can be very beneficial because they are powerful tools. They provide you with leverage and risk management opportunities that your average financial instruments don't offer. If you can harness the power of these instruments, you can dramatically increase your leverage — and performance — in the markets. Book III explains investing in futures and options.

Commodities

Commodities are the raw materials humans use to create a livable world: the agricultural products, mineral ore, and energy that are the essential building blocks of the global economy. The commodities markets are broad and deep, presenting both challenges and opportunities. For example, how do you decide whether to trade crude oil or gold, sugar or palladium, natural gas or frozen concentrated orange juice, soybeans or aluminum? What about corn, feeder cattle, and silver — should you trade these commodities as well? And if you do, what is the best way to invest in them? Should you go through the futures markets, through the equity markets, or buy the physical stuff (such as silver coins or gold bullion)? And do all commodities move in tandem, or do they perform independently of each other? To start your search for answers, turn to Book IV.

A lot of folks equate (incorrectly) commodities exclusively with the futures markets. There is no doubt that the two are inextricably linked: The futures markets offer a way for commercial users to hedge against commodity price risks and a means for investors and traders to profit from this price risk. But equity markets are also deeply involved in commodities, as are a number of investment vehicles, such as master limited partnerships (MLPs), exchange-traded funds (ETFs), and commodity mutual funds.

Foreign currency trading

When you get involved in foreign currency trading (sometimes called *forex* trading), you're essentially speculating on the value of one currency versus another. You "buy" a currency just as you'd buy an individual stock, or any other financial security, in the hope that it will make a profitable return. But the value of your security is particularly volatile because of the many factors that can affect a currency's value and the amazingly quick timeframe in which these values can change. Nevertheless, if you're an active trader looking for alternatives to trading stocks or futures, the forex market is hard to beat. Online trading innovations over the past decade have made it accessible, both technologically and financially. Find out more in Book V.

Trading foreign currencies is a challenging and potentially profitable opportunity *for educated and experienced investors.* Before deciding to participate in the forex market, carefully consider your investment objectives, level of experience, and risk appetite. Most important, don't invest money you can't afford to lose. The leveraged nature of forex trading means that any market movement will have an equally proportional effect on your deposited funds; this may work against you as well as for you.

Hedge funds

In a nutshell, hedge funds are lightly regulated private partnerships that pursue high returns through multiple strategies. A hedge fund manager may invest in almost any opportunity in the market where he or she foresees favorable risk to reward. Through hedge funds, you can net some high returns for your portfolio — if you don't mind the risk and have *a lot* of money to invest.

Because of the risk and the investment criteria, hedge funds aren't open to most investors. In fact, to participate, you have to meet strict limits put in place by the Securities and Exchange Commission regarding your worth (a net worth of at least $1 million and/or an annual income exceeding $200,000 in each of the two most recent years).

A hedge fund differs from so-called "real money" — traditional investment accounts like mutual funds, pensions, and endowments — because it has more freedom (read: little to no regulatory oversight) to pursue aggressive investment strategies, which can lead to huge gains or huge losses. To find out more about hedge funds, head to Book VI.

Studying Investment Strategies

No matter how much money an investor has to invest, how tolerant she is of high-risk investments, or how willing she is to absorb some losses for a higher gain, no investor likes losing money. Regardless of what investment vehicle you choose — whether traditional, high-end, or a combination — you want to invest smart. And that means making good decisions about where to put your money and when to make a trade.

The strategy you use depends on the particular investment vehicle. Sometimes, the dividing line between success and failure is knowing the value of the business or company you're putting your money in. Other times, the key component is recognizing a trend — what the market is doing or getting ready to do — so you can beat the crowd. The following sections explain.

Value investing: It's fundamental!

What is something really worth? Regardless of what you buy — or invest in — this nagging question ruins sleep for value types. You pay six figures for a house and know that its value is a whole lot greater than the sum of the parts. Not only does it include the nails or two-by-fours or roof shingles and the work required to put everything together, but also what the house returns to you as a living space now, in the future, and compared to alternatives.

Investments can be looked at in much the same way. You can round up all the buildings, trucks, pallet jacks, and PCs that a company owns, assign a value to each, and add it all up, but that still doesn't tell what's really important about the business. What you want is a way to evaluate a business's intrinsic value. Finding *intrinsic valuation* is the art and science of placing a fair value on current and future investment returns. When assets are deployed productively, you don't care about the value of pallet jacks. The return is the main thing!

Value investing is about figuring out the intrinsic value of a business so that you can recognize when a business is undervalued: That's where the potential is. Book VII has the details.

Technical analysis

Technical analysis (sometimes called *charting, market timing,* and *trend-following)* is a set of forecasting methods that can help you make better trading decisions and manage market risk. Technical analysis is the study of how securities prices behave and how to exploit that information to make money while avoiding losses. With technical analysis, your goal is to identify price trends for a certain time period and/or forecast the price of a security in order to buy and sell that security to make a cash profit. Technical analysis is ideal for *traders* (those who make profits from trading), not *investors* (those who view securities as savings vehicles).

As a technical trader, you devise rules for dealing with price developments as they occur. But how you analyze prices can take many different forms — from drawing lines on a chart by hand to using high-powered computer software to calculate the most likely path of a price out of a zillion randomly generated paths. You can find the details in Book VIII.

Recognizing and Managing Investment Risks

As an investor, you face many risks. The most obvious is financial risk. Companies go bankrupt, trading decisions go south, the best laid investment plans go awry, and you can end up losing your money — all or some of it, whether the economy is strong or weak. What puts your finances at risk? Here are some types of risk:

- ✔ **Interest rate risk:** Interest rates, set by banks and influenced by the Federal Reserve, change on a regular basis. When the Fed raises or lowers interest rates, banks raise or lower interest rates accordingly. Interest rate changes affect consumers, businesses, and, of course, investors. Whether rising or falling interest rates are good or bad depends on the type of investment.

- ✔ **Market risk:** No matter how modern our society and economic system, you can't escape the laws of supply and demand. When masses of people want to buy a particular stock, it becomes in demand, and its value rises. That value rises higher if the supply is limited. Conversely, if no one's interested in buying a stock, its value falls. This is the nature of market risk. The value of your stock can rise and fall on the fickle whim of market demand. For that reason, what the market does (goes up or goes down) and its mood (bullish or bearish) impact your investments.

- ✔ **Inflation risk:** *Inflation* is the growth of the money supply without a commensurate increase in the supply of goods and services. To consumers, inflation shows up in the form of higher prices for goods and services. Inflation risk frequently is also referred to as *purchasing power risk* because your money doesn't buy as much as it used to.

✔ **Tax risk:** Taxes don't affect your investments directly, but they do affect how much of your money you get to keep. To minimize tax risk, be aware of the tax implications and obligations associated with the different types of investments. Because the tax rules are complex, differ for different investment vehicles and scenarios, and change regularly, talk to your accountant, tax advisor, or tax attorney for guidance.

✔ **Political and governmental risks:** If investment vehicles were fish, politics and government policies (such as taxes, laws, and regulations) would be the pond. In the same way that fish die in a toxic or polluted pond, politics and government policies greatly influence the financial stability of companies and commodities, the value of currencies — you name it.

✔ **Emotional risk:** Emotions are important risk considerations because the main decision-makers are human beings. Logic and discipline are critical factors in investment success, but even the best investor can let emotions take over the reins of money management and create loss. For any kind of investing, the main emotions that can sidetrack you are fear and greed.

Despite this rather lengthy list of all the ways your investments can be at risk, the good news is there are steps you can take to minimize risk.

Diversify, diversify, diversify

One of the best ways to manage risk is through *diversification,* a strategy for reducing risk by spreading your money across different investments. It's a fancy way of saying, "Don't have all your eggs in one basket." But how do you go about divvying up your money and distributing it among different investments? The easiest way to understand proper diversification may be to look at what you should *not* do:

✔ **Don't put all your money in just one investment vehicle.** One of the benefits of using commodities to minimize your overall portfolio risk, for example, is that commodities tend to behave differently than stocks and bonds.

✔ **Don't tie up all your money in one type of asset class.** In order for diversification to have the desired effect on your portfolio (to minimize risk), you want to spread the wealth among different asset classes: large cap and small cap, for example.

✔ **Don't put all your money in one industry.** If a problem hits an entire industry, you'll get hurt.

Research your investment

One way to minimize risk is to research all aspects of the investment you're about to undertake — before you undertake it. Too often, investors won't start doing research until after they invest.

A large number of investors jump in on hype; they hear a certain thing mentioned in the press, and they leap in just because everyone else is. Acting on impulse is one of the most detrimental habits you can develop as an investor or a trader. Before you put your money in anything, find out as much as possible about this potential investment.

Of course, simply knowing about the investment — its pros and cons and so forth — isn't enough. You have to stay up to speed on all the things that can affect your industry of choice in general and your specific investments or trades in particular.

Practice before you jump in

Before you actually put money in any type of new investment or make your first trade, make a few dry runs. For example, pick a few stocks that you think will increase in value and then track them for a while to see how they perform. Watch a few trades online and see how the process works. Create a few technical charts and see how accurately you're able to identify trends.

Noting the Role of the SEC

Long before you invest your first dollar, get to know the Securities and Exchange Commission (SEC). It's there primarily to protect investors from fraud and other unlawful activity designed to fleece them. The SEC was created during the early 1930s by the federal government to crack down on abuses that continued to linger from the speculative and questionable trading practices that were in high gear during the 1920s. It continues to this day to be the most important watchdog of the investment industry.

The SEC has an excellent Web site at www.sec.gov. The site offers plenty of great articles and resources for both novice and experienced investors to help you watch out for fraud and better understand the financial markets and how they work. Look up the telephone numbers for regional offices, and feel free to call with your questions about dubious investments and broker/dealers. The SEC carries on a number of activities designed to help you invest with confidence. It maintains a database on file about complaints lodged against brokers and companies that have committed fraud or other abuses against the investing public. Your tax dollars pay for this important agency. Find out about its free publications, services, and resources before you invest. If you've already been victimized by unscrupulous operators, call the SEC for assistance.

Other than stipulations regarding who can invest in a hedge fund, the SEC provides little or no oversight for this very high-end investment vehicle. The presumption is that folks who can actually qualify to participate in hedge funds are also fairly experienced investors and knowledgeable about the risks associated with these funds. If you invest in hedge funds, you're pretty much on your own.

Going for Brokers

Many investment options require that you negotiate your trades or buy and sell through a broker. A broker is essentially an intermediary between you and the investing world. Brokers can be organizations (Charles Schwab, Merrill Lynch, E*TRADE, and so on) and individuals. Although the primary task of brokers is to act as the intermediary, they can perform other tasks as well:

- ✔ **Providing advisory services:** Investors pay brokers a fee for investment advice.
- ✔ **Offering limited banking services:** Brokers can offer features such as interest-bearing accounts and check writing.

Brokers make their money through various fees, including the following:

- ✔ **Brokerage commissions:** This is a fee for buying and/or selling stocks and other securities.
- ✔ **Margin interest charges:** This is interest charged to investors for borrowing against their brokerage account for investment purposes.
- ✔ **Service charges:** These are charges for performing administrative tasks and other functions. For example, brokers charge fees to investors for individual retirement accounts (IRAs) and for mailing stocks in certificate form.

Any broker you deal with should be registered with the Financial Industry Regulatory Authority (FINRA) and the Securities and Exchange Commission (SEC). In addition, to protect your money after you've deposited it into a brokerage account, that broker should be a member of Securities Investor Protection Corporation (SIPC). SIPC doesn't protect you from market losses; it protects your money in case the brokerage firm goes out of business. To find out whether the broker is registered with these organizations, contact FINRA, the SEC, and SIPC.

Full-service or discount?

There are two basic categories of brokers: full-service and discount. The type you choose really depends on what type of investor you are. In a nutshell, full-service brokers are suitable for investors who need some guidance, while discount brokers are better for those who are sufficiently confident and knowledgeable about investing to manage with minimal help.

Full-service brokers

Full-service brokers are just what the name indicates. They try to provide as many services as possible for investors who open accounts with them. When you open an account at a brokerage firm, a representative is assigned to your account. This representative is usually called an *account executive,* a *registered rep,* or a *financial consultant* by the brokerage firm. This person usually has a securities license and is knowledgeable about stocks in particular and investing in general.

Your account executive is responsible for assisting you, answering questions about your account and the securities in your portfolio, and transacting your buy and sell orders. Here are some things that full-service brokers can do for you:

- ✔ **Offer guidance and advice:** The greatest distinction between full-service brokers and discount brokers is the personal attention you receive from your account rep. You get to be on a first-name basis, and you disclose much information about your finances and financial goals. The rep is there to make recommendations about stocks and funds that are suitable for you.

  Brokers and account reps are salespeople. No matter how well they treat you, they're still compensated based on their ability to produce revenue for the brokerage firm. They generate commissions and fees from you on behalf of the company. (In other words, they're paid to sell you things.)

- ✔ **Provide access to research:** Full-service brokers can give you access to their investment research department, which can give you in-depth information and analysis on a particular company.

- ✔ **Help you achieve your investment objectives:** Beyond advice on specific investments, a good rep gets to know you and your investment goals and *then* offers advice and answers your questions about how specific investments and strategies can help you accomplish your wealth-building goals.

- ✔ **Make investment decisions on your behalf:** Many investors don't want to be bothered when it comes to investment decisions. Full-service brokers can actually make decisions for your account with your authorization. This service may be fine, but be sure to require the broker to explain his or her choices to you.

Handing over decision-making authority to your rep can be a possible negative because letting others make financial decisions for you is always dicey — especially when they're using *your* money. If they make poor investment choices that lose you money, you may not have any recourse because you authorized them to act on your behalf. More egregious is a practice called *churning:* buying and selling securities for the sole purpose of generating commissions.

Before you deal with any broker, full-service or otherwise, get a free report on the broker from the Financial Industry Regulatory Authority by calling 800-289-9999 or visiting its Web site at www.finra.org (click on "FINRA BrokerCheck"). The report can indicate whether any complaints or penalties have been filed against that brokerage firm or the individual rep.

Discount brokers

Perhaps you don't need any hand-holding from a broker. You know what you want, and you can make your own investment decisions. All you want is someone to transact your buy/sell orders. In that case, go with a discount broker. Discount brokers, as the name implies, are cheaper to engage than full-service brokers. They don't offer advice or premium services, though — just the basics required to perform your transactions.

If you choose to work with a discount broker, you must know as much as possible about your personal goals and needs. You have a greater responsibility for conducting adequate research to make good stock selections, and you must be prepared to accept the outcome, whatever that may be. Because you're advising yourself, you can save on costs that you would have incurred had you paid for a full-service broker.

There are two types of discount brokers: conventional discount brokers and Internet discount brokers. Conventional discount brokers (such as Charles Schwab) have national offices where you walk in and speak to the customer service staff face-to-face. You can transact in person, over the phone, or through the Internet. Internet discount brokerage firms (such as E*TRADE) have essentially the same services except for the walk-in offices and face-to-face communication.

Both conventional and Internet-based discount brokers share many of the same primary advantages over full-service brokers, including the following:

- ✔ **Lower cost:** This lower cost is usually the result of lower commissions.

- ✔ **Unbiased service:** Because discount brokers offer you the ability to transact your buys and sells only without advice, they have no vested interest in trying to sell you any particular security.

- ✔ **Access to information:** Established discount brokers offer extensive educational materials at their offices or on their Web sites.

Choosing a broker

Before you choose a broker, you need to analyze your personal investing style. After you know yourself and the way you invest, you can proceed to finding the kind of broker that fits your needs. Keep the following points in mind:

- ✔ Match your investment style with a brokerage firm that charges the least amount of money for the services you're likely to use most frequently.

- ✔ Compare all the costs of buying, selling, and holding stocks and other securities through a broker. Don't compare only commissions. Compare other costs, too, such as margin interest and other service charges.

- ✔ Use broker comparison services such as Gomez Advisors at www.gomez.com and read articles that compare brokers in publications such as *SmartMoney* and *Barron's*.

Picking among types of brokerage accounts

Most brokerage firms offer investors several different types of accounts, each serving a different purpose. The three most common are presented in the following sections. The basic difference boils down to how particular brokers view your "creditworthiness" when it comes to buying and selling securities. If your credit isn't great, your only choice is a cash account. If your credit is good, you can open either a cash account or a margin account.

Cash accounts

A *cash account* (also referred to as a *Type 1* account) is just what you think it is: You deposit a sum of money with the new account application to begin trading. The amount of your initial deposit varies from broker to broker. Some brokers have a minimum of $10,000, while others let you open an account for as little as $500.

With a cash account, your money has to be deposited in the account before the closing (or *settlement*) date for any trade you make. The closing occurs three business days after the date you make the trade (the *date of execution*).

If you have cash in a brokerage account (remember, all accounts are brokerage accounts, and "cash" and "margin" are simply types of brokerage accounts), see whether the broker will pay you interest on it and how much. Some offer a service in which uninvested money earns money-market rates.

Margin accounts

A *margin account* (also called a *Type 2* account) gives you the ability to borrow money against the securities in the account to buy more stock. After you're approved, your brokerage firm gives you credit. A margin account has all the benefits of a cash account plus this ability of buying on margin. A margin account is also necessary if you plan on doing short-selling.

The interest rate that you pay varies depending on the broker, but most brokers generally charge a rate that is several points higher than their own borrowing rate.

Option accounts

An *option account* (also referred to as a *Type 3* account) gives you all the capabilities of a margin account (which in turn also gives you the capabilities of a cash account) plus the ability to trade stock and index options. To open an options account, the broker usually asks you to sign a statement that you are knowledgeable about options and are familiar with the risks associated with them.

Chapter 2

Indexes and Exchanges

. . . .

In This Chapter

▶ Defining indexes and exchanges

▶ Exploring the Dow, the S&P 500, and other key indexes

▶ Looking at important market exchanges

. . . .

"**H**ow's the market doing today?" is probably the most common question that investors ask about the stock market. "What did the Dow do?" "How about NASDAQ?" Invariably, people asking those questions are expecting the performance number of an index. "Well, the Dow fell 57 points to 13,100, while NASDAQ was unchanged at 2,375." Indexes can be useful, general gauges of stock market activity. They give investors a basic idea of how well (or how poorly) the overall market is doing. *Exchanges* — the places (physical or electronic) where the buying and selling actually take place — are important too. This chapter gives you the lowdown on both.

Indexes: Tracking the Market

Indexes, which measure and report changes in the value of a selected group of securities, give investors an instant snapshot of how well the market is doing. Through them, you can quickly compare the performance of your portfolio with the rest of the market. If the Dow goes up 10 percent in a year and your portfolio shows a cumulative gain of 12 percent, you know that you're doing well.

Indexes are *weighted;* that is, their calculations take into account the relative importance of the items being evaluated. There are several kinds of indexes:

▸ **Price-weighted index:** This index tracks changes based on the change in the individual stock's price per share. Suppose that you own two stocks: Stock A worth $20 per share and Stock B worth $40 per share. In a price-weighted index, the stock at $40 is allocated a greater proportion of the index than the one at $20.

✔ **Market value–weighted index:** This index tracks the proportion of a stock based on its market capitalization (or market value). Say that in your portfolio the $20 stock (Stock A) has 10 million shares and the $40 stock (Stock B) has only 1 million shares. Stock A's market cap is $200 million, while Stock B's market cap is $40 million. In a market value–weighted index, Stock A represents 83 percent of the index's value because of its much larger market cap.

This sample portfolio shows only two stocks — obviously not a good representative index. Most investing professionals (especially money managers and mutual fund firms) use a broad-based index as a benchmark to compare their progress. A *broad-based index* is an index that represents the performance of the entire market, such as the S&P 500.

✔ **Composite index:** This type of index is a combination of several indexes. An example is the New York Stock Exchange (NYSE) Composite, which tracks the entire exchange by combining all the stocks and indexes that are included in it.

Dow Jones Industrial Average

The oldest and most famous stock market index is the Dow Jones Industrial Average (DJIA or, more commonly, *the Dow*). It is most frequently the index quoted when someone asks how the market is doing. The Dow is price-weighted and tracks a basket of 30 of the largest and most influential public companies in the stock market.

The Dow has survived as a popular gauge of stock market activity for over a century. Although it is an important indicator of the market's progress, it does have one major drawback: It tracks only 30 companies. Regardless of their status in the market, the companies in the Dow represent a limited number, so they don't communicate the true pulse of the market. Nor is the Dow a pure gauge of industrial activity because it also includes a hodgepodge of nonindustrial issues such as JPMorgan Chase and Citigroup (banks), Home Depot (retailing), and Microsoft (software).

Serious investors are better served by looking at broad-based indexes, such as the S&P 500 and the Wilshire 5000, and industry or sector indexes, which better gauge the growth (or lack thereof) of specific industries and sectors.

For more information, visit www.djindexes.com.

Standard & Poor's 500

The Standard & Poor's 500 (S&P 500) is an index that tracks the 500 largest (measured by market value) publicly traded companies. Because it contains 500 companies, the S&P is more representative of the overall market's performance than the Dow. Money managers and financial advisors watch the S&P 500 more closely than the Dow. Mutual funds especially like to measure their performance against the S&P 500 rather than against any other index.

The S&P 500 includes companies that are widely held and widely followed. The companies are also leaders in a variety of industries, including energy, technology, healthcare, and finance. It is a market value–weighted index.

Although it is a reliable indicator of the market's overall status, the S&P 500 also has some limitations. Despite the fact that it tracks 500 companies, the top 50 companies encompass 50 percent of the index's market value. This situation can be a drawback because those 50 companies have a greater influence on the S&P 500 index's price movement than any other segment of companies. In other words, 10 percent of the companies have an equal impact to 90 percent of the companies on the same index. Therefore, the index may not offer an accurate representation of the general market.

The 500 companies in the S&P are not set in stone. They can be added or removed as market conditions change. A company can be removed if it is not doing well or goes bankrupt. A company in the index can be replaced by another company that is doing better. For more information, visit www. standardandpoors.com.

QQQ

QQQ (or *Qubes*) is the index that tracks NASDAQ-100: the top 100 stocks traded on the NASDAQ, an exchange that's discussed later in this chapter. This index is for investors who want to concentrate on the largest companies, which tend to be especially weighted in technology issues. QQQ is a favorite index among day-traders — much more so than the S&P 500 or the Dow — because it tends to be much more volatile.

Russell 1000, 2000, and 3000

The Russell 3000 index includes the 3,000 largest publicly traded companies (nearly 98 percent of publicly traded stocks). The Russell 3000 is important because it includes many mid cap and small cap stocks. Most companies covered in the Russell 3000 have an average market value of a billion dollars or less.

The Russell 3000 index was created by the Frank Russell Company, which computes a series of indexes including the Russell 1000 and the Russell 2000. The Russell 2000 contains the smallest 2,000 companies from the Russell 3000, while the Russell 1000 contains the largest 1,000 companies. The Russell indexes do not cover *microcap* stocks (companies with a market capitalization under $250 million).

Even though the largest 1,000 U.S. stocks are in the Russell 1000, this index remains relatively obscure because the Dow and the S&P 500 hog the spotlight when it comes to measuring large cap performance. For more information, visit www.russell.com.

Dow Jones Wilshire 5000

The Wilshire 5000, which is often referred to as the *Wilshire Total Market Index,* is probably the largest stock index in the world. Created in 1974 by Wilshire Associates, it started out tracking 5,000 stocks and has ballooned to cover more than 7,500 stocks. The advantage of the Wilshire 5000 is that it's very comprehensive, covering nearly the entire market. (At the very least, the stocks tracked are the largest publicly traded stocks.) It includes all the stocks that are on the major stock exchanges (NYSE, AMEX, and the largest issues on NASDAQ), which by default also include all the stocks covered by the S&P 500. The Wilshire 5000 is a market value–weighted index. For more information, visit www.wilshire.com.

Morgan Stanley Capital International

With indexes of all kinds — stocks, bonds, hedge funds, U.S. and international securities — Morgan Stanley Capital International (MSCI), although not quite a household name, has been gaining ground as the indexer of choice for many exchange-traded fund (ETF) providers. MSCI indexes are the backbone of domestic and international Vanguard ETFs, as well as Barclays iShares individual country ETFs. For more information, visit www.msci.com.

International indexes

The whole world is a vast marketplace that interacts with and exerts tremendous influence on individual national economies and markets. Whether you have one stock or a mutual fund or multiple investment vehicles, keep tabs on how your portfolio is affected by world markets. The best way to get a snapshot of international markets is, of course, with indexes. Here are some of the more widely followed international indexes:

  ✔ **Nikkei (Japan):** This is considered Japan's version of the Dow. If you're invested in Japanese stocks or in stocks that do business with Japan, you can bet that you want to know what's up with the Nikkei.

  ✔ **FTSE 100 (Great Britain):** Usually referred to as the *footsie,* this is a market value–weighted index of the top 100 public companies in the United Kingdom.

  ✔ **CAC 40 (France):** This index tracks the 40 public stocks that trade on the Paris Stock Exchange.

  ✔ **DAX (Germany):** This index tracks the 30 largest and most active stocks that trade on the Frankfurt Exchange.

You can track these international indexes (among others) at major financial Web sites, such as www.bloomberg.com and www.marketwatch.com.

Lehman Brothers

Yeah, I know it sounds like a clothing shop in Brooklyn, but Lehman Brothers is actually the world's leading provider of fixed income benchmarks. Barclays iShares uses Lehman Brothers indexes for five of its six fixed-income ETFs. For more information, visit www.lehman.com.

Exchanges: Securities Marketplaces

Stock exchanges are organized marketplaces for the buying and selling of stocks and other securities. The main exchanges for most stock investors are these three:

  ✔ New York Stock Exchange: www.nyse.com

  ✔ American Stock Exchange: www.amex.com

  ✔ NASDAQ: www.nasdaq.com

New York Stock Exchange

Tracing its origins to 1792, the New York Stock Exchange today lists nearly 2,700 securities and trades about 1.5 billion shares a day. Many of the member companies are among the largest in the United States. All together, New York Stock Exchange companies represent over three-quarters of the total market capitalization in the nation. Trading occurs on the floor of the exchange with specialists and floor traders running the show. The Web site for the New York Stock Exchange is www.nyse.com.

The specialist

Specialists are the workers who are responsible for matching buyers to sellers. The specialists' role is to be certain that the stocks for which they're responsible are traded in a fair, competitive, orderly, and efficient market, ensuring that all customers have an equal opportunity to buy shares while receiving the best prices. The specialist seeks to avoid large or unreasonable price fluctuations between consecutive sales and usually is fairly successful.

The four critical roles that specialists serve on the floor of the exchange are

- ✔ **Auctioneer:** The specialist serving in the capacity of an auctioneer shows the best bids and offers throughout the trading day. This information is disseminated electronically through the NYSE systems and reaches a worldwide audience almost instantaneously. The specialist maintains order and interacts with agents whose customers want to buy the stock.

- ✔ **Agent:** The specialist is the agent for SuperDOT (electronically routed) orders. Floor brokers also may leave an order with a specialist with instructions for the specialist to execute the order at a later time when the stock is available at a specified price. When specialists take on this role, they have the same fiduciary responsibilities as a broker.

  Fiduciary responsibility in this situation means that someone has voluntarily agreed to act as a caretaker of another person's assets and must carry out those responsibilities in good faith with honesty and integrity, and in a way that benefits the asset owner for which the agent has taken the responsibility.

- ✔ **Catalyst:** Specialists serving as catalysts actually become conduits for the flow of orders, keeping track of all known interest in the stock, because not all buyers and sellers are always represented on the floor of the exchange.

- ✔ **Principal:** Specialists must place and execute all orders ahead of their own. Three out of four transactions at the NYSE actually take place between customers without the capital participation of the specialist. In the small minority of trades in which specialists do participate, their role is to provide capital and add liquidity to the market. This capital bridges temporary gaps in supply or demand, which in turn helps reduce price volatility.

The floor trader

The guys you see on the floor of the stock exchange waving their hands wildly to make trades are the *floor traders.* They're actually members of the NYSE who trade exclusively for their own accounts. Floor traders also can act as floor brokers for others and sell their services.

The NYSE is the last big stock exchange to use the *open outcry system,* in which stocks are sold like a public auction with verbal bids and offers shouted in trading pits. This system may soon become history because the Securities and Exchange Commission (SEC) is pushing for changes after bowing to pressure exerted by investor groups. Major players such as Fidelity and AIG have joined the voices of individual investors who want to see a change in this antiquated system to a more modern system similar to that used by NASDAQ. If the SEC succeeds, this change would be the biggest shake-up in the more than 200-year history of the NYSE.

Book I

Investment
Basics

The SuperDOT (Designated Order Turnaround) system

Orders from brokers not on the floor of the exchange reach specialists through the SuperDOT system. SuperDOT is a stock order entering system that can handle daily trading volume that exceeds 2 billion shares. The system sends brokers messages through a common message switch to the proper specialist's trading-floor workstation. Specialists handle these trades as buyers or sellers as particular stocks and orders become available, and they send acknowledgements to the originating brokerage firms, using the same switching system.

American Stock Exchange

The Amex lists roughly 1,350 securities and has a daily trading volume of about 83 million shares. Amex lists stocks that are smaller in size than those on the NYSE yet still have a national following. Many firms that first list on Amex work to meet the listing requirements of the NYSE and then switch over.

Trades on the Amex are executed using an automated or manual order processing system. In the automated system, orders are routed electronically to specialists, virtually eliminating the use of paper on the trading floor. Using a system called the Booth Automated Routing System (BARS), transactions are electronically captured, and reports to member firms are generated. Rather than the specialist's order books, Amex uses a New Equity Trading System (NETS) to collect information about the trades and automate the process of updating and matching orders, quoting and reporting trades, and regulating and researching order details.

Orders also can be placed manually by calling the floor broker by phone. Manual order processes usually are initiated for large or complex orders. Specialists in a stock help to assemble the buyers or sellers for these orders. See www.amex.com for more details.

NASDAQ

No bricks and mortar here. The NASDAQ, which lists over 3,200 securities and trades about 2 billion shares a day, is a uniquely electronic exchange and the fastest growing stock market today. (The acronym NASDAQ stands for National Association of Securities Dealers Automated Quotation system.)

The market was formed after an SEC study in the early 1960s concluded that the sale of over-the-counter securities (those that aren't traded on the existing stock exchanges) was fragmented and obscure. The report called for the automation of the OTC market and gave the responsibility for implementing that system to the National Association of Securities Dealers (NASD). NASD began construction of the NASDAQ system in 1968, and its first trades were made beginning February 8, 1971, when NASDAQ became the world's first electronic stock market.

Market makers

Unlike the specialist structure of the NYSE, in which one specialist represents a particular stock, NASDAQ market makers compete with each other to buy and sell the stocks they choose to represent. More than 500 member firms act as market makers for NASDAQ. Each uses its own capital, research, and system resources to represent a stock and compete with other market makers.

Market makers compete for customers' orders by displaying buy and sell quotations on an electronic exchange for a guaranteed number of shares at a specific price. After market makers receive orders, they immediately purchase or sell stock from their own inventories or seek out the other side of the trades so they can be executed, usually in a matter of seconds. The four types of market makers are

- **Retail market makers:** They serve institutional and individual investors through brokerage networks that provide a continuous flow of orders and sales opportunities.

- **Wholesale market makers:** They serve primarily institutional clients and other brokers or dealers who aren't registered market makers in a particular company's stock but need to execute orders for their customers.

- **Institutional market makers:** They execute large block orders for institutional investors, such as pension funds, mutual funds, insurance companies, and asset management companies.

- **Regional market makers:** They serve companies and individuals of a particular region. By focusing regionally, these market makers offer their customers more extensive coverage of the stocks and investors in a particular area of the country.

NASDAQ listing requirements

To be listed on the NASDAQ stock exchange, a company must meet certain financial and liquidity standards. The financial requirements relate to pre-tax earnings, cash flows, market capitalization, revenue, bid price, the number of market makers, and corporate governance standards. The liquidity requirements involve the number of beneficial shareholders, the average monthly trading volume over the past 12 months, and the market value of publicly held shares and shareholder equity.

Over-the-counter and bulletin-board stocks

Stocks that do not meet the minimum requirements to be listed on NASDAQ are traded as over-the-counter or bulletin-board stocks (OTCBB). The OTCBB is a regulated quotation service that displays real-time quotes, last-sale prices, and volume information for the stocks traded OTCBB. These stocks generally don't meet the listing qualifications for NASDAQ or other national securities exchanges, and fewer than two (and sometimes even no) market makers trade in these stocks, making buying and selling them more difficult.

The SOES system

NASDAQ's Small Order Execution (market) System (SOES) was introduced in 1985 and became mandatory for all market makers after the 1987 stock market crash. Small traders using this system can execute trades directly without worry or fear of market-maker misconduct. Available stocks are posted on an electronic bulletin board and trades are executed electronically. All market makers list the stocks they have available for sale with their *bid* price (the current price at which the market maker will buy) and *ask* price (the current price at which the market maker will sell). Traders pick the bid/ask price that looks best and execute their trades in a matter of seconds using the SOES system.

Regional exchanges

Stock exchanges that focus on listing stocks of corporations from specific geographic regions of the country are called *regional exchanges.* In the United States, the major regional exchanges include Boston, Chicago, Pacific, and Philadelphia stock exchanges. These regional markets are smaller than the NYSE, NASDAQ, and Amex. Although they list mostly regional stocks not on the national exchanges, regional exchanges sometimes list stocks of companies located in their regions even if they're listed on one of the national exchanges.

Each regional exchange offers its own unique blend of services. Boston serves a financial community where trillions of dollars that are invested in mutual funds are managed, so that exchange focuses on serving those clients. Chicago trades stocks listed regionally but also trades stocks from other exchanges, including the NYSE, Amex, and NASDAQ, so it also serves the needs of its regional financial institutions.

The Pacific Exchange focuses on buying and selling options, and thus is known as one of the world's leading derivatives markets. The Philadelphia Stock Exchange focuses on trading options of various sectors including oil service, precious metals (gold and silver), semiconductors, banks, and utilities. The exchange also manages a market structure for trading currency options.

Electronic communications networks (ECNs)

A new system of electronic trading that is developing is called the *electronic communications network* (ECN). The SEC reports that about 30 percent of the total share volume in NASDAQ-listed securities and 40 percent of the dollar volume is traded using ECNs. Likewise, about 96 percent of the trades on ECNs are shares of NASDAQ-listed stocks.

ECNs enable buyers and sellers to meet electronically to execute trades. The trades are entered into the ECN systems by market makers at one of the exchanges or by an OTC market maker. Transactions are completed without a broker-dealer, saving users the cost of commissions normally charged for more traditional forms of trading.

Subscribers to ECNs include retail investors, institutional investors, market makers, and broker-dealers. ECNs are accessed through a custom terminal or by direct Internet dial-up. Orders are posted by the ECN for subscribers to view. The ECN then matches orders for execution. In most cases, buyers and sellers maintain their anonymity and do not list identifiable information in their buy or sell orders.

More than a dozen ECNs operate in the U.S. securities markets, including Archipelago Exchange, Brut, Instinet, Island, and SelectNet.

Book II
Basic Investments: Stocks, Bonds, Mutual Funds, and More

The 5th Wave   By Rich Tennant

"Perhaps you'd like to buy these magic beans, or this charm that will give you good luck, or this stock that promises a 200% return using the buy-and-hold approach."

In this book . . .

*E*very month, it seems, Wall Street comes up with some newfangled investment idea. The array of financial products (replete with 164-page prospectuses) is now so dizzying that the old lumpy mattress is starting to look like a more comfortable place to stash the cash. As a high-end investor, you're more capable than most of weeding through all the promises and potential and figuring out what's real (and what isn't) and what belongs in your portfolio (and what doesn't).

But sometimes you need to take a step back to realize that you don't always need newfangled investment ideas to create a smart portfolio — one that's diversified enough to offer some protection from risk. That's where traditional investment vehicles, like stocks and bonds, can come into play.

Chapter 1

Playing the Market: Stocks

In This Chapter
▶ Getting some stock basics
▶ Making sense of stock tables
▶ Investing in stocks for growth or income

The stock market is a centerpiece of the U.S. financial scene. Stocks are one of the most traditional investment vehicles — one that many Americans are familiar with. But just because stocks are familiar doesn't mean you don't have to make an effort to understand them. Successfully investing in stocks requires a realistic approach and quite a bit of know-how. This chapter gives you an overview.

Starting with the Basics

Stocks represent ownership in companies, and stock markets are the places where stocks are bought and sold. Those places may be made of bricks and mortar, like the New York Stock Exchange, or they may be computer networks, like the NASDAQ. In years past, when someone bought stock in a company, he would receive a physical certificate that proved how many shares he owned. These days, if you buy stock in a company, you don't get a pretty piece of paper to prove it; you generally get electronic confirmation of the trade.

Connecting economics to the stock market

While no one is asking you to understand "the inelasticity of demand aggregates" or "marginal utility," having a working knowledge of basic economics is crucial (and I mean *crucial*) to your success as a stock investor. The stock market and the economy are joined at the hip. The good or bad things that happen to one have a direct effect on the other.

Understanding basic economics can help you filter financial news to separate relevant information from the irrelevant in order to make better investment decisions. Here are a few important economic concepts to be aware of:

- ✔ **Supply and demand:** Supply and demand can be simply stated as the relationship between what's available (the supply) and what people want and are willing to pay for (the demand). This equation is the main engine of economic activity and is extremely important for your stock investing analysis and decision-making process.

- ✔ **Cause and effect:** Considering cause and effect is an exercise in logical thinking. If you were to pick up a prominent news report and read, "Companies in the table industry are expecting plummeting sales," would you rush out and invest in companies that sell chairs or manufacture tablecloths? When you read business news, play it out in your mind. What good (or bad) can logically be expected given a certain event or situation?

- ✔ **Economic effects from government actions:** Nothing has a greater effect — good or bad — on investing and economics than government, which controls the money supply, credit, and all public securities markets. Government actions usually manifest themselves as taxes, laws, or regulations. They also can take on a more ominous appearance, such as war or the threat of war. A single government action can have a far-reaching effect that can have a direct or indirect economic impact on your stock investments.

Reading stock tables

The stock tables in major business publications, such as *The Wall Street Journal* and *Investor's Business Daily,* are loaded with information that can help you become a savvy investor. You use this information not only to select promising investment opportunities but also to monitor your stocks' performance.

Table 1-1 shows a sample stock table for you to refer to as you read the sections that follow. Each item gives you some clues about the current state of affairs for a particular company.

Table 1-1		Deciphering Stock Tables						
52-Wk High	52-Wk Low	Name (Symbol)	Div	Vol	Yld	P/E	Day Last	Net Chg
21.50	8.00	SkyHigh Corp (SHC)		3143		76	21.25	+.25
47.00	31/75	LowDown Inc (LDI)	2.35	2735	5.7	18	41.00	−.50
25.00	21.00	ValueNow Inc (VNI)	1.00	1894	4.5	12	22.00	+.10
83.00	33.00	DoinBadly Corp (DBC)		7601			33.50	−.75

Here's what each column means:

- **52-week high:** This column gives you the highest price that particular stock has reached in the most recent 52-week period. This is important info if you want to gauge where the stock is now versus where it has been recently.

- **52-week low:** This column gives you the lowest price that particular stock has reached in the most recent 52-week period. Again, this information is crucial to your ability to analyze stocks over a period of time.

  The high and low prices just give you a range for how far that particular stock's price has moved, up or down, within the past 52 weeks. Interesting information, but to understand what it means or how (or whether) you should act on it, you need to get more information.

- **Name and symbol:** This column tells you the company name (usually abbreviated) and the stock symbol assigned to it. When you have your eye on a stock for potential purchase, get familiar with its symbol. Financial tables list stocks in alphabetical order by symbol, and you need to use them in all stock communications, from getting a stock quote at your broker's office to buying stock over the Internet.

- **Dividend:** A value in this column indicates that payments have been made to stockholders. The amount you see is the annual dividend quoted as if you owned one share of that stock. If you look at LowDownInc (LDI) in Table 1-1, you can see that you would get $2.35 as an annual dividend for each share of stock that you own.

Book II

Basic Investments: Stocks, Bonds, Mutual Funds, and More

✔ **Volume:** This column tells you how many shares of that particular stock were traded that day. If only 100 shares are traded in a day, the trading volume is 100.

You can't necessarily compare one stock's volume against that of any other company. The large cap stocks like IBM or Microsoft typically have trading volumes in the millions of shares almost every day, while less active, smaller stocks may have average trading volumes in far, far smaller numbers. The key thing to remember is that trading volume that's far in excess (either positively or negatively) of the stock's normal range is a sign that something is going on with that stock. Be sure to check out what's happening when you hear about heavier than usual volume (especially if you already own the stock).

✔ **Yield:** This column refers to what percentage that particular dividend is to the stock price. Yield, which is most important to income investors, is calculated by dividing the annual dividend by the current stock price. Yield reported in the financial pages changes daily as the stock price changes and is always reported as if you're buying the stock that day.

✔ **P/E:** This column indicates the ratio between the price of the stock and the company's earnings. This ratio (also called the *earnings multiple* or just *multiple*) is frequently used to determine whether a stock is a good value. Value investors (see Book VII) find P/E ratios to be essential to analyzing a stock as a potential investment.

In the P/E ratios reported in stock tables, *price* refers to the cost of a single share of stock. *Earnings* refers to the company's reported earnings as of the most recent four quarters.

✔ **Day last:** This column tells you how trading ended for a particular stock on the day represented by the table. Some newspapers report the high and low for that day in addition to the stock's ending price.

✔ **Net change:** This column answers the question "How did the stock price end today compared with its trading price at the end of the prior trading day?"

Investing for Growth

Obviously, not all stocks perform the same way. If they did, investing in the stock market would be pretty dull. Instead, certain types of stocks tend to be more risky than others. And, as a rule, those that carry more risk also tend to carry more potential for growth. In this section, I focus on those stocks that fall into the higher risk/return category. In the next section, I turn the focus to those stocks that tend to involve lower risk, lower return, and a different set of pros and cons than growth stocks.

A lesson from the late '90s

Because most investors ignored some basic observations about economics in the late 1990s, they lost trillions in their stock portfolios. In the late 1990s, the United States experienced the greatest expansion of debt in history, coupled with a record expansion of the money supply. (Both are controlled by the Federal Reserve, the U.S. government central bank referred to as *the Fed*.) This growth of debt and money supply resulted in more consumer (and corporate) borrowing, spending, and investing. This activity hyperstimulated the stock market and caused stocks to rise 25 percent per year for five straight years. Sounds great, but such a return can't be sustained and encourages speculation.

This artificial stimulation by the Fed resulted in more and more people depleting their savings, buying on credit (it's cheap — why not?), and borrowing against their homes. All this spending (on big ticket discretionary items, vacations, and so on) prompted businesses to expand (by borrowing money, of course, or by going public). But such high-level spending can't go on forever.

When the inevitable slowdown came, companies were caught in a financial bind. Too much debt and too many expenses in a slowing economy mean one thing: Profits shrink or disappear. To stay in business, companies cut expenses, and the biggest expense in a company is payroll. So companies started laying off employees.

And when you don't have a job — or are afraid of losing one — and you have little in the way of savings and too much in the way of debt, you start selling your stock to pay the bills. This was a major reason that stocks started to fall in 2000. Earnings started to drop because of shrinking sales from a sputtering economy. As earnings fell, stock prices also fell.

The lessons from the 1990s are important ones for investors today:

✔ Stocks aren't a replacement for savings accounts. Always have some money in the bank.

✔ Stocks should never occupy 100 percent of your investment funds.

✔ When anyone (including an "expert") tells you that the economy will keep growing indefinitely, be skeptical and read diverse sources of information.

✔ If stocks do well in your portfolio, consider protecting your stocks (both your original investment and any gains) with stop-loss orders.

✔ Keep debt and expenses to a minimum.

✔ Remember that if the economy is booming, a decline is sure to follow as the ebb and flow of the economy's business cycle continues.

Book II

Basic Investments: Stocks, Bonds, Mutual Funds, and More

Choosing growth stocks

A stock is considered a *growth stock* when it's growing faster and higher than stocks of other companies with similar sales and earnings figures. I say *higher than stocks of other companies* because you have to measure growth against something. Usually, you compare the growth of a company with growth from other companies in the same industry or compare it with the stock market in general. In practical terms, when you measure the growth of a stock against the stock market, you're actually comparing it against a generally accepted benchmark, such as the Dow Jones Industrial Average (DJIA) or the Standard & Poor's 500 (S&P 500). For more on the DJIA or S&P 500, see Book I.

If a company has earnings growth of 15 percent per year over three years or more and the industry's average growth rate over the same time frame is 10 percent, then this stock qualifies as a growth stock. A growth stock is called that not only because the company is growing but also because the company is performing well with some consistency. Just because your earnings did great versus the S&P 500's average in a single year doesn't cut it. Growth must be consistently accomplished.

Although comparison is a valuable tool for evaluating a stock's potential, you don't want to pick growth stocks on the basis of comparison alone. You should also scrutinize the stock to make sure that it has other things going for it to improve your chance of success, as the following sections explain.

When choosing growth stocks, invest in a company only if it makes a profit and only if you understand *how* it makes that profit. You need to know such information so that you can monitor the industry and more accurately predict whether the company you choose to invest in will continue to make money based on the likelihood that its customers, in turn, will be making money.

Checking out a company's fundamentals

When you hear the word *fundamentals* in the world of stock investing, it refers to the company's financial condition and related data. When investors do *fundamental analysis,* they look at the company's fundamentals: its balance sheet, income statement, cash flow, and other operational data, along with external factors such as the company's market position, industry, and economic prospects. Essentially, the fundamentals should indicate to you that the company is in strong financial condition: It has consistently solid earnings, low debt, and a commanding position in the marketplace.

Deciding whether a company is a good value

You already know that a *growth stock* is the stock of a company that is performing better than its peers in categories such as sales and earnings. *Value stocks* are stocks that are priced lower than the value of the company and its assets. You can identify a value stock by analyzing the company's fundamentals and looking at some key financial ratios, such as the price-to-earnings ratio. If the stock's price is lower than the company's fundamentals indicate it should be (in other words, it's undervalued), then it's a good buy — a bargain — and the stock is considered a great value. For more on value investing, see Book VII.

Looking for leaders and megatrends

What's the current megatrend, and how does the company you're investigating fit into it? A *megatrend* is a major development that has huge implications for most (if not all) of society and for a long time to come. A good example of a megatrend is the aging of America. Federal government studies tell us that senior citizens will be the fastest-growing segment of our population during the next 20 years. How does the stock investor take advantage of a mega-trend? By identifying a company that's poised to address the opportunities that such trends reveal. A strong company in a growing industry is a common recipe for success.

Considering a company with a strong niche

Companies that have established a strong niche are consistently profitable. Look for a company with one or more of the following characteristics:

- ✔ **A strong brand:** Companies that have a positive, familiar identity — such as Coca-Cola and Microsoft — occupy a niche that keeps customers loyal. Other companies have to struggle to overcome that loyalty if they want a share of the market.

- ✔ **High barriers to entry:** United Parcel Service and Federal Express have set up tremendous distribution and delivery networks that competitors can't easily duplicate. High barriers to entry offer an important edge to companies that are already established.

- ✔ **Research & development (R&D):** Companies such as Pfizer and Merck spend a lot of money researching and developing new pharmaceutical products. This investment becomes a new product with millions of consumers who become loyal purchasers, so the company's going to grow.

Noticing who's buying and/or recommending the stock

You can invest in a great company and still see its stock go nowhere. Why? Because what makes the stock go up is demand — there need to be more buyers than sellers of the stock. If you pick a stock for all the right reasons and the market notices the stock as well, that attention will cause the stock price to climb. The things to watch for include the following:

- ✔ **Institutional buying:** Are mutual funds and pension plans buying up the stock you're looking at? If so, this type of buying power will exert tremendous upward pressure on the stock's price.

- ✔ **Analysts' attention:** Are analysts talking about the stock on the financial shows? As much as you should be skeptical about an analyst's recommendation, it offers some positive reinforcement for your stock. A single recommendation by an influential analyst can be enough to send a stock skyward.

- ✔ **Newsletter recommendations:** Newsletters are usually published by independent researchers (or so we hope). If influential newsletters are touting your choice, that praise is also good for your stock.

- ✔ **Consumer publications:** Publications such as *Consumer Reports* regularly look at products and services and rate them for consumer satisfaction. If a company's offerings are well received by consumers, that's a strong positive for the company. This kind of attention will ultimately have a positive effect on that company's stock.

Exploring small caps

Everyone wants to get in early on a hot new stock. Who wouldn't want to buy a stock that could become the next IBM or Microsoft? This is why investors are attracted to small cap stocks.

Small cap (or *small capitalization*) is a reference to the company's market size. Small cap stocks are stocks from companies that have market capitalization (the number of shares outstanding multiplied by the price per share) of under $1 billion. Investors may face more risk with small caps, but they also have the chance for greater gains.

Out of all the types of stocks, small cap stocks continue to exhibit the greatest amount of growth. In the same way that a tree planted last year will have more opportunity for growth than a mature 100-year-old redwood, small caps have greater growth potential than established large cap stocks. Of course, a small cap will not exhibit spectacular growth just because it's small. It will grow when it does the right things, such as increasing sales and earnings by producing goods and services that customers want. As you consider small caps, keep these things in mind:

- ✔ **An IPO is not a sure thing.** An initial public offerings (IPO) is the first offering to the public of a company's stock. The IPO is also referred to as "going public." Because a company that is going public is frequently an unproven enterprise, investing in an IPO can be risky.

- ✔ **If it's a small cap stock, make sure it's making money.** When you evaluate a company for stock investing, make sure that the company is established (being in business for at least three years is a good minimum) and that it's profitable. These rules are especially important for investors in small stocks. Plenty of start-up ventures lose money but hope to make a fortune down the road. A good example is a company in the biotechnology industry. Biotech is an exciting area, but it's esoteric, and at this early stage, companies are finding it difficult to use the technology in profitable ways. You may say, "But shouldn't I jump in now in anticipation of future profits?" You may get lucky, but understand that when you invest in small cap stocks, you're speculating.

- ✔ **Investing in small cap stocks requires analysis.** You need to do more research on small cap stocks than on large caps. Plenty of information is available on large cap stocks because they're widely followed. Small cap stocks don't get as much press, and fewer analysts issue reports on them.

Investing for Income

Investing for income means investing in stocks that will provide you with regular money payments (dividends). Income stocks may not offer stellar growth, but they're good for a steady infusion of money. What type of person is best suited to income stocks? Income stocks can be appropriate for many investors, but they are especially well suited for the following individuals:

- ✔ **Conservative and novice investors:** These investors like to see a slow-but-steady approach to growing their money while getting regular dividend checks. Novice investors who want to start slowly also benefit from income stocks.

- ✔ **Retirees:** Growth investing is best suited for long-term needs, while income investing is best suited to current needs. Retirees may want some growth in their portfolios, but they're more concerned with regular income that can keep pace with inflation.

- ✔ **Dividend reinvestment plan (DRP) investors:** A DRP is a program that a company may offer to allow investors to accumulate more shares of its stock without paying commissions. For those who like to compound their money with DRPs, income stocks are perfect.

If you have a low tolerance for risk or if your investment goal is anything less than long term, income stocks are your best bet.

Book II

Basic Investments: Stocks, Bonds, Mutual Funds, and More

Analyzing income stocks

When we talk about gaining income from stocks, we're usually talking about dividends. A *dividend* is nothing more than money paid out to the owner of a stock. A good income stock is a stock that has a higher-than-average dividend (typically 4 percent or higher) and is purchased primarily for income — not for spectacular growth potential.

A dividend is quoted as an annual number but is usually paid on a quarterly, pro-rata basis. In other words, if the stock is paying a dividend of $4, you would probably be paid $1 every quarter. If, in this example, you had 200 shares, you would be paid $800 every year (if the dividend isn't changed during that period), or $200 per quarter. Getting that regular dividend check every three months for as long as you hold the stock can be a nice perk.

Dividend rates are not guaranteed; they can go up or down or, in some extreme cases, the dividend can be discontinued. Fortunately, most companies that issue dividends continue them indefinitely and actually increase dividend payments from time to time. Historically, dividend increases have equaled or exceeded the rate of inflation.

Look at income stocks in the same way that you do growth stocks when assessing the financial strength of a company. Getting a nice dividend can come to a screeching halt if the company can't afford to pay them. If your budget depends on dividend income, then monitoring the company's financial strength is that much more important.

Considering yield

The main thing to look for in choosing income stocks is *yield:* the percentage rate of return paid on a stock in the form of dividends. Looking at a stock's dividend yield is the quickest way to find out how much money you'll earn from a particular income stock versus other dividend-paying stocks (or even other investments, such as a bank account). Dividend yield is calculated in the following way:

Dividend yield = dividend income ÷ stock investment

When you see a stock listed in the financial pages, the dividend yield is provided along with the stock's price and annual dividend. The dividend yield in the financial pages is always calculated as if you bought the stock on that given day.

Based on supply and demand, stock prices change every day (almost every minute!) that the market's open. If the stock price changes every day, the yield changes as well. Take a look at Table 1-2. If you bought stock in Smith Co. a month ago at $20 per share with an annual dividend of $1, your yield is 5 percent. But if Smith Co. is selling for $40 per share today, the yield quoted would be 2.5 percent. Did the dividend get cut in half?! Not really. You're still getting 5 percent because you bought the stock at $20 instead of the current $40; the quoted yield is for investors who purchase Smith Co. today. Investors who buy Smith Co. stock today would pay $40 and get the $1 dividend; the yield has changed to 2.5 percent, which is the yield that they lock into. So, while Smith Co. may have been a good income investment for you a month ago, it's not such a hot pick today because the price of the stock doubled, cutting the yield in half. Even though the dividend hasn't changed, the yield has changed dramatically because of the stock price change.

Table 1-2	Comparing Yields			
Investment	Type	Investment Amount	Annual Investment Income (Dividend)	Yield (Annual Investment Income ÷ Investment Amount)
Smith Co.	Common stock	$20 per share	$1.00 per share	5%
Jones Co.	Common stock	$30 per share	$1.50 per share	5%
Wilson Bank	Savings account	$1,000 deposit	$40	4%

You can't stop scrutinizing income stocks after you acquire them. You may have made a great choice that gives you a great dividend, but that doesn't mean it will be that way indefinitely. Monitor the company's progress for as long as it is in your portfolio. Use resources such as www.bloomberg.com and www.marketwatch.com to track your stock and to monitor how well that particular company is continuing to perform.

Checking the payout ratio

The *payout ratio* is simply a way to figure out what percentage of the company's earnings are being paid out in the form of dividends. People concerned about the safety of their dividend income should regularly watch the payout ratio. Generally, a dividend payout ratio of 60 percent or less is safe. Obviously, the lower the percentage is, the safer the dividend.

Say that the company Urn More Corp. (UMC) has annual earnings of $1 million dollars. Total dividends of $500,000 are to be paid out, and the company has 1 million outstanding shares. Using those numbers, you know that UMC has earnings per share (EPS) of $1.00 ($1 million in earnings divided by 1 million shares) and that it pays an annual dividend of 50 cents per share ($500,000 divided by 1 million shares). The dividend payout ratio is 50 percent (the 50 cents dividend is 50 percent of the $1.00 EPS). This is a healthy dividend payout ratio because even if the company's earnings were to fall by 10 percent or 20 percent, it would still have plenty of room to pay dividends.

Keep in mind that a company's earnings aren't necessarily cash. Looking at cash flow from operations versus earnings is another way to measure dividend safety.

Examining a company's bond rating

A company's bond rating is very important to income stock investors. The bond rating offers insight into the company's financial strength. Bonds get rated for quality for the same reasons that consumer agencies rate products such as cars or toasters. Standard & Poor's (S&P) is the major independent rating agency that looks into bond issuers. It looks at the issuer of a bond and asks the question "Does the bond issuer have the financial strength to pay back the bond and the interest as stipulated in the bond indenture?"

If the bond rating is good, the company is strong enough to pay its obligations, which include expenses, payments on debts, and dividends. If a bond rating agency gives the company a high rating (or if it raises the rating), that's a great sign for anyone holding the company's debt or receiving dividends. Conversely, a lowered rating indicates the company's financial health is deteriorating, while a bad bond rating means the company is having difficulty paying its obligations.

The highest rating issued by S&P is AAA. The grades AAA, AA, and A are considered "investment grade" or of high quality. Bs and Cs indicate a poor grade, while anything lower than that is considered very risky (the bonds are referred to as *junk bonds*).

Looking at typical income stocks

Income stocks tend to be in established industries with established cash flows and less emphasis on financing or creating new products and services. When you're ready to start your search for a great income stock, start looking at utilities and real estate trusts — two established industries with proven track records — for high-dividend stocks.

You won't find too many dividend-paying income stocks in the computer or biotech industry; odds are you won't even find one! The reason is that these types of companies need a lot of money to finance expensive research and development (R&D) projects to create new products. Without R&D, the company can't create new products to fuel sales, growth, and future earnings. Computer, biotech, and other innovative industries are better for growth investors.

Utilities

Utilities generate a large cash flow, which includes money from income (sales of products and/or services) and other items (such as the selling of equipment, for example). This cash flow is needed to cover things such as expenses, including dividends. Utilities are considered the most common type of income stocks, and many investors have at least one in their portfolios. Investing in your own local utility isn't a bad idea. At least you know that when you pay your energy bill, you're helping out at least one investor.

Real estate investment trusts (REITs)

Real estate investment trusts (REITs) are a special breed of stock. A REIT is an investment that has the elements of both a stock and a *mutual fund* (a pool of money received from investors that is managed by an investment company). It's like a stock in that it's a company whose stock is publicly traded on the major stock exchanges, and it has the usual features that you expect from a stock — it can be bought and sold easily through a broker, income is given to investors as dividends, and so on. A REIT resembles a mutual fund in that it doesn't make its money selling goods and services; it makes its money by buying, selling, and managing an investment portfolio — in the case of a REIT, the portfolio is full of real estate investments. It generates revenue from rents and property leases as any landlord would. In addition, some REITs own mortgages, and they gain income from the interest.

REITs are called *trusts* only because they meet the requirements of the Real Estate Investment Trust Act of 1960. This act exempts REITs from corporate income tax and capital gains taxes as long as they meet certain criteria, such as dispensing 95 percent of their net income to shareholders. There are other criteria, but this is the one that interests income investors. This provision is the reason REITs generally issue generous dividends. Beyond this status, REITs are, in a practical sense, like any other publicly traded company.

Chapter 2

Many Happy Returns: Bonds

In This Chapter

▶ Understanding bond ratings, maturity levels, and yields

▶ Stabilizing your portfolio with low-risk investments

▶ Selecting the right types of bonds for your investment needs

*B*onds are investments for people who prefer predictability to volatility and income to capital gains. They're the sweethearts that may have saved your grandparents from selling apples on the street during the hungry 1930s. They are the babies that may have saved your 401(k) from devastation during the three growly bear-market years on Wall Street that started this century. Bonds belong in nearly every portfolio. Whether they belong in *your* portfolio is something this chapter helps you decide.

Getting Your Bond Basics

Just what are bonds? The word *bond* basically means an IOU. When you buy a bond, you're lending your money to Uncle Sam, to General Electric, to Procter & Gamble, to the city in which you live — to whatever entity issues the bonds — and that entity promises to pay you a certain rate of interest in exchange for borrowing your money. Bond investing is very different from stock investing, where you purchase shares in a company, become an alleged partial owner of that company, and then pray that the company churns a profit and the CEO doesn't pocket it all.

By and large, bonds' most salient characteristic — and the one thing that most, but not all bonds share — is a certain stability and steadiness well above and beyond that of most other investments. Because you are, in most cases, receiving a steady stream of income, and because you expect to get your principal back in one piece, bonds tend to be more conservative invest- ments than, say, stocks, commodities, or collectibles.

Some key things to know about bonds:

- A bond is always issued with a certain *face amount* (also called the *principal* or the *par value* of the bond). Most often, bonds are issued with face amounts of $1,000. So in order to raise $50 million, the entity issuing the bonds would have to issue 50,000 of them, each selling at $1,000 par.

- After a bond is issued, it may sell on the secondary market for more or less than its face amount. If it sells for more than its face amount, the bond is said to sell at a *premium*. If it sells for less than its face amount, the bond is said to sell at a *discount*. Many factors determine the price of a bond in the secondary market.

- Every bond pays a certain rate of interest, and typically (but not always) that rate is fixed over the life of the bond (that's why some people call bonds *fixed-income* securities). The life of the bond is known as the bond's *maturity*. The rate of interest is a percentage of the face amount and is typically paid out twice a year. For example, if a corporation or government issues a $1,000 bond paying 6 percent, that corporation or government promises to fork over to the bondholder $60 a year — or, in most cases, $30 twice a year. Then, when the bond matures, the corporation or government gives the bondholder the original $1,000 back.

- In some cases, you can buy a bond directly from the issuer and sell it back directly to the issuer, but in most cases, bonds are bought and sold through a brokerage house or a bank. Oh, yes, these brokerage houses take a piece of the pie, sometimes a quite sizeable piece. For information on choosing brokers, refer to Book I.

- The issuance of bonds is regulated by the Securities and Exchange Commission (and other regulatory authorities). Again, you can find information on the SEC and other regulatory agencies in Book I.

Maturity choices

Almost all bonds these days are issued with life spans (maturities) of up to 30 years. Any bond with a maturity of less than five years is called a *short bond*. Bonds with maturities of 5 to 12 years are called *intermediate bonds*. Bonds with maturities of 12 years or more are called *long bonds*.

In general, the longer the maturity, the greater the interest rate paid. That's because bond buyers generally demand more compensation the longer they agree to tie up their money. At the same time, bond issuers are willing to fork over more interest in return for the privilege of holding onto your money longer.

The difference between the rates you can get on short bonds versus intermediate bonds versus long bonds is known as the *yield curve*. *Yield* simply refers to the annual interest rate.

Investment-grade or junk-grade bonds

When choosing a bond, you may think that the bonds that offer the best interest rates are the best investments. But that's not necessarily the case. When it comes to bonds, a higher rate of interest isn't always the best deal. Why? Because when you fork your money over to buy a bond, your principal is guaranteed only by the issuer of the bond, which means that it's only as solid as the issuer itself.

Bond issuers with the shakiest reputations pay higher interest rates. If you had to decide between U.S. Treasury bonds (guaranteed by the U.S. government), General Electric bonds, and General Motors bonds, you'd expect that you'd get the highest rate of interest from General Motors because it's currently on shaky footing. Lending your money to GM involves more risk than lending it to either of the other two. If GM were to go bankrupt, you might lose a good chunk of your principal. That risk requires GM to pay a higher rate of interest. Without paying some kind of *risk premium,* the manufacturer of gas-guzzling cars simply would not be able to attract any people to lend it money to make more gas-guzzling cars. Conversely, the U.S. government, which has the power to levy taxes and print money, is not going bankrupt any time soon. Therefore, U.S. Treasury bonds, which are said to carry no risk of default, tend to pay relatively modest interest rates.

Bonds that carry a relatively high risk of default are commonly called *high-yield* or *junk* bonds. Bonds issued by solid companies and governments that carry very little risk of default are commonly referred to as *investment-grade* bonds.

The major creators of bonds

Every year, millions — yes, literally millions — of bonds are issued by thousands of different governments, government agencies, municipalities, financial institutions, and corporations. The following list gives an overview of things to consider about each major kind of bond.

- ✔ **U.S. Treasury:** Politicians like raising money by selling bonds, as opposed to raising taxes, because voters hate taxes. Of course, when the government issues bonds, it promises to repay the bond buyers over time. The more bonds the government issues, the greater its debt. Voters don't seem to care much about debt. In the later section "'Risk-free' Investing: U.S Treasury Bonds," you can read about the many kinds of Treasury bonds.

- ✔ **Agencies:** Federal agencies such as Federal Home Loan Mortgage Corporation (Freddie Mac) and Federal National Mortgage Association (Fannie Mae) issue a good chunk of the bonds on the market. Such agencies aren't quite government and aren't quite private concerns. They are government "sponsored" and, in theory, Congress and the Treasury would serve as protective big brothers if one of these agencies were to take a financial beating and couldn't pay off its debt obligations. You can find out about these types of bonds in the later section "Lots of Protection: Agency Bonds."

✔ **Corporate bonds:** Bonds issued by for-profit companies are riskier than government bonds but tend to compensate for that added risk by paying higher rates of interest. In recent history, corporate bonds in the aggregate have tended to pay about a percentage point higher than Treasuries of similar maturity. Find out about the corporate bond world in the section "Industrial Returns: Corporate Bonds."

✔ **Municipalities:** Municipal bonds (*munis*) issued by cities, states, and counties are used to raise money either for general day-to-day needs of the citizenry (schools, roads, sewer systems) or for specific projects (a new bridge, a sports stadium). The section "(Almost) Tax-free Havens: Municipal Bonds" offers basic information on municipal bonds.

Individual bonds vs. bond funds

One of the big questions about bond investing is whether to invest in individual bonds or bond funds. I'm a big advocate of bond funds — both bond mutual funds and exchange-traded funds. Mutual funds and exchange-traded funds both represent baskets of securities (usually stocks or bonds, or both) and allow for instant and easy portfolio diversification.

Here's a very broad overview of the pros and cons of owning individual bonds versus bond funds.

Individual bonds

Individual bonds offer you the opportunity to really fine-tune a fixed-income portfolio. With individual bonds, you can choose exactly what you want in terms of bond quality, maturity, and taxability. For larger investors — especially those doing their homework — investing in individual bonds may also be more economical than investing in a bond fund. That's especially true for those investors up on the latest advances in bond buying and selling.

Bond funds

Investors now have a choice of more than 5,000 bond mutual funds or exchange-traded funds. All have the same basic drawback: management expenses. But even so, some make for very good potential investments, particularly for people with modest portfolios.

I'm a strong proponent of buying *index funds* — mutual funds or exchange-traded funds that seek to provide exposure to an entire asset class (such as bonds or stocks) with very little trading and very low expenses. I believe that such funds are the way to go for most investors to get the bond exposure they need.

Various types of yield

Yield is what you want in a bond. Yield is income. Yield contributes to return. Yield is confusion! People (and that includes overly eager bond salespeople) often misuse the term or use it inappropriately to gain an advantage in the bond market. Don't be a yield sucker! Understand what kind of yield is being promised on a bond or bond fund, and know what it really means.

Coupon yield

The coupon yield, or the coupon rate, is part of the bond offering. A $1,000 bond with a coupon yield of 5 percent is going to pay $50 a year. A $1,000 bond with a coupon yield of 7 percent is going to pay $70 a year. Usually, the $50 or $70 or whatever will be paid out twice a year on an individual bond.

Bond funds don't really have coupon yields, although they have an average coupon yield for all the bonds in the pool. That average tells you something, for sure, but you need to remember that a bond fund may start the year and end the year with a completely different set of bonds — and a completely different average coupon yield.

Current yield

Current yield is derived by taking the bond's coupon yield and dividing it by the bond's price. Suppose you had a $1,000 face value bond with a coupon rate of 5 percent, which would equate to $50 a year in your pocket. If the bond sells today for 98 (meaning that it is selling at a discount for $980), the current yield is $50 divided by $980 = 5.10 percent. If that same bond rises in price to a premium of 103 (meaning it's selling for $1,030), the current yield is $50 divided by $1,030 = 4.85 percent.

The current yield is a sort of snapshot that gives you a very rough (and possibly entirely inaccurate) estimate of the return you can expect on that bond over the coming months. If you take today's current yield (translated into nickels and dimes) and multiply that amount by 30, you'd think that would give you a good estimate of how much income your bond will generate in the next month, but that's not the case. The current yield changes too quickly for that kind of prediction to hold true. The equivalent would be taking a measure of today's rainfall, multiplying it by 30, and using that number to estimate rainfall for the month. (Well, the current yield would be *a bit* more accurate, but you get the point.)

Yield-to-maturity

A much more accurate measure of return, although still far from perfect, is the *yield-to-maturity*. Yield-to-maturity factors in not only the coupon rate and the price you paid for the bond, but also how far you have to go to get your principal back, and how much that principal will be.

Yield-to-maturity calculations make a big assumption that may or may not prove true: They assume that as you collect your interest payments every six months, you reinvest them at the same interest rate you're getting on the bond. To calculate the yield-to-maturity, you'd either need to use a terribly long formula with all kinds of horrible Greek symbols and lots of multiplication and division, or (thank goodness) you can use a financial calculator. (I like the calculator on MoneyChimp.com, a great financial Web site that features all sorts of cool calculators.) You put in the par (face) value of the bond (almost always $1,000), the price you are considering paying for the bond, the number of years to maturity, and the coupon rate, and press "calculate."

Unscrupulous bond brokers have been known to tout current yield, and only current yield, when selling especially premium-priced bonds. The current yield may look great, but you'll take a hit when the bond matures by collecting less in principal than you paid for the bond. Your yield-to-maturity, which matters more than current yield, may, in fact, stink.

Yield-to-call

If you buy a *callable* bond, the company or municipality that issues your bond can ask for it back, at a specific price, long before the bond matures. Premium bonds, because they carry higher-than-average coupon yields, are often called. What that means is that your yield-to-maturity is pretty much a moot point. What you're likely to see in the way of yield is yield-to-call. It's figured out the same way that you figure out yield-to-maturity (use MoneyChimp.com if you don't have a financial calculator), but the end result — your actual return — may be considerably lower.

Keep in mind that bonds are generally called when market interest rates have fallen. In that case, not only is your yield on the bond you're holding diminished, but your opportunity to invest your money in anything paying as high an interest rate has passed. From a bondholder's perspective, calls are not pretty, which is why callable bonds must pay higher rates of interest to find any buyers. (From the issuing company's or municipality's perspective, callable bonds are just peachy; after the call, the company or municipality can, if it wishes, issue a new bond that pays a lower interest rate.)

Certain hungry bond brokers may "forget" to mention yield-to-call and instead quote you only current yield or yield-to-maturity numbers. In such cases, you may pay the broker a big cut to get the bond, hold it for a short period, and then have to render it to the bond issuer, actually earning yourself a *negative* total return. Ouch.

Usually a callable bond will not have one possible call date, but several. *Worst-case basis yield* (or *yield-to-worst-call*) looks at all possible yields and tells you what your yield would be if the company or municipality decides to call your bond at the worst possible time.

The 30-day SEC yield

Because there are so many ways of measuring yield, and because bond mutual funds were once notorious for manipulating yield figures, the Securities and Exchange Commission (SEC) requires that all bond funds report yield in the same manner. The 30-day SEC yield, which attempts to consolidate the yield-to-maturity of all the bonds in the portfolio, exists so the mutual-fund bond shopper can have some measure with which to comparison shop. It isn't a perfect measure, in large part because the bonds in your bond fund today may not be the same bonds in your bond fund three weeks from now. Nonetheless, the 30-day SEC yield can be helpful in choosing the right funds.

Total Return: THIS is what matters most!

Total return is the entire pot of money you wind up with after the investment period has come and gone. In the case of bonds or bond funds, that involves not only your interest, but also any changes in the value of your original principal. Ignoring for the moment the risk of default (and losing all your principal), here are other ways in which your principal can shrink or grow.

Figuring in capital gains and losses

In the case of a bond fund, your principal is represented by a certain number of shares in the fund multiplied by the share price of the fund. As bond prices go up and down (usually in response to prevailing interest rates), so too will the share price of the bond fund go up and down. Because of bond volatility, the share price of a bond fund may go up and down quite a bit, especially if the bond fund is holding long-term bonds, and doubly-especially if those long-term bonds are of questionable quality (junk bonds).

In the case of individual bonds, your principal will come back to you whole — but only if you hold the bond to maturity or if the bond is called. If, on the other hand, you choose to sell the bond before maturity, you'll wind up with whatever market price you can get for the bond at that point. If the market price has appreciated (the bond sells at a premium), you can count your capital gains as part of your total return. If the market price has fallen (the bond sells at a discount), the capital losses will offset any interest you've made on the bond.

Factoring in reinvestment rates of return

Total return of a bond can come from three sources:

- ✔ Interest on the bond

- ✔ Any possible capital gains (or losses)

- ✔ Whatever rate of return you get, if you get any, when you reinvest the money coming to you every six months

Believe it or not, on a very long-term bond, the last factor — your so-called *reinvestment rate* — will probably be the most important of the three! That's because of the amazing power of compound interest.

The only kind of bond where the reinvestment rate is not a factor is a *zero-coupon* bond, or a bond where your only interest payment comes at the very end when the bond matures. In the case of zero-coupon bonds, there is no compounding. The coupon rate of the bond is your actual rate of return, not accounting for inflation or taxes.

Allowing for inflation adjustments

Your truest total rate of return needs to account for inflation. To account for inflation when determining the real rate of return on an investment, you can simply take the nominal rate of return (perhaps 5 or 6 percent) and subtract the annual rate of inflation (which has been about 3 percent in recent years). That will give you a very rough estimate of your total real return.

Weighing pre-tax versus post-tax

Taxes almost always eat into your bond returns. For most bonds, the interest payments are taxed as regular income, and any rise in the value of the principal, if the bond is sold (and sometimes even if the bond is not sold), is taxed as capital gain. For most people these days, long-term capital gains (more than one year) on bond principal are taxed at 15 percent. Any appreciated fixed-income asset bought and sold within a year is taxed at your normal income-tax rate, whatever that is. (Most middle-income Americans today are paying somewhere around 30 percent in income tax.)

Here are two exceptions:

- ✔ Tax-free municipal bonds where there is neither a capital gain nor a capital loss, nor is the bondholder subject to any alternative minimum tax.

- ✔ Bonds held in a tax-advantaged account, such as an IRA or a 529 college savings plan.

"Risk-free" Investing: U.S Treasury Bonds

There are umpteen different kinds of debt securities issued by the U.S. Treasury. *Savings bonds,* which can be purchased for small amounts and come in certificate form (making for nice bar mitzvah and birthday gifts), are but one kind. In fact, when investment people speak of *Treasuries,* they usually are not talking about savings bonds. Rather, they're talking about larger-denomination bonds known formerly as *Treasury bills, Treasury notes,* and *Treasury bonds* that are issued only in electronic (sometimes called *book-entry*) form.

All U.S. Treasury debt securities, whether a $50 savings bond or a $1,000 Treasury note, share four things in common:

✔ Every bond, an IOU of sorts from Uncle Sam, is backed by the "full faith and credit" of the United States government and, therefore, is considered by most investors to be the safest bet around.

✔ Because it is assumed that any principal you invest is absolutely safe, Treasury bonds, of whatever kind, tend to pay relatively modest rates of interest — lower than other comparable bonds, such as corporate bonds, that may put your principal at some risk.

✔ True, the United States government is very unlikely to go bankrupt anytime soon, but Treasury bonds are nonetheless still subject to other risks inherent in the bond market. Prices on Treasury bonds, especially those with long-term maturities, can swoop up and down like hungry hawks in response to such things as prevailing interest rates and investor confidence in the economy.

✔ All interest on U.S. government bonds is off-limits to state and local tax authorities (just as the interest on most municipal bonds is off-limits to the Internal Revenue Service). But you do pay federal tax.

Beyond these four similarities, the differences among U.S. government debt securities are many and, in some cases, like night and day.

Savings bonds for beginning investors

U.S. savings bonds make for popular gifts, in part because they are, unlike other Treasury debt securities, available in pretty certificate form. You can buy them from just about any bank or directly from the Treasury at www.treasurydirect.gov. You don't have to buy them in certificate form; from the Web site, you can also buy an electronic savings bond, which is registered online (no paper involved).

Book II

Basic Investments: Stocks, Bonds, Mutual Funds, and More

Savings bonds are a natural for small investors because you can get started with as little as $25. With that money, you can buy a bond that has $50 printed on it but won't actually be worth $50 for some time to come. At the current interest rate that savings bonds are paying (3.60 percent), you would have to wait 20 years until the true value caught up with the face amount.

Aside from the (optional) certificates and the ability to invest a small amount, a third thing that makes savings bonds unique among Treasury debt securities is that they are strictly non-marketable. When you buy a U.S. savings bond, either direct from the government or from a bank, you either put your own name and Social Security number on the bond or the name and Social Security number of someone you're gifting it to. You or that person is then entitled to receive interest from that bond. The bond itself cannot be sold to another buyer. This is in stark contrast to Treasury bills and bonds that can, and often do, pass hands more often than poker chips.

Among savings bonds, there are two kinds sold today: EE (or Patriot) bonds and I bonds.

EE (Patriot) bonds

EEs and Patriot bonds are one and the same. The word *Patriot* was added to some, but not all, EE bonds in 2001. Whatever you want to call them, EE bonds are the most traditional kind of savings bond. Series EE bonds carry a face value of twice what you purchase them for. They are *accrual bonds,* which means that they accrue interest as the years roll on even though you aren't seeing any cash. You can pay taxes on that interest as it accrues, but in most cases it makes more sense to defer paying the taxes until you decide to redeem the bond. Uncle Sam allows you to do that.

EE bonds are nonredeemable for the first year you own them, and if you hold them fewer than five years, you surrender three months of interest. EEs are available in eight different denominations, from $50 up to $10,000. Any individual can buy up to $30,000 in EE savings bonds a year (or a face amount of $60,000).

If you use your savings bonds to fund an education, the interest may be tax-free.

I bonds

These babies are built to buttress inflation. Issued in the very same denominations as EE bonds, the I Series bonds offer a fixed rate of return plus an adjustment for rising prices. Every May 1 and November 1, the Treasury announces both the fixed rate for all new I bonds and the inflation adjustment for all new and existing I bonds. After you buy an I bond, the fixed rate is yours for the life of the bond. The inflation rate adjusts every six months. You collect all your interest only after cashing in the bond. (That is called *accrual* interest.)

The dinosaurs: Old bonds

Other kinds of savings bonds pre-date today's EE and I bonds. Each series of the past has its own peculiarities, but since you won't be buying any of them, there's no need to get into detail. Suffice to say that some of the older bonds are still paying interest, and others are not. If you have any questions on the status of a savings bond you have tucked away in the back of your sock drawer, you can simply type the serial numbers into the Savings Bond Calculator at www.treasurydirect.gov, or jot down the serial number and write a letter to

Bureau of the Public Debt
P.O. Box 7012
Parkersburg, WV 26106-7012

The Bureau of the Public Debt needs a written and signed request from the owner of the bond, at which point it will tell you whether the bond is still earning interest, when it will stop paying interest, and how much you could redeem it for today.

Book II

Basic Investments: Stocks, Bonds, Mutual Funds, and More

The rules and parameters for I bonds are pretty much the same as they are for EEs: You have to hold them a year, and if you sell within five years, you pay a penalty. There's a limit to how many I bonds you can invest in — $30,000 a year, per person. And in certain circumstances, the proceeds may become tax-free if used for education expenses.

If you plan to hold I bonds as a long-term investment (longer than a year or two), you should be more concerned with the fixed rate, which will be in effect throughout the life of the bond, than the inflation adjustment, which will vary. You can purchase I Bonds at your bank or by visiting www.treasury direct.gov.

Treasury bills, notes, and bonds for more serious investing

About 98 percent of the approximately $5 trillion in outstanding Treasury debt is made up not of savings bonds but of *marketable* (tradable) securities known as bills, notes, and bonds. This "bills, notes, and bonds" stuff can be a little confusing because technically they are all bonds. They are all backed by the full faith and credit of the U.S. government. They are all issued electronically (you don't get a fancy piece of paper as you do with savings bonds). They can all be purchased either directly from the Treasury or through a broker. They can all trade like hotcakes. The major difference among them is the time you need to wait to collect your principal:

- ✔ Treasury bills have maturities of a year or less.

- ✔ Treasury notes are issued with maturities from two to ten years.

- ✔ Treasury bonds are long-term investments that have maturities of 10 to 30 years from their issue date.

The bills, like savings bonds, are sold at a discount from their face value. You get the full amount when the bill matures. The notes and bonds, on the other hand, are sold at their face value, have a fixed interest rate, and kick off interest payments once every six months. The minimum denomination for all three is $1,000, and you can buy them all in any increment of $1,000.

Keep in mind that you don't have to hold any of these securities (bills, notes, or bonds) till maturity. You can, in fact, cash out at any point. The longer until the maturity of the bond, however, the more its price can fluctuate and, therefore, the more you risk losing money.

Treasury Inflation-Protected Securities (TIPS)

Like the I bonds, Treasury Inflation-Protected Securities (TIPS) receive both interest and a twice-yearly kick up of principal for inflation. As with interest on other Treasury securities, interest on TIPS is free from state and local income taxes. Federal income tax, however, must be coughed up each year on both the interest payments and the growth in principal.

TIPS, unlike I bonds, are transferable. You can buy TIPS directly from the Treasury or through a broker. They are currently being issued with terms of 5 and 10 years, although there are plenty of 20-year term TIPS in circulation. The minimum investment is $1,000.

One of the sweet things about TIPS is that if inflation goes on a rampage, your principal moves north right along with it. If *deflation,* a lowering of prices, occurs (which it hasn't since the 1930s), you won't get any inflation adjustment, but you won't get a deflation adjustment, either. You'll get back at least the face value of the bond.

TIPS sound great, and in many ways they are. But be aware that the coupon rate on TIPS varies with market conditions and tends to be minimal — perhaps a couple of percentage points. If inflation is calmer than expected moving into the future, you will almost certainly do better with traditional Treasuries. If inflation turns out to be higher than expected, your TIPS will be the stars of your fixed-income portfolio.

Industrial Returns: Corporate Bonds

When it comes to adding stability to a portfolio — the number one reason that bonds belong in your portfolio — Treasuries and investment-grade (high quality) corporate bonds are your two best choices. If you look at some of the worst economic times in our nation's history, corporate investment-grade (high quality) bonds have held up remarkably well. By including both Treasuries *and* corporate bonds in your portfolio you get the best of both worlds. Of course, the key is knowing which corporate bonds to consider and which to steer clear of.

Keep in mind that corporate bonds are not without their challenges. To put it bluntly, corporate bonds can be something of a pain in the pants, especially when compared to Treasury bonds. The following sections outline the issues you need to think about when investing in corporate bonds.

Giving credit ratings their due

If the company goes down, you may lose some or all of your money. Even if the company doesn't go down but merely limps, you can lose some or all of your money. For that reason, you need to pay attention to some crucial credit ratings.

Appropriately weighing potential risk and return is what good investing is all about. As for the risk and return on corporate bonds, the potential return (always something of a guessing game) is quoted in terms of yield, and there are many kinds of yield. The most oft-quoted kind of yield, used for example by *The Wall Street Journal* and most other business papers, is the *yield-to-maturity* (refer to the earlier section "Various types of yield").

The largest determinant of the risk and return you take on a bond is the fiscal muscle of the company behind the bond. That fiscal muscle is measured by a company's credit ratings.

Revisiting your ABCs

There's an entire industry devoted to rating companies by their financial strength. The most common ratings come from Moody's and Standard & Poor's, but there are other rating services, such as Fitch Ratings, Dominion, and A.M. Best. Your broker, I assure you, subscribes to at least two of these services and will be happy to share the ratings with you.

The highest ratings — Moody's Aaa and Standard & Poor's AAA — are the safest of the safe among corporate bonds, and those ratings are given to few corporations. If you lend money to one of these stellar companies, you should expect in return a rate of interest only modestly higher than Treasuries. As you progress from these five-star companies down the ladder, you can expect higher rates of interest to compensate you for your added risk. Table 2-1 shows how Moody's, Standard and Poor's, and Fitch define corporate bond credit quality ratings.

Table 2-1	Corporate Bond Credit Quality Ratings		
Credit Risk	*Moody's*	*Standard & Poor's*	*Fitch*
Investment grade			
Tip-top quality	Aaa	AAA	AAA
Premium quality	Aa	AA	AA
Near-premium quality	A	A	A
Take-home-to-Mom quality	Baa	BBB	BBB
Not investment grade			
Borderline ugly	Ba	BB	BB
Ugly	B	B	B
Definitely don't-take-home-to-Mom quality	Caa	CCC	CCC
You'll be extremely lucky to get your money back	Ca	CC	CC
Interest payments have halted or bankruptcy is in process	C	D	C
Already in default	C	D	D

If you are going to invest in individual bonds, diversification through owning multiple bonds becomes more important as you go lower on the quality ladder. There's a much greater risk of default down there, so you'd be awfully foolish to have all your eggs in a basket rated Caa or CCC. (*Default* in bond-talk means that you bid adieu to your principal.)

One risk inherent to corporate bonds is that they may be downgraded, even if they never default. Say a bond is rated A by Moody's. If Moody's gets moody and later rates that bond a Baa, the market will respond unfavorably. Chances are, in such a case, that the value of your bond will drop. Of course, the opposite is true, as well. If you buy a Baa bond and it suddenly becomes an A bond, you'll be sitting pretty. If you wish to hold your bond to maturity, such downgrades and upgrades are not going to much matter. But should you decide to sell your bond, they can matter very much.

It's a very good idea to diversify your bonds not only by company but also by industry. If there is a major upheaval in, say, the utility industry, the rate of both downgrades and defaults is sure to rise. In such a case, you would be better off not having all utility bonds.

Gauging the risk of default

How often do defaults occur? According to a study by the folks at Moody's covering the years 1970 to 2005, the odds of a corporate bond rated Aaa defaulting were rather miniscule: 0.36 percent within 10 years and 0.64 percent within 20 years. Of all corporate bonds, only about 2 percent are given that gloriously high rating.

As you move down the ladder, as you would expect, the default numbers jump. Bonds rated A can be expected to default at a rate of 0.87 percent over 10 years and 1.55 percent over 20 years. Among Baa bonds, 11.40 percent can be expected to go belly up within a decade, and 13.84 percent within two decades.

By the time you get down to Caa bonds, the rate of default is generally expected to be about 40 times that of Aaa bonds — approximately 14 percent within one decade and 26 percent within two decades. (Of course, these rates can vary greatly with economic conditions.)

Going for high-yield bonds (or not)

There is no distinct line between investment-grade and high-yield bonds, sometimes known as *junk* bonds. But generally, if a bond receives a rating less than a Baa from Moody's or a BBB from Standard & Poor's, the market considers it high-yield.

High-yield bonds offer greater excitement for the masses. The old adage that risk equals return is clear as day in the world of bonds. High-yield bonds offer greater yield than investment-grade bonds, and they are more volatile. But they are also one other thing: much more correlated to the stock market. In fact, Treasuries and investment-grade corporate bonds aren't correlated to the stock market at all. So if bonds are going to serve as ballast for your portfolio, which is what they do best, why would anyone want high-yield bonds? In my opinion, you wouldn't, regardless of whether good times or bad times are coming:

> ✔ **If the economy is strong,** then companies are making money, the public is optimistic, and stocks are going to sail. So may high-yield bonds, but stocks historically return much more than high-yield bonds. Stocks have a century-old track record of returning about five percentage points more than high quality bonds. And, unless you have those bonds in a retirement account, you're going to pay income tax on the interest. Most of the gain

Book II

Basic Investments: Stocks, Bonds, Mutual Funds, and More

in your stocks, however, won't be taxed at all until you sell the stock. Even then, it will most likely be taxed as capital gains — 15 percent — which is probably lower than your income tax.

✔ **If the economy starts to sour** and companies start closing their doors, then stocks will fall and high-yield bonds very likely will too. In 2000, for example, when the stock market started to crumble, a basket of high-yield bonds would have lost between 3 and 4 percent. That's not a tragedy, but the last thing you want is for your bonds to turn south right along with your stocks.

If you *really* want junk bonds in your portfolio, take a serious look at foreign high-yield bonds, especially the bonds of emerging-market nations, which can make a lot of sense. That's because they don't have much, if any, correlation to the ups and downs on Wall Street. And if you're wealthy (or not-so-wealthy but you choose to ignore my advice) and decide to invest in individual high-yields anyway, know that the broker markups can sometimes kill you.

Calculating callability

One consideration that pertains to corporate bonds but not to Treasuries is the nasty issue of *callability*. There's a chance that the issuing company may call in your bond and spit your money back in your face at some terribly inopportune moment, such as when prevailing interest rates have just taken a tumble. Treasuries aren't called. Corporate bonds, as well as municipal bonds and agency bonds, often are. And that can make a huge difference in the profitability of your investment.

If you own a callable bond, chances are that it will be called at the worst moment — just as interest rates are falling and the value of your bond is on the rise. At that moment, the company that issued the bond, if it has the right to issue a call, no doubt will. And why not? Interest rates have fallen. The firm can pay you off and find someone else to borrow money from at a lower rate.

Because calls aren't fun, callable bonds must pay higher rates of interest.

If you're inclined to go for that extra juice that comes with a callable bond, I say fine. *But,* you should always do so with the assumption that your callable bond will be called. With that in mind, ask the broker to tell you how much (*after* taking his markup into consideration) your yield will be between today and the call date. Consider that a worst-case-yield. (It is often referred to as *yield-to-worst-call,* sometimes abbreviated YTW.) Consider it the yield you'll get. And compare that to the yield you'll be getting on other comparable bonds. If you choose the callable bond and it winds up not being called, hey, that's gravy.

Some squirrelly bond brokers, to encourage you to place your order to buy, will assure you that a certain callable bond is unlikely to be called. They may be right in some cases, but you should never bank on such promises.

Coveting convertibility

The flip side of a callable bond is a *convertible* bond. Some corporate bond issuers sell bonds that can be converted into a fixed number of shares of common stock. With a convertible bond, a lender (bondholder) can become a part owner (stockholder) of the company by converting the bond into company stock. Having this option is a desirable thing (options are always desirable, no?), and so convertible bonds generally pay lower interest rates than do similar bonds that are not convertible.

If the stock performs poorly, there is no conversion. You are stuck with your bond's lower return (lower than what a nonconvertible corporate bond would get). If the stock performs well, there is a conversion. So you win, so to speak.

Convertible bonds, which are fairly common among corporate bonds, introduce a certain measure of unpredictability into a portfolio. Perhaps the most important investment decision you can make is how to divide your portfolio between stocks and bonds. With convertibles, whatever careful allotment you come up with can be changed overnight. Your bonds suddenly become stocks. You are rewarded for making a good investment. But just as soon as you receive that reward, your portfolio becomes riskier. It's the old trade-off in action.

Book II

Basic Investments: Stocks, Bonds, Mutual Funds, and More

Lots of Protection: Agency Bonds

You've no doubt heard the story of the three blind, er, sight-impaired men and the elephant . . . how the first man touches the tail and assumes the elephant is like a snake; the second touches the tusk and assumes the elephant is like a spear; and the third touches the side of the animal and assumes the elephant is like a wall. Welcome to the touch-me, feel-me, open-to-wide-interpretation world of agency bonds! Don't get me wrong. There are some good investments to be had here. All you have to do is figure out the tusk from the tail. The following sections give you an overview.

Slurping up your alphabet soup

Who or what issues agency bonds? Governmental agencies or quasi-governmental agencies, like the Federal Farm Credit Banks (FFCB), the Federal Home Loan Mortgage Corporation (FHLMC), the General Services Administration (GSA), the Small Business Administration (SBA), the Tennessee Valley Authority (TVA), and the U.S. Agency for International Development (USAID).

The first thing to know about these (and the many other) government agencies is that they fit under two large umbrellas. Some of them really are U.S. federal agencies; they are an actual part of the government just as are Congress, the jet engines on Air Force One, and the fancy silverware at the White House. Such official agencies include the General Services Administration, the Government National Mortgage Association, and the Small Business Administration. The U.S. Post Office also once issued bonds but has not done so lately.

Most of the so-called agencies, however, aren't quite parts of the government. They are, technically speaking, *government-sponsored enterprises* (GSEs): corporations created by Congress to work for the common good but then set out more or less on their own. Many of these are publicly held, issuing stock on the major exchanges. Such pseudo-agencies include the Federal Home Loan Mortgage Corporation and the Federal National Mortgage Association.

What's the difference between the two groups, especially with regard to their bonds? The first group (the official-government group) issues bonds that carry the full faith and credit of the U.S. government. The second group, well, their bonds carry a mysterious implicit guarantee that the U.S. government will bail them out in times of trouble. Because this second group is much larger than the first — both in terms of the number of agencies and the value of the bonds they issue — when investment experts speak of "agency bonds," they are almost always talking about the bonds of the GSEs.

Because of the very small risk of default inherent in agency bonds and the greater risk of price volatility due to public sentiment, agency bonds tend to pay higher rates of interest than Treasury bonds, although not a heck of a lot more. The spread between Treasuries and the faux-agency bonds is typically within half a percentage point, if even that much. As for the real government agencies, such as the Small Business Administration, which issue bonds backed by the full faith and credit of the U.S. government, the difference in yield between their bonds and Treasuries would be so small as to be almost immeasurable.

Introducing the agency biggies

To give you an idea of what GSEs are and what they do, this section describes the three largest (and most popular with retail investors) issuers of agency bonds: the Federal National Mortgage Association (known colloquially as *Fannie Mae*), the Federal Home Loan Mortgage Corporation (*Freddie Mac*), and the Federal Home Loan Banks.

Federal National Mortgage Association (Fannie Mae)

Fannie Mae, which dates back to 1968, raises money by selling bonds. It then turns some of that money over to banks. The banks use the money to make loans, mostly to homebuyers (believe it or not, 63 million homebuyers and counting).

Most Fannie Mae bonds (generally available in increments of $1,000) are purchased by institutions: insurance companies, other nation's central banks (especially China's), university endowments, and so on. But individual investors are certainly welcome to join in the fun, too. The agency issues bonds of varying maturities; and, naturally, there's a large secondary market where you can find any maturity from several months to many years down the pike. Fannie Mae sounds like a public agency, but it is really a private corporation with government oversight. For more information, see `www.fannie mae.com`.

If you believe that agency debt belongs in your portfolio (it certainly isn't a necessity, but it's a good option for many investors), Fannie Mae bonds may be an okay choice. It all depends on the price your broker offers you. Note that Fannie Mae bonds may be traditional interest-bearing bonds, or they may be mortgage-backed bonds.

Federal Home Loan Mortgage Corporation (Freddie Mac)

This agency (which is also, technically, a private corporation tied to the government) was formed in 1970 and is very similar to Fannie Mae. So are its multitude of bond issues with their many maturities, denominations of $1,000, and choice of traditional or mortgage-backed.

Freddie Mac buys one residential mortgage every seven seconds and, by so doing, helps to finance one in six homes in the United States. Most of the mortgages are purchased from primary lenders (such as your neighborhood bank). With the money those lenders get from Freddie Mac, they can go out and make more loans. Like Fannie Maes, most Freddie Macs are bought by institutions. For more information, see `www.freddiemac.com`.

Book II

Basic Investments: Stocks, Bonds, Mutual Funds, and More

Federal Home Loan Banks

This is not a single agency but a coalition of 12 regional banks formed in 1932. Its mission is to fund low-income housing and housing projects. The money used for the funding comes from — you guessed it — selling bonds. *Lots* of bonds.

This coalition is far and away the largest issuer of so-called agency bonds. These bonds are a bit more popular with individual investors than Freddies and Fannies — as well they should be, at least for those in higher tax brackets: The interest earned is exempt from state and local taxes. For more information, see www.fhlbanks.com.

Like Fannies and Freddies, the FHLB bonds come in many different flavors as far as denominations and maturities.

Comparing agency bonds

All agency bonds are considered high quality with very little risk of default. The honest-and-true federal agencies, such as the Small Business Administration (SBA), are said to have no risk of default; therefore, their bonds pay more or less what Treasuries do. You may get a smidgen more interest (maybe 5 basis points, or 5/100 of 1 percent) to compensate you for the lesser *liquidity* of such agency bonds (the lesser ability to sell them in a flash).

The majority of agency bonds are issued by government-sponsored enterprises (GSEs), and the risk of default, although real, is probably next to nothing. You get a higher rate of interest on these bonds than you do with Treasuries to compensate you for the fact that the risk of default does exist.

With all agency bonds, you pay a markup when you buy and sell, which you don't with Treasuries if you buy them directly from the government. If you're not careful, that markup could easily eat up your first several months of earnings. It also could make the difference between agency bonds and Treasury bonds a wash.

Most agency bonds pay a fixed rate of interest twice a year. About 25 percent of them are *callable,* meaning that the agencies issuing the bonds have the right to cancel the bond and give you back your principal. The other 75 percent are non-callable bonds (sometimes referred to as *bullet* bonds). Callable bonds tend to pay somewhat higher rates of interest, but your investment takes on a certain degree of uncertainty.

Investing in individual agency bonds, or individual bonds of any kind, for that matter, is not an activity for poor people. Although you may be able to get into the game for as little as $1,000, bond brokers typically mark up such small transactions to the point that they simply don't make sense. I wouldn't suggest even looking at individual agency bonds unless you've got at least $50,000 to invest in a pop. Otherwise, you should be looking at bond funds, or individual Treasuries that you can buy without paying any markup whatsoever.

When choosing among different agencies, you want to carefully compare yields-to-maturity and make sure that you know full well whether you are buying a traditional bond or a mortgage-backed security. They are totally different animals.

The taxes you pay on agency bonds vary. Interest from bonds issued by Freddie Mac and Fannie Mae is fully taxable. The interest on most other agency bonds — including the king of agency bonds, the Federal Home Loan Banks — is exempt from state and local tax.

Book II
Basic Investments: Stocks, Bonds, Mutual Funds, and More

(Almost) Tax-free Havens: Municipal Bonds

If not for the fact that municipal bonds are exempt from federal income tax, they would likely be about as popular as buttermilk at a college keg party. On the day I'm writing this chapter, for example, high quality munis with maturities of five years out are yielding an average of 3.75 percent. Five-year Treasuries, meanwhile, are currently yielding 4.75 percent — about one-quarter more the return. (Keep in mind that Treasuries aren't exactly world-famous for their high returns.) And while the munis carry some (limited) risk, the Treasuries do not. But of course, munis *are* tax-exempt.

The issuers of municipal bonds include, of course, municipalities (duh), such as cities and towns. But they also include counties, public universities, certain private universities, airports, not-for-profit hospitals, public power plants, water and sewer administrations, various and sundry nonprofit organizations, bridge and tunnel authorities, housing authorities, and an occasional research foundation.

Any government, local agency, nonprofit, or what-have-you that is deemed to serve the public good, with a blessing from the Securities and Exchange Commission and the IRS (and sometimes voters), may have the honor of issuing a municipal bond.

Comparing and contrasting with other bonds

The tax-exempt status of munis is unquestionably their most notable and easily recognizable characteristic — the equivalent of Kojak's cue ball or Groucho Marx's mustache.

Like most bonds, munis come with differing maturities. Some mature in a year or less, others in 20 or 30 years. Unlike most bonds, munis tend to be issued in minimal denominations of $5,000 and multiples of $5,000 (not a minimum of $1,000 and multiples of $1,000, like corporate bonds and Treasuries).

Like many corporate bonds, but unlike Treasuries, many municipal bonds are *callable,* meaning the issuer can kick back your money and sever your relationship before the bond matures. Like other bonds, the interest rate on munis is generally fixed, but the price of the bond can go up and down; unless you hold your bond to maturity, you may or may not get your principal returned whole. If the maturity is many years off, the price of the bond can go up and down considerably.

The tax-exempt status of munis isn't the only reason they may belong in your portfolio. Municipal bonds also offer a fair degree of diversification, even from other bonds. Because they are the only kind of bond more popular with households than with institutions, the muni market is swayed more by public demand than the markets for other bonds. For example, when the stock market tanks and individual investors get butterflies in their stomachs, they tend to sell out of their stock holdings (often a mistake) and load up on what they see as less risky investments, such as munis. When the demand for munis goes up, it tends to drive prices higher. Popular demand or lack of demand for munis typically affects their prices more than it does the price of corporate bonds and Treasuries. Those taxable bonds, in contrast, tend to be more interest-rate sensitive than munis.

Realizing that all cities (or bridges or hospitals) are not created equal

Like the corporations that issue corporate bonds, the entities (cities, hospitals, universities, and so on) that issue municipal bonds are of varying economic strength — although the degree of variance isn't nearly as large as it is in the corporate world. One study looked at bond defaults between the years 1970 and 2000. Of all the muni bonds rated by credit-rating agency Moody's during that 30-year period (about 80 percent of the dollar volume of all municipal offerings), only 18 defaults occurred. That compares to 819 corporate-bond defaults during the same period.

Of those 18 municipal defaults reported in the study, 10 were healthcare facilities. All the defaulted bonds were revenue bonds; none were general obligation bonds. *General obligation bonds* are secured by the full faith and credit of the issuer and are typically supported by that issuer's power to tax the hell out of the citizenry, if necessary. *Revenue bonds'* interest and principal are secured only by the revenue derived from a specific project. If the project goes bust, so does the bond.

Enjoying low risk

The same study from Moody's also found a huge difference in recovery rates of munis as compared to other bonds. The *recovery rate* is the amount of money bondholders get back after the dust of a default settles. On defaulted munis from 1970 to 2000, the recovery rate was 66 percent of the face value of the bonds. In contrast, the poor corporate bondholders got back only 42 percent of the face value on their defaulted bonds.

So by and large, municipal bonds are very safe animals — at least those rated by the major rating agencies (such as Moody's), which are the vast majority of munis. If the mild nature of the beast weren't enough to put your investing soul at ease, know that roughly two-thirds of municipal bonds issued today come insured; you can't lose your principal unless the issuer *and* its insurance company go under, which is very unlikely! And even if the insurance company were to fail, the general feeling among industry insiders is that most states would be very, very reluctant to allow one of their cities to default on a general obligation bond.

Rating munis

Municipal bonds, like corporate bonds, are rated by the major bond-rating agencies. But they have their very own rating system. (If municipalities were rated using the corporate ratings, almost all would hug the very top of the scale.) Table 2-2 shows the ratings used by three major bond-rating agencies: Moody's, Standard & Poor's, and Fitch.

Book II

Basic Investments: Stocks, Bonds, Mutual Funds, and More

Table 2-2	Municipal Bond Credit Quality Ratings		
Credit Risk	*Moody's*	*Standard & Poor's*	*Fitch*
Prime	Aaa	AAA	AAA
Excellent	Aa	AA	AA
Upper medium	A	A	A
Lower medium	Baa	BBB	BBB
Speculative	Ba	BB	BB
Very speculative	B	B	B
Very, very speculative	Caa	CCC	CCC
In default	Ca, C	CC, C, D	CC, CCC, D

Choosing from a vast array of possibilities

You definitely want munis that are rated. Some municipal offerings are not rated, and these can be risky investments or very *illiquid* (you may not be able to sell them when you want, if at all). I suggest going with the top-rated munis: Moody's Aaa or Aa. The lower rated munis may give you a wee bit extra yield but probably are not worth the added risk. (Keep in mind that a lower rated bond can be more volatile than a high rated bond. Default isn't the only risk.)

Of course, you also want to choose a municipal bond that carries a maturity you can live with. If the bond is callable, well, is that something you can live with and be happy with? Callable bonds pay slightly higher coupon rates but are less predictable than noncallable bonds.

But perhaps most importantly, because the tax-free status of the muni is undoubtedly a prime motivation for buying a muni in the first place, you want to consider whether you want to buy a national muni or a state muni, and if you buy a state muni, do you want double- or triple-tax-free? Here's the scoop:

✔ *National munis* are exempt from federal tax but are not necessarily exempt from state income tax. (Some states tax bond coupon payments and others do not.)

✔ *State munis,* if purchased by residents of the same state, are typically exempt from state tax, if there is one. Some, but not all, state munis are also exempt from all local taxes.

✔ Munis that are exempt from both federal and state tax are called *double-tax-free* bonds. Those exempt from federal, state, and local tax are often referred to as *triple-tax-free* bonds.

To decide which kind of muni — national or state, double- or triple-tax-free — consult your tax adviser before laying out any big money on munis. The tax rules are complicated and forever changing. Some states impose taxes on you if you invest in other states' munis; others do not. Some states even tax you if you invest in munis in your own state. Certain bonds issued in Puerto Rico and other U.S. territories are free from almost all taxation regardless of where you live. It's a jungle out there!

Municipal bonds, like any tax-free investment, make most sense in a taxable account. In fact, I'd say that putting a muni into any kind of tax-advantaged account, such as an IRA or Roth IRA, makes about as much sense as putting a kidney pie on a vegetarian buffet. If you're looking to fill your IRA with fixed-income investments, don't be looking at munis. Taxable bonds provide greater return, and if the taxes can be postponed (as in an IRA) or avoided (as in a Roth IRA), then taxable bonds are almost always the way to go.

Book II

Basic Investments: Stocks, Bonds, Mutual Funds, and More

Taxes you may pay, even for a muni

There are instances, rare as they may be, where taxes can grab you from behind and make you not want to wake up on the morning of April 15.

✔ **The AMT tax:** The alternative minimum tax is a federal tax that exists in a parallel universe, which you enter unwillingly when you make a fair chunk of change, claim too many exemptions, or take too many deductions. Ask your tax guru if you are likely to be smacked by AMT at any point in the near future. If so, you may want to hand-pick your munis (and muni funds) to include only those that are exempt from the AMT.

✔ **Capital gains taxes:** If you buy a security at a certain price and then sell it at a higher price, that's a good thing! But you may be subject to pay capital gains tax to the IRS . . . even if the security you sold is a tax-exempt municipal bond. (The tax rules governing municipal zero-coupon bonds bought at a discount and then sold at a lesser discount or a premium can be complicated; talk to your tax advisor.) What pertains to individual bonds also pertains to municipal bond mutual funds. Sell your shares for more than you purchased them, and you'll have to pay capital gains. Of course, if you sell at a loss, whether a bond or a bond fund, you may then declare a capital-gains tax loss, which is usually used to write off capital gains.

Chapter 3

Getting to Know Mutual Funds

- -

In This Chapter

▶ Finding out what mutual funds are

▶ Sorting through the many types of mutual funds

▶ Understanding sales loads

▶ Researching your fund and its features

- -

*A*lthough most people should have exposure to the stock market, it's really hard for an individual investor to make money trading single stocks. To reduce portfolio risk, you should hold about 30 different stocks, and it takes a lot of money and time to accumulate that. You could buy individual bonds, as well, but minimum prices start at $1,000, making it costly to build a diversified portfolio of those. What if you don't have a lot of money to get started? What if you don't have a lot of time to spend analyzing securities and making trades? What if there were easier ways to invest?

Well, there is an easier way. It's called the mutual fund, and in this chapter, I cover all you need to get started making money with this popular, powerful investment vehicle.

Defining the Mutual Fund

A mutual fund is an investment company registered with the U.S. Securities and Exchange Commission under the Investment Company Act of 1940. Simple, huh? Each individual mutual fund is a stand-alone company that contracts with an investment manager who takes the money of all the fund investors and buys securities on their behalf.

Because thousands of different shareholders in the fund pool their money together, the investment manager can buy a diverse portfolio of securities. And because managing money is her full-time job, she can do lots of research that may help her to choose securities that collectively will beat the market. Alternatively, she may decide to simply invest in the market, or a big slice of it, and not pick securities. Such funds, which tend to be the least expensive, are known as *index* funds, and I discuss them later in this chapter.

Mutual funds are popular investments. At the end of 2006, the Investment Company Institute, which is the industry's largest trade organization, reported that Americans held $10.4 trillion in 8,726 different open-end mutual funds. This represents 23.2 percent of household financial assets.

Each of the thousands of mutual funds falls into two main categories: open-end and closed-end. Which type you choose affects your rights and your costs of buying and selling, as well as your potential profit, so you'll want to know the difference.

Open-end funds

Most mutual funds sold in the United States are *open-end mutual funds*. This means that you buy and sell shares directly from the fund, and the fund company continually issues and redeems new shares. If you invest $1,000 in the fund, the total fund size grows by $1,000. If you cash in $1,000 of your shares, the fund shrinks by $1,000. This means that there is always a market for the fund shares. If the fund doesn't have enough cash to meet its redemptions, the portfolio manager — the person who invests the money — sells some of the securities to raise the funds.

In an open-end fund, the share value is its *net asset value* (NAV), which is the total value of all the securities in the fund divided by the total number of shares that the fund has issued. Shares never trade for more or less than the NAV. There may be an additional sales charge, called a *load,* which I discuss in more detail later in this chapter.

Closed-end funds

Closed-end funds are relatively rare, with only about 650 of them compared to the almost 9,000 open-end funds on the market. These funds do not buy and sell their shares continuously. Instead, the fund organizers collect money from investors all at once and then do an initial public offering of stock (just like a regular company would). The fund's portfolio managers invest the money, and investors who want to buy or sell shares in the fund do so through the exchange, trading the closed-end fund shares just as they would the shares of any other public company.

Now, if markets were truly efficient, a closed-end fund's share price would be its net asset value (NAV): the value of all the securities divided by the total number of shares outstanding. After all, you know what the securities are worth because the fund company has to report it every day. Why would you pay more than that, and why would someone else let you get away with paying less? Well, it turns out that closed-end funds rarely trade at NAV. Instead, they usually trade at a discount. (And yes, this irritates the heck out of academics who hold a fervent belief in market efficiency.)

Some investors like to buy closed-end funds just for the bargain. They wait until the share price is well below the NAV, then they swoop in. In some cases, closed-end fund shareholders have forced the fund managers to either disband the fund or convert it to an open-ended fund in order to eliminate the discount.

Knowing How Big Fund Companies Fit In

Legally, each mutual fund is its own company. So what about the big brand-name fund companies like Fidelity, T. Rowe Price, and Vanguard? What do they do? Well, legally, these firms are money management companies that handle the investment, marketing, and sales of the different mutual funds that use their name, and they are often known as *fund complexes* or *families of funds*. They come up with new fund ideas, then form mutual fund companies that will pay a fee to the money management company for these services. When you buy a mutual fund, you become a shareholder in the mutual fund, not in the fund management complex.

Although each fund has its own board of directors, the board of directors usually goes along with the fund management company's decisions. But not always. It's rare, but boards have on occasion become fed up with the management company's services, dropping the arrangement and giving the management contract to a different firm.

Meeting Myriad Types of Mutual Funds

Mutual fund managers don't just invest willy-nilly. Instead, they take your money and invest it in specific types of securities to meet a specific investment objective, which is described in the fund's *prospectus*. That's a legal document that an open-end fund must keep on file at the Securities and Exchange Commission (SEC) and make available to anyone who wants to buy shares in the fund. (Closed-end funds issue a prospectus when they are organized; after that, they must file annual reports with the SEC.)

The investment objective gives you a sense of the fund's expected return — and the expected amount of risk that the fund will take. That information helps you make decisions about whether the fund is right for you. Because the prospectus also tells you about the fund's investments, you'll have a sense of how it works with other investments you have. After all, one way to reduce your total risk is to diversify (see Book I, Chapter 1).

Book II

Basic Investments: Stocks, Bonds, Mutual Funds, and More

Return is your reward for taking risk. The higher the expected return, the higher the amount of risk that an investment has.

Stock funds

Stock funds, also called *equity funds,* invest in shares of stock of different companies. These represent partial ownership in the companies, and they should go up in price when the company does well and down in price when it does not. Stock funds make it easy for investors to get exposure to a wide range of companies, helping them get better long-term performance than they can probably get on their own. Stock funds are usually designed to generate capital gains, which mean that they try to rate profits by buying the stock at one price and selling it at a higher one.

Stock funds fall into many different styles, because the fund managers usually concentrate on specific market sectors or types of stocks. There are lots of different categories of stock funds, and it seems like more emerge each year as markets change and fund managers get great new ideas. Following are descriptions of some that you may come across.

Growth funds

Growth funds invest in growth stocks. They look for companies that are developing new products and new markets, that have good control over their expenses, and that are expected to grow their profits faster than the average company trading in the stock market. Investors choose growth funds when they are looking to get a high return on their money, especially if they are saving their money for a long time, as for retirement. That way, the investors can live through the downside risk to reap gains in the great years.

Some growth fund managers specialize in small, medium, or large companies. In general, small company stocks offer greater long-term returns (with greater risk), while larger company stocks have lower returns and lower risk.

Value funds

Many companies and stocks do not perform well. They may have problems with a product, the management may not be doing a good job, or maybe the companies are great but no one seems to know it. These stocks may be great bargains, and that's what value fund managers look for. They want to buy companies when they are cheap, then collect the profits when the business is sold or when it improves. Value investors have to be patient, as it can take a while for the rest of the market to see that these stocks are underpriced. But when and if that happens, the value fund will be sitting pretty.

Index funds

Market returns are measured by indexes, which hold a large number of stocks and are designed to demonstrate the performance of the market in general. One of the best known of these is the Standard & Poor's 500 index (S&P 500), which aggregates the prices of 500 large U.S. companies. Others include the Dow Jones Industrial Average, which has 30 very large companies in it, and the Russell 3000, which is an average of the prices of the 3,000 largest public companies in the United States. See Book I, Chapter 2 for more details on indexes.

An index fund is designed to mimic the performance of one of the indexes, performing no better and no worse. The fund manager buys all the securities in the index in equal proportion, using futures (contracts designed to generate the same return as the index) to help if it is difficult to buy the right securities on any given day while also handling purchases and redemptions.

 Most investors find that index funds are an easy, low-cost way to match market performance. They are popular with novice investors who are uncertain about making choices among all the funds out there, as well as with experienced investors who appreciate the inexpensive way to get good performance.

Sector (or specialty) funds

Want a mutual fund that invests just in electric utilities, health care companies, or real estate? If so, you want a specialty fund. These invest in specific industries, to the exclusion of all others. The fund managers tend to know what's happening in their sectors inside and out. The downside is that these funds offer less diversification; if technology stocks are out of favor, your technology fund probably won't be doing very well even if the rest of the stock market is going gangbusters.

International funds

Many great investment opportunities can be found outside of the United States, and that's the appeal of international funds. Some of these funds specialize in a specific region, like Europe, or in specific types of markets, like developing economies. International funds give you exposure to returns available in other countries, and you don't have to learn a new language, figure out the currency issues, or master different accounting systems — the international fund manager does that for you.

A variant, the global fund, invests anywhere in the world, at home or abroad.

Bond funds

Want to take on less risk than the stock market in exchange for a more predictable return? Then maybe a bond fund is right for you. Bonds are essentially loans in which the issuing company, government, or agency is borrowing money from the bond investor. In exchange, the investor receives a regular interest payment. See Chapter 2 in this book for the details about bonds.

Bond funds pool money from many investors to buy a diversified portfolio of bonds, often with different maturities and interest rates. But few bond managers want to buy everything that comes out, so they specialize. Read on for descriptions of some of the most common types of bond funds.

U.S. government bond funds

The U.S. government is running a huge deficit at the time I write this chapter, and most likely, it will still have a deficit when you read it. To finance this deficit, the government borrows money. But no matter how big the deficit gets, these bonds are free from bankruptcy risk. The U.S. government owns printing presses and can print off money. This means that it is almost impossible for the government to default on its loans.

Some U.S. government bond funds invest in all sorts of securities issued by the government and its agencies, while others specialize. Most government issues are known as *Treasuries,* and Treasury is often shortened to *T. T bonds* are those that mature in ten years or more. *T notes* mature in less than ten years but more than one year. Those treasuries that mature in less than one year are known as *T bills.*

In addition to Treasuries, the U.S. government backs bonds issued by entities that are affiliated with the government. These are known as *agency securities,* and they are often issued by such mortgage guarantee agencies as Fannie Mae, Freddie Mac, and Ginnie Mae. See Chapter 2 in this book for much more detail.

Corporate bond funds

Corporations often borrow money to build new factories, make acquisitions, or simply finance continuing operations. They often do this by issuing bonds. Corporate bonds have some risk because the company can go bankrupt and refuse to pay back the money that it borrowed. Many rating services evaluate a company's financial performance and assign a rating that affects the interest rate that the company pays, just as the credit bureaus evaluate an individual's financial performance and assign a credit score that affects the interest rate you pay on your mortgage. Some funds invest only in higher-quality bonds, while others look for opportunities among less credit-worthy bond offerings (known as *junk bonds* or *high-yield bonds*), trading off the higher risk for the higher interest rates.

Municipal bond funds

Many state and local governments need to raise money, and the federal government gives them a nice little advantage to help them do so at relatively low interest costs: It exempts the interest income on these bonds from federal taxes. Many states also give a tax break on income from these bonds, known as *municipal bonds* (often shortened to *munis*), even if they are issued by a state entity. Municipal bonds are of most interest to individual investors in a high tax bracket looking for high current income. They are not appropriate for retirement or college savings accounts because those accounts usually have their own tax advantages.

Most municipal bond funds invest all over the country, but a few specialize only in the bonds from certain states, especially New York and California. (No surprise, these are populous states with high income tax rates.) State-specific funds rarely make sense for people who live elsewhere.

International bond funds

Companies and governments around the world need to borrow money, and international bond funds are happy to loan it to them. Investors may find better returns and increased diversification benefits from international bond funds, especially if exchange rates happen to move in favorable ways.

Many international investments offer great returns in the foreign currency that disappear when converted back to U.S. dollars. Many fund managers use hedging techniques to reduce this risk, but exchange rate risk can have a real effect on your return — positive or negative.

Some international bond funds organize themselves around a currency or region, buying both corporate and government bonds from the area. Others invest only in corporate bonds or only in government bonds.

Total return funds

Most stock fund managers look to get capital gains, while bond fund managers try to generate interest income. But suppose you want an investment that offers both income and appreciation? That's the goal of a total return fund, also called a *balanced fund*. These funds invest in a mix of stocks and bonds to get a better return than is available with most bond funds with less risk than with most stock funds.

Many fund companies offer a type of total return fund called a *target fund*. It's designed for investors who are saving money for retirement or other long-term goals. The fund managers adjust the investment strategy over time, generally investing in riskier investments in the earlier years and more conservative ones as the fund gets closer to the target date.

Money market funds

Are you looking for a safe investment that pays a higher return than you can get from a bank CD or savings account? You may want to consider a money market mutual fund. These funds invest in such short-term investments as one-month jumbo bank CDs, Treasury bills, and corporate overnight securities, which are one-day loans to companies that may have a temporary mismatch between when their bills are due and when their customers pay them. The short time frame means that the risk is very low, so money market funds effectively function like cash. In fact, many mutual fund management companies allow their money market fund customers to write checks on their accounts.

A money market mutual fund is not federally insured, so your investment is not guaranteed. That being said, the risk is extremely low, and money market investors have rarely lost money. The funds are managed to maintain a net asset value of $1.00 per share; some fund management companies have added their own money to poorly performing funds in order to avoid "breaking the buck."

Keeping a Close Eye on Sales Charges

A *load* is a sales charge, and many mutual funds have them. Sometimes this charge compensates a broker or financial planner for helping you manage your money, and other times it's just pure profit to the fund company for services that they need to provide anyway. Because loads reduce the amount of money that you invest, they affect your total investment return. I describe different types of loads here so that you know what you are up against.

If you are getting good advice from a broker or a financial planner before you buy the fund, it may be worth your while to pay a load. If you are making the entire investment decision yourself, you should seek funds that do not have loads. Why compensate someone else for the work you've done?

No-load funds

A no-load fund is a fund with no sales charge. These are becoming rare as more investors use outside advisors and as more fund companies look for ways to increase profits. With a no-load fund, you may buy and sell shares directly from the fund company, or from a brokerage house. You make the decisions and take the responsibility for your choices. In exchange for investigating the fund yourself, you save the sales fee.

If you buy a mutual fund in your 401(k) or other employer retirement plan, you probably won't pay a load, no matter how the fund is sold to other types of accounts. You may pay a 12b-1 fee, though, which is similar to a load and is described in an upcoming section.

Front-end load funds

With a front-end load fund, the investor pays a sales charge at the time the investment is made. In most cases, the charge is shared between the fund management company and the broker or financial planner who recommended the fund. If you are buying a mutual fund through one of these advisors, you will almost definitely pay a front-end load. And that may not be the only load you pay.

Some good funds carry high front-end loads because they are sold through brokers and financial planners. However, the fund companies may also allow customers of discount brokerage firms to buy these funds directly at a lower, or even no, sales charge. One such operation is the Charles Schwab Mutual Fund OneSource (www.schwab.com). If you like to make your own decisions, consider buying funds that way.

Most load funds have breakpoints, which means that the percentage of the sales charge goes down as you invest more money. For example, the load may be 4 percent of the first $1,000 invested, 3 percent of the second $1,000, and 1 percent on amounts over $2,000. Some unscrupulous advisors have been known to charge the highest load on the entire investment. Check to make sure this doesn't happen to you.

Back-end load funds

Some funds levy a sales charge when you take money out of the fund. This way, you get to put all of your money to work up front, so it may be cheaper for you than a front-end load.

In some cases, the load is charged only if the money is in the fund for a short period of time, in which case, it's known as a *contingent deferred sales charge.* This contingent load compensates the fund company for the upfront costs of opening the account, and it discourages fund investors from trading in and out of their accounts. (And that's as it should be, because mutual funds aren't really appropriate for traders with short time horizons.) After the customer has proven that he or she is a long-term investor, no sales charge will be levied on redemption.

12b-1 fees

In 1980, the SEC decided to allow mutual fund companies to charge an ongoing sales charge. The paragraph of the law is Rule 12b-1, and hence the fees are known as 12b-1 fees. And doesn't that sound nicer than "license to print money"?

Most funds charge 12b-1 fees these days, and that's why there are so few true no-load funds anymore. These fees are usually small — maybe 0.25 percent per year — but they come out of your investment performance. They compensate the fund company for its ongoing marketing costs, meaning that you pay for the fund company to clog your mailbox with ads to get you to invest more money. If you work with a financial advisor, part of the 12b-1 fee will go toward paying an ongoing commission for keeping you up-to-date on the fund.

To be honest, I think that 12b-1 fees are vaguely immoral. I don't see why I should pay for ads that I don't want, nor do I see why customer service from the fund company is an extra frill requiring a special charge. After all, it's already making plenty of money from me. Furthermore, I don't use a financial advisor! But here's the thing: 12b-1 fees are hard to avoid. That's why you need to pay attention to a fund's performance after all fees are paid, not the amount charged in any one fee category.

Some funds charge very high 12b-1 fees — as much as 1.25 percent. It's difficult to generate enough performance to offset that amount, especially in a low-risk, low-return investment like a bond fund. There are very few cases where a 1.25 percent 12b-1 fee is worth the money.

Being a Savvy Mutual Fund Investor

Mutual fund investing is one of the easiest ways for an individual investor to set up a cost-effective, diversified portfolio that will help generate returns to meet long-term financial goals. While it may be easier to get started in mutual funds than in other types of financial vehicles, you should still do some work to make sure that the fund you invest in is right for you right now. You also want to understand the effects of fees and the rights you may have. All the fun stuff is in the fine print, and here, I help you navigate it.

Doing the research

Before you buy a mutual fund, you want to do some upfront research on the fund, its investment style, and its historical performance to make sure it fits your risk and return objectives. How are you going to do that?

The fund company will give you some information, and you can find more yourself. (If you are using a broker or financial planner, he or she should help with the research.) Different research services, magazines, and newspapers evaluate mutual funds and offer information on news and trends that affect mutual fund investors. Here are a few of the many that you should check out:

- ✔ *The Wall Street Journal:* No newspaper covers U.S. finance as thoroughly as *The Wall Street Journal,* so its mutual fund information is detailed. Every quarter, the *Journal* publishes a special mutual funds section. Almost every day, it publishes news about funds. And its Web site, www.wsj.com, includes searchable databases and screens that can help you make fund decisions.

- ✔ **Morningstar:** Morningstar is an investment research company that makes its data available to investors at its Web site, www.morningstar.com. The company was founded to cover mutual funds, and it continues to offer thorough news and research, including rankings of fund performance relative to the market and relative to the funds' investment style.

- ✔ **Lipper:** Although its services are primarily for fund companies, not for individual investors, Lipper (www.lipper.com) has news and performance information that you may find useful.

The goal of investing is to buy low and sell high. Unfortunately, many mutual fund investors get this all wrong: they *chase return.* They buy the fund that was last year's top-performing fund in the top-performing sector, hoping that the performance will continue; inevitably, they buy at the very high and watch the fund go down. When evaluating performance, look for a fund and fund manager who offer consistent performance relative to their sector, not relative to the market as a whole. Sometimes, the right fund to buy is one that performed poorly last year.

Reading the prospectus

Under Federal law, anyone soliciting your money for a mutual fund must give you a *prospectus,* which is a legal document describing how the fund will invest its money, listing all the fees, and laying out any rights you may have. Your financial advisor will give you a prospectus when making fund recommendations, and fund companies that sell shares directly to investors will put the prospectus on their Web sites.

It will look dull. You will be tempted to push it aside to read later, and of course, "later" will never arrive. Instead, pull it out and take a look. Once you read it, you'll understand the mutual fund better and have a good sense of whether or not it is a good one for your situation.

Although you should read the whole thing, pay particular attention to two sections: the fees and the share classes.

Fees

All mutual funds charge fees, but some charge higher fees than others. You need to know what they are to see if you are getting your money's worth. These fall into several categories:

- ✔ **Management fees:** Management fees go to the investment advisor to cover the costs of research services and the salaries of the investment analysts and portfolio managers who work on the fund. In general, these fees will be higher for actively-managed equity funds and lower for bond funds and index funds.

- ✔ **Distribution charges, loads, and 12b-1 fees:** These fees, described earlier in the chapter, compensate the fund and brokers and financial planners who recommend it for their sales and advisory services.

- ✔ **Other expenses:** These include legal costs, auditing fees, and fees paid to fund directors, and they are usually quite low.

When these costs are added together, you end up with the *expense ratio,* which is the total percentage of the fund that is charged to expenses each year. Expenses come off the top to reduce your performance, so in general, the lower the expense ratio, the better for you. However, there are funds that perform well enough to justify a high expense ratio, so be sure to consider the expense ratio along with the performance.

Share classes

Many mutual fund companies divide their portfolio up into different classes of shares. Every investor buys into the same underlying investments, but holders of different share classes are charged different fees and may have different rights for reinvestment and redemption. For example, investors who buy shares directly from the fund buy one class of shares, those who work with a financial planner buy a different class, and those who are buying shares through a qualified retirement plan at work buy yet another class.

When you read the prospectus, make sure you check the expenses and features for the share class that applies to you.

Making the investment

So how do you actually make an investment in a mutual fund? Well, if you are buying shares from the fund company directly, you fill out a paper form and mail in a check, or you fill out an online form and transfer money from your bank account. If you buy from a broker or financial planner, the process is similar, but you may be transferring money from your brokerage account or writing the check to the planning firm.

After you make that initial investment, you may want to consider adding more money to the fund. You can do this by simply writing another check or making another transfer from your bank account. Or, you can set up an automatic withdrawal program where the fund company takes a set amount of money from your bank account every month. That way, you never even consider spending the money.

I think the main advantage of an automatic withdrawal program is that it forces you to take care of your own financial needs and to spend less money than you make now. Sure, some months you are buying shares at higher prices than other months, but over the long run, the consistent investment habit should pay off handsomely for you.

Handling the taxes

Mutual funds themselves are exempt from paying federal taxes. Neat, huh? But there's a catch: The funds push the tax obligations on to you.

Now, if your mutual fund investment is part of such qualified retirement plans as IRAs or 401(k)s, you won't have to pay taxes on the fund until you withdraw the money, if you even have to then. (It depends on how your plan is set up, and that information is beyond the scope of this chapter!) Many qualified college savings plans that use mutual funds have similar tax benefits, so investigate those before you open the account.

If your mutual fund investment is not part of a retirement or college account, you'll probably have to pay taxes on the fund's income and capital gains. If you do, in January the mutual fund company will send you a year-end tax form that tells you the fund's dividends and its capital gains distributions. If the fund had any of these, you will need to put the amounts on your own tax return and pay the taxes accordingly.

When you cash in shares in the fund, you'll trigger another tax event, which is the capital gain. In general, this is the percentage change between the net asset value when you bought the fund and the net asset value when you sold the fund, and your fund company will probably send you a form before your tax return is due telling you how much of a gain you have. (You may also have a capital loss, in which case, you'll likely qualify for a tax write-off.)

These taxes may not be onerous; right now in the United States, the tax rate on dividends and long-term capital gains is just 15 percent. Of course, this could well change when you are doing your taxes, so be sure to check on the most recent rates and regulations before April 15 of whatever year you are in.

Book II

Basic Investments: Stocks, Bonds, Mutual Funds, and More

Chapter 4

The ABCs of ETFs

*T*here are, no doubt, a good number of pinstriped ladies and gentlemen in and around Wall Street who froth heavily at the mouth when they hear the words *exchange-traded fund.* In a world of very pricey investment products and very lucratively paid investment-product salespeople, ETFs are the ultimate killjoys.

Since their arrival on the investment scene in the early 1990s, more than 600 ETFs have been created, and they have grown faster in asset accumulation than any other investment product. And that is a good thing. ETFs have allowed the average American investment opportunities that do not involve shelling out fat commissions or paying layers of ongoing, unnecessary fees. And they've saved investors oodles and oodles in taxes.

Hallelujah.

Defining ETFs

Just as a deed shows that you have ownership of a house, and a share of common stock certifies ownership in a company, a share of an ETF represents ownership (most typically) in a basket of company stocks. Originally, ETFs were developed to mirror various indexes:

  ✔ The SPDR 500 (ticker SPY) represents stocks from the S&P 500, an index of the 500 largest companies in the United States.

  ✔ The DIAMONDS Trust Series 1 (ticker DIA) represents the 30 underlying stocks of the Dow Jones Industrial Average index.

  ✔ The NASDAQ-100 Trust Series 1, otherwise known as *Qubes* (ticker QQQQ), represents the 100 stocks of the NASDAQ-100 Index.

Since ETFs were first introduced, many others, tracking all kinds of things, have emerged.

Okay, so why buy a basket of stocks rather than individual stock? Quick answer: You'll sleep better. Compared to the world of individual stocks, the stock market as a whole is as smooth as a morning lake. If you're not especially keen on roller coasters, then you are advised to put your nest egg into not one stock, not two, but many. If you have a few million sitting around, hey, no problem diversifying. Maybe individual stocks are for you. But for most of us commoners, the only way to effectively diversify is with ETFs or mutual funds (which you can read about in Chapter 3 of this book).

Advantages of ETFs

Mutual funds also represent baskets of stocks or bonds, but ETFs offer quite a few advantages that mutual funds don't. Table 4-1 compares ETFs and mutual funds (with stocks thrown in for good measure), and the following sections explain the key differences — and advantages — in more detail.

Table 4-1 ETFs Versus Mutual Funds Versus Individual Stocks			
	ETFs	*Mutual Funds*	*Individual Stocks*
Priced, bought, and sold throughout the day?	Yes	No	Yes
Offer some investment diversification?	Yes	Yes	No
Is there a minimum investment?	No	Yes	No
Purchased through a broker or online brokerage?	Yes	Yes	Yes
Do you pay a fee or commission to make a trade?	Yes	Sometimes	Yes
Can you buy/sell options?	Yes	No	Sometimes
Indexed (passively managed)?	Usually	Not usually	No
Can you make money or lose money?	Yes	Yes	You bet

Lower fees

In the world of mutual funds, the average management fee at present, according to Morningstar, is 1.67 percent (of the account balance) annually. That may not sound like a lot of money, but it is a very substantial sum. In the world of ETFs, the expenses are much, much lower, averaging 0.40 percent, and many of the more traditional domestic indexed ETFs cost no more than 0.20 percent a year in management fees. A handful are under 0.10 percent.

Lower capital gains taxes

Unless your money is in a tax-advantaged retirement account, making money in the markets means that you have to fork something over to Uncle Sam at year's end. Before there were ETFs, individual securities had a big advantage over funds in that you were only required to pay capital gains taxes when you actually enjoyed a capital gain. With mutual funds, that isn't so. The fund itself may enjoy a capital gain by selling off an appreciated stock, but you pay the capital gains tax regardless of whether you sell and regardless of whether the share price of the mutual fund increased or decreased since the time you bought it.

Because ETFs are index-based, there is generally little turnover to create capital gains. To boot, ETFs are structured in a way that insulates shareholders from having to pay capital gains tax, as mutual fund shareholders must often do, when other shareholders cash in their chips.

What you see is what you get

A key to building a successful portfolio, right up there with low costs and tax efficiency, is diversification. You cannot diversify optimally unless you know exactly what's in your portfolio. With a mutual fund, you often have little idea of what stocks (if any) the fund manager is holding. When you buy an ETF, you get complete transparency. You know exactly what you are buying. No matter what the ETF, you can see on the prospectus or on the ETF provider's Web site (or on any number of independent financial Web sites) a complete picture of the ETF's holdings.

Index advantage

Index funds, which buy and hold a fixed collection of stocks or bonds, consistently outperform actively managed funds. Here are some reasons that index funds (both mutual funds and ETFs) are hard to beat:

- They typically carry much lower management fees, sales loads, or redemption charges.
- Hidden costs — trading costs and spread costs — are much lower when little trading is done.
- They don't have cash sitting around idle as the manager waits for what he thinks is the right time to enter the market.

Book II

Basic Investments: Stocks, Bonds, Mutual Funds, and More

Why the big boys prefer ETFs

When ETFs were first introduced, they were primarily of interest to institutional traders — insurance companies, hedge fund people, banks — who often have investment needs considerably more complicated than yours and mine.

Trading in large lots: Prior to the introduction of ETFs, there was no way for a trader to instantaneously buy or sell, in one fell swoop, hundreds of stocks or bonds. Because they trade both during market hours and, in some cases, after market hours, ETFs made that possible. Institutional investors also found other things to like about ETFs. For example, ETFs are often used to quickly put cash to productive use or to fill gaps in a portfolio by allowing immediate exposure to an industry sector or geographic region.

Savoring the versatility: ETFs, unlike mutual funds, can also be purchased with limit, market, or stop-loss orders, taking away the uncertainty involved with placing a buy order for a mutual fund and not knowing what price you're going to get until several hours after market close. And because ETFs can be sold short, they provide an important means of risk management. If, for example, the stock market takes a dive, *shorting* ETFs — selling them now at a locked-in price with an agreement to purchase them back (cheaper) later on — may help keep a portfolio afloat. For that reason, ETFs have become a darling of hedge fund managers who offer the promise of investments that won't tank should the stock market tank.

Other things to know about ETFs

Okay, so on the plus side of ETFs we have ultra-low management expenses, super tax efficiency, transparency, and a lot of fancy trading opportunities, such as shorting, if you are so inclined. What about the negatives? Here are some other facts about ETFs that you should consider before parting with your precious dollars.

Calculating commissions

You have to pay a commission every time you buy and sell an ETF. Here's the good news: Trading commissions for stocks and ETFs (it's the same commission for either) have been dropping faster than the price of desktop computers. What once would have cost you a bundle, now — if you trade online, which you definitely should — is really pin money, perhaps as low as $4 a trade. However, you can't simply ignore trading commissions. They aren't always that low, and even $4 a pop can add up.

Moving money in a flash

The fact that ETFs can be traded throughout the day like stocks makes them, unlike mutual funds, fair game for day-traders and institutional wheeler-dealers. For the rest of us common folk, there isn't much about the way that ETFs are bought and sold that makes them especially valuable. Indeed, the ability to trade throughout the day may make you more apt to do so, perhaps selling or buying on impulse, which (although it can get your endorphins pumping) is generally not the most profitable investing strategy.

Getting in on the Action

Buying ETFs isn't all that difficult. You find a brokerage house (or supplier), open an account, and place an order, either by phone or online. The following sections have the details.

Choosing a brokerage house

You — you personally — can't just buy a share of an ETF as you would buy, say, a negligee. You need someone to actually buy it for you and hold it for you. That someone is a broker, sometimes referred to as a *brokerage house* or a *broker-dealer*.

Here are the some things you want from any broker who is going to be holding your ETFs:

- ✔ Reasonable prices. Comparing the prices at brokerage houses is anything but easy because each house identifies its own pricing criteria: Some base prices on how much money you have in your account or how many trades you make per quarter; others use that criteria but also consider the number of shares you trade at any particular point, and so on.

- ✔ Good service (they pick up the phone without putting you through voicemail hell) and good advice (if you think you're going to need advice).

- ✔ A user-friendly Web site (or, if you like doing business with real human beings, a service center near you).

- ✔ Incentives for opening an account, which can run the gamut from a certain number of free trades to laptop computers.

The following sections give an overview of some of the major brokerage houses and a brief look at their pricing. Before choosing, always look at the entire brokerage package, which includes not only the price of trades but total account fees.

The Vanguard Group

At Vanguard, the trading commissions are middle of the road, and the service is middle of the road. What really shines about Vanguard is its broad array of top-rate index mutual funds. I know, I know, this is a chapter about ETFs. But index mutual funds and ETFs are close cousins, and sometimes it makes a lot of sense to have both in a portfolio. If you do wish to hold Vanguard index mutual funds alongside your ETFs, Vanguard is a logical place to hold them because you can buy and sell Vanguard funds, provided you don't do it often, at no charge. You can find Vanguard at `www.vanguard.com` or 800-992-8327.

Fidelity Investments

Fidelity has great service, and the price of trades is competitive. Fidelity also has some excellent low-cost index funds of its own, which you may wish to keep alongside your ETF portfolio. And the Fidelity Web site has some really good tools — some of the best available — for analyzing your portfolio and researching new investments. You can find Fidelity at `www.fidelity.com` or 800-343-3548.

T. Rowe Price

This Baltimore-based shop has several claims to fame, including its bend-over-backward friendliness to small investors and its plethora of really fine financial tools, especially for retirement planning, available to all customers at no cost. The price of trading is a wee bit higher than average. The service is excellent (reps tend to be very chummy). Go to `www.troweprice.com` or call 800-225-5132.

TD AMERITRADE

The trading prices at TD are just about middle of the pack, and the service is reputedly quite high. The Web site has a very clean and crisp feel to it. On the down side (in my opinion, of course), the TD culture and many of the articles on the Web site promote frequent trading, as opposed to, say, Vanguard, where the culture is decidedly more buy-and-hold. Find TD at `www.tdameritrade.com` or 800-454-9272.

What happens if your brokerage house collapses?

Brokerage houses, as part of their registration process with the federal government, are automatically insured through the Securities Investor Protection Corporation (SIPC). Each individual investor's securities are protected up to $500,000 should the brokerage house go belly up. Larger brokerage houses generally carry supplemental insurance that protects customers' account balances beyond the half-million that SIPC covers. TD AMERITRADE, for example, has insurance through Lloyd's of London that protects each customer's account up to $150 million.

Note: Neither SIPC coverage nor any kind of supplemental insurance will protect the value of your account from a market downfall! For additional information on SIPC, you can order the free brochure by calling 1-800-934-4448 or checking out its Web site at `www.sipc.org`.

ShareBuilder

At an unheard-of $4 a trade, or even less if you're willing to pay a monthly fee, you can't beat ShareBuilder for price. The catch is that you have to commit to regular trades. You need to make trades (investing as little as $25) once a week or once a month. Find out more at www.sharebuilder.com or 800-747-2537.

Other major brokerage houses

Here are a few more to consider:

- ✔ **Charles Schwab:** 866-232-9890; www.schwab.com. I've never liked Schwab, because of its high trading costs, but just as I was writing this chapter, the firm lowered its fees across the board.

- ✔ **E*TRADE:** 800-387-2331; www.etrade.com. Not only can you house your ETFs with E*TRADE, but you can refinance the mortgage on your house, as well.

- ✔ **TIAA-CREF:** 800-842-2776; www.tiaa-cref.org. I've heard pretty good things about TIAA, but I can't work with them directly because I'm not a teacher. This brokerage house works only with people who have chalk under their nails. (If you're married to someone with chalk under the nails, you qualify, too.)

Opening an account

When you open an account with a brokerage house. you'll be asked a zillion questions:

- ✔ **Retirement or non-retirement account?** If you want a retirement account, you need to specify what kind (IRA? Roth IRA? SEP?).

- ✔ *Margin* **account or** *cash* **account?** A margin account is somewhat similar to a checking account with overdraw protection. It means that you can borrow from the account or make purchases of securities (such as ETFs, but generally not mutual funds) without actually having any cash to pay for them on the spot. Cool, huh?

Unless you have a gambling addiction, go with margin. You never know when you may need a quick and potentially tax-deductible loan. But, before you blithely begin to buy on margin, read the next paragraph for dire warnings!

Margin buying is very dangerous business. The stock market is risky enough. Don't ever compound that risk by borrowing money to invest. You may wind up losing not only your nest egg but your home. In addition, the brokerage house can usually change the rate of interest you're paying without notice, and if your investments dip below a certain percentage of your margin loan, the brokerage house can sell your stocks and bonds from right under you. Margin only with great caution.

✔ **Beneficiaries and titling (or registration)?** Be certain that who you name is who you want to receive your money if you die. Beneficiary designations supercede your will.

✔ **Your employment, your wealth, and your risk tolerance?** Don't sweat them! Federal securities regulations require brokerage houses to know something about their clients, but honestly, I don't think anyone ever looks at the personal section of the forms.

Placing an order to buy

After your account is in place, you're ready to buy your first ETF. ETFs are usually traded just as stocks are traded. Same commissions. Mostly the same rules. Same hours (generally 9:30 a.m. to 4:00 p.m., Manhattan Island time). Through your brokerage house, you can buy 1, 2, or 10,000 shares.

Most brokerage houses give you a choice: Call in your order, or do it yourself online. Calling is typically much more expensive; place all your orders online. If you need help, a representative of the brokerage house will walk you through the process step-by-step — at no expense to you.

Keep in mind when trading ETFs that the cost of the trades, if substantial enough, can nibble seriously into your holdings. To avoid such nibbling, don't trade often (buy and hold, buy and hold, buy and hold!) and don't bother with ETFs if the trade is going to cost you more than half of 1 percent.

Managing risk with ETFs

Asking how risky, or how lucrative, ETFs are is like trying to judge a soup knowing nothing about the soup itself, only that it is served in a blue china bowl. The bowl — or the ETF — doesn't create the risk; what's inside it does. Thus stock and real estate ETFs tend to be more volatile than bond ETFs. Short-term bond ETFs are less volatile than long-term bond ETFs. Small-stock ETFs are more volatile than large-stock ETFs. And international ETFs often see more volatility than U.S. ETFs.

To minimize risk and maximize return, diversify. Include both stocks and bonds and both domestic and international holdings in your portfolio. You also need to diversify the domestic stock part of a portfolio, and that part's a bit trickier since not even the experts agree on how to accomplish that. Two competing methods predominate, and either is fine (as is a mixture of both for those with good-sized portfolios):

✔ Divide the portfolio into domestic and foreign, and then into different styles: large cap, small cap, mid cap, value, and growth.

✔ Divide the portfolio up by industry sector: healthcare, utilities, energy, financials, and so on.

Exploring ETF Options Galore

As of this writing, more than 600 ETFs are available. To help you wade through the choices, the following sections introduce a few that may be worth a look, divided according to style or type of ETF.

Today, all competent investment pros develop their portfolios with at least some consideration given to the cap size and growth or value orientation of their stock holdings. *Capitalization* or *cap* refers to the combined value of all shares of a company's stock. The following divisions are generally accepted:

✔ **Large caps:** Companies with over $5 billion in capitalization

✔ **Mid caps:** Companies with $1 billion to $5 billion in capitalization

✔ **Small caps:** Companies with $250 million to $1 billion in capitalization

Anything from $50 million to $250 million would usually be deemed a *micro cap*. And your local pizza shop, if it were to go public, might be called a *nano cap (con aglio)*. There are no nano cap ETFs. For all the other categories, there are ETFs to your heart's content.

Blended options for large cap exposure

All the expense ratios, average cap sizes, price/earnings ratios, and top five holdings listed here (and elsewhere) are subject to change. Before making a purchase, be sure to get the most recent data.

Among the *blended* (large cap value and growth) options for smaller portfolios ($10,000 to $20,000), consider these ETFs.

Vanguard Large Cap ETF (VV)

Indexed to: MSCI U.S. Prime Market 750 Index (750 corporate biggies from both the value and growth sides of the grid)

Expense ratio: 0.07 percent

Average cap size: $44.8 billion

P/E ratio: 17.6

Top five holdings: Exxon Mobil Corp., General Electric, Microsoft, Citigroup, Bank of America

iShares S&P 500 (IVW)

Indexed to: S&P 500 (500 of the biggest and most stable U.S. companies)

Expense ratio: 0.09 percent

Average cap size: $47.0 billion

P/E ratio: 16.0

Top five holdings: General Electric, Exxon Mobil Corp., Citigroup, Microsoft, Procter & Gamble

Rydex S&P 500 Equal Weight (RSP)

Indexed to: S&P 500, but each of the 500 companies in the index is given equal weight rather than the traditional market weighting

Expense ratio: 0.40 percent

Average cap size: $11.5 billion

P/E ratio: 16.3

Top five holdings: 500 stocks share equal weights (each about 0.25 of the portfolio)

Strictly large growth

For large growth and large growth alone (complimented by large value, of course) — a position for people with adequate assets ($20,000+) — the four options listed here all provide good exposure to the asset class at very reasonable cost. You may also want to consider an offering from Rydex.

Vanguard Growth ETF (VUG)

Indexed to: MSCI U.S. Prime Market Growth Index (400 of the nation's largest growth stocks)

Expense ratio: 0.11 percent

Average cap size: $41.8 billion

P/E ratio: 22.2

Top five holdings: Microsoft, Procter & Gamble, General Electric, Johnson & Johnson, International Business Machines

iShares Morningstar Large Growth (JKE)

Indexed to: Morningstar Large Growth Index (105 of the largest and most growthy U.S. companies)

Expense ratio: 0.25 percent

Average cap size: $30.75 billion

P/E ratio: 28.9

Top five holdings: Microsoft, Johnson & Johnson, Cisco Systems, Intel, PepsiCo

iShares S&P 500 Growth (IVW)

Indexed to: S&P 500/Citigroup Growth Index (300 of the largest growth companies in the land, chosen from the S&P 500 universe)

Expense ratio: 0.18 percent

Average cap size: $19.1 billion

P/E ratio: 18.3

Top five holdings: Microsoft, Exxon Mobil Corp., Procter & Gamble, Pfizer, Johnson & Johnson

Rydex S&P 500 Pure Growth (RPG)

Indexed to: Approximately 140 of the most growthy of the S&P 500 companies

Expense ratio: 0.35 percent

Average cap size: $23.4 billion

P/E ratio: 19.1

Top five holdings: International Game Technology, Nvidia, XTO Energy, Forest Laboratories, Express Scripts

Book II

Basic Investments: Stocks, Bonds, Mutual Funds, and More

Large value stock best buys

In the past 77 years, large value stocks have enjoyed an annualized growth rate of 11.4 percent, versus but 9.5 percent for large growth stocks — with roughly the same volatility. Thanks to ETFs, investing in value was never easier.

Vanguard Value ETF

Indexed to: MSCI U.S. Prime Market Value Index (400 or so of the nation's largest value stocks)

Expense ratio: 0.11 percent

Average cap size: $45.1 billion

P/E ratio: 14.6

Top five holdings: Exxon Mobil Corp., Citigroup, Bank of America, Pfizer, General Electric

iShares Morningstar Large Value (JKF)

Indexed to: Morningstar Large Value Index (94 of the largest U.S. value stocks)

Expense ratio: 0.25 percent

Average cap size: $37.6 billion

P/E ratio: 12.7

Top five holdings: Exxon Mobil Corp., Citigroup, Bank of America, Pfizer, Altria Group

iShares S&P 500 Value (IVE)

Indexed to: S&P 500/Citigroup Value Index (355 large value candidates plucked from the companies that make up the S&P 500)

Expense ratio: 0.18 percent

Average cap size: $15.7 billion

P/E ratio: 15.6

Top five holdings: Citigroup, General Electric, Bank of America, JPMorgan Chase & Co., Exxon Mobil Corp.

Rydex S&P 500 Pure Value (RPV)

Indexed to: Approximately 150 of the most valuey of the S&P 500 companies

Expense ratio: 0.35 percent

Average cap size: $17.7 billion

P/E ratio: 30.9

Top five holdings: Ryder Systems, Dillard's, United States Steel, Ford Motor Company, Albertsons

Small cap blend funds

Some pretty good ETF options for people with limited portfolios include the following.

Vanguard Small Cap ETF (VB)

Indexed to: MSCI U.S. Small Cap 1750 Index (1,750 broadly diversified smaller U.S. companies)

Expense ratio: 0.10 percent

Average cap size: $1.6 billion

P/E ratio: 23.8

Top five holdings: Western Digital Corp., Martin Marietta Materials, AMR Corporation, Vertex Pharmaceuticals, Oshkosh Truck Corp.

iShares Morningstar Small Core (JKJ)

Indexed to: 383 companies from the Morningstar Small Core Index that fall somewhere between growth and value

Expense ratio: 0.25 percent

Average cap size: $865 million

P/E ratio: 19.8

Top five holdings: Integrated Device Technology, Walter Industries, Manitowoc Co., Jones Lang Lasalle, Sierra Pacific Resources

Book II

Basic Investments: Stocks, Bonds, Mutual Funds, and More

iShares S&P Small Cap 600 (IJR)

Indexed to: Roughly 600 companies that make up the S&P Small Cap 600 Index

Expense ratio: 0.20

Average cap size: $883 million

P/E ratio: 17.5

Top five holdings: Oshkosh Truck Corp., NVR, Cimarex Energy Co., Frontier Oil Corp., Resmed

Strictly small cap growth funds

If you have enough assets to warrant splitting up small value and small growth, go for it.

Vanguard Small Cap Growth ETF (VBK)

Indexed to: MSCI U.S. Small Cap Growth Index (approximately 970 small growth capitalization companies in the United States)

Expense ratio: 0.12 percent

Average cap size: $1.6 billion

P/E ratio: 28.8

Top five holdings: Western Digital Corp., AMR Corp., Vertex Pharmaceuticals, Oshkosh Truck Corp., The Corporate Executive Board

iShares Morningstar Small Growth Index (JKK)

Indexed to: Approximately 370 companies from the Morningstar Small Growth Index

Expense ratio: 0.30 percent

Average cap size: $850 million

P/E ratio: 28.3

Top five holdings: Rambus, Silicon Laboratories, PMC-Sierra, Hologic, Trimble Navigation Ltd.

iShares S&P Small Cap 600 Growth (IJT)

Indexed to: 354 holdings from the S&P Small Cap/Citigroup Growth Index

Expense ratio: 0.25 percent

Average cap size: $734 million

P/E ratio: 16.7

Top five holdings: NVR, Cimarex Energy Co., Global Payments, Frontier Oil Corp., Resmed

Rydex S&P 600 Small Cap Pure Growth (RZG)

Indexed to: Approximately 140 of the smallest and most growthy of the S&P 600 companies

Expense ratio: 0.35

Average cap size: $1.2 billion

P/E ratio: 27.5

Top five holdings: Coinstar, Biolase Technology, Ceradyne, Christopher & Banks Corp., Odyssey HealthCare

Diminutive dazzlers: Small value ETFs

Look at the list of some the top ten companies represented in the Vanguard Small Value ETF and you probably won't recognize them. If you wanted to pick one of these companies to sink a wad of cash into, I would tell you that you're crazy. But if you wanted to sink that cash into the entire small value index, well, that's another matter. Assuming you can handle some risk, your odds of making money are pretty darned good — at least if history is our guide.

Whatever your total allocation to domestic small cap stocks, I recommend that 60 to 75 percent of that amount be allocated to small value.

Vanguard Small Cap Value ETF (VBR)

Indexed to: MSCI U.S. Small Cap Value Index (about 950 small value domestic companies)

Expense ratio: 0.12 percent

Average cap size: $1.6 billion

P/E ratio: 20.1

Top five holdings: Camden Property Trust REIT, Conseco, Federal Realty Investment Trust REIT, Harsco, Ryder System

iShares Morningstar Small Value Index (JKL)

Indexed to: 338 of Morningstar's Small Value Index

Expense ratio: 0.30 percent

Average cap size: $910 million

P/E ratio: 15.5

Top five holdings: Foster Wheeler Ltd., Trinity Industries, Ciena Corp., Brandywine Realty Trust, New Century Financial Corp.

iShares S&P Small Cap 600 Value Index (IJS)

Indexed to: 457 of the S&P Small Cap 600/Citigroup Value Index

Expense ratio: 0.25 percent

Average cap size: $592 million

P/E ratio: 19.1

Top five holdings: Commercial Metals Co., Shurgard Storage Centers, Reliance Steel & Aluminum Co., Energen Corp., Standard Pacific Corp.

Micro caps

Micro caps are companies larger than the corner delicatessen, but not by much. They're volatile little suckers, but as a group they offer impressive long-term performance figures. In terms of diversification, micro caps — in conservative quantity — are a nice addition to most portfolios.

iShares Russell Microcap Index (IWC)

Indexed to: 1,240 of the smallest publicly traded companies, all culled from the Russell 3000 Index

Expense ratio: 0.60 percent

Average cap size: $425 million

P/E ratio: 21

Top five holdings: Trident Microsystems, Brightpoint, Nuance Communications, Cubist Pharmaceuticals, Stratasys

PowerShares Zacks Microcap Index (PZI)

Indexed to: The proprietary ZAX Index, which includes roughly 400 micro cap stocks chosen for "investment merit criteria, including fundamental growth, stock valuation, investment timeliness . . . ." In other words, someone behind the scenes is stock picking.

Expense ratio: 0.60 percent

Average cap size: $342 million

P/E ratio: 19.7

Top five holdings: Biogen IDEC, Applera Applied Biosystems, Gilead Sciences, Sigma-Aldrich, Amgen

Bond ETFs

For the most part, bonds are less volatile than stocks, and their returns over time tend to be less. But they're a key stabilizing force in a portfolio (refer to Chapter 2 of this book to find out why).

Treasuries: Uncle Sam's IOUs

If the creator/issuer of a bond is a national government, the issue is called a *sovereign* bond. The vast majority of sovereign bonds sold in the United States are Uncle Sam's own Treasuries.

iShares Lehman 1–3 Year Treasury Bond Fund (SHY)

Indexed to: The Lehman Brothers 1–3 Year U.S. Treasury Index, an index tracking the short-term sector of the United States Treasury market. The fund uses a representative sampling — typically around 30 individual bond issues.

Expense ratio: 0.15 percent

Current yield: 3.96 percent

Average weighted maturity: 1.8 years

iShares Lehman 7–10 Year Treasury Bond Fund (IEF)

Indexed to: The Lehman Brothers 7–10 Year U.S. Treasury Index, an index tracking the intermediate-term sector of the United States Treasury market. The fund uses a representative sampling — typically around 20 individual bond issues.

Expense ratio: 0.15 percent

Current yield: 4.40 percent

Average weighted maturity: 8.4 years

iShares Lehman 20+ Year Treasury Bond Fund (TLT)

Indexed to: The Lehman Brothers 20+ Year U.S. Treasury Index, an index tracking the long-term sector of the United States Treasury market. The fund uses a representative sampling — typically around 15 individual bond issues.

Expense ratio: 0.15 percent

Current yield: 4.73 percent

Average weighted maturity: 23.1 years

Inflation-protected securities

Technically, U.S. Treasury Inflation-Protected Securities (TIPS) are Treasuries, but they play a distinctly different role in your portfolio than the other Treasuries do. The gig with TIPS is this: They pay you only a nominal amount of interest (currently about 2.5 percent), but they also kick in an adjustment for inflation. So, for example, if inflation is running at 4 percent, all things being equal, your TIPs will yield 6.5 percent.

iShares Lehman TIPS Bond Fund (TIP)

Indexed to: The Lehman Brothers U.S. Treasury Inflation-protected sector of the United States Treasury market. The fund uses a representative sampling of roughly 15 bond issues.

Expense ratio: 0.20 percent

Current yield: 6.7 percent

Average weighted maturity: 10.5 years

Corporate bond ETFs

Logically enough, corporations issue bonds called *corporate* bonds, and you can buy a dizzying array of them with varying maturities, yields, and ratings. Or you can buy a representative sampling through an ETF.

iShares GS $ InvesTop Corporate Bond Fund (LQD)

Indexed to: The GS $ InvesTop Index — an index of bond issues sponsored by a chorus line of companies rated "investment grade" (which means highly unlikely to go bankrupt any time soon) or above

Expense ratio: 0.15 percent

Current yield: 5.33 percent

Average credit quality: A

Average weighted maturity: 9.7 years

Investing in the entire U.S. bond market

The broadest fixed-income ETF is an all-around good bet.

iShares Lehman Aggregate Bond Fund (AGG)

Indexed to: The Lehman Aggregate Bond Index, which tracks the performance of the total U.S. investment grade bond market, including both government bonds and the highest quality corporate bonds. More than 6,000 bonds are in the index, but AGG uses a representative sampling of roughly 120 holdings. The average credit quality — AAA — indicates that there is very little chance any of the bonds in the index will default. (Even if one or two did, with 120 holdings, it wouldn't kill you.)

Expense ratio: 0.20 percent

Current yield: 4.6 percent

Average credit quality: AAA

Average weighted maturity: 6.9 years

Real estate investing (REITs)

In a nutshell, *real estate investment trusts,* popularly known as *REITs* (rhymes with "Pete's"), are companies that hold portfolios of properties, such as shopping malls, office buildings, hotels, amusement parks, or timberland. Or they may hold certain real estate related assets, such as commercial mortgages. Via a handful of ETFs, you can buy a bevy of REITs.

The tax efficiency of ETFs will help cap any capital gains you enjoy on your REIT fund, but it can't do anything to diminish the taxes you'll be paying on the dividends. For that reason, all REIT funds — ETFs or otherwise — are best kept in tax-advantaged retirement accounts.

iShares Cohen & Steers Realty Majors Index Fund (ICF)

Indexed to: Cohen & Steers Realty Majors Index, which tracks 30 of the largest and most liquid REITs in the U.S. market

Expense ratio: 0.35 percent

Number of holdings: 31

Top five holdings: Simon Property Group, Vornado Realty Trust, ProLogis, Equity Residential, Boston Properties

Top sectors: Retail, office buildings, and residential (accounting for 72 percent of total assets)

iShares Dow Jones U.S. Real Estate Index Fund (IYR)

Indexed to: Dow Jones U.S. Real Estate Index, a subset of the Dow Jones U.S. Financials Index that uses about 90 REIT stocks to track the U.S. commercial real estate market

Expense ratio: 0.60 percent

Number of holdings: 88

Top five holdings: Simon Property Group, Equity Office Properties Trust, Equity Residential, ProLogis, Vornado Realty Trust

Top sectors: Retail and office buildings (accounting for 43 percent of total assets)

Vanguard REIT ETF (VNQ)

Indexed to: The Morgan Stanley U.S. REIT index, which tracks roughly 105 U.S. REITs — representing about half of all publicly traded REITS and roughly two-thirds the value of the total U.S. REIT market

Expense ratio: 0.12 percent

Number of holdings: 107

Top five holdings: Simon Property Group, Equity Office Properties Trust, Equity Residential, ProLogis, Vornado Realty Trust

Top sectors: Retail, apartments, and office buildings (accounting for roughly 62 percent of total assets)

Chapter 5

Annuities

A few years ago, public policy wonks, finance professors, and insurance executives realized that 77 million Baby Boomers will soon begin to retire. Together, they will have saved trillions of dollars in their 401(k) and 403(b) plans, but few will have a strategy for stretching that money over what could be 20, 25, or even 30 years of retirement.

Annuities will be the answer, the experts decided. Annuities will help Baby Boomers (especially those without traditional pensions) protect their savings and/or convert it into guaranteed lifelong income. If Boomers don't buy annuities, the wonks predict, they'll blow their retirement money on bass boats, golf balls, spa makeovers, and ranch land in Wyoming.

It'll be a few years before anyone will know whether these prognosticating scolds were right, but annuities can be a viable investment option for folks who want to protect their income in their later years. This chapter gives you an overview of what annuities are, what they offer (both good and bad), and the general types of annuities you can choose from.

Introducing Annuities

You may think of annuities as the duck-billed platypuses of the financial world. They are neither pure investments nor pure insurance. Instead, they have one foot in the investment world and one foot in the insurance world.

✔ An annuity is an *investment* in the sense that you give a sum of money to a financial institution with the hope that you'll get back more than what you put in. Your investment — or, in this case, a *premium* — can range in size from $2,000 to over $2 million. The financial institution — usually an insurance company — puts your money in its own general account (if you bought a fixed annuity) or in what's called a separate account (if you bought a variable annuity).

✔ An annuity is *insurance* in the sense that a small portion of your premium buys a guarantee. The exact nature of the guarantee varies with the type of annuity. In fixed annuity contracts, for instance, your rate of return is guaranteed for a certain number of years. In the latest variable annuity contracts, you can lock in a guaranteed rate of return and get a guaranteed payout in retirement. With an immediate annuity, you get guaranteed income.

In fact, guaranteeing you a pension-like income for life is what annuities do better than any other financial product. There is no more efficient tool for converting a specific sum of money into a monthly income that lasts as long you live — even if you live to 105.

Annuities are all about tradeoffs between risk and return. The guarantees reduce your risk of losing money. But the fee you pay for the guarantee generally reduces the potential growth of your investment. (That's not always the case, but the principle holds true: Lower risk brings lower returns.)

Looking at how annuities work

Annuities are intended to help you save for retirement and supplement your retirement income. Various types of annuities can make your retirement more secure by helping you do the following:

✔ **Save for retirement:** Before you retire, fixed deferred annuities — which include CD-type annuities, market value–adjusted fixed annuities, and indexed annuities — allow you to earn a specific (or adjustable) rate of interest on your money for a specific number of years, tax-deferred. They're also a safe place to park money during retirement.

✔ **Invest for retirement:** Before you retire, variable deferred annuities — baskets of mutual funds, essentially — allow you to invest your savings in stocks or bonds while deferring taxes on all the capital gains, dividends, and interest that mutual funds usually throw off every year.

✔ **Distribute your savings:** Most Baby Boomers who retire with six-figure balances in their employer-sponsored retirement plans won't know how fast or slow to spend their savings. An immediate annuity or a variable deferred annuity with "guaranteed lifetime benefits" can provide structure to the process.

✔ **Insure you against longevity risk:** Just as life insurance insures you and your family from the risk of dying early, an income annuity or an advanced life deferred annuity (ALDA) can insure you against the risk of living so long that you run out of money.

✔ **Manage your taxes:** Everybody with a big 401(k) or 403(b) plan will retire with a massive income tax debt to the government. A life income annuity allows you spread that tax liability evenly across your entire retirement.

To encourage saving, Uncle Sam lets you defer taxes on the growth of your investment in an annuity. To discourage you from spending your savings before retirement, the IRS exacts a penalty for withdrawals taken from annuities (as well as from other tax-deferred investments) before you reach age 59½.

Getting to know the participants

Every annuity has an owner, an annuitant, beneficiaries, and an issuer.

✔ **The owner:** The owner of an annuity is the person who pays the premiums, signs the application, and agrees to abide by the terms of the contract. The owner decides who the other parties of the contract will be. Depending on the type of contract owned or what stage it is in, the owner can withdraw money or even sell the annuity. The owner is liable for any taxes that are due.

✔ **The annuitant:** The annuitant is the person on whose life expectancy the annuity payments will be calculated. If and when the owner decides to start taking a guaranteed lifetime income from the annuity, the size of the annuity payments will be based on the annuitant's age and life expectancy — not the owner's! (Although, in most cases, the owner and annuitant are the same person.)

✔ **The beneficiaries:** On the contract application, you need to name an owner's beneficiary and an annuitant's beneficiary. The owner and annuitant can be each other's beneficiary, which can help keep things simple, but no one can be his or her own beneficiary.

✔ **The issuer:** The insurance company that issues the contract and puts itself on the hook for any guarantees in the contract is the issuer (also sometimes called the *carrier*).

You should always look for an issuer that's rated "excellent," "superior," or "very good" by the ratings agencies, such as A.M. Best and Fitch. A high rating suggests — but doesn't guarantee — that the issuer will fulfill its promises to you and that you'll get your money back.

Book II

Basic Investments: Stocks, Bonds, Mutual Funds, and More

Noting common elements of all (or most) annuities

All annuities have a free look period, a death benefit, guarantees, and annuitization options. Most have surrender periods. Deferred variable annuities have AUVs, or accumulated unit values. The following list provides basic information about these elements:

- **Free look period:** Whoever buys an annuity has between 10 and 30 days after receiving the contract in the mail to cancel the contract. Some immediate annuity contracts offer a rider that lets you cancel your contract within the first six months. Some fixed annuity contracts let you opt out during a brief "window" at the beginning of each contract year.

- **Death benefit:** In most annuities, the owner and annuitant are the same person. If that person dies, the insurance company pays a death benefit to his or her beneficiary. The death benefit may be more than simply the value of the contract when the owner dies. Depending on whether the owner bought the standard death benefit or an enhanced death benefit, the death benefit may be equal to the original premium or equal to the maximum value of the contract on any contract anniversary.

- **Guarantees:** Annuities offer one or more of the following guarantees: a guarantee of a particular return; a guarantee against loss of principal; a guarantee that, if the owner dies during a bear market, his or her heirs won't suffer financially; or a guarantee of lifetime income. This is one of the reasons that annuities cost more than investments. You're paying for the guarantee.

- **Annuitization option:** Whether you do so or not (and more than 90 percent of owners do not), all deferred annuities allow you to annuitize. To *annuitize* is to relinquish control over your money to the issuer in return for a guarantee that the issuer will pay you a fixed or variable income for a specific period, for the rest of your life, or as long as either you and your spouse are living.

- **Surrender period:** Most, but not all, annuities have surrender periods during which the issuer may levy a contingent deferred sales charge, or CDSC, if you withdraw too much of your money from the contract too soon. All deferred fixed annuities have CDSCs, and so do most deferred variable annuities that are purchased from agents or brokers.

- **Accumulation unit value (AUV):** The most important unit of measure for mutual fund shares is the net accumulation value, or NAV. After the financial markets close every business day, when the traders go home and the final prices are fixed for the evening (except for after-hours trading), a mutual fund manager tallies up the value of all his investments and divides those millions or billions of dollars by the number of mutual fund shares outstanding. The result is the NAV.

In the parallel universe of deferred variable annuities, mutual funds are called *subaccounts* and NAVs are called *accumulation unit values* (AUVs). A subaccount and a mutual fund may be managed by the same manager and invest in the same securities, but they will have different daily values. Certain fees are deducted every day from the subaccounts that are not deducted from the mutual fund accounts. Also, the mutual fund makes taxable distributions and the subaccount does not. Thus the NAV of a mutual fund and the AUV of a variable annuity are typically different, even when they own the same basket of securities.

Deciding If An Annuity Is Right for You

Annuities aren't for everyone. The very poor or the ultra-rich, for example, won't find much use for them. Those lucky devils who can look forward to both Social Security and a handsome company pension in retirement probably won't need the extra guaranteed income that annuities offer. Cockeyed optimists, who buy every dip in the Dow and revel in volatility, won't bother with annuities because annuities can blunt or buffer their potential returns.

Nor is every type of annuity right for everybody. But certain annuities will appeal to certain types of people:

- ✔ People in high tax brackets often like deferred annuities, because they can contribute virtually any amount of money to an annuity and defer taxes on the gains for as long as they like.

- ✔ Middle-class couples in their 50s, earning $100,000 or less, with savings of $250,000 or more but no pension, should like income annuities. There's a 50 percent chance that one of the two will live to age 90, and that's when income annuities provide the most value.

- ✔ Pessimists — otherwise known as Cassandras, doomsayers, and bears — who believe that the gigantic, highly leveraged house of cards (i.e., our financial system) might collapse at any time, should like the guarantees that annuities provide.

- ✔ Women are much more likely to need annuities than men. They live significantly longer and are therefore at greater risk of running out of savings. Single or widowed women are more likely to be poor in old age than single or widowed men. The retirement financing crisis that's looming in all the developed countries of the world will have its greatest impact on women.

Evaluating the pluses

Annuities offer a number of benefits, such as tax deferral, unlimited contributions, and the opportunity for guaranteed income. Some of these benefits are a result of federal tax law. Others come from the fact that annuities are insurance products as well as investments. Different types of annuities offer different types of advantages, as the following sections explain.

Guaranteeing income after age 59½

Annuities are the only financial product that can guarantee you an income for life (or two lives) or for a specific number of years. All annuities offer you the option to convert savings to income, and new types of annuities are making it easier to buy future income.

Deferring taxes

When you buy a deferred annuity, you can let the money grow and not pay taxes on the growth until years later — ordinarily after you reach age 59½. This is called *tax deferral,* and the IRS allows it in order to encourage you to save for retirement. Assuming that your tax rate during retirement will be lower than your tax rate while you're still working, you'll ultimately pay less in taxes. (Note: You can't deduct your contributions to a deferred annuity from your taxable income, the way you can deduct contributions to a traditional IRA or employer-sponsored retirement account.)

The more you can afford to put in an annuity, the longer you can leave it there, and the higher your tax bracket today (relative to what it will be in retirement), the more you can benefit from tax deferral.

Allowing unlimited contributions

You can contribute as much as you want to a deferred annuity. Most insurance companies reserve the right to review contributions over $1 million in advance — to prevent large-scale money laundering, in part — but they don't specifically discourage large deposits.

Reducing investment risk

You'll often hear it said that annuities are *contracts,* not investments. There's an important difference between the two. When you invest in a bond mutual fund, for instance, you can lose money if interest rates go up and the prices of the fund's existing bonds fall. Investments involve risk. When you put your savings in a fixed deferred annuity, there's virtually no risk. Your contract guarantees you a specific return for at least one year and maybe more, and it promises that, no matter what, you won't lose money and you'll make a certain minimum amount. Contracts involve guarantees.

Paying death benefits

When you buy a deferred annuity, you pay a small annual fee for a death benefit. This benefit ensures that, if you die while the annuity contract is in force, your beneficiaries will receive a certain minimum. The more you pay for the death benefit (you may have as many as three or four options), the richer the benefit.

Distributing survivorship credits

The concept of mortality pooling forms the basis of a classic life annuity (also known as an *income annuity* or *immediate annuity*). A cohort of 65-year-olds buys life annuities, and each receives — spread more or less evenly over their lifetimes — a payout consisting of three components: returned principal, investment gains, and a share of the money relinquished by those who die before them. It's simply the insurance principle at work.

If you own an income annuity, to the extent that you'll rely on all or part of your savings to generate basic income in retirement (as opposed to relying on it for splurges or reserving it for your children or other beneficiaries), and to the extent that you're "at risk" for living a very long life, mortality pooling is arguably the most efficient way to maximize your retirement income and to guarantee an income for life.

Obtaining peace of mind!

People who own income annuities say they like the security that comes from a regular paycheck — just as they like the peace of mind that Social Security and traditional company pensions can provide. When proposals were made to change and possibly undermine the Social Security system a few years ago, many middle class people protested. Most people don't like the ongoing disappearance of traditional pensions either, but they can't do much about it. Annuities can provide the safety and security that many people yearn for in retirement.

Providing a retirement distribution method

You may be one of the millions of Americans who, after compiling a six-figure nest egg in your employer's retirement plan, don't know how to begin converting it into an income. An income annuity, which pays out a blend of principal, earnings, and survivorship credits more or less evenly over your entire future, is a smart way to turn your savings into income.

Book II

Basic Investments: Stocks, Bonds, Mutual Funds, and More

Recognizing the minuses

For every one of the benefits of annuities, there's a corresponding drawback. When you buy an annuity, you're usually buying a guarantee, and guarantees always cost money and usually come with restrictions written in type that's small enough to require bifocals or reading glasses. It's to be expected.

You already own an income annuity

Anyone who has worked in the United States and paid payroll taxes for a sufficient number of years owns an annuity provided by the Social Security Administration. Although it is financed differently from individually purchased annuities and pays proportionately more to those in the lower income tax brackets, Social Security provides almost everyone with a true annuity.

Higher expenses than mutual funds

Although inexpensive products do exist, high fees are very common in the world of deferred variable annuities — especially if you buy your contract from a broker or other commission-earning intermediary. The insurance fees, distribution costs, investment fees, and rider fees can easily amount to more than 3 percent per year. The average annual expense ratio for variable annuities is about 2.4 percent.

High fees also contribute to the cost of immediate (income-generating) annuities, though the fees are not as apparent because they are built into the price you pay for your lifelong income stream. Depending on the insurance company's costs and perhaps its desire to make a sale, it may charge you from $140,000 to $150,000 for a $1,000-a-month lifelong income that starts at age 65. You won't receive an explanation why.

Reduced liquidity and control

Annuities offer guaranteed benefits. Insurance companies can't provide those guarantees unless they can count on possessing your money long enough to collect fees and earn interest on it. For that reason, annuities offer less flexibility and access to your money (*liquidity*) than conventional risky investments such as mutual funds.

Annuity earnings are taxed as ordinary income

Eventually you'll have to pay income taxes on the gains in your deferred annuity contract. If your taxable income is higher than about $160,000, the annuity profits will be taxed at the rate of 33 or 35 percent. By contrast, your profit on that single stock or mutual fund that you bought 20 years ago and sold last year will be taxed at the capital gains rate of only 15 percent.

Lack of transparency and moving parts

Insurance is a proverbial "black box." No one but the managers and actuaries are privy to the many different formulas and factors that go into the pricing of products. When an issuer of income annuities offers you, at age 65, $671 per month for life in return for a premium of $100,000, you don't know how the carrier arrived at that figure.

Then there are the "moving parts" in deferred annuities. When you buy a fixed deferred annuity that guarantees a rate for only the first year, you don't know exactly what the rate will be during subsequent years. An issuer of indexed annuities (also known as *fixed indexed* or *equity-indexed* annuities) also reserves the right to change the formula for crediting gains to you.

The benefits of today's popular deferred variable annuity contracts — which offer guaranteed lifetime income and access to your principal if you need it — require some very complex financial engineering and entail many different restrictions. The rules are described in the prospectus, but they can be extremely difficult or even impossible for the average person to understand.

Book II

Basic Investments: Stocks, Bonds, Mutual Funds, and More

Purchasing Annuities

You will probably buy your annuity from a licensed insurance agent, broker, or financial adviser. Standing directly behind these intermediaries are brokerage firms (for brokers and financial advisers), marketing organizations (for independent insurance agents), or the insurance companies themselves (in the case of career insurance agents). (Note: Insurance agents aren't licensed to sell variable annuities.)

The transaction begins when you meet with the agent or broker who discusses your finances with you. After you choose a suitable product, the agent or broker will submit the application for approval. You will eventually send the contract issuer — the insurance company — a check for at least the minimum amount (every carrier sets its own minimum initial premiums). Then the carrier sends you your contract. You will have 10 to 30 days to reconsider your decision and send the contract back for a refund.

Important participants in the annuity food chain include the following:

- **Annuity issuers:** Only insurance companies issue annuities. There are hundreds of issuers, but the 25 largest firms — household names like The Hartford, MetLife, and Prudential — account for about 90 percent of all annuities sold each year.

Some insurers are publicly owned, and some are mutually owned. Publicly owned firms are owned by their stockholders, and mutually owned firms are owned by their customers. The two types may have different cultures and attitudes, and slightly different products. Look for a company whose view of risk and reward matches your own. Personally, I like mutual companies — they're more customer-oriented and not under pressure to impress Wall Street with ever-larger quarterly earnings.

✔ **Annuity distributors:** Distributors include big brokerages (known as *wirehouses*) like Merrill Lynch and Morgan Stanley, as well as independent broker-dealers like Raymond James and LPL. Banks like Bank of America and Wachovia also distribute annuities through their branches. Distributors serve as middlemen between the carriers and the producers. In many cases, they employ or supervise producers (see the next bullet), making sure they comply with insurance and investment laws.

✔ **Annuity producers:** Years ago, most insurance companies employed an army of career agents to represent and sell their products. While companies like AXA, Ameriprise, MetLife, and others still have these agents, many annuities are sold by independent agents, brokers, and bank officers.

"Independents" can recommend any annuity they wish. In practice, they may steer you toward their list of preferred products or carriers. Be aware that a producer may earn a higher commission or a free trip to Cancun for selling certain products.

✔ **Direct marketers.** If you're the self-reliant type and you don't need an agent or broker to explain annuities to you, you can buy your annuity direct. Some but not all insurance companies will sell a no-load (that is, no sales commission) contract directly to you. No-load mutual fund companies like Vanguard, Fidelity, and T. Rowe Price also sell no-load annuity contracts directly to the public over the phone or Internet or by mail. In the case of Vanguard and T. Rowe Price, their contracts are issued by third-party insurance companies. Relatively few people buy annuities direct, however.

The Main Types of Annuities

If you prefer a safety net, and if you're willing to pay for one, you may consider an annuity. This section's primary purpose is explain the basic annuities options that are available.

Annuities in themselves are neither good nor bad. Like other forms of insurance, they may or may not seem worth the price. Ultimately, the decision to buy an annuity or not depends on the amount of financial risk you're willing to tolerate.

Fixed deferred annuities

Years ago, before credit cards and mutual funds, people saved. If they wanted to buy something big — a house, a diamond, or a dream vacation — they put money in a savings account, where it earned interest. The money grew, and when the day of purchase finally arrived, voila — they paid cash. A fixed annuity is the insurance industry's version of a savings account. It helps you save. Technically, fixed annuities are *deferred* annuities. Their owners defer their right to convert the annuity's value to a retirement income stream for at least several years. In truth, few people ever convert them. Most people use them to save or to increase the stability of their investment portfolios.

Like all investments, fixed annuities represent a mixture of trade-offs. On the plus side, they offer the following:

- ✔ **Safety:** Buying a fixed annuity with a multi-year guarantee (MYG) and holding it for the entire term is a safe, conservative way to grow your money. It's even safer than buying a bond or shares in a bond fund, because a bond's price or the share prices of a bond fund can fall in response to rising interest rates.

- ✔ **Tax deferral:** Annuities, like investments that are held in IRAs and 401(k) plans, grow tax deferred. You earn interest each year, but you don't receive a 1099 form in January advising you to report it and pay taxes on it. The advantage is that your annuity grows faster than it would if taxes were deducted from it every year.

- ✔ **Stable rates:** When you buy a MYG fixed annuity, you know what interest rate return you'll receive and you know exactly what your investment will be worth at the end of the term. As long as you don't make withdrawals, you have complete peace of mind.

- ✔ **Higher returns when the bond yield curve is steep:** A steep bond *yield curve* occurs when bonds of longer maturities (ten-year Treasury bonds, say) pay higher rates of interest than bonds of shorter maturities (a three-month Treasury bill, for instance). At such times, fixed annuities often pay higher interest rates than certificates of deposit.

- ✔ **No probate:** It's hard to get excited about a benefit that you can enjoy only by dying, but annuities are famous for them. In this case, if you die while owning a fixed annuity, your money goes straight to the beneficiaries you named on your contract. The money doesn't become part of your estate and therefore doesn't go through the legal process known as *probate,* where creditors and relatives can lay claim to it.

- ✔ **The option to annuitize:** Like all annuity contracts, a fixed annuity can be converted to a retirement income stream. Although this option is the defining feature of annuities, few people know about it and even fewer use it.

Book II

Basic Investments: Stocks, Bonds, Mutual Funds, and More

Fixed annuities also have their fair share of negatives:

- ✔ **Low liquidity:** If you take more than 10 percent of your money out of your fixed annuity during the surrender period, you'll pay a charge. You can avoid charges by buying a fixed annuity with a short surrender period or by using other sources of cash for emergencies. Contracts with longer surrender periods typically pay higher rates, but don't be lured into tying up your money for longer than you can afford to.

- ✔ **Uncertain returns:** With single-year guarantee fixed annuities, you don't know exactly what the interest rate will be after the first year. From what I have seen of renewal rate histories, the rates on single-year guarantee contracts either stay the same or decline gradually after the first year. Rates are especially likely to fall if the annuity offers a first-year bonus.

- ✔ **Lower returns when the bond yield curve is flat:** When the yield curve is flat — when long-term interest rates are the same as or lower than short-term rates — you may be able to get a better rate from a certificate of deposit.

- ✔ **Federal penalty for early withdrawal:** If you withdraw money from a fixed annuity before you reach the age of 59½, you may have to pay a penalty to the IRS. The penalty, equal to 10 percent of the earnings withdrawn, is Uncle Sam's way of discouraging Americans from using annuities and other tax-favored investments for anything but saving for retirement. Early withdrawals from tax-deductible IRAs and employer-sponsored retirement plans are penalized in a similar way, but in those cases the entire withdrawal is subject to the 10 percent penalty. However, under certain circumstances, such as illness, you can withdraw money from an annuity before age 59½ without a penalty.

Single-year guarantee fixed annuity

In this type of annuity, the insurance company promises to pay you a certain rate of interest for one year. Each year, for the rest of the surrender period, the insurance company can raise or reduce the interest rate it pays you. The rates after the first year are known as *renewal rates*.

Single-year guarantee fixed annuities often offer big first-year *bonus rates*. A bonus rate is an interest rate that lasts only for the first year. It will be anywhere from 1 to 10 percent higher than the rate your money will earn in any other year of the contract. After that, the rate generally falls slightly from year to year, enabling the company to recover the cost of the bonus.

Multi-year guarantee (MYG) fixed annuity

In an MYG fixed annuity, you give a specific amount of money to an insurance company, and the insurer guarantees that your investment will earn a specific rate of compound interest for a specific number of years. MYG annuities are often called *CD-type* annuities or *tax-deferred CDs* because they serve the same purpose as a certificate of deposit.

The beauty of MYGs is their transparency: What you see is what you get. You know the interest rate your money will earn and how long it will earn it. If you want to buy a $30,000 boat in ten years, you can plunk down $19,500 today in a ten-year MYG annuity paying 4.5 percent. In ten years you can pay cash for the boat and have enough left over for dinner for two at the marina.

Market value–adjusted (MVA) fixed annuities

With a *market value–adjusted* fixed (MVA) annuity, you, not the insurer, assume the interest rate risk. In return, the insurance company pays you a slightly higher interest rate than it pays on non-MVA annuities, which are known as *book value* annuities.

If you withdraw too much of your money (over 10 percent, in most cases) from your MVA annuity during the surrender period, typically two things will happen. First, you'll pay a surrender charge (a percentage equal to the number of years left in the surrender period, in many cases). Second, your account value will either be adjusted downward (if interest rates have risen since you bought your annuity) or upward (if rates have declined).

In addition to paying higher rates, MVA fixed annuities tend to have longer terms than other fixed annuities. So, if you want to lock in current interest rates for a long time, an MVA fixed annuity may be right for you.

Floating rate and pass-through rate contracts

A few fixed annuity contracts offer an interest rate that *floats* from month to month. If interest rates go up a bit, you earn a little more that month. If interest rates go down, you earn less. Certain floating-rate fixed annuities will give you a 30-day window once a year to take withdrawals without charging you a penalty or a market value adjustment.

You may also come across annuities that offer *pass-through* rates of interest. Instead of paying you a fixed rate and keeping the rest of what it earns on its bonds, the insurance company pays itself a fixed spread — perhaps 2 percent — and gives you the rest of what it earns. These annuities can be attractive because there's no upper limit on the amount of interest you can earn.

In these contracts, the insurance company will typically try for the highest possible returns by investing in *junk bonds.* Junk bonds offer higher interest rates because there's a risk that the bond's issuer — the borrower — won't repay the lender, which in this case is the insurance company. Typically, a borrower with weak credit can attract investors (lenders) only by offering a higher interest rate. Each of these two types of fixed annuities offers the potential for higher returns than conventional fixed annuities, as well as higher risk. But why *add* risk to a fixed annuity, whose principal virtue is safety? If you want more risk (and potentially more reward), consider investing a larger percentage of your money in stocks.

Book II

Basic Investments: Stocks, Bonds, Mutual Funds, and More

Variable annuities

Variable annuities (VAs) are mutual fund investments that have certain insurance-related guarantees, such as living benefits and death benefits.

Guaranteed living benefits

Guaranteed living benefits (GLBs) are what draw most people to VAs these days. GLBs can be used as investment insurance or as a retirement income strategy. Because they can protect you from so-called sequence-of-returns risk — the chance that a bear market early in your retirement will permanently wreck your portfolio — they're worth your attention.

GLBs are designed to let investors have it all: protection from catastrophic loss, the potential for growth, and the assurance that if they die, their beneficiaries won't be left empty-handed. There are various kinds of GLBs:

- ✔ **Guaranteed minimum income benefit (GMIB):** This option guarantees that you can annuitize (convert to a regular income) whichever is greater: the market value of your investments or a guaranteed minimum amount based on your principal plus a minimum guaranteed annual growth rate.

- ✔ **Guaranteed minimum withdrawal benefit (GMWB):** This option protects your principal and guarantees that you will receive it in equal installments (for example, 7 percent of the principal amount per year for 14.3 years) until it is exhausted.

- ✔ **Guaranteed minimum withdrawal benefit — for life (GMWB for life):** This option guarantees that you can withdraw a certain percentage (typically 5 percent) of a guaranteed amount (known as the *benefit base*) every year for life, even if a market crash wipes out the value of your investments after payments begin. You can dip into your principal if you need to, but you may reduce your future annual income by doing so.

    GMWBs for life can be confusing because they involve real money and hypothetical money. There's your *account balance,* which is the market value of your subaccount investments (a value that can move up or down). That's real money, which you may withdraw. Then there's the *guaranteed minimum value* or *guaranteed benefit base.* It is not real money, and you can't withdraw it. It is simply the amount on which your 5 percent annual lifetime withdrawals will be based. Don't fall into the trap of thinking that the guaranteed minimum value or benefit base is your money.

- ✔ **Guaranteed minimum accumulation benefit (GMAB):** This option guarantees that, after a seven- to ten-year investment period, your investments will not lose money. Some GMABs guarantee a certain amount of growth over ten years, and a GMAB may be combined with a GMWB for life.

- ✔ **Guaranteed account value (GAV):** This option guarantees your principal over the course of a specific investment period and may automatically lock in any gains at the end of each quarter or year.

- ✔ **Guaranteed payout annuity floor (GPAF):** This option guarantees that your monthly income payment will never be less than a certain percentage — from 85 to 100 percent — of the first payment. (Note: GPAF applies only to contract owners who annuitize their contracts and opt for a variable monthly payment for life.)

VA pros and cons

There are several pros and cons of VA ownership that you need to carefully weigh before deciding on your investment strategy. The pros include:

- ✔ Deferred taxes on dividends and capital gains

- ✔ Lifetime income options, including annuitization and GLBs

- ✔ A death benefit that protects heirs from market losses

- ✔ Investment options that provide control over retirement savings

- ✔ No limit on the contribution of pre-tax money

The cons of VA ownership include:

- ✔ High fees relative to no-load mutual funds, especially if sold by commissioned brokers or agents.

    When you add up the insurance fees, fund management fees, death benefit fees, and rider fees of today's VAs, you'll find yourself paying 3 percent a year, on average. Even as these fees put a safety net below you, they can act as a significant drag on the earnings of your investments. And you may end up never even using the benefits you paid for.

- ✔ Earnings are taxed as income rather than as capital gains.

- ✔ Withdrawals of earnings before age 59½ may be subject to a 10 percent federal penalty, in addition to income tax.

- ✔ Investment risks are usually greater than with fixed-rate annuities.

Immediate income annuities

Income annuities enable you to convert a large sum of cash into a monthly, quarterly, or annual paycheck. You give the lump sum to a reputable insurance company, and the insurer issues a contract that promises to pay you (or someone you choose) an income for an agreed-upon length of time. Income annuities are attractive to many people for two basic reasons: First, they deliver more income than a comparably safe investment in U.S. government bonds. Second, they provide an income that you can't outlive.

In this way, income annuities protect you from *timing risk* (that just before or after you start drawing down your savings, a sharp market downturn will take a huge bite out of your portfolio and increase the chances you'll run out of money too soon), *investment risk* (the possibility that the returns on your portfolio won't be enough to support you in retirement), and *longevity risk* (that you'll outlive your income). An income annuity transfers these risks to an insurance company. In return for your purchase payment — usually $100,000 or more — you receive an income (monthly, quarterly, or annual) that's immune to bond defaults, resistant to stock market crashes, and can last for as long as you live.

A "life" annuity *guarantees* that you will receive an income as long as you live (or as long as either you or your spouse is living). But this guarantee assumes that the insurance company will remain financially strong enough to meet its obligations for the next 30 years or more. If the insurer fails, your payments will be in jeopardy. That's why you must buy your annuity from a gilt-edged, A-rated company.

The simplest type of income annuity is known as a SPIA (spee-ah). Income from a SPIA begins no later than one year after you purchase it. When brokers and advisers talk about SPIAs — and they rarely do — they usually mean annuities that offer a fixed payment every month. But you can also buy a SPIVA (a single premium immediate *variable* annuity) whose payout rate fluctuates with the stock market.

People tend to be wary of income annuities because they feel that "if I die the insurance company will get my money." That's a healthy fear. But buying an income annuity doesn't necessarily mean losing control over all your money, or even all the money in your annuity. Most issuers of income annuities offer options that allow you to tailor your annuity to your own needs and comfort level.

Insurance company actuaries have created a variety of sweeteners to overcome the public's historic reluctance to buy life annuities. For instance, you can decide to keep some of your money in stocks, or you can provide coverage for two people. You can arrange to leave something for your heirs. You can even arrange cost-of-living increases.

In short, there are dozens of possible combinations of options. And each of them will produce a different monthly payment from the same initial premium. Keep in mind, however, that you'll get the highest monthly payment if you relinquish all control over your money. The more control you retain, the lower your income will be.

Advanced life deferred annuities

This section covers the most intriguing annuity of all: the advanced life deferred annuity (ALDA), also called *pure longevity insurance*. Typically people who purchase an ALDA

- ✔ Are between the ages of 50 and 60.
- ✔ Use 10 to 30 percent of their retirement savings to fund it.
- ✔ Begin receiving guaranteed monthly income at age 80 or 85.

If that sounds like a terrible investment to you, your instincts are spot-on. In fact, an ALDA isn't an investment at all. It's insurance *against* longevity — the risk that you may outlive your savings. And because your chance of living really, really long is only so-so, the insurance companies can afford to make ALDAs fairly cheap.

The world isn't quite ready for ALDAs. Not many people have heard of them let alone purchased one. And as far as I know, only three insurance companies (MetLife, Hartford Life, and New York Life) currently market them with any enthusiasm. But, when you crunch the numbers, you see that ALDAs may be the most cost-effective way to cure one huge retirement headache: figuring out how much money to put in reserve just in case you happen to live a long, long time.

If you're married, take a serious look at ALDAs. Would you buy flood insurance if your house had a 50 percent chance of being flooded over the next 20 years? Probably. Well, on average, one member of a couple has a 75 percent chance of living to age 85 and a 50 percent chance of living to age 90. In short, you or your spouse will probably be knee-deep in longevity some day.

In a simple, no frills ALDA, your decision to take income at age 85 is unchangeable; if you and your spouse die before payments begin, you forfeit your initial payment. However, because insurance carriers know that most people will balk at those terms, the carriers are likely to offer one or more of the following features:

- ✔ **Cash refund:** If and your spouse both die before collecting the amount of your initial payment, the insurance company pays your beneficiaries the unpaid balance.
- ✔ **Death benefit:** If you die before you receive any income, your beneficiaries may receive a death benefit.

  One company offers a death benefit equal to your initial payment growing at a compound interest rate of 3 percent. If you pay $20,000 for your ALDA at age 60 and die at age 81, your heirs will receive $37,206.

Book II

Basic Investments: Stocks, Bonds, Mutual Funds, and More

Book III
Futures and Options

The 5th Wave   By Rich Tennant

"I was so into futures that one day she came in and told me she was running away with the pool boy. Now there's an option I didn't see coming."

In this book . . .

In the past, investors could afford the luxury of buying and holding stocks or mutual funds for the long term, but today's world calls for a more active and even a speculative investor. The new world calls for a trader. And futures and options markets, although high-risk, offer some of the best opportunities to make money when trading in volatile times.

Risk and uncertainty go hand in hand with opportunities to make money. That's why learning how to trade futures and options is important for investors who not only want to diversify their portfolios but also want to find ways to protect and grow their money when times are hard in traditional investment venues, such as the stock market.

After you read this part, you'll know how trading futures and options is done and how to stay in the game as long as you want.

Chapter 1

Futures and Options Fundamentals

• •

• •

*B*efore you trade in futures and options, there's quite a bit you need to know. For starters, you need to understand what, exactly, futures and options trading is! Then you need to know how the futures and options markets work and who the major players are. And because futures trading involves speculating (more akin to gambling than investing), you absolutely need to know about volatility and risk. This chapter gives you just that kind of information. And because trading futures and options isn't for everyone, I also help you decide whether being a trader is the right move for you.

Defining Futures and Options

Futures markets are the hub of capitalism. They provide the bases for prices at wholesale and eventually retail markets for commodities ranging from gasoline and lumber to key items in the food chain, such as cattle, pork, corn, and soybeans.

A *futures contract* is a security, similar in concept to a stock or a bond while being significantly different. Whereas a stock gives you equity and a bond makes you a debt holder, a futures contract is a legally binding agreement that sets the conditions for the delivery of commodities or financial instruments at a specific time in the future.

Futures contracts are available for more than just mainstream commodities. You can contract stock index futures, interest rate products — bonds and Treasury bills, and lesser known commodities like propane. Some futures contracts are even designed to hedge against weather risk.

Futures markets emerged and developed in fits and starts several hundred years ago as a mechanism through which merchants traded goods and services at some point in the future, based on their expectations for crops and harvest yields. Now virtually all financial and commodity markets are linked, with futures and cash markets functioning as a single entity on a daily basis.

Just like stocks and futures contracts, *options* are securities that are subject to binding agreements. The key difference between options and futures contracts is that options give you the *right* to buy or sell an underlying security or asset without being obligated to do so, as long as you follow the rules of the options contract. In addition, options are derivatives. A *derivative* is a financial instrument that gets its value not from its own intrinsic value but rather from the value of the underlying security and time. Options on the stock of IBM, for example, are directly influenced by the price of IBM stock.

Getting the Lowdown on Futures Trading

Futures contracts are by design meant to limit the amount of time and risk exposure experienced by speculators and hedgers. As a result, futures contracts have several key characteristics that enable traders to trade them effectively:

- **Expiration:** All futures contracts are time-based; they *expire,* which means that at some point in the future they will no longer exist. From a trading standpoint, the expiration of a contract forces you to make one of the following decisions: sell the contract or roll it over; sell the contract (taking your profits or losses) and just stay out of the market; or take delivery of the commodity, equity, or product represented by the contract.

- **Daily price limits:** Because of their volatility and the potential for catastrophic losses, futures contracts include limits that freeze prices but don't freeze trading. Daily price limits are stated in terms of the previous day's closing price plus and minus so many cents or dollars per trading unit. After a futures price has increased by its daily limit, there can be no trading at any higher price until the next day of trading. After a futures price has decreased by its daily limit, there can be no trading at any lower price until the next day of trading.

  Limits are meant to let markets cool down during periods of extremely active trading. (Keep in mind that the market can trade at the limit price but not beyond it.) Some contracts have *variable limits,* meaning the limits change if the market closes at the limit. (For example, if the cattle markets close at the limit for two straight days, the limit is raised on the third day.)

- **Size of account:** Most brokers require individuals to deposit a certain amount of money in a brokerage account before they can start trading. A fairly constant figure in the industry is $5,000.

Depositing only $5,000 with the brokerage firm probably is not enough to provide you with a good trading experience. Some experienced traders will tell you that $100,000 is a better figure to have on hand, and $20,000 is probably the least amount you can actually work with. These are not hard and fast rules, though.

Futures exchanges: Where the magic happens

Several active futures and options exchanges exist in the United States. Each has its own niche, but some overlaps occur in the types of contracts that are traded. Here are the names to know:

- **Chicago Board Options Exchange (CBOE, www.cboe.com):** The premier options exchange market in the world, the CBOE specializes in trading options on individual stocks, stock index futures, interest rate futures, and a broad array of specialized products such as exchange-traded funds. The CBOE is not a futures exchange but is included here to be complete, because futures and options can be traded simultaneously, as part of a single strategy.

- **CME Group: A CME/Chicago Board of Trade Company (www.cmegroup .com):** In 2007, the Chicago Mercantile Exchange (CME) and the Chicago Board of Trade (CBOT) merged, creating this new entity.

  The CBOT brings to the table trades made in futures contracts for the agriculturals, interest rates, Dow Indexes, and metals. The CME was already the largest futures exchange in North America, trading a wide variety of instruments, including commodities, stock index futures, foreign currencies, interest rates, TRAKRS, and environmental futures. (TRAKRS, or *total return asset contracts,* are designed to track an index that can be composed of stocks, bonds, currencies, or other financial instruments. Environmental futures are principally weather contracts initially based upon temperature.)

  Futures contracts for the Goldman Sachs Commodity Index and options on the futures contracts that the CME listed also are traded here, along with real estate futures.

- **Intercontinental Exchange (ICE, www.theice.com):** This exchange was established in 2000 and through mergers and acquisitions, most notably that of the New York Board of Trade, has become a key electronic 24-hour trading platform. ICE offers trading for crude oil, both Brent and West Texas Light Sweet contracts, as well as heating oil, jet fuel, electric power, and soft commodities such as coffee, sugar, cocoa, and frozen orange juice.

Book III

Futures and Options

- ✔ **Kansas City Board of Trade (KCBT, www.kcbt.com):** The KCBT is a regional exchange that specializes in wheat futures and offers trading on stock index futures for the Value Line Index, a broad listing of 1,700 stocks.

- ✔ **Minneapolis Grain Exchange (MGEX, www.mgex.com):** MGEX is a regional exchange that trades three kinds of seasonally different wheat futures, and offers futures and options on the National Corn Index and the National Soybeans Index.

- ✔ **New York Mercantile Exchange (NYMEX, www.nymex.com):** The NYMEX is the hub for trading in energy futures and metals.

E-mini contracts are smaller-value versions of the larger contracts. They trade for a fraction of the price of the full value instrument and thus are more suitable for small accounts. The attractive feature of e-mini contracts is that you can participate in the market's movements for lesser investment amounts. Be sure to check commissions and other prerequisites before you trade, though.

Futures trading systems: How trading actually takes place

Around the world, most futures exchanges now use electronic trading. In the United States, we still use the *open outcry system* of futures trading for many physical commodities, such as agriculturals and oil. This means that traders on a trading floor or in a trading pit shout and use hand signals to make transactions or trades with each other. However, most U.S. futures markets also offer electronic trading.

In the open outcry system, here's how a trade takes place: When you call your broker, he relays a message to the trading floor, where a runner relays the message to the floor broker, who then executes the trade. The runner then relays the trade confirmation back to your broker, who tells you how it went. Trade reporters on the floor of the exchange watch for executed trades, record them, and transmit these transactions to the exchange, which, in turn, transmits the price to the entire world almost simultaneously.

The order of business is similar when you trade futures online, except that you receive a trade confirmation via an e-mail or other online communiqué.

In the futures market, your daily trading activity is *marked to market,* which means that your net gain or net loss from changes in price of the outstanding futures contracts open in your account are calculated and applied to your account each day at the end of the trading day. Your gains are available for use the following day for additional trading or withdrawal from your account.

Your net losses are removed from your account, reducing the amount you have to trade with or that you can withdraw from your account.

One key difference between open outcry and electronic trading is the length of the trading day. Regular market hours usually run from 8:30 a.m. to 4:15 p.m. eastern time. Globex, the major electronic data and trading system, extends futures trading beyond the pits and into an electronic overnight session. Globex is active 23 hours per day.

When you turn to the financial news on CNBC before the stock market opens, you see quotes for the S&P 500 futures and others taken from Globex as traders from around the world make electronic trades. Globex quotes are real, meaning that if you keep a position open overnight, and you place a *sell stop* (defined in the next section) under it or you place a buy order with instructions to execute in Globex, you may wake up the next morning with a new position, or out of a position altogether.

Globex trading overnight tends to be thinner than trading during regular market hours. It's also more volatile in some ways than trading during regular hours.

You can monitor Globex stock index futures, Eurodollars, and currency trades on a delayed basis overnight free of charge at `www.cme.com/trading/dta/del/globex.html`.

Futures lingo

If you're going to trade futures, you have to know trader talk. Key terms include the following:

- ✔ **Going long:** You're *bullish,* or positive on the market, and you want to buy something. When I say "I'm long oil," in the context of futures trading, it means that I own oil futures.

- ✔ **Being short:** You're *bearish,* or negative on the market, and your goal is to make money when the price of the futures contract that you choose to short falls in price.

- ✔ **Locals:** The people in the trading pits. They're usually among the first to react to news and other events that affect the markets.

- ✔ **Front month:** The futures contract month nearest to expiration. This time frame may not always feature the most widely quoted futures contract. As one contract expires, the next contract in line becomes the front month.

✔ **Orders:** Instructions that lead to the completion of a trade. They can be placed in a variety of ways, including the following:

- A *stop-loss order* means that you want to limit your losses at or above a certain price. A stop-loss order becomes a market order (see the next entry) to buy or sell at the prevailing market price after the market touches the *stop price,* or the price at which you've instructed the broker to sell. A *buy stop* is placed above the market. A *sell stop* is placed below the market. Stop orders can also be used to initiate a long or short position, not just to close (offset) an open position.

- A *market order* means that you'll take the prevailing price the market has to offer.

- A *trailing stop* is a self-adjusting stop order. When you place a trailing stop, it changes automatically depending on the price of the underlying asset.

✔ **Hedging:** A trading technique used to manage risk. It may mean that you're setting up a trade that can go either way, and you want to be prepared for whichever way the market breaks. In the context of large producers of commodities, *hedging* means that they put strategies in place in case the market does the opposite of what's expected.

✔ **The pit:** Where all futures contracts are traded during a regular-hours trading session in the futures markets.

✔ **Speculators:** Traders (usually small- to medium-sized) who are trying to make money only from the fluctuation of prices without intending to take delivery of the contract.

✔ **Floor brokers:** Agents (generally futures commission merchants) who receive a commission to buy and sell futures contracts for their clients.

✔ **Bid:** The highest price a buyer is willing to pay.

✔ **Offer:** The lowest price a seller is willing to accept.

✔ **Taking delivery:** Taking the product on which you were speculating.

✔ **Supply-and-demand equation:** Trader talk referring to whether buyers outnumber sellers. When there are more sellers than buyers, the equation tilts toward supply, and vice versa.

✔ **Expiration:** The date at which a contract expires, or is no longer trading.

✔ **Delivery:** What futures contracts are all about — someone actually delivering or handing something to someone else in exchange for money.

The individual players: Hedgers and speculators

The two major categories of traders are hedgers and speculators. The two groups enter the futures market trying to accomplish different objectives.

Hedgers trade not only in futures contracts but also in the commodity, equity, or product represented by the contract. They trade futures to secure the future price of the commodity of which they will take delivery and then sell later in the cash market. By buying or selling futures contracts, they protect themselves against future price risks. *Speculators* bet on the price change potential for one reason only — profit.

The interaction between speculators and hedgers is what makes the futures markets efficient. This efficiency and the accuracy of the supply-and-demand equation increase as the underlying contract gets closer to expiration and more information about what the marketplace requires at the time of delivery becomes available.

A hedger may try to take the speculator's money, and vice versa. A speculator, for example, may buy a contract from a hedger at a low price, anticipating that it will be worth more. The hedger sells at that low price because he expects the price to decline further. Hedgers transfer the risk of price variability to others in exchange for the cost of the hedge. Speculators assume price variability risk, thus making the transfer possible in exchange for the potential to gain. A hedger and a speculator can both be very happy from the outcome of price variability in the same market.

Futures contracts are attractive to *longs* (people looking to buy at the lowest possible price and sell at the highest possible price) and *shorts* (people selling commodities in the hope that prices fall) because they provide price and time certainty and reduce the risk associated with *volatility,* or the speed at which prices change up or down. Hedging can help lock in an acceptable *price margin,* or difference between the futures price and the cash price for the commodity, and improve the risk between the cost of the raw material and the retail cost of the final product by covering for any market-related losses. Note: Hedge positions don't always work, and in some cases, they can make losses worse.

Duarte Air: A hedging example

Let's say that Duarte Air is projecting a need for large amounts of jet fuel for the summer season, based on the trends in travel during the past decade. The airline also knows that demand for gasoline tends to rise in the summer; thus prices for the jet fuel it needs are also likely to rise because of refinery usage issues — refineries switch a major portion of their summer production to gasoline.

Wanting to hedge costs for crude oil in the summer, Duarte Air starts buying July crude oil and gasoline futures a few months ahead of time, hoping that, as the prices rise, the profits from the trades can offset the costs of the expected rise in jet fuel. So Duarte Air buys July crude futures at $50 per barrel in December, and by June they are trading at $60 per barrel. As the prices continue to rise, Duarte starts unloading the contracts, pocketing the $10-per-barrel profit and using it to offset the higher costs of its fuel in the spot market (during the summer travel season).

Getting Up to Speed on Options

The options market goes hand in hand with the futures markets. When used properly, options give you an opportunity to diversify your holdings beyond traditional investments and to hedge your portfolio against risk. The key is discovering how to use options the right way.

Here's some basic information about options:

- **Option buyers are also known as *holders*, and option sellers are known as *writers*.** *Call* option holders have the right to buy a stipulated quantity of the underlying asset specified in the contract. *Put* option holders have the right to sell a specified amount of the underlying asset in the contract. Call and put holders can exercise these rights at the *strike price,* the predetermined price at which an option will be delivered when it is exercised.

  Call option writers have the potential obligation to sell. Put option buyers have the potential obligation to buy.

- **Options, like futures contracts, have expiration dates.** All stock options expire on the third Friday of the month. Options on futures expire on different days depending on the contract. Sometimes different classes of options expire on the same day. These days are known as double-, triple-, and quadruple-witching days:

  - **Double-witching days:** When any two of the different classes of options (stock, stock index options, and stock index futures options) expire.

- **Triple-witching days:** When all three classes expire simultaneously, which happens on the third Friday at the end of a quarter.

- **Quadruple-witching days:** When all three classes of options expire along with single stock futures options.

✔ **Options trade during the trading hours of the underlying asset.**

✔ **Owning an option doesn't give the holder any share of the underlying security.** The right to buy or sell that security is what options are all about.

✔ **Options are a (slightly less than) zero-sum game.** For every dollar someone makes, someone loses a dollar. Options, like futures, have both a seller and a buyer. When you make a losing trade, someone else gets an amount equal to your losses transferred to his or her account, and you get charged commission. The exchanges also get a fee.

✔ **If you win, you'll probably owe taxes.** The treatment of options in the tax code is complex, and much of it deals with whether you have short-term or long-term gains. The details are provided in the option disclosure statement, which is required reading before you ever trade options. The statement is part of the packet of information your broker gives you along with the account application. Be sure to read that document carefully and discuss the tax-related details with your accountant before trading.

Some traders trade options (and do it well) purely as a vehicle of speculation. However, the primary function of a listed option is risk management, not speculation, even though options (when applied properly) do offer limited risk and unlimited reward potential and can be more compelling than straight futures, especially for people who want to speculate with less than $30,000.

Options usually trade at a fraction of the price of the underlying asset, making them attractive to investors with small accounts. Before you trade, visit the Commodity Futures Trading Commission (CFTC) Web site Education Center, www.cftc.gov/educationcenter/. It's an excellent resource that provides you with a summary of what you need to know before you open a trading account and what to avoid after you open one.

American- and European-style options

Two major categories of options exist and are based on the way they can be exercised:

✔ *American-style options* can be exercised, or acted upon, if your intent is to do what the option gives you the right to do on or before the expiration date. The person holding the option decides.

The advantage of American-style options is that you have more flexibility regarding when and how to exercise them. Most individual stock options and some index options are traded under American-style options exercise rules.

✔ *European-style options* can be exercised only on the date of expiration. European-style options are traded on many of the cash-based indexes. For example, options based on the S&P 500 and the Dow Jones Industrial indexes are European-style.

The advantage of European-style options is that you are certain about the timeline you have until the option is exercised.

All options can be exercised only once.

Types of options: Calls and puts

Two types of options are traded. One kind lets you speculate on prices of the underlying asset rising, and the other lets you bet on their fall.

Calls

A *call option* gives you the right to buy a defined amount of the underlying asset at a certain price before a certain amount of time expires. (Think of it as a bet that the underlying asset is going to rise in value.) If you don't buy the asset by the time the option expires, you lose only the money that you spent on the call option. You can always sell your option prior to expiration to avoid exercising it, to avoid further loss, or to profit if it has risen in value. Call options usually rise in price when the underlying asset rises in price.

When you buy a call option, you put up the option premium for the right to exercise an option to buy the underlying asset before the call option expires. When you exercise a call, you're buying the underlying stock or asset at the *strike price,* the predetermined price at which an option will be delivered when it is exercised.

The attractiveness of buying call options is that the upside potential is huge, and the downside risk is limited to the original premium — the price you pay for the option.

Puts

Put options are bets that the price of the underlying asset is going to fall. Puts are excellent trading instruments when you're trying to guard against losses in stocks, futures contracts, or commodities that you already own. Buying a put option gives you the right to sell a specific quantity of the underlying asset at a predetermined price (the strike price) during a certain amount of time. Like calls, if you don't exercise a put option, your risk is limited to the option premium, or the price you paid for it.

When you exercise a put option, you're exercising your right to sell the underlying asset at the strike price. Puts are sometimes thought of as portfolio insurance, because they give you the option of selling a falling stock at a predetermined strike price. You can also sell puts.

Option quotes

When you trade options, you have to look at quote boards on your computer, even if you're using a broker. Figure 1-1 shows you a good generic example of a quote board provided by the Chicago Board of Options Exchange (www.cboe.com).

Call Quote	XYZ	Put Quote
* 6.50-7.00	* APR25	* 0.15-0.25 *
* 1.55-1.90	* APR30	* 0.15-0.25 *
* 0.15-0.25	* APR35	* 3.10-3.50 *
* 6.50-7.00	* MAY25	* 0.05-0.15 *
* 4.10-4.50	* MAY27$\frac{1}{2}$	* 0.15-0.25 *
* 1.75-2.00	* MAY30	* 0.20-0.45 *
* 0.45-0.70	* MAY32$\frac{1}{2}$	* 1.15-1.40 *
* 0.15-0.25	* MAY35	* 3.10-3.50 *
* 6.90-7.40	* AUG25	* 0.15-0.25 *
* 2.75-3.10	* AUG30	* 0.90-1.00 *
* 0.50-0.75	* AUG35	* 3.40-3.80 *

Figure 1-1: A sample options quote board, courtesy of CBOE. The circled price is the premium paid in the example described.

Book III

Futures and Options

On this quote board, which shows the May 30 call option for XYZ, you find information about option classes, series, and pricing. XYZ is the option class, while May 30 is the *option series,* a grouping of puts or calls of the same underlying asset with the same strike price and expiration date. If you look above and below the May 30 series, you find other option series listed, such as the May 25 puts and calls, listed two sections above the circled series. The *premium,* or the price, on the May 30 XYZ is two points. If this was a call to buy XYZ stock, you'd pay $200, because options for stocks give you the right to control 100-share lots of the stock.

The all-important volatility

Volatility, a measure of how fast and how much prices of the underlying asset move, is key to understanding why option prices fluctuate and act the way they do. In fact, volatility is the most important concept in options trading. There are two kinds of volatility: implied volatility (IV) and historical (or statistical) volatility (HV). Whereas HV measures the rate of movement in the price of the underlying asset, IV measures the price movement of the option itself:

- ✔ **Implied volatility (IV):** This is the estimated volatility of a security's price in real time, or as the option trades. Values for IV come from formulas that measure the options market's expectations, offering a prediction of the volatility of the underlying asset over the life of the option. Another way of looking at it is that IV is the volatility implied by the market price of the option based on an option pricing model. In other words, it is the volatility that, given a particular pricing model, yields a theoretical value for the option equal to the current price. It usually rises when the markets are in downtrends and falls when the markets are in uptrends.

  Most of the time, IV is computed using a formula based on something called the *Black-Scholes model.* The goal of the Black-Scholes model, which is highly theoretical for actual trading, is to calculate a fair market value of an option by incorporating multiple variables such as historical volatility, time premium, and strike price. Here's a little secret: Although the number it produces, IV, is central to options trading, the Black-Scholes formula alone isn't very practical as a trading tool because trading software automatically calculates the necessary measurements.

- ✔ **Historical volatility (HV):** Also known as *statistical volatility* (SV), this is a measurement of how fast prices of the underlying asset have been changing over time. Because HV is always changing, it has to be calculated on a daily basis. It's stated as a percentage and summarizes the recent movements in price. In general, the bigger the HV, the more an option is worth.

Volatility can be difficult to grasp unless taken in small bites. Fortunately, trading software programs provide a great deal of the information needed to keep track of volatility. Bare-bones screening software is available for free from The Options Industry Council (go to www.888options.com). For more sophisticated analysis, you have to spend some money. Many good options-trading programs are available. Among the most popular programs is Option Vue 5 Options Analysis Software, which has just about everything you could want to analyze options and find trades. Many traders use OptionVue and consider it the benchmark program.

Options mispricing

In a perfect world, HV and IV should be fairly close together, given the fact that they are supposed to be measures of two financial assets that are intrinsically related to one another, the underlying asset and its option. In fact, sometimes IV and HV actually are very close together. Yet the differences in these numbers at different stages of the market cycle can provide excellent trading opportunities. This concept is called *options mispricing,* and if you can understand how to use it, options mispricing can help you make better trading decisions.

When HV and IV are far apart, the price of the option is not reflecting the actual volatility of the underlying asset. For example, if IV rises dramatically and HV is very low, the underlying stock may be a possible candidate for a takeover. Under those circumstances, the stock probably has been stuck in a trading range as the market awaits news. At the same time, option premiums may remain high because of the potential for sudden changes with regard to the deal.

The bottom line is that HV and IV are useful tools in trading options. Most software programs will graph out these two variables. When they are charted, big spreads become easy to spot, and that enables you to look for trading opportunities.

Using volatility to make trading decisions

Think of decreasing volatility as a coiled spring that is about to explode. As a trader, you want to be able to predict when changes in volatility — and thus changes in prices — are coming. One way to do that is to keep tabs on HV. You can chart 10-, 20-, 50-, and 100-day volatility figures. Watch the trends during each of the four periods. If the 100-day volatility was 60 percent and the 10-day volatility was 10 percent, the volatility in price of the underlying asset is slowing. When prices begin to congregate in narrower trading ranges, volatility begins to decrease, and it can be a sign that a big move is coming. That's when you can

✔ Start paying closer attention to the option series and making potential trading plans.

✔ Decide whether IV is cheap or expensive, no matter what you may think the prospects of the underlying asset are.

✔ Play the momentum, which is also a good strategy with options, regardless of volatility. A couple of simple but powerful algorithms are buying calls or selling puts in stocks currently trending higher, or buying puts and selling calls in markets currently trending lower. In other words, paying attention to strong price trends can outweigh all volatility considerations.

When the majority of traders expects the underlying asset to be nonvolatile, as indicated by low volatility measurements, or wide spreads between HV and IV appear, you need to be buying volatility. That means when everyone else is selling options, you need to analyze the situation and pick the options with the best potential to buy, always knowing that you can be wrong and making plans to get out of the positions before you lose a whole lot of money.

Selling expensive options and buying cheap ones

The first step to trading options based on implied volatility is to buy and sell them correctly at the best possible price. This may sound difficult but can be made relatively easy by option trading software. A simple method is to list a series of options on your screen, and to look at two particular numbers, the actual price of the option (the ask price) and the theoretical value of the option, which is derived from the Black-Sholes formula, the benchmark equation for valuing options. Black-Sholes values are based on underlying price, option strike price, option premium, historical volatility, expiration date, interest rate, and dividend rate.

The difference between the ask price and the theoretical price is the key, with the largest difference between the two numbers giving you the "largest discount" and leading you to the least expensive option in the series. To find the most expensive option, you would rank the series in reverse and look for the smallest difference in the two prices, or the "smallest discount." An excellent example of this technique can be found at www.optionstar.com/art/art1.htm.

It is always useful to keep an eye on options trading activity, because market makers often smell that something is up and start buying options for their own accounts to cover their short positions. Market makers tend to be short more often than not to protect themselves, because with access to all the trading activity data, they have better information than the public in general.

When option volume and IV pick up, look at the underlying assets and at the action in other option series. If the underlying asset doesn't make a move and the action in other options doesn't start to pick up, what's probably happening is that a hedge fund or other market mover is putting on a big hedge or establishing a large position to protect its portfolio.

Rising options prices combined with the propagation of high volume and/or implied volatility, with or without a rise in the price of the underlying asset, are signs that the options market makers are on the move. These smart guys usually can tell when someone is putting on a hedge or when something else is really up. Most of the time, market makers are in risky positions against the market trend. When the action starts to pick up, the first thing they do is try to figure out whether the spike in activity is something major or just a hedge. If market makers determine that something major is going on, they try to buy all the options they can find on the other side of their current positions. If they can't find options, they start buying the underlying assets — stocks or futures contracts.

When you see big rises in trading volume and implied volatility in an option, it's a fairly good sign that somebody knows something that few others know. Staying away from such trades, or at least not selling in volatility, is a good idea. These can be highly risky situations that can turn on a dime and can make you lose money very quickly.

Measurements of risk: It's Greek to me

Options require you to pick up a bit of the Greek language, but don't panic; you need to learn only four words: *delta, gamma, theta,* and *vega.* Each is important. *The Greeks,* as they are commonly called, are measurements of risk. They explain several variables that influence option prices:

- ✔ **Amount of volatility:** An increase in volatility usually is positive for put and call options, if you're long in the option. If you're the writer of the option, an increase in volatility is negative. (See the preceding section for details about volatility.)

- ✔ **Changes in the time to expiration.** The closer you get to the time of expiration, the more negative the time factor becomes for a holder of the option and the less your potential for profit. Time value shrinks as an option approaches expiration and is zero upon expiration of the option.

- ✔ **Changes in the price of the underlying asset.** An increase in the price of the underlying asset usually is a positive influence on the price of a call option. A decrease in the price of the underlying instrument usually is positive for put options and vice versa.

- ✔ **Interest rates:** Interest rates are less important than the other factors most of the time. Higher interest rates make call options more expensive and put options less expensive, in general.

Delta

Delta measures the effect of a change in the price of the underlying asset on the option's premium. Delta is best understood as the amount of change in the price of an option for every one-point move in the underlying asset, or the percentage of the change in price of the underlying asset that is reflected in the price of an option. Delta is positive for calls and negative for puts. Values range from 0 to 100 for calls and from 0 to –100 for puts.

Puts have a negative delta number because of their inverse or negative relationship to the underlying asset. Put premiums fall when the underlying asset rises in price, and they rise when the underlying asset falls. Call options have a positive relationship to the underlying asset and thus a positive delta number. As the price of the underlying asset goes up, so do call premiums, unless other variables change, such as implied volatility, time to expiration, and interest rates. Call premiums generally go down as the price of the underlying asset falls, as long as no other influences are putting undue pressure on the option.

Book III

Futures and Options

Here is how it works: An at-the-money call has a delta value of 0.5 or 50, which tells you that the option's premium will rise or fall by half a point with a one-point move in the underlying asset. If an at-the-money call option for wheat has a delta of 0.5 and the wheat futures contract associated with the option goes up 10 cents, the premium on the option will rise approximately by 5 cents, or $0.5 \times 10 = 5$. The actual gain will be $250 because each cent in premium is worth $50 in the contract.

The further into the money the option premium advances, the closer the relationship between the price of the underlying asset and the price of the option becomes. When delta approaches 1 for calls, or –1 for puts, the price of the option and the underlying asset move the same, assuming all the other variables remain under control.

Gamma

Gamma measures the rate of change of delta in relation to the change in the price of the underlying asset, and it enables you to predict how much you're going to make or lose based on the movement of the underlying position.

The best way to understand this concept is to look at an example like the one in Figure 1-2, which shows the changes in delta and gamma as the underlying asset changes in price. The example features a short position in the S&P 500 September $930 call option as it rises in price from $925 on the left to $934 on the right and is based on trader John Summa's explanation of the Greeks. (Summa runs a Web site called OptionsNerd.com.) The chart was prepared using OptionVue 5 Options Analytical Software (www.optionvue.com).

Figure 1-2:
Summary of risk measures for the short September S&P 500 930 call option.

P/L	425	300	175	50	-75	-200	-325	-475	-600	-750
Delta	-48.36	-49.16	-49.96	-50.76	-51.55	-52.34	-53.13	-53.92	-54.70	-55.49
Gamma	-0.80	-0.80	-0.80	-0.80	-0.79	-0.79	-0.79	-0.79	-0.78	-0.78
Theta	45.01	45.11	45.20	45.28	45.35	45.40	45.44	45.47	45.48	45.48
Vega	-96.30	-96.49	-96.65	-96.78	-96.87	-96.94	-96.98	-96.99	-96.96	-96.91

The first line in Figure 1-2 is a calculation of the profit or loss for the S&P 500 Index futures 930 call option — $930 is the strike price of the S&P 500 Index futures option that expires in September. The –200 line is the at-the-money strike of the 930 call option, and each column represents a one-point change in the underlying asset. The at-the-money gamma of the underlying asset for the 930 option is –0.79, and the delta is –52.34. What this tells you is that for every one-point move in the depicted futures contract, delta will increase by exactly 0.79. If you move one column to the right, you see the delta changes to –53.13, which is an increase of 0.79 from –52.34.

The position depicts a short call position that is losing money. The P/L line is measuring Profit/Loss. The more negative the P/L numbers become, the more in the red the position is. Note also that delta is increasingly negative as the price of the option rises. Finally, with delta being at –52.34, the position is expected to lose 0.5234 points in price with the next one-point rise in the underlying futures contract.

The further out of the money that a call option declines, the smaller the delta, because changes in the underlying asset cause only small changes in the option premium. The delta gets larger as the call option advances closer to the money, which is a result of an increase in the underlying asset's price. Other important aspects of gamma are that it

✔ Is smallest for deep out-of-the-money and in-the-money options.

✔ Is highest when the option gets near the money.

✔ Is positive for long options and negative for short options.

Theta

Theta measures the rate of decline of the *time premium* (the effect on the option's price of the time remaining until option expiration) with the passage of time. Understanding premium erosion due to the passage of time is critical to being successful at trading options. Often the effects of theta will offset the effects of delta, resulting in the trader being right about the direction of the move and still losing money.

It helps to remember that option premiums consist of time premium plus intrinsic value. If the option is not in the money, all the premium is considered time premium. Time premium reflects the price for the remaining life of the option and the volatility component.

As time passes and option expiration grows near, the value of the time premium decreases, and the amount of decrease grows faster as option expiration nears. Theta rises sharply during the last few weeks of trading and can do a considerable amount of damage to a long holder's position, which is made worse when the option's implied volatility is falling at the same time.

The following mini-table shows the theta values for the featured example of the short S&P 500 Index futures 930 call option (refer to Figure 1-2).

	T+0	T+6	T+13	T+19
Theta	45.4	51.85	65.2	93.3

Book III

Futures and Options

To see how theta affects the price of an option, look in the fourth column of the table, where the figure for T+19 measures theta six days before the option's expiration. The value 93.3 tells you that the option is losing $93.30 per day, a major increase in time-influenced loss of value compared with the figure for T+0, where the option's loss of value attributed to time alone was only $45.40 per day.

Vega

Vega measures risk exposure to changes in implied volatility and tells traders how much an option's price will rise or fall as the volatility of the option varies. Put another way, vega is an estimate of how much the theoretical value of an option changes when volatility changes 1 percent.

Vega is expressed as a value; refer to Figure 1-2, which shows that the short call option has a negative vega value — this tells you that the position will gain in price if the implied volatility falls. The value of vega tells you by how much the position will gain in this case. If the at-the-money value for vega is –96.94, for example, you know that for each percentage-point drop in implied volatility, a short call position will gain by $96.94.

Here are a few other vega facts to keep you out of the poorhouse:

✔ Vega can rise or fall without the price changes of the underlying asset.

✔ It can increase if the price of the underlying asset moves quickly, especially when the stock market declines fast or a commodity makes a big move.

✔ It falls as expiration of the option nears.

Should Futures or Options Be in Your Future?

Futures traders, at least the ones who survive the initial stages of torment and can ride out the inevitable and discouraging down periods, are by nature risk takers. And options are an integral part of the trading game that futures traders play, although it is worth noting that options and futures are viable stand-alone vehicles for trading. But is trading in futures or options right for *you?* The following sections help you answer that question.

How much money do you have?

Many experienced traders say that you need $100,000 to get started, but the truth is that there are many talented traders who have made fortunes after starting out with significantly less than $100,000. However, it would be irresponsible for me to lead you astray by giving you the impression that the odds are in your favor if you start trading at a very low level.

The reality is that different people fare differently depending on their trading ability, at any level of experience. A trader with $1 million in equity can lose large amounts just as easily as you and I with $10,000 worth of equity in our account.

If you don't have that much money and are not sure how to proceed, you need to either reconsider trading altogether, develop a stout trading plan and the discipline required to heed its tenets, or consider managed futures contracts.

How involved are you?

Futures trading is risky business and requires active participation. It can be plied successfully only if you're serious about it and committed to it. That means you must be able to develop your trading craft by constantly reviewing and modifying your plan and strategies.

Trading is not investing; it's *speculating,* assuming a business risk with the hope of profiting from market fluctuations. Successful speculating requires analyzing situations, predicting outcomes, and putting your money on one side of a trade based on which way you think the market is going to go, up or down. To be a successful futures and options trader, you're going to have to become connected with the world through the Internet, television, and other news sources so you can be up-to-date and intimately knowledgeable with regard to world events. And I don't mean just picking up on what you get from occasionally watching the evening or headline news shows.

Book III

Futures and Options

Before You Begin

If you decide that futures and options trading is right for you, you need to amass a few things. In addition to a sufficient amount of money, you need a computer, trading program, and brokerage account of some sort. This section explains the details.

Setting up shop: Technology

When it comes to technology, you need an efficient computer system with enough memory to enable you to look at large amounts of data and run either multiple, fully loaded browsers or several monitors at the same time. You also need a high-speed Internet connection. If you get serious about trading, you also need to consider having two modes of high-speed Internet access.

For a home office, a full-time trader often has high-speed Internet through the cable television service and through DSL (digital subscriber line), with one or the other serving as a backup.

Knowing what you're getting into

Not all options are created equal. In his book *Starting Out In Futures Trading* (McGraw-Hill), author Mark Powers offers the following checklist of what you need to know before you start trading, which I'm paraphrasing:

✔ **Are you trading a U.S. or a foreign option? And is it an exchange-traded or dealer-traded option?** U.S. options are easily followed, and they're regulated by the CFTC and so are all the parties involved in issuing the contract. Exchange-traded options are standardized contracts that are more liquid and can be hedged better against risk. That isn't always the case with other, dealer-traded options.

✔ **Who is guaranteeing the transaction?** U.S. exchanges and firms are constantly monitored for liquidity and solvency. Foreign institutions are not necessarily as well monitored, so their futures and options contracts need to be checked individually, especially in the case of foreign options or options that are not exchange-traded.

✔ **How much of the premium that you pay is actually the value of the option?** In some cases, the fees involved when you deal with independent options dealers can be very high and can hurt your transaction. Also keep the following in mind: commission versus cost of the option versus its theoretical value versus intrinsic value, all of which can be vastly different. You pay the option premium plus a commission charge; the commission is not imbedded in the option premium.

✔ **What is the break-even price for your option?** In other words, how much price appreciation will be needed before you make money?

✔ **How much in commissions are you paying, and what kind of service are you getting for what you're paying?** Part of the answer here is to consider where you are with regard to your trade. Prior to expiration if long or short an option, your breakeven is the cost of your option. (If initially long and you paid $5 and you sell it for $5, you break even. If initially short an option and you sold for $5 and you buy it back for $5, you break even.) At expiration it gets a little more complicated. For calls, your breakeven is the strike price plus the premium paid or received by the writer. For puts, your breakeven is the strike price minus the premium paid or received by the writer.

✔ **Will your advisor/broker check several independent sources to find out what expectations are with respect to the future price of the underlying asset?** If there is a widespread expectation that price will change very little in the future, the premium that you pay should be low.

✔ **How will you and your advisor/broker exercise your option, and what will you receive when you do?** Always know how you and your broker will communicate. That means that you have to read and understand the terms of the management contract carefully before you put any money down.

✔ **How will your broker let you know when your options contract has been executed and what the status of your account is?** Online brokers usually let you know this information automatically after your trade is executed. Some traditional brokers call you sometime after the order is executed. You have to do what is most comfortable for you. It's important to keep in mind, though, that options trading can be very short-term oriented; the more you know and the faster you know it, the better your chances are of keeping up with your account, and the better the set of decisions you can make.

Choosing an options broker

If you are interested in trading options but aren't sure about your own ability to trade them, you need to find a good options broker/advisor to help you out. A broker can assist with strategy development, research, monitoring open positions, and working orders. A futures broker usually can handle your options activity as it relates to futures and may be able to handle stock option transactions. If you want to do all that stuff yourself, then you just want to get access to the markets through the lowest cost medium, usually an online discount broker.

Con artists and unscrupulous advisors lurk around every corner and prey on the unsuspecting and uninformed options trader, so do homework. When selecting a broker/advisor, be sure to ask these important questions, which are applicable to broker and advisor candidates for online and managed accounts:

✔ **What kinds of services does the brokerage firm offer?** If you decide to establish a managed account, make sure early on that you're getting your money's worth. Aside from getting good results, you're paying for customer service. Most advisors will meet with you at least on a yearly basis. Many meet with you on a quarterly basis. If you're an active trader and your advisor calls you with trades frequently, make sure that he's giving you winning trades. Otherwise, he's probably churning your account.

✔ **What commissions and other costs are charged and under what circumstances?** As part of your search, compare fees and services between the different advisor/broker candidates, and match their results with their costs.

✔ **How experienced in options trading is the broker who was assigned to me?**

Book III

Futures and Options

✔ **Is my broker registered with the Commodities Futures Trading Commission (CFTC) or National Futures Association (NFA)?** This is applicable to options on futures only. For stock options, the Financial Industry Regulatory Authority (FINRA) and CBOE memberships are critical.

If the broker is registered with one of these organizations, contact it to find out whether the firm or the broker is in good standing or if public records of previous disciplinary actions exist. If disciplinary actions have been taken, ask for audited results (and check out the auditor because they may have had their own problems!).

✔ **What kind of results can I expect from the broker assigned to me?** Be careful of financial advisors that advertise instant riches based on small amounts of money and promise that they will return all of your money. No one can make such a promise. Also get to know who's doing the trading and what methods they're using before you give them any of your money.

In addition to asking questions, make sure that you tell your advisor how much risk you are willing to take and how involved you want to be. If he or she does things that make you uncomfortable despite your wishes regarding the amount of risk you're willing to take, it's time to say goodbye to that advisor. A good advisor tells you whether (or not) you're a good customer-match for the methods he's accustomed to using. When I meet with clients whose risk tolerance is different from my own, I never take on their accounts. Avoiding discomfort before money changes hands is the best course.

Completing the necessary paperwork

You have to sign an options agreement with your options broker to be able to trade options. An options agreement, by the way, is separate from a margin agreement. You actually need to sign both before you can trade options, which trade mainly from margin accounts. (A margin agreement is similar to a promissory note when you get a loan from the bank. Basically, you are promising to repay the loan, and the borrowed stock is collateral for the loan.)

Option trading agreements are pretty stout, spelling out the risks of options trading above your signature and not only holding you liable for knowing the stuff on the agreement but also expecting you to make good on the promises you make in the agreement.

Chapter 2

Being a Savvy Futures and Options Trader

In This Chapter

▶ Understanding the fiat system

▶ Eyeing the relationship between central banks and the money supply

▶ Studying key economic reports

Successful futures and options traders can anticipate market movement. You can also be successful by following established trends and cutting losses. To understand what the markets are doing or anticipate where they're heading, you need to be familiar with the global economy, the conflicting pressures that can impact it (money supply, interest rates, and inflation, for example), and the role of central banks in stabilizing those forces — all topics covered in this chapter.

Being a savvy futures and options trader also means being able to recognize economic trends early. To that end, this chapter also explains how to read and make sense of key economic reports.

Maneuvering Money Matters: The Fiat System

Throughout the world, governments use what's called the *fiat system:* A government mandates that the paper currency it prints is legal tender for making financial transactions. Fiat money has no value in and of itself, but it is accepted as money because a government says that it's money, and the public has enough confidence and faith in the money's ability to serve as a storage medium for purchasing power.

Fiat money is the opposite of *commodity money,* money based on a valuable commodity. This method of valuation was used in the past. At times, the commodity itself actually was used as money. For instance, the use of gold, grain, and even furs and other animal products as commodity money preceded the current fiat system.

Realizing where money comes from

Central banks, such as the Federal Reserve ("the Fed") in the United States, create fiat money either by printing it or by buying bonds in the Treasury market. When the economy slows down and the Fed wants to jumpstart it, the Fed can inject money into the system by buying bonds from the banks, which tends to lower interest rates. When the Fed wants to tighten credit and slow down the economy, it might sell bonds to banks, thus draining money from the system.

Instead of using gold as the basis for the monetary system — as was the custom until 1971 — the Fed requires its member banks to keep certain specific amounts of money on reserve as a means of keeping a lid on the uncontrolled expansion of fiat money. These reserve requirements are the major safeguard of the system.

To curb inflation, the Fed limits how much banks can actually lend by using a bank reserve management system. If the current formula calls for a 10 percent reserve ratio, for every dollar that a bank keeps in reserve, it can lend ten dollars. Under the same scenario (a formula that calls for a 10 percent reserve ratio), if the Fed buys $500 million in bonds in the open market, it creates $5 billion in new money that makes its way to the public via bank loans.

Putting fiat to work for you

As a futures trader, the fiat concept is the center of your universe. If you can figure out which way interest rates are headed and where money is flowing, most of what happens in the markets in general will fall into place, and you can make better decisions about which way to trade. Keep these relationships in mind:

✔ Futures markets often move based on the relationship between the bond market and the Fed. When either the Fed or the bond market moves interest rates in one direction, the other eventually will follow.

✔ Higher interest rates tend to eventually slow economic growth, while lower interest rates tend to spur economies.

Normally, you begin to see these markets come to life at some point before or after the Fed makes a move. So get in the habit of watching all the markets together. When the Fed starts to ease rates, you want to look at what happens to commodities like copper, gold, oil, and so on. The commodities markets provide you with confirmation of what the markets in general are expecting as the Fed makes its move.

Respecting the Role of Central Banks

Central banks are designed to make sure that their respective domestic economies run as smoothly as possible. They buy and sell bonds and inject or extract money from the banking system they control. In most countries, central banks are expected at the very least to combat inflationary pressures.

To understand the role of central banks, consider the U.S. economy and the actions of the Federal Reserve. The U.S. economy is dependent upon a series of intertwined relationships. Consumers drive the U.S. economy, and consumers need jobs to buy things and keep the economy going. Economic activity is driven up or down by the ebb and flow between the degree of joblessness and full employment, how easy or difficult it is to get credit, and how much the supply of goods and services is in demand.

As a rule, steady job growth, easy-enough credit, and a balance between supply and demand of goods and services are what the Fed likes to see. When one or more of these factors teeters off balance, the Fed has to act by raising or lowering interest rates with the intention of

- ✔ Tightening or loosening the consumer's ability to obtain credit.
- ✔ Reining in unemployment.
- ✔ Increasing or decreasing the supply side of goods and services to bring it in line with demand.

After a central bank starts down a certain policy route, it usually stays with it for months, creating an intermediate-term trend on which to base the direction of trading. After September 11, 2001, for example, the Fed lowered interest rates 14 times and left them at 1 percent until the summer of 2004, when it began to raise them until the summer of 2006. In September 2007, the Federal Reserve lowered the Discount rate and the Fed Funds rate in response to the subprime mortgage crisis, and followed with another cut in the Fed Funds rate in October.

Book III

Futures and Options

The overarching goal of central banks is to keep in check the boom and bust cycles in the global economy. So far this goal is only an intention, because boom and bust cycles remain in place and are now referred to as the *business cycle*. Nevertheless, the actions of the Fed and other central banks have served to lengthen the amount of time between boom and bust cycles to the extent that they've smoothed out volatile trends.

Following the Money Supply

The *money supply* is how much money is available in an economy to buy goods, services, and securities. The money supply is as important as the supply of goods in determining the direction of the futures and options markets. The four money supply figures to watch are

- ✔ **M0:** This figure refers to all the cash and coins in circulation.

- ✔ **M1:** This figure represents M0 *plus* the amount of money housed in all checking and savings accounts.

- ✔ **M2:** This figure represents M1 *plus* money housed in other types of savings accounts, such as money-market funds and certificates of deposit (CDs) of less than $100,000.

- ✔ **M3:** This figure represents M2 *plus* all other CDs, deposits held in euros, and all *repurchase agreements* (repos, which are essentially secured loans) in which one party sells securities to another party and agrees to buy them back at a later date.

The multiplier effect

The wildest thing about money is how one dollar counts as two dollars whenever it goes around the loop enough times in an interesting little concept known as the *multiplier effect*. For example, say the Fed buys $1 worth of bonds from Bank X, and Bank X lends it to Person 1. Person 1 buys something from Person 2, who deposits the dollar in Bank 1. Bank 1 lends the money to Person 3, who deposits it in Bank 2, where the $1, in terms of money supply, is now $2 because it's been counted twice. By multiplying this little exercise by billions of transactions, you can arrive at the massive money supply numbers in the United States.

Grasping the monetary exchange equation

The *monetary exchange equation* explains the relationship between money supply and inflation:

Velocity × Money Supply = Gross Domestic Product (GDP) × GDP Deflator

Velocity is a measure of how fast money is changing hands, recording how many times per year the money actually is exchanged. *GDP* is the sum of all the goods and services produced by the economy. The *GDP deflator* is a measure of inflation, or a sustained rise in prices.

Here's what's important about the money supply as it relates to futures and options trading: A rising money supply, usually spawned by lower interest rates, tends to spur the economy and eventually fuels demand for commodities. Whenever the money supply rises to a key level, which differs in every cycle, inflationary pressures eventually begin to appear, and the Fed starts reducing the money supply. The more money that's available, the more likely that some of it will make its way into the futures and options markets.

Linking money supply and commodity tendencies

As a general rule, futures prices respond to inflation. Some, such as gold, tend to rise; others, such as the U.S. dollar, tend to fall. Here is a quick-and-dirty guide to general money supply/commodity tendencies:

- Metals, agricultural products, oil, and livestock contracts generally tend to rise along with money supply.

- Generally, bond prices fall, and interest rates or bond yields rise in response to inflation.

- Stock index futures are more variable in their relationship with the money supply, but eventually, they tend to rise when interest rates are falling, and they tend to fall when interest rates reach a high enough level.

- Currencies tend to fall with inflation.

In a global economy, many of these dynamics occur simultaneously or in close proximity to each other, which is why an understanding of the global economy is more important when trading futures than when trading individual stocks.

Putting money supply info to good use

The key to making money by using money supply information is to have a good grip on whether the Fed actually is putting money into the system or taking it out. What's even more important is how fast the Fed is doing whatever it's doing at the time.

I have a quick-and-dirty formula that I use to figure out how fast the money supply is growing or shrinking. Every week I check Barron's Web site (www.barrons.com). From the home page, I click on Market Lab, and then I look for a Money Supply table that can be found under the "Economy & Money" heading. Figure 2-1 is a reproduction of one of the tables. Because I'm not an economist, I ignore the seasonal adjustments and go straight to the raw data in the table, calculating a ratio of the growth rate. Although it isn't scientific, it works.

Money Supply

Money Supply (Bil. $ sa)		Latest	Prev.	Yr. Ago
Week ended 3/21				
M1	(seas. adjusted)	1380.1	1352.9	1343.5
M1	(not adjusted)	1382.1	1338.7	1341.1
M2	(seas. adjusted)	6477.6	r6447.4	6183.3
M2	(not adjusted)	6471.4	r6472.9	6176.8
M3	(seas. adjusted)	9509.8	r9491.9	9001.0
M3	(not adjusted)	9530.7	r9547.5	9019.3
Monthly Money Supply				
Month Ended February				
M1	(seas. adjusted)	1366.9	1358.5	1311.9
M2	(seas. adjusted)	r6456.4	6442.2	6129.0
M3	(seas. adjusted)	r9502.6	9485.3	8930.6

Figure 2-1: Money supply weekly summary from www.barrons.com.

For example, I plug the M2 numbers for the same time frame this year and last into this simple equation:

[(This year's M2 ÷ Last year's M2) − 1] × 100 = percentage growth

With the numbers from Figure 2-1 plugged in, the equation looks like this:

[(6,471.4 ÷ 6,176.8) − 1] × 100 = 4.7 percent

The 4.7 percent growth rate is what I care about, because that's how fast the M2 money supply grew during the past year and that means that on a yearly basis, as of the date in the figure, 4.7 percent more money was in circulation than the year before.

The money supply growth rate, when put together with other market indicators such as consumer prices and the Commodity Research Bureau (CRB) Index (a measure of global commodities markets), can be a useful trading tool. So don't limit your observations to just what the Fed is doing.

Don't get bogged down with the esoteric aspects of money supply. The key is to understand the following concept: At some point in the future, it may come to pass that global central banks have put so much money into circulation that money supply may become as important an indicator as it was in decades past. If and when that time comes, the inflation-sensitive markets, such as gold, energy, and grains, are likely to become very active. When that happens, you need to be able to trade them effectively.

Connecting money flows to financial markets

When central banks buy bonds from banks and dealers, they're putting money into circulation, making it easier for people and businesses to borrow. When money becomes easier to borrow, the potential for commodity markets to become explosive reaches its zenith because commodity markets thrive on money. The commodity markets' actions are directly related to interest rates; underlying supply; and the perceptions and actions of the public, governments, and traders as they react to *supply* (how much is available and how fast it's going to be used up) and, to a lesser degree, *demand* (how long this period of rising demand is likely to last).

The higher the money supply, the easier it is to borrow, and the higher the likelihood that commodity markets will rise. As more money chases fewer goods, the chances of inflation rise, and the central banks begin to make it more difficult to borrow money. Keep good tabs on the rate of growth of the money supply, and you'll probably be ahead of the curve on what future trends in the markets are going to be.

To make big money in all financial markets, futures and options included, you have to find out how to spot changes in the trend of how easy or difficult it is to borrow money. The perfect time to enter positions is as near as possible to those inflection points in the flow of money — when they appear on the charts as changes in the direction of a long-standing trend. These moves can come before or after any changes in money supply or adjustments to borrowing power appear. However, when a market trends in one direction (up or down) for a considerable amount of time and suddenly changes direction after you notice a blip in the money supply data, you know that something important is happening, and you need to pay close attention to it.

Digesting Economic Reports

Each month the U.S. government and the private sector generate and release a steady flow of economic data. These reports are a major influence on how the futures and the financial markets move in general. They're also a source of the *cyclicality,* or repetitive nature, of market movements. These reports provide futures and options traders with a major portion of the road map they need to decide which way the prices in their respective markets are generally headed.

Economic reports provide you with sources of new information. As a trader, you can best use them as

✔ **Risk management tools:** You can place your money at risk if you ignore any of the reports. Each has the potential for providing important information that can create key turning points in the market.

✔ **Harbingers of more important information:** Individual headlines about economic reports are only part of the important data. The markets explore more data beyond what's contained in the initial release. Sometimes data hidden deep within a report become more important than the initial knee-jerk reaction characterized within the headlines and cause the market to reverses its course.

✔ **Trend-setters:** Current reports may not always be what matters. The trend of the data from reports during the last few months, quarters, or years, in addition to expectations for the future, also can be powerful information that moves the markets up or down.

✔ **Planning tools:** Trading solely on economic reports can be very risky and requires experience and thorough planning on your part.

Cable news outlets, major financial Web sites, and business radio networks — CNBC and Bloomberg are two that I follow — broadcast every major report as it is released, and the wire services send out alerts regarding the reports to all major financial publishers not already covering the releases. The government agencies and companies that are responsible for the reports also post them on their respective Web sites immediately.

As a trader, your world is highly dependent on the *economic calendar,* the listing of when reports will be released for the current month. You can get access to the calendar in many places. Most futures brokers post the calendar on their Web sites and can mail you a copy along with key information on their margin and commission rates. *The Wall Street Journal,* Marketwatch.com, and other major news outlets also publish the calendar, either posted for the month or for a particular day or week.

The employment report

The U.S. Department of Labor's employment report is the first piece of major economic data. It's released on the first Friday of every month and is formally known as the Employment Situation Report. Bond, stock index, and currency futures are keyed upon the release of the number at 8:30 a.m. eastern time. The report is so important that it can set the trend for overall trading in the entire arena of the financial markets for several weeks after its release. The employment report is most important when the economy is shifting gears, similar to the way it did after the events of September 11, 2001, and during the 2004 presidential election.

When consecutive reports show that a dominant trend is in place, the trend of the overall market tends to remain in the same direction for extended periods of time. The reversal of such a dominant trend can often be interpreted as a signal that bonds, stock indexes, and currencies are going to change course.

Traders use the employment report as one of several important clues to predict the future of interest rates. For trading purposes, there are two major components of the employment report:

- ✔ **The number of new jobs created:** This number tends to predict which way the strength of the economy is headed. Large numbers of new jobs usually mean that the economy is growing. When the number of new jobs begins to fall, it's usually a sign that the economy is slowing.

- ✔ **The unemployment rate:** The rate of unemployment is more difficult to interpret, but the trend in the rate is more important than the actual monthly number. Full employment usually is a sign that interest rates are going to rise, so the markets begin to factor that into the equation.

Be ready to make trades based on the reaction to the report and not necessarily on the report itself. As with all economic and financial reports, the report may not be as important as the market's reaction in terms of a trader making or losing money.

Book III

Futures and Options

The Consumer Price Index (CPI)

The CPI is the main inflation report for the futures and financial markets. Unexpected rises in this indicator usually lead to falling bond prices, rising interest rates, and increased market volatility. Consumer prices are important because consumer buying drives the U.S. economy. No consumer demand at the retail level means no demand for products along the other steps in the chain of manufacturers, wholesalers, and retailers. Following are some key factors to consider regarding the CPI:

- ✔ **Prices at the consumer level are not as sensitive to supply and demand as they are to the ability of retailers to pass their own costs on to consumers.** Clothing retailers, for example, can't always or immediately pass their wholesale costs for fabric components or labor to consumers, because consumers will start buying discount clothing if premium apparel is too expensive.

- ✔ **Supply tends to be more important than demand.** When enough of something is available, prices tend to stay down. Scarcities, however, don't necessarily mean inflation (but they certainly can accompany it).

- ✔ **Inflationary expectations and consumer prices are related.** Inflationary expectations are built into the cost of borrowing money.

  The relationship between prices and interest rates is key to developing an intuitive feeling for futures trading. The true return on an investment is the percentage of the investment that you gain after accounting for inflation. If your portfolio gains 20 percent for five years and inflation is running at 10 percent during that period, you actually gain only 10 percent per year.

- ✔ **By the time prices begin to rise at the consumer level, the supply-and-demand equation, price discovery, and pressure on the system have been ongoing at other levels of the price chain for some time.**

- ✔ **As a trader, you want to know what the core CPI number is — that is, prices at the consumer level without food and energy factored in.** For example, the April 2005 CPI was a classic report. The initial line from the Labor Department quoted consumer prices as rising 0.7 percent, a number that, if it stood alone, would have caused a big sell-off in the bond market. However, as the report revealed, the core number was unchanged. As a result, bonds and stock futures had a big rally, which spilled over into the stock market that day.

The release of the CPI usually moves the markets for interest-rate, currency, and stock index futures, and it's one of the best reports with which to trade option strategies, such as straddles. (For more about options strategies, see Chapters 3 and 4.)

The Producer Price Index (PPI)

The PPI is an important report, but it doesn't usually cause market moves as big as the CPI and the employment report create. The PPI measures prices at the producer level (the cost of raw materials to companies that produce goods). The market is interested in two things contained in this report:

- ✔ **How fast these prices are rising:** If a rise in PPI is significantly large in comparison to previous months, the market checks to see where it's coming from. For example, the May 2005 PPI report pegged prices at the producer level as rising 0.6 percent in April, following a 0.7-percent increase in March and a 0.4-percent hike in February. At first glance, the market viewed the April increase (compared to the previous two months) as a negative number. However, market makers discovered a note deeper in the report indicating that if you didn't measure food and energy — in this case (especially) oil prices — producer prices at the so-called core level rose only 0.1 percent. The market looked at the core level, and bonds rallied.

- ✔ **Whether producers are passing along any price hikes to their consumers:** If prices at the core level are tame, as they seemed to be in the April 2005 report, traders will conduct business based on the information they have in hand at least until the CPI is released — usually one or two days after the PPI is released. In this case, based only on the PPI, inflation at the core producer level was tame, so traders wagered that producers were not passing any added costs onto the consumer.

The ISM and purchasing managers' reports

The Institute for Supply Management's (ISM) Report on Business, which measures the health of the manufacturing sector in the United States, is a market mover. It's based on the input of purchasing managers surveyed across the country and is compiled by the ISM. The Report on Business is different from regional purchasing managers' reports. (The regional reports aren't used as a basis for the national report.) However, some regional reports, such as the Chicago-area report, often serve as good predictors of the national data.

The report addresses 11 categories, including the widely watched headline, the purchasing managers' index (PMI). The data for the entire report are included with a summary of the economy's current state and pace near the headline.

Here are a couple key questions to ask when looking at the ISM report:

- ✔ **Are the main index and subsector numbers above or below 50?** A number above 50 on the PMI means that the economy is growing.

- ✔ **Is the pace of growth slowing or picking up speed?** You can get this information at the ISM Web site, `www.ism.ws/ISMReport/ROB052005.cfm`.

Consumer confidence reports

Consumer confidence reports come from two sources: The Conference Board, Inc., a private research group, and the University of Michigan. The Conference Board publishes a monthly report based on survey interviews of 5,000 consumers. Here are the key components of The Conference Board survey:

- ✔ The monthly index
- ✔ Current conditions
- ✔ Consumers' outlook for the next six months

The University of Michigan conducts its own survey of consumer confidence, and it publishes several preliminary reports and one final report per month. Here are the key components of the University of Michigan survey:

- ✔ The Index of Consumer Confidence
- ✔ The Index of Consumer Expectations
- ✔ The Index of Current Economic Conditions

The Beige Book

The Summary of Commentary on Current Economic Conditions, otherwise known as the *Beige Book,* is released eight times per year. In each tome, the Fed produces a summary of current economic activity in each of its 12 federal districts, based on anecdotal information from Fed bank presidents, key businesses, economists, and market experts, among other sources. The Beige Book is released to the members of the Federal Open Market Committee (FOMC) before each of its meetings on interest rates, so it's an important source of information for the committee members when they're deciding in what direction they'll vote to take interest rates.

The 12 Federal Reserve District Banks are located in Boston, New York, Philadelphia, Cleveland, Richmond, Atlanta, Chicago, St. Louis, Minneapolis, Kansas City, Dallas, and San Francisco.

Traders look for any mention of labor shortages and wage pressures in the Beige Book. If any such trends are mentioned, bonds may sell off, as rising wage pressures are taken as a sign of building inflation in the pipeline.

Here's a good habit to get into so you can capitalize on knowledge from one area of the market as you apply it to another: After the initial headlines and market reactions, I like to read through the report on the Internet. You can find links to it on the Fed's Web site, `www.federalreserve.gov`, or you can do a Google or Yahoo! search for "Beige Book." What I look for when I scan the full text on the Web is what the Beige Book says about individual sectors of the economy. Under manufacturing in April 2005, the Beige Book said that although little pickup was reported in the growth for electronics, slightly rising demand was noted for networking switches and other related products in telecommunications. If you see something like that, you can start looking at the action of key stocks in that sector. Interestingly, the stock of Cisco Systems, the leader in switches and related products, made a good bottom in the month of April, and on April 21, a day after the Beige Book was released, it began to rally. By May 20, the stock was up 13.26 percent.

The Beige Book usually is released in the afternoon, one or two hours before the stock market closes. The overall trend of all markets can reverse late in the day when the data in the report surprise traders.

Housing starts

Bond and stock traders like housing starts, because housing is a central portion of the U.S. economy, given its dependence on credit and the fact that it uses raw materials and provides employment for a significant number of people in related industries, such as banking, the mortgage sector, construction, manufacturing, and real-estate brokerage. Big moves often occur in the bond market after the numbers for housing starts are released. Released every month, housing starts are compiled by the U.S. Commerce Department and reported in three parts:

- ✔ Building permits
- ✔ Housing starts
- ✔ Housing completions

The markets focus on the percentage of rise or fall in the numbers from the previous month for each component.

This data can be greatly affected by weather, so this report is also seasonally adjusted and includes a significant amount of revised data within each of the internal components. For example, when winter arrives, snow storms and cold weather tend to halt or slow new and ongoing construction projects, so housing permits and housing starts can decline. If you don't know that, you can make trading mistakes by betting that interest rates are going to fall. Markets look at the seasonally adjusted numbers, which are smoothed out by statistical formulas used by the U.S. Department of Commerce. Even then, this set of numbers is tricky. The Commerce Department disclaimer notes that it can take up to four months of data to come up with a reliable set of indicators.

Index of Leading Economic Indicators

The Index of Leading Economic Indicators is a lukewarm indicator that sometimes moves the markets and other times doesn't. It is more likely to move the markets whenever it clearly diverges from data provided by other indicators. In calculating its Index of Leading Economic Indicators, the Conference Board looks at ten key indicators:

- ✔ Index of consumer expectations
- ✔ Real money supply
- ✔ Interest-rate spread
- ✔ Stock prices
- ✔ Vendor performance
- ✔ Average weekly initial claims for unemployment insurance
- ✔ Building permits
- ✔ Average weekly manufacturing hours
- ✔ Manufacturers' new orders for nondefense capital goods
- ✔ Manufacturers' new orders for consumer goods and materials

Gross Domestic Product (GDP)

The report on Gross Domestic Product (GDP) measures the sum of all the goods and services produced in the United States. Although GDP can yield confusing and mixed results on the trading floor, it sometimes is a big market mover whenever it's far above or below what the markets are expecting it to be. At other times, GDP is not much of a mover. Multiple revisions of previous GDP data accompany the monthly release of the GDP and tend to dampen the effect of the report. Although the GDP is not a report to ignore, by any means, it usually isn't as important as the employment report, CPI, and PPI.

GDP has a component called the *deflator,* which is a measure of inflation. The deflator can be the prime mover whenever it is above or below market expectations.

Oil supply data

The Energy Information Administration (EIA), a part of the U.S. Department of Energy, and the American Petroleum Institute (API) release oil supply data for the previous week at 10:30 a.m. eastern time every Wednesday. Traders want to know the following:

✔ **Crude oil supply:** The crude oil supply is the basis for the oil markets and is important year-round. Every week, oil experts and commentators guess what the number will be.

 A *build* occurs when the stockpiles of crude oil in storage are increasing. Such increases are considered *bearish* or negative for the market because large stockpiles generally mean lower prices at the pump. A *drawdown,* on the other hand, is when the supply shrinks. Traders like drawdown situations because prices tend to rise after the news is released.

✔ **Gasoline supply:** Gasoline supplies are more important as the summer driving season approaches.

✔ **Distillate supply:** Distillate supply figures are more important in winter because they essentially represent a measure of the heating oil supply.

Although the experts and commentators are almost never right in their predictions, the fact that they're wrong sets the market up for more volatility when the numbers come out and give you a trading opportunity if you're set up to take advantage of it.

Other factors affecting the volatility of this market include the following:

✔ **Changes in the market due to problems with refinery capacity:** In the United States, we saw this factor have a big impact after hurricanes Katrina and Rita in 2005.

✔ **Inaccurate interpretation of the data by reporters:** Although this scenario is not frequent, I've seen it happen, and I've seen it have an effect on trading.

A good way to set up for the oil report, or any report, is to set up an options strategy called a *straddle,* which I discuss in Chapter 3.

A bevy of other reports

The hodgepodge of data that trickles out of the woodwork throughout the month about retail sales, personal income, industrial production, and the balance of trade sometimes causes a bit of commotion in the futures markets. However, these individual reports mostly cause only a few daily ripples — unless, of course, the effect of the data is dramatic.

Book III

Futures and Options

As a futures and options trader, you need to know that these reports are coming, but a good portion of the time, they come and go without fanfare or trouble unless the economy is at a critical turning point and one of these reports happens to be the missing piece to the puzzle.

Adding Technical Analysis to Your Toolbox

After you become better acquainted with the basic drivers and influences of a particular market and how that information — key market-moving reports, the major players involved, and the general fundamentals of supply and demand — fits into the big picture of the marketplace in general, the next logical step is to become acquainted with how the fundamentals are combined with the data that is compiled in price charts. And that leads you to the field of *technical analysis:* the use of price charts, moving averages, trend lines, volume relationships, and indicators for identifying trends and trading opportunities in underlying financial instruments.

Technical analysis is the key to success in the futures and options markets. The more you know about reading charts, the better your trading results are likely to be. Aside from its key role in decision-making, technical analysis is also a tool that leads you toward exploring more information about why the pattern suggests that you need to buy, sell, or sell short the underlying instrument.

By becoming proficient at reading the charts of various security prices, you gain quick access to significant amounts of information, such as prices, general trends, and info about whether a market is sold out and ready to rally or *overbought,* meaning few buyers are left and prices can fall. By combining your knowledge of the markets and trading experiences with excellent charting skills, you vastly improve your market reaction time and your ability to make informed trades.

Book VIII is devoted to technical analysis. Head there for the nuts and bolts of how to use technical analysis to chart and recognize patterns.

Chapter 3

Basic Trading Strategies

*T*he four mainstream groups of options available to trade are options on stocks, index options, options on futures, and long-term options on stocks. Each has its own particular quirks but still is dependent on the basic rules of volatility and the action of the underlying asset (refer to Chapter 2). This chapter deals mainly with stock options, the most popular set of options.

This chapter covers the basic option strategies in the stock market. It isn't meant to cover every possible permutation of this complex style of investing; however, it does cover the more commonly used strategies and offers plenty of examples to get you going. The first strategy, trading on margin, is a key concept to futures and options trading.

Paper trading — simulating or practicing trades on paper before you make real trades — is *never* a bad idea. If you're a beginner who insists on trading real money, trade only in small lots or small amounts of money, one contract at a time. Finding a good options advisor/broker, one with a conscience who can run your option strategies for you — at least until you get your feet wet — is another worthy consideration.

Trading on Margin

To be a successful futures and options trader, you need to understand the ins and outs of trading on margin. Margin is what makes futures trading so attractive, because it adds leverage to futures contract trades. Trading on margin enables you to *leverage* your trading position — that is, control a larger amount of assets with a smaller amount of money. Margins in the futures market generally are low; they tend to be near the 10 percent range, so you can control, or trade,

$100,000 worth of commodities or financial indexes with only $10,000 or so in your account. The downside is that if you don't understand how trading on a margin works, you can take on some big losses in a hurry.

You can reduce the risk of buying futures on margin by

- Trading contracts that are lower in volatility.

- Using advanced trading techniques such as *spreads,* or positions in which you simultaneously buy and sell contracts in two different commodities or the same commodity for two different months, to reduce the risk. An example of an *intramarket spread* is buying March crude oil and selling April crude. An example of an *intermarket spread* is buying crude oil and selling gasoline.

Trading on margin in the stock market is a different concept than trading on margin in the futures market:

- In the stock market, the Federal Reserve sets the allowable margin at 50 percent; to trade stocks on margin, you must put up 50 percent of the value of the trade. Futures margins are set by the futures exchanges and are different for each different futures contract. Margins in the futures market can be raised or lowered by the exchanges, depending on current market conditions and the volatility of the underlying contract.

  Futures markets margins by design are lower than other margins, because futures contracts are meant to be highly leveraged trading instruments, and their main attraction is the potential they have for yielding large profits with small cash requirements. The flip side, of course, is the risk involved.

  The Securities and Exchange Commission (SEC), which governs the trading of stocks and options on stocks, changed margin requirements for options trading in 1999 and now allows brokers to lend up to 25 percent of the required margin to options traders, which means you must keep 75 percent of the value of your positions in your account to be able to continue trading options on margin. That amount is important because the amount of money that the broker is allowed to lend you to trade options is less than the amount of money he can lend you for trading stocks. In other words, options already have a great deal of leverage and risk built into them, and the SEC is trying to keep traders from taking risks to levels that can lead to losing the entire value of their account.

  Also, you can't purchase options on margin, as you can stocks, if the life of the option is nine months or less. However, if the option has a life of greater than nine months, the broker can lend you 25 percent.

- Generally, when you deposit a margin on a stock purchase, you buy partial equity of the stock position and owe the balance as debt. In the futures market, a margin acts as a security deposit that protects the exchange from default by the customer or the brokerage house.

> ✔ When you trade futures on margin, in most cases you buy the right to participate in the price changes of the contract. Your margin is a sign of good faith, or a sign that you're willing to meet your contractual obligations with regard to the trade.

Margin requirements for different options and strategies sometimes are difficult to calculate and may vary among different brokers. Before setting up an account, read the options and margin agreements from your broker carefully so that you fully understand margin requirements for each individual class of options you're trading.

Writing Calls

When you *write a call,* you sell someone the right to buy an underlying stock from you at a strike price that's specified by the option series. As the writer, you are now *short* the option. The buyer of your call is *long* the option. You also are obligated to deliver the stock if the buyer decides to exercise the call option.

As a call writer, you are hoping that

> ✔ The stock goes nowhere.
>
> ✔ You collect the premium.
>
> ✔ The option expires worthless so you don't have to come up with a hundred shares of the stock to settle when the holder exercises the call, which is what can happen with naked call writing.

Choosing to be naked or covered

When you write a *naked call option,* you're selling someone else a chance to bet that the underlying stock is going to go higher in price. The catch is that you don't own the stock, so if the buyer exercises the option, you need to buy the stock at the market price to meet your obligation. When you write a *covered call option,* you already own the shares. If you're exercised against, you just sell your shares at the strike price.

Covered call writing is a perfect strategy if you're looking to smooth out your portfolio's performance and collect the extra income from the call premiums. When the call expires worthless, you get to keep the stock (which you already own) and collect all the dividends that accrued during the time the call was in play. When you write naked calls (in which you don't own the stock), if the call expires worthless, you still keep the premium.

Writing covered calls is a safer strategy than writing naked calls. If the holder exercises a naked call option, you have to buy the stock before you can deliver it to him. If the stock price has risen in the interim, you could sustain a serious loss in meeting the exercise. You can get around losing a lot of money when writing naked calls by figuring out your break-even point and unwinding the position if the price reaches that point. Getting out of the trade at your break-even point enables you to decide what you're willing to lose before ever making a trade.

Doing your homework

When you write calls, think of your stock and your option as two different parts of one single position. Each part has its own role to play and is dependent on the other to perform a complete job for your portfolio. Each part also has its own cost, so you need to know the price of the stock when you bought it and add in the price of the premium that you gain when you sell the call.

Before you write a call, figure out how much you get from the strike price and the premium if the call option is exercised against you. Always know your worst-case scenario before you hit the trade button. Here are some additional tips to keep in mind about writing calls:

- ✔ A low volatility stock is perfect for call option writing.

- ✔ Writing in-the-money options generally lets you collect a better premium than writing out-of-the-money options; however, the profit potential is greater when you write out-of-the-money call options.

- ✔ For the covered-call strategy to work best, try to execute the trades — buy the stock and write the call option — at the same time by establishing a *net position* in which your goal is to achieve your *net price,* or the price you set as your investment goal for the order. You can establish a net position by placing a *contingent order* with your broker, which stipulates how you want the order executed.

  Contingent orders — also referred to as *net orders* — are not guaranteed by the broker. They're also referred to as *not-held orders,* because if the broker thinks the order is too difficult to fill, you'll receive a "nothing done" report, and the order won't be filled.

- ✔ If you're unwilling to sell the stock against which you're writing the covered call, you shouldn't even consider writing the option. You'll probably get hurt if someone exercises a call against you.

- ✔ If you change your mind after selling an option, you can buy it back in the marketplace. The buyer can also sell his options to the marketplace. This rule applies to both puts and calls.

Protecting your trade by diversification

A diversification strategy is pretty simple, and it works best when you own more than a couple hundred shares of a stock. In this strategy, you sell more than one covered call at different strike prices and for different time frames. Again, the goal is to spread out your risk against volatility and your risk against the call you sold being exercised. You accomplish this strategy by writing in-the-money calls on some stocks and out-of-the-money calls on other stocks in your portfolio.

Setting up this strategy is difficult because writing out-of-the-money calls theoretically works better when you write them against stocks that do well. In other words, you're forced to decide which stocks you think are likely to do better than others, which is difficult to do in a simple stock-picking strategy without the option strategy. Conversely, writing in-the-money calls works better for stocks with low volatility. One way to get around this problem is to write half of the position against in-the-money and half against out-of-the-money on the same stock.

Writing a covered call: An example

Here's an example of writing a covered call, loosely adapted from Lawrence G. McMillan's *Options as a Strategic Investment*. Buy 500 shares of ABC stock, at $38, in January, and sell five July $40 call options at 3, for a total of $1,500. With this strategy, you've established a covered-call position with a six-month duration. Selling the options gives you $1,500, or 3 points per share of downside protection on your 500 shares of ABC. (In options language, a point, as it pertains to this example, is worth $100.)

You lose money on your overall position if the price of your stock falls more than the amount of downside protection you gained by selling the call option. In other words, if ABC drops below $35, you've lost money on the overall position. (This is why you really need to do the math before you ever write a call.)

Think about it. If the price of ABC falls 3 points ($3 per share) and you still own the stock, you've lost $1,500 of the value of that portion of the position. However, because you wrote call options, you had $1,500 worth of downside protection, so at the $35 price level, you're essentially breaking even. In other words, by using the call-writing strategy, you're essentially back where you started on the overall position. The alternative would have been a $1,500 loss (in the value of the stock — at least on paper) had you not written the call option and held the stock without the protection of the option strategy.

Following up after writing a call

Your job as an options trader starts when you make the transaction. The heavy lifting is what lies ahead — managing the position, which is more difficult in some ways than opening the position. Here are two important factors in managing the position:

- What to do if a stock falls after you've written a covered call
- What to do as the covered call approaches expiration

Knowing what to do when the stock rises

If your stock goes up, you can just let the buyer have it at the higher price. You made your premium, and you sold your stock at a price that you were comfortable with. If you want to be aggressive, you can buy back your option and *roll up,* or write another call at a higher strike price. When you do, though, you incur a debit in your trade, because you have to put up more money into the account.

Rolling up can be risky, because you can end up with a loss. Lawrence McMillan, author of *Options as a Strategic Investment* (Prentice-Hall Press), suggests that you shouldn't roll up whenever you can't withstand a 10-percent correction in the stock's price.

When the expiration time nears: Rolling forward

Rolling forward is what you may want to do as your option's expiration time nears. When you roll forward, you buy back your option and sell a new one with a longer term but the same strike price. Although you could let the stock be called away, if your stock has low volatility and your option strategy has been working for you, rolling forward usually is best. How you make your decision is based on your projected costs of commissions and fees, and what your break-even point will be for the position.

If you're writing calls, make sure you're willing to let the underlying stock get called away. Otherwise, you're likely to become sorry at some point. If the position is going against you and you keep rolling up and forward, you're probably only making matters worse. At some point, you will hit the panic button and buy back your calls at a loss. You'll probably start selling put options to generate some credits, but you'll also end up placing yourself in a position that can wipe out your whole account.

Buying Calls

Call buying is different from call writing, because it isn't usually used by traders as a hedge against risk. Instead, call buying is used to make money on stocks that are likely to go up in price. Call buying is the most common technique used by individual investors, but beware that success in this form of trading requires good stock-picking skills and a sense of timing.

The main attraction of buying call options is the potential for making large sums of money in short amounts of time, while limiting downside risk to only the original amount of money that you put up when you bought the option. Here are two reasons for buying call options:

- ✔ **You expect the stock to rise.** ABC stock is selling at $50, and you buy a six-month call, the December 55, at $3. You pay $300 for the position. For the next six months you have a chance to make money if the stock rises in price. If the stock goes up 10 points, or 20 percent, your option also will rise, and because of leverage, the option will be worth much more. If the price drops below $55 by the expiration date, all you lose is your original $300 if you didn't sell back the option prior to that.

- ✔ **You expect to have money later and don't want to miss a move up in a stock.** Say, for example, that you expect a nice sum of money in a couple of weeks, and a stock you like is starting to move. You can buy an option for a fraction of the price of the stock. When you get your money, if you're still interested, you can exercise your option and buy the stock. If you're wrong, you lose only a fraction of what you would have by owning the stock.

When you buy a call option, you pay for it in full. You have to post no margin.

Here's some advice to keep in mind when buying call options:

- ✔ Choose the right stock. Buy call options on stocks that look ready to break out. That means that you need to become familiar with charting techniques and technical analysis (see Book VIII).

- ✔ Use charts over fundamentals when you trade call options.

- ✔ Out-of-the-money calls have greater profit potential and greater risk.

- ✔ In-the-money calls may perform better when the stock does not move as you expected.

- ✔ Don't buy cheap call options just because they're cheap.

- ✔ Near-term calls are riskier than far-term calls.

- ✔ Intermediate-term calls may offer the best risk/reward ratio.

Book III

Futures and Options

Calculating the break-even price for calls and puts

Before you buy any call option, you must calculate the break-even price by using the following formula:

> Strike price + Option premium cost + Commission and transaction costs = Break-even price

So if you're buying a December 50 call on ABC stock that sells for a $2.50 premium and the commission is $25, your break-even price would be

> $50 + $2.50 + 0.25 = $52.75 per share

That means that to make a profit on this call option, the price per share of ABC has to rise above $52.75.

To calculate the break-even price for a put option, you subtract the premium and the commission costs. For a December 50 put on ABC stock that sells at a premium of $2.50, with a commission of $25, your break-even point would be

> $50 − $2.50 − 0.25 = $47.25 per share

That means the price per share of ABC stock must fall below $47.25 for you to make a profit.

Make sure that you understand the fee structure used by your broker before making any option trades. Fees differ significantly from one broker to the next. Brokers frequently charge *round-trip fees,* which refer to the fees that you're charged on the way in and on the way out of an options trading position. To figure out round-trip commission fees in the break-even formula, simply double the commission cost.

Using delta to time call-buying decisions

Delta (which I explain in Chapter 1) measures the amount by which the price of the call option will change, up and down, every time the underlying stock moves 1 point.

In a day-trading situation, McMillan recommends trading the underlying stock. This strategy follows the key concept of using *delta:* The shorter the term of the strategy, the greater your delta should be. The delta of the underlying stock is 1.0. Thus, the stock is the most volatile instrument and is best suited for day-trading.

How long you expect to hold an option determines in part which option to buy. Here are some general rules to follow when using delta to time your call buying:

- For trades that you expect to hold for a week or less, use the highest delta option you can find, because its moves will correlate the closest with the underlying asset. In this case, short-term, in-the-money options are the best bet.

- For intermediate-term trading, usually weeks in duration, use options with smaller deltas. McMillan recommends using at-the-money options for this time frame.

- For longer-term trading, choose low-delta options, either slightly out-of-the-money or longer-term at-the-money options.

Following up after buying a call option

Keep these rules in mind after you buy a call option:

- If the underlying stock tanks, the best course is to sell the call option and cut your losses.

- If the option rises in price, especially if it doubles in a short period of time, take some profits.

- It's better to sell a call than to exercise it because the commission costs to buy the stock when you exercise the call are usually more than what it costs to sell the option. Also, if you then turn around and sell the stock, you'll pay more of a commission at that time as well.

- If you buy several options and the stock rises significantly, you can take partial profits by selling a portion of your overall position. For example, if you bought five calls and the position is profitable, you can sell three calls and ride the profit train with the remaining ones.

- If you decide to do nothing, you can lose everything at expiration. But if you sell your profitable initial position and stay out of the options in that particular stock, you can keep your profit. (For my money, a good profit in my pocket is better than a great one that may never come.) So remember: At the beginning of an options trading strategy, keeping it simple is the best way to go. As you become more experienced, you can start making more sophisticated bets.

Book III

Futures and Options

Considering Basic Put Option Strategies

When you buy a put option, you're hoping that the price of the underlying stock falls. You make money with puts when the price of the option rises, or when you exercise the option to buy the stock at a price that's below the strike price and then sell the stock in the open market, pocketing the difference. By buying a put option, you limit your risk of a loss to the premium that you paid for the put.

If, for example, you bought an ABC December 50 put, and ABC falls to $40 per share, you can make money either by selling a put option that rises in price or by buying the stock at $40 on the open market and then exercising the option, thus selling your $40 stock to the writer for $50 per share, which is what owning the put gave you the right to do.

Put options are used either as pure speculative vehicles or as protection against the potential for stock prices to fall. When you buy a put option, you are accomplishing essentially the same thing as short selling without some of the more complicated details. Put options also give you leverage because you don't have to spend as much money as you would trying to short-sell a stock.

Making the most of your put option buys

Out-of-the-money puts are riskier but offer greater reward potential than in-the-money puts. The flip side is that if a stock falls a relatively small amount, you're likely to make more money from your put if you own an in-the-money option.

McMillan points out an important point: Call options tend to move more dramatically than puts. You can buy the right put option, and the underlying stock may have fallen significantly. Still, the market decided that the put option should rise only 1 or 2 points. In an ideal world, you'd expect to be greatly rewarded for buying a put option on a stock that collapses. But, in the world of options pricing, things are not always what you'd expect them to be because of the vagaries of trading, the time to expiration, and other major influences on option pricing. To avoid disappointment, you're better off buying in-the-money puts unless the probability that the underlying stock is going to fall by a significant amount is extremely high.

In contrast to call options, you may be able to buy a longer-term put option for a fairly good price. Doing so is a good idea, because it gives you more time for the stock to fall. Buying the longer-term put also protects you if the stock rises, because its premium will likely drop less in price.

Dividends make put options more valuable, and the larger the dividend, the more valuable the put becomes. When stocks go ex-dividend, the day the dividend gets paid out, the amount of the dividend reduces the price of the stock. As the stock falls, the put increases in value. The prices of puts and calls are not reduced by dividends. Instead, the price reflects the effect of the dividend on the stock. Call prices fall as the stocks pay out their dividends. Put prices rise as of the ex-dividend date.

Buying put options — fully dressed

Buying a put option without owning the stock is called *buying a naked put*. Naked puts give you the potential for profit if the underlying stock falls. But if you own a stock and buy a put option on the same stock, you're protecting your position and limiting your downside risk for the life of the put option.

A good time to buy a put on a stock that you own is when you've made a significant gain, but you're not sure you want to cash out. You can also use puts to protect against short-term volatility in long-term holdings. In the first instance, your put option acts as an insurance policy to protect your gains. In the second instance, if your put goes up in value, you can sell it and decrease the paper losses on your stock. You decide which put option to buy by calculating how much profit potential you're willing to lose if the stock goes up.

Out-of-the-money puts are cheap, but they won't give you as much protection as in-the-money puts until the stock falls to the strike price. In-the-money puts are more expensive but can provide better insurance.

Selling naked and covered puts

Selling naked put options is similar to buying a call option, because you make money when the underlying stock goes up in price. Selling naked puts means you're selling a put option without being short the stock, and in the process, you're hoping that the stock goes nowhere or rises, which enables you to keep the premium without being assigned. If the stock falls in a big way, and you get assigned, you can face big losses from having to buy the stock in the open market to sell it to the party exercising the put you sold.

You need to put up collateral to write naked puts, usually in an amount that is equal to 20 percent of the current stock price plus the put premium minus any out-of-the-money amount. Here is how it works: ABC is selling at $40 per share, and a four-month put with a striking price of $40 is selling for 4 points. You have the potential to make $400 here or the potential for a huge loss if the stock falls. Your loss is limited only because the stock can't go below zero.

The amount of collateral you'd need to put up would be $400, plus 20 percent of the price of the stock, or $800. The minimum you'd have to put up, though, would be 10 percent of the strike price plus the put premium, even if the amount is smaller than what you just calculated.

Selling covered puts is not particularly recommended for beginners. A put sale is *covered*, not by owning the stock, but rather by having an open short position on the underlying stock. Your margin is covered if you're also short the stock. This strategy has unlimited upside risk and limited profit potential if the underlying stock rises because the short sale will accrue losses. The position is equivalent to a naked call write, except the covered put writer has to pay out the dividend of the underlying stock if the stock pays a dividend.

Exercising your put option

Put and call options rarely are exercised in the stock market. Most option traders take the gains on the options if they have them or cut their losses short as early as possible if the market goes against them. But if you're the holder of a put option and you decide to exercise it, you're selling the underlying stock at the striking price, and you can sell the stock at the strike price any time during the life of the option. If you write, or sell, the put, you're assigned the obligation of buying the stock at the strike price.

You can sell stock that you own at the strike price or buy stock in the open market if you don't own it, as in the case of a naked strategy, and then sell it at the strike price. You notify your broker how you'll deliver or receive the stock. You must make sure that you can satisfy any margin or other requirement involved, and the exercise procedure and share transfer will be handled by the broker.

Dealing with a huge profit in a put option

If you're lucky enough to get a nice drop in a stock on which you own a put option, you can do several things:

- ✔ **Do nothing.**
- ✔ **Take profits.** Doing so guarantees that you lock in a gain if you execute the trade in a timely manner.
- ✔ **Sell your in-the-money put and buy an out-of-the money put.** By opting for this strategy, you're taking partial profits and then extending your risk and your profit potential if the stock continues to fall.

✔ **Create a spread strategy by selling an out-of-the-money put against the one you already own.** This strategy adds an important new wrinkle to the possible strategies you can use. Your options:

- Sell a different put option than the one you already own. You can, for instance, sell a December 45 put to offset the already profitable December 50 put that you own, all so that you make some money off the sale and lock in some of the costs of having bought the original December 50 put. If the stock goes above 50, you lose everything. But if the stock falls below 45 and stabilizes, you make the 5-point maximum profit from the spread, which is the best of all worlds in this strategy.

- Buy a call option. You can buy a December 45 call to limit your risk if the stock rises. See the previous sections about writing calls. Again your cost would be 5 points. This spread guarantees you 5 points no matter where the stock closes at expiration.

Spreads get the best results when the stock stabilizes in price after the spread is put on. But it is more important that the stock price stays in the profit range of the spread.

The IRS taxes short-term and long-term profits on every sale of every trade you make, except in a retirement account for which it taxes you later on, when you withdraw the money. Some tax-specific details you need to know if you're trading put options include the following:

✔ Buying put options has no tax consequences if you're a long-term holder, usually greater than six months.

✔ If you forfeit any accrued time during the holding period, or if you're a short-term holder of the stock and you buy a put option, holding time won't begin to accrue again until you sell the put, or it expires.

Be sure to consult with your accountant before you trade any options.

Creating Straddles and Strangles

You can create a *straddle* when you simultaneously buy a put and a call for the same stock at the same strike price and of the same duration. With a straddle, if the underlying stock moves far enough, you can make large potential profits and limit your losses to the amount of your initial investment.

Straddles are expensive because you are buying equal numbers of puts and calls.

You want to build straddles on stocks that are likely to be volatile but that are in price consolidation patterns at the current time, and you'd like to give yourself some time before a news announcement or another event is expected from the company. Buying the straddle two weeks ahead of the announcement is a decent time frame used by some experienced traders.

If the announcement comes and there is no major move, it's better to exit both sides of the straddle within the first one or two days, just in case it takes a little time for the news to move the stock.

If there is a big move in one direction, you can sell the profitable side of the trade and hold on to the losing side since the price could retrace. Then you can sell the other side.

The chances of losing all your money in a straddle are small, but the chances of making money in this strategy when you hold the position until the expiration date also are small.

Taking small profits in a straddle can cost you money in the long run. You may have to take a few small losses before you hit a big win. This particular gut-wrenching quality about straddle strategy is what makes it more suitable for experienced investors. If you're interested in straddles, using an experienced options broker/advisor who truly understands this strategy, at least during your early trading experiences, may be your best option.

You build a *strangle* with a put and a call that usually have the same expiration date but different strike prices. Strangles work best when the put and the call are out-of-the-money. Strangles are a risky strategy because you can lose money anywhere along the spread, as opposed to straddles where you can lose money only at the strike price.

Chapter 4

Advanced Speculation Strategies

*T*his chapter is where you get into the big money, starting with interest-rate futures and taking stock of stock index futures. These markets, in addition to the currency market (which you can read about in Book V), often set the tone for the trading day in all markets because they form a focal point or hub for the global financial system. What's good about these markets is that they're great places for you to get started in futures trading, so I provide you with tips for doing just that.

Thinking Like a Contrarian

Contrarians trade against the grain at key turning points when shifts in market sentiment become noticeable. A contrarian, for example, may start looking for reasons to sell when everyone else is bullish or may consider it a good time to buy when pessimism about the markets is so thick that you can cut it with a knife. In this section, I take you through the major aspects of contrarian thinking and explain how to know when to use it and how to make it part of your trading arsenal.

Picking apart popular sentiment surveys

Sentiment surveys are used to gauge when a particular market is at an extreme point with either too much bullishness or too much bearishness. Their major weakness is that they're now so popular that their ability to truly mark major turning points is not as good as it was even in the late 1980s or early 1990s. Still, when used within the context of good technical and fundamental analysis, they can be useful. Two popular sentiment surveys affect the futures markets: Market Vane (www.marketvane.net) and Consensus, Inc. (www.consensus-inc.com). Both offer sentiment data on items such as the following:

- ✔ **Precious metals:** Silver, gold, copper, and platinum
- ✔ **Financial instruments:** Eurodollars, U.S. dollar, Treasury bills (T-bills), and Treasury bonds (T-bonds)
- ✔ **Currencies:** The U.S. dollar, Euro FX, British pound, Deutschemark, Swiss franc, Canadian dollar, and Japanese yen
- ✔ **Agricultural products:** Soybean products, meats, grains, other foods (such as sugar, cocoa, and coffee), and more
- ✔ **Stock indexes:** The S&P 500 and NASDAQ-100 stock indexes
- ✔ **Energy complex:** Crude oil, natural gas, gasoline, and heating oil

Snapshots of both surveys for stocks, bonds, Eurodollars, and Euro currency are available weekly in *Barron's* magazine under the Market Laboratory section or at Barron's Online, www.barrons.com. What you'll find when reading *Barron's* or another such publication are percentages of market sentiment, such as oil being 75 percent bulls, or bullish, which simply means that 75 percent of the opinions surveyed by the editors of Market Vane or Consensus are bullish on oil.

After you find out the market sentiment, you need to perform a bit of technical analysis. A high bullish reading in terms of sentiment, for example, should alert you to start looking for technical signs that a top is in place, checking whether key support levels or trend lines have been breached, or checking whether the market is struggling to make new highs.

Sentiment survey readings must be at extreme levels to be useful. Sentiments below 35 to 40 percent for any given category usually are considered bullish, for example, because few advisors are left to recommend selling. Even so, when using sentiment to help guide your decision-making, avoid trading on sentiment data alone, which can be too risky. Always check sentiment tendencies against technical and fundamental analyses, even though it may make you a little late in executing your entry or exit trades.

Reading trade volume as a sentiment indicator

Trading volume is a direct, real-time sentiment indicator. As a general rule, high trading volume is a sign that the current trend is likely to continue. Still, good volume analysis takes other market indicators into account. When analyzing volume, be sure that you

✔ Put the current volume trends in the proper context with relationship to the market in which you're trading, rather than thinking about hard-and-fast rules. It's important to note that trends tend to either start or end with a volume spike climax (typically twice the 20- or 50-day moving average of daily volume).

✔ Remember the differences in the way that volume is reported and interpreted in the futures market compared with the stock market.

✔ Check other indicators to confirm what volume is telling you.

✔ Ask yourself whether the market is vulnerable to a trend change.

✔ Consider key support and resistance levels.

✔ Protect your portfolio by being prepared to make necessary changes.

Figure 4-1, which shows the S&P 500 e-mini futures contract for September 2005, portrays an interesting relationship between volume, sentiment, and other indicators. In April, the market made a textbook bottom. Notice how the volume bars at the bottom of the chart rose as the market was reaching a selling climax, as signified by the three large candlesticks, or trading bars. This combination of signals — large price moves and large volumes when the market is falling — is often the prelude to a classic market bottom, because traders were panicking and selling at any price just to get out of their positions.

Book III

Futures and Options

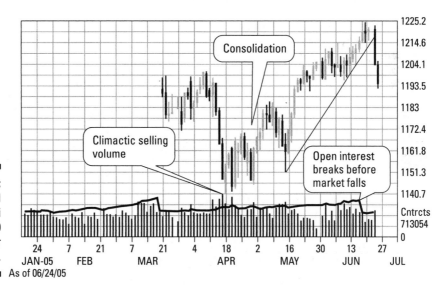

Figure 4-1:
Volume and the e-mini S&P 500 September 2005 futures.

As of 06/24/05

Notice how the volume trailed off as the market consolidated, or started moving sideways, making a complex bottom that took almost two weeks to form. *Consolidation* is what happens when buyers and sellers are in balance. When markets consolidate, they're catching their breath and getting set up for their next move. Consolidation phases are unpredictable and can last for short periods of time, such as hours or days, or longer periods, even months to years.

A third important volume signal occurred in late May and early June as the market rallied. Notice how volume faded as the market continued to rise. Eventually, the market fell and moved significantly lower as it broke below key trend-line support. Finally, note that open interest fell during the last stage of the rally in late June, which usually is a sign that more weakness is likely, because fewer contracts remain open, suggesting that traders are getting exhausted and are less willing to hold on to open positions.

Using volume indicators in the futures markets has limitations. The example in Figure 4-1 needs to be viewed within the context of these limitations:

✔ The release of volume figures in the futures market is delayed by one day.

✔ Higher volume levels steadily migrate toward the closest *delivery month,* or the month in which the contract is settled and delivery of the underlying asset takes place. That migration is important for traders, because the chance of getting a better price for your trade is higher when volume is better. In June, for example, the trading volume is higher in the S&P 500 futures for the September contract than for other months, because September is the next delivery month. Volume for the delivery-month contract increases for a while as traders move their positions to the *front month,* or the commonly quoted (price) contract at the time.

✔ *Limit days* (especially limit up days), or days in which a particular contract makes a big move in a short period of time, can have very high volume, thus skewing your analysis. Limit up or limit down days tend to happen in response to a single or related series of events, external or internal, such as a very surprising report. A *limit up day,* when the market rises to the limit in a short period of time, usually is a signal of strength in the market. When markets crash, you can see limit down moves that then trigger *trading collars* (periods when the market trades but prices don't change) or complete stoppages of trading.

Viewing open interest as a sign of trend reversal

One of the most useful tools you can have when trading futures, *open interest* is the total number of options and/or futures contracts that are not closed or delivered on a particular day. It is the most useful tool for analyzing potential trend reversals in futures markets. Open interest applies to futures and options but not to stocks and does the following:

- ✔ Measures the total number of short and long positions (*shorts* and *longs*). In the futures markets, the number of longs always equals the number of shorts. So when a new buyer buys from an old buyer who is cashing in, no change occurs in open interest.

- ✔ Varies based on the number of new traders entering the market and the number of traders leaving the market.

- ✔ Rises by one whenever one new buyer and one new seller enter the market, thus marking the creation of one new contract.

- ✔ Falls by one when a long trader closes out a position with a trader who already has an open short position.

The exchanges publish open-interest figures daily, but the numbers are delayed by one day, so the volume and open-interest figures on today's quotes are only estimates. Nevertheless, charting open interest on a daily basis in conjunction with a price chart helps you keep track of the trends in open interest and how they relate to market prices. Barchart.com (www.barchart.com) offers excellent free futures charts that give you a good look at open interest.

Rising markets

In a rising trend, open interest is fairly straightforward:

- ✔ **Bullish open interest:** When open interest rises along with prices, it signals that an uptrend is in place and can be sustained. This bullish sign also means that new money is moving into the market. Extremely high open interest in a bull market, however, usually is a danger signal.

- ✔ **Bearish open interest:** Rising prices combined with falling open interest signal a short-covering rally in which short sellers are reversing their positions so that their buying actually is pushing prices higher. In this case, higher prices are not likely to last, because no new buyers are entering the market.

- ✔ **Bearish leveling or decline:** A leveling off or decrease in open interest in a rising market often is an early warning sign that a top may be nearing.

Sideways markets

In a sideways market, open interest gets trickier, so you need to watch for the following:

- ✔ **Rising open interest during periods when the market is moving sideways (or in a narrow trading range).** This usually leads to an intense move after prices break out of the trading range — up or down.

Book III

Futures and Options

When dealing with sideways markets, be sure to confirm open-interest signals by checking them against other market indicators.

- **Down-trending price breakouts (breakdowns).** Some futures traders use breakouts on the downside to set up short positions, thus leaving the public wide open for a major sell-off.

- **Falling open interest in a trader's market.** When it happens, traders with weak positions are throwing in the towel, and the pros are covering their short positions and setting up for a market rally.

Falling markets

In falling markets, open-interest signals also are a bit more complicated to decipher:

- **Bearish open interest:** Falling prices combined with a rise in open interest indicate that a downtrend is in place and being fueled by new money coming in from short sellers.

- **Bullish open interest:** Falling prices combined with falling open interest signal that traders who had not sold their positions as the market broke — hoping the market would bounce back — are giving up. In this case, you need to start anticipating, or even expecting, a trend reversal toward higher prices after this give-up phase ends.

- **Neutral:** If prices rise or fall but open interest remains flat, a trend reversal is possible. You can think of these periods as preludes to an eventual change in the existing trend. Neutral open-interest situations are good times to be especially alert.

- **Trending down:** A market trend that shifts downward at the same time open interest reaches high levels can be a sign that more selling is coming. Traders who bought into the market right before it topped out are now liquidating losing positions to cut their losses.

Combining open interest and volume

You can combine open interest and volume to predict a trend change. Generally, volume and open interest need to be heading in the same direction as the market. When the market starts rising, for example, you want to see volume and open interest expanding. A rising market with shrinking volume and falling open interest usually is one that is heading for a correction. This is an important concept. Rising markets should have rising volume and open interest accompanying the rise of prices. That is a sign of strength. Table 4-1 summarizes the relationship between volume and open interest.

Table 4-1	The Relationship Between Volume and Open Interest		
Price	*Volume*	*Open Interest*	*Market Trend*
Rising	Up	Up	Strong
Rising	Down	Down	Weak
Declining	Up	Up	Weak
Declining	Down	Down	Strong

Looking at put/call ratios as sentiment indicators

The *put/call ratio* is the most commonly used sentiment indicator for trading stocks, but it can also be useful in trading stock index futures because with it you can pinpoint major inflection points in trader sentiment. At extremes, put/call ratios can be signs of excessive fear (a high level of put buying relative to call buying) and excessive greed (a high level of call buying relative to put buying). However, these indicators aren't as useful as they once were because of the more sophisticated hedging strategies now used in the markets.

As a futures trader, put/call ratios can help you make several important decisions about

- ✔ Tightening your stops on open positions.
- ✔ Setting new entry points if you've been out of the market.
- ✔ Setting up hedges with options and futures.
- ✔ Taking profits.

The Chicago Board Options Exchange (CBOE) updates the put/call ratio throughout the day at its Web site, www.cboe.com/data/IntraDayVol.aspx, and provides final figures for the day after the market closes (5 p.m. central time). Check the put/call ratios after the market closes.

Put/call ratios are best used as alert mechanisms for potential trend changes and in conjunction with technical analysis. So be sure to look at your charts and take inventory of your own positions during the time frame in which you're trading futures contracts. The sections that follow describe important ratios you need to become familiar with when trading stock index futures.

Book III

Futures and Options

Total put/call ratio

The total put/call ratio is calculated using the following equation:

Total put options purchased ÷ Total call options purchased

The total ratio includes options on stocks, indexes, and long-term options bought by traders on the CBOE. Although you can make sense of this ratio in many ways, I've found it useful when the ratio rises above 1.0 and when it falls below 0.5. Above 1.0, the ratio usually means too much fear is in the air and the market is trying to make a bottom. Readings below 0.5 usually mean that too much bullishness is in the air and the market may fall.

Index put/call ratio

The index put/call ratio is a good measure of what futures and options players, institutions, and hedge-fund managers are up to. Above 2.0, this indicator traditionally is a bullish sign; below 0.90, it becomes bearish and traditionally signals that some kind of correction is coming. Because these numbers are not as reliable as they used to be, consider them only as reference points and never base any trades on them alone. Don't forget that put/call ratios need to be correlated with chart patterns.

A word about abnormal ratios

Don't ignore abnormal put/call ratio readings. Doing so can cost you significant amounts of money in a hurry. When you see abnormally high or low put/call ratios, make sure you're ready to handle dramatic changes and immediately look for weak spots in your portfolio. Abnormal activity should trigger ideas about hedging. When you see abnormal put/call ratio numbers, consider

✔ Tightening stops on your open stock index futures positions.

✔ Exploring options strategies, such as straddles and strangles (see Chapter 3).

✔ Reversing positions. If you have a short position in the market, make sure you're ready to reverse and go long, or vice versa if you have a long position.

✔ Looking to the bond, currency, and oil markets for other trading opportunities with a goal of both hedging any problems in your stock index futures and options and possibly expanding your profits in those areas.

Using soft sentiment signs

Soft sentiment signs usually are subtle, nonquantitative factors that most people tend to ignore. They can be anything from the shoeshine boy giving stock tips or a wild magazine cover (classic signs of a top) to people jumping out of windows during a market crash (a classic sign of the other extreme). These signs can be anywhere from humorous to dramatic. By no means should you make them a mainstay of your trading strategy, but they can be helpful. You can find soft sentiment signs in the following places:

✔ **Magazine covers and Web site headlines:** Every time crude oil rallies, I start looking for crazy headlines. When crude oil reached an all-time high on June 17, 2005, *Time's* cover featured the late Mao Tse-tung, *BusinessWeek* had senior citizens, and *Newsweek* had dinosaurs. None of them even mentioned oil — a good soft sentiment sign that the oil market still had some room to rise.

✔ **Congressional investigations and activist protests:** Political activity and outrage are usually a sign that things are at a fever pitch, and the trend can change, possibly in a hurry.

✔ **The Drudge Report:** All good traders need to keep an eye on the Drudge Report, which is a barometer of public opinion (or at least Matt Drudge's current attempts to influence public opinion). As a contrary sign for the markets, the Drudge Report is a useful tool.

As with put/call ratios, wild headlines, Congressional hearings, and plenty of attention on cable and local news channels are an alert that something dramatic is going to happen.

Exploring Interest Rate Futures

The bond market rules the world. Everything that anyone does in the financial markets anymore is built upon interest rate analysis. When interest rates are on the rise, at some point doing business becomes difficult. When interest rates fall, eventually economic growth is energized. The relationship between rising and falling interest rates makes the markets in interest rate futures, Eurodollars, and Treasuries (bills, notes, and bonds) important for all consumers, speculators, economists, bureaucrats, and politicians.

Book III

Futures and Options

Bonding with the universe

At the center of the world's financial universe is the bond market. And at the center of the bond market is its relationship with the United States Federal Reserve (the Fed) and the way the Fed conducts interest rate policies. (See Chapter 2 for more information on the Fed.)

When you buy a bond, you get a fixed return as long as you hold that bond until it matures or, in the case of some corporate or municipal bonds, until it's called in. If you're getting a 5 percent return on your bond investment and inflation is growing at a 6-percent clip, you're already 1 percent in the hole, which is why bondholders hate inflation.

Grasping the connection between the bond market, the Fed, and the rest of the financial markets is fundamental to understanding how to trade futures and options and how to invest in general. In the next section, I discuss the most important aspects of how they all work together.

The Fed and bond market roles

The Fed cannot directly control the long-term bond rates that determine how easy (or difficult) it is to borrow money to buy a new home or to finance long-term business projects. What the Fed *can* do is adjust short-term interest rates, such as the interest rate on *Fed funds,* the overnight lending rate used by banks to square their books, and the *discount rate,* the rate at which the Fed loans money to banks to which no one else will lend money. As the Fed senses that inflationary pressures are rising, it starts to raise interest rates. When the Fed raises the Fed funds and/or the discount rates, banks usually raise the *prime rate,* the rate that targets their best customers. At the same time, credit card companies raise their rates.

As the bond market senses inflationary pressures are rising, bond traders sell bonds and market interest rates rise. Rising market interest rates usually trigger rate increases for mortgages and car loans, which usually are tied to a bond market benchmark rate.

When it comes to recognizing when inflation is lurking, sometimes the bond market takes action ahead of the Fed. When that happens, bond prices fall, market rates rise (such as the yield on the U.S. ten-year T-note), and the Fed raises rates if its indicators agree with the bond market's analysis. Whenever the Fed disagrees with the markets, it signals those disagreements usually through speeches from Fed governors or even the chairman of the Fed.

Interest rates are a two-way street: The bond market sometimes disagrees with the Fed, and the Fed sometimes disagrees with the markets. Disagreements between the Fed and the bond market usually occur at the beginning or at the end of a trend in interest rates. Say, for example, that the Fed continually raises interest rates for an extended period of time. At some point, long-term rates, which are controlled by the bond market, begin to drop, even though short-term rates are on the rise. Falling long-term bond rates usually are a sign — from the bond market to the Fed — that the Fed needs to consider pausing its interest rate increases. The opposite also is true: When the Fed goes too far in lowering short-term rates, bond yields begin to creep up and signal the need for the Fed to consider a pause in its lowering of the rates.

Interest rate futures and you

Interest rate futures serve one major function: They enable large institutions to neutralize or manage their price risks. As an investor or speculator who trades interest rate futures, you look at the markets differently than banks and other commercial borrowers. For you, it's a way to make money based on the system's inefficiencies, which often are created by the current relationship between large hedgers, the Fed, and other major players, such as foreign governments. Generally, you want to watch for the following:

✔ Opportunities to trade the long-term issues when interest rates are falling

✔ Opportunities to stay on the shorter-term side of the curve when interest rates are rising

Going global with interest rate futures

Globalization has increased the number of short-term interest rate contracts that trade at the Chicago Mercantile Exchange (CME) and around the world. Just about every country with a convertible currency has some kind of bond or bond futures contract that trades on an exchange somewhere around the world. The following are not complete lists, but they offer snapshots of some of the more liquid contracts.

Fed funds futures

Fed funds futures trade on the CME and are an almost pure bet on what the Federal Reserve is expected to do with future interest rates. Fed funds measure interest rates that private banks charge each other for overnight loans of excess reserves. The rates often are quoted in the media as a means of pricing the probability of the Fed raising or lowering interest rates at an upcoming meeting into the market.

Book III

Futures and Options

Each Fed funds contract lets you control $5 million and is cash settled. The tick size as described by the Chicago Board of Trade (CBOT) is "$20.835 per ½ of one basis point (½ of ¹⁄₁₀₀ of 1 percent of $5 million on a 30-day basis rounded up to the nearest cent)." Margins are variable, depending on the tier in which you trade, and they range from $104 to $675. A *tier* is just a time frame. The longer the time frame before expiration, the higher the margin. For full information, you can visit the CBOT's margin page at www.cbot.com/cbot/pub/page/0,3181,2142,00.html#1b. Fed funds contracts are quoted in terms of the rate that the market is speculating on by the time the contract expires, and they're based on the formula found at the CBOT: "100 minus the average daily Fed funds overnight rate for the delivery month (for example, a 7.25 percent rate equals 92.75)."

LIBOR futures

LIBOR futures are one-month interest rate contracts based on the London Interbank Offered Rate (LIBOR), the interest rate charged between commercial banks. LIBOR futures have 12 monthly listings. Each contract is worth $3 million. The role of LIBOR futures is to offer professionals a way to hedge their interest portfolio in a similar fashion to that offered by Eurodollars.

The minimum increment of price movement is "0.0025 (¼ tick = $6.25) for the front month expiring contract and 0.005 (½ tick = $12.50) for all other expirations." The major difference: Margin requirements are less for LIBOR, at $473 for initial and $350 for margin maintenance, compared with margins of $945 and $700 for respective Eurodollar contracts.

If you're new to trading, a good way to choose between the highly liquid and popular Eurodollar and LIBOR contracts — which offer essentially the same type of trading opportunities — is to paper trade both contracts after doing some homework on how each contract trades.

Eurodollar contracts

A *Eurodollar* is a dollar-denominated deposit held in a non-U.S. bank. Eurodollars are the most popular futures trading contract in the world because they offer reasonably low margins and the potential for fairly good return in a short period of time. A Eurodollar contract gives you control of $1 million Eurodollars and is a reflection of the LIBOR rate for a three-month, $1 million offshore deposit. Eurodollars are popular trading instruments. Following are some facts about Eurodollars that you need to know:

- ✔ In the case of Eurodollars, a point = one tick = 0.1 = $25. If you own a Eurodollar contract and it falls or rises four ticks, or 0.4, you either lose or gain $100. Eurodollars can trade in ¼ or ½ points, which are worth $6.25 and $12.50, respectively.

- ✔ Eurodollar prices are a central rate in global business and are quoted in terms of an index. If the price on the futures contract is $9,200, for example, the yield is 8 percent.

✔ Eurodollars trade on the CME with contract listings in March, June, September, and December. Different Eurodollar futures contracts suit different time frames. Some enable you to trade more than two years from the current date. This kind of long-term betting on short-term interest rates is rare, but sometimes large corporations use it. For full details, it's always good to check with your broker about which contracts are available, or go to the CME Web site.

✔ Trading hours for Eurodollars are from 7:20 a.m. to 2 p.m. central time on the trading floor, but they can be traded almost 24/7 on Globex. For Eurodollars, Globex is shut down only between 4 and 5 p.m. daily.

✔ The initial margin, or the minimum you need in your account (as of this writing) to trade a single Eurodollar contract at CME, is $743 for non-exchange members. The maintenance margin, or the minimum you need in your account to keep the trade going, is $550. But remember that the exchange minimum is a *guideline*. More important to you as a trader is what your broker offers. This amount can vary, and it does not have to be the exchange minimum. In fact, it is often greater and varies with the assets' volatility. This is true for every futures contract.

You want to trade Eurodollars when events are occurring that are likely to influence interest rates. If you grasp the concept of trading Eurodollars, you're also set to trade other types of interest rate futures, as long as you understand that each individual contract is going to have its own special quirks and idiosyncrasies. The CME has a good help page that you can find at www.cme.com/edu/res/bro/cmeinterestrate.

Book III

Futures and Options

Treasury bill futures

A 13-week T-bill contract is considered a risk-free obligation of the U.S. government. In the cash market, T-bills are sold in $10,000 increments; if you pay $9,600 for a T-bill in the cash market, an annualized interest rate of 4 percent is implied. At the end of the three months (13 weeks), you get $10,000 in return.

Risk-free means that if you buy the T-bills, you're assured of getting paid by the U.S. government. Trading T-bill futures, on the other hand, is not risk-free. Instead, T-bill futures trades essentially are governed by the same sort of risk rules that govern Eurodollar trades.

T-bill futures are 13-week contracts based on $10,000 U.S. Treasury bills and have a face value at maturity of $1,000,000. In addition, T-bill futures move in ½-point increments (½ point = 0.005 = $12.50) with trading months of March, June, September, and December.

Bonds and Treasury notes

The 10-year U.S. Treasury note has been the accepted benchmark for long-term interest rates since the United States stopped issuing the long bond (30-year U.S. Treasury bond) in October 2001. Thirty-year bond futures and

30-year T-bonds (issued before 2001) still are actively traded, and new 30-year T-bonds hit the market in early 2006.

Bond and note futures are big-time trading vehicles that move fast. Each tick or price quote, especially when you hold more than one contract and the market is moving fast, can be worth several hundred dollars. Some other facts about 10- and 30-year interest rate futures that you need to know:

- ✔ They're traded under the symbols *TY* for pit trading and *ZN* for electronic trading in the 10-year contract.

- ✔ U.S. note and bond futures have no price limits.

- ✔ They're valued at $100,000 per contract, the same as for a 30-year bond contract (which is traded under the symbol *US* for pit trading and *ZB* for electronic trading).

- ✔ They're longer-term debt futures that have higher margin requirements than Eurodollars. As of this writing, the initial and maintenance margins for the 10-year were $1,148 and $850. Initial and maintenance margins for the 30-year bond were $1,755 and $1,300 per contract.

- ✔ They're quoted in terms of 32nds. One point is $1,000, and one tick must be at least

  - ½ of ½₃₂, or $15.625, for a 10-year issue.

  - ½₃₂, or $31.25, for a 30-year issue.

  When a price quote is "84-16," it means the price of the contract is 84 and ¹⁶⁄₃₂ for both, and the value is $84,500.

- ✔ They're traded on the CME from 7:20 a.m. to 2 p.m. central time Monday through Friday. Electronic trades can be made from 7 a.m. to 4 p.m. central time Sunday through Friday.

  Trading in expiring contracts closes at noon central time (Chicago time) on the *last trading day,* which is the seventh business day before the last business day of the delivery month.

Taking delivery of T-bonds

If you take delivery, your contract will be wired to you on the last business day of the delivery month via the Federal Reserve book-entry wire-transfer system. What you get delivered to you, as of November 2007, is a series of U.S. Treasury bonds that either cannot be retired for at least 15 years from the first day of the delivery month or that are not callable with a maturity of at least 15 years from the first day of the delivery month. The *invoice price,* or the amount that you'll have to tender, equals the futures settlement price multiplied by a conversion factor with accrued interest added. The *conversion factor* used is the price of the delivered bond ($1 par value) to yield the interest rate that is pertinent to the contract. For full details, you can read these important chapters of the CBOT rulebook: Chapter 18 for Treasury bond futures, Chapter 23 for two-year Treasury note futures, Chapter 24 for ten-year Treasury note futures, and Chapter 25 for five-year Treasury note futures. The CBOT Rulebook can be viewed at www.cbot.com.

Bonds that are not callable remain in circulation until full maturity, which means that the holder receives all the interest payments until the bond expires, when the principle is returned. Callable bonds put the holder at risk of receiving less interest because of an earlier retirement of the bond than the holder had planned.

Taking delivery of T-notes

If you take delivery of T-notes, you receive a package of U.S. Treasury notes that mature from 6½ to 10 years from the first day of the delivery month. The price is calculated by using a formula you can find on the CBOE Web site. As a small speculator, your chances of getting a delivery are nil.

Euroyen contracts

Euroyen contracts represent Japanese yen deposits held outside of Japan. Open positions in these contracts can be held at CME or at the SIMEX exchange in Singapore. Euroyen contracts are listed quarterly, trade monthly, and offer expiration dates as far out as three years. That long-term time frame can be useful to professional hedgers with specific expectations about the future.

CETES futures

These 28-day and 91-day futures contracts are based on Mexican Treasury bills. These instruments are denominated and paid in Mexican pesos, and they reflect the corresponding benchmark rates of interest rates in Mexico.

Small traders usually trade Eurodollars, while pros with large sums and more experience tend to trade LIBOR. No matter what contract you trade, though, think in terms of short holding periods. Consider how much you may actually have to pay up (if you're long) if you don't sell before the contract rolls over (the amount specified by the contract — $3 million).

Eurobond futures

Longer-term global plays include Eurobond futures. The Eurobond market is composed of bonds issued by the Federal Republic of Germany and the Swiss Confederation. Eurobonds come in four different categories: Euro Shatz, Euro Bobl, Euro Bund, and Euro Buxl. The duration on each respective category is 1.75 years, 4.5 to 5.5 years, 8.5 to 10.5 years, and 24 to 35 years. The contract size is for 100,000 euros or 100,000 Swiss francs, depending on the issuer. Eurobonds can be traded in the United States. The basic strategies are similar to U.S. bonds because they trade on economic fundamentals and inflationary expectations, and they respond to European economic reports similar to the way U.S. bonds respond to U.S. reports.

Book III

Futures and Options

Yielding to the curve

The *yield curve* is a graphical representation comparing the entire spectrum of interest rates available to investors. Several informative shapes can be seen on the yield curve. Three important ones are

- ✔ **Normal curves:** The *normal curve* rises to the right, and short-term interest rates are lower than long-term interest rates. Economists usually look at this kind of movement as a sign of normal economic activity, where growth is ongoing and investors are being rewarded for taking more risks by being given extra yield in longer-term maturities.

- ✔ **Flat curves:** A *flat curve* is when short-term yields are equal or close to long-term yields. This type of graph can be a sign that the economy is slowing down or that the Federal Reserve has been raising short-term rates.

- ✔ **Inverted curves:** An *inverted curve* shows long-term rates falling below short-term rates, which can happen when the market is betting on a slowing of the economy or during a financial crisis when traders are flocking to the safety of long-term U.S. Treasury bonds.

Figures 4-2 and 4-3 are excellent illustrations of the U.S. Treasury yield curve and rate structure at a time when inflationary expectations are under control and the economy is growing steadily. The curve and the table are from July 1, 2005, just two days after the Federal Reserve raised interest rates for the ninth consecutive time in a 12-month period. Figure 4-3 depicts a standard, table-style snapshot of all market maturities for the U.S. Treasury. You can view an up-to-date version at `bonds.yahoo.com/rates.html`.

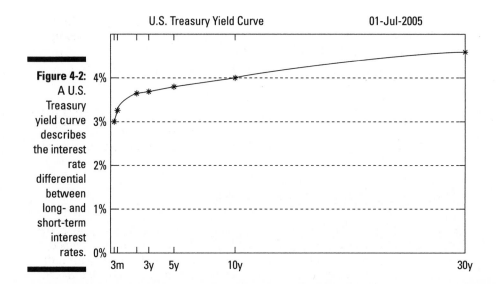

Figure 4-2:
A U.S. Treasury yield curve describes the interest rate differential between long- and short-term interest rates.

U.S. Treasury Bonds				
Maturity	Yield	Yesterday	Last week	Last month
3 Month	3.00	2.96	2.93	2.81
6 Month	3.21	3.18	3.12	2.98
2 Year	3.73	3.62	3.56	3.46
3 Year	3.76	3.64	3.60	3.50
5 Year	3.82	3.69	3.68	3.61
10 Year	4.04	3.91	3.91	3.88
30 Year	4.29	4.18	4.21	4.23

Figure 4-3: A U.S. Treasury summary shows all the common maturity listings and the price changes.

As you review Figures 4-2 and 4-3, notice the following:

- ✓ **The longer the maturity, the higher the yield:** That relationship is normal for interest-paying securities because you're lending your money to someone for an extended period of time, and you want them to pay you a premium for the extra risk.

- ✓ **The yields on all securities rose:** Starting with the 3-month Treasury bill (T-bill) and ending with the 30-year bond, all yields rose (compared with the previous week and month) after the Fed raised interest rates.

By keeping track of the yield curve, you're achieving several goals that Mark Powers describes in *Starting Out In Futures Trading* (Probus Publishing). By checking out the yield curve, you can

- ✓ Focus on the cash markets. Doing so enables you to put activity in the futures markets in perspective and provides clues to the relationship between prices in the futures markets.

- ✓ Watch for prices rising or falling below the yield curve. This can indicate good opportunities to buy or sell a security.

- ✓ Know that prices above the yield curve point to a relatively underpriced market.

- ✓ Know that prices below the curve point to a relatively overpriced market.

Book III

Futures and Options

Deciding your time frame

From a trader's standpoint, you want to consider trading the short term, the intermediate term, or the long term. Each position has its own time, place, and reasoning, ranging from how much money you have to trade, your individual risk tolerance, and whether your analysis leads you to think that the particular area of the curve can move during any particular period of time. The general rule is that the longer the maturity, the greater the potential reaction to good or bad news on inflation. In other words, the further out you go on the curve, the greater the chance for volatility.

Eurodollars are the best instrument for trading the short term because they are *liquid* investments, meaning that they're easy to buy and sell. Eurodollars are well suited for small traders because margin requirements tend to be smaller and the movements can be less volatile; however, don't consider those attractive factors a guarantee of success by any means. Any futures contract can be a quick road to ruin if you become careless.

For long- and intermediate-term trading, you can use the 10-year T-note and 30-year T-bond futures. Ten-year T-note and T-bond futures can be quite volatile because large traders and institutions usually use them for direct trading and for complicated hedging strategies.

Sound interest rate trading rules

When trading international interest rate contracts, you must consider the effects of currency conversion. If you just made a 10-percent profit trading Eurobonds but the Euro fell 10 percent, your purchasing power hasn't grown. When getting ready to trade, make sure that you do the following:

- ✔ **Calculate your margin requirements.** You need to know how much of a cushion for potential losses you have available before you get a margin call and are required to put up more money to keep a position open. Here's a good rule used by professionals: *Never risk more than 50 percent of your total account equity when trading.*

- ✔ **Never put yourself in a position to receive a margin call.** Make sure you have enough money in your account, never risking more than 10 percent of your equity on any one position (5 percent if your account's small), and calculating your maximum risk while keeping it below the amount that results in a margin call.

- ✔ **Price in how much of your account's equity you plan to risk before you make your trade.** As a general rule, you should never risk any more than 5 percent of your equity on any one trade with a small account. The bare minimum requirement for trading futures as an individual small speculator is widely accepted to be no less than $20,000.

- ✔ **Canvass your charts.** You want to know support and resistance levels on each of the markets that you plan to trade, and then you can set your entry points above or below those levels, depending, of course, on which way the market breaks.

- ✔ **Understand what the economic calendar has in store on any given day.** Knowing the potential for economic indicators of the day to move the market in either direction prepares you for the major volatility that can occur on the day they're released.

- ✔ **Pick your entry and exit points.** Include your worst-loss scenario — the possibility of taking a margin call.

- ✔ **Use trailing stops when trading all futures contracts.** That way, even when you aren't sure whether a top was reached, you are stopped out when the price falls below the three moving averages.

- ✔ **Decide what your options are if your trade goes well and you have a significant profit to deal with.**

Focusing on Stock Index Futures

Stock index futures are futures contracts based on indexes that are composed of stocks. For example, the S&P 500 futures contract is based on the popular market benchmark of the same name — the S&P 500 stock index, a group of 500 commonly traded stocks. When you trade stock index futures, you're betting on the direction of the contract's value, *not* on the individual stocks that make up the index.

Stock index futures are an integral part of the stock market's daily activity. As a percentage of the total number of futures contracts traded, stock index futures are by far the largest category of futures contracts traded. That dominance clearly speaks of the major role that stock index futures play in risk management for the entire stock market.

I can think of several major reasons for trading stock index futures. Here are some of the more common ones:

- ✔ **Speculation:** When you speculate, you're making an educated guess about the direction of a market. You can deliver trading profits to your accounts by going long or short on index futures, or by betting on prices rising or falling, respectively.

- ✔ **Hedging:** A *hedge* is when you use stock index futures and options to protect an individual security in your portfolio or, in some cases, your entire portfolio from losing value.

- ✔ **Tax consequences:** Short-term gains in the futures markets may be taxed at lower rates than stock-market capital gains.

  The IRS has a complex set of rules for taxing gains in the futures markets and specific forms (such as IRS Form 4797 Part II for securities or Form 6781 for commodities) that you must become familiar with. To be safe and stay on the right side of tax law, check with your accountant *before* you start trading.

Book III

Futures and Options

✔ **Lower commission rates:** Many futures brokerages offer lower commission rates. This practice is not as widespread as it was before online discount brokers for stocks became a mainstay of the business. But you still can find low commission rates in the futures markets, a factor that becomes more important as you trade large blocks or quantities of stocks.

✔ **Time factors:** If something happens overnight, when the stock market is closed, and you want to hedge your risk, you can trade futures on Globex, a 24-hour electronic trading system, while Wall Street sleeps.

You don't need to trade every major index contract in the world to be successful; you just need to find one or two with which you're comfortable — the ones that enable you to implement your strategies. In this section, I focus on the S&P 500 stock index futures. Any of the lessons that I describe with respect to the S&P 500 can be applied to just about any contract.

Looking into fair value

Fair value is the theoretically correct value for a futures contract at a particular point in time. You calculate fair value using a formula that includes the current index level, index dividends, number of days to contract expiration, and interest rates. Without getting caught up in the details, the important thing for you to remember is that fair value is a benchmark that can be a helpful tool for your analysis of the markets. When a stock index futures contract trades below its fair value, for example, it's trading at a *discount.* When it trades above fair value, it's trading at a *premium.*

Knowing the fair value is most helpful in gauging where the market is headed. Because stock index futures prices are related to spot-index prices, changes in fair value can trigger price changes. Here's how it works:

✔ If the futures contract is too far below fair value, the index (cash) is sold and the futures contract is bought.

✔ If the futures contract is too high versus its fair value, the futures contract is sold and the index (cash) is bought.

✔ If enough sell programs hit the market hard enough over an extended period of time, you can see a *crash,* or a situation where market prices fall dramatically.

✔ If enough buy programs kick in, the market tends to rally.

Fair value is the number that the television stock analysts refer to when discussing the action in futures before the market opens.

Considering major stock index futures contracts

You can trade many different stock index contracts, but they all share the same basic characteristics. I describe many of these general issues in the section that follows, and I address any particular differences with descriptions of other individual contracts throughout the rest of this section.

S&P 500 futures (SP)

The biggest stock index futures contract is the S&P 500, which trades on the Chicago Mercantile Exchange (CME). This index is made up of the 500 largest stocks in the United States. It's a *weighted* index, which means that component companies that have bigger *market capitalizations,* or market values, can have a much larger impact on the movements of the index than components with smaller market capitalizations.

Some of the particulars about the S&P 500 Index include the following:

- ✔ **Composition:** The S&P 500 is made up of 400 industrial companies, 40 financial companies, 40 utilities, and 20 transportation companies, offering a fairly diversified view of the U.S. economy.

- ✔ **Valuation:** The S&P 500 Index is valued in ticks worth 0.1 index points or $25.

- ✔ **Contracts:** S&P 500 index futures contracts are worth 250 times the value of the index. That means that when the index value is at 1,250, a contract is worth $250 \times \$1,250$, or $312,500. A move of a full point is worth $250.

- ✔ **Trading times:** Regular trading hours for S&P 500 index futures are from 8:30 a.m. to 3:15 p.m., but S&P 500 index futures contracts are another example of how 24-hour-a-day trading enables traders to respond to economic news and releases in the premarket and aftermarket sessions. The evening session starts 15 minutes after the close (at 3:30 p.m.) and continues in the overnight until 8:15 a.m. on Globex.

- ✔ **Contract limits:** Individual contract holders are limited to no more than 20,000 net long or short contracts at any one time.

- ✔ **Price limits:** *Price limits* halt trading above or below the price specified by the limit. A price limit is how far the S&P 500 index can rise or fall in a single trading session. The limits are set on a quarterly basis. If the index experiences major declines or increases beyond these limits, a procedure is in place to halt trading. You can find the price limits detailed on the CME's Web site (www.cme.com).

Book III

Futures and Options

✔ **Circuit breakers:** Circuit breakers halt trading briefly in a coordinated manner between exchanges. The limits that trigger circuit breakers are calculated and agreed upon on a quarterly basis by the different exchanges.

✔ **Final settlement:** For all stock index futures, settlement on the CME is based on a Special Opening Quotations (SOQ) price, which is calculated based on the opening prices for each of the stocks in an index on the day that the contract expires. Don't confuse the SOQ with the opening index value, which is calculated right after the opening. Note: Some stocks may take a while to establish opening prices.

✔ **Margin requirements:** Margin values for S&P 500 index contracts are variable. In November 2007, the initial margin for the S&P 500 contract was $19,688, and the maintenance margin was $15,750.

✔ **Cash settlement:** Stock index futures are settled with cash, a practice known as *cash settlement.* That means if you hold your contract until expiration, you have to either pay or receive the amount of money the contract is worth as determined by the SOQ price. Cash settlement applies to all stock index futures.

Overnight and premarket trading can be thin and dangerous, especially during slow seasons in the stock market, such as in summer, fall, and around winter holidays.

NASDAQ-100 futures (ND)

The NASDAQ-100 index futures contract is similar to the S&P 500 futures contract. Here's what you need to know about it:

✔ **Composition:** The NASDAQ-100 stock index is made up of the 100 largest stocks traded on the NASDAQ system, including large technology and biotech stocks.

✔ **Valuation:** The ND is valued in minimum ticks of 0.25 that are worth $25.

✔ **Contract limits:** No more than 10,000 net long or short contracts can be held by any individual at any one time.

✔ **Margin requirements:** Margins required for NASDAQ-100 index futures are similar to the S&P 500 index futures. In November 2007, the initial margin for the ND contract was $12,500, and the maintenance margin was $10,000.

e-mini S&P 500 (ES) and e-mini NASDAQ-100 (NQ)

The e-mini S&P 500 (ES) contract and the e-mini NASDAQ-100 (NQ) are among the most popular stock index futures contracts because they enable you to trade the market's trend with only a fifth of the requirement. The e-mini S&P is a favorite of day-traders because of its high intraday volatility and major price swings on a daily basis. The mini contracts are marketed to small investors, and they offer some advantages. However, they also carry significant risks because they're volatile and still have fairly high margin requirements.

The ES and NQ e-mini contracts are based on the same makeup as the respective S&P 500 and NASDAQ-100 index contracts, and they can be very volatile and can move even more aggressively during extremely volatile market environments. Other particulars about the e-mini contracts:

- ✔ **Valuation:** One tick on ES is 0.25 of an index point and is worth $12.50. One tick on NQ is 0.50 of an index point and is worth $10.

- ✔ **Contracts:** The value of an ES contract is $50 multiplied by the value of the S&P 500 index. The value of an NQ contract is $20 multiplied by the value of the NASDAQ-100 index.

- ✔ **Trading times:** The e-mini contracts trade nearly 24 hours per day, with a 30-minute maintenance break in trading from 4:30 to 5:00 p.m. daily.

- ✔ **Monthly identifiers:** Monthly identifiers for both mini contracts are *H* for March, *M* for June, *U* for September, and *Z* for December.

- ✔ **Margin requirements:** Margins for the ES and NQ contracts are less than for the normal-sized contracts. As of November 2007, the ES required $3,938 for initial margin and $3,150 for maintenance, and the NQ required $2,500 and $2,000, respectively.

Book III

Futures and Options

The day-trading margin is less than the margin to hold an overnight position in S&P 500 e-mini futures. Traders, though, are obligated to pay for the difference between the margins for entry and exit points, which means that if you lose, you're likely to pay up in a big way at the end of the day.

When you own normal-sized contracts and e-mini contracts in one or the other of the underlying indexes, position limits apply to both positions, meaning that each of the contracts is counted as an individual part of the overall position. The combined number of contracts can't exceed the 20,000 contract limit for the S&P 500-based index and the 10,000 contract limit for the NASDAQ-100-based index.

Book IV
Commodities

"Precious metals? Energy futures? Cocoa beans? I say we stick the money in the ground like always, and then feed this guy to the sharks."

In this book . . .

Savvy investors always keep their fingers on the pulse of the markets and seek to develop investment strategies that take advantage of the market fundamentals. One of the biggest trends in the global investment game in the beginning of the 21st century is the increasing popularity of commodities in investor portfolios. Driven by high commodity prices, many investors are looking for ways to profit in this sector. This book tells you what you need to know about key commodities markets — energy, metals, and agriculture — so that you can decide whether to put some of your investment dollars in commodities, and, if so, where.

Chapter 1

A Commodities Overview

In This Chapter

▶ Distinguishing commodities from other investment options

▶ Identifying ways to invest in the commodity markets

▶ Understanding risks specific to commodities

▶ Determining whether commodities should be part of your portfolio

*F*or whatever reason, investors have often shunned commodities in favor of what they think are more "prudent" investments, such as stocks. This is quite baffling because the performance of commodities in recent years has been superior to that of stocks. Between 2002 and 2005, for example, the Dow Jones Industrial Average returned a respectable 7 percent. Meanwhile, the Dow Jones-AIG Commodity Index, which tracks a basket of commodities, was up more than 21 percent! In 2002 alone, while the Dow Jones Industrial Average had negative returns (–7 percent), the Dow Jones-AIG Commodity Index had returns of 26 percent.

Many investors are afraid of commodities because they don't know much about them. The goal of this chapter is to shed some light on commodities so you can invest with confidence.

Defining Commodities

Just what, exactly, are commodities? Put simply, commodities are the raw materials humans use to create a livable world. We humans have been exploiting the Earth's natural resources since the beginning of time. We use energy to sustain ourselves, metals to build weapons and tools, and agricultural products to feed ourselves. These resources — energy, metals, and agricultural products — are the three classes of commodities, and they are the essential building blocks of the global economy.

Energy

Energy, whether fossil fuels or renewable energy sources, can make a great investment; the world has a seemingly unquenchable thirst for this resource. In Chapter 4, I cover investment opportunities in each of these major forms of energy:

- ✔ **Crude oil:** Crude oil is the undisputed heavyweight champion in the commodities world. In terms of volume, more crude oil is traded every day (85 million barrels and growing) than any other commodity. Accounting for 40 percent of total global energy consumption, it provides some terrific investment opportunities.

- ✔ **Natural gas:** Natural gas, the gaseous fossil fuel, is a major commodity in its own right. It's used for everything from cooking food to heating houses during the winter.

- ✔ **Coal:** Coal accounts for more than 20 percent of total world energy consumption. In the United States, the largest energy market, 50 percent of electricity is generated through coal. Because of abundant supply, coal is making a resurgence.

- ✔ **Uranium/nuclear power:** Because of improved environmental standards within the industry, nuclear power use is on the rise.

- ✔ **Electricity:** Electricity is a necessity of modern life, and the companies responsible for generating this special commodity have some unique characteristics.

- ✔ **Solar power:** Due to a number of reasons ranging from environmental to geopolitical, demand for renewable energy sources such as solar power is increasing.

- ✔ **Wind power:** Wind power is getting a lot of attention from investors as a viable alternative source of energy.

- ✔ **Ethanol:** Ethanol, produced primarily from corn or sugar, is an increasingly popular fuel additive that offers investment potential.

There are other commodities in the energy complex, such as heating oil, propane, and gasoline. Although I do provide insight into some of these other members of the energy family in Chapter 4, I focus primarily on the resources mentioned in this list.

Metals

Metallurgy has been essential to human development since the beginning of time. Societies that have mastered the production of metals have been able to survive and thrive. Similarly, investors who have incorporated metals into their portfolios have been able to generate significant returns. In Chapter 5, I discuss investment opportunities for all the major metals:

✔ **Gold:** For centuries, people have been attracted to its quasi-indestructibility and have used it as a store of value. Folks invest in gold to hedge against inflation and to protect their assets during times of global turmoil.

✔ **Silver:** Silver, like gold, has monetary applications. The British currency, the pound sterling, is still named after this metal. Silver also has applications in industry (such as electrical wiring).

✔ **Platinum:** The rich man's gold is one of the most valuable metals in the world, used for everything from jewelry to the manufacture of catalytic converters.

✔ **Steel:** Created by alloying iron and other materials, steel is the most widely used metal in the world, helping to create everything from cars to buildings.

✔ **Aluminum:** Perhaps no other metal has the versatility of aluminum; it's lightweight yet surprisingly robust. That's probably why it's the second most used metal (right behind steel).

✔ **Copper:** Copper, the third most widely used metal, is the metal of choice for industry because it's a great conductor of heat and electricity.

✔ **Zinc:** The fourth most widely used metal in the world, zinc is sought for its resistance to corrosion. It's used in the process of *galvanization,* where zinc coating is applied to other metals to prevent rust.

✔ **Palladium:** Almost half the palladium that's mined goes toward building automobile catalytic converters. As the number of cars with these emission-reducing devices increases, the demand for palladium increases as well.

✔ **Nickel:** Nickel is in high demand because of its resistance to corrosion and oxidation. Because steel is usually alloyed with nickel to create stainless steel, nickel will have an important role to play for years to come.

Agricultural products

Food is the most essential element of human life, and the production of food presents solid money-making opportunities. Following are some major agricultural products, which I discuss further in Chapter 6:

✔ **Coffee:** Coffee is the second most widely produced commodity in the world in terms of physical volume, behind only crude oil.

✔ **Cocoa:** Cocoa is a major agricultural commodity primarily because it's is used to create chocolate.

✔ **Sugar:** Sugar can be a sweet investment. In industry lingo, *Sugar #11* represents a futures contract for global sugar. *Sugar #14* is specific to the United States and is a widely traded commodity.

- **Frozen concentrated orange juice:** There are two types of frozen concentrated orange juice: Type A (FCOJ-A) and Type B (FCOJ-B). FCOJ-A, the benchmark for North American orange juice prices, is grown in the hemisphere's two largest regions: Florida and Brazil. FCOJ-B represents global orange juice prices and gives you exposure to orange juice activity on a world scale.

- **Corn:** Corn's use for culinary purposes is perhaps unrivaled by any other grain.

- **Wheat:** Wheat was one of the first agricultural products grown by man and is still a staple.

- **Soybeans and their derivatives (soybean oil and soybean meal):** Soybeans have many applications, and the soybean market is large. Soybean oil, also known as vegetable oil, has become very popular in recent years. Soybean meal is used as feedstock for poultry and cattle.

- **Cattle:** There are two types of cattle commodities: live cattle and feeder cattle. Using the live cattle futures contract (which tracks adult cows) to hedge against price volatility is a good idea for investors involved in agriculture. The feeder cattle contract is used to hedge against the risk associated with growing calves. This area is not widely followed in the markets, but it's important to figure out how it works.

- **Lean hogs:** They may not be the sexiest commodity out there, but lean hogs are an essential.

- **Frozen pork bellies:** Frozen pork bellies are essentially just good old bacon. This industry is subject to wild price swings, which provides unique arbitrage trading opportunities.

Chewing on Characteristics of Commodities

As an asset class, commodities have unique characteristics that separate them from other asset classes and make them attractive, whether as independent investments or as part of a broader based investment strategy. I go through these unique characteristics in the following sections.

Savoring the inelasticity

In economics, *elasticity* seeks to determine the effects of price on supply and demand. The calculation can get pretty technical but, essentially, elasticity quantifies how much supply and demand will change for every incremental change in price.

Goods that are elastic tend to have a high correlation between price and demand, which is usually inversely proportional: When the price of a good increases, demand tends to decrease. This makes sense because you're not going to pay for a good that you don't need if it becomes too expensive. Capturing and determining that spread is what elasticity is all about.

Inelastic goods, however, are goods that are so essential to consumers that changes in price tend to have a limited effect on supply and demand. Most commodities fall in the inelastic goods category because they are essential to human existence.

For instance, if the price of ice cream were to increase by 25 percent, chances are you'd buy less ice cream because it's not a necessity. However, when the price of unleaded gasoline increases by 25 percent, you may not be happy, but you still fill your tank because gas is a necessity. Of course, the demand for gasoline isn't *absolutely* inelastic; a point will come when you decide that it's simply not worth paying the amount you're paying at the pump, and you'll begin looking for alternatives. But the truth remains that you're willing to pay more for gasoline than for other products you don't need (such as ice cream); that's the key to understanding price inelasticity.

Most commodities are fairly inelastic because they are the raw materials that allow us to live the lives we strive for; they allow us to maintain a decent (and, in some cases, extravagant!) standard of living. Without these precious raw materials, you wouldn't be able to heat your home in the winter; actually, without cement, copper, and other basic materials, you wouldn't even have a house to begin with! And then, of course, there's the most essential commodity of all: food. Without food we would not exist.

Offering a safe haven for investors

During times of turmoil, commodities tend to act as safe havens for investors. Certain commodities, such as gold and silver, are viewed by investors as reliable stores of value, so investors flock to these assets when times aren't good. When currencies slide, when nations go to war, when global pandemics break out, you can rely on gold, silver, and other commodities to provide you with financial safety.

Have part of your portfolio in gold and other precious metals so that you can protect your assets during times of turmoil. Turn to Chapter 5 for more on investing in precious metals.

Hedging against inflation

One of the biggest things you need to watch out for as an investor is the ravaging effects of inflation. Inflation can devastate your investments, particularly

Book IV

Commodities

paper assets such as stocks. The central bankers of the world — smart people all — spend their entire careers trying to tame inflation, but despite their efforts, inflation can easily get out of hand. You need to protect yourself against this economic enemy.

Ironically, one of the only asset classes that actually *benefits* from inflation is — you guessed it — commodities. Perhaps the biggest irony of all is that increases in the prices of basic goods (commodities such as oil and gas) actually contribute to the increase of inflation. For example, there's a positive correlation between gold and the inflation rate (see Figure 1-1). During times of high inflation, investors load up on gold because it is considered a good store of value.

Bringing new sources online takes time

The business of commodities is a time- and capital-intensive business. Unlike high tech or other "new economy" start-ups (such as e-commerce), bringing commodity projects online takes a lot of time. It can take up to a decade, for example, to bring new sources of oil online. First, a company must identify potentially promising areas to explore for oil. Then the company has to start drilling and prospecting for the oil (a process that, if it's lucky, will take only three to five years). After discovering significantly recoverable sources of oil, the company must then develop infrastructure and bring in machinery to extract the oil, which must then be transported to a refining facility to be transformed into consumable energy products such as gasoline or jet fuel. After the oil goes through the lengthy refining stage, it must finally be transported to consumers!

What does this mean to you as an investor? When you're investing in commodities, you have to think long term. If you're used to investing in tech stocks or if you're an entrepreneur involved in e-commerce, you need to radically change the way you think about investing when you approach commodities. If you're able to recognize the long-term nature of commodities, you're on your way to becoming a successful commodities investor.

Moving in different cycles

"Sell in May and go away" is an old Wall Street adage referring to stocks; because the stock market doesn't perform well during the summer months, the thinking goes, you should sell your stocks and get back into the game in the fall. This adage doesn't apply to commodities because commodities move in different cycles than stocks. Some commodities perform really well during the summer months. Gasoline products see an increase in demand during the summer months (due to increased driving); all things equal, unleaded gasoline tends to increase in price during the summer.

Figure 1-1:
The relationship between gold and inflation.

Choosing the Right Investment Vehicle

One of the most critical questions you should ask yourself before getting started in commodities is the following: How do I invest in commodities? The following sections give you some answers. (The other critical question is what to invest in. You find a plethora of possibilities in Chapters 4 through 6.)

The futures markets

In the futures markets, individuals, institutions, and sometimes governments transact with each other for price hedging and speculating purposes. An airline company, for instance, may want to use futures to enter into an agreement with a fuel company to buy a fixed amount of jet fuel for a fixed price for a fixed period of time. This transaction in the futures markets allows the airline to hedge against the volatility associated with the price of jet fuel. Although commercial users are the main players in the futures arena, the futures markets are also used by traders and investors who profit from price volatility through various trading techniques.

Book IV

Commodities

The futures markets are administered by the various commodity exchanges, such as the Chicago Mercantile Exchange (CME) and the New York Mercantile Exchange (NYMEX). I discuss the major exchanges, the role they play in the markets, and the products they offer in Chapter 2.

Investing through the futures markets requires a good understanding of futures contracts, options on futures, forwards, spreads, and so on. The most direct way of investing in the futures markets is by opening an account with a futures commission merchant (FCM). The FCM is very much like your traditional stock brokerage house (such as Schwab, Fidelity, or Merrill Lynch), except that it's allowed to offer products that trade on the futures markets. Here are some other ways to get involved in futures:

- **Commodity trading advisor (CTA):** The CTA is an individual or company licensed to trade futures contracts on your behalf.

- **Commodity pool operator (CPO):** The CPO is similar to a CTA except that the CPO can manage the funds of multiple clients under one account. This provides additional leverage when trading futures.

- **Commodity indexes:** A commodity index is a benchmark, similar to the Dow Jones Industrial Average or the S&P 500, which tracks a basket of the most liquid commodities. You can track the performance of a commodity index, which allows you in effect to "buy the market." A number of commodity indexes are available, such as the Goldman Sachs Commodity Index and the Reuters/Jefferies CRB Index.

The futures markets are regulated by a number of organizations, such as the Securities and Exchange Commission (SEC) and the Commodity Futures Trading Commission (CFTC). These organizations monitor the markets to prevent market fraud and manipulation and to protect investors from such activity. For more information about the nuts and bolts of futures trading, go to Book III.

Trading futures is not for everyone. By their very nature, futures markets, contracts, and products are extremely complex and require a great deal of mastery even by the most seasoned investors. If you don't feel you have a good handle on all the concepts involved in trading futures, don't jump into futures or you could lose a lot more than your principal (because of the use of leverage and other characteristics unique to the futures markets). If you're not comfortable trading futures, don't sweat it. You can invest in commodities in multiple other ways.

If you are ready to start investing in the futures markets, you need to have a solid grasp of technical analysis, which is discussed in Book VIII.

The equity markets

Although the futures markets offer the most direct investment gateway to the commodities markets, the equity markets also offer access to these raw materials. You can invest in companies that specialize in the production, transformation, and distribution of these natural resources. If you're a stock investor familiar with the equity markets, this may be a good route for you to access the commodities markets. The only drawback of the equity markets is that you have to take into account external factors, such as management competence, tax situations, debt levels, and profit margins, which have nothing to do with the underlying commodity. That said, investing in companies that process commodities still allows you to profit from the commodities boom.

Publicly traded companies

The size, structure, and scope of the companies involved in the business are varied. Here's a sampling:

- **Integrated energy companies:** These companies, such as Exxon Mobil Corp. (NYSE: XOM) and Chevron (NYSE: CVX), are involved in all aspects of the energy industry, from the extraction of crude oil to the distribution of liquefied natural gas (LNG). They give you broad exposure to the energy complex (see Chapter 4).

- **Diversified mining companies:** A number of companies focus exclusively on mining metals and minerals. Some of these companies, such as Anglo American PLC (NASDAQ: AAUK) and BHP Billiton (NYSE: BHP), have operations across the spectrum of the metals complex, mining metals that range from gold to zinc. Head to Chapter 5 for more details.

- **Electric utilities:** Utilities are an integral part of modern life because they provide one of life's most essential necessities: electricity. They're also a good investment because they have historically offered large dividends to shareholders. Read Chapter 4 to figure out whether these companies are right for you.

This list is only a small sampling of the commodity companies I cover in these pages. I also analyze highly specialized companies, such as coal mining companies and oil refiners (Chapter 4), platinum mining companies (Chapter 5), and purveyors of gourmet coffee products (Chapter 6).

Master limited partnerships

Master limited partnerships (MLPs) invest in energy infrastructure, such as oil pipelines and natural gas storage facilities. I'm a big fan of MLPs because

Book IV

Commodities

they're publicly traded partnerships. This means they offer the benefits of trading like a corporation on a public exchange while offering the tax advantages of a private partnership. MLPs are required to transfer all cash flow back to shareholders, which makes them an attractive investment. You can find more information about MLPs in Chapter 3.

Managed funds

Sometimes it's easier to have someone else manage your investments for you. Luckily, you can count on professional money managers that specialize in commodity trading to handle your investments. Here are two options:

- ✔ **Mutual funds:** If you've previously invested in mutual funds and are comfortable with them, look into adding a mutual fund that gives you exposure to the commodities markets. A number of funds are available that invest solely in commodities. You can find more information on commodity mutual funds in Chapter 3.

- ✔ **Exchange-traded funds (ETFs):** ETFs are an increasingly popular investment because they are managed funds that offer the convenience of trading like stocks. A plethora of ETFs that track everything from crude oil and gold to diversified commodity indexes have appeared in recent years. Find out how to benefit from these vehicles in Chapter 3.

An outright commodity purchase

The most direct way of investing in certain commodities is by buying them outright. Precious metals such as gold, silver, and platinum are a great example of this. When the price of gold and silver skyrockets, you may see ads on TV or in newspapers from companies offering to buy your gold or silver jewelry. As gold and silver prices increase in the futures markets, they also cause prices in the spot markets to rise (and vice versa). You can cash in on this trend by buying coins, bullion, or even jewelry. I present this unique investment strategy in Chapter 5.

Obviously, this investment strategy is suitable only for a limited number of commodities, mostly precious metals. Unless you own a farm, keeping live cattle or feeder cattle to profit from price increases doesn't make much sense. And I won't even mention commodities like crude oil or uranium!

Putting Risk in Perspective

Commodities have a reputation for being a risky asset, and many investors are scared of investing in this asset class. Of course, investing in commodities does present risks — all investments do. This section explains what the risks are and how you can minimize and manage them.

The pitfalls of using leverage

In finance, *leverage* refers to the act of magnifying returns through the use of borrowed capital. Leverage is a powerful tool that gives you the opportunity to control large market positions with relatively little upfront capital. However, leverage is the ultimate double-edged sword because both your profits and losses are magnified to outrageous proportions.

If you invest in stocks, you know that you are able to trade on margin. You have to qualify for a margin account but, after you do, you are able to use leverage (margin) to get into stock positions. You can also trade commodities on margin. However, the biggest difference between using margin with stocks and with commodities is that the margin requirement for commodities is much lower than margins for stocks, which means the potential for losses (and profits) is much greater in commodities.

If you qualify for trading stocks on margin, you have to have at least 50 percent of the capital in your account before you can enter into a stock position on margin. The minimum margin requirements for commodity futures vary but are, on average, lower than that for stocks. For example, the margin requirement for soybeans in the Chicago Board of Trade is 4 percent. This means that with only $400 in your account, you can buy $10,000 worth of soybeans futures contracts! If the trade goes your way, you're a happy camper. But if you're on the losing side of a trade on margin, you can lose much more than your principal.

 When you're trading on margin, you may get a *margin call* from your broker requiring you to deposit additional capital in your account to cover the borrowed amount. The balance on futures accounts is calculated at the end of the trading session. This means that if you get a margin call, you need to take care of it immediately. So if you're trading commodities on margin, you may have to come up with a nice chunk of change — even more than if you're trading stocks on margin.

Book IV

Commodities

Because of the use of margin and the extraordinary amounts of leverage you have at your disposal in the futures markets, you should be extremely careful when trading commodity futures contracts. In order to be a responsible investor, I recommend using margin only if you have the necessary capital reserves to cover any subsequent margin calls you may receive if the market moves adversely.

The real risks behind commodities

Investing is all about managing the risk involved in generating returns. In this section, I lay out some common risks you face when investing in commodities and some small steps you can take to minimize these risks.

Geopolitical risk

One of the inherent risks of commodities is that the world's natural resources are located in various continents and the jurisdiction over these commodities lies with sovereign governments, international companies, and many other entities. International disagreements over the control of natural resources are quite commonplace. Sometimes a host country will simply kick out foreign companies involved in the production and distribution of the country's natural resources. In 2006, Bolivia, which contains South America's second largest deposits of natural gas, nationalized its natural gas industry and kicked out the foreign companies involved. In a day, a number of companies such as Brazil's Petrobras and Spain's Repsol were left without a mandate in a country where they had spent billions of dollars in developing the natural gas industry. Investors in Petrobras and Repsol paid the price.

One way to minimize the risk associated with geopolitical uncertainty is to invest in companies with experience and economies of scale. If, for example, you're interested in investing in an international oil company, go with one with an established international track record. A company like Exxon Mobil Corp., for instance, has the scale, breadth, and experience in international markets to manage the geopolitical risk it faces. A smaller company without this sort of experience is going to be more at risk than a bigger one. In commodities, size does matter.

Speculative risk

The commodities markets, just like the bond and stock markets, are populated by traders whose primary interest is in making short-term profits by speculating whether the price of a security will go up or down. Because speculators are simply interested in making profits, they tend to move the markets in different ways. Although speculators provide much-needed liquidity to the markets (particularly in commodity futures markets), they also tend to increase market volatility, especially when they begin exhibiting what Alan Greenspan termed "irrational exuberance." Because speculators can get out of control, as they did during the dot-com bubble, always be aware of the amount of speculative activity going on in the markets. The amount of speculative money involved in commodity markets is in constant fluctuation, but as a general rule, most commodity futures markets contain about 75 percent commercial users and 25 percent speculators.

Although I'm bullish on commodities because of the fundamental supply and demand story, too much speculative money coming into the commodities markets can have detrimental effects when speculators drive the prices of commodities in excess of the fundamentals. If you see too much speculative activity, it's probably a good idea to simply get out of the markets.

If you trade commodities, find out as much as possible about who the market participants are so that you can distinguish between the commercial users and the speculators. Check out the Commitment of Traders report, put out by the Commodity Futures Trading Commission (CFTC) and available online at www.cftc.gov/cftc/cftccotreports.htm.

The risk of fraud

As if there weren't enough things to worry about, you should always watch out for plain and simple fraud. Although the Commodity Futures Trading Commission (CFTC) and other regulatory bodies do a decent job of protecting investors from market fraud, there is always the possibility that you will become a victim of fraud. Your broker may hide debts or losses in offshore accounts, for example.

One way to prevent being taken advantage of is to be extremely vigilant about who you do business with. Make sure that you thoroughly research a firm before handing over your money. I go through the due diligence process you should follow when selecting managers in Chapter 2. Unfortunately, there are times when no amount of research or due diligence is able to protect you from fraud — it's just a fact of the investment game.

Chapter 2

Understanding How Commodity Exchanges Work

*T*he first image that usually comes to mind when you think of a commodity exchange is a group of brokers standing in a large circle, wearing bright-colored jackets, and shouting at each other while making funny gestures. Behind all this apparent chaos is a very rational, efficient, and orderly process that is responsible for setting global benchmark prices for the world's most important commodities. The prices established in the exchanges have a direct impact on our lives, from the price we pay to fill our gas tanks to how much we pay to heat our homes.

This chapter gives you a tour of a typical commodity exchange, explains the role that exchanges play in global capital markets, and introduces some of the players who are part of this fascinating world. It also examines some of the products traded on the exchanges and shows you how you can get involved in the buying and selling of exchange-traded commodities.

The Role of Commodity Exchanges

Commodity exchanges provide investors and traders with the opportunity to invest in commodities by trading futures contracts, options on futures, and other derivative products. By their very nature, these products are extremely sophisticated financial instruments used by only the savviest investors and the most experienced traders. They also serve a very important role in establishing global benchmark prices for crucial commodities such as crude oil, gold, copper, orange juice, and coffee.

Although independent traders, like you and me, can and do trade the futures markets, the majority of players in the futures markets are large commercial entities who use the futures markets for price hedging purposes. Hershey Foods Corporation, for example, is an active participant in cocoa futures because it wants to hedge against the price risk of cocoa, a primary input for making its chocolates. If you decide to trade cocoa futures contracts, you should remember that you're up against some large and experienced market players.

At the end of the day, the commodity futures exchanges are your gateway to the futures markets; in fact, they *are* the commodity futures markets. However, because of the fierce competition in these markets and because of the complexity of exchange-traded products, you should trade directly in the commodity futures markets only if you have an iron clad grasp of the technical aspects of the markets and have a rock solid understanding of the market fundamentals. If you don't have either, I recommend staying out of these markets because you could subject yourself to disastrous losses. That said, you can hire a trained professional with experience trading commodity futures to do the trading for you.

A number of commodity exchanges operate worldwide, specializing in all sorts of commodities. In the following sections, I identify the major commodity exchanges and list the commodities traded in them.

The Major Commodity Exchanges

Many commodity exchanges operate worldwide, and each exchange specializes in certain commodities. In the following sections, I introduce you to some of the key players in the United States and abroad.

Key U.S. players

The main commodity exchanges in the United States are located in New York and Chicago, with a few other exchanges in other parts of the country. Table 2-1 lists the major commodity exchanges in the United States along with some of the commodities traded in each one.

Table 2-1	The Major U.S. Commodity Exchanges	
Exchange Name	*Web Site*	*Commodities Traded*
Chicago Board of Trade (CBOT)	www.cbot.com	Corn, ethanol, gold, oats, rice, silver, soybeans, wheat
Chicago Mercantile Exchange (CME)	www.cme.com	Butter, milk, feeder cattle, frozen pork bellies, lean hogs, live cattle, lumber
Intercontinental Exchange* (ICE)	www.theice.com	Crude oil, electricity, natural gas
Kansas City Board of Trade (KCBT)	www.kcbt.com	Wheat, natural gas
Minneapolis Grain Exchange (MGE)	www.mgex.com	Corn, soybeans, wheat
New York Board of Trade (NYBOT)	www.nybot.com	Cocoa, coffee, cotton, ethanol, frozen concentrated orange juice, sugar
New York Mercantile Exchange (NYMEX)	www.nymex.com	Aluminum, copper, crude oil, electricity, gasoline, gold, heating oil, natural gas, palladium, platinum, propane, silver

* The Intercontinental Exchange is one of the only exchanges without a physical trading floor — all orders are routed and matched electronically. It is, in fact, one of the only all-electronic exchanges.

Keep in mind that this table offers only a small sampling of the commodities that these exchanges offer. The CME, for example, offers more than 100 futures products. I recommend visiting the exchange Web sites for a comprehensive listing of their product offerings.

 When a commodity is traded on more than one exchange, you want to trade the most liquid market. You can find out where the most liquid market for a commodity is by consulting the Commodity Futures Trading Commission (CFTC), which keeps information on all the exchanges and their products.

 The technical name for a commodity exchange is *designated contract market* (DCM). DCM is a designation handed out by the CFTC to exchanges that offer commodity products to the public. If an exchange does not have the designation DCM, stay away from it!

Book IV

Commodities

A sampling of international exchanges

Although the bulk of commodity trading is done in the United States — the largest consumer market of commodities — there are commodity exchanges located in other countries. Table 2-2 lists some of these international commodity exchanges.

Table 2-2	International Commodity Exchanges	
Exchange Name	*Country*	*Commodities Traded*
European Energy Exchange	Germany	Electricity
London Metal Exchange	United Kingdom	Aluminum, copper, lead, nickel, tin, zinc
Natural Gas Exchange	Canada	Natural gas
Tokyo Commodity Exchange	Japan	Aluminum, crude oil, gasoline, gold, kerosene, palladium, platinum, rubber, silver

Regulatory organizations for commodity exchanges

Commodity exchanges are under strict oversight in order to protect all market participants and to ensure transparency in the exchanges. Here are the main regulatory organizations that have oversight of commodity exchanges in the United States:

✓ **Commodity Futures Trading Commission (CFTC):** The CFTC is a federal regulatory agency created by Congress in 1974. Its main purpose is to regulate the commodity markets and to protect all market participants from fraud, manipulation, and abusive practices. Any exchange that conducts business with the public must be registered with the CFTC. You can visit its Web site at www.cftc.gov.

✓ **National Futures Association (NFA):** The NFA is the industry's self-regulatory body. It conducts audits, launches investigations to root out corrupt practices in the industry, and enforces the rules relating to the trading of commodities on the various exchanges. It also regulates every single firm or individual who conducts business with you as an investor — including floor traders and brokers, futures commission merchants, commodity trading advisors, commodity pool operators, and introducing brokers. You can check out the work of the NFA, as well as research individual commodities professionals, at the NFA Web site: www.nfa.futures.org.

If you're in the United States, you may want to consider investing in overseas exchanges for liquidity purposes. For example, aluminum futures contracts are offered on both the American NYMEX and the British London Metal Exchange (LME). However, the aluminum contract in the LME is more liquid, so you could get a better price by buying aluminum contracts in London as opposed to New York.

Ready, Set, Invest: Opening an Account and Placing Orders

When you decide you're ready to start trading exchange-traded products, you have to choose the most suitable way for you to do so. Unless you're a member of an exchange or have a seat on the exchange floor, you have to open a trading account with a commodity broker who's licensed to conduct business on behalf of clients at the exchange.

The technical term for a commodity broker is a *futures commission merchant* (FCM). The FCM is licensed to solicit and execute commodity orders and accept payments for this service. Before choosing a commodity broker who will handle your account, perform a thorough and comprehensive analysis of its trading platform. You want to get as much information as possible about the firm and its activities. A few things you should consider are firm history, firm clients, licensing information, trading platform, regulatory data, and employee information.

Choosing the right account

After you select a commodity brokerage firm you're comfortable with, it's time to open an account and start trading! You can choose from a number of different brokerage accounts. Most firms will offer you at least two types of accounts, depending on the level of control you want to exercise over the account:

Book IV

Commodities

✔ **Self-directed accounts:** If you feel confident about your trading abilities, have a good understanding of market fundamentals, and want to get direct access to commodity exchange products, then a self-directed account is for you. In this type of account, also known as a *non-discretionary individual account,* you call the shots and make all the trading decisions.

Before you open a self-directed account, talk to a few commodity brokers because each firm offers different account features. Specifically, ask about any minimum capital requirements the firm has (some commodity brokers require that you invest a minimum amount of $10,000 or more), account maintenance fees, and the commission scale the firm uses.

✔ **Managed accounts:** In a managed account, you're essentially transferring the responsibility of making all buying and selling decisions over to a trained professional. This type of account is ideal if you don't follow the markets on a regular (i.e. daily) basis, are unsure about which trading strategy will maximize your returns, or simply don't have the time to manage a personal account.

Before you open a managed account, first determine your investment goals, time horizon, and risk tolerance, and find a commodity trading advisor (CTA) who will manage your account based on your personal risk profile. Before contracting with anyone, however, find out about any minimum capital requirements, commissions, or management fees you may face.

Selecting a commodity trading advisor

If you are trading commodities through a managed account, you need to select a commodity trading advisor (CTA). A CTA is a securities professional who is licensed by the Financial Industry Regulatory Authority (FINRA) and the National Futures Association (NFA) to offer advice on commodities and to accept compensation for investment and management services. Here are a few things to find out about your CTA:

✔ How many years of market experience does he have?

✔ What is his long-term performance record?

✔ What is his trading strategy and does it square with your investment goals?

✔ Does he have any complaints filed against him? (This information is publicly available through the NFA.)

✔ How many accounts is he currently managing? If the number seems high, your account may not be a high priority for him.

A CTA is allowed by law to manage more than one account and have more than one client. However, a CTA must keep all managed accounts separate. That means there is no commingling of funds allowed and no transferring of profits or losses between accounts. A managed account is very different from a *commodity pool,* where your funds are pooled with those of other investors. In a commodity pool, the manager, who is known as a *commodity pool operator* (CPO), pools all the funds, and all profits or losses are shared by all investors.

✔ Does he have a criminal record? If so, find out the details of any arrests or convictions. This information is also available through the NFA.

Before you select a CTA, perform a rigorous background check. Because a CTA is required to register with the NFA to transact with the public, you can find out a lot about a CTA by simply visiting the NFA Web site (www.nfa.futures.org).

After you perform due diligence on your CTA and feel comfortable with him, you're ready to turn over trading privileges to him. How do you do that? You sign a power of attorney document, which gives your CTA full trading discretion and complete control over the buying and selling of commodities in your account. That means he makes all the decisions, and you have to live with them. The main benefit of the managed account is that you get a trained professional managing your investments. The drawback is you can't blame anyone but yourself if you incur any losses.

Placing orders

Your trading account is your link to a commodity exchange. The broker's trading platform gives you access to the exchange's main products such as futures contracts, options on futures, and other derivative products. Because the products traded on commodity exchanges are fairly sophisticated financial instruments, you need to specify a number of parameters in order to purchase the product you want.

Establishing contract parameters

The lifeblood of the exchange is the contract. As an investor, you can choose from a number of different contracts — from plain vanilla futures contracts to exotic swaps and spreads. Whichever contract(s) you choose, there are specific entry order procedures you need to follow. Here is a list of the parameters you need to indicate to place an order at the exchange:

- ✔ **Action:** Indicate whether you are buying or selling.

- ✔ **Quantity:** Specify the number of contracts you're interested in either buying or selling.

- ✔ **Time:** By definition, commodity futures contracts represent an underlying commodity traded at a specific price for delivery at a specific point in the future. Futures contracts have delivery months, and you must specify the delivery month. Additionally, you should also specify the year because many contracts represent delivery points for periods of up to five years (or more).

- ✔ **Commodity:** This is the underlying commodity that the contract represents. It could be crude oil, gold, or soybeans. Sometimes, it's also helpful to indicate on which exchange you want to place your order. (This is fairly significant as more and more of the same commodities are being offered on different exchanges.)

- ✔ **Price:** This could be the most important piece of the contract: the price at which you're willing to buy or sell the contract. Unless you're placing a *market order* (which is executed at current market prices), indicate the price at which you want your order to be filled.

Book IV

Commodities

✔ **Type of order:** This is where you indicate how you want to buy or sell the contract. Several types of orders are available, from plain vanilla market orders to more exotic ones such as *Fill or Kill* (FOK). The next section lists the different types of orders.

✔ **Day or open order:** This item relates to how long you want your order to remain open. In a *day order,* your order expires if it isn't filled by the end of the trading day. An *open order,* however, remains open unless you cancel the order, the order is filled, or the contract expires.

Defining different types of orders

One of the most important pieces of information you need to indicate is the order type. This indicates how you want your order to be placed and executed:

✔ **Fill or Kill (FOK):** Your order is to be filled right away at a specific price. If a matching offer is not found within three attempts, your order will be cancelled, or "killed."

✔ **Limit (LMT):** Your order is to be filled only at a specified price or better. If you're on the buy side of a transaction, you want your limit buy order placed at or below the market price. If you're on the sell side, you want your limit sell order at or above market price.

✔ **Market (MKT):** Your order will be filled at the current market price.

✔ **Market if Touched (MIT):** You specify the price at which you want to buy or sell a commodity. When that price is reached (or "touched"), your order is automatically filled at the current market price. A buy MIT order is placed below the market; a sell MIT order is placed above the market.

✔ **Market on Close (MOC):** You select a specific time to execute your order, and your order will be executed at whatever price that particular commodity is commanding at the end of the trading session.

✔ **Stop (STP):** Your order is placed when trading occurs at or through a specified price. A buy stop order is placed above the market, and a sell stop order is placed below market levels.

✔ **Stop Close Only (SCO):** Your stop order will be executed only at the closing of trading and *only* if the closing trading range is at or through your designated stop price.

✔ **Stop Limit (STL):** After the stop price is reached, the order will become a limit order and the transaction will be executed only if the specified price at which you want the order to go through has been reached.

Here are a couple sample orders:

✔ *Buy ten June 2008 COMEX Gold at $550 Limit Day Order.* This means you're buying ten contracts for gold on the COMEX (the metals complex of the NYMEX) with the delivery date of June 2008. You are willing to pay $550 per troy ounce per contract, or better. (A *troy ounce* is the measurement unit for gold at the COMEX.) Because this is a day order, if your order isn't filled by the end of the trading day, it will expire.

✔ *Sell 100 September 2009 NYMEX Crude at Market Open Order.* Through this order, you're selling 100 contracts of crude oil on the NYMEX with the delivery date of September 2009. You are willing to sell them at the current market price. Because this is an open order, your order will remain open for multiple trading sessions until it is filled.

Tracking your order from start to finish

When you pick up the phone or log into your online account and place an order, it's sometimes easy to forget that your order isn't placed in a vacuum. You place the order and wait for the confirmation number. Seems simple, right? Not quite. In this section, I shed some light on how your orders are executed and introduce you to some of the people who make this possible.

The information that follows details what happens in the *open outcry system* — the system where brokers physically stand in a trading pit filling and executing orders manually. However, this system faces ever-increasing competition from electronic trading platforms, where orders are matched electronically. Of the major exchanges in the United States, only the NYMEX, COMEX, and NYBOT still rely heavily on the open outcry system to conduct business. Most exchanges now use a combination of electronic and open outcry, and many people believe that the open outcry system will soon be retired altogether.

Following are some of the players involved in the open outcry system:

✔ **The clerk:** At the exchange, the first point of contact with the outside world is the clerk. Employed by the various commodity brokers licensed to conduct business at the exchange, the clerk works the phones and is responsible for taking down client orders. When the clerk receives an order by phone or e-mail, he fills out an order ticket, which he passes on to the floor broker.

✔ **The floor broker (FB):** The FB — the person in the large ring shouting and making funny gestures — is licensed to buy and sell commodities on behalf of clients. It's his job to execute the order. When the FB receives the order ticket from the clerk, it's his responsibility to find a matching offer and to fill the order. After he finds a broker or trader willing to fill his order, he writes down on the order ticket the time the agreement was entered into.

✔ **The floor trader (FT):** The FT may only trade on behalf of his personal account. Sometimes known as a "local," she provides much-needed liquidity to the exchange. An FT may be the person who will sell or buy a contract from the FB.

Book IV

Commodities

Owning a piece of an exchange

Commodity exchanges are becoming popular vehicles through which investors access the commodity markets. Because of their unique position, commodity exchanges stand to gain tremendously from this interest from the investing public. Interested in cashing in on this trend without trading a single contract on a single commodity exchange?

Sometimes, with all the commotion associated with the trading floors on commodity exchanges, it's easy to forget that an exchange is a business like any other business. Exchanges have employees, board members, revenues, earnings, expenses, and so on. While a car manufacturer sells cars to customers, commodity exchanges sell commodity contracts to customers. Of course, they charge fees for this service.

For most of their existence, exchanges have been privately held companies whose business side remained under close wraps. However, because of the increasing popularity of commodities and the rise of the electronic trading platform, many commodity exchanges are now becoming public companies with shareholders and outside investors.

In 2003, the Chicago Mercantile Exchange (the nation's largest commodity exchange in terms of volume) went public. Its shares are traded on the New York Stock Exchange under the ticker symbol CME. CME went public at a price of $43 a share. By March 2006, the stock price of CME reached an astonishing $435 a share! That's more than a 1,000 percent increase in a period of three years. Encouraged by these results, a number of other commodity exchanges went public soon after, and more are following suit. Other exchanges that have gone public include Chicago Board of Trade (CBOT) and Intercontinental Exchange (ICE).

You can cash in on this trend by becoming a shareholder in one of these exchanges. But before you purchase equity (stock) in one of the commodity exchanges, make sure you perform a thorough analysis of the stock and the company fundamentals. A stock will never go up in a straight arrow — it always retreats before reaching new highs. Sometimes, it doesn't reach new highs at all. I recommend you follow a stock on paper — that is, follow its movements without actually owning the stock — for a period of at least two weeks. That way you can get a feel for how the stock moves with the rest of the market. This will allow you to pinpoint the right entry and exit points.

When both buyer and seller at the exchange agree on price and other contractual terms, both must write down that the transaction went through on their tickets. However, only the *seller* is responsible for notifying the exchange that the transaction went through. He does so by filling out an order ticket (with the price, quality, and quantity of the contract, along with the time the transaction took place) and physically throwing the ticket order to the card clocker.

✔ **The card clocker:** This person, who is employed by the exchange, sits in the middle of the ring, literally at the center of the action. The responsibility of the clocker is to time stamp every ticket order and record the time of each transaction that takes place on the exchange floor. Because brokers and traders are throwing order tickets at him, he must wear eye goggles to protect himself.

✔ **The floor runner:** The *floor runner,* also employed by the exchange, is responsible for gathering all time-stamped ticket orders from the card clocker and handing them to the data-entry folks at the exchange. She is called a floor runner because she has to literally run between the card clocker and data-entry to deliver the ticket orders. Data-entry is responsible for recording the exact time and nature of the contract for the exchange's internal compliance records.

✔ **The price reporter:** The price reporter is a major link between the exchange and the outside world. She's responsible for noting the price and time of every transaction that takes place inside a trading ring. The price reporter notes this information in a hand-held computer that is directly linked to the exchange's floor board. The price the reporter notes flashes directly and instantaneously on the board, where it is then disseminated to the public via news and wire services.

✔ **The ring supervisor:** Every ring (or pit) where specific commodity contracts are bought and sold during the open outcry sessions has a supervisor who is responsible for overseeing trading activity and maintaining orderly conduct.

Book IV

Commodities

Chapter 3

Welcoming Commodities into Your Portfolio

. . . .

In This Chapter

▶ Determining how prominent a role commodities should play in your portfolio

▶ Gaining exposure to commodities in a variety of ways

▶ Researching before you invest

. . . .

*T*he goal of this chapter is to help you figure out how much of your portfolio you should devote to commodities and introduce you to the vehicles that let you invest in them — from index funds to master limited partnerships. If you've ever wondered how to get commodities into your portfolio, you can't afford not to read this chapter!

Making Room in Your Portfolio for Commodities

One of the most common questions I get from investors is, "How much of my portfolio should I have in commodities?" My answer is usually very simple: It depends. You have to take into account a number of factors to determine how much capital to dedicate to commodities.

Many investors who like the way commodities anchor their portfolios have about 15 percent exposure to commodities. But if you're new to commodities, start out with a relatively modest amount, anywhere between 3 and 5 percent, to see how comfortable you feel with this new member of your financial family. Test out how commodities contribute to your overall portfolio's performance. If you're satisfied with what you see, gradually increase the percentage.

Modern Portfolio Theory and the benefits of diversification

The idea that diversification is a good strategy in portfolio allocation is the cornerstone of the Modern Portfolio Theory (MPT). MPT is the brainchild of Nobel Prize–winning economist Harry Markowitz. In a paper he wrote in 1952 for his doctoral thesis, Markowitz argued that investors should look at a portfolio's overall risk/reward ratio. While this sounds like common sense today, it was a groundbreaking idea at the time.

Up until Markowitz's paper, most investors constructed their portfolios based on a risk/reward ratio analysis of individual securities. Investors chose a security based on its individual risk profile and ignored how that risk profile would fit within a broader portfolio. Markowitz argued (successfully) that investors could construct more profitable portfolios if they looked at the overall risk/reward ratio of their portfolios.

Therefore, when you are considering an individual security, you should not only assess its individual risk profile, but also take into account how that risk profile fits within your general investment strategy. Markowitz's idea that holding a group of different securities reduces a portfolio's overall volatility is one of the most important ideas in portfolio allocation.

Choosing Your Method(s) for Investing in Commodities

You have several methods at your disposal, both direct and indirect, for getting exposure to commodities. In this section, I go through the different ways you can invest in commodities.

Having a diversified portfolio is important because it helps reduce the overall volatility of your market exposures. Holding unrelated assets in your portfolio increases your chances of maintaining good returns when a certain asset underperforms. (See the sidebar "Modern Portfolio Theory and the benefits of diversification.")

Buying commodity futures

The futures markets are the most direct way to get exposure to commodities. Futures contracts allow you to purchase an underlying commodity for an agreed-upon price in the future. You can find in-depth information about futures contracts in Book III. In this section, I list some ways you can play the futures markets.

Commodity indexes

Commodity indexes track baskets of commodity futures contracts. Each index uses a different methodology, and the performance of the each is different from its peers. Commodity indexes are known as passive, long-only investments because they aren't actively managed, and they can only buy the underlying commodity; they can't short it. Here are the five major commodity indexes you can choose from:

- Goldman Sachs Commodity Index (GSCI)
- Reuters/Jefferies Commodity Research Bureau Index (R/J-CRBI)
- Dow Jones-AIG Commodity Index (DJ-AIGCI)
- Rogers International Commodity Index (RICI)
- Deutsche Bank Liquid Commodity Index (DBLCI)

Futures commission merchants

To buy futures contracts, options, and other derivatives, you probably want to open an account with a futures commission merchant (FCM). Don't be intimidated by the name — an FCM is very much like your regular stockbroker, except he doesn't buy and sell stocks. Opening an account with an FCM gives you the most direct access to the commodity futures markets.

If you're going to trade futures contracts directly, you should have a solid grasp of technical analysis, discussed in Book VIII.

Commodity trading advisors

If you're interested in investing in commodities through the futures markets or on a commodity exchange, getting advice from a trained professional is always a good idea. One option is to hire the services of a commodity trading advisor (CTA). Like an FCM, a CTA can help you open a futures account and trade futures contracts. But she also can help you develop an investment strategy based on your personal financial profile.

Make sure you research a CTA's track record and investment philosophy to make sure it squares with yours. Refer to Chapter 2 to identify key elements to look for when shopping for a CTA.

Book IV

Commodities

CTAs have to pass a rigorous financial, trading, and portfolio management exam called the Series 3. Administered by the Financial Industry Regulatory Authority (FINRA), this exam tests the candidate's knowledge of the commodities markets inside and out. By virtue of passing this exam and working at a commodities firm, most CTAs have a good fundamental understanding of the futures markets. CTAs are also licensed by the Commodity Futures Trading Commission (CFTC) and registered with the National Futures Association (NFA).

Commodity pools

Another way you can get access to the commodities futures markets is by joining a *commodity pool*. As its name suggests, it is a pool of funds that trades in the commodities futures markets. The commodity pool is managed and operated by a designated *commodity pool operator* (CPO) who is licensed with the NFA and registered with the CFTC. All investors share in the profits (and losses) of the commodity pool based on how much capital they've contributed to the pool.

Investing in a commodity pool has two main advantages over opening an individual trading account with a CTA. First, because you're joining a pool with a number of different investors, your purchasing power increases significantly. You get a lot more leverage and diversification if you're trading a $1 million account as opposed to a $10,000 account.

The second benefit, which may not seem obvious at first, is that commodity pools tend to be structured as limited partnerships. This means that, as an investor with a stake in the pool, the most you can lose is the principal you invested in the first place. Losing your entire principal may seem like a bad deal, but for the futures markets this is pretty good!

The CPO acts a lot like a CTA except that, instead of managing separate accounts, the CPO has the authority to "pool" all client funds in one account and trade them as if she were trading one account.

A good place to start looking for commodity pools is the Web site www. commodities-investor.com.

Investing in commodity mutual funds

Commodity mutual funds are exactly like your average, run-of-the-mill mutual funds except that they focus specifically on investing in commodities. You have a number of such funds to choose from, but the two biggest ones are offered by PIMCO and Oppenheimer.

To find out more about commodity mutual funds, a very useful tool is the Morningstar Web site (www.morningstar.com). This is an all-around excellent resource for investors and includes lots of information related to commodity mutual funds, such as the latest news, load charges, and expense ratios. It also uses a helpful five-star ratings system to rate mutual funds.

PIMCO

With more than $12 billion in assets under management, the PIMCO Commodity Real Return Strategy Fund (PCRAX) is the largest commodity-oriented fund in the market. Although the fund is actively managed, it seeks to broadly mirror the performance of the Dow Jones-AIG Commodity Index. As such, the fund invests directly in commodity-linked instruments such as futures contracts, forward contracts, and options on futures.

Because these contracts are naturally leveraged, the fund also invests in bonds and other fixed-income securities to act as a collateral to the commodity instruments. This fund offers three classes of shares — A, B, and C — and I encourage you to examine each class carefully in order to choose the best one for you. For example, if you invest in Class A shares, there is a minimum investment amount of $5,000, a front load of 5.5 percent, and an expense ratio of 1.24 percent. When you invest in Class B shares, there is no front load, but there is a deferred sales charge of 5 percent and an expense ratio of 1.99 percent.

A recent SEC ruling changed the way that mutual funds account for qualifying income, and this has put some pressure on funds, particularly PIMCO, to come up with different accounting methods. Make sure you find out how such rulings affect your investments.

Oppenheimer

With a little under $2 billion in assets, the Oppenheimer Real Asset Fund (QRAAX) is considerably smaller than the PIMCO fund. It tracks the performance of the Goldman Sachs Commodity Index, an index that tracks a broad basket of 24 commodities.

With $1,000 as its minimum investment requirement, Oppenheimer requires a little less capital upfront than PIMCO's fund. It offers five classes of shares (A, B, C, N, and Y), Class A being the most popular among average individual investors. Class A shares have no deferred sales charge, although they have a front load of 5.75 percent and an expense ratio of 1.32 percent. So even though you need less initial capital to invest in the Oppenheimer fund, it is slightly more expensive than the PIMCO fund because of the front load charges and its expense ratio.

Book IV

Commodities

Other funds

Although Oppenheimer and PIMCO offer the two most popular commodity funds, a number of other firms are starting to offer similar products to satisfy the growing demand from investors for funds that have wide exposure to the commodities markets. Two relative newcomers to the market are the Merrill Lynch Real Investment (MDCDX) and the Credit Suisse Commodity Return Strategy Fund (CRSCX). As more investors seek exposure to commodities, expect more funds of this nature to crop up in the future. This is good news because you have more funds to choose from!

Tapping commodity-based exchange-traded funds

Driven by a growing demand for commodities, many financial institutions are now offering commodities-based exchange-traded funds (ETFs). This breed of fund offers the diversification inherent in a mutual fund with the added benefit of being able to trade that fund like a regular stock, giving you the powerful combination of diversification and liquidity.

Unlike a regular mutual fund, where the net asset value is generally calculated at the end of the trading day, the ETF allows you to trade throughout the day. Furthermore, you can go both long and short on the ETF, something you can't do with regular mutual funds. (For more on ETFs in general, head to Book II, Chapter 4.)

The first commodity ETF in the United States was launched by Deutsche Bank in February 2006. The Deutsche Bank Commodity Index Tracking Fund (DBC) is listed on the American Stock and Options Exchange (AMEX) and tracks the Deutsche Bank Liquid Commodity Index (DBLCI). The DBLCI in turn tracks a basket of six liquid commodities: light sweet crude oil (35 percent), heating oil (20 percent), gold (10 percent), aluminum (12.5 percent), corn (11.25 percent), and wheat (11.25 percent).

The DBC ETF invests directly in commodity futures contracts. In order to capture additional yields, the energy contracts are rolled monthly, while the rest of the contracts are rolled on an annual basis. The fund also invests in fixed-income products, including the three-month Treasury bill. This provides an additional yield. With an expense ratio of 1.5 percent, it is a reasonably priced investment.

One of the downsides of investing in ETFs is that they can be fairly volatile because they track derivative instruments that trade in the futures markets. A downside of the DBC specifically is that it tracks a basket of only six commodities. However, more commodity ETFs are in the pipeline that will offer even greater diversification benefits. A number of ETFs that track individual commodities have launched fairly recently, such as

✔ **United States Oil Fund (USO):** This is an ETF that seeks to mirror the performance of the West Texas Intermediate (WTI) crude oil futures contract on the New York Mercantile Exchange (NYMEX). Although the ETF doesn't reflect the movement of the WTI contract tick by tick, it does a good job of broadly mirroring its performance. It's a good way to get exposure to crude oil without going through the futures markets.

✔ **streetTRACKS Gold Shares (GLD):** This ETF seeks to mirror the performance of the price of gold on a daily basis. The fund actually holds physical gold in vaults located in secure locations to provide investors with the ability to get exposure to physical gold without actually holding gold bullion.

✔ **iShares Silver Trust (SLV):** This is the first ETF to track the performance of the price of physical silver. Like the gold ETF, the silver ETF holds actual physical silver in vaults. This is a safe way to invest in the silver markets without going through the futures or physical markets.

Make sure you examine all fees associated with the ETF before you invest.

Taking stock in commodity companies

Another route you can take to get exposure to commodities is to buy stocks of commodity companies. These companies are generally involved in the production, transformation, and/or distribution of various commodities.

This is perhaps the most indirect way of accessing the commodity markets because in buying a company's stock, you're getting exposure not only to the performance of the underlying commodity the company is involved in, but also other factors such as the company's management skills, creditworthiness, and ability to generate cash flow and minimize expenses.

Publicly traded companies

Publicly traded companies can give you exposure to specific sectors of commodities, such as metals, energy, or agricultural products. Within these three categories, you can choose companies that deal with specific methods or commodities, such as refiners of crude oil into finished products or gold mining companies.

Book IV

Commodities

If you're considering an equity stake in a commodity company, you should determine how the company's stock performs relative to the price of the underlying commodity that company is involved in.

Although no hard fast rule exists, there is a relatively strong correlation between the performance of commodity futures contracts and the performance of companies that use these commodities as inputs. So investing in the stock of commodity companies actually gives you pretty good exposure to the underlying commodities themselves. However, be extra careful to perform a thorough due diligence before you invest your money in these companies.

Master limited partnerships

If you're interested in investing in companies that are involved in the production, transformation, and distribution of commodities, one of the best ways to do so is by investing in a master limited partnership (MLP). MLPs are a great investment because of their tax advantage and high cash payouts. When you invest in an MLP, you are essentially investing in a public partnership. This partnership is run by a *general partner* (which can be an individual or a corporate entity) for his/its benefit and, more importantly, for the benefit of the *limited partners* (which you become when you buy MLP units).

One of the biggest advantages of MLPs is that, as a unit holder, you are taxed only at the individual level. This is different than if you invest in a corporation, where cash back to shareholders (in the form of dividends) is taxed both at the corporate level and the individual level. MLPs do not pay any corporate tax! This is a huge benefit for your bottom line.

In order for an MLP to qualify for these tax breaks, it must generate 90 percent of its income from qualifying sources that relate to commodities, particularly in the oil and gas industry. Some of the popular assets that MLPs invest in include oil and gas storage facilities and transportation infrastructure such as pipelines.

Investing in an MLP is actually quite simple. Because MLPs are publicly traded, you can purchase any of them on the exchanges on which they're traded; call your broker to purchase MLP units or buy them through an online trading account. Either way, buying MLP units is as simple as buying stocks. Table 3-1 lists some MLPs along with the exchanges they're traded on.

Table 3-1	Exchange-Traded MLPs	
MLP Name	*Investments*	*Exchange*
Kinder Morgan (KMP)	Energy transportation, storage, and distribution	NYSE
Enterprise Products (EPD)	Oil and gas pipelines, storage, and drilling platforms	NYSE
Enbridge Energy Partners (EEP)	Energy pipelines	NYSE
Alliance Resources (ARLP)	Coal production and marketing	NASDAQ

Although a majority of MLPs in the United States trade on the NYSE, a few trade on the NASDAQ as well as the AMEX. Check whether your brokerage firm has published any research on MLPs you're interested in.

Looking Before You Leap: Researching Potential Investments

A large number of investors buy on hype; they hear a certain commodity mentioned in the press, and they buy just because everyone else is buying. Buying on impulse is one of the most detrimental habits you can develop as an investor. Before you put your money in anything, you should find out as much as possible about this potential investment.

Because you have a number of ways you can invest in commodities, the type of research you perform depends on what approach you take. The following sections go over the due diligence you should perform for each investment methodology.

Asking some fundamental questions

Whether you decide to invest through futures contracts, managed funds, or commodity companies, you need to gather as much information as possible about the underlying commodity itself. This is perhaps the most important piece of the commodities puzzle because the performance of any investment vehicle you choose depends on what the actual fundamental supply and demand story of the commodity is.

Here are a few questions you should ask yourself before you start investing in any commodity:

- ✔ Which country/countries hold the largest reserves of the commodity?
- ✔ Is that country politically stable or is it vulnerable to turmoil?
- ✔ How much of the commodity is actually produced on a regular basis? (Ideally, you want to get data for daily, monthly, quarterly, and annual basis.)
- ✔ Which industries/countries are the largest consumers of the commodity?
- ✔ What are the primary uses of the commodity?
- ✔ Are there any alternatives to the commodity? If so, what are they and do they pose a significant risk to the production value of the target commodity?
- ✔ Are there any seasonal factors that affect the commodity?
- ✔ What is the correlation between the commodity and comparable commodities in the same category?
- ✔ What are the historical production and consumption cycles for the commodity?

Book IV

Commodities

These are only a few questions you should ask before you invest in any commodity. Ideally you want to be able to gather this information before you start trading.

Inquiring about futures contracts

If you are interested in investing through commodity futures, you need to ask a lot of questions before you get started. Here are some:

- ✔ On what exchange is the futures contract traded?
- ✔ Is there an accompanying option contract for the commodity?
- ✔ Is the market for the contract liquid or illiquid? (You want it to be liquid.)
- ✔ Who are the main market participants?
- ✔ What is the expiration date for the contract you're interested in?
- ✔ What is the open interest for the commodity?
- ✔ Are there any margin requirements? If so, what are they?

To find out more about trading futures contracts, as well as options, make sure you read Book III.

Getting to know your managers

Before you work with a commodity trading advisor or a commodity pool operator, or before you trust your money to the manager of a commodity mutual fund, you need to find out as much as you can about these people. Here are a few questions you should ask:

- ✔ What is the manager's track record?
- ✔ What is his investing style? Is it conservative or aggressive?
- ✔ Does he have any disciplinary actions against him?
- ✔ What do clients have to say about him? (It's okay to ask to speak to one of his existing clients.)
- ✔ Is he registered with the appropriate regulatory bodies?
- ✔ What fees does he charge, and are there any undisclosed fees? (Always watch out for hidden fees!)

✔ How much assets does he have under management?

✔ What are his after-tax returns? (Make sure you specify *after*-tax returns because many managers post returns before taxes are considered.)

✔ Are there minimum time commitments?

✔ Are there penalties if you choose to withdraw your money early?

✔ Are there minimum investment requirements?

Inspecting commodity companies

Here are a few questions you should ask before you buy a company's stock:

✔ What are the company's assets and liabilities?

✔ How effective is the management with the firm's capital?

✔ Where will the firm generate future growth from?

✔ Where does the company actually generate its revenue from?

✔ Has the company run into any regulatory problems in the past?

✔ What is the company's structure? (Some commodity companies are corporations, while others act as limited partnerships.)

✔ How does the company compare with competitors?

✔ Does the company operate in regions of the world that are politically unstable?

✔ What's the company's performance across business cycles?

Of course, these are only a few questions you should ask before making an equity investment. I go through a series of other facts and figures you should gather about commodity companies in Chapter 4 (for energy companies) and Chapter 5 (for mining companies).

You can get the answers to some of these questions by looking through the company's annual report (Form 10-K) and/or quarterly reports (Form 8-K).

Book IV

Commodities

Chapter 4

The Power House: Making Money in Energy

*E*nergy is the largest commodities asset class and presents some solid investment opportunities. This chapter helps you discover the ins and outs of the energy markets and shows you ways to profit in this sector, from trading crude oil futures contracts to investing in diversified electric utilities.

Investing in Crude Oil

Crude oil is undoubtedly the king of commodities, in terms of both its production value and its importance to the global economy. It's the most traded nonfinancial commodity in the world, and it supplies 40 percent of the world's total energy needs — more than any other single commodity. As of this writing, about 87 million barrels of crude oil are traded on a daily basis.

Crude oil's importance also stems from the fact that it is the base product for a number of indispensable goods. Gasoline, jet fuel, plastics, and a number of other essential products are derived from it. Because of its preeminent role in the global economy, crude oil makes for a great investment.

Crude oil by itself isn't very useful; it derives its value from its derivative products. Only after it is processed and refined into consumable products such as gasoline, propane, and jet fuel does it become so valuable.

Facing the crude realities

Having a good understanding of global consumption and production patterns is important if you're considering investing in the oil industry, especially when misconceptions abound. Following are a couple key (and perhaps surprising) facts:

- ✔ The United States is the third largest producer of crude oil in the world, producing more than 7 million barrels a day (this includes oil products), behind only Saudi Arabia and Russia.

- ✔ The United States imports about 65 percent of its oil. The biggest oil exporter to the United States isn't a Middle Eastern country but our friendly northern neighbor. That's right: Canada is the largest exporter of crude oil to the United States! Persian Gulf oil makes up about 20 percent of imported oil.

Global oil reserves and production

As an investor, knowing which countries have large crude oil deposits is an important part of your investment strategy. As demand for crude oil increases, countries that have large deposits of this natural resource stand to benefit tremendously. One way to benefit from this trend is to invest in countries and companies with large reserves of crude oil. To determine which countries are exploiting their reserves adequately, you also need to look at actual production. Having large reserves is meaningless if a country isn't tapping those reserves to produce oil.

Table 4-1 lists the countries with the largest proven crude oil reserves, as well as the top ten producers of crude oil. Note that the reserve figures may change as new oilfields are discovered and as new technologies allow for the extraction of additional oil from existing fields.

Table 4-1		Oil Reserves and Production by Country		
		Oil Reserves		*Production*
Rank	*Country*	*Proven Reserves (Billion Barrels)*	*Country*	*Daily Production (Million Barrels)*
1	Saudi Arabia	264	Saudi Arabia	10.7
2	Iran	132	Russia	9.6
3	Iraq	115	United States	8.3
4	Kuwait	101	Iran	4.1

		Oil Reserves	Production	
Rank	Country	Proven Reserves (Billion Barrels)	Country	Daily Production (Million Barrels)
5	United Arab Emirates	98	Mexico	3.7
6	Venezuela	79	China	3.6
7	Russia	60	Norway	3.1
8	Libya	39	Canada	3.1
9	Nigeria	36	Venezuela	2.9
10	United States	21	United Arab Emirates	2.7

Oil Reserves Source: Oil & Gas Journal.

Although Canada does not appear on the reserve list, it has proven reserves of 4.7 billion barrels of *conventional* crude oil — crude that is easily recoverable and accounted for. In addition to conventional crude, Canada is rich in unconventional crude oil located in oil sands, which is much more difficult to extract and, therefore, generally not included in the calculation of official and conventional reserve estimates. If Canada's oil sands were included, Canada would jump to number two with a grand total of 178 billion barrels.

If you're an active oil trader with a futures account, it's crucial that you follow the daily production numbers, available through the Energy Information Administration (EIA) Web site at www.eia.doe.gov. The futures markets are particularly sensitive to these numbers, and any event that takes crude off the market can have a sudden impact on crude futures contracts. To keep up on updated figures and statistics on the oil industry, you can also check out the following organizations:

- ✔ International Energy Agency (IEA): www.iea.org
- ✔ BP Statistical Review (BP): www.bp.com
- ✔ *Oil & Gas Journal:* www.ogj.com

Demand figures

Demand figures are important because they indicate a steady and sustained increase in crude demand for the mid- to long term, which is likely to maintain increased pressure on crude prices. Table 4-2 lists the top ten consumers of crude oil in the world.

Book IV

Commodities

Table 4-2	Largest Consumers of Crude Oil	
Rank	**Country**	**Daily Consumption (Million Barrels)**
1	United States	20.5
2	China	7.2
3	Japan	5.4
4	Russia	3.1
5	Germany	2.6
6	India	2.5
7	Canada	2.2
8	Brazil	2.1
9	South Korea	2.1
10	Saudi Arabia	2.0

The United States and China are currently the biggest consumers of crude oil in the world, and this trend will continue throughout the 21st century, with global consumption expected to increase to 120 million barrels a day by 2025.

Always design an investment strategy that will profit from long-term trends. The steady increase in global demand for crude oil is a good reason to be bullish on oil prices.

Imports and exports

Another pair of numbers you need to keep close tabs on is export and import figures. Identifying the top exporting countries is helpful because it allows you to zero in on the countries that are actually generating revenues from the sale of crude oil to other countries. You can get in on the action by investing domestically in these countries.

Imports are as important as exports in your calculations. Countries that are main importers of crude oil are primarily advanced, industrialized societies like Germany and the United States, which are rich enough that they can absorb crude oil price increases. As a general rule, however, importers face a lot of pressure during any price increases, which sometimes translates into lower stock market performances in the importing countries. Be careful if you're exposed to the domestic stock markets of these oil importers. Table 4-3 shows the top oil-exporting and importing countries.

Table 4-3	Top Ten Oil Exporters and Importers			
	Exports		Imports	
Rank	Country	Daily Oil Exports (Million Barrels)	Country	Daily Oil Imports (Million Barrels)
1	Saudi Arabia	8.7	United States	11.8
2	Russia	6.6	Japan	5.3
3	Norway	2.542	China	2.9
4	Iran	2.519	Germany	2.5
5	UAE	2.515	South Korea	2.1
6	Venezuela	2.203	France	2.0
7	Kuwait	2.150	Italy	1.7
8	Nigeria	2.146	Spain	1.6
9	Mexico	1.8	India	1.5
10	Algeria	1.6	Taiwan	1.0

Crude quality

Crude oil is classified into two broad categories: light and sweet, and heavy and sour. There are other classifications, but these are the two major ones. The two criteria most widely used to determine the quality of crude oil are density and sulfur content:

- **Density** usually refers to how much a crude oil will yield in terms of products, such as heating oil and jet fuel. A crude oil with lower density, known as a *light crude,* for example, tends to yield higher levels of products. A crude oil with high density, commonly referred to as a *heavy crude,* will have lower product yields.

- **Sulfur content** is another key determinant of crude oil quality. Sulfur is a corrosive material that decreases the purity of a crude oil. Crude oil with high sulfur content, which is known as *sour,* is much less desirable than a crude oil with low sulfur content, known as *sweet* crude.

If you want to invest in the oil industry, you need to know what kind of oil you're going to get for your money. A company involved in the production of light, sweet crude will generate more revenue than one involved in the processing of heavy, sour crude. This doesn't mean you shouldn't invest in companies with exposure to heavy, sour crude; you just have to factor the type into your investment strategy.

Making big bucks with big oil

The price of crude oil has skyrocketed during the first years of the 21st century (see Figure 4-1); if this trend is any indication of what's in store for oil, you definitely want to develop a winning game plan to take advantage of it.

The integrated oil companies, sometimes known as *big oil, the majors,* or *integrated oil companies,* are involved in all phases of the oil production process — from exploring for oil, to refining it, to transporting it to consumers. ExxonMobil, Chevron Texaco, and BP are all "big oil" companies.

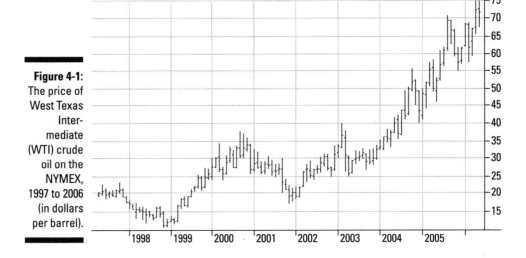

Figure 4-1:
The price of West Texas Intermediate (WTI) crude oil on the NYMEX, 1997 to 2006 (in dollars per barrel).

Big oil companies aren't the only players in the oil business. A number of other companies are involved in specific aspects of the transformational process of crude oil. For example, you have companies like Valero that are primarily involved in refining, and others such as General Maritime that own fleets of tankers that transport crude oil and products. I discuss how to invest in these companies — the refiners, transporters, and explorers — later in the chapter in the section "Putting Your Money in Energy Companies."

Buying into individual oil companies

The major oil companies have been posting record profits. In 2005, Exxon Mobil announced the largest annual corporate profit in history as it earned a staggering $36.1 billion on revenues of $371 billion! Exxon's 2005 profits were 20 percent higher than its 2004 profits, which were over 10 percent higher than the previous year's! Another big oil company, ConocoPhillips, raked in $13.53 billion in profits for 2005, up 66 percent from the previous year. Chevron Corp., meanwhile, posted $14.1 billion in earnings for 2005. These announcements are a direct result of the increased global demand for crude oil and its products.

As global demand continues and supplies remain limited, big oil companies are likely to keep generating record revenues and profits. Table 4-4 lists some of the companies that you may want to include in your portfolio. For a more comprehensive list, check out Yahoo! Finance's section on integrated oil companies at `http://biz.yahoo.com/ic/120.html`.

Table 4-4	Major Integrated Oil Companies, 2005 Figures			
Oil Company	**Ticker**	**Market Cap**	**Revenues**	**Earnings**
ExxonMobil	XOM	$518 billion	$366 billion	$40 billion
PetroChina	PTR	$387 billion	$101 billion	$19 billion
Shell	RDS-B	$266 billion	$318 billion	$27 billion
BP	BP	$241 billion	$264 billion	$21 billion
Chevron	CVX	$195 billion	$190 billion	$19 billion
Eni	E	$55 billion	$118 billion	$12 billion
Repsol	REP	$44 billion	$66 billion	$4 billion

Most of these traditional oil companies have now moved into other areas in the energy sphere. These companies not only process crude oil into different products, but they also have vast petrochemicals businesses as well as growing projects involving natural gas and, increasingly, alternative energy sources. Investing in these oil companies gives you exposure to other sorts of products in the energy industry as well.

Choosing oil company ETFs

If you can't decide which oil company you want to invest in, you have several other options at your disposal, which allow you to buy the market, so to speak. One option is to buy exchange-traded funds (ETFs) that track the performance of a group of integrated oil companies. (ETFs are discussed in detail in Book II, Chapter 4.) Here are a few oil company ETFs to consider:

- ✔ **iShares S&P Global Energy Index Fund (AMEX: IXC):** This ETF mirrors the performance of the Standard & Poor's Global Energy Sector index. Buying this ETF gives you exposure to companies such as ExxonMobil, Chevron, ConocoPhillips, and Royal Dutch Shell.

- ✔ **Energy Select Sector SPDR (AMEX: XLE):** The XLE ETF is the largest energy ETF in the market. It is part of the S&P's family of Standard & Poor's Depository Receipts (SPDRs), commonly referred to as *spiders,* and tracks the performance of a basket of oil company stocks. Some of the stocks it tracks include the majors ExxonMobil and Chevron; however, it also tracks oil services companies such as Halliburton and Schlumberger. You get a nice mix of integrated oil companies as well as other independent firms by investing in the XLE.

- ✔ **iShares Goldman Sachs Natural Resources Index Fund (AMEX: IGE):** The IGE ETF mirrors the performance of the Goldman Sachs Natural Resources Sector index, which tracks the performance of companies like ConocoPhillips, Chevron, and BP, as well as refiners such as Valero and Suncor. Although a majority of this ETF is invested in integrated oil companies, it also provides you with a way to play a broad spectrum of energy companies.

Investing overseas

Another great way to capitalize on oil profits is to invest in an emerging-market fund that invests in countries that sit on large deposits of crude oil and that have the infrastructure in place to export crude oil.

Here are a couple of emerging-markets funds that give you an indirect exposure to booming oil-exporting countries:

- ✔ **Fidelity Emerging Markets** (FEMKX)
- ✔ **Evergreen Emerging Markets Growth I** (EMGYX)

Trading Natural Gas

Natural gas is an important source of energy both in the United States and around the world, accounting for approximately 25 percent of energy consumption. Because of its importance as a source of energy, natural gas makes for a good investment.

Although natural gas is sometimes used as a transportation fuel, the gasoline you buy at the gas station and natural gas have nothing to do with each other. The gasoline your car consumes is a product of crude oil, while natural gas is an entirely different member of the fossil fuel family used primarily for heating, cooling, and cooking purposes.

Liquefied natural gas, or LNG, is nothing but natural gas in a liquid state. LNG is easy to transport — an important characteristic as meeting increasing demand requires transporting natural gas across vast distances, like continents and oceans.

The majority of natural gas in the United States is transported through pipelines in a gaseous state. LNG is usually transported in specially designed tankers to consumer markets. Some of the major operators of natural gas pipelines that transport both natural gas and LNG are entities known as *master limited partnerships* (MLPs). You can profit from moving natural gas across the United States by investing in MLPs.

Recognizing natural gas applications

Because it is one of the cleanest-burning fossil fuels, natural gas has become increasingly popular as an energy source. In the United States alone, natural gas accounts for nearly a quarter of total energy consumption. It's second only to petroleum when it comes to generating energy in the United States. The primary consumers of this commodity are the industrial sector, residences, commercial interests, electricity generators, and the transportation sector. Figure 4-2 shows the consumption ratio of these sectors.

Figure 4-2:
Primary
consumers
of natural
gas in the
United
States.

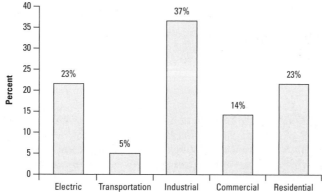

Source: U.S. Department of Energy

Industrial uses

The industrial sector is the largest consumer of natural gas, accounting for almost 40 percent of total consumption, using it for processing food, melting glass and metal, incinerating waste, fueling industrial boilers, and more.

While industrial uses of natural gas have always played a major role in the sector, their significance has increased over the last several years. As you can see in Figure 4-3, the industrial sector's demand for natural gas use is projected to continue. (Actually, demand for natural gas products as a whole is going to increase throughout the first quarter of the 21st century.) This increased demand should put upward price pressures on natural gas.

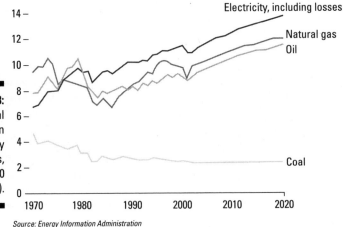

Figure 4-3:
Industrial consumption of energy products, 1970 to 2020 (projected).

Source: Energy Information Administration

Residential uses

Residential usage accounts for almost a quarter of total natural gas consumption, with a large portion of homes in the United States and other countries using natural gas for both cooking and heating needs. About 70 percent of households in the United States have natural gas ovens in the kitchen. More than 50 percent of homes in the United States use natural gas for heating purposes.

One way to benefit from the use of natural gas as a heating fuel is to identify peak periods of natural gas consumption. Specifically, demand for natural gas for heating increases in the northern hemisphere during the winter seasons. One way to profit in the natural gas markets is to calibrate your strategy to this cyclical, weather-related trend.

Commercial uses

Commercial users, such as hospitals and schools, account for almost 15 percent of total natural gas consumption, using it for space and water heating, lighting, cooling, cooking, and so on. Because commercial users also include restaurants, movie theaters, malls, and office buildings, demand for natural gas from these key drivers of the economy will rise during times of increasing economic activity. This means that, all things being equal, you should be bullish on natural gas during times of economic growth.

One place to look for important economic clues that affect demand for natural gas is the Energy Information Administration (EIA), a division of the U.S. Department of Energy (DOE). The EIA provides a wealth of information regarding consumption trends of key energy products, such as natural gas, from various economic sectors. For information on the commercial usage of natural gas, visit www.eia.doe.gov/oiaf/aeo/aeoref_tab.html.

Electricity generation

Natural gas is quickly becoming a popular alternative to generate electricity; just under 25 percent of natural gas usage goes toward generating electricity. In the United States, natural gas is used to support approximately 10 percent of electricity generation, a figure that is expected to increase dramatically in the coming years (see Figure 4-4). Such an increased demand from a critical sector will keep upward pressures on natural gas prices over the long term.

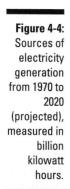

Figure 4-4: Sources of electricity generation from 1970 to 2020 (projected), measured in billion kilowatt hours.

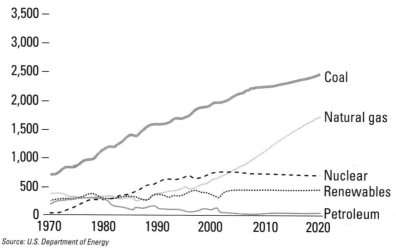

Source: U.S. Department of Energy

Book IV

Commodities

Transportation uses

Natural gas is used in approximately 3 million vehicles worldwide as a source of fuel. These *natural gas vehicles* (NGVs) run on a grade of natural gas called *compressed natural gas* (CNG). While this usage accounts for only about 5 percent of total natural gas consumption, demand for NGVs could increase as they become a viable (cheaper) alternative to vehicles that use gasoline (a crude oil derivative).

Keep a close eye on technological developments that affect natural gas usage in the transportation sector. If natural gas were to grab a slice of the transportation market, which now accounts for almost two-thirds of crude oil consumption, prices for natural gas could increase dramatically. One place to check out the latest info on NGVs is the International Association for Natural Gas Vehicles; the Web site is www.iangv.org.

Choosing how to invest in natural gas

The future for natural gas looks bright. The total natural gas consumption on a global scale in 2006 was approximately 110 trillion cubic feet (110 Tcf). By 2025, that figure is estimated to increase more than 50 percent — at a rate of 2.3 percent annually — to a total of 156 Tcf. More important than knowing that demand for natural gas will remain steady until 2025 is figuring out which countries and companies will be meeting this demand. Table 4-5 lists the countries with the largest reserves of natural gas in the world.

Table 4-5	Top Ten Natural Gas Reserves by Country, 2006 Figures		
Rank	**Country**	**Proven Reserves (Tcf)**	**Percent of World Total**
1	Russia	1680	27.5%
2	Iran	971	15.9%
3	Qatar	911	14.9%
4	Saudi Arabia	241	3.9%
5	United Arab Emirates	212	3.5%
6	United States	193	3.1%
7	Nigeria	185	3.0%
8	Algeria	161	2.6%
9	Venezuela	151	2.5%
10	Iraq	112	1.8%

Global natural gas reserves are estimated at 6112 Tcf, which is the equivalent of approximately 6 quadrillion cubic feet. You can get exposure to the huge natural gas market in a couple of ways: by trading futures contracts or by investing in companies that are involved in the production and development of natural gas fields in the countries listed in Table 4-5.

Trading natural gas futures

The most direct method of investing in natural gas is by trading futures contracts on one of the designated commodities exchanges. On the New York Mercantile Exchange (NYMEX), the preeminent exchange for energy products, you can buy and sell natural gas futures and options. The natural gas (Nat Gas) futures contract is the second most popular energy contract right behind crude oil. Traded under the ticker symbol NG, it trades in increments of 10,000 Mmbtu. You can trade it during all the calendar months, to periods up to 72 months after the current month.

The NYMEX offers a mini version of this contract for individual hedgers and speculators. Check out the Nat Gas section of the NYMEX Web site for more on this contract: `www.nymex.com/ng_pre_agree.aspx`.

Trading natural gas futures contracts and options is not for the faint hearted. Even by commodities standards, natural gas is a notoriously volatile commodity subject to wild price fluctuations. If you're not an aggressive investor willing to withstand the financial equivalent of a wild roller coaster ride, then natural gas futures may not be for you.

Investing in natural gas companies

Investing in companies that process natural gas offers you exposure to this market through the expertise and experience of industry professionals, without the volatility of the futures market. Some natural gas companies are involved in the production of natural gas fields, while others are responsible for delivering natural gas directly to consumers. Following are *fully integrated* natural gas companies, which means they are involved in all the production, development, transportation, and distribution phases of natural gas. Investing in these companies provides you with a solid foothold in this industry:

- **Alliant Energy (NYSE: LNT):** Provides consumers with natural gas and electricity derived from natural gas throughout the United States. A good choice if you want exposure to the North American natural gas market.

- **Allegheny Energy (NYSE: AYE):** Provides natural gas–based electricity to consumers in the eastern United States, primarily in Pennsylvania, Virginia, and Maryland. A good option if you want regional exposure to natural gas production.

Book IV

Commodities

✔ **Nicor Inc. (NYSE: GAS):** Provides natural gas to more than 2 million consumers, primarily centered in the Illinois area. Another good regional investment.

For a complete listing of companies involved in natural gas production and distribution, look at the American Gas Association Web site: www.aga.org.

Looking at Other Energy Sources

While crude oil and natural gas are always in the spotlight, they aren't the only energy commodities you can consider. The following sections touch on coal, nuclear power, and other sectors of the energy market that may be worth your investment dollars.

Bowing to Ol' King Coal

Coal, which accounted for 28 percent of total fossil fuel consumption in the United States in 2006, is used primarily for electricity generation (steam coal) and steel manufacturing (metallurgical coal). It's an increasingly popular fossil fuel because of its large reserves. Companies in the United States have long touted the benefits of moving toward a more coal-based economy because the United States has the largest coal reserves in the world.

Demand for coal is expected to increase dramatically during the first quarter of the 21st century. Most of this growth will come from the emerging-market economies, particularly the economies of China and India which will account for approximately 75 percent of the demand increase for coal. (China is currently the largest consumer of coal in the world, ahead of the United States, India, and Japan.) The coal markets have already started reacting to this increased demand for the product. From 2002 to 2005, the price of coal in the spot market rose from approximately $25 per short ton in January 2002 to reach a high of more than $60 per short ton by January 2005.

Considering coal reserves and production

If you're going to invest in coal, you need to know which countries have the largest coal reserves. Just because a country has large deposits of a natural resource, however, doesn't mean that it exploits them to full capacity. Therefore, there is a significant gap between countries with large coal reserves and those that produce the most coal on an annual basis. Table 4-6 lists the top ten countries with the largest coal reserves, as well as the top coal-producing countries.

Table 4-6	Coal Reserves and Production by Country, 2006 Figures			
	Reserves		*Production*	
Rank	*Country*	*Reserves (Million Short Tons)*	*Country*	*Production (Million Short Tons)*
1	United States	246,643	China	1,212.3
2	Russia	157,010	United States	595.1
3	China	114,500	India	209.7
4	India	92,445	Australia	203.1
5	Australia	78,500	South Africa	144.8
6	South Africa	48,750	Russia	144.5
7	Ukraine	34,153	Indonesia	119.9
8	Kazakhstan	31,279	Poland	67.0
9	Poland	14,000	Germany	50.3
10	Brazil	10,113	Kazakhstan	49.2

Reserve Source: World Energy Council

Coal is measured in short tons. One *short ton* is the equivalent of 2,000 pounds. In terms of energy, one short ton of *anthracite,* the coal of highest quality, contains approximately 25 million Btu of energy.

If you're going to invest in a company that processes coal, select a company with a heavy exposure in one of the countries listed in Table 4-6. Because the United States, Russia, and China collectively hold more than 55 percent of the world's total coal reserves, investing in a coal company with large operations in any of these countries will provide you with exposure to this important segment of the market.

Before you invest in companies involved in the coal business, find out which type of coal they produce, which can help you better understand the company's business and profit margins. You can find this type of information in a company's annual and quarterly reports.

Book IV

Commodities

Investing in coal

You can get access to the coal markets by either trading coal futures or investing in coal companies:

- ✔ **Coal futures:** Coal has an underlying futures contract that trades on a commodity exchange, in this case the New York Mercantile Exchange (NYMEX). The coal futures contract on the NYMEX tracks the price of the high quality Central Appalachian coal (CAPP), sometimes affectionately called *the big sandy.* The CAPP futures contract is the premium benchmark for coal prices in the United States. It trades under the ticker symbol QL and is tradable during all the calendar months of the current year, in addition to all calendar months in the subsequent three years. Additional information on this futures contract is available on the NYMEX Web site: www.nymex.com/coa_fut_descri.aspx.

  Most of the traders in this market represent large commercial interests that transact with each other, which means that you may not be able to get involved directly in this market without large capital reserves to compete with the commercial interests.

- ✔ **Coal companies:** One of the best ways to invest in coal is by investing in a company that mines it. The following three companies are among the best:

  - *Peabody Energy (NYSE: BTU):* This is the largest coal company in the United States with approximately 10.2 billion short tons of coal reserves. The coal that Peabody produces is responsible for generating approximately 10 percent of the electricity in the United States. The company has mining operations in the United States, Australia, and Venezuela.

  - *Consol Energy (NYSE: CNX):* Headquartered in Pittsburgh, Consol Energy has significant operations in the coal mines of Pennsylvania and the neighboring coal-rich states of West Virginia and Kentucky. As of 2006, it controlled 4.5 billion short tons of coal reserves, with operations in over 17 mines across the United States. CNX is well positioned to take advantage of the booming domestic coal market.

  - *Arch Coal (NYSE: ACI):* Smaller in size than Peabody or Consol, Arch Coal operates more than 20 mines on the continental United States and controls more than 3 billion short tons of reserves.

If you want to invest in coal companies with a more international exposure to markets in Russia, China, and other coal-rich countries, consult the World Coal Institute (www.worldcoal.org).

Embracing nuclear power

Civilian and commercial nuclear power is an integral part of the global energy supply chain and is a valuable energy source for residential, commercial, and industrial consumers worldwide. Nuclear power generates more than 20 percent of the electricity in the United States; in countries like France, nuclear power generates over 75 percent of electricity! Accounting for about 5 percent of total global energy consumption, nuclear power is expected to remain at stable levels until 2030. But if the price of fossil fuels (oil, natural gas, and coal) rises dramatically enough to start affecting demand, nuclear may play an important role in picking up the slack.

One way you can profit from increased interest in nuclear power is to invest in uranium, the most widely used fuel in nuclear power plants. There's been a bull market in uranium from 2000 to 2007, and this shows no sign of slowing. Because uranium isn't a widely tradable commodity, the best way to profit from this trend is to invest in companies that specialize in mining, processing, and distributing uranium for civilian nuclear purposes. A few companies in this sector include:

- ✔ **Cameco Corp. (NYSE: CCJ):** Cameco operates four uranium mines in the United States and Canada. It's also involved in refining and converting the uranium into fuel sold to nuclear power plants to generate electricity.

- ✔ **UEX Corp. (Toronto: UEX):** This Canada-based mining company specializes in the exploration and mining of uranium in the Athabasca basin. The Athabasca basin in Canada is an important region in global uranium mining that accounts for about 30 percent of total world production. UEX is currently still in exploration phases, but it could become a real money-maker if it comes across large deposits of uranium. The company trades on the Toronto Stock Exchange.

- ✔ **Strathmore Minerals Corp. (Toronto: STM):** Strathmore — another Canadian company — specializes in the mining of uranium. The company, which trades on the Toronto Stock Exchange, operates in the Athabasca region in Canada and in the United States.

For more information on nuclear power, the Energy Information Administration (EIA) has an excellent Web site with all sorts of practical information on this industry at www.eia.doe.gov/fuelnuclear.html. Another great source for everything regarding uranium and nuclear power is The Ux Consulting Company (www.uxc.com).

Book IV

Commodities

Trading electricity

Investing in coal and in nuclear power are ways to invest in electricity. But there are also several ways you can invest directly in the power industry, as the following sections explain.

Plugging into the electricity futures market

The New York Mercantile Exchange (NYMEX) offers a futures contract that tracks the price of electricity as administered by PJM Interconnection, a regional transmission organization (RTO) that oversees the largest electric grid system in the world and services more than 50 million customers in the United States. It's responsible for generating more than 700 million megawatt hours of electricity across 55,000 miles of transmission lines. Because of its dominance in the U.S. electricity market, the PJM electricity futures contract on the NYMEX provides you with a widely recognizable and tradable electricity benchmark.

The PJM contract (traded under the symbol JM) offers you the option of trading both *on-peak* and and *off-peak* electricity hours:

- ✓ **On-peak:** Monday through Friday between 7:00 a.m. and 11:00 p.m.
- ✓ **Off-peak:** Monday through Friday from midnight to 7:00 a.m. local time; all day Saturday and Sunday

On-peak hours are usually more liquid because that's when most electricity is consumed. For more information on this specific contract, check out the NYMEX Web site at www.nymex.com/JM_desc.aspx.

Although most of the market participants in the electricity futures market are local and regional power providers and suppliers, the futures contract lends itself to being traded by individual speculators as well. In recent years, as interest in commodities as an asset class has increased, the number of speculative participants in the electricity market has grown.

Investing in utilities

Electric utilities are the companies responsible for providing electricity to millions of folks in the United States and around the world, and they offer sound investment opportunities. There are several reasons to like utilities, but the main reason is their very high dividend payout. The industry has on average a 3 percent dividend yield, one of the highest of any industry.

Dividends are a taxable source of income. Because of recent tax relief legislation, taxes on income generated through dividends are usually capped at 15 percent. However, Congress is considering an overhaul of the dividend tax in 2008 that may result in an increase in the dividends tax rate. Make sure to keep a close eye on these dividend tax issues because they will have a direct impact on your utility investments.

Tapping into renewable energy sources

Currently, renewable sources of energy make up about 8 percent of total energy use in the world. This figure pales compared to the 87 percent share of fossil fuels, but it has the potential to grow as nonrenewable energy sources are depleted. The field of renewable energy is getting a lot of attention, and there is certainly potential to make some money in this field.

If you're interested in keeping up-to-date on the latest developments in the renewable energy space, check out the U.S. Department of Energy's Energy Efficiency and Renewable Energy (EERE) initiative (www.eere.energy.gov).

Spotlighting solar energy

Solar power is the process by which energy from the sun is harnessed and channeled into a usable energy form, generally heat or electricity. Solar power can be transformed using two different processes:

- **Solar thermal energy** transforms the sun's energy into heat, which can be used for a number of different purposes, such as interior space heating or water heating. Flat panel solar collectors mounted on homes or buildings are used for solar thermal energy purposes.

- **Solar photovoltaic energy** is the method whereby energy from the sun is captured and transformed into electricity.

In 2007, solar power accounted for a little less than 0.10 percent of total energy consumed in the United States. This doesn't mean, however, that you can't make any money investing in this sector. Because of technological advancements, the future looks bright for solar energy. Of the many companies that have entered the field of solar power, two companies stand out:

- **Evergreen Solar (Nasdaq: ESLR):** Evergreen Solar has operations in Germany and the United States and is engaged in the production and distribution of photovoltaic cells. It has a patented system that allows for direct transformation from solar to consumable electricity, and it sells its electricity directly to residential, commercial, and industrial consumers.

- **Suntech Power Holdings (NYSE: STP):** This company, headquartered in China, is involved in producing photovoltaic cells and panels for electricity generation. It's attractive because it has a foothold in China, which could be a huge market for solar power.

Book IV

Commodities

Eyeing the potential of wind energy

Wind energy — generated by huge wind machines (similar to traditional wind mills) that are placed side by side in *wind farms* — is getting increasing attention from investors, even though it is extremely difficult to invest in wind energy at this stage. Currently very few publicly traded companies deal specifically in wind power. However, with rising energy prices, wind energy may get more focus. If you are interested in investing in wind power and want to keep on top of any emerging trend, check out the American Wind Energy Association (www.awea.org), which keeps a database of private companies involved in wind energy that may go public one day.

Investing in ethanol

Ethanol, an alcohol fuel that can be used as a transportation fuel, can be made from corn, sugar, wheat, and other agricultural products. In Brazil, the world's largest producer of ethanol fuel, ethanol is the primary automotive fuel. The United States has seen an increase in the use of ethanol as a transportation fuel, a trend that's likely to increase. One company involved in the production of ethanol that you may want to check out is Pacific Ethanol (NASDAQ: PEIX).

Putting Your Money in Energy Companies

One way to play the energy markets is to invest in the companies involved in the production, transformation, and distribution of the world's most important energy commodities. Each of the companies operating in these segments of the market offers unique money-making investment opportunities. Finding out about specialized energy and oil companies that are critical links in the global crude oil supply chain can help you develop a targeted investment strategy.

Profiting from oil exploration and production

The exploration and discovery of oil is a very lucrative segment in the oil business. Fortunately, to strike it rich by discovering oil, you don't have to go prospecting for oil in the Texas heartland yourself. You can invest in companies that specialize in the exploration and production of oilfields, known in the business as *E&P*. Oil wells are found in one of two places: on land or on sea.

Among industry insiders, exploring for oil and gas is affectionately called *wildcatting.* Most wildcatting expeditions end up without any oil discoveries. When wildcatters drill a hole in the ground and no oil comes out, that is known as having a *dry hole,* the unfortunate opposite of a gusher.

Going offshore

In recent years, offshore drilling has generated a lot of interest among investors, and a flurry of activity has been taking place in this sector as oil on land becomes more and more scarce. Here are some of the leading offshore drilling companies:

- ✔ **Transocean Inc. (NYSE: RIG):** Transocean, with more than 90 offshore drilling units at its disposal, is an expert in operating under harsh and extreme weather conditions. It has offshore operations in the U.S. Gulf of Mexico, Brazil, South Africa, the Mediterranean Sea, the North Sea, Australia, and Southeast Asia. If you're looking for the most diversified company in the group, this is it.

- ✔ **GlobalSantaFe Corp. (NYSE: GSF):** GSF is a global offshore drilling contractor, operating a fleet of more than 60 vessels in locations stretching from Canada to the Middle East. It operates in three major segments: the leasing of drilling equipment, services, and crews (contract drilling); engineering and project services where it teams up with clients to provide offshore engineering solutions; and turnkey services where it assumes full control and responsibility of drilling projects from the design to the implementation phase. GSF offers an array of full offshore services to its clients, which include independent and integrated oil companies as well as foreign governments and oil companies.

- ✔ **Noble Corp. (NYSE: NE):** Noble is one of the oldest drilling contractors in the world. With a fleet of more than 60 vessels and operations stretching from Brazil to the North Sea, it has an edge in implementing technologically oriented solutions to meet customer demands.

If you'd like to dig deeper into this sector, check out www.rigzone.com, which includes up-to-date information on the offshore industry as well as the oil industry as a whole.

Staying on dry land

While most industry insiders agree that a majority of onshore oil wells have been discovered, you can still benefit by investing in companies that are involved in the exploitation and production of onshore oilfields. Here are a couple of companies to consider:

Book IV

Commodities

✔ **Nabors Industries (NYSE: NBR):** One of the largest land drilling contractors in the world, Nabors has a division that can perform heavy-duty and horizontal drilling activities.

✔ **Patterson-UTI Energy Inc. (NASDAQ: PTEN):** Patterson-UTI, an onshore oilfield drilling contractor that has extensive operations in North America, operates in a number of segments, including the drilling of new wells and the servicing and maintenance of existing oil wells.

Servicing oilfields

You can also invest in companies that focus on oilfield maintenance and services. These companies seek to maximize an oilfield's output and are generally hired by major integrated oil companies or national oil companies for general oilfield and oil well maintenance and extraction solutions. The added value of the oilfield services companies is that they can improve oil recovery rates on existing fields and recover previously untapped oil pockets in old fields. As fewer and fewer oilfields are discovered, the world's major oil companies are looking for ways to maximize existing oilfields. Therefore, the role of the oilfield services companies will become increasingly important in the future. Here is your hit list of top companies if you're looking to invest in the oilfield services space:

✔ **Schlumberger Ltd. (NYSE: SLB):** Schlumberger, one of the most technologically savvy services companies, can provide solutions regarding all aspects of oilfield management services, from exploration and extraction to maintenance and abandonment.

✔ **Halliburton Co. (NYSE: HAL):** The Houston-based company makes a lot of headlines (sometimes not very positive ones) because of the political nature of its work with the U.S. government and military. Besides its governmental contracts — which make up only a fraction of its revenues — the company is a leader in oil and gas field maintenance. It helps customers extract as much energy from existing wells as possible while maintaining low costs.

✔ **Baker Hughes Inc. (NYSE: BHI):** Baker Hughes, also headquartered in Houston, operates both in the United States and internationally, with operations stretching from the Persian Gulf to West Africa. Baker Hughes provides technologically oriented solutions to its customers to maximize oilfield output efficiency.

For more information on the oilfield services sector and all the companies involved in it, check out the Yahoo! Finance Web site at `http://biz.yahoo .com/ic/124.html`.

Investing in refineries

To be useful, crude oil must be refined into consumable products such as gasoline, diesel and jet fuel, automotive lubricating oil, propane and kerosene, and a myriad of other products. For this reason, refineries are a critical link in the crude oil supply chain. Given the importance of the crude oil derivative products, you can make a lot of money investing in refineries.

When considering investing in companies that operate refineries, pay attention to three criteria (included in a company's annual or quarterly reports):

- **Refinery throughput:** The capacity for refining crude oil over a given period of time, usually expressed in barrels.

- **Refinery production:** Actual production of crude oil products, such as gasoline and heating oil.

- **Refinery utilization:** The difference between production capacity (the throughput) and what's actually produced.

Most major integrated oil companies, like ExxonMobil and BP, have large refining capacity. ExxonMobil, for example, operates the largest refinery in the United States, with a refining capacity of 557,000 barrels per day. One way to get exposure to the refining space is by investing in these major companies. Another, more direct, way to profit from refining activity is by investing in independent refineries, such as the following:

- **Valero Energy Corp. (NYSE: VLO):** Valero is the largest independent refining company in North America, with a throughput capacity of 3.3 million barrels per day.

- **Sunoco Inc. (NYSE: SUN):** The second largest refiner in terms of total refinery throughput, Sunoco refines approximately 1 million barrels of crude a day. It distributes its products primarily in the eastern United States.

- **Tesoro Corp. (NYSE: TSO):** Tesoro is one of the leading refiners in the mid-continental and western United States. Its refineries transform crude oil into gasoline distributed through a network of about 500 retail outlets in the western United States.

The Energy Information Administration compiles data on all U.S. refineries at www.eia.doe.gov/neic/rankings/refineries.htm.

Book IV

Commodities

Banking on the shipping industry

The shipping industry plays a crucial role in the integrated oil business. Two out of every three barrels of oil that are transported are moved around in ships (the remaining one-third are transported via pipelines). Fortunately, as an investor, this provides you with fertile ground to make money in the transportation of commodities.

Grasping transportation supply and demand

If you invest in shipping, you need to understand the relationship between the price of crude oil and oil tanker profit margins (tanker spot rates), which is affected by a number of variables.

Tanker spot rates — the bread and butter of the shipping industry — are determined by supply and demand. The supply side consists of how many ships are available to transport crude and products to the desired destinations around the world. On the demand side is how much crude oil and products need to be shipped. In the global shipping business, you need to watch these two factors closely.

Oil import dependency is another important demand factor. The lifeblood of the global oil tanker business is the flow of oil across countries and continents, or the dependence on oil imports. One key metric to help you gauge the level of activity in this area is global import and export data, which is monitored by the Energy Information Administration's energy statistics division (www.eia.doe.gov/oil_gas/petroleum/info_glance/petroleum.html).

To the extent that crude oil prices affect the demand of crude oil worldwide, crude oil prices will have an effect on tanker spot rates. If crude oil prices go so high that folks are no longer willing to buy crude, thus reducing demand, the demand for shipping crude oil worldwide will also decrease, causing tanker spot rates to go down as well.

As with most things that have to do with commodities, tanker spot rates and fixed rates, which provide the bulk of a shipping company's revenue stream, are highly cyclical. It's not out of the ordinary for shipping rates to fluctuate by 60 or 70 percent on a daily basis. To protect yourself from these extreme price volatilities, you may want to invest in one of the large oil tanker stocks mentioned in the upcoming section "Listing key petroleum shipping companies"; these companies have been in the business a long time and have substantial experience managing the wild price swings.

Ships ahoy!

Before you invest in a tanker stock, closely examine the fleet of vessels it operates. The following list of vessels used in the global crude oil shipping industry can help you with this examination:

- **Ultra Large Crude Carrier (ULCC):** The largest vessels in the market, ULCCs are used for long haul voyages. They offer economies of scale because they can carry large amounts of oil across long distances.

- **Very Large Crude Carrier (VLCC):** VLCCs are ideally suited for intercontinental maritime transportation; their areas of operation include the Persian Gulf to East Asia and West Africa to the United States, among other routes.

- **Suezmax:** The size and design of this vessel allow it to transit through the Suez Canal in Egypt. Ideally suited for medium haul voyages, these vessels transport oil from the Persian Gulf to Europe, as well as to other destinations.

- **Aframax:** The workhorse in the tanker fleet, the Aframax is capable of transporting crude and products to most ports around the world. Because of its smaller size, it is ideally suited for short haul voyages.

- **Panamax:** Named for its ability to transit the Panama Canal, this vessel is sometimes used for short haul voyages between the ports in the Caribbean, Europe, and the United States.

Besides their catchy names, these vessels are also identified by how much crude oil and products they can transport on sea. The unit of measurement, known as the *dead weight ton,* or DWT, measures the weight of the vessel including all cargo. Most ships are constructed in such a way that one DWT is the equivalent of 6.7 barrels of oil. Table 4-7 lists the DWT capacities of the vessels, along with their equivalent in barrels of oil.

Table 4-7	Vessel Capacity in DWT and Oil Equivalents	
Vessel Type	*Dead Weight Tons*	*Oil Equivalent (Barrels)*
ULCC	320,000 and up	2+ million
VLCC	200,000–320,000	2 million
Suezmax	120,000–200,000	1 million
Aframax	80,000–120,000	600,000
Panamax	50,000–80,000	300,000

Listing key petroleum shipping companies

The companies responsible for transporting crude oil and petroleum products are a diverse bunch. Some companies concentrate their operations regionally; others transport oil and products all around the globe. Some operate a small group of VLCC vessels, while others operate a large number of smaller vessels. Some specialize in shipping only crude oil; others focus primarily on petroleum products such as gasoline. With so many options to choose from, trying to identify which company to invest in can be confusing. Here are all the major publicly traded oil shipping companies to help you decide:

- **Teekay Corp. (NYSE: TK):** Teekay, one of the world's largest seaborne transporters of crude oil and crude oil products, operates a fleet of more than 130 vessels, including one VLCC that transports crude from the Persian Gulf and West Africa to Europe, the United States, and Asia; about 15 Suezmax vessels that connect producers in North Africa (Algeria) and West Africa to consumers in Europe and the United States; and more than 40 Aframax vessels that operate in the North Sea, the Black Sea, the Mediterranean Sea, and the Caribbean. In addition to conventional tankers, Teekay operates a fleet of offshore tankers to transport crude from offshore locations to onshore facilities. If you're interested in a truly global and diversified oil shipping company, consider this one.

- **Frontline Ltd. (NYSE: FRO):** One of the largest tanker companies in the world in terms of transportation capacity, Frontline operates a fleet of more than 44 VLCCs and more than 35 Suezmax vessels in the Persian Gulf, Europe, the United States, and Asia. In addition to its tanker fleet, Frontline offers shareholders very high dividend payouts.

- **Overseas Shipholding Group, Inc. (NYSE: OSG):** Although OSG has an international presence, it's the only company with a large presence in the American shipping market. Its U.S. vessels are mainly engaged in the transportation of crude oil from Alaska to the continental United States, and products from the Gulf of Mexico to the East Coast. Additionally, OSG has one of the highest profit margins in the industry: a whopping 45 percent in 2006.

- **General Maritime Corp. (NYSE: GMR):** General Maritime focuses on the small and mid-size segment of the tanker market, operating a fleet of Suezmax and Aframax vessels primarily focused in the Atlantic basin. General Maritime links producers and consumers from Western Africa, the North Sea, the Caribbean, the United States, and Europe.

The preceding is a snapshot of global tanker activities. If you decide to invest in the global oil shipping business, dig deeper into a target company's operations. Most of the information you need is found in a company's annual report (Form 10K) or quarterly report (Form 10Q). You can also obtain additional information through third parties, such as analyst reports.

Book IV

Commodities

Chapter 5

Pedal to the Metal: Investing in Metals

- -

In This Chapter

▶ Investing in precious metals: gold, silver, and platinum

▶ Mapping out a strategy to invest in steel, aluminum, and copper

▶ Looking at other metals: palladium, zinc, and nickel

▶ Examining mining companies as an investment option

- -

*I*nvestors who have been able to master the fundamentals of the metals markets have been handsomely rewarded. Gold, silver, and platinum have industrial applications, but their primary value comes from their ability to act as stores of value, in addition to their use in jewelry. Steel, aluminum, and copper, while not as glamorous as their precious metal counterparts, are perhaps even more precious to the global economy. Other important metals, like palladium, zinc, and nickel, are also essential building blocks of the global economy. In this chapter, I cover all these metals that can play an important role in your portfolio.

Metals are classified into two broad categories: *precious metals* and *base metals*. This classification is based on a metal's resistance to corrosion and oxidation: Precious metals have a high resistance to corrosion, whereas base metals have a lower tolerance.

Going for the Gold

Perhaps no other metal — or commodity — in the world has the cachet and prestige of gold. For centuries, gold has been coveted and valued for its unique metallurgical characteristics. It is such a desirable commodity that a number of currencies used to be based on its value. In addition, gold has a number of applications in industry and jewelry that have increased its demand. Here are the characteristics that make gold such a hot commodity:

- ✔ **Quasi-indestructibility:** Corrosive agents such as oxygen and heat have almost no effect on gold, which can retain its luster over thousands of years. (The only chemical that affects gold is cyanide.)

- ✔ **Rarity:** Gold is one of the rarest natural resources on earth. All the gold in the world would not even fill up four Olympic-size swimming pools!

- ✔ **Malleability:** Pure gold (24 karat) is very malleable and prized by craftsmen around the world. One ounce of gold can be transformed into more than 96 square feet of gold sheet!

- ✔ **Ductility:** *Ductility* measures how much a metal can be drawn out into a wire, and gold is a very ductile metal. One ounce of gold can be converted into more than 50 miles of gold wire, which can then be applied in electronics.

Recognizing the gold standard

To profit from the demand for gold, you need to be familiar with the fundamentals of the gold market. First, you should know what gold is used for:

- ✔ **Jewelry:** Jewelry is the most important consumer use of gold in the world, accounting for more than 70 percent of gold's total consumption.

- ✔ **Electronics:** Because of its ability to efficiently conduct electricity, gold is a popular metal in electronics.

- ✔ **Dentistry:** Because gold resists corrosion, it has wide application in dentistry, where it's alloyed with other metals to create dental fixtures.

- ✔ **Monetary:** Gold has many monetary uses: Many central banks hold reserves of gold; it's one of the only commodities that the investing public holds in its physical form; and it's used in coinage.

You also need to know how it's measured. Gold, like most metals, is measured and weighed in *troy ounces* (oz). One troy ounce is the equivalent of 31.10 grams. When you buy gold for investment purposes, such as through exchange-traded funds or gold certificates, troy ounces is the measurement of choice. When you want to refer to large quantities of gold, such as the amount of gold a bank holds in reserve or the amount of gold produced in a mine, the unit of measurement you use is *metric tons.* One metric ton is equal to 32,150 troy ounces.

If you've ever bought gold jewelry (or heard a jewelry ad on TV), you've certainly heard of the measurement call *karats* (sometimes spelled *carats*). This measurement indicates the purity of gold. The purest form of gold is 24 karat gold (24K). Everything below that number denotes that the gold is *alloyed,* or mixed, with another metal. The purer the gold, the higher its value:

Karats	Purity
24K	100%
22K	91.67%
18K	75%
14K	58.3%
10K	41.67%
9K	37.5%

Buying into the gold market

You can invest in gold in a number of ways: physical gold, gold ETFs, gold mining companies, and gold futures contracts.

Getting physical

Gold is one of the few commodities that can be physically stored to have its value preserved or increased over time, so one way to invest in gold is to actually buy it. You can purchase gold coins or bars and store them in a safe location as an investment.

To purchase physical gold, or even gold certificates (which I explain in a moment), you need to go through a gold dealer such as Kitco (www.kitco. com). Before doing business with any gold dealer, find out as much information about the business and its history as possible. You can check out different gold dealers by going through the Better Business Bureau at www.bbb.org.

Gold coins

One of the easiest ways to invest in physical gold is by buying gold coins. Here are the most popular types of gold coins:

- ✔ **Gold Eagle:** Issued by the United States government, the 22 karat Gold Eagle comes in various sizes including 1 ounce, ½ ounce, ¼ ounce, and ⅒ ounce

- ✔ **Gold Maple Leaf:** Issued by the Royal Canadian Mint, this 24 karat coin is the purest gold coin on the market.

- ✔ **Gold Krugerrand:** Issued by the South African government, this is one of the oldest gold coins issued in the world and has a fineness of 0.916. (*Fineness* is the ratio of the primary metal to any additives or impurities.)

Gold bars

Gold bars have an undeniable allure. While gold coins are more suited for smaller purchases, gold bars are ideal if you're interested in purchasing larger quantities of gold. Gold bars come in all shapes and sizes. They can be as small as 1 gram or as large as 400 troy ounces. Most gold bars are high quality with a fineness of 0.999 and above (24 karats). For a comprehensive listing of gold bars, peruse *The Industry Catalogue of Gold Bars Worldwide* at www.grendon.com.au/goldbarscat.htm.

FYI, the term *gold bullion* simply refers to large gold bars.

Gold certificates

Gold certificates enable you to own physical gold without actually taking possession of it. Gold certificates certify that you own a certain amount of gold, which is usually stored in a safe location by the authority that issues the gold certificates. The gold standard of gold certificates is the Perth Mint Certificate Program (PMCP). Administered by The Perth Mint, Australia's oldest and most important mint, the PMCP issues you a certificate and stores your gold in a secure government vault. You may retrieve or sell your gold at any point. For more on this program, check out The Perth Mint's Web site at www.perthmint.com.au.

Purchasing gold through ETFs

Currently you have two gold ETFs to choose from:

- **streetTRACKS Gold Shares (NYSE: GLD):** The streetTRACKS gold ETF is the largest gold ETF on the market today. Launched in late 2004, it holds about 12 million ounces of physical gold in secured locations. The price per ETF unit is calculated based on the average of the bid/ask spread in the gold spot market. This fund is a good way of getting exposure to physical gold without actually owning it.

- **iShares COMEX Gold Trust (AMEX: IAU):** The iShares gold ETF holds a little more than 1.3 million ounces of gold in its vaults. The per-unit price of the ETF seeks to reflect the current market price in the spot market of the ETF gold.

Because both ETFs track the price of gold on the spot market, their performance is remarkably similar — at times, it's actually identical. If you're struggling to decide between the two, consider that streetTRACKS holds more physical gold and, more importantly, offers you more liquidity than the iShares ETF.

Holding stock in gold companies

Another way to get exposure to gold is by investing in gold mining companies. A number of companies specialize in mining, processing, and distributing gold. A few recommendations:

✔ **Newmont Mining Corp. (NYSE: NEM):** Newmont is one of the largest gold mining companies in the world, with operations in Australia, Indonesia, Uzbekistan, the United States, Canada, Peru, and Bolivia. It is the largest gold producer in South America and has exploration programs in Ghana that could turn out to be very promising for the company.

✔ **Barrick Gold Corp. (NYSE: ABX):** Barrick, a Canadian company, is a premier player in the gold mining industry. It has operations in Canada, the United States, Argentina, Peru, Chile, Tanzania, South Africa, Australia, and Papua New Guinea, as well as a foothold in the potentially lucrative Central Asian market, where it has joint operations in Turkey, Russia, and Mongolia. Barrick also has one of the lowest production costs per ounce of gold in the industry.

✔ **AngloGold Ashanti Ltd. (NYSE: AU):** AngloGold, listed in five different stock exchanges around the world, operates more than 20 mines and has significant operations in Africa and South America, particularly in South Africa, Namibia, Tanzania, Ghana, Mali, Brazil, Argentina, and Peru, which all have major gold deposits. It has additional operations in Australia and North America. It is a wholly owned subsidiary of Anglo American PLC, a global mining giant that I cover at the end of the chapter in "Putting Stock in Diversified Mining Companies."

These companies don't give you direct exposure to gold, as gold certificates or bars do, for example. Also, by investing in these stocks, you're exposing yourself to regulatory, managerial, and operational factors. Research the company before you invest.

Getting in the game through gold futures contracts

With gold futures contracts, you invest in gold directly through the futures markets. Two gold futures contracts are widely traded in the United States:

✔ **COMEX Gold (COMEX: GC):** The most liquid gold contract in the world, this contract is traded on the COMEX division of the New York Mercantile Exchange (NYMEX). Although large commercial consumers and producers, such as jewelry manufacturers and mining companies, use these contracts primarily for price hedging purposes, you can also purchase the contract for investment purposes. Each contract represents 100 troy ounces of gold.

✔ **CBOT Mini-Gold (CBOT: YG):** Launched in 2004, this gold contract is a relative newcomer to the North American gold futures market, but it's very attractive because you can trade it online through the Chicago Board of Trade's electronic trading platform. In addition, at a contract size of 33.2 troy ounces, the mini is popular with investors and traders who prefer to trade smaller size contracts.

Book IV

Commodities

Although the CBOT also offers the more traditional, full-size 100-ounce gold ontract, the COMEX's 100-ounce contract is currently the more liquid of the two.

Taking a Shine to Silver

Silver has a number of uses that make it an attractive investment. Here are the most important ones, which account for more than 95 percent of total demand for silver:

- **Industrial:** The industrial sector is the single largest consumer of silver products, accounting for almost 47 percent of total silver consumption in 2006. Silver has a number of applications in the industrial sector, including creating control switches for electrical appliances and connecting electronic circuit boards.

- **Jewelry and silverware:** Silver plays a large role in creating jewelry and silverware, accounting for 16 percent of total silver consumption in 2006.

- **Photography:** The photographic industry is a major consumer of silver, accounting for about 24 percent of total consumption. (In photography, silver is compounded with halogens to form *silver halide,* which is used in photographic film.) The demand for silver by the photo industry is slowly decreasing, however, because digital cameras, which don't use silver halide, are becoming more popular than traditional cameras.

Monitor the commercial activity in each of these market segments to look for signs of strength or weakness, because a demand increase or decrease in one of these markets will have a direct impact on the price of silver.

Because of its precious metal status, you can use silver as a hedge against inflation and to preserve part of your portfolio's value. And because it has important industrial applications, you can use it for capital appreciation opportunities. Whether for capital preservation or appreciation purposes, there's room in any portfolio for some exposure to silver.

If you're interested in finding out more about silver and its investment possibilities, The Silver Institute (`www.silverinstitute.org`), a trade association for silver producers and consumers, maintains a comprehensive database on the silver market.

Buying physical silver

Like gold, you can invest in silver by actually buying the stuff. Most dealers that sell gold generally offer silver coins and bars as well. Here are two products to consider as investments:

- **Silver Maple Coins:** These coins, a product of the Royal Canadian Mint, are the standard for silver coins around the world. Each coin represents 1 ounce of silver and has a purity of 99.99 percent, making it the most pure silver coin on the market.

✔ **100 oz. Silver Bar:** These bars are what their name indicates: 100-ounce bars of silver. Before buying, check the bar to make sure it's pure silver. (You want 99 percent purity or above.)

Pure silver is sometimes alloyed with another metal, such as copper, in order to make it stronger and more durable. The term *sterling silver* refers to a specific silver alloy that contains 92.5 percent silver and 7.5 percent copper or other base metals. Just remember that if you're considering silver jewelry as an investment, sterling silver won't provide you with as much value in the long term as buying pure silver.

Considering a silver ETF

One of the most convenient ways of investing in silver is by going through an exchange-traded fund (ETF). Barclays Global Investors (a subsidiary of the investment bank) launched an ETF through its iShares program in 2006 to track the price of silver. The iShares Silver Trust (AMEX: SLV) holds silver bullion in a vault and seeks to mirror the spot price of that silver based on current market prices.

Looking at silver mining companies

Another alternative investment route is to go through companies that mine silver. Although some of the larger mining companies (covered in the later section "Putting Stock in Diversified Mining Companies") have silver mining operations, you can get a more direct exposure to the silver markets by investing in companies that *specialize* in mining this precious metal. These companies may not be household names, but they are a potentially good investment nevertheless. Here are a couple of them:

✔ **Pan American Silver Corp. (NASDAQ: PAAS):** This well-managed company, based in Vancouver, operates six mines in some of the most prominent locations in the world, including Peru, Mexico, and Bolivia.

✔ **Silver Wheaton Corp. (NYSE: SLW):** Silver Wheaton, one of the few companies focusing exclusively on developing and mining silver, has operations in geographically diverse areas that stretch from Mexico to Sweden.

Book IV

Commodities

Tapping into silver futures contracts

The silver futures contracts, like gold futures, provide you with the most direct access to the silver market. Following are the most liquid silver futures contracts:

- ✓ **COMEX Silver (COMEX: SI):** This silver contract is the standard futures contract for silver. It is traded on the COMEX division of the New York Mercantile Exchange (NYMEX) and represents 5,000 troy ounces of silver per contract.

- ✓ **CBOT Mini-Silver (CBOT: YI):** The Mini-Silver contract that trades on the Chicago Board of Trade (CBOT) represents a stake in 1,000 troy ounces of silver with a purity of 99.9 percent. This contract is available for electronic trading.

Putting Your Money in Platinum

Platinum, sometimes referred to as "the rich man's gold," is one of the rarest and most precious metals in the world. Perhaps no other metal or commodity carries the same cachet as platinum, and for good reason. If you were to put all the platinum that has ever been mined in an Olympic-size swimming pool, it wouldn't even cover your ankles! Platinum has superior characteristics to most metals: It is more resistant to corrosion, doesn't oxidize in the air, and has stable chemical properties.

Platinum is also the name of the group of metals that includes platinum, palladium, rhodium, ruthenium, osmium, and iridium. In this section, I talk about the metal only — not the group of metals. (I do cover palladium later in the chapter in the section "Appreciating Palladium.")

Poring over some platinum facts

Deposits of platinum ore are extremely scarce and, more important, are geographically concentrated in a few regions around the globe, primarily in South Africa, Russia, and North America. South Africa has the largest deposits of platinum in the world and, by some accounts, may contain up to 90 percent of the world's total reserve estimates. Russia is also a large player in the production of platinum, currently accounting for 20 percent of total global production (2006 figures). North America also contains some commercially viable platinum mines, located mostly in Montana. Platinum's rarity is reflected in its price per troy ounce. For example, the price of platinum in October 2007 was $1,415 per troy ounce! By comparison, silver during the same period cost $13.77 per troy ounce.

Platinum has several uses. Here are the most important ones:

- ✔ **Catalytic converters:** Platinum's use in catalytic converters accounts for more than 45 percent of total platinum demand. As environmental fuel standards become more stringent, expect the demand from this sector to increase.

- ✔ **Jewelry:** Jewelry once accounted for more than 50 percent of total demand for platinum. Although that number has decreased, the jewelry industry is still a major purchaser of platinum metals.

- ✔ **Industrial:** Platinum has wide applications in industry, being used in everything from personal computer hard drives to fiber optic cables.

 A change in demand from one of these industries will affect the price of platinum. The International Platinum Association (www.ipa-news.com) maintains an updated database of the uses of platinum. Check out the site for more information on platinum supply and demand.

Going platinum

Platinum's unique characteristics as a highly sought-after precious metal with industrial applications make it an ideal investment. Fortunately, you can invest in platinum in a number of ways. I list a couple in the following sections.

Purchasing a platinum futures contract

The most direct way of investing in platinum is by going through the futures markets. The New York Mercantile Exchange (NYMEX) offers a platinum futures contract. Because of increased demand from the industrial sector and other fundamental supply and demand reasons, the price of the NYMEX platinum futures contract has experienced a significant upward shift in recent years. The NYMEX platinum futures contract represents 50 troy ounces of platinum and is available for trading electronically. It trades under the ticker symbol PL.

Book IV

Commodities

Buying into platinum mining companies

Here are a couple of companies you can check out that will give you direct exposure to platinum mining activities:

- ✔ **Stillwater Mining Company (NYSE: SWC):** Stillwater Mining, headquartered in Billings, Montana, owns the rights to the Stillwater mining complex in Montana, which contains one of the largest commercially viable platinum mines in North America. This is a good play on North American platinum mining activities.

- ✔ **Anglo American PLC (NASDAQ: AAUK):** Anglo American is a diversified mining company that has activities in gold, silver, platinum, and other precious metals. It's worth a look because it has significant interests in South African platinum mines, the largest mines in the world.

Adding Some Steel to Your Portfolio

Steel, iron alloyed with other compounds (usually carbon), is still the most widely produced metal in the world today. In a high-tech world dominated by software and technological gadgets, this age-old metal is making a resurgence as advanced developing countries — China, India, and Brazil — barrel down a path toward rapid industrialization.

Getting the steely facts

Steel production today is dominated by China, which produces three times more steel than Japan, the second largest producer. The United States is still an important player in the steel industry, and other countries worth mentioning include Russia, Germany, and South Korea.

If you're interested in exploring additional statistical information relating to steel production and manufacturing, check out these resources: International Iron and Steel Institute (www.worldsteel.org), Iron and Steel Statistics Bureau (www.issb.co.uk), and the Association for Iron & Steel Technology (www.aist.org).

Holding stock in steel companies

Currently, no underlying futures contract for steel exists. However, a number of exchanges have expressed interest in developing a steel futures contract, so keep an eye out for such a development. For now, the best way to get exposure to steel is by investing in companies that produce steel, specifically globally integrated steel companies. Following, I list good investments that are not only the best-run companies but also show the greatest potential for future market dominance:

- ✔ **U.S. Steel (NYSE: X):** U.S. Steel, formed as a result of the consolidation of Andrew Carnegie's steel holdings in the early 20th century, is one of the oldest and largest steel companies in the world. Today it's the seventh largest steel-producing company worldwide, involved in all aspects of the steel-making process from iron ore mining and processing to the marketing of finished products.

- ✔ **Nucor Corp. (NYSE: NUE):** Nucor operates almost exclusively in the United States, offering exposure to the U.S. steel market. It's also one of the only companies to operate mini-mills domestically, which many people argue are more cost-efficient than the traditional blast furnaces.

- ✔ **ArcelorMittal (NYSE: MT):** In 2006, the two largest steel companies in the world merged. The newly formed company controls more than 10 percent of the world's steel market (in terms of output) and produces approximately 120 million metric tons of steel annually.

Inviting Aluminum to Your Investments

Aluminum, generally measured in *metric tons* (MT), is lightweight, resistant to corrosion, durable, and sturdy. It's the second most widely used metal in the world, right after steel, and is used in the following sectors:

- ✔ **Transportation (26 percent of total aluminum consumption):** Aluminum is used in car bodies, axles, and, in some cases, engines. It's also used in large commercial aircraft.

- ✔ **Packaging (22 percent):** Almost a quarter of aluminum is used to make aluminum wrap and foil, along with beverage cans and rivets.

- ✔ **Construction (22 percent):** Aluminum's industrial uses include construction of buildings, oil pipelines, and even bridges.

- ✔ **Other:** Aluminum is also used in electrical (8 percent), machinery (8 percent), and consumer goods (7 percent).

The underlying demand from rapidly industrializing nations such as China and India has resulted in upward price pressures on the metal.

To find out more about the aluminum industry, check out these organizations: International Aluminium Institute (www.world-aluminium.org), the Aluminum Association (www.aluminum.org), and aluNET International (www.alunet.net).

Book IV

Commodities

Trading aluminum futures

You can invest in aluminum through the futures markets. Currently, two major contracts for aluminum are available:

- ✔ **LME Aluminum (LAH):** The London Metal Exchange's aluminum contract is the most liquid in the world. The LME aluminum contract represents a size of 25,000 tons, and its price is quoted in U.S. dollars.

- ✔ **COMEX Aluminum (COMEX: AL):** The aluminum contract traded on the COMEX division of the NYMEX trades in units of 44,000 pounds, with a 99.7 percent purity. The contract is tradable during the current calendar month as well as for the next 25 consecutive months. It's also available for trade electronically.

If you start investing in futures and something goes wrong, you need to know who to turn to. NYMEX, located in the United States, is regulated by the Commodity Futures Trading Commission (CFTC). LME, located in the United Kingdom, falls under the jurisdiction of the Financial Services Authority (FSA), the British regulator.

Considering aluminum companies

Another way to invest in aluminum is to invest in companies that produce and manufacture aluminum products. Here are a few companies that make the cut:

- ✔ **Alcoa (NYSE: AA):** The world leader in aluminum production, Alcoa is involved in all aspects of the aluminum industry and produces primary aluminum, fabricated aluminum, and alumina. The company has operations in more than 40 countries and services a large number of industries, from aerospace to construction. Alcoa is a good choice if you're looking to get the broadest exposure to the aluminum market.

- ✔ **Alcan (NYSE: AL):** Alcan, headquartered in Canada, is a leading global manufacturer of aluminum products. It has operations that cover the spectrum of aluminum processing, from mining and refining to smelting and recycling. Alcan provides you with wide exposure to aluminum.

- ✔ **Aluminum Corporation of China (NYSE: ACH):** ACH is primarily engaged in the production of aluminum in the Chinese market. This company, which trades on the New York Stock Exchange, provides a foothold in the aluminum Chinese market, which has the potential to be the biggest such market in the future. Besides of this competitive advantage, ACH boasts profit margins that, during the writing of this book, were in excess of 16 percent.

Seeing the Strengths of Copper

Copper, the third most widely used metal in the world, has applications in many sectors and is sought after because of its high electrical conductivity, resistance to corrosion, and malleability. Because of the current trends of industrialization and urbanization across the globe, demand for copper has been — and will remain — very strong.

Copper is used for a wide variety of purposes, from building and construction to electrical wiring, engineering, and transportation. To find out more about copper usage, consult the Copper Development Association (www.copper.org).

Copper is often alloyed with other metals, usually with nickel (to make copper) and zinc (to make brass). Ironically, the U.S. penny, the only U.S. coin that's a reddish-brown color (the color of copper), uses only 2.5 percent copper; the other 97.5 percent of the penny is made from zinc. The other coins in U.S. currency, which are all silvery-white colors, contain more than 90 percent copper.

Buying copper futures contracts

A futures market is available for copper trading. Most of this market is used by large industrial producers and consumers of the metal, although you can also use it for investment purposes. You have two copper contracts to choose from:

✔ **LME Copper (LME: CAD):** The copper contract on the London Metal Exchange (LME) accounts for more than 90 percent of total copper futures activity. It represents a lot size of 25 tons.

✔ **COMEX Copper (COMEX: HG):** This copper contract trades in the COMEX division of the New York Mercantile Exchange (NYMEX). The contract, which trades during the current month and subsequent 23 calendar months, is traded both electronically and through the open outcry system. It represents 25,000 pounds of copper.

Demand for copper from China, India, and other advanced developing countries is increasing, which has put upward pressure on the price of copper.

Investing in copper companies

You can invest in copper by getting involved in companies that specialize in mining and processing copper ore. An industry leader involved in all aspects of the copper supply chain is **Freeport McMoRan Copper & Gold Inc.** (NYSE:

FCX). Freeport-McMoRan is one of the lowest cost producers of copper in the world. It has copper mining and smelting operations across the globe and has a significant presence in Indonesia and Papua New Guinea. The company specializes in the production of highly concentrated copper ore, which it then sells on the open market. FCX also has some operations in gold and silver. The company acquired Phelps Dodge, one of the oldest mining companies in the United States, in 2007.

Appreciating Palladium

Palladium, which belongs to the group of platinum metals, is a popular alternative to platinum in the automotive and jewelry industries. Its largest use is in the creation of pollution-reducing catalytic converters. Because of palladium's malleability, corrosion resistance, and price (it's less expensive than platinum: $380 per ounce versus $1,415 per ounce in October 2007), it's increasingly becoming the metal of choice for the manufacture of these devices. Palladium is also used in dentistry and electronics.

When pollution-reducing regulation was established in the United States in the 1970s, demand for palladium skyrocketed. All things equal, if emissions standards are further improved and require a new generation of catalytic converters, demand for palladium will increase again. Another reason to be bullish on palladium is that the number of automobiles, trucks, and other vehicles equipped with platinum- and palladium-made catalytic converters is increasing, particularly in China. So if you invest in palladium, make sure you keep an eye on automobile manufacturing patterns.

The palladium market is essentially dominated by two countries: Russia and South Africa. These two countries account for more than 85 percent of total palladium production. Any supply disruption from either country has a significant impact on palladium prices.

One of the best — albeit indirect — methods of getting exposure to the palladium markets is by investing in companies that mine the metal. A number of companies specialize in this activity; following are the two largest companies that trade publicly on U.S. exchanges:

- **Stillwater Mining Company (NYSE: SWC):** Stillwater Mining is the largest producer of palladium outside South Africa and Russia. It produces approximately 500,000 ounces of palladium a year, primarily through North American mines.

- **North American Palladium (AMEX: PAL):** North American Palladium, headquartered in Toronto, has a significant presence in the Canadian palladium ore mining business. It is the largest producer of palladium in Canada, with production in 2006 totaling more than 237,000 ounces.

Several international companies have significantly larger palladium mining activities than these two. Here are a couple of international palladium companies to consider. (Before investing, make sure you're aware of the many regulatory differences between U.S. and overseas markets.)

- ✔ **Anglo Platinum Group (South Africa):** Anglo Platinum Group, one of the largest producers of palladium in the world, produced more than 2.5 million ounces of palladium in 2005 and is estimated to have reserves of more than 200 million ounces (this includes other platinum group metals). With its operations located primarily in South Africa, Anglo Platinum Group is your gateway to South African palladium. Its shares are traded on the Johannesburg Stock Exchange (JSE), as well as the London Stock Exchange (LSE).

- ✔ **Norilsk Nickel (Russia):** Norilsk Nickel, the largest producer of palladium in the world, dominates the Russian palladium industry. While the company has large palladium mining activities, it's also a major player in copper and nickel ore mining. The company's shares are available through the Moscow Inter-bank Currency Exchange (MICEX).

For folks who are comfortable in the futures markets, the New York Mercantile Exchange (NYMEX) offers a futures contract that tracks palladium. This contract represents 100 troy ounces of palladium and trades both electronically and during the open outcry session. It trades under the symbol PA.

Keeping an Eye on Zinc

Zinc is the fourth most widely used metal, right behind iron/steel, aluminum, and copper. Zinc, which has unique abilities to resist corrosion and oxidation, is used for metal *galvanization,* the process of applying a metal coating to another metal to prevent rust and corrosion. Galvanization is by far the largest application of zinc (accounting for 47 percent of zinc usage), but zinc has other applications as well: brass and bronze coatings and zinc alloying, for example.

The best way to invest in zinc is by going through the futures markets. The London Metal Exchange (LME) offers a futures contract for zinc, which has been trading since the early 1900s and is the industry benchmark for zinc pricing. The contract trades in lots of 25 tons and is available for trading during the current month and the subsequent 27 months.

Book IV

Commodities

Noting the Merits of Nickel

Nickel is sought-after for its ductility, malleability, and resistance to corrosion. Although there are a number of important uses for nickel, the creation of stainless steel remains its primary application (accounting for 65 percent of its market consumption). Nickel is also used in non-ferrous alloys, ferrous alloys, and electroplating, among other things.

Australia has the largest reserves of nickel, and its proximity to the rapidly industrializing Asian center — China and India — is a strategic advantage. Another major player in the nickel markets is Russia; the Russian company Norilsk Nickel (covered in the section on palladium) is the largest producer of nickel in the world. Nickel mining is a labor-intensive industry, but those countries that have large reserves of this special metal, listed in Table 5-1, are poised to do very well.

Table 5-1	Largest Nickel Reserves, 2004 Figures	
Country	*Reserves (Thousand Tons)*	*Percentage of Total*
Australia	48,611	25.1%
Russia	24,625	12.7%
Indonesia	22,491	11.6%
New Caledonia	13,863	7.1%
Canada	13,074	6.7%
Cuba	11,640	6.0%
Philippines	9860	5.1%
Papua New Guinea	8903	4.6%
Brazil	6960	3.6%
China	550	2.8%

Source: U.S. Geological Survey

The London Metal Exchange (LME) offers a futures contract for nickel. The nickel futures contract on the LME provides you with the most direct access to the nickel market. It trades in lots of 6 tons, and its tick size is $5.00 per ton. It trades during the first month and in 27 subsequent months.

Putting Stock in Diversified Mining Companies

Trading metals outright — through the futures markets — can be tricky for the uninitiated trader. You have to keep track of a number of moving pieces, such as contract expiration dates, margin calls, trading months, and other variables. In addition, metals on the futures markets can be subject to extreme price volatility, and you can set yourself up for disastrous losses. So it's understandable if you'd rather not trade metals futures contracts. But this doesn't mean that you should ignore the metals sub-asset class altogether because you could be missing out on some tasty returns.

One possible avenue for opening up your portfolio to metals is investing in companies that mine metals and minerals. A number of such companies exist, and their performance has been stellar recently. This section looks at the top diversified companies. For information about specialized mining companies, refer back to the section that covers the metal you're interested in.

Diversified mining companies are involved in *all* aspects of the metals production process. These companies, which often employ tens of thousands of people, have operations in all four corners of the globe. They're involved in the excavation of metals, as well as the transformation of these metals into finished products and subsequent distribution of the end products to consumers. Investing in one of these companies gives you exposure not only to a wide variety of metals, but also to the whole mining supply chain.

BHP Billiton

BHP Billiton is one of the largest mining companies in the world. Headquartered in Melbourne, Australia, it has mining operations in more than 25 countries including Australia, Canada, the United States, South Africa, and Papua New Guinea. The company processes a large number of metals, including aluminum, copper, silver, and iron; it also has small oil and natural gas operations in Algeria and Pakistan. The company is listed on the New York Stock Exchange (NYSE) under the symbol BHP.

In recent years, the company has benefited handsomely from the increasing prices of commodities such as copper and aluminum. As a result, BHP Billiton's profit increased by a staggering 108 percent between 2005 and 2006.

Book IV

Commodities

Rio Tinto

Rio Tinto was founded in 1873 by the Rothschild banking family to mine ore deposits in Spain. Today, Rio Tinto boasts operations in Africa, Australia, Europe, the Pacific Rim, North America, and South America. The company is involved in the production of a number of commodities, including iron ore, copper, aluminum, and titanium. In addition, Rio Tinto has interests in diamonds, manufacturing almost 30 percent of global natural diamonds, processed primarily through its mining activities in Australia.

Rio Tinto trades on the New York Stock Exchange (NYSE) under the ticker symbol RTP.

Anglo American

Anglo American PLC began mining gold in South Africa in 1917. Ever since, it has played an important role in the development of South Africa's gold mining industry. Today, Anglo American has operations in all four corners of the globe and operates in more than 20 countries. It is involved in the production and distribution of a wide array of metals, minerals, and natural resources including gold, silver, and platinum but also diamonds and paper packaging. (It owns 45 percent of De Beers, the diamond company.)

The company is listed in the London Stock Exchange under the ticker symbol AAL. In addition, it has American Depository Receipts listed in the NASDAQ National Market that trade under the symbol AAUK.

Chapter 6

Down on the Farm: Trading Agricultural Products

*F*ood is the most essential resource in human life. Investing in this sector can also help improve your bottom line. This chapter introduces the major sectors in this sub-asset class and shows you how to profit from grains such as corn and wheat; tropical commodities like coffee and orange juice; and livestock.

Profiting from the Softs: Coffee, Cocoa, Sugar, and OJ

The commodities I present in this section — coffee, cocoa, sugar, and frozen concentrated orange juice — are known as *soft commodities*. Soft commodities are those commodities that are usually grown, as opposed to those that are mined, such as metals, or those that are raised, such as livestock. The *softs,* as they are sometimes known, represent a significant portion of the commodities markets. They are indispensable and cyclical, just like energy and metals, but they are also unique because they're edible and seasonal. *Seasonality* is actually a major distinguishing characteristic of soft commodities because they can be grown only during specific times of the year and in specific geographical locations — usually in tropical areas. (This is why these commodities are also known as *tropical commodities*.) In this section, I show you that there's nothing soft about these soft commodities.

Feeling the buzz from coffee

Coffee is the second most widely traded commodity in terms of physical volume, behind only crude oil (see Chapter 4). Like a number of other commodities, coffee production is dominated by a handful of countries. Brazil, Colombia, and Vietnam are the largest producing countries, as you can see in Table 6-1.

Table 6-1	Top Coffee Producers, 2006 Figures
Country	*Production (Thousands of Bags)*
Brazil	42,512
Vietnam	15,500
Colombia	12,200
Indonesia	6,973
India	4,750
Ethiopia	5,000

Source: International Coffee Organization

Just like choosing the right flavor when buying your cup of coffee, knowing the different types of coffees available for investment is important. The world's coffee production is pretty much made up of two types of beans:

- ✔ **Arabica:** Arabica coffee accounts for more than 60 percent of global coffee production. It's grown in countries as diverse as Brazil and Indonesia and is the premium coffee bean, adding a richer taste to any brew. As a result, it's the most expensive coffee bean. It serves as the benchmark for coffee prices all over the world.

- ✔ **Robusta:** Robusta accounts for about 40 percent of total coffee production. Because it's easier to grow than Arabica coffee, it's also less expensive.

You can invest in coffee production by buying coffee in the futures markets or by investing in companies that specialize in running gourmet coffee shops.

To find out more about coffee markets, consult these resources: International Coffee Organization (www.ico.org) and the National Coffee Association of the U.S.A. (www.ncausa.org).

A number of organizations that offer information on specific commodities are specialized lobby groups whose agenda — alongside providing information to the public — includes promoting the consumption of the products they represent. Keep this in mind as you consult any outside resource for research purposes.

The coffee futures contract: It could be your cup of tea

The coffee futures markets are used to determine the future price of coffee and, more importantly, to protect producers and purchasers of coffee from wild price swings and to allow individual investors to profit from coffee price variations. The most liquid coffee futures contract is available on the New York Board of Trade (NYBOT).

The NYBOT coffee futures contract is one of the oldest futures contracts in the market today. Here are its contract specs:

- **Contract ticker symbol:** KC
- **Contract size:** 37,500 pounds
- **Underlying commodity:** Pure Arabica coffee
- **Price fluctuation:** $0.0005/pound ($18.75 per contract)
- **Trading months:** March, May, July, September, December

Because of seasonality, cyclicality, and geopolitical factors, coffee can be a volatile commodity subject to extreme price swings. Make sure to research the coffee markets inside and out before investing.

Investing in gourmet coffee shops

Coffee is serious business, and you can profit from the coffee craze that has gripped the United States (the largest consumer of coffee in the world) and is spreading throughout Europe and newly-developing countries like India and China by investing in the companies that are capitalizing on the gourmet coffee shop trend. Find out where your $4.50 for a cup of coffee is going and profit from it:

- **Starbucks Corp. (NASDAQ: SBUX):** Starbucks is a cultural phenomenon, but, more important, it's also a financial Juggernaut. With more than $7 billion in revenue, Starbucks dominates the entire coffee supply chain, from purchasing and roasting to selling and marketing. It has more than 10,000 stores worldwide, primarily in the United States and Europe but also in China, Singapore, and even one in Saudi Arabia.
- **Peet's Coffee and Tea, Inc. (NASDAQ: PEET):** Peet's Coffee operates only about 100 coffee shops, but its strength lies in distribution. The company sells a large selection of coffees, produced in countries as diverse as Guatemala and Kenya, to customers across the United States, including restaurants and grocery stores.

✔ **Green Mountain Coffee Roasters, Inc. (NASDAQ: GMCR):** Green Mountain Coffee, headquartered in Vermont, operates in the distribution of specialized coffee products to a number of entities, such as convenience stores, specialty retailers, and restaurants. It has a large presence in the East Coast and has a partnership with Paul Newman's *Newman's Own* company to provide organic coffee to customers. This is a good company if you want exposure to the high-end coffee distribution market in the Northeast.

Heating up your portfolio with cocoa

Cocoa is a fermented seed from the cacao tree, which is usually grown in hot and rainy regions around the equator. The first cacao tree is said to have originated in South America, but today the cocoa trade is dominated by African countries, as you can see in Table 6-2.

Table 6-2	Top Cocoa Producers, 2006 Figures
Country	*Production (Thousands of Tons)*
Ivory Coast	1,350
Ghana	670
Indonesia	445
Nigeria	170
Brazil	160
Cameroon	160

Source: *International Cocoa Organization*

For a more nuanced understanding of the cocoa market and the companies that control it, check out these resources: World Cocoa Foundation (www. worldcocoafoundation.org), International Cocoa Organization (www.icco. org), and Cocoa Producers' Alliance (www.copal-cpa.org).

The New York Board of Trade (NYBOT) offers a futures contract for cocoa. Here is some useful information regarding this cocoa futures contract, which is the most liquid in the market:

✔ **Contract ticker symbol:** CC

✔ **Contract size:** 10 metric tons

✔ **Underlying commodity:** Generic cocoa beans

✔ **Price fluctuation:** $1.0/ton ($10.00 per contract)

✔ **Trading months:** March, May, July, September, December

Like coffee, the cocoa market is subject to seasonal and cyclical factors that have a large impact on price movements, which can be pretty volatile.

Being sweet on sugar

Although sugar production began more than 9,000 years ago in southeastern Asia, today, Latin American countries dominate the sugar trade. Brazil is the largest sugar producer in the world, as you can see in Table 6-3.

Table 6-3	Top Sugar Producers, 2005 Figures
Country	*Production (Thousands of Tons)*
Brazil	33,591
India	27,174
China	11,630
United States	7,661
Thailand	7,011
Mexico	5,543

Source: United States Department of Agriculture

If you're interested in investing in sugar, head over to the New York Board of Trade (NYBOT), which offers two futures contracts that track the price of sugar: *Sugar #11* (world production) and *Sugar #14* (U.S. production). Here are the contract specs for these two sugar contracts:

	Sugar #11 (World)	*Sugar #14 (U.S. production)*
Ticker symbol	SB	SE
Contract size	112,000 pounds	112,000 pounds
Underlying commodity	Global sugar	Domestic (U.S.) sugar
Price fluctuation	$0.01/pound ($11.20 per contract)	$0.01/pound ($11.20 per contract)
Trading months	March, May, July, October	January, March, May, July, September, November

Book IV

Commodities

Historically, Sugar #14 tends to be more expensive than Sugar #11. However, Sugar #11 accounts for most of the volume in the NYBOT sugar market.

Getting healthy profits from OJ

Orange juice is one of the only actively traded contracts in the futures markets that's based on a tropical fruit. Oranges are widely grown in the western hemisphere, particularly in Florida and Brazil. As you can see in Table 6-4, Brazil is by far the largest producer of oranges, although the United States — primarily Florida — is also a major player.

Table 6-4	Top Orange Producers, 2005 Figures
Country	*Production (Tons)*
Brazil	17,804,600
United States	8,266,270
Mexico	3,969,810
India	3,100,000
Italy	2,533,535
China	2,412,000

Source: United Nations Statistical Database

Because oranges are perishable, the futures contract tracks *frozen concentrated orange juice* (FCOJ). This particular form is suitable for storage and fits one of the criteria for inclusion in the futures arena: that the underlying commodity be deliverable. This contract is available for trade on the New York Board of Trade (NYBOT). The NYBOT includes two versions of the FCOJ contract: one that tracks the Florida/Brazil oranges (FCOJ-A) and another one based on global production (FCOJ-B). Here are the contract specs for both:

	FCOJ-A (Florida/Brazil)	*FCOJ-B (World)*
Ticker symbol	OJ	OB
Contract size	15,000 pounds	15,000 pounds
Underlying commodity	FCOJ from Brazil and/or Florida only	FCOJ from any producing country
Price fluctuation	$0.0005/pound ($7.50 per contract)	$0.0005/pound ($7.50 per contract)
Trading months	January, March, May, July, September, November	January, March, May, July, September, November

The production of oranges is very sensitive to weather. The hurricane season common in the Florida region, for example, can have a significant impact on the prices of oranges both on the spot market and in the futures market. Make sure to take into consideration weather and seasonality when investing in FCOJ futures.

Trading Ags: Corn, Wheat, and Soybeans

The major agricultural commodities that trade in the futures markets, sometimes simply known as *ags,* are a unique component of the broader commodities markets. They are very labor intensive and are subject to volatility because of underlying market fundamentals. However, they also present solid investment opportunities.

For additional information on agricultural commodities in general, check out the following resources: National Grain and Feed Association (www.ngfa.org), U.S. Department of Agriculture (USDA) (www.usda.gov), USDA National Agriculture Library (www.nal.usda.gov), and USDA National Agricultural Statistics Service (www.nass.usda.gov).

Fields of dreams: Corn

Corn is definitely big business. In 2006, world corn production stood at almost 700 million metric tons. Approximately 35 million hectares of land are used exclusively for the production of corn worldwide, a business that the U.S. Department of Agriculture values at over $20 billion a year.

The most direct way of investing in corn is by going through the futures markets. A corn contract exists, courtesy of the Chicago Board of Trade (CBOT), to help farmers, consumers, and investors manage and profit from the underlying market opportunities. Here are the contract specs:

- ✔ **Contract ticker symbol:** C
- ✔ **Electronic ticker:** ZC
- ✔ **Contract size:** 5,000 bushels
- ✔ **Underlying commodity:** High grade No. 2 or No. 3 yellow corn
- ✔ **Price fluctuation:** $0.0025/bushel ($12.50 per contract)
- ✔ **Trading hours:** 9:05 a.m. to 1:00 p.m. open outcry; 6:30 p.m. to 6:00 a.m. electronic (Chicago Time)
- ✔ **Trading months:** March, May, July, September, December

Both high-grade number 2 and number 3 yellow corn are traded in the futures markets. In addition, corn futures contracts are usually measured in bushels. Large scale corn production and consumption is generally measured in metric tons.

Historically, the United States has dominated the corn markets, and still does due to abundant land and helpful governmental subsidies. China is also a major player and exhibits a lot of potential for being a market leader in the coming years. Other notable producers include Brazil, Mexico, Argentina, and France, listed in Table 6-5.

Table 6-5	Top Corn Producers, 2006 Figures
Country	*Production (Tons)*
United States	282,300,000
China	139,400,000
Brazil	41,700,000
Mexico	19,500,000
Argentina	15,800,000
France	13,200,000

Source: U.S. Department of Agriculture

Like other agricultural commodities, corn is subject to seasonal and cyclical factors that have a direct, and often powerful, effect on prices. Prices for corn can go through roller coaster rides, with wild swings in short periods of time.

 For more information on the corn markets, check out the following sources: National Corn Growers Association (www.ncga.com), Corn Refiners Association (www.corn.org), and USDA Economic Research Service (www.ers.usda.gov/briefing/corn).

The bread basket: Wheat

Wheat is the second most widely produced agricultural commodity in the world (on a per volume basis), right behind corn and ahead of rice. World wheat production was more than 600 million metric tons in 2006, according to the USDA.

Unlike other commodities that are dominated by single producers — Saudi Arabia and oil, the Ivory Coast and cocoa, Russia and palladium — no one country dominates wheat production. As a matter of fact, as you can see from Table 6-6, the major wheat producers are a surprisingly eclectic group. The advanced developing countries of China and India are the two largest producers, while industrial countries like Canada and Germany also boast significant wheat production capabilities.

Table 6-6	Top Wheat Producers, 2006 Figures
Country	**Production (Thousand Tons)**
China	97,500
India	68,000
United States	50,970
Russia	42,000
France	36,500
Canada	26,000

Source: U.S. Department of Agriculture

Book IV

Commodities

Wheat is measured in bushels for investment and accounting purposes. Each bushel contains approximately 60 pounds of wheat. As with most other agricultural commodities, metric tons are used to quantify total production and consumption figures on a national and international basis.

The most direct way of accessing the wheat markets, short of owning a wheat farm, is by trading the wheat futures contract. The Chicago Board of Trade (CBOT) offers a futures contract for those interested in capturing profits from wheat price movements — whether for hedging or speculative purposes. Here are the specs for the CBOT futures contract:

- ✔ **Contract ticker symbol:** W

- ✔ **Electronic ticker:** ZW

- ✔ **Contract size:** 5,000 bushels

- ✔ **Underlying commodity:** Premium wheat

- ✔ **Price fluctuation:** $0.0025/bushel ($12.50 per contract)

- ✔ **Trading hours:** 9:30 a.m. to 1:15 p.m. open outcry; 6:32 p.m. to 6:00 a.m. electronic (Chicago Time)

- ✔ **Trading months:** March, May, July, September, December

Wheat production, like that of corn and soybeans, is a seasonal enterprise subject to various output disruptions. For instance, Kazakhstan, an important producer, has faced issues with wheat production in the past due to underinvestment in machinery and the misuse of fertilizers. This mismanagement of resources has an impact on the acreage yield, which in turn impacts prices. Such supply side disruptions can have a magnified effect on futures prices.

To find out more about the wheat market, check out these sources: Wheat Foods Council (www.wheatfoods.org), National Association of Wheat Growers (www.wheatworld.org), and U.S. Wheat Associates (www.uswheat.org).

Masters of Versatility: Soybeans

Soybeans are a vital crop for the world economy, used for everything from poultry feedstock to the creation of vegetable oil. You can trade soybeans themselves, soybean oil, and soybean meal.

To get more background information on the soybean industry, check out these resources: American Soybean Association (www.soygrowers.org), Iowa Soybean Association (www.iasoybeans.com), Soy Stats Reference Guide (www.soystats.com), and Soy Protein Council (www.spcouncil.org).

Soybeans

Although most soybeans are used for the extraction of soybean oil (used as vegetable oil for culinary purposes) and soybean meal (used primarily as an agricultural feedstock), whole soybeans are also a tradable commodity. Soybeans are edible, and if you've ever gone to a sushi restaurant you may have been offered soybeans as appetizers, under the Japanese name *edamame*.

The United States dominates the soybean market, accounting for more than 50 percent of total global production. Brazil is a distant second, with about 20 percent of the market. The crop in the United States begins in September, and the production of soybeans is cyclical.

The most direct way for you to trade soybeans is through the Chicago Board of Trade (CBOT) soybean futures contract:

- **Contract ticker symbol:** S
- **Electronic ticker:** ZS
- **Contract size:** 5,000 bushels
- **Underlying commodity:** Premium No. 1, No. 2, and No. 3 yellow soybean bushels
- **Price fluctuation:** $0.0025/bushel ($12.50 per contract)
- **Trading hours:** 9:30 a.m. to 1:15 p.m. open outcry; 6:31 p.m. to 6:00 a.m. electronic (Chicago Time)
- **Trading months:** January, March, May, July, August, September, November

Soybean oil

Soybean oil, more commonly known as vegetable oil, is an extract of soybeans. Soybean oil is the most widely used culinary oil in the United States and around the world, partly because of its healthy, nutritional characteristics. Soybean oil is also becoming an increasingly popular additive in alternative energy sources technology, such as biodiesel. An increasing number of cars in the United States and abroad, for example, are being outfitted with engines that allow them to convert from regular diesel to soybean oil during operation.

Demand for soybean oil has increased in recent years as demand for these cleaner-burning fuels increases and as the automotive technology is more able to accommodate the usage of such biodiesels. According to the Commodity Research Bureau (CRB), production of soybean oil increased from an average of 15 billion pounds in the mid-1990s to more than 22 billion pounds in 2003.

If you want to trade soybean oil, you need to go through the Chicago Board of Trade (CBOT), which offers the standard soybean oil contract. Here is the contract information:

- **Contract ticker symbol:** BO
- **Electronic ticker:** ZL
- **Contract size:** 60,000 pounds
- **Underlying commodity:** Premium crude soybean oil
- **Price fluctuation:** $0.0001/pound ($6.00 per contract)
- **Trading hours:** 9:30 a.m. to 1:15 p.m. open outcry, 6:31 p.m. to 6:00 a.m. electronic (Chicago Time)
- **Trading months:** January, March, May, July, August, September, October, December

For more info, take a look at the National Oilseed Processors Association, an industry group (www.nopa.org).

Soybean meal

Soybean meal is another extract of soybeans. Soybean meal is a high protein, high energy-content food used primarily as a feedstock for cattle, hogs, and poultry.

To invest in soybean meal, you can trade the soybean meal futures contract on the Chicago Board of Trade (CBOT). Here is the information to help you get started trading this contract:

- **Contract ticker symbol:** SM
- **Electronic ticker:** ZM
- **Contract size:** 100 tons
- **Underlying commodity:** 48% protein soybean meal
- **Price fluctuation:** $0.10/ton ($10.00 per contract)
- **Trading hours:** 9:30 a.m. to 1:15 p.m. open outcry; 6:31 p.m. to 6:00 a.m. electronic (Chicago Time)
- **Trading months:** January, March, May, July, August, September, October, December

You can get more information regarding soybean meal from the Soybean Meal Information Center (www.soymeal.org).

Making Money Trading Livestock

Like the tropical and grain commodities, livestock is a unique category in the agricultural commodities sub-asset class. It's not a widely followed area of the commodities markets — unlike crude oil, for example, you're not likely to see feeder cattle prices quoted on the nightly news — but this doesn't mean you should ignore this area of the markets. That said, raising livestock is a time-consuming and labor-intensive undertaking, and the markets are susceptible and sensitive to minor disruption. This section covers the markets for cattle (both live cattle and feeder cattle), lean hogs, and frozen pork bellies.

Even by agricultural futures standards, livestock futures are notoriously volatile and should be traded only by traders with a high level of risk tolerance. Keep in mind that trading agricultural futures requires an understanding of the cyclicality and seasonality of the underlying commodity as well as large capital reserves to help offset any margin calls that may arise from a trade gone bad. If your risk tolerance is not elevated or you are not comfortable in the futures arena, then I recommend you don't trade these contracts because you could be setting yourself up for disastrous losses. Venture into this area of the market only if you have an iron-clad grasp on the concepts behind futures trading — and a high tolerance for risk.

One resource that provides fundamental data relating to the consumption and production patterns of pork bellies, livestock, and other commodities is the *CRB Commodity Yearbook,* compiled by the Commodity Research Bureau (www.crbtrader.com). This book includes a large number of data on some of the most important commodities, including the identification of seasonal and cyclical patterns affecting the markets.

Staking a claim on cattle

Throughout the ages, cows have been valued not only for their dietary value, but also their monetary worth. Cows are literally a special breed because they are low maintenance animals with high products output: They eat almost nothing but grass yet they are used to produce milk, provide meat, and, in some cases, create leather goods. This input to output ratio means that cows occupy a special place in the agricultural complex.

Two futures contracts exist for the cattle trader and investor: the live cattle and the feeder cattle contracts, which both trade on the Chicago Mercantile Exchange (CME).

Book IV

Commodities

Live cattle

The live cattle futures contract is widely traded by various market players, including cattle producers, packers, consumers, and independent traders. Here are the specs of this futures contract:

- ✔ **Contract ticker symbol:** LC
- ✔ **Electronic ticker:** LE
- ✔ **Contract size:** 40,000 pounds
- ✔ **Underlying commodity:** Live cattle
- ✔ **Price fluctuation:** $0.00025/pound ($10.00 per contract)
- ✔ **Trading hours:** 9:05 a.m. to 1:00 p.m. (Chicago Time), electronic and open outcry
- ✔ **Trading months:** February, April, June, August, October, December

One of the reasons for the popularity of the live cattle contract is that it allows all interested parties to hedge their market positions in order to reduce the volatility and uncertainty associated with livestock production in general, and live cattle growing in particular.

If you do trade this contract, keep the following market risks in mind: seasonality, fluctuating prices of feedstock, transportation costs, changing consumer demand, and the threat of diseases (such as mad cow disease).

Feeder cattle

The feeder cattle contract is for calves that weigh in at the 650- to 849-pound range, which are sent to the feedlots to get fed, fattened, and then slaughtered.

Because the CME feeder cattle futures contract is settled on a cash basis, the CME calculates an index for feeder cattle cash prices based on a seven-day average. This index, known in the industry as the *CME Feeder Cattle Index,* is an average of feeder cattle prices from the largest feeder cattle producing states in the United States, as compiled by the U.S. Department of Agriculture (USDA). You can get information on the CME Feeder Cattle Index through the CME Web site at www.cme.com.

To get livestock statistical information, you should check out the U.S. Department of Agriculture's statistical division. Its Web site is www.market news.usda.gov/portal/lg.

Here are the specs of this futures contract:

- ✔ **Contract ticker symbol:** FC
- ✔ **Electronic ticker:** GF
- ✔ **Contract size:** 50,000 pounds
- ✔ **Underlying commodity:** Feeder cattle
- ✔ **Price fluctuation:** $0.00025/pound ($12.50 per contract)
- ✔ **Trading hours:** 9:05 a.m. to 1:00 p.m. (Chicago Time), electronic and open outcry
- ✔ **Trading months:** January, March, April, May, August, September, October, November

Seeking fat profits on lean hogs

The lean hog futures contract (which is a contract for the hog's carcass) trades on the Chicago Mercantile Exchange (CME) and is used primarily by producers of lean hogs — both domestic and international — and pork importers/exporters. Here are the contract specs for lean hogs:

- ✔ **Contract ticker symbol:** LH
- ✔ **Electronic ticker:** HE
- ✔ **Contract size:** 40,000 pounds
- ✔ **Underlying commodity:** Lean hogs
- ✔ **Price fluctuation:** $0.0001 per hundred pounds ($4.00 per contract)
- ✔ **Trading hours:** 9:10 a.m. to 1:00 p.m. (Chicago Time), electronic and open outcry
- ✔ **Trading months:** February, April, May, June, July, August, October, December

Perhaps no other commodity, agricultural or otherwise, exhibits the same level of volatility as the lean hogs futures contract (see Figure 6-1). One of the reasons is that, compared to other products, this contract is not very liquid because it is primarily used by commercial entities seeking to hedge against price risk. Other commodities, say, crude oil, that are actively traded by individual speculators as well the commercial entities are far more liquid and thus less volatile. If you are intent on trading this contract, keep in mind that you're up against some very experienced and large players in this market.

Figure 6-1:
The price of
lean hogs
futures on
the CME
from 1997 to
2006.

Warming up to frozen pork bellies

Essentially, the term *pork bellies* is the traders' way of saying "bacon."
Physically, pork bellies come from the underside of a hog and weigh approximately 12 pounds. These pork bellies are generally stored frozen for
extended periods of time, pending delivery to consumers.

As with most other livestock products, the Chicago Mercantile Exchange
offers a futures contract for frozen pork bellies. Here are the specs for the
CME frozen pork bellies futures contract:

- ✔ **Contract ticker symbol:** PB

- ✔ **Electronic ticker:** GPB

- ✔ **Contract size:** 40,000 pounds

- ✔ **Underlying commodity:** Pork bellies, cut and trimmed

- ✔ **Price fluctuation:** $0.0001/ pound ($4.00 per contract)

- ✔ **Trading hours:** 9:10 a.m. to 1:00 p.m. (Chicago Time), electronic and
  open outcry

- ✔ **Trading months:** February, March, May, July, August

The pork bellies market is a seasonal market subject to wild price fluctuations. Although production of pork bellies is a major determining factor of market prices, other variables also have a significant impact on prices. A buildup in pork belly inventories usually takes place in the beginning of the calendar year, resulting in lower prices. But as inventories are depleted, the market moves to a supply side bias, thereby placing upward pressure on market prices. On the other side of the equation, consumer demand for bacon and other meats is not easily predictable and fluctuates with the seasons. Because of the cyclicality of the supply side model, coupled with the seasonality of the demand model, pork belly prices are subject to extreme volatility. As a matter of fact, the pork bellies futures contract is one of the more volatile contracts trading in the market today.

Book V
Foreign Currency Trading

The 5th Wave   By Rich Tennant

Looks like another new exotic investment strategy to me.

In this book . . .

The foreign exchange *(forex)* market was once the private domain of hedge funds, global banks, multinational corporations, and wealthy private investors. But this all changed a few years ago when the revolution of online trading spread to the forex markets. Today, tens of thousands of individual traders and investors all over the world are discovering the excitement and challenges of trading in the forex market.

No question about it, forex markets can be one of the fastest and most volatile financial markets to trade. Money can be made or lost in a matter of seconds or minutes. At the same time, currencies can display significant trends lasting several days to weeks and even years. This book shows you how the forex market really works, what moves it, and how you can actively trade it. It also provides the tools you need to develop the structured game plan required for trading in the forex market without losing your shirt.

Chapter 1

Your Forex Need-to-Know Guide

In This Chapter

▶ Understanding currency trading and the forex market

▶ Recognizing what impacts currency rates

▶ Identifying key participants

▶ Tracking markets as they open and close during a trading day

*T*he foreign exchange (*forex*) market has exploded onto the scene and is the hot new financial market. It's been around for years, but advances in electronic trading have made it available to individual traders on a scale unimaginable just a few years ago. Because it's relatively new, a lot of people are still in the dark when it comes to exactly what the currency market is: how it's organized, who's trading it, and what a trading day looks like when the market never closes. This chapter sheds a bit of light on these topics.

What Is Currency Trading?

Currency trading is speculation, pure and simple. The securities you're speculating with are the currencies of various countries. For that reason, currency trading is both about the dynamics of market speculation, or trading, and the factors that affect the value of currencies. Put them together and you've got the largest, most dynamic, and most exciting financial market in the world.

Speculating is all about taking on financial risk in the hope of making a profit. But it's not gambling (playing with money even when you know the odds are stacked against you) or investing (minimizing risk and maximizing return, usually over a long time period). Speculating, or active trading, is about taking calculated financial risks to attempt to realize a profitable return, usually over a very short time horizon.

The forex market is the largest financial market in the world, at least in terms of daily trading volumes. To be sure, the forex market is unique in many respects:

- ✔ Because the volumes are huge, liquidity is ever present.

- ✔ The forex market operates around the clock six days a week, giving traders access to the market any time they need it.

- ✔ Few trading restrictions exist — no daily trading limits up or down, no restrictions on position sizes, and no requirements on selling a currency pair short.

- ✔ There are anywhere from 15 to 20 different currency pairs — pitting the U.S. dollar (USD) against other countries' currencies or pitting two non-USD currencies against each other — depending on which forex brokerage you deal with. Chapter 2 discusses these pairs in detail.

- ✔ Most individual traders trade currencies via the Internet through a brokerage firm. Online currency trading is typically done on a margin basis, which allows individual traders to trade in larger amounts by leveraging the amount of margin on deposit.

- ✔ The *leverage,* or margin trading ratios, can be very high, sometimes as much as 200:1 or greater, meaning a margin deposit of $1,000 could control a position size of $200,000. But trading on margin carries its own rules and requirements and is the backdrop against which all your trading will take place. See Chapter 4 for details.

Risk management is the key to any successful trading plan. Without a risk-aware strategy, margin trading can be an extremely short-lived endeavor. With a proper risk plan in place, you stand a much better chance of surviving losing trades and making winning ones. You can find information on risk management in Chapter 4.

The Foreign Currency Market

Often called the *forex market* (or FX market), the foreign exchange market is the largest and most liquid of all international financial markets. It's the crossroads for international capital, the intersection through which global commercial and investment flows have to move. International trade flows, such as when a Swiss electronics company purchases Japanese-made components, were the original basis for the development of the forex markets.

Today, however, global financial and investment flows dominate trade as the primary nonspeculative source of forex market volume. Whether it's an Australian pension fund investing in U.S. Treasury bonds, or a British insurer allocating assets to the Japanese equity market, or a German conglomerate purchasing a Canadian manufacturing facility, each cross-border transaction passes through the forex market at some stage.

Firms such as FOREX.com, Saxo Bank, and MF Global have made the forex market accessible to individual traders and investors. You can now trade the same forex market as the big banks and hedge funds.

Entering the interbank market

When people talk about the "currency market," they're referring to the *interbank market,* whether they realize it or not. The interbank market is where the really big money changes hands. Minimum trade sizes are one million of the base currency, such as €1 million of EUR/USD or $1 million of USD/JPY. Much larger trades of between $10 million and $100 million are routine and can go through the market in a matter of seconds. Even larger trades and orders are a regular feature of the market. For the individual trading FX online, the prices you see on your trading platform are based on the prices being traded in the interbank market.

As the prefix suggests, the *interbank* market is "between banks," with each trade representing an agreement between the banks to exchange the agreed amounts of currency at the specified rate on a fixed date. The interbank market is alternately referred to as the *cash market* or the *spot market* to differentiate it from the currency futures market, which is the only other organized market for currency trading.

Currency futures markets operate alongside the interbank market, but they are definitely the tail being wagged by the dog of the spot market. As a market, currency futures are generally limited by exchange-based trading hours and lower liquidity than is available in the spot market.

The interbank market developed without any significant governmental oversight and remains largely unregulated. In most cases, there is no regulatory authority for spot currency trading apart from local or national banking regulations.

The interbank market is a network of international banks operating in financial centers around the world. Currency trading today is largely concentrated in the hands of about a dozen major global financial firms, such as UBS, Deutsche Bank, Citibank, JPMorgan Chase, Barclays, Goldman Sachs, and Royal Bank of Scotland, to name just a few. Hundreds of other international banks and financial institutions trade alongside the top banks, and all contribute liquidity and market interest.

These banks maintain trading operations to facilitate speculation for their own accounts, called *proprietary trading* (or *prop trading* for short), and to provide currency trading services for their customers. Banks' customers can range from corporations and government agencies to hedge funds and wealthy private individuals.

Trading in the interbank market

The interbank market is an over-the-counter (OTC) market, which means that each trade is an agreement between the two counterparties to the trade. There are no exchanges or guarantors for the trades, just each bank's balance sheet and the promise to make payment.

The bulk of spot trading in the interbank market is transacted through electronic matching services, such as EBS and Reuters Dealing. Electronic matching services allow traders to enter their bids and offers into the market, *hit bids* (sell at the market), and *pay offers* (buy at the market). Price spreads vary by currency pair and change throughout the day depending on market interest and volatility.

The matching systems have prescreened credit limits, and a bank will only see prices available to it from approved counterparties. Pricing is anonymous before a deal, meaning you can't tell which bank is offering or bidding, but the counterparties' names are made known immediately after a deal goes through.

The rest of interbank trading is done through currency brokers, referred to as *voice brokers* to differentiate them from the electronic ones. Traders can place bids and offers with these brokers the same as they do with the electronic matching services. Prior to the electronic matching services, voice brokers were the primary market intermediaries between the banks.

Introducing currency pairs

Forex markets refer to trading currencies by pairs, with names that combine the two different currencies being traded against each other, or exchanged for one another. Additionally, forex markets have given most currency pairs nicknames or abbreviations, which reference the pair and not necessarily the individual currencies involved. The following sections give you a brief overview of the currency pairs; go to Chapter 2 for in-depth information.

The bulk of spot currency trading, about 75 percent by volume, takes place in the so-called major currencies. Trading in the major currencies is largely free from government regulation and takes place outside the authority of any national or international body. Trading in the currencies of smaller, less-developed economies, such as Thailand or Chile, is often referred to as *emerging-market* or *exotic* currency trading, and may involve currencies with local restrictions on convertibility or limited liquidity, both of which limit access and inhibit the development of an active market.

Major currency pairs

The major currency pairs all involve the U.S. dollar on one side of the deal. The designations of the major currencies are expressed using International Standardization Organization (ISO) codes for each currency. Table 1-1 lists the most frequently traded currency pairs, what they're called in conventional terms, and what nicknames the market has given them.

Table 1-1	The Major U.S. Dollar Currency Pairs		
ISO Currency Pair	*Countries*	*Long Name*	*Nickname*
EUR/USD	Eurozone*/ United States	Euro-dollar	N/A
USD/JPY	United States/ Japan	Dollar-yen	N/A
GBP/USD	United Kingdom/ United States	Sterling-dollar	Sterling or Cable
USD/CHF	United States/ Switzerland	Dollar-Swiss	Swissy
USD/CAD	United States/ Canada	Dollar-Canada	Loonie
AUD/USD	Australia/ United States	Australian-dollar	Aussie or Oz
NZD/USD	New Zealand/ United States	New Zealand-dollar	Kiwi

* The Eurozone is made up of all the countries in the European Union that have adopted the euro as their currency. As of this printing, the Eurozone countries are Austria, Belgium, Finland, France, Germany, Greece, Ireland, Italy, Luxembourg, the Netherlands, Portugal, Slovenia, and Spain.

Currency names and nicknames can be confusing when you're following the forex market or reading commentary and research. Be sure you understand whether the writer or analyst is referring to the individual currency or the currency pair.

✔ If a bank or a brokerage is putting out research suggesting that the Swiss franc will weaken in the future, the comment refers to the *individual* currency, in this case CHF, suggesting that USD/CHF will move *higher* (USD stronger/CHF weaker).

✔ If the comment suggests that Swissy is likely to weaken going forward, it's referring to the currency *pair* and amounts to a forecast that USD/CHF will move *lower* (USD weaker/CHF stronger).

Cross-currency pairs

A cross-currency pair (*cross* or *crosses* for short) is any currency pair that does not include the U.S. dollar. Cross rates are derived from the respective USD pairs but are quoted independently and usually with a narrower spread than you could get by trading in the dollar pairs directly. (The *spread* refers to the difference between the bid and offer, or the price at which you can sell and buy. Spreads are applied in most financial markets.)

Cross trades can be especially effective when major cross-border mergers and acquisitions (M&A) are announced. If a UK conglomerate is buying a Canadian utility company, the UK company is going to need to sell GBP and buy CAD to fund the purchase. The key to trading on M&A activity is to note the cash portion of the deal. If the deal is all stock, you don't need to exchange currencies to come up with the foreign cash.

The most actively traded crosses focus on the three major non-USD currencies (EUR, JPY, and GBP) and are referred to as *euro crosses, yen crosses,* and *sterling crosses.* The remaining currencies (CHF, AUD, CAD, and NZD) are also traded in cross pairs. Tables 1-2, 1-3, and 1-4 highlight the key cross pairs in the euro, yen, and sterling groupings, respectively, along with their market names. (Nicknames never quite caught on for the crosses.) Table 1-5 lists other cross-currency pairs.

Table 1-2	Euro Crosses	
ISO Currency Pair	*Countries*	*Market Name*
EUR/CHF	Eurozone/Switzerland	Euro-Swiss
EUR/GBP	Eurozone/United Kingdom	Euro-sterling
EUR/CAD	Eurozone/Canada	Euro-Canada
EUR/AUD	Eurozone/Australia	Euro-Aussie
EUR/NZD	Eurozone/New Zealand	Euro-Kiwi

Table 1-3	Yen Crosses	
ISO Currency Pair	*Countries*	*Market Name*
EUR/JPY	Eurozone/Japan	Euro-yen
GBP/JPY	United Kingdom/Japan	Sterling-yen
CHF/JPY	Switzerland/Japan	Swiss-yen
AUD/JPY	Australia/Japan	Aussie-yen
NZD/JPY	New Zealand/Japan	Kiwi-yen
CAD/JPY	Canada/Japan	Canada-yen

Table 1-4	Sterling Crosses	
ISO Currency Pair	*Countries*	*Market Name*
GBP/CHF	United Kingdom/ Switzerland	Sterling-Swiss
GBP/CAD	United Kingdom/Canada	Sterling-Canadian
GBP/AUD	United Kingdom/ Australia	Sterling-Aussie
GBP/NZD	United Kingdom/ New Zealand	Sterling-Kiwi

Table 1-5	Other Crosses	
ISO Currency Pair	*Countries*	*Market Name*
AUD/CHF	Australia/Switzerland	Aussie-Swiss
AUD/CAD	Australia/Canada	Aussie-Canada
AUD/NZD	Australia/New Zealand	Aussie-Kiwi
CAD/CHF	Canada/Switzerland	Canada-Swiss

Identifying base and counter currencies

When you look at currency pairs, you may notice that the currencies are combined in a seemingly strange order. For instance, if sterling-yen (GBP/JPY) is a yen cross, why isn't it referred to as "yen-sterling" and written "JPY/GBP"? The answer is that these quoting conventions evolved over the years to reflect traditionally strong currencies versus traditionally weak currencies, with the strong currency coming first.

It also reflects the market quoting convention where the first currency in the pair is known as the *base currency.* The base currency is what you're buying or selling when you buy or sell the pair. It's also the *notional,* or *face,* amount of the trade. So if you buy 100,000 EUR/JPY, you've just bought 100,000 euros and sold the equivalent amount in Japanese yen. If you sell 100,000 GBP/CHF, you just sold 100,000 British pounds and bought the equivalent amount of Swiss francs.

The second currency in the pair is called the *counter currency,* or the *secondary currency.* Hey, who said this stuff isn't intuitive? Most important for you as an FX trader, the counter currency is the denomination of the price fluctuations and, ultimately, what your profit and losses will be denominated in. If you buy GBP/JPY, it goes up, and you take a profit, your gains are not in pounds but in yen.

Getting Inside the Numbers

Average daily currency trading volumes exceed $2 trillion per day — a mind-boggling number and a lot of zeros ($2,000,000,000,000) no matter how you slice it. To give you some perspective on that size, it's about 10 to 15 times the size of daily trading volume on all the world's stock markets *combined.* That $2-trillion-a-day number, which you may have seen in the financial press or other books on currency trading, actually overstates the size of what the forex market is all about: spot currency trading.

What affects currency rates?

Information drives every financial market, but the forex market has its own unique roster of information inputs. Many different cross-currents are at play in the currency market at any given moment. After all, the forex market is setting the value of one currency relative to another, so at the minimum, you're looking at the things affecting two major international economies. Add in half a dozen or more other national economies, and you've got a serious amount of information flowing through the market.

Fundamentals

Fundamentals, outlined in Chapter 3, are the broad grouping of news and information that reflect the macroeconomic and political fortunes of the countries whose currencies are traded. Most of the time, when you hear someone talking about the fundamentals of a currency, he's referring to the economic fundamentals, which are based on economic data reports, interest rate levels, monetary policy, international trade flows, and international investment flows.

There are also political and geopolitical fundamentals. An essential element of any currency's value is the faith or confidence that the market places in the value of the currency. If political events, such as an election or scandal, are seen to be undermining the confidence in a nation's leadership, the value of its currency may be negatively affected.

Gathering and interpreting all this information is just part of a currency trader's daily routine.

Technicals

The term *technicals* refers to *technical analysis,* a form of market analysis most commonly involving chart analysis, trend-line analysis, and mathematical studies of price behavior, such as momentum or moving averages, to mention just a couple. We don't know of too many currency traders who don't follow some form of technical analysis in their trading. If you've been an active trader in other financial markets, chances are you've engaged in some technical analysis or at least heard of it.

If you're not aware of technical analysis but you want to trade actively, we strongly recommend that you familiarize yourself with some of its basics (see Book VIII).

Technical analysis is especially important in the forex market because of the amount of fundamental information hitting the market at any given time. Currency traders regularly apply various forms of technical analysis to define and refine their trading strategies, with many people trading based on technical indicators alone. (See Chapter 6 for how traders really use technicals.)

Something else

Many cross-currents are at play in the forex market at any given time. That means that in addition to understanding the currency-specific fundamentals, and familiarizing yourself with technical analysis, you also need to have an appreciation of the market dynamics (see Chapter 4).

Book V

Foreign Currency Trading

Liquidity in the currency market

The vast majority of currency trading volume is based on speculation: traders buying and selling for short-term gains based on minute-to-minute, hour-to-hour, and day-to-day price fluctuations. The depth and breadth of the speculative market means that the liquidity of the overall forex market is unparalleled among global financial markets.

From a trading perspective, liquidity is a critical consideration because it determines how quickly prices move between trades and over time. A highly liquid market like forex can see large trading volumes transacted with relatively minor price changes. An illiquid, or *thin,* market will tend to see prices move more rapidly on relatively lower trading volumes. A market that trades only during certain hours (futures contracts, for example) also represents a less liquid, thinner market. Liquidity, liquidity considerations, and market interest are among the most important factors affecting how prices move, or *price action.*

Although the forex market offers exceptionally high liquidity on an overall basis, liquidity levels vary throughout the trading day and across various currency pairs. For individual traders, variations in liquidity are more of a strategic consideration than a tactical issue. For example, if a large hedge fund needs to make a trade worth several hundred million dollars, it needs to be concerned about the tactical levels of liquidity, such as how much its trade is likely to move market prices depending on when the trade is executed. For individuals, who generally trade in smaller sizes, the amounts are not an issue, but the strategic levels of liquidity are an important factor in the timing of when and how prices are likely to move.

Key Players

Participants in the forex market generally fall into one of two categories: financial transactors and speculators. *Financial transactors,* including hedgers and financial investors, are active in the forex market as part of their overall business but not necessarily for currency reasons. (Don't confuse hedgers with *hedge funds.* Despite the name, a hedge fund is typically 100 percent speculative in its investments; go to Book VI for details on hedge funds.)

Financial transactors are important to the forex market for several reasons:

- ✔ Their transactions can be extremely sizeable, typically hundreds of million or billions.
- ✔ Their deals are frequently one-time events.
- ✔ They are generally not price sensitive or profit maximizing.

Speculators — hedge funds and day traders — are in it purely for the money. In contrast to hedgers, who enter the market to neutralize or reduce risk and have some form of existing currency market risk, speculators have no currency risk until they enter the market, and they embrace risk-taking as a means of profiting from long-term or short-term price movements.

The lion's share of forex market turnover — upwards of 90 percent — comes from speculators (*specs* for short), who are the ones that really make a market efficient. They add liquidity to the market by infusing it with their views and, more important, their capital. That liquidity is what smoothes out price movements, keeps trading spreads narrow, and allows a market to expand.

The following sections look at all these main players.

Hedgers

Hedging is about eliminating or reducing risk. In financial markets, hedging refers to a transaction designed to insure against an adverse price move in some underlying asset. In the forex market, hedgers are looking to insure themselves against an adverse price movement in a specific currency rate.

Say, for example, that you're a widget maker in Germany and you just won a large order from a UK-based manufacturer to supply it with a large quantity of widgets. To make your bid more attractive, you agreed to be paid in British pounds (GBP). But because your production cost base is denominated in euros (EUR), you face the exchange rate risk that GBP will weaken against the EUR, which would make the amount of GBP in the contract worth fewer EUR back home, reducing or even eliminating your profit margin on the deal. To insure, or *hedge,* against that possibility, you would seek to sell GBP against EUR in the forex market. If the pound weakens against the euro, the value of your market hedge will rise, compensating you for the lower value of the GBP you'll receive. If the pound strengthens against the euro, your loss on the hedge is offset by gains in the currency conversions. (Each pound would be worth more euros.)

Financial investors

Financial investors are the other main group of nonspeculative players in the forex market. As far as the forex market is concerned, financial investors are mostly just passing through on their way to other investments. More often than not, financial investors look at currencies as an afterthought because they're more focused on the ultimate investment target, be it Japanese equities, German government bonds, or French real estate.

When a company seeks to buy a foreign business, there can be a substantial foreign exchange implication from the trade. When large merge and acquisitions (M&A) deals are announced, note the answers to the following two questions:

- ✔ **Which countries and which currencies are involved?** If a French electrical utility buys an Austrian power company, there are no currency implications because both countries use the euro (EUR). But if a Swiss pharmaceutical company announces a takeover of a Dutch chemical firm, the Swiss company may need to buy EUR and sell Swiss francs (CHF) to pay for the deal.

- ✔ **How much of the transaction will be in cash?** Again, if it's an all stock deal, there are no forex market implications. But if the cash portion is large, forex markets will take note and begin to speculate on the currency pair involved.

Hedge funds

Hedge funds are a type of *leveraged fund,* which refers to any number of different forms of speculative asset management funds that borrow money for speculation based on real assets under management. For instance, hedge funds with $100 million under management can *leverage* those assets (through margin agreements with their trading counterparties) to give them trading limits of anywhere from $500 million to $2 billion. Hedge funds are subject to the same type of margin requirements as you are, just with a whole lot more zeroes involved.

The other main type of leveraged fund is known as a *commodity trading advisor* (CTA). A CTA is principally active in the futures markets. But because the forex market operates around the clock, CTAs frequently trade spot FX as well.

In the forex market, leveraged funds can hold positions anywhere from a few hours to days or weeks. When you hear that leveraged names are buying or selling, it's an indication of short-term speculative interest that can provide clues as to where prices are going in the near future.

Day-traders, big and small

This is where you fit into the big picture of the forex market. If the vast majority of currency trading volume is speculative in nature, then most of that speculation is short-term in nature. *Short-term* can be minute-to-minute or hour-to-hour, but rarely is it longer than a day or two. From the interbank traders who are scalping EUR/USD (high frequency in-and-out trading for few pips — the smallest price increments in the currency) to the online trader looking for the next move in USD/JPY, short-term day-traders are the backbone of the market.

Intraday trading was always the primary source of interbank market liquidity, providing fluid prices and an outlet for any institutional flows that hit the market. Day-traders tend to be focused on the next 20 to 30 pips in the market, which makes them the source of most short-term price fluctuations.

Around the World in a Trading Day

The forex market is open and active 24 hours a day from the start of business hours on Monday morning in the Asia-Pacific time zone straight through to the Friday close of business hours in New York. At any given moment, depending on the time zone, dozens of global financial centers — such as Sydney, Tokyo, and London — are open, and currency trading desks in those financial centers are active in the market.

In addition to the major global financial centers, many financial institutions operate 24-hour-a-day currency trading desks, providing an ever-present source of market interest. It may be a U.S. hedge fund in Boston that needs to monitor currencies around the clock, or it may be a major international bank with a concentrated global trading operation in one financial center.

Currency trading doesn't even stop for holidays when other financial markets, like stocks or futures exchanges, may be closed. Even though it's a holiday in Japan, for example, Sydney, Singapore, and Hong Kong may still be open. It may be the Fourth of July in the United States, but if it's a business day, Tokyo, London, Toronto, and other financial centers will still be trading currencies. About the only holiday in common around the world is New Year's Day, and even that depends on what day of the week it falls on.

Opening the trading week

There is no officially designated starting time to the trading day or week, but for all intents the market action kicks off when Wellington, New Zealand, the first financial center west of the international dateline, opens on Monday morning local time. Depending on whether daylight saving time is in effect in your own time zone, it roughly corresponds to early Sunday afternoon in North America, Sunday evening in Europe, and very early Monday morning in Asia.

The Sunday open represents the starting point where currency markets resume trading after the Friday close of trading in North America (5 p.m. eastern time [ET]). This is the first chance for the forex market to react to news and events that may have happened over the weekend. Prices may have closed New York trading at one level, but depending on the circumstances, they may start trading at different levels at the Sunday open. The risk that currency prices open at different levels on Sunday versus their close on Friday is referred to as the *weekend gap risk* or the *Sunday open gap risk*. A *gap* is a change in price levels where no prices are tradable in between.

As a strategic trading consideration, you need to be aware of the weekend gap risk and know what events are scheduled over the weekend. There's no fixed set of potential events, and there's never any way of ruling out what may transpire, such as a terror attack, a geopolitical conflict, or a natural disaster. You just need to be aware that the risk exists and factor it into your trading strategy. Of typical scheduled weekend events, the most common are quarterly Group of Seven (G7) meetings and national elections or referenda. Just be sure you're aware of any major events that are scheduled.

On most Sunday opens, prices generally pick up where they left off on Friday afternoon. The opening price spreads in the interbank market will be much wider than normal, because only Wellington and 24-hour trading desks are active at the time. Opening price spreads of 10 to 30 points in the major currency pairs are not uncommon in the initial hours of trading. When banks in Sydney, Australia, and other early Asian centers enter the market over the next few hours, liquidity begins to improve and price spreads begin to narrow to more normal levels.

Because of the wider price spreads in the initial hours of the Sunday open, most online trading platforms do not begin trading until 5 p.m. ET on Sundays, when sufficient liquidity enables the platforms to offer their normal price quotes. Make sure you're aware of your broker's trading policies with regard to the Sunday open, especially in terms of order executions.

Trading in the Asia-Pacific session

The principal financial trading centers in the Asia-Pacific session are Wellington, New Zealand; Sydney, Australia; Tokyo, Japan; Hong Kong; and Singapore. In terms of the most actively traded currency pairs, that means news and data reports from New Zealand, Australia, and Japan are going to be hitting the market during this session. New Zealand and Australian data reports are typically released in the early morning local time, which corresponds to early evening hours in North America. Japanese data is typically released just before 9 a.m. Tokyo time, which equates to roughly 7 or 8 p.m. ET. Some Japanese data reports and events also take place in the Tokyo afternoon, which equates to roughly midnight to 4 a.m. ET.

The overall trading direction for the NZD, AUD, and JPY can be set for the entire session depending on what news and data reports are released and what they indicate. In addition, news from China, such as interest rate changes and official comments or currency policy adjustments, may also be released. Occasionally as well, late speakers from the United States, such as

Federal Reserve officials speaking on the West Coast of the United States, may offer remarks on the U.S. economy or the direction of U.S. interest rates that affect the value of the U.S. dollar against other major currencies.

Because of the size of the Japanese market and the importance of Japanese data to the market, much of the action during the Asia-Pacific session is focused on the Japanese yen currency pairs, such as USD/JPY and the JPY crosses, like EUR/JPY and AUD/JPY. Of course, Japanese financial institutions are also most active during this session, so you can frequently get a sense of what the Japanese market is doing based on price movements.

Trading in the European/London session

About midway through the Asian trading day, European financial centers begin to open up and the market gets into its full swing. The European session overlaps with half of the Asian trading day and half of the North American trading session, which means that market interest and liquidity is at its absolute peak during this session.

News and data events from the Eurozone (and individual countries like Germany and France), Switzerland, and the United Kingdom are typically released in the early-morning hours of the European session. As a result, some of the biggest moves and most active trading take place in the European currencies (EUR, GBP, and CHF) and the euro cross-currency pairs (EUR/CHF and EUR/GBP).

Asian trading centers begin to wind down in the late-morning hours of the European session, and North American financial centers come in a few hours later, around 7 a.m. ET.

Trading in the North American session

Because of the overlap between North American and European trading sessions, the trading volumes are much more significant. Some of the biggest and most meaningful directional price movements take place during this crossover period.

The North American morning is when key U.S. economic data is released and the forex market makes many of its most significant decisions on the value of the U.S. dollar. Most U.S. data reports are released at 8:30 a.m. ET, with others coming out between 9 and 10 a.m. ET. Canadian data reports are also released in the morning, usually between 7 and 9 a.m. ET. There are also a few U.S. economic reports that variously come out at noon or 2 p.m. ET, livening up the New York afternoon market.

London and the European financial centers begin to wind down their daily trading operations around noon eastern time each day. The London close (or *European close,* as it's known) can frequently generate volatile flurries of activity.

On most days, market liquidity and interest fall off significantly in the New York afternoon, which can make for challenging trading conditions. On quiet days, the generally lower market interest typically leads to stagnating price action. On more active days, when prices may have moved more significantly, the lower liquidity can spark additional outsized price movements, as fewer traders scramble to get similarly fewer prices and liquidity. Lower liquidity and the potential for increased volatility are most evident in the least-liquid major-currency pairs, especially USD/CHF and GBP/USD.

North American trading interest and volume generally continue to wind down as the trading day moves toward the 5 p.m. New York close, which also sees the change in value dates take place. (See Chapter 3 for more on rollovers and value dates.) But during the late New York afternoon, Wellington and Sydney have reopened and a new trading day has begun.

Noting key daily times and events

In addition to the ebb and flow of liquidity and market interest during the global currency trading day, you need to be aware of the following daily events, which tend to occur around the same times each day.

Expiring options

Currency options are typically set to expire either at the Tokyo expiry (3 p.m. Tokyo time) or the New York expiry (10 a.m. ET). The New York option expiry is the more significant one, because it tends to capture both European and North American option market interest. When an option expires, the underlying option ceases to exist. Any hedging in the spot market that was done based on the option being alive suddenly needs to be unwound, which can trigger significant price changes in the hours leading up to and just after the option expiry time.

Setting the rate at currency fixings

There are several daily currency fixings in various financial centers, but the two most important are the 8:55 a.m. Tokyo time and the 4 p.m. London time fixings. A *currency fixing* is a set time each day when the prices of currencies for commercial transactions are set, or fixed.

From a trading standpoint, these fixings may see a flurry of trading in a particular currency pair in the run-up (generally 15 to 30 minutes) to the fixing time that abruptly ends exactly at the fixing time. A sharp rally in a specific currency pair on fixing-related buying, for example, may suddenly come to an end at the fixing time and see the price quickly drop back to where it was before.

Squaring up on the currency futures markets

The Chicago Mercantile Exchange (CME), one of the largest futures markets in the world, offers currency futures through its International Monetary Market (IMM) subsidiary exchange. Daily currency futures trading closes each day on the IMM at 2 p.m. central time (CT), which is 3 p.m. ET. Many futures traders like to square up or close any open positions at the end of each trading session to limit their overnight exposure or for margin requirements.

The 30 to 45 minutes leading up to the IMM closing occasionally generate a flurry of activity that spills over into the spot market. Because the amount of liquidity in the spot currency market is at its lowest in the New York afternoon, sharp movements in the futures markets can drive the spot market around this time.

Chapter 2

Major and Minor Currency Pairs

· ·

In This Chapter

▶ Looking at the trading fundamentals of the major currency pairs

▶ Getting to know the small dollar pairs: USD/CAD, AUD/USD, and NZD/USD

▶ Finding opportunities in cross-currency trading

▶ Modifying trading strategies to fit the currency pair

· ·

*T*he vast majority of trading volume takes place in the *major* currency pairs: EUR/USD, USD/JPY, GBP/USD, and USD/CHF. These currency pairs account for about two-thirds of daily trading volume in the market and are the most watched barometers of the overall forex market. When you hear about the dollar rising or falling, it's usually referring to the dollar against these other currencies.

Of course, speculative trading opportunities extend well beyond just the four major *dollar pairs* (currency pairs that include the USD). For starters, three other currency pairs — commonly known as the *minor* or *small* dollar pairs — round out the primary trading pairs that include the USD. Then there are the *cross-currency* pairs, or *crosses* for short, which pit two non-USD currencies against each other.

This chapter takes a closer look at the major and minor dollar pairs and cross-currency pairs to show how they fit into the overall market. You can also find an additional array of speculative trading opportunities. Although the USD is frequently the driving force in the currency market, you're going to want to know where the opportunities are when the spotlight isn't on the greenback.

The Big Dollar: EUR/USD

EUR/USD is by far the most actively traded currency pair in the global forex market. Everyone and his brother, sister, and cousin trades EUR/USD. The same can be said for the big banks. Every major trading desk has at least one, and probably several, EUR/USD traders. All those EUR/USD traders add up to vast amounts of market interest, which increases overall trading liquidity.

EUR/USD is the currency pair that pits the U.S. dollar against the single currency of the Eurozone, the euro. The *Eurozone* refers to a grouping of countries in the European Union (EU); as of this printing, they are Austria, Belgium, Finland, France, Germany, Greece, Ireland, Italy, Luxembourg, the Netherlands, Portugal, Slovenia, and Spain. All together, the Eurozone constitutes a regional economic bloc roughly equal to the United States in both population and total GDP.

Trading fundamentals of EUR/USD

Standard market convention is to quote EUR/USD in terms of the number of USD per EUR. For example, a EUR/USD rate of 1.3000 means that it takes $1.30 to buy €1.

EUR/USD trades inversely to the overall value of the USD, which means when EUR/USD goes up, the euro is getting stronger and the dollar weaker. When EUR/USD goes down, the euro is getting weaker and the dollar stronger. If you believed the U.S. dollar was going to move higher, you'd be looking to sell EUR/USD. If you thought the dollar was going to weaken, you'd be looking to buy EUR/USD.

EUR/USD has the euro as the base currency and the U.S. dollar as the secondary or counter currency. That means

- ✔ **EUR/USD is traded in amounts denominated in euros.** In online currency trading platforms, standard lot sizes are €100,000, and mini lot sizes are €10,000.

- ✔ **The pip value, or minimum price fluctuation, is denominated in USD.**

- ✔ **Profit and loss accrue in USD.** For one standard lot position size, each pip is worth $10; for one mini lot position size, each pip is worth $1.

- ✔ **Margin calculations in online trading platforms are typically based in USD.** At a EUR/USD rate of 1.3000, to trade a one-lot position worth €100,000, it'll take $1,300 in available margin (based on 100:1 leverage). That calculation will change over time, of course, based on the level of the EUR/USD exchange rate. A higher EUR/USD rate will require more USD in available margin collateral, and a lower EUR/USD rate will need less USD in margin.

Having a sense of which currency is driving EUR/USD at any given moment is important so you can better adapt to incoming data and news. If it's a EUR-based move higher, for instance, and surprisingly positive USD news or data is released later in the day, guess what? You've got countertrend information hitting the market, which could spark a reversal lower in EUR/USD (in favor of the dollar). By the same token, if that U.S. data comes out weaker than expected, it's likely to spur further EUR/USD gains, because EUR-buying interest is now combined with USD-selling interest.

Swimming in deep liquidity

Liquidity in EUR/USD is unmatched by other major currency pairs. This is most evident in the narrower trading spreads regularly available in EUR/USD. Normal market spreads are typically around 2 to 3 pips versus 3 to 5 pips in other major currency pairs.

The euro also serves as the primary foil to the U.S. dollar when it comes to speculating on the overall direction of the U.S. dollar in response to U.S. news or economic data. If weak U.S. economic data is reported, traders are typically going to sell the dollar, which begs the question, "Against what?" The euro is the first choice for many, simply because it's there. It also helps that it's the most liquid alternative, allowing for easy entry and exit.

This is not to say that EUR/USD reacts only to U.S. economic data or news. On the contrary, Eurozone news and data can move EUR/USD as much as U.S. data moves the pair. But the overall tendency still favors U.S. data and news as the driving force of short-term price movements.

Watching the data reports

Here's a list of the major European data reports and events to keep an eye on:

- ✔ European Central Bank (ECB) interest rate decisions and press conferences after ECB Central Council meetings
- ✔ Speeches by ECB officials and individual European finance ministers
- ✔ EU-harmonized consumer price index (CPI), as well as national CPI and producer price index (PPI) reports
- ✔ EU Commission economic sector confidence indicators
- ✔ Consumer and investor sentiment surveys separately issued by three private economic research firms known by their acronyms: Ifo, ZEW, and GfK
- ✔ Industrial production
- ✔ Retail sales
- ✔ Unemployment rate

Trading behavior of EUR/USD

The deep liquidity and tight trading spreads in EUR/USD make the pair ideal for both shorter-term and longer-term traders. The price action behavior in EUR/USD regularly exhibits a number of traits you should be aware of.

Trading tick by tick

In normal market conditions, EUR/USD tends to trade tick by tick, as opposed to other currency pairs, which routinely display sharper short-term price movements of several pips. In trading terms, if EUR/USD is trading at 1.2910/13, there are going to be traders looking to sell at 13, 14, and 15 and higher, while buyers are waiting to buy at 9, 8, 7 and lower.

Fewer price jumps and smaller price gaps

The depth of liquidity in EUR/USD also reduces the number of *price jumps* or *price gaps* in short-term trading. A price *jump* refers to a quick movement in prices over a relatively small distance (roughly 10 to 20 pips) in the course of normal trading. A price *gap* means prices have instantaneously adjusted over a larger price distance, typically in response to a news event or data release.

Price jumps/gaps do occur in EUR/USD, as anyone who has traded around data reports or other news events can attest. But price jumps/gaps in EUR/USD tend to be generated primarily by news/data releases and breaks of significant technical levels, events which can usually be identified in advance.

Backing and filling

When it comes to EUR/USD price action, backing and filling, in which prices moving rapidly in one direction tend to reach a short-term stopping point when opposite interest enters the market, is quite common. It tends to be more substantial than in most currency pairs, meaning a greater amount of the directional move is retraced. Look at Figure 2-1 to get a visual idea of what backing and filling looks like. When EUR/USD is not backing and filling the way you would expect, it means the directional move is stronger and with greater interest behind it.

Prolonged tests of technical levels

When it comes to trading around technical support and resistance levels, EUR/USD can try the patience of even the most disciplined traders because EUR/USD can spend tens of minutes (an eternity in forex markets) or even several hours undergoing tests of technical levels. (See Book VIII for a primer on technical analysis.) This goes back to the tremendous amount of interest and liquidity that defines the EUR/USD market. All those viewpoints come together in the form of market interest (bids and offers) when technical levels come into play. The result is a tremendous amount of market interest that has to be absorbed at technical levels, which can take time.

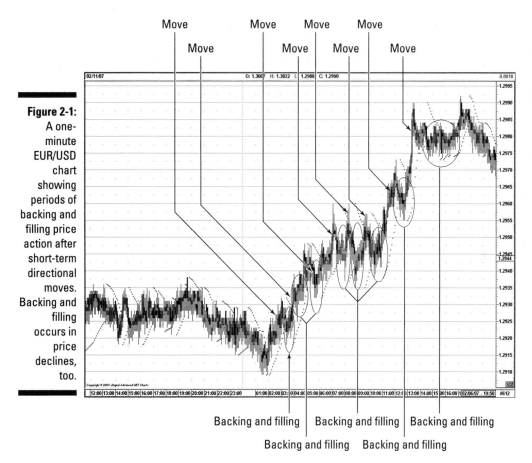

Figure 2-1: A one-minute EUR/USD chart showing periods of backing and filling price action after short-term directional moves. Backing and filling occurs in price declines, too.

Looking at GBP/USD and USD/CHF as leading indicators

Given the tremendous two-way interest in EUR/USD, it can be very difficult to gauge whether a test of a technical level is going to lead to a breakout or a rejection. To get an idea of whether a test of a technical level in EUR/USD is going to lead to a break, professional EUR/USD traders always keep an eye on GBP/USD and USD/CHF, as they tend to be leading indicators for the bigger EUR/USD and dollar moves in general.

If GBP/USD and USD/CHF are aggressively testing (trading at or through the technical level with very little pullback) similar technical levels to EUR/USD (for example, daily highs or equivalent trend-line resistance), then EUR/USD is likely to test that same level. If GBP/USD and USD/CHF break through their technical levels, the chances of EUR/USD following suit increase. By the same token, if GBP/USD and USD/CHF are not aggressively testing the key technical level, EUR/USD is likely to see its similar technical level hold.

GBP/USD and USD/CHF lead times can be anywhere from a few seconds or minutes to several hours and even days. Just make sure you're looking at the equivalent technical levels in each pair.

EUR/USD trading considerations

The preceding sections look at the major trading attributes of EUR/USD. This section looks at how those elements translate into real-life trading tactics. After all, that's where the real money is made and lost.

Being patient in EUR/USD

Earlier in this chapter we explore why EUR/USD can spend hours trading in relatively narrow ranges or testing technical levels. The key in such markets is to remain patient based on your directional view and your technical analysis. You should be able to identify short-term support that keeps an upside test alive or resistance that keeps a down-move going. If those levels fail, the move is stalling at the minimum and may even be reversing.

Taking advantage of backing and filling

Because EUR/USD tends to retrace more of its short-term movements, you can usually enter a position in your desired direction by leaving an order to buy or sell at slightly better rates than current market prices may allow. If the post–08:30 ET U.S. data price action sees EUR/USD move lower, and you think getting short is the way to go, you can leave an offer slightly (roughly 5 to 10 pips) above the current market level and use it to get short, instead of reaching out and hitting the bid on a down-tick.

If your order is executed, you've got your desired position at a better rate than if you went to market, and you're probably in a better position rhythm-wise with the market (having sold on an up-tick). Alternatively, you can take advantage of routine backing and filling by dealing at the market by selling on up-ticks and buying on down-ticks.

Allowing for a margin of error on technical levels

When it comes to determining whether EUR/USD has broken a technical level, use a 10- to 15-pip margin of error. (Shorter-term traders may want to use a smaller margin of error.) Some very short-term traders and technical purists like to pinpoint an exact price level as support or resistance. If the market trades above or below their level, they'll call it a break and that's that. But the spot forex market rarely trades with such respect for technical levels to make such a clear and pinpointed distinction. And given the amount of interest in EUR/USD, it's especially prone to hazy technical lines in the sand.

The key point to take away from this is that all sorts of interest emerges around technical levels, and it's still going through the market even though the pinpointed level may have been breached. And this is where our margin of error comes in. Again, it's not a hard and fast rule, but generally speaking, EUR/USD will have chewed through most of the market interest around a technical level within about 10 to 15 points beyond the level.

East Meets West: USD/JPY

USD/JPY is one of the more challenging currency pairs among the majors. Where other currency pairs typically display routine market fluctuations and relatively steady, active trading interest, USD/JPY seems to have an on/off switch. It can spend hours and even days in relatively narrow ranges and then march off on a mission to a new price level. The key to developing a successful trading game plan in USD/JPY is to understand what drives the pair and the how price action behaves.

Trading fundamentals of USD/JPY

The Japanese yen is the third major international currency after the U.S. dollar and the European single currency, the euro. USD/JPY accounts for 17 percent of daily global trading volume, according to the 2004 Bank for International Settlements (BIS) survey of foreign exchange markets. Japan stands as the second largest national economy after the United States in terms of GDP.

Standard market convention is to quote USD/JPY in terms of the number of JPY per USD. For example, a USD/JPY rate of 115.35 means that it takes ¥115.35 to buy $1.

USD/JPY trades in the same direction as the overall value of the USD, and inversely to the value of the JPY. If the USD is strengthening and the JPY is weakening, the USD/JPY rate will move higher. If the USD is weakening and the JPY is strengthening, the USD/JPY rate will move lower.

USD/JPY has the U.S. dollar as the base currency and the JPY as the secondary or counter currency. This means

 ✔ **USD/JPY is traded in amounts denominated in USD.** In online currency trading platforms, standard lot sizes are $100,000, and mini lot sizes are $10,000.

 ✔ **The pip value, or minimum price fluctuation, is denominated in JPY.**

- ✔ **Profit and loss accrue in JPY.** For one standard lot position size, each pip is worth ¥1,000; for one mini lot position size, each pip is worth ¥100. To convert those amounts to USD, divide the JPY amount by the USD/JPY rate. Using 115.00 as the rate, ¥1,000 = $8.70 and ¥100 = $0.87

- ✔ **Margin calculations are typically calculated in USD.** So it's a straightforward calculation using the leverage rate to see how much margin is required to hold a position in USD/JPY. At 100:1 leverage, $1,000 of available margin is needed to open a standard-size position of 100,000 USD/JPY.

It's politically sensitive to trade

USD/JPY is the most politically sensitive currency pair among the majors. Japan remains a heavily export-oriented economy, accounting for more than 40 percent of overall economic activity. This means the JPY is a critical policy lever for Japanese officials to stimulate and manage the Japanese economy — and they aren't afraid to get involved in the market to keep the JPY from strengthening beyond desired levels.

The Japanese Ministry of Finance (MOF) engages in routine verbal intervention in not-so-subtle attempts to influence the level of the JPY. The chief spokesman on currencies is, of course, the Minister of Finance, but the Vice Finance Minister for International Affairs is the more frequent commentator on forex market developments.

The Japanese financial press devotes a tremendous amount of attention to the value of the JPY, similar to how the U.S. financial media cover the Dow or S&P 500. Press briefings by MOF officials are routine. During times of forex market volatility, expect near-daily official comments. These statements move USD/JPY on a regular basis.

The MOF has also been known to utilize covert intervention through the use of sizeable market orders by the pension fund of the Japanese Postal Savings Bank, known as Kampo. This is sometimes referred to as *semiofficial intervention* in various market commentaries.

JPY as a proxy for other Asian currencies

The JPY is sometimes considered a proxy for other Asian currencies that are not freely convertible or have poor liquidity or other trading restrictions, such as the Korean won, Chinese yuan, or Taiwan dollar. Speculation that the Chinese government would *revalue* (strengthen) the Chinese yuan relative to the USD in early 2005 led to speculation that the JPY would also strengthen.

Japanese asset managers tend to move together

If Americans are the ultimate consumers, the Japanese are the consummate savers. The Japanese savings rate (the percentage of disposable income that's not spent) is around 15 percent. (Compare that with the U.S. savings rate at around –1 percent!) As a result, Japanese financial institutions control trillions of dollars in assets, many of which find their way to investments outside of Japan. The bulk of assets are invested in fixed income securities, and this means Japanese asset managers are on a continual hunt for the best yielding returns.

This theme has taken on added prominence in recent years due to extremely low domestic yields in Japan. The continual off-shoring of JPY-denominated assets leads to continual selling of JPY to buy the currencies of the ultimate investment destination. This makes domestic interest-rate yields in Japan a key long-term determinant of the JPY's value.

Japanese financial institutions also tend to pursue a highly collegial approach to investment strategies. The result for forex markets is that Japanese asset managers tend to pursue similar investment strategies at the same time, resulting in tremendous asset flows hitting the market over a relatively short period of time. This situation has important implications for USD/JPY price action (see the section "Price action behavior of USD/JPY").

Important Japanese data reports

The key data reports to focus on coming out of Japan are

- Bank of Japan (BOJ) policy decisions, monthly economic assessments, and Monetary Policy Committee (MPC) member speeches
- Tankan report (a quarterly sentiment survey of Japanese firms by the BOJ — the key is often planned capital expenditures)
- Industrial production
- Machine orders
- Trade balance and current account
- Retail trade
- Bank lending
- Domestic Corporate Goods Price Index (CGPI)
- National CPI and Tokyo-area CPI
- All-Industry Activity Index and Tertiary Industry (service sector) Activity Index

Price action behavior of USD/JPY

As noted earlier, USD/JPY seems to have an on/off switch when compared to the other major currency pairs. Add to that the fact that USD/JPY liquidity can be similarly fickle. Sometimes, hundreds of millions of USD/JPY can be bought or sold without moving the market noticeably; other times, liquidity can be extremely scarce. This phenomenon is particularly acute in USD/JPY owing to the large presence of Japanese asset managers. The Japanese investment community tends to move en masse into and out of positions. Of course, they're not the only ones involved in USD/JPY, but they do tend to play the fox while the rest of the market is busy playing the hounds.

Prone to short-term trends, followed by sideways consolidations

The result of this concentration of Japanese corporate interest is a strong tendency for USD/JPY to display short-term trends (several hours to several days) in price movements, as investors pile in on the prevailing directional move. This tendency is amplified by the use of standing market orders from Japanese asset managers.

For example, if a Japanese pension fund manager is looking to establish a long position in USD/JPY, he's likely to leave orders at several fixed levels below the current market to try to buy dollars on dips. If the current market is at 116.00, he may buy a piece of the total position there, but then leave orders to buy the remaining amounts at staggered levels below, such as 115.75, 115.50, 115.25, and 115.00. If other investors are of the same view, they'll be bidding below the market as well.

If the market begins to move higher, the asset managers may become nervous that they won't be able to buy on weakness and raise their orders to higher levels, or buy at the market. Either way, buying interest is moving up with the price action, creating a potentially accelerating price movement. Any countertrend move is met by solid buying interest and quickly reversed.

Such price shifts tend to reach their conclusion when everyone is onboard — most of the buyers who wanted to buy are now long. At this point, no more fresh buying is coming into the market, and the directional move begins to stall and move sideways. The early buyers may be capping the market with profit-taking orders to sell above, while laggard buyers are still buying on dips. This leads to the development of a consolidation range, which can be as wide as ¥1 or ¥2, or as narrow as 40 to 50 pips.

Short-term traders can usually find trading opportunities in such consolidation ranges, but medium- and longer-term traders may want to step back and wait for a fresh directional movement.

Technical levels are critical in USD/JPY

If you're a regular trader or investor and you don't work at a Japanese bank, you can tell where the orders are by focusing on the technical levels. Perhaps no other currency pair is as beholden to technical support and resistance as USD/JPY. In large part, this has to do with the prevalence of substantial orders, where the order level is based on technical analysis. USD/JPY displays a number of other important trading characteristics when it comes to technical trading levels:

- ✔ USD/JPY tends to respect technical levels with far fewer false breaks.

- ✔ USD/JPY's price action is usually highly directional (one-way traffic) on breaks of technical support and resistance.

- ✔ Spike reversals (sharp — 20- to 50-pip — price movements in the opposite direction of the prior move) from technical levels are relatively common.

- ✔ Orders frequently define intraday highs and lows and reversal points (see Figure 2-2).

Figure 2-2: USD/JPY highs and lows are frequently defined by institutional orders left at round-number price levels.

Source: www.eSignal.com

USD/JPY trading considerations

USD/JPY's tendency is to either be active directionally or consolidating — the on/off switch. A good way to approach USD/JPY is on a more strategic, hit-and-run basis — getting in when you think a directional move is happening and standing aside when you don't. Look for breaks of trend lines, spike reversals, and candlestick patterns as your primary clues for spotting a pending directional move.

Actively trading trend-line and price-level breakouts

One trigger point for jumping into USD/JPY is breaks of trend lines and key price levels, such as daily or weekly highs/lows. It usually takes a significant amount of market interest to break key technical levels. So look at the actual breaks as concrete evidence of sizeable interest, rather than normal back-and-forth price action.

Jumping on spike reversals

After USD/JPY has seen a relatively quick (usually within two to three hours) move of more than 70 to 80 pips in one direction, be on the lookout for any sharp reversals in price. Spike reversals of 30 to 40 pips that occur in very short timeframes (5 to 20 minutes) are relatively common in USD/JPY. But you pretty much have to be in front of your trading screen to take advantage of these, because they're a short-term phenomenon by their very nature.

Monitoring EUR/JPY and other JPY crosses

USD/JPY is heavily influenced by cross flows and can frequently take a back seat to them on any given day. In evaluating USD/JPY, always keep an eye on the JPY crosses and their technical levels as well. A break of important support in GBP/JPY, for instance, could unleash a flood of short-term USD/JPY selling, because GBP/JPY is mostly traded through the dollar pairs.

EUR/JPY is the most actively traded JPY cross, and its movements routinely drive USD/JPY on an intraday basis. Be alert for when significant technical levels in the two pairs coincide, such as when both USD/JPY and EUR/JPY are testing a series of recent daily highs or lows. A break by either can easily spill into the other and provoke follow-through buying/selling in both.

The Other Majors: GBP/USD and USD/CHF

GBP/USD (affectionately known as *sterling* or *cable*) and USD/CHF (called *Swissy* by market traders) are counted as major currency pairs, but their trading volume and liquidity are significantly less than EUR/USD or USD/JPY. As a result, their trading characteristics are very similar to each other.

The British pound: GBP/USD

Trading in cable presents its own set of challenges, because the pair is prone to sharp price movements and seemingly chaotic price action. But it's exactly this type of price behavior that keeps the speculators coming back — when you're right, you'll know very quickly, and the short-term results can be significant.

Trading fundamentals of GBP/USD

The UK economy is the second largest national economy in Europe, after Germany, and the pound is heavily influenced by cross-border trade and mergers and acquisitions (M&A) activity between the United Kingdom and continental Europe. Upwards of two-thirds of UK foreign trade is conducted with EU member states, making the EUR/GBP cross one of the most important trade-driven cross rates.

The 2004 BIS survey of foreign exchange turnover showed that GBP/USD accounted for 14 percent of global daily trading volume, making cable the third most active pairing in the majors. But you may not believe that when you start trading cable, where liquidity seems always to be at a premium. Relatively lower liquidity is most evident in the larger bid-offer spread, which is usually 3 to 5 pips compared to 2 to 4 pips in EUR/USD and USD/JPY.

GBP/USD is quoted in terms of the number of dollars it takes to buy a pound, so a rate of 1.8515 means it costs $1.8515 to buy £1. The GBP is the primary currency in the pair and the USD is the secondary currency. That means

- ✔ **GBP/USD is traded in amounts denominated in GBP.** In online currency trading platforms, standard lot sizes are £100,000, and mini lot sizes are £10,000.
- ✔ **The pip value, or minimum price fluctuation, is denominated in USD.**
- ✔ **Profit and loss accrue in USD.** For one standard lot position size, each pip is worth $10; for one mini lot position size, each pip is worth $1.

✔ **Margin calculations are typically calculated in USD in online trading platforms.** Because of its high relative value to the USD, trading in GBP pairs requires the greatest amount of margin on a per-lot basis. At a GBP/USD rate of 1.9000, to trade a one-lot position worth £100,000, it'll take $1,900 in available margin (based on 100:1 leverage). That calculation will change over time, of course, based on the level of the GBP/USD exchange rate. A higher GBP/USD rate will require more USD in available margin collateral, and a lower GBP/USD rate will need less USD in margin.

Trading alongside EUR/USD, but with a lot more zip!

Cable is similar to the EUR/USD in that it trades inversely to the overall USD, except that it exhibits much more abrupt volatility and more extreme overall price movements. If U.S. economic news disappoints, for instance, both sterling and EUR/USD will move higher. But if EUR/USD sees a 60-point rally on the day, cable may see a 100+ point rally.

This goes back to liquidity and a generally lower level of market interest in cable. In terms of daily global trading sessions (see Chapter 1), cable volume is at its peak during the UK/European trading day, but that level of liquidity shrinks considerably in the New York afternoon and Asian trading sessions. During those off-peak times, cable can see significant short-term price moves simply on the basis of position adjustments (for example, shorts getting squeezed out).

Another important difference between cable and EUR/USD comes in their different reactions to domestic economic/news developments. Cable tends to display more explosive reactions to unexpected UK news/data than EUR/USD does to similar Eurozone news/data.

Important UK data reports

Key UK data reports to watch for are

✔ Bank of England (BOE) Monetary Policy Committee (MPC) rate decisions, as well as speeches by MPC members and the BOE governor

✔ BOE MPC minutes (released two weeks after each MPC meeting)

✔ Inflation gauges, such as consumer price index (CPI), producer price index (PPI), and the British Retailers Consortium (BRC) shop price index

✔ Retail sales and the BRC retail sales monitor

✔ Royal Institution of Chartered Surveyors (RICS) house price balance

✔ Industrial and manufacturing production

✔ Trade balance

✔ GfK (a private market research firm) UK consumer confidence survey

Safe haven or panic button: USD/CHF

The Swiss franc has, or we should say *had*, a reputation for being a safe-haven currency — a reputation that is largely a relic of the Cold War, when fears of a European ground war between the United States and the Soviet Union meant most European financial centers could be out of business in short order. In practical terms, this is no longer the case, but plenty of people in the market continue to refer to the CHF as a safe-haven currency.

Knee-jerk buying of CHF frequently occurs in response to geopolitical crises or terrorism. But those market reactions are increasingly very short-lived, usually only a few minutes or hours now, before preexisting trends reassert themselves. Instead of portraying it as a safe-haven currency pair, we prefer to view USD/CHF as the panic button of forex markets. When unexpected geopolitical news hits the proverbial fan, USD/CHF usually reacts the fastest and the farthest.

Trading fundamentals of USD/CHF

In terms of overall market volume, USD/CHF accounts for only 4 percent of global daily trading volume according to the 2004 BIS survey. With such a small share of market turnover, you'd be right in wondering why it's considered a major pair in the first place. And that's probably the key takeaway from this section: In terms of liquidity, Swissy is not a major.

USD/CHF is quoted in terms of the number of CHF per USD. At a USD/CHF rate of 1.2545, it costs CHF 1.2545 to buy $1. USD/CHF trades in the overall direction of the U.S. dollar and inversely to the CHF. If the USD/CHF rate moves higher, the USD is strengthening and the CHF is weakening. The USD is the primary currency in the pairing, and the CHF is the secondary currency. That means

- ✔ **USD/CHF is traded in amounts denominated in USD.** In online currency trading platforms, standard lot sizes are $100,000, and mini lot sizes are $10,000.

- ✔ **The pip value, or minimum price fluctuation, is denominated in CHF.**

- ✔ **Profit and loss accrues in CHF.** For one standard lot position size, each pip is worth CHF 10; for one mini lot position size, each pip is worth CHF 1. To convert those amounts to USD, divide the CHF amount by the USD/CHF rate. Using 1.2500 as the rate, CHF 10 = $8 and CHF 1 = $0.80. The pip value will change over time as the level of the USD/CHF exchange rate fluctuates, with a lower USD/CHF rate giving a higher pip value in USD terms, and vice versa.

- ✔ **Margin calculations are typically calculated in USD.** So it's a straightforward calculation using the leverage rate to see how much margin is required to hold a position in USD/JPY. At 100:1 leverage, $1,000 of available margin is needed to open a standard-size position of 100,000 USD/CHF.

Keeping the focus on Europe

Switzerland conducts the vast share (about 80 percent) of its foreign trade with the Eurozone and remaining EU countries. When it comes to the value of the CHF, the Swiss are most concerned with its level against the EUR as opposed to the USD. The Swiss National Bank (SNB), the Swiss central bank, tends to get involved in the forex market only when the Swiss franc is either too strong or too weak against the euro.

The SNB typically prefers to use verbal intervention to influence the value of the CHF, and SNB comments frequently stir up USD/CHF and EUR/CHF trading. Since the introduction of the euro in 1999, EUR/CHF has been confined mostly to a relatively narrow range of 1.5000 to 1.6200, but as of this writing it's pushing toward 1.65, drawing increased criticism from the SNB.

Important Swiss economic reports

Swiss data tends to get lost in the mix of data reports out of the United States and the Eurozone, with many in the market looking at Switzerland as a de facto Eurozone member. In that sense, market reactions to Swiss data and events primarily show up in EUR/CHF cross rates. The important Swiss data to keep an eye on are

- SNB rate decisions and speeches by directorate members
- KOF Index of Globalization
- Retail sales
- Trade balance
- PPI and CPI
- Unemployment rate

Price action behavior in GBP/USD and USD/CHF

The GBP/USD and USD/CHF share similar market liquidity and trading interest, which are the main drivers of price action. In both pairs, liquidity and market interest tend to be the thinnest among the majors, especially outside of European trading hours. As a result, both pairs typically trade with wider 3- to 5-pip prices relative to narrower spreads in EUR/USD and USD/JPY. The most important trading characteristics of cable and Swissy are as follows:

- **Price action tends to be jumpy, even in normal markets.** Cable and Swissy are like long-tailed cats in a room full of rocking chairs — extremely nervous. In a relatively calm market, you can see prices in these two pairs jump around by routine 2- to 3-pip increments (say, from 20/25 to 22/27 or 23/28, back to 21/26, and then 24/29).

When prices are moving in response to news or data, those price jumps can be even more pronounced, frequently changing by 3 to 5 pips between prices. Online traders are also likely to get more "rates changed" responses when trying to deal on the current market price. That response means the price changed by the time your trade request was received and the attempted trade was not completed. The subsequent price may be 2 to 3 pips higher or lower than where you first tried to deal.

✔ **Price action tends to see one-way traffic in highly directional markets.** When news or data move the market, the price changes in Swissy and cable are apt to be the most abrupt. On top of that, cable and Swissy will remain highly directional and tend to see minimal pullbacks or backing and filling.

✔ **Look at cable and Swissy as leading indicators for EUR/USD.** One of the ways that experienced traders judge the level of buying or selling interest, how *bid* or *offered* a market is, during a directional move is by looking at how cable and Swissy are trading. For example, if bids in USD/CHF keep appearing in a relatively orderly fashion, say every 1 to 2 pips on a downswing, it's a sign that the move is not especially extreme. On the other hand, if the prices are dropping by larger increments and displaying very few bounces, it's a strong indication that a larger move is unfolding.

✔ **False breaks of technical levels occur frequently.** Cable and Swissy have a nasty habit of breaking beyond technical support and resistance levels, only to reverse course and then trade in the opposite direction. And we're not talking about just a few points beyond the level here, but more like 25 to 30 pips in many cases.

✔ **Spike reversals are very common.** The tendency of cable and Swissy to overshoot in extreme directional moves and to generate false breaks of technical levels means that spike reversals appear frequently on short-term charts. Though the size of the spikes will vary depending on the market circumstances and current events, spike reversals of more than 30 to 40 points on an hourly closing basis should alert you to a potentially larger reversal taking place. The bigger the spike reversal (and it's not uncommon to see 50- to 70-pip spikes in cable and Swissy), the more significance it holds for the future direction.

GBP/USD and USD/CHF trading considerations

The routine short-term volatility of cable and Swissy suggests several important tactical trading refinements. The overarching idea here is to adjust your trading strategies to weather the erratic price action and higher overall volatility in these pairs in comparison to the larger EUR/USD.

Reducing position size relative to margin

This first consideration is especially important in cable, due to its high relative value to the USD. With GBP/USD trading around 1.90 to the dollar (£1 = $1.90) a one-lot position (£100,000) eats up $1,900 in required margin at 100:1 leverage. A similar-size position in EUR/USD (at 1.30) takes up only $130,000 and costs $1,300 in margin. If you're going to trade in cable, you need more margin than if you stay with EUR/USD, USD/JPY, or Swissy.

Cable and Swissy's higher volatility also argue for overall smaller position sizes. A smaller position allows you to better withstand their short-term volatility and gives you greater staying power relative to margin.

Allowing a greater margin of error on technical breaks

In cable and Swissy, tests of technical levels frequently result in false breaks as stops are triggered. If your stop loss is too close to the technical level, it's ripe for the picking by the market. Factoring in a margin of error when placing stop-loss orders can help — it allows you to withstand any short-term false break. Using a margin of error may also require you to reduce your position size to give you greater flexibility and margin staying-power.

Anticipating overshoots and false breaks for position entry

When you're looking to enter a position by selling on rallies or buying on dips, you're probably focused on selling at resistance and buying on support. You can take advantage of cable and Swissy's tendency to overshoot or make false breaks of technical levels by placing your limit order behind the technical level (above resistance, below support). If cable and Swissy break through the level, you'd be able to enter at a better price than you would have if you'd adhered to the technical level alone.

Alternatively, you can enter a portion of your desired position at the technical level and enter the rest at better prices if the level is breached, improving the average rate of your position. Worst-case scenario, the market only fills you for half of your desired position and then reverses. Best-case scenario, you establish your full desired position at a better rate than you expected and the market reverses. If the market keeps going against you, at least your average position rate is better than it otherwise would have been.

Being quick on the trigger

Cable and Swissy tend to move very quickly and may not spend a lot of time around key price levels. This favors traders who are decisive and quick on the trigger in terms of entering and exiting positions. Another way you can take advantage of the short-term volatility of cable and Swissy is by using resting orders to get in and out. You may not be in front of your trading screen, or your click-and-deal trade may not have made it through on a rapid price fluctuation. A standing limit order will accomplish the same trade — only automatically and instantly if the price deals. Trailing stops are especially useful when you have a position that's moving the right way.

Resisting the contrarian urge following large directional moves

After an extended directional price move, many traders may feel inclined to trade in the opposite direction, if only for a short-term correction. Maybe you missed the big move and think it's ripe for a pullback. Or maybe it looks like the move has gone too far, too fast. Resist that urge in cable and Swissy. On days with large directional price moves of more than 100 pips, cable and Swissy often finish out the trading day at the extremes of the price move (meaning at the highs on an up-move and at the lows on a decline). So even if you sell the high of a move up, you're unlikely to get any joy on the day.

Picking your spots wisely

Instead of simply jumping into cable or Swissy, the way you may in EUR/USD, you're going to need to do a fair amount of watching and studying to get a handle on where appropriate entry points may be. Short-term volatility in cable and Swissy make for treacherous short-term trading conditions. You'll greatly improve your chances of catching a favorable move if you step back and look at the medium and longer-term pictures (four-hour and daily) instead of getting caught up in the short-term volatility.

Trading the Minor Pairs: USD/CAD, AUD/USD, and NZD/USD

The minor dollar pairs are USD/CAD (the U.S. dollar versus the Canadian dollar), AUD/USD (the Australian dollar versus the U.S. dollar), and NZD/USD (the New Zealand dollar versus the U.S. dollar). The minor currency pairs are also commonly referred to as the *commonwealth currencies* or the *commodity currencies.*

Commonwealth refers to the commonwealth of former colonies of the United Kingdom. The *commodity currencies* nickname stems from the key role that oil, metals, and mining industries play in the national economies of Canada, Australia, and New Zealand.

The minor currency pairs each account for around 5 percent of global daily trading volume, according to the 2004 Bank for International Settlements (BIS) survey of forex market volumes. But they can offer significant trading opportunities, both for short-term traders and medium- to longer-term speculators.

Trading fundamentals of USD/CAD

The Canadian dollar (nicknamed the *Loonie,* after the local bird pictured on domestic currency notes) trades according to the same macroeconomic fundamentals as most other major currencies. That means you'll need to closely follow Bank of Canada (BOC) monetary policy developments, current economic data, inflation readings, and political goings-on, just as you would with any of the other majors.

As goes the U.S. economy, so goes the Canadian economy. The trajectory of the Canadian economy is closely linked to the overall direction of the U.S. economy. The United States and Canada are still each other's largest commercial trading partners, and the vast majority of Canadians live within 100 miles of the U.S./Canadian border. Even the BOC regularly refers to the U.S. economic outlook in its forecasts of Canadian economic prospects. It's a long-term dynamic, making for plenty of short-term trading opportunities.

Trading USD/CAD by the numbers

The standard market convention is to quote USD/CAD in terms of the number of Canadian dollars per USD. A USD/CAD rate of 1.1800, for instance, means it takes CAD 1.18 to buy USD 1. The market convention means that USD/CAD trades in the same overall direction of the USD, with a higher USD/CAD rate reflecting a stronger USD/weaker CAD and a lower rate showing a weaker USD/stronger CAD.

USD/CAD has the USD as the primary currency and the CAD as the counter currency. This means

- ✔ **USD/CAD is traded in amounts denominated in USD.** For online currency trading platforms, standard lot sizes are USD 100,000, and mini lot sizes are USD 10,000.

- ✔ **The pip value, or minimum price fluctuation, is denominated in CAD.**

- ✔ **Profit and loss register in CAD.** For a standard lot position size, each pip is worth CAD 10, and each pip in a mini-lot position is worth CAD 1. Using a USD/CAD rate of 1.1800 (which will change over time, of course), that equates to a pip value of USD 8.47 for each standard lot and USD 0.85 for each mini-lot.

- ✔ **Margin calculations are typically based in USD, so to see how much margin is required to hold a position in USD/CAD it's a simple calculation using the leverage ratio.** At 100:1 leverage, for instance, $1,000 of available margin is needed to trade 100,000 USD/CAD, and $100 is needed to trade 10,000 USD/CAD.

USD/CAD is unique among currency pairs in that it trades for spot settlement only one day beyond the trade date, as opposed to the normal two days for all other currency pairs. The difference is due to the fact that New York and Toronto, the two nations' financial centers, are in the same time zone, allowing for faster trade confirmations and settlement transfers. For spot traders, the difference means that USD/CAD undergoes the extended weekend (three-day) rollover after the close of trading on Thursdays, instead of on Wednesdays like all other pairs, assuming no holidays are involved.

Canadian events and data reports to watch

On top of following U.S. economic data to maintain an outlook for the larger economy to the south, you need to pay close attention to individual Canadian economic data and official commentaries. In particular, keep an eye on the following Canadian economic events and reports:

- ✔ Bank of Canada (BOC) speakers, rate decisions, and economic forecasts
- ✔ Employment report
- ✔ Gross domestic product (GDP) reported monthly
- ✔ International securities transactions
- ✔ International merchandise trade
- ✔ Leading economic indicators
- ✔ Wholesale and retail sales
- ✔ Consumer price index (CPI) and BOC CPI
- ✔ Manufacturing shipments
- ✔ Ivey Purchasing Managers Index

Trading fundamentals of AUD/USD

The Australian dollar is commonly referred to as *Aussie* (pronounced *aw-zee*), or even just *Oz* for short. These terms refer to both the AUD/USD pair and Australian dollar cross pairs. Aussie trading volume accounts for a little over 5 percent of daily global spot turnover, but it's still a regular mover, both against the U.S. dollar and on the crosses, so it makes an active currency pair for speculators.

In trading AUD/USD, you need to factor in all the usual macroeconomic suspects, like monetary policy rhetoric, interest-rate levels, and all the domestic economic data that determine them. Comments by officials from the Reserve Bank of Australia (RBA), the central bank, and the finance minister can move the Aussie market sharply.

The boom in Asian regional growth over the past decade and high levels of global economic growth have benefited the Australian economy in recent years. Those high levels of growth have brought with them relatively high levels of inflation, prompting the RBA to repeatedly hike interest rates. As a result, nominal interest rates in Australia are currently the second highest among the dollar pairs, with only New Zealand interest rates higher. That means the interest-rate outlook is especially critical to the value of the Aussie.

Aussie trading is heavily influenced by cross trading, especially against the yen, because the AUD/JPY cross captures one of the highest interest differentials between major currencies, as of this writing. AUD/JPY has been a favorite among traders pursuing the carry trade, so you'll want to monitor important AUD/JPY technical levels.

Aussie trading is also regularly influenced by New Zealand economic data, but the flow is usually more significant in the opposite direction, where Aussie data will exert a larger pull on NZD prices, given the larger size of the Australian economy. Still, when trading Aussie, it helps to be aware of upcoming NZD data, because the two tend to move together in regional sympathy. Occasionally, though, divergent economic data can produce sharp swings in the AUD/NZD cross rate, where NZD may be sold on weaker NZ data, for instance, and AUD bought if Aussie prospects remain more buoyant.

Trading AUD/USD by the numbers

Market quoting conventions for trading in AUD/USD are to quote the pair in terms of the number of USD per AUD. An AUD/USD rate of 0.7800 means it takes USD 0.78 (or 78¢) to buy AUD1. This is the same convention as GBP/USD.

AUD/USD trades in the opposite direction of the overall value of the USD and in the same direction as the value of the AUD. A higher AUD/USD rate means AUD is stronger/USD weaker, and a lower AUD/USD rate means AUD is weaker/USD stronger. If you think the AUD should strengthen, for example, you'd be looking to buy AUD/USD. Alternatively, if you think the USD is in an overall strengthening trend, you'd be looking to sell AUD/USD (buy USD).

AUD is the primary currency in the pair, and USD is the counter currency, which means

- ✔ **AUD/USD is traded in amounts denominated in AUD.**

- ✔ **The pip value is denominated in USD.**

- ✔ **Profit and loss accrue in USD.** For a 100,000 AUD/USD position size, each pip is worth USD 10, and each pip on a 10,000 AUD/USD position is worth USD 1.

✔ **Margin calculations are typically in USD on online trading platforms.** Because of AUD's lower relative value to USD, the amount of margin required per lot of AUD/USD is one of the lowest of the dollar pairs. At an AUD/USD rate of 0.7800, for example, a 100,000 AUD/USD position size requires USD 780 of margin, and a 10,000 AUD/USD position needs only USD 78. Compare that to the USD 1,300 of margin needed for a 100,000 EUR/USD position (at 1.3000) or USD 1,900 needed for a 100,000 GBP/USD position (at 1.9000), and you can see that AUD/USD provides a lot of pip bang for your margin buck. But don't trade Aussie solely on its lower relative margin cost. The margin cost will change over time based on changes in the AUD/USD exchange rate, with a lower AUD/USD rate requiring less USD in margin and a higher AUD/USD rate requiring more margin USD.

Australian events and data reports to watch

Australian data and events regularly transpire during the New York late afternoon or early evening, which is early morning the next day in the land down under. Keep an eye on the following:

✔ Reserve Bank of Australia (RBA) and treasury speakers, RBA rate decisions, and monetary policy outlooks

✔ Trade balance (monthly) and current account balance (quarterly)

✔ Employment report

✔ Consumer and business confidence indices

✔ Consumer price index (CPI) and producer price index (PPI) reports

✔ Retail sales and housing market data

Trading fundamentals of NZD/USD

The New Zealand dollar is nicknamed the *Kiwi,* which refers to both the NZD and the NZD/USD pair. Given the relatively small size of the New Zealand economy, Kiwi is probably the most interest-rate sensitive of all the currencies and, therefore, heavily influenced by investment and speculation.

The New Zealand economy has undergone a virtual transformation over the past two decades, moving from a mostly agricultural export orientation to a domestically driven service and manufacturing base. The rapid growth has seen disposable incomes soar; with higher disposable incomes have come persistently high levels of inflation. The Reserve Bank of New Zealand (RBNZ), the central bank, has responded by raising official interest rates to over 7 percent, the highest nominal interest rate among the major currencies (as of this writing).

Kiwi trading is heavily influenced by interest-rate levels and expectations, with international investors able to reap several percentage points in higher yields on high credit-quality New Zealand government bonds. The primary fundamental force driving Kiwi, then, is near-term interest-rate outlook and inflation environment. The RBNZ has shown a determined willingness to tighten monetary policy to stamp out inflation, even at the risk of unsettling domestic growth, reinforcing the value of Kiwi along the way.

In addition to all the standard New Zealand economic data and official pronouncements you need to monitor, Kiwi trading is closely tied to Australian data and prospects, due to a strong trade and regional relationship. No set formula exists to describe the currencies' relationship, but a general rule is that when it's a USD-based move, Aussie and Kiwi will tend to trade in the same direction as each other relative to the USD. But when Kiwi or Aussie news comes in, the AUD/NZD (Aussie/Kiwi) cross will exert a larger influence.

Trading NZD/USD by the numbers

Kiwi is another of the commonwealth currencies and is quoted in similar fashion to GBP/USD and AUD/USD, or the number of USD per NZD. An NZD/USD rate of 0.6800 means it costs USD 0.68 (or 68¢) to buy NZD 1. Kiwi trades in the opposite direction of the overall value of the USD, so a weaker USD means a higher Kiwi rate, and a lower Kiwi rate represents a stronger USD.

The NZD is the primary currency in the pair, and the USD is the counter currency, which means

- ✔ **NZD/USD is traded in position sizes denominated in NZD.**

- ✔ **The pip value is denominated in USD.**

- ✔ **Profit and loss accrues in USD.** On a 100,000 NZD/USD position, each pip is worth USD 10; on a 10,000 Kiwi position size, each pip is worth USD 1. At current exchange rates, that makes Kiwi pips the most expensive of the dollar pairs on a percentage-of-margin basis.

- ✔ **Margin calculations are typically based in USD on margin trading platforms.** Because of Kiwi's lower value relative to the USD, NZD/USD currently requires the least amount of margin dollars on a per-lot basis. Using an NZD/USD rate of 0.6800 and a leverage ratio of 100:1, a 100,000 Kiwi position requires only USD 680 in margin, while a 10,000 NZD/USD position would need only USD 68 in margin. In relation to the other dollar pairs, this makes Kiwi the cheapest to trade on a margin basis and, together with the high pip value, provides the highest pip-per-margin ratio.

Don't trade Kiwi solely based on the lower margin cost basis. No relationship exists between the margin cost of a position and the likelihood of a positive outcome.

New Zealand events and data reports to watch

RBNZ commentary and rate decisions are pivotal to the value of Kiwi, given the prominence of the interest-rate differential in favor of NZD at the moment. Finance ministry comments are secondary to the rhetoric of the independent RBNZ but can still upset the Kiwi cart from time to time. Additionally, keep an eye on the following:

✔ Consumer prices, housing prices, and food prices

✔ Retail sales and credit-card spending

✔ Trade balance and current account

✔ Nonresident bond holdings

✔ Business confidence surveys from National Bank of New Zealand (NBNZ) and Australia and New Zealand Banking Group (ANZ), and the quarterly business sentiment survey issued by the private New Zealand Institute of Economic Research (NZIER)

Trading considerations in USD/CAD, AUD/USD, and NZD/USD

These three currency pairs share many of the same trading traits and even travel as a pack sometimes — especially Aussie and Kiwi, given their regional proximity and close economic ties. Whether they're being grouped as the commodity currencies, the commonwealth currencies, or just smaller regional currencies versus the U.S. dollar, they can frequently serve as a leading indicator of overall USD market direction.

Liquidity and market interest are lower

One of the reasons these pairs tend to exhibit leading characteristics is due to the lower relative liquidity of the pairs, which amplifies the speculative effect on them. If sentiment is shifting in favor of the U.S. dollar, for example, the effect of speculative interest — the fast money — is going to be most evident in lower-volume currency pairs.

In general, you need to be aware that overall liquidity and market interest in these pairs is significantly lower than in the majors. On a daily basis, liquidity in these pairs is at its peak when the local centers (Toronto, Sydney, and Wellington) are open. London market makers provide a solid liquidity base to bridge the gap outside the local markets, but you can largely forget about USD/CAD during the Asia-Pacific session, and the Aussie and Kiwi markets are problematic after the London/European session close until their financial centers reopen a few hours later. The net result is a concentration of market interest in these currency pairs among the major banks of the currency countries, which has implications of its own (see the "Technical levels can be blurry" section, later in this chapter).

Price action is highly event driven

As a result of the overall lower level of liquidity in these currency pairs, in concert with relatively high levels of speculative positioning (at times), you've got the ultimate mix for explosive reactions after currency-specific news or data comes out. Significant data or news surprises, especially when contrary to expectations and likely market positioning, tend to have an out-sized impact on the market. Traders positioning in these currencies need to be especially aware of this and to recognize the greater degree of volatility and risk they're facing if events don't transpire as expected.

A data or event surprise typically leads to a price gap when the news is first announced. If the news is sufficiently at odds with market expectations and positioning, subsequent price action tends to be mostly one-way traffic, as the market reacts to the surprise news and exits earlier positions. If you're caught on the wrong side after unexpected news in these pairs, you're likely better off getting out as soon as possible rather than waiting for a correction to exit at a better level. The lower liquidity and interest in these currency pairs mean you're probably not alone in being caught wrong-sided, which tends to see steady, one-way interest, punctuated by accelerations when additional stop-loss order levels are hit.

All politics (and economic data) is local

Domestic political developments in these smaller-currency countries can provoke significant movements in the local currencies. National elections, political scandals, and abrupt policy changes can all lead to upheavals in the value of the local currency. The effect tends to be most pronounced on the downside of the currency's value (meaning that bad news tends to hurt a currency more than good news — if there ever is any in politics — helps it). Of course, every situation is different, but the spillover effect between politics and currencies is greatest in these pairs, which means you need to be aware of domestic political events if you're trading in them.

In terms of economic data, these currency pairs tend to participate in overall directional moves relative to the U.S. dollar until a local news or data event triggers more concentrated interest on the local currency. If the USD is under pressure across the board, for instance, USD/CAD is likely to move lower in concert with other dollar pairs. But if negative Canadian news or data emerges, USD/CAD is likely to pare its losses and may even start to move higher if the news is bad enough. If the Canadian news is CAD-positive (say, a higher CPI reading pointing to a potential rate hike), USD/CAD is likely to accelerate to the downside, because USD selling interest is now amplified by CAD buying interest.

Technical levels can be blurry

The relatively lower level of liquidity and market interest in these currency pairs makes for sometimes-difficult technical trading conditions. Trend lines and retracement levels in particular are subject to regular overshoots. Prices may move beyond the technical level — sometimes only 5 to 10 pips, other times for extensive distances or for prolonged periods — only to reverse course and reestablish the technical level later.

If the price break of a technical level is quickly reversed, it's a good sign that it was just a position-related movement. If fresh news is out, however, you may be seeing the initial wave of a larger directional move.

Cross-Currency Pairs

A *cross-currency pair* (or *cross,* for short) is any currency pair that doesn't have the U.S. dollar as one of the currencies in the pairing. The catch is that cross rates are derived from the prices of the underlying USD pairs. For example, one of the most active crosses is EUR/JPY, pitting the two largest currencies outside the U.S. dollar directly against each other. But the EUR/JPY rate at any given instant is a function (the product) of the current EUR/USD and USD/JPY rates.

The most popular cross pairs involve the most actively traded major currencies, like EUR/JPY, EUR/GBP, and EUR/CHF. According to the 2004 BIS survey of foreign-exchange market activity, direct cross trading accounted for a relatively small percentage of global daily volume — less than 10 percent for the major crosses combined.

But that figure significantly understates the amount of interest that is actually flowing through the crosses, because large interbank cross trades are typically executed through the USD pairs instead of directly in the cross markets. If a Japanese corporation needs to buy half a billion EUR/JPY (*half a yard,* in market parlance), for example, the interbank traders executing the order will alternately buy EUR/USD and buy USD/JPY to fill the order. Going directly through the EUR/JPY market would likely be impractical and would tend to tip off too many in the market and drive the rate away from them. (We look at how large cross flows can drive the dollar pairs in the "Stretching the legs" section, later in this chapter.)

For individual traders dealing online, however, the direct cross pairs offer more than ample liquidity and narrower spreads than can be realized by trading through the dollar pairs. Additionally, most online platforms do not net out positions based on overall dollar exposure, so you'd end up using roughly twice the amount of margin to enter a position through the dollar pairs to create the same net market position you'd have if you'd gone through the direct cross market. The advances in electronic trading technology even make relatively obscure crosses like NZD/JPY and GBP/CHF easily accessible to individual online traders.

Why trade the crosses?

Cross pairs represent entirely new sets of routinely fluctuating currency pairs that offer another universe of trading opportunities beyond the primary USD pairs. In particular, cross trading offers the following advantages:

- ✔ **You can pinpoint trade opportunities based on news or fundamentals.** If negative Japanese news or data is released, you may be looking to sell the JPY. But against what? If the USD is currently weakening, buying USD and selling JPY may not yield any results. Selling JPY against another currency with better immediate prospects (such as buying EUR/JPY or AUD/JPY) may yield a more appreciable return.

- ✔ **You can take advantage of interest-rate differentials.** Selling low-yielding currencies against higher-yielding currencies is known as a *carry trade*. Carry trades seek to profit from both interest-rate differentials and spot price appreciation, and can form the basis of significant trends.

- ✔ **You can exploit technical trading opportunities.** The majors may be range bound or showing no actionable technical signals, but a cross rate may be set to stage a directional price breakout. Survey charts of cross rates to spot additional technical trading setups.

- ✔ **You can expand the horizon of trading opportunities.** Instead of looking at only four to seven dollar pairs, cross rates offer another dozen currency pairs that you can look to for trading opportunities.

- ✔ **You can go with the flow.** Speculative flows are ever-present in the currency market, but they don't always involve the dollar pairs. Today's speculative flow may be focused on the JPY crosses or selling CAD across the board on the back of surprisingly weak CAD data. The more attuned you are to cross-currency pairs, the more likely you are to identify and capitalize on the speculative move du jour.

Calculating cross rates

Cross rates are a function of the prices of the underlying USD pairs. Depending on how the dollar pairs are quoted (that is, whether the USD is the primary or the secondary currency), the cross rate is going to be either the product of multiplying the rates of two dollar pairs or the quotient of dividing the rates of two dollar pairs. But each currency quote has two sides: the bid and the offer.

Calculating the cross rate is a messy business. Fortunately, online traders don't really need to know how cross rates are calculated, because the online trading platforms are doing it for you and narrowing the spread to boot.

Different cross pairs have different spreads depending on the spreads of the underlying USD pairs, with less-liquid and more-volatile pairs resulting in wider cross spreads. For instance, GBP/JPY is going to have a wider spread than EUR/JPY because of the lower liquidity and higher volatility of GBP/USD relative to EUR/USD. But because the components of wider-spread crosses are more volatile, the cross rates themselves will also be more volatile, allowing the spread to be recouped, typically in relatively short order.

Stretching the legs

A lot of interbank cross trading volume does not go through the direct cross market, because institutional traders have a vested interest in hiding their operations from the rest of the market. In many cases, too, standing liquidity is simply not available in less-liquid crosses (GBP/JPY or NZD/JPY, for example). So they have to go through the *legs,* as the dollar pairs are called with respect to cross trading, to get the trade done. They also have an interest in maximizing the prices at which they're dealing — to sell as high as possible and to buy as low as possible.

One of the ways they're able to do that is to alternate their trading in the dollar legs. If you have to sell a large amount of EUR/JPY, for example, you can alternate selling EUR/USD, which may tend to drive down EUR/USD but also push USD/JPY higher (because U.S. dollars overall are being bought). You now (you hope) have a higher USD/JPY rate at which to sell the JPY leg of the order. But selling USD/JPY may push USD/JPY lower or cap its rise, leading EUR/USD to stop declining and recover higher, because U.S. dollars are now being bought. Now you have a slightly better EUR/USD rate to keep selling the EUR leg of the order. By alternating the timing of which U.S. dollar leg you're selling, you have (you hope) executed the order at better rates than you could have directly in the cross and likely managed to obscure your market activity in the more active dollar pairs.

Of course, it doesn't always work out as neatly and cleanly as just described. The net result in the market is a steady directional move in the cross rate, while the USD pairs remain relatively stagnant or within recent ranges. Be alert for such dollar-based movement, and consider that it may be a cross-driven move and a potential trading opportunity.

Cross-rate movements can also have a pronounced effect on how individual dollar pairs move in an otherwise dollar-based market reaction. Say some very USD-positive news or data has just been released, and the market starts buying USD across the board. If USD/JPY happens to break a key technical resistance level, it may accelerate higher and prompt EUR/JPY to break a similarly significant resistance level, bringing in EUR/JPY buyers. The net effect in this case is that EUR/USD will not fall as much or as rapidly as USD/JPY will rally, because of the EUR/JPY cross buying. If you went short EUR/USD on the positive U.S. news, you may not get as much joy. But the legs also tend to move in phases, and continued EUR/USD selling may eventually break through support, sending EUR/JPY lower and capping USD/JPY in the process.

As you can see, crosses can affect the market in virtually limitless ways, and there's no set way these things play out.

When the U.S. dollar is not the primary focus of the market's attention, or if major U.S. news is approaching (like a non-farm payrolls [NFP] report or a Federal Open Market Committee [FOMC] decision in a few days), sending market interest to the sidelines, speculative interest frequently shifts to the crosses. Always consider that the market's focus may be cross-driven rather than centered on the USD or any other single currency. Some days it's a dollar market, and other days it's a cross market. GBP may be weakening across the board on weak UK data, but if the USD is similarly out of favor, the pound's weakness is likely to be most evident on the crosses.

When looking at cross-trade opportunities, you may be tempted to translate the cross idea into a USD-based trade. You may think that AUD/JPY is forming a top, for example. If you're right, you may be thinking that one of two moves is likely — USD/JPY will move lower or AUD/USD will move lower — and you may be tempted into selling one of the legs (AUD/USD or USD/JPY) because you don't want to get involved in a cross. But there's another possibility: One leg may go down precipitously while the other moves higher, sending the cross lower, as you expected. But if you went short the wrong leg, you missed the boat.

When you spot a trade opportunity in a cross, trade the cross. Don't try to out-guess the market and pick which component will make the cross move. Trust that if your trade analysis is correct, the cross will move the way you expect.

Trading the JPY crosses

The JPY crosses constitute one of the primary cross families and basically pit the JPY against the other major currencies. EUR/JPY is the highest volume of the JPY crosses, but the prominence of the carry trade, where the low-yielding JPY is sold and higher-yielding currencies are bought, has seen significant increases in GBP/JPY, AUD/JPY, and NZD/JPY trading volume. Those currencies offer the highest interest-rate differentials against the JPY.

JPY crosses have their pip values denominated in JPY, meaning profit and loss will accrue in JPY. The margin requirement will vary greatly depending on which primary currency is involved, with GBP/JPY requiring the greatest margin and NZD/JPY requiring the least.

In terms of JPY-cross fundamentals, JPY-based news and events tend to have the greatest impact, but trying to pin down which leg is going to cause the JPY crosses to move is a risky game. When trading in the JPY crosses, you need to keep an eye on USD/JPY in particular, due to its relatively explosive tendencies and its key place as an outlet for overall JPY buying or selling. Be alert for similar technical levels between USD/JPY and the JPY crosses, as a break in either could spill over into the other.

Trading the EUR crosses

Outside of EUR/JPY, EUR cross action tends to be concentrated in EUR/GBP and EUR/CHF, where the cross direction is largely determined by changing outlooks between the Eurozone economy relative to the UK and Swiss economies. Reactions to Eurozone and Swiss news or data are most likely to be felt in the EUR crosses as opposed to EUR/USD or USD/CHF, whereas UK news/data is going to explode all over GBP/USD and EUR/GBP.

Sharp USD-driven moves will also affect these crosses, with the brunt of the USD move being felt in GBP/USD and USD/CHF, frequently biasing those legs to drive their EUR cross in the short run. That means frequently (but not always) that a sharp move higher in the USD will tend to see a higher EUR/CHF and EUR/GBP, while a rapid USD move lower will tend to see lower EUR/CHF and EUR/GBP.

The pip values of these EUR crosses will be denominated in either GBP or CHF, with GBP significantly more expensive on a pip basis than CHF (as of this writing). Typical daily ranges in the EUR crosses are relatively small on a pip basis — roughly 20 to 40 pips on average — but they're still substantial on a pip-value basis and roughly equivalent to daily EUR/USD ranges.

Chapter 3

The Mechanics of Currency Trading

The currency market has its own set of market trading conventions and related lingo, just like any other financial market. If you're new to currency trading, the mechanics and terminology may take some getting used to. But at the end of the day, you'll see that most currency trade conventions are pretty straightforward.

Not as straightforward is figuring out in what direction the major currencies are likely to move. Because so many things impact whether currencies strengthen or weaken, currency traders have to have a bit of detective in them. Not only do they have to find the necessary information, but they often have to interpret it, too.

The Nuts and Bolts of Currency Trading

The biggest mental hurdle facing newcomers to currencies, especially traders familiar with other markets, is the idea that each currency trade consists of a simultaneous purchase and sale. The purchase of one currency involves the simultaneous sale of another currency. This is the *exchange* in *foreign exchange*. To put it another way, if you're looking for the dollar to go higher, the question is "Higher against what?" The answer has to be another currency. In relative terms, if the dollar goes up against another currency, it also means that the other currency has gone down against the dollar. To think of it in stock-market terms, when you buy a stock, you're selling cash, and when you sell a stock, you're buying cash. The following sections outline the other conventions fundamental to currency trading.

Grasping the long, short, and square of it

Forex markets use the same terms to express market positioning as most other financial markets do. But because currency trading involves simultaneous buying and selling, being clear on the terms helps — especially if you're totally new to financial market trading.

Going long

A *long position,* or simply a *long,* refers to a market position in which you've bought a security. In the currency market, it refers to having bought a currency pair. When you're long, you're looking for prices to move higher, so you can sell at a higher price than where you bought. When you want to close a long position, you have to sell what you bought. If you're buying at multiple price levels, you're *adding to longs* and *getting longer.*

Getting short

A *short position,* or simply a *short,* refers to a market position in which you've sold a security that you never owned. In the stock market, selling a stock short requires borrowing the stock (and paying a fee to the lending brokerage) so you can sell it. In forex markets, it means you've sold a currency pair: You've sold the base currency and bought the counter currency. So you're still making an exchange, just in the opposite order and according to currency pair quoting terms. When you've sold a currency pair, it's called *going short* or *getting short,* and it means you're looking for the pair's price to move lower so you can buy it back at a profit. If you sell at various price levels, you're *adding to shorts* and *getting shorter.*

Because currencies can fall or rise relative to each other, both in medium- and long-term trends and minute-to-minute fluctuations, currency pair prices are as likely to be going down at any moment as they are up. Therefore, in currency trading, going short is as common as going long. "Selling high and buying low" is a standard currency trading strategy.

Squaring up

If you have no position in the market, it's called being *square* or *flat.* If you have an open position and want to close it, it's called *squaring up.* If you're short, you need to buy to square up. If you're long, you need to sell to go flat. The only time you have no market exposure or financial risk is when you're square.

Understanding rollovers

One market convention unique to currencies is *rollovers.* A rollover is a transaction where an open position from one *value date* (settlement date) is rolled over into the next value date. Rollovers represent the intersection of interest-rate markets and forex markets.

Rollovers and interest rates

Rollover rates are based on the difference in interest rates of the two currencies in the pair you're trading. That's because what you're actually trading is good old-fashioned cash. When you're long a currency (cash), it's like having a deposit in the bank. If you're short a currency (cash), it's like having borrowed a loan. Just as you would expect to earn interest on a bank deposit or pay interest on a loan, you should expect an interest gain/expense for holding a currency position over the change in value.

The catch in currency trading is that if you carry over an open position from one value date to the next, you have two bank accounts involved. Think of it as one account with a positive balance (the currency you're long) and one with a negative balance (the currency you're short). But because your accounts are in two different currencies, the two interest rates of the different countries will apply.

The difference between the interest rates in the two countries is called the *interest-rate differential.* The larger the interest-rate differential, the larger the impact from rollovers. The narrower the interest-rate differential, the smaller the effect from rollovers. You can find relevant interest-rate levels of the major currencies from any number of financial-market Web sites, but www. marketwatch.com and www.fxstreet.com have especially good resources. Look for the base or benchmark lending rates in each country.

If you're going to be trading a relatively large account with an online forex broker (say, over $25,000 in margin deposited), you'll probably be able to negotiate a tighter rollover spread with your broker. This will enable you to capture more of the gains if you're positioned the right way, or to reduce your cost of carry if you're not.

Rollovers and value dates

In forex markets, *spot* refers to trade settlement in *two* business days, which is called the *value date.* That time is needed to allow for trade processing across global time zones and for currency payments to be wired around the world.

The forex market operates on a 24-hour trade date basis beginning at 5 p.m. eastern time (ET) and ending the next day at 5 p.m. ET. So if it's a Monday, spot currencies are trading for value on Wednesday (assuming no holidays). At 5 p.m. ET on Monday, the trade date becomes Tuesday and the value date is shifted to Thursday. If you have an open position on Monday at 5 p.m. ET closing, your position will be rolled over to the next value date, in this case from Wednesday to Thursday, or a *one-day rollover.* If you close your position the next day (Tuesday) and finish the trade date square, there are no rollovers because you have no position. The same is true if you never carry a position through the daily 5 p.m. ET close. Sounds simple enough, but things get a bit more complicated when you consider weekends and holidays, when banks are closed:

- ✔ **Weekend rollovers:** On Wednesday trade dates, spot currencies are normally trading for a Friday value date. At 5 p.m. ET on Wednesday, the value date changes from Friday to Monday, a *weekend rollover.* In rollover calculations, that's a *three-day rollover* (Saturday, Sunday, and Monday), which means the rollover costs/gains are going to be three times as much as any other day.

  The one exception to the two-day spot convention in currency trading is trades in USD/CAD, which settle in one business day. The weekend rollover for USD/CAD takes place on Thursday after the 5 p.m. ET close, when the value date shifts from Friday to Monday. This applies only to USD/CAD and not to other pairs involving CAD, such as CAD/JPY or EUR/CAD.

- ✔ **Holidays:** Rollover periods can be longer if there is a banking holiday in one of the countries whose currency is part of the trade. For example, if it's Wednesday and you're trading GBP/USD, the normal spot value date would be Friday. But if UK banks aren't open on Friday because of a holiday, the value date would change to Monday, skipping Friday's holiday. That's a *four-day rollover* (Friday, Saturday, Sunday, and Monday). A few times each year (mostly around Christmas, New Year's, and Golden Week spring holidays in Japan), when multiple banking holidays in various countries coincide over several days, rollover periods can be as long as seven or eight days. So you may earn or pay rollovers of seven or eight times normal on one day, but then not face any rollovers for the rest of the holiday period.

Applying rollovers

Rollover transactions are usually carried out automatically by your forex broker if you hold an open position past the change in value date. Rollovers are applied to your open position by two offsetting trades that result in the same open position. Some online forex brokers apply the rollover rates by adjusting the average rate of your open position. Other forex brokers apply rollover rates by applying the rollover credit or debit directly to your margin balance.

Reading currency prices

Online brokerages display currency prices. Although different online forex brokers use different formats to display prices on their trading platforms, the info is the same.

Two prices appear for each currency pair. The price on the left-hand side is called the *bid,* and the price on the right-hand side is called the *offer* (some call this the *ask*). Some brokers display the prices above and below each other, with the bid on the bottom and the offer on top. The easy way to tell the difference is that the bid price will always be lower than the offer price.

The price quotation of each bid and offer you see has two components: the big figure and the dealing price. The *big figure* refers to the first three digits of the overall currency rate and is usually shown in a smaller font size or even in shadow. The *dealing price* refers to the last two digits of the overall currency price and is brightly displayed in a larger font size (see Figure 3-1).

Book V

Foreign Currency Trading

Figure 3-1:
A dealing box from the FOREX.com trading platform for EUR/USD.

A *spread* is the difference between the bid price and the offer price. Most online forex brokers use spread-based trading platforms for individual traders. Think of it as the commission that the online brokers charge for executing your trades. Spreads will vary from broker to broker and by currency pairs at each broker as well. Generally, the more liquid the currency pair, the narrower the spread; the less liquid the currency pair, the wider the spread. This is especially the case for some of the less-traded crosses.

Executing a trade

There are two main ways of executing trades in the currency market: live trades and orders.

Live trades

Live dealing is how you access the market to buy or sell at current market rates. Knowing exactly what you want to do is important, because when you make a live deal, it's a *done* deal. If you make a mistake, you'll have to make another trade to correct your erroneous trade, and that is very likely going to cost you real money.

Online dealing

Most forex brokers provide live streaming prices that you can deal on with a simple click of your computer mouse. To execute a trade, simply specify the amount of the trade you want to make and then click on the Buy or Sell button. The forex trading platform will respond back, usually within a second or two, to let you know whether the trade went through. If the trade goes through, you have a position in the market and you'll see your unrealized profit and loss (P&L) begin updating according to market price fluctuations.

Some online brokers advertise narrower trading spreads as a way to attract traders. If your click-and-deal trade attempts frequently fail, and the platform then asks if you'd like to make the trade at a worse price, you're probably being re-quoted. *Re-quoting* is when brokers offer you a worse price to make your trade, meaning you end up paying a larger spread than you bargained for.

Phone dealing

Placing live trades over the phone is available from most online forex brokers. You need to find out from your broker whether it offers this service and exactly what its procedures are before you can be ready to use it. When you place a trade over the phone, make sure you have your trading account number and password and that you know what your position is. (If you're not sure, your broker will be able to give you this info, but be prepared for time delays.) Then do the following:

1. **Ask what the current price is for the currency pair you're trading.**

   The broker's representative will quote you a two-way bid/offer price, such as "EUR/USD is trading at 1.3213/15."

2. **If you don't want the price, say, "No, thank you"; if you *do* want the price, specify *exactly* what trade you would like to make.**

   Note the direction (buy or sell), the amount (don't use lots — use the real amounts), and the currency pair. For example, "I would like to sell 140,000 EUR/USD."

   The broker should then say "Done" or "That's agreed."

3. **Confirm with your broker exactly what trade you just made.**

   For example, say, "To confirm, I just sold 140,000 EUR/USD at 1.3213."

   Be sure the broker confirms the trade. You can double-check that the trade was correct by asking the broker to input the trade and update your position.

4. **Get the name of the broker's representative you just made the trade with in case you have to call back.**

Orders: Trading in absentia

If you're not a full-time trader, then you've probably got a full-time job that requires your attention when you're at work. (At least your boss *hopes* he has your attention.) Orders are how you can act in the market without being there. Not all order types are available at all online brokers, so add order types to your list of questions to ask your prospective forex broker.

Using orders helps you capitalize on short-term market movements, as well as limit the impact of any adverse price moves. A disciplined use of orders also helps you quantify the risk you're taking and, with any luck, gives you peace of mind in your trading.

- **Take-profit orders:** You use *take-profit orders* to lock in gains when you have an open position in the market. If you're short USD/JPY at 117.20, your take-profit order will be to buy back the position and be placed somewhere below that price, say at 116.80 for instance. If you're long GBP/USD at 1.8840, your take-profit order will be to sell the position somewhere higher, maybe 1.8875. *Partial take-profit orders* are take-profit orders that close only a portion of your open position, enabling you to take some money off the table and lock in some gains. With two partial take-profit orders, you can close the whole position at two different levels.

- **Limit orders:** A limit order is any order that triggers a trade at more favorable levels than the current market price. Think "Buy low, sell high." If the limit order is to buy, it must be entered at a price below the current market price. If the limit order is to sell, it must be placed at a price higher than the current market price.

- **Stop-loss orders:** Stop-loss orders are critical to trading survival. The traditional stop-loss order stops losses by closing out an open position that's losing money. If you're long, your stop-loss order will be to sell, but at a lower price than the current market price. If you're short, your stop-loss order will be to buy, but at a higher price than the current market.

Most online forex brokers guarantee that your stop-loss order will be executed at the order rate. To do so, they rely on the spread: Stop-loss orders to sell are triggered if the broker's *bid* price reaches your stop-loss order rate; stop-loss orders to buy are triggered if the platform's *offer* price reaches your stop-loss rate. The benefit of this practice is that some firms will guarantee against slippage on your stop-loss orders in normal trading conditions. The downside is that your order will likely be triggered earlier than stop-loss orders in other markets, so add in some extra cushion when placing them on your forex platform.

- **Trailing stop-loss orders:** A trailing stop-loss order is a stop-loss order that you set at a fixed number of pips from your entry rate. The trailing stop adjusts the order rate as the market price moves, *but only in the direction of your trade.* For example, if you're long EUR/CHF at 1.5750 and you set the trailing stop at 30 pips, the stop will initially become active at 1.5720 (1.5750 – 30 pips). Essentially it lets you cut losing positions quickly and let winning positions run.

✔ **One-cancels-the-other orders:** A *one-cancels-the-other order* (more commonly referred to as an OCO order) is a stop-loss order paired with a take-profit order. It's the ultimate insurance policy for any open position. Your position will stay open until one of the order levels is reached by the market and closes your position. When one order level is reached and triggered, the other order automatically cancels. OCO orders are highly recommended for every open position.

✔ **Contingent orders:** A *contingent order* is a fancy term for combining several types of orders to create a complete currency trade strategy. You use contingent orders to put on a trade while you're asleep, or otherwise indisposed, knowing that your contingent order has got all the bases covered and your risks are defined. Contingent orders are also referred to as *if/then orders*. If/then orders require the *if* order to be done first, and *then* the second part of the order becomes active, so they're sometimes called *if done/then* orders.

Online forex brokers accept your orders according to their trading policies, which are spelled out in detail in the fine print in the contract you'll have to sign to open up an online trading account. The key feature of most brokers' order policies is that your orders will be executed based on the *price spread* of the trading platform. A limit order to buy, for example, will be filled only if the trading platform's offer price reaches your buy rate. A limit order to sell will be triggered only if the trading platform's bid price reaches your sell rate.

Profit and loss, up close and personal

If you're going to trade currencies actively, you need to get up close and personal with P&L. Understanding how P&L works is especially critical to online margin trading, where your P&L directly affects the amount of margin you have to work with. Changes in your margin balance will determine how much you can trade and for how long you can trade if prices move against you.

Margin balances and liquidations

When you open an online currency trading account, you need to pony up cash as collateral to support the margin requirements established by your broker. That initial margin deposit becomes your opening *margin balance* and is the basis on which all your subsequent trades are collateralized. Unlike futures markets or margin-based equity trading, online forex brokerages do not issue *margin calls* (requests for more collateral to support open positions). Instead, they establish ratios of margin balances to open positions that must be maintained at all times.

Be sure you completely understand your broker's margin requirements and liquidation policies. Some brokers' liquidation policies allow for all positions to be liquidated if you fall below margin requirements. Others close out the biggest losing positions or portions of losing positions until the required ratio is satisfied again. You can find the details in the fine print of the account opening contract that you sign.

Unrealized and realized profit and loss

Most online forex brokers provide real-time mark-to-market calculations showing your margin balance. Your margin balance is the sum of your initial margin deposit, your unrealized P&L, and your realized P&L. *Mark-to-market* is the calculation that shows your unrealized P&L based on where you could close your open positions in the market at that instant. *Realized P&L* is what you get when you close out a trade position, or a portion of a trade position.

Your unrealized P&L will continue to fluctuate based on the remaining open positions and so will your total margin balance. If you've got a winning position open, your unrealized P&L will be positive and your margin balance will increase. If the market is moving against your positions, your unrealized P&L will be negative and your margin balance will be reduced. Currency prices are constantly changing, so your mark-to-market unrealized P&L and total margin balance will also be constantly changing.

Calculating profit and loss with pips

Profit-and-loss calculations are pretty straightforward in terms of math — it's all based on position size and the number of pips you make or lose. A *pip* (or point) is the smallest increment of price fluctuation in currency prices. In the five-digit currency quote, the pip is the last itty-bitty digit:

- **EUR/USD:** 1.2853
- **USD/CHF:** 1.2267
- **USD/JPY:** 117.23
- **GBP/USD:** 1.9285
- **EUR/JPY:** 150.65

Looking at EUR/USD, if the price moves from 1.2853 to 1.2873, it's just gone up by 20 pips. If it goes from 1.2853 down to 1.2792, it's just gone down by 61 pips.

Pips provide an easy way to calculate the P&L. To turn that pip movement into a P&L calculation, all you need to know is the size of the position. For a 100,000 EUR/USD position, the 20-pip move equates to $200 (EUR 100,000 × 0.0020 = $200). For a 50,000 EUR/USD position, the 61-point move translates into $305 (EUR 50,000 × 0.0061 = $305).

True, online currency trading platforms calculate the P&L for you automatically, but they do so only *after* you enter a trade. To structure your trade and manage your risk effectively (How big a position? How much margin to risk?), you need to calculate your P&L outcomes *before* you enter the trade.

Forces behind Forex Rates

On a daily basis, currency traders have to sort through myriad economic reports, interpret the comments of political and financial officials from around the world, take stock of geopolitical developments, and assess movements in other financial markets. They do all this to help them determine what direction major currencies are likely to move.

Currencies and interest rates

In currency trading, the guiding principle is "interest rates, interest rates, interest rates." Interest rates are important to currencies because they influence the direction of global capital flows and serve as benchmarks for what investors expect to earn investing in a particular country. Currencies with higher yields (higher interest rates) tend to go up, and currencies with lower yields (lower interest rates) tend to weaken. The most significant overall determinant of a currency's value relative to other currencies is the nature and direction of monetary policy set by a country's central bank (explained in the next section).

The future is now: Interest rate expectations

When it comes to currencies and interest rates, forex markets are focused more on the direction of future interest rate moves (higher or lower) than they are on the current levels because the current levels are already priced in by the market. So even though a currency may have a low interest rate, market expectations of higher interest rates in the future frequently will cause the currency to appreciate. The opposite is also true: A currency with a relatively high interest rate frequently weakens if the market expects interest rates in that country to move lower in the future.

The *outlook period,* or the time frame in which markets are expecting interest rates to change, can span several months or quarters into the future. The farther out the expected changes are on the horizon, however, the more limited the impact on the currencies in the here and now. Speculation on interest rate levels six months out tends to prompt relatively small adjustments that are frequently lost in the day-to-day noise. But as the timing for anticipated interest rate changes nears, currency speculation will reach a crescendo in the immediate run-up (weeks and days) to the anticipated change.

Relative interest rates

You may be tempted to focus strictly on the level of a currency's interest rate as the basis for deciding whether the currency should move up or down. But currency traders usually pay very little attention to absolute interest rates and prefer to home in on one currency's interest rate in relation to other currencies' interest rates:

- ✔ **Interest-rate differentials:** In currency trading, markets are always focused on *currency pairs,* or one currency's value relative to another currency. In this case, the difference between the interest rates of the two currencies, known as the *interest-rate differential,* is the key spread to watch. An increasing interest-rate differential will generally favor the higher-yielding currency, while a narrowing interest-rate differential will tend to favor the lower-yielding currency.

- ✔ **Nominal and real interest rates:** The interest rate to focus on is not always just the *nominal interest rate* (the base interest rates you see, such as the yield on a bond). Markets focus on *real interest rates* (inflation-adjusted rates, which is the nominal interest rate minus the rate of inflation [usually consumer price index]). So even though a bond may carry a nominal yield of, say, 8.5 percent, if the annual rate of inflation in the country is 4.5 percent, the real yield on the bond is closer to 4 percent.

One of the more popular (though potentially risky) long-term trade strategies, known as a *carry trade,* is based on relative interest rates.

Monetary policy

Monetary policy is the set of policy actions that central banks use to achieve their legal mandates. Most central banks function under legislative mandates that focus on two basic objectives:

- ✔ Promoting price stability (a.k.a. restraining inflation)
- ✔ Promoting sustainable economic growth, sometimes with an explicit goal of promoting maximum employment

Although it's a no-brainer that promoting economic growth is more important to those of us who work for a living, central bankers like to focus primarily on inflation, and the primary lever of monetary policy is changes to benchmark interest rates, such as the federal funds rate in the United States or the refinance rate in the Eurozone.

Expansionary or restrictive?

Changes in interest rates effectively amount to changes in the cost of money, where higher interest rates increase the cost of borrowing and lower interest rates reduce the cost of borrowing. The benchmark rates set by central banks apply to the nation's banking system and determine the cost of borrowing between banks. Banks in turn adjust the interest rates they charge to firms and individual borrowers based on these benchmark rates, affecting domestic retail borrowing costs.

The main thrust (or *bias*, as markets call it) of monetary policy generally falls into two categories: expansionary and restrictive. An expansionary monetary policy aims to expand or stimulate economic growth, while a restrictive bias aims to slow economic growth, usually to fight off inflation.

- ✔ **Expansionary monetary policy:** Expansionary monetary policy (also known as *accommodative* or *stimulative* monetary policy) is typically achieved through lowering interest rates (that is, reducing the costs of borrowing in the hope of spurring investment and consumer spending). Cutting interest rates is also known as *easing* interest rates and is frequently summed up in the term *easy monetary policy.*

- ✔ **Restrictive monetary policy:** Restrictive monetary policy (also known as *contractionary* or *tighter* monetary policy) is achieved by raising, or "tightening," interest rates. Higher interest rates increase the cost of borrowing and work to reduce spending and investment with the aim of slowing economic growth.

Identifying monetary policy cycles

Changes in monetary policy usually involve many small shifts in interest rates (because central bankers are increasingly reluctant to shock an economy by adjusting interest rates too drastically) that play out over extended periods of time, ranging from quarters to years. Still, given the significance of monetary policy to currencies, currency traders devote a great deal of attention trying to divine the intentions of central bankers. Fortunately, central bankers communicate with the markets in a number of ways: rate decisions, policy statements or guidance, and public speeches.

Currency traders need to be aware of and constantly follow the current market thinking on the direction of interest rates because of the strong relationship between interest rates and currency values. The best way to do this is to follow market commentaries in print and online news media, always keeping in mind that such outlets (especially print) are usually one step behind the current market. This makes online news commentaries that much more relevant. Some of the best sites for timely insights and market reporting are Bloomberg.com, Reuters.com, and MarketWatch.com. Best of all, these sites are free.

Interpreting monetary policy communications

Central bankers are keenly aware that their comments have the ability to move, and potentially disrupt, financial markets all over the world. So they choose their words very carefully, leaving traders to act as interpreters. Before you start interpreting monetary policy statements and commentary, it helps to know the following:

- When the head of the central bank gives an update on the economy or the outlook for interest rates, listen up. A scheduled speech by the chair of the Fed, for instance, is likely to be preceded by market speculation similar to that of a major economic data report. And the reaction to his comments can be equally sharp.

- Markets typically refer to central bankers in terms of being hawks or doves: A *hawk* is someone who generally favors an aggressive approach and tends to be fixated on fighting inflation. A *dove* tends to stress growth and employment. If a hawk is slated to speak on the outlook for monetary policy, and he downplays the threats from inflation or suggests that inflationary pressures may be starting to recede, pay attention. Markets will jump all over dovish comments coming from a hawk, and vice versa with hawkish comments made by a dove.

Official currency policies and rhetoric

After considering monetary policy and interest rates, the next biggest influences on currency values are government policies or official stances regarding the value of individual currencies. National governments have a great deal at stake when it comes to the value of their currencies. After all, in a sense, a nation's currency is the front door to its economy and financial markets. If the currency is viewed as unstable or too volatile, it's tantamount to slamming the front door shut. And no major economy can afford to do that today.

Currency market intervention

In every big-bank currency trading room in major financial centers, there is a direct line to the open market trading desk of the central bank. When that line lights up, the whole dealing room erupts. That line is reserved for open market intervention by the central bank, and when it rings, it usually means only one thing: The central bank is intervening in the market.

Intervention refers to central banks buying or selling currencies in the open market to drive currency rates in a desired direction. Direct intervention in the market is usually taken only as a last resort. It also may be a stopgap measure to stabilize markets upset by extreme events, such as a terrorist attack or rumors of a financial institution's failure. When it's not necessitated by emergency circumstances, markets are generally aware of the increasing risks of intervention.

Some of the more subtle forms of intervention are

- ✔ **Verbal intervention or jawboning:** These are efforts by finance ministry or central bank officials to publicly suggest that current market directions are undesirable. Basically, it amounts to trying to talk up or talk down a particular currency's value.

- ✔ **Checking rates:** This is the central bank's open market desk ringing in on the direct line to major currency banks' trading desks. The traders don't know if it's going to be a real intervention or not, but they still react instinctively based on previously indicated preferences. Even rumors of a central bank checking rates are enough to trigger a significant market reaction.

In terms of actual open market intervention, there are several different forms it can take, all depending on which and how many central banks are participating. The more the merrier; better still, there's strength in numbers.

- ✔ **Unilateral intervention:** This is intervention by a single central bank to buy or sell its own currency. Unilateral intervention is generally the least effective form of intervention, because the government is perceived (usually correctly) to be acting alone and without the support of other major governments. Markets will typically revert to the earlier direction after the intervention has run its course to test the central bank's resolve and to see if it's intent on stopping the move or simply slowing it.

- ✔ **Joint intervention:** This is when two central banks intervene together to shift the direction of their shared currency pair. This is a clear sign to markets that the two governments are prepared to work together to alter the direction of that pair's exchange rate.

- ✔ **Concerted intervention:** This is when multiple central banks join together to intervene in the market simultaneously. This is the most powerful and effective type of intervention, because it suggests unity of purpose by multiple governments. Concerted intervention is not done lightly by major central banks — and markets don't take it lightly either. It's the equivalent of a sledgehammer to the head. Concerted intervention frequently results in major long-term trend changes.

In terms of the impact of intervention, different governments are given different degrees of respect by the market. Due to the frequency of past interventions and constant threats of it, the Japanese tend to get the least respect. The Bank of England, the Swiss National Bank, and the European Central Bank (ECB) are treated with considerably more respect by markets, with the ECB being the linchpin of credibility for the Eurozone. Finally, when the U.S. Treasury (via the Fed) intervenes, it's considered a major event, and the market usually respects the intervention.

Geopolitical risks and events

Geopolitics is nothing more than a fancy word used to describe what's going on in the world at large. As it's applied to the currency markets, geopolitics tends to focus on political, military/security, or natural disruptions to the global economy or individual regions or nations. Because currency markets are the conduits for international capital flows, they're usually the first to react to international events, as global investors shift assets in response to geopolitical developments.

As important as geopolitical issues are to the market's overall assessment of a currency's value, they tend to have relatively short-run implications and must be interpreted in light of other prevailing economic fundamentals.

Chapter 4

Gathering and Interpreting Economic Data

*A*ny number of real-world forces are at work in the forex market at any given moment: economic data, interest rate decisions, and geopolitical events, to name just a few. And they all get filtered through the market's collective consciousness and translated into price movements. So, with a whole raft of active participants and a whole slew of factors that impact it, how can you make any sense at all of economic data you rely on to make sound trading decisions?

First, you become familiar with the key economic reports. Then you figure out how to interpret the information the reports contain. Not necessarily easy tasks, but vital — and the ones that this chapter focuses on. The goal of this chapter is to give you a better understanding of the types of information that move the market and a solid foundation to interpret the information and apply it. In other words, by the end of this chapter, not only will you know what reports to read, but *how* to read them.

First Up: A Model for Absorbing Economic Data

The sooner you're able to make sense of what a specific report means and factor it into the bigger picture, the sooner you'll be able to react in the market. But, given the deluge of economic indicators you'll encounter in the forex market, it's all too easy to get swept away in the details. The key is staying focused on these areas:

✔ **The labor market:** Jobs and job creation are the keys to the medium- and long-term economic outlook for any country or economic bloc. No matter what else is going on, always have a picture of the labor market in the back of your mind. If jobs are being created, more wages are being paid, consumers are consuming more, and economic activity expands. If job growth is stagnant or weak, long-run economic growth will typically be constrained, and interim periods will show varying degrees of strength and weakness. Signs of broader economic growth will be seen as tentative or suspect unless job growth is also present.

From the currency market point of view, labor market strength is typically seen as a currency positive, because it indicates positive growth prospects going forward, along with the potential for higher interest rates based on stronger growth or wage-driven inflation.

✔ **The consumer:** The economies of the major currencies are driven overwhelmingly by personal consumption, accounting for 65 to 70 percent or more of overall economic activity. *Personal consumption* (also known as *private consumption, personal spending,* and similar impersonal terms) refers to how people spend their money. In a nutshell, are they spending more, or are they spending less?

✔ **The business sector:** Businesses and firms contribute directly to economic activity through *capital expenditures* (for example, building factories, stores, and offices; buying software and telecommunications equipment) and indirectly through growth (by hiring, expanding production, and producing investment opportunities). Look at the data reports coming from the corporate sector. (Keep in mind that manufacturing and export sectors are more significant in many non-U.S. economies than they are in the United States.)

Market-Moving Reports

This section gets down to the nitty-gritty data, explaining the major economic data reports that you need to be familiar with. Each report is classified in terms of its usual impact on the market.

The significance of individual reports rises and falls depending on the environment, the market's current focus, and a host of other factors. See the section "Understanding Market Info and Anticipating Market Reactions" for factors to consider as you try to make sense of it all.

Rumors: Where there's smoke, there's fire

All financial markets love rumors. They tend to come out after relatively extensive directional moves or attempts to break through important technical levels — attempts that subsequently fail and see prices reverse direction. Here are some of the forex market's favorites:

✔ **Whisper numbers:** These are generally unfounded rumors of economic data anywhere from a few minutes to a few hours before the scheduled release time. They tend to roil short-term positions opened in anticipation of a report and influence the market's subsequent reaction to the report. Whisper numbers are one reason to consider avoiding the market going into a data release.

✔ **Large market orders:** These rumors frequently do hold water, but not always. They're typically associated with central

banks or large institutional players buying or selling, and they usually mention a price level.

✔ **Terrorism rumors:** Everything from suspicious packages to building evacuations sends a shudder through the market. These rumors tend to have relatively small and short-lived impacts on the currencies involved (like GBP dipping on a London subway evacuation). The USD tends to dip slightly regardless of the location of the rumored terror scare.

The trouble with rumors is that you have no easy way to determine whether they're true, and even if you can, you have no way of being certain of the price reaction. Just be aware that an intraday move or test of a technical level is underway, and have a relatively tight exit strategy if the market turns tail.

Major U.S. reports

The United States is the world's largest national economy, and the U.S. dollar is on one side of 80 percent of currency trades. But that's not why U.S. reports come first. Nope, the aim here is to introduce the major economic reports issued by every major currency country, using U.S. data as the example.

The main data reports of other major national economies essentially mirror the U.S. data reports, but with some minor differences in calculation methods or reporting. The upcoming section "Major international data reports" highlights other reports that are important in non-U.S. economies.

Labor market reports

Various labor market reports let you keep tabs on the job market. The monthly U.S. employment report, the highlight of which is the non-farm payrolls (NFP) report, gets the most attention. *Non-farm Fridays,* as they're semi-affectionately known, are among the most volatile trading days each month.

Non-farm payroll report (Relevance: High)

The NFP report, also referred to as the *establishment survey* (because it's based on responses from companies), is the government's primary report assessing the overall labor market in the prior month. The main components of the report are

- ✔ **Change in non-farm payrolls:** This NFP number accounts for 75 to 80 percent of total U.S. employment, excluding government, self-employed, and farm workers, among other categories. The going wisdom is that the U.S. economy needs to add an average of 100,000 to 150,000 jobs each month to keep the unemployment rate steady. The market's initial reaction is based on the difference between the actual and the forecast change in non-farm payroll workers.

- ✔ **Unemployment rate:** The unemployment rate measures unemployed individuals seeking work as a percentage of the civilian labor force. Increases in the unemployment rate are typically interpreted as a sign of weakness in the labor market and the economy overall, while declines in the rate are considered a positive indicator of the job situation.

- ✔ **Change in manufacturing payrolls:** Measures the number of jobs added or lost in manufacturing industries and is looked at as a gauge of near-term production activity.

- ✔ **Average hourly earnings:** Measures the change in employee wages and is viewed as an indicator of whether incomes are rising or falling and the implications for consumer spending.

- ✔ **Average weekly hours:** Measures the average number of hours worked each week and is looked at as a rough gauge of the demand for labor, with increasing weekly hours seen as a positive for the labor market.

ADP national employment report (Relevance: Medium)

The ADP report is intended to serve as an alternative measurement of the labor market, but it's a relative newcomer, having debuted in mid-2006. Early discrepancies between the ADP report and the NFP report have left market participants uncertain about how much weight to give the ADP report. At the moment, it produces little market reaction on its own. Instead, the market may adjust its forecasts for the NFP depending on what the ADP indicates.

Weekly initial unemployment claims (Relevance: Low)

Initial jobless claims represent first-time filings for unemployment insurance. The changes in initial claims can be volatile on a week-to-week basis, so analysts look at a four-week moving average of initial claims to factor out one-off events. Still, sharp increases or declines in initial claims data will get the market's attention. A second part of the weekly claims report is *continuing claims,* which is a measure of the total number of people receiving unemployment benefits, excluding first-time filers. The market looks at continuing claims as another gauge of labor market conditions, with increases in continuing claims typically suggesting deterioration in the job market and declines in continuing claims suggesting an improvement.

Inflation gauges

Inflation reports are used to monitor overall changes in price levels of goods and services. Increases in inflation are likely to be met with higher interest rates (as central-bank policy makers seek to stamp out inflation), while moderating or declining inflation readings suggest generally lower interest-rate expectations.

There are a number of different inflation reports, with each focused on a different source of inflation or stage of the economy where the price changes are appearing. The main inflation reports to keep an eye on are

- ✔ **Consumer price index (CPI) (Relevance: High):** The CPI measures the cost of a basket of goods and services at the consumer or retail level — the prices we're paying. The CPI is looked at as the final stage of inflation.

- ✔ **Producer price index (PPI) (Relevance: Medium):** The PPI measures the change in prices at the producer or wholesale level, or what firms are charging one another for goods and services. The PPI may serve as a leading indicator of overall inflation.

- ✔ **Personal consumption expenditure (PCE) (Relevance: High):** The PCE is roughly equivalent to the CPI in that it measures the changes in price of a basket of goods and services at the consumer level, but it's preferred by the Federal Reserve as its main inflation gauge because the composition of items in the PCE basket changes more frequently than in CPI, reflecting evolving consumer tastes and behavior.

- ✔ **Institute for Supply Management (ISM) prices paid index (Relevance: Medium):** The national and regional purchasing managers indices have subcategories reporting on the level of prices paid and the level of prices received by firms. The prices-paid component usually gets the most attention as another corporate-level indication of price pressures, likely to be mirrored by the PPI.

Gross domestic product (Relevance: High)

Gross domestic product (GDP) measures the total amount of economic activity in an economy over a specified period, usually quarterly and adjusted for inflation. The percentage change in GDP from one period to the next is looked at as the primary growth rate of an economy. GDP is frequently calculated on a quarterly basis but reported in *annualized* terms. That means a 0.5 percent quarterly GDP increase would be reported as a 2 percent annualized rate of growth for the quarter (0.5 percent × 4 quarters = 2 percent). The use of annualized rates is helpful for comparing relative growth among economies.

In most countries, GDP is reported on a quarterly basis, so it's taken as a big-picture reality check on overall economic growth. The market's economic outlook will be heavily influenced by what the GDP reports indicate. Better-than-expected growth may spur talk of the need for higher interest rates, while steady or slower GDP growth may suggest easier monetary policy ahead. At the same time, though, GDP reports cover a relatively distant economic past — a quarter's GDP report typically comes out almost midway through the next quarter and is looking back at economic activity three to four months ago. As a result, market expectations continue to evolve based on incoming data reports, so don't get too caught up in GDP for too long after its initial release.

Trade and current account balances

Two of the most important reports for the forex markets are trade balance and current account balance:

- ✓ **Trade balance (Relevance: High)** measures the difference between a nation's exports and its imports. If a nation imports more than it exports, it's said to have a *trade deficit;* if a nation exports more than it imports, it's said to have a *trade surplus.*

- ✓ **Current account balance (Relevance: High)** is a broader measure of international trade and includes financial transfers as well as trade in goods and services. Current accounts are also either in deficit or surplus, reflecting whether a country is a net borrower or lender to the rest of the world. Nations with current account deficits are net borrowers; those with current account surpluses are net lenders.

Countries with persistently large trade or current account deficits tend to see their currencies weaken relative to other currencies, while currencies of countries running trade surpluses tend to appreciate.

Leading economic indicators (Relevance: Low)

The index of leading economic indicators (LEI) is based on ten components that typically lead overall economic developments, such as initial unemployment claims, average hourly wages, and consumer sentiment, to single out just a few. The LEI index is looked at as a gauge of the economy's direction over the next six to nine months. Increases in the index point to stronger growth in the months ahead, while declines in the index point to likely future weakness. Because eight of the ten components in the index are known in advance of its release, the LEI index tends to have a subdued market impact, but it's still useful to guide future expectations.

Institute for Supply Management and purchasing managers reports

The Institute for Supply Management (ISM) calculates several regional and national indices of current business conditions and future outlooks based on surveys of purchasing managers. ISM readings are based on a boom/bust scale with 50 as the tipping point: A reading above 50 indicates expansion, while a reading below 50 signals contraction.

The main ISM reports to keep an eye on are

- **Chicago Purchasing Managers Index (PMI) (Relevance: Low):** The Chicago PMI is the first of the national PMIs to be reported, and the market frequently views it as a leading indicator of the larger national ISM manufacturing report, which is released a few days after the Chicago PMI.

- **ISM manufacturing report (Relevance: Medium):** This report includes a prices-paid index, which is viewed as an interim inflation reading, along with other key subsector measurements, like the employment situation. The market tends to react pretty aggressively to sharp changes in the report or if the ISM is moving above or below 50, but because the manufacturing sector accounts for a relatively small portion of overall U.S. economic activity, the importance of the ISM manufacturing gauge tends to be exaggerated.

- **ISM nonmanufacturing report (Relevance: Medium):** The ISM non-manufacturing report is the monthly ISM report that covers the other 80 percent of the U.S. economy. The ISM manufacturing report may get more attention, but the ISM nonmanufacturing report is the one to focus on.

Consumer sentiment and spending reports

Consumer psychology is at the heart of the market's attempts to interpret future consumer activity and, with it, the overall direction of the economy. The theory is that if you feel good, you'll spend more, and if you feel lousy, you'll stop spending. The market likes to pay attention to consumer confidence indicators even though there is little correlation between how consumers tell you they feel and how they'll actually go on to spend.

Consumer sentiment reports

The key confidence gauges are

- **Consumer confidence index (Relevance: Medium):** A monthly report issued by the Conference Board comprised of the expectations index (looking six months ahead) and the present-situation index. The surveys ask households about their outlooks for overall economic conditions, employment, and incomes.

- **University of Michigan consumer sentiment index (Relevance: Medium):** Comes out twice a month: a preliminary reading in the middle of the month and a final reading at the start of the next month.

Personal income and personal spending (Relevance: Medium)

Personal income includes all wages and salaries, along with transfer payments (like Social Security or unemployment insurance) and dividends. *Personal spending* is based on personal consumption expenditures for all types of individual outlays. The market looks at these two monthly reports to get an update on the health of the U.S. consumer and the outlook for personal consumption going forward.

Personal income is watched as a leading indicator of personal spending on the basis that future spending is highly correlated with personal income. The greater the increases in personal income, the more optimistic the consumption outlook will be, and vice versa. But it's important to note that inflation-adjusted incomes are the key. If incomes are just keeping pace with inflation, the outlook for spending is less positive.

Retail sales (Relevance: High)

The monthly advance retail sales report is the primary indicator of personal spending in the United States, covering most every purchase Americans make, from gas station fill-ups to dinner out and a night at the movies. These reports are subject to a variety of distorting effects, most commonly from weather. Stretches of bad weather, such as major storms or bouts of unseasonable cold or heat, can impair consumer mobility or alter shopping patterns, reducing retail sales in the affected period. Sharp swings in gasoline prices can also create illusory effects, such as price spikes leading to an apparent increase in retail sales due to the higher per-gallon price, while overall non-gas retail sales are reduced or displaced by the higher outlays at the pump.

Durable goods orders (Relevance: Medium)

Durable goods reports measure the amount of orders received by manufacturers that produce items made to last at least three years. Durables are generally bigger-ticket purchases, such as washing machines and furniture, so they're also looked at as a leading indicator of overall consumer spending. If consumers are feeling flush with cash and confidence, big-ticket spending is more common. If consumers are uncertain, or times are tight, high-cost purchases are the first to be postponed.

Housing-market indicators

There's a raft of monthly housing market reports to monitor the sector, based on whether the homes are new or existing:

✔ **Existing-home sales (Relevance: High)** is reported by the National Association of Realtors (NAR). Sales of preexisting homes (condos included) account for the lion's share of residential real estate activity — about 85 percent of total home sales. Existing-home sales are reported on an annualized rate, and the market looks at the monthly change in that rate. Median home prices and the inventory of unsold homes are important clues to how the housing market is evolving. Existing-home sales are counted after a closing. (Pending home sales are a separate report viewed as a leading indicator of existing home sales and are counted when a contract is signed to buy an existing home.)

✔ **New-home sales (Relevance: Medium),** reported on an annualized basis, account for about 15 percent of residential home sales. New home sales are counted when a contract is signed to purchase the new home, which means that contract cancellations (not reported) may result in lower actual sales than originally reported.

✔ **Housing starts (Relevance: Medium)** measure the number of new-home construction starts that took place in each month, reported on an annualized rate. Housing starts are considered a leading indicator of new-home sales but more recently have been looked at as an indication of home builder sentiment, as builders try to reduce inventories of unsold new homes.

✔ **Building permits (Relevance: Medium)** are reported alongside housing starts each month. Building permits are viewed as another leading indicator of housing starts and new-home sales.

Regional Federal Reserve indices

A number of the Federal Reserve district banks issue monthly surveys of business sentiment in their regions, usually concentrated on the manufacturing sector. Responses above zero indicate that conditions are improving, and readings below zero indicate deterioration. The main regional Fed indices to watch are

✔ **Philadelphia Fed index (Relevance: Medium):** Usually the first of the major Fed indices to be reported each month, covering the manufacturing sector in Pennsylvania, New Jersey, and Delaware.

✔ **New York Empire State index (Relevance: Medium):** Assesses New York state manufacturers' current and six-month outlooks.

✔ **Richmond Fed manufacturing index (Relevance: Low):** A composite index based on new orders, production, and employment, covering the Middle Atlantic states.

The Fed's Beige Book (Relevance: High)

The Beige Book is a compilation of regional economic assessments from the Fed's 12 district banks, issued about two weeks before every Federal Open Market Committee (FOMC) policy-setting meeting. The regional Fed banks develop their summaries based on surveys and anecdotal reporting of local business leaders and economists, and the report is then summarized by one of the Fed district banks, all of which take turns issuing the report. The Beige Book is designed to serve as the basis of economic discussions at the upcoming FOMC meeting. Markets look at the Beige Book's main findings to get a handle on how the economy is developing:

✔ Is the economy expanding or contracting? How fast and how widespread?

✔ Which sectors are strongest, and which sectors are weakest?

✔ Are there any signs of inflation?

✔ How does the labor market look?

Major international data reports

Plenty of national data reports don't have an equivalent in the United States, and others are followed more closely in local markets and require extra attention. The next few sections highlight the main data reports of other national economies.

Eurozone

The main data reports out of the Eurozone are remarkably similar to those of the United States. The key difference is that individual European countries report national economic data, which comes out alongside Eurozone-wide reports from the European Commission or other pan-European reporting agencies, like the European Central Bank (ECB). Don't panic, though — you don't have to start monitoring Irish CPI and Dutch retail sales unless you're trading securities of those countries.

Because the Eurozone has a common currency and central bank, the forex market focuses primarily on Eurozone indicators that cover the entire region, such as Eurozone industrial production and trade balance. Among individual national reports, the market concentrates on the key reports from the largest Eurozone economies: Germany; France; and, to a lesser extent, Italy. Keep a close eye on all the major data reports coming out of those countries.

The only European reports that may escape your attention due to unusual names are the principal European confidence indicators, which go by the acronyms of the groups that put them together. These reports can generate sizeable reactions when they're out of line with expectations:

- ✔ **ZEW and GfK sentiment surveys (Relevance: Medium)** are two separate consumer confidence gauges issued by private research firms known by their initials (ZEW and GfK). They're reported for Germany and France and on a Eurozone-wide basis.

- ✔ **IFO sentiment survey (Relevance: Medium)** is a corporate sentiment survey that queries businesses across Germany on current sentiment and how business is expected to develop over the next six months. The IFO survey is put out by the IFO Institute, a private think tank in Munich, and covers only Germany.

Japan

In addition to following all the usual reports, pay special attention to industrial production and manufacturing data because of their large role in the Japanese economy (which is heavily export-oriented). Outside the standard reports to watch, keep an eye on the following:

- ✔ **Tankan index (Relevance: High):** This is the big corporate sentiment survey in Japan, issued by the Bank of Japan (BOJ) after surveying some 10,000+ Japanese firms on their outlook. The Tankan is reported as a *diffusion index,* where negative responses are subtracted from positive responses, resulting in a net reading — the higher the Tankan index, the more optimistic the outlook. The Tankan survey produces four readings: current conditions and future outlook from both large manufacturers and large nonmanufacturers. The large all-industry capital expenditures survey is an important gauge of capital spending and is often the focus of the entire Tankan survey.

- ✔ **Trade balance (Relevance: High):** Japan's monthly trade balance is nearly always in surplus. The size of that surplus carries indications for the health of the export sector as well as potential political repercussions against excessive JPY weakness when the trade surplus is seen to be too large.

- ✔ **All-industry and tertiary industry (services) indices (Relevance: Medium):** These are monthly sentiment gauges of industrial and service-sector firms.

United Kingdom

Be alert for the following reports that can trigger sharp reactions in GBP:

- ✔ **Bank of England minutes (Relevance: High):** Released two weeks after each Monetary Policy Committee (MPC) meeting, they show the voting results for the most recent decision. Market expectations and GBP are frequently upended when the policy vote shows dissent (not all members voted for the action) or unanimity.

- ✔ **GfK consumer confidence and Nationwide consumer confidence (Relevance: Medium):** These are two separate consumer-sentiment gauges put out by GfK, a UK/European marketing agency, and the Nationwide Building Society, a UK mortgage lender.

- ✔ **Royal Institution of Chartered Surveyors (RICS) house price balance (Relevance: Medium):** This monthly housing market survey shows the proportion of real-estate agents reporting a rise in housing prices minus those indicating a decline.

- ✔ **CBI distributive trades survey and industrial trends survey (Relevance: Medium):** These two monthly reports are put out by the Confederation of British Industry, a private trade group. The distributive trades survey is a measure of retail sales, and the industrial trends survey is a survey of manufacturers' current and future outlook.

- ✔ **British Retail Consortium (BRC) retail sales monitor and shop price index (Relevance: Medium):** These two monthly reports are put out by the British Retail Consortium, a private trade organization. The retail sales monitor is another measure of retail sales, and the shop price index measures inflation at the retail level.

Canada

Canadian data mirrors U.S. data in many respects, but here are few other important Canadian indicators to watch:

- ✔ **International securities transactions (Relevance: High):** This is roughly the equivalent of the U.S. Treasury's TIC report, showing net investment flows into and out of Canada on a monthly basis. High inflows typically support the CAD, and outflows tend to hurt it.

- ✔ **International merchandise trade (Relevance: Medium):** Canada's trade balance is especially significant due to the size of the manufacturing and export sectors.

- ✔ **Ivey purchasing managers index (Relevance: Medium):** This key monthly sentiment gauge of Canadian businesses is issued by the Richard Ivey Business School.

Australia

Australian data reports exert a strong influence on Aussie, similar in many respects to how UK data affects the pound. In particular, keep an eye on

- ✔ **Westpac consumer confidence and National Australia Bank (NAB) business confidence (Relevance: Medium):** These two monthly sentiment gauges are put out by two of Australia's leading banks.

- ✔ **Trade balance (Relevance: Medium):** Australia's trade balance is critical due to the significance of the export sector and the relatively small size of the economy, which means that trade deficits tend to hurt the AUD more than surpluses support it.

Switzerland

Swiss data reports are generally fewer but fit the standard data bill of fare. Swiss data tends to have the greatest impact on EUR/CHF, especially if the two economies are seen to be diverging, either in economic growth or interest rates. The most important Swiss data report outside the usual suspects is the **KOF Swiss Leading Indicator (Relevance: Medium).** The KOF is an index of six indicators intended to forecast the outlook over the next six to nine months. The index is calculated by the KOF Technical Institute in Zurich.

Book V

Foreign Currency Trading

New Zealand

New Zealand data is similarly provocative for the Kiwi, and inflation reports are among the most significant due to the relatively high level of benchmark interest rates. In addition to the other main data reports, keep an eye on the following Kiwi-specific data:

- ✓ **Australia New Zealand (ANZ) business New Zealand (NZ) purchasing managers index (PMI) (Relevance: Medium):** A monthly survey of purchasing managers' (corporate) sentiment issued by ANZ Banking Group.

- ✓ **Trade balance (Relevance: High):** New Zealand's trade balance is also critical due to the relatively small size of the economy and the importance of exports.

- ✓ **Westpac New Zealand consumer confidence (Relevance: Medium):** A monthly consumer sentiment index released by Westpac Banking Corporation.

Understanding Market Info and Anticipating Market Reactions

Fundamental economic data reports are among the more significant information inputs because policy makers and market participants alike use them to gauge the state of the economy, set monetary policy, and make investment decisions. While you may have a decent idea of what certain economic reports mean, you may not feel comfortable that you can really make sense of what you read and hear. The following sections can help you out by not only explaining the prism through which market info is filtered, but also explaining how the market tends to react.

Deciphering market themes

At any given moment in the forex market, several *themes* dominate the market's attention. Market themes are the essence of the real-world forces currently driving the market. Themes are what market commentators and analysts are talking about when they explain what's happening. But most important, themes are the filters through which new information and data are absorbed by the market. Or to put it another way, they're the lenses through which the market sees events and data.

Market themes come in all shapes and sizes; some are long-term themes that can color the market's direction for months and years; others may hold sway for only a few hours, days, or weeks. Market themes come in two main forms that coexist in parallel universes and also frequently overlap:

- **Fundamental themes:** Each currency has its own set of fundamental circumstances in which it's being evaluated by the market. The basic fundamental environment is ever-present, but it's also subject to change over time, just as economic conditions will change in the course of business cycles. Fundamental themes will also shift in relative importance to one another, with certain themes being pushed to the side for a period when news or events focus the market's attention on other, more pressing themes. The following sections explain the main fundamental themes.

- **Technical themes:** The prevalence of technical analysis as the basis for many trading decisions can add weight to existing fundamental-driven moves, generating yet another theme to propel the move: the technical theme. It may be a trending market movement that attracts trend-following traders who don't give a hoot about the underlying fundamentals. As long as the technical trend is in place, they keep pushing the market in the direction it's going, prolonging the price adjustment perhaps far beyond what the fundamentals would dictate. For information on technical analysis, see Book VIII.

Rising or falling interest rates

Because interest rates are usually the single most important determinant of a currency's value, markets are constantly speculating about their direction. But it's not just about where interest rate levels are now, though that's still important (higher interest rate currencies tend to do better against lower-yielding currencies). What matters most is their overall direction (whether they're going up or down), their future level (how high or low they're likely to go), and the timing of any changes (how fast rates are likely to change). The effect of interest rate themes is most powerful when the interest rates of two currencies are diverging — when one currency's interest rate is expected to move higher and the other lower.

When you're looking at economic data or monetary policy rhetoric, always assess information first in terms of what it means for the interest rates of the nation's currency. A currency that's expected to see lower rates in the near future, for example, is likely to stop declining and may even rebound if an economic growth report or an inflation reading comes in higher than expected. The market will pause to consider whether its outlook for lower rates is correct.

Looking for growth

Economic growth prospects are the linchpin to a host of currency value determinants, from the interest rate outlook to the attractiveness of a nation's investment climate (stocks and bonds). Strong economic growth increases the likelihood of higher interest rates down the road. Weaker growth data increases the prospect of potentially lower interest rates, as well as dampening the outlook for the investment environment.

There's no set recipe for how growth data will impact a currency's value, but when the interest rate outlook is generally neutral, as in no solid conviction on the direction of two countries' rates, the growth theme becomes more important.

Be aware that many growth data reports reflect only a particular sector of a nation's larger economy, such as the manufacturing sector or the housing market. How significant the information is interpreted to be depends on how significant that sector is to the larger national economy.

Fighting inflation

Inflation is *the* bogeyman to all central bankers. Even when inflation is low, they still worry about it — it's just part of the job. As a currency trader attuned to monetary policy developments, you need to monitor inflation readings as well.

When factoring inflation data into the interest rate theme, be aware of how the overall growth theme is holding up. If growth is good, and inflation is high because of economic strength, higher inflation readings will be currency supportive. If growth is slowing, and inflation is still too high, the currency impact will be decidedly less positive and very likely downright negative. (You may be wondering why currencies are so fickle, liking higher interest rates some, but not all, of the time. The reason is the low-/slow-growth scenario coupled with high/higher interest rates increases the risks of an economy dropping into recession, which would ultimately result in interest rate cuts farther down the road.)

Gauging the strength of structural themes

Structural themes (the big-picture elements of how an economy is performing or national events are playing out) are the most fleeting; they can be in full force one day or for several weeks or months and then drop from the radar screen altogether. These themes are also usually secondary to the interest rates, growth, and inflation, but they can still exert significant influence on a currency. More important, they can amplify the impact of the primary themes. Following are frequently recurring structural themes:

- **Employment:** Employment is the key to an economy's long-run expansion and a primary driver of interest rates. Sharp increases in unemployment are among the fastest triggers to interest rate cuts by central bankers, going back to the primary interest rate theme.

- **Deficits:** Both fiscal and trade deficits are typically currency negatives. During times of low/slow growth, the impact of deficits can be magnified, as the very credibility of a currency can be questioned. During times of steady/high growth, their impact tends to be more muted, but they are still a negative hanging over the outlook.

- **Geopolitical issues:** The USD is the currency most vulnerable to geopolitical issues, given the size of the U.S. economy, its reliance on world trade, and the potential for military involvement. After geopolitical tensions subside, the market is quick to revert to preexisting themes.

- **Political elections or uncertainty:** Changes of government and political uncertainty in the major-currency countries can certainly dent the market's sentiment toward the affected currency. The impact on the currency will usually be felt on the margins, hurting a softening currency and restraining an appreciating one. But shortly after the political situation is resolved, political issues tend to fade quickly into the background.

Recognizing reporting conventions

The data that you find in economic textbooks is very neat and clean, but the data as it actually arrives in the market can be anything *but* neat and clean. We're talking here not only about the imperfections of economic data gathering, which relies heavily on statistical sampling methods, but also about how the market interprets individual data reports.

In the following sections, we look at important data-reporting conventions and how they can affect market reactions. When currencies don't react to the headlines of a data report as you would expect, odds are that one of the following elements is responsible, and you need to look more closely at the report to get the true picture.

Comparing past and present: Data history

When you're looking at upcoming economic data events, not only do you need to be aware of what's expected, but it also helps to know what, if any, trends are evident in the data series. The key is to first be aware of prior-period revisions and to then view them relative to the incoming data. Things to keep in mind:

- ✔ The more pronounced or lengthy the trend is, the more likely the reactions to out-of-line economic reports will prove short lived. The more ambiguous or fluid the recent data has been, the more likely the reaction to the new data will be sustained.

- ✔ See whether the data in the new report revises the data from the prior period, in which case the market tends to look at the two reports together. If a current report comes out worse than expected, and the prior report is revised lower as well, the two together are likely to be interpreted as very disappointing. If a current report comes out better than expected, but the prior period's revision is negative, the positive reaction to the most recent report will tend to be restrained by the downgrade to the earlier data.

- ✔ The larger the revision to the prior report, the more significance it will carry into the interpretation of the current release.

- ✔ Current data reports tend to receive a higher weighting by the market if only because the data is the freshest available, and markets are always looking ahead.

Getting to the core

A number of important economic indicators are issued on a headline basis and a core basis. The *headline* reading is the complete result of the indicator, while the *core* reading is the headline reading minus certain categories or excluding certain items. In the case of inflation reports, for example, many reporting agencies strip out or exclude highly volatile components, such as food and energy. The rationale for ignoring those items is that they're prone to market, seasonal, or weather-related disruptions. By leaving them out, the core reading is believed to paint a more accurate picture of structural, long-term price pressures, which is what monetary-policy makers are most concerned with.

Whenever you see a data report "ex-something," it's short for "excluding" that something. In the United States, for instance, the consumer price index (CPI) is reported on a core basis <u>ex</u>cluding <u>f</u>ood and <u>e</u>nergy, commonly cited as *CPI ex-F&E*.

Markets tend to focus on the core reading over the headline reading in most cases, especially where a known preference for the core reading exists on the part of monetary-policy makers. The result can be large discrepancies between headline data and the core readings, resulting in market reactions that are similarly disjointed, with an initial reaction based on the headline reading frequently followed by a different reaction to the core.

Watching early moves: Consensus expectations and pricing in and out

Data reports and news events don't happen in a vacuum. Forex markets evaluate incoming data reports relative to market forecasts, commonly referred to as *consensus expectations* or simply the *consensus.* Consensus expectations are the average of economic forecasts made by economists from the leading financial institutions, banks, and securities houses. News agencies like Bloomberg and Reuters survey economists for their estimates of upcoming data and collate the results. The resulting average forecast is what appears on market calendars indicating what is expected for any given data report.

The consensus becomes the baseline against which incoming data will be evaluated by the market. In the case of economic data, the market will compare the *actual* result — the economic figure that's actually reported — with what was expected (the consensus). The actual data is typically interpreted by the market as *expected* (or *in line with expectations*), *better than expected,* or *worse than expected.* The degree to which a data report is better or worse than expected is important. The farther off the mark the data report is, the greater the likelihood and degree of a subsequent price shift following the data release.

Players in the currency market don't typically wait for news to actually be released before they start trading on it. Currency traders begin to price consensus expectations into the market anywhere from several days to several hours before a report is scheduled. The more significant the report, the sooner markets are likely to start pricing in expectations. *Pricing in* is the practice of trading as though the data were already released and, usually, as though it has come out as expected. But not always. Keep these things in mind:

✔ Sometimes the market doesn't always price in an as-expected result. Market sentiment may have soured (or improved) in the run-up to the release, leading the market to price in a worse-than-expected (or better-than-expected) report.

✔ Consensus estimates can sometimes change in the days leading up to the report, based on other interim reports. This can lead to *pricing out* of consensus expectations, depending on to what degree the consensus was priced in.

✔ *Data miss* is the market euphemism for when a data report comes in outside expectations. If the consensus was for an improvement in a particular indicator, and the actual report is worse than expected or disappointing, the result may be a sharp reversal in price direction. The same thing can happen in reverse if negative expectations are met by a surprisingly positive data report.

To get a sense of how much the market has priced in any forecast, follow market commentaries and price action in the hours and days before a scheduled report. Stay on top of the market reports to get a handle on the mood.

It frequently helps to think through the likely reactions to major data releases to prepare for how the market may react in the very likely case that the data surprises one way or the other. It's a thoroughly academic exercise, but it may just give you a significant leg up on the rest of the market if you're inclined to trade around data reports.

Chapter 5

Advice for Successful Forex Trading

Sun Tzu, author of the ancient *The Art of War,* a book of military strategy, observed that every battle is won or lost before it even begins. That same rationale applies to trading. And just as an army must know its strengths and weaknesses to succeed, you have to get to know yours, too. This chapter looks at various trading styles, provides tips to develop trading discipline, and offers a practical plan for analyzing markets with an eye to spotting trade opportunities. It also takes a hard look at risks beyond just losing money, so you can be prepared for bumps in the road.

Finding a Trading Style That Suits You

We're frequently asked, "What's the best way to trade the forex market?" Unfortunately, there is no easy answer. Better put, there is no *standard* answer: one that applies to everyone. The forex market's trading characteristics have something to offer every trading style (long-term, medium-term, or short-term) and approach (technical, fundamental, or a blend). In deciding what style or approach, the starting point is not the forex market itself, but your own individual circumstances and way of thinking.

Step 1: Know thyself

Before you can begin to identify a trading style and approach that works best for you, you need to give some serious thought to what resources you have available to support your trading. In other words, forex trading takes time and money: What can you afford?

 ✔ **Money:** When it comes to money, trading capital has to be *risk capital:* money that, if lost, will not materially affect your standard of living. Obviously, borrowed money is *not* risk capital — never use borrowed money for speculative trading.

   When you determine how much risk capital you have available for trading, you'll have a better idea of what size account you can trade and what position size you can handle. Most online trading platforms typically offer generous leverage ratios that allow you to control a larger position with less required margin. But just because they offer high leverage doesn't mean you have to fully utilize it.

 ✔ **Time:** If you're a full-time trader, you have lots of time to devote to market analysis and actually trading the market. But if your full-time job is something other than trading, you have to do your market research in your free time. Be realistic when you think about how much time you'll be able to devote on a regular basis, keeping in mind family obligations and other personal circumstances.

Step 2: Technical or fundamental analysis?

Ask yourself on what basis you'll make your trading decisions: fundamental analysis, which relies on evaluating the underlying value and future potential of the security, or technical analysis, which uses the tracking of price fluctuations to predict or identify market trends? (For details on the different styles, go to Books VII and VIII respectively.)

Sometimes forex markets seem to be more driven by fundamental factors, such as current economic data or comments from a central bank official. In those times, fundamentals provide the catalysts for technical breakouts and reversals. At other times, technical developments seem to be leading the charge. So rather than take sides, why not follow an approach that *blends* the two disciplines? Approaching the market with a blend of fundamental and technical analysis can improve your chances of both spotting trade opportunities and managing your trades more effectively.

Step 3: Pick a style, any style

After you've given some thought to the time and resources you're able to devote to currency trading and which approach you favor (technical, fundamental, or a blend), the next step is to settle on a trading style that best fits those choices. The next sections explain three main trading styles, with degrees of exposure to market risk. Keep in mind that styles frequently overlap, and you can adopt different styles for different trade opportunities or different market conditions.

The two main elements of market risk are time and relative price movements. The longer you hold a position, the more risk you're exposed to. The more of a price change you're anticipating, the more risk you're exposed to.

Short-term, high-frequency day trading

Short-term trading in forex typically involves holding a position for only a few seconds or minutes and rarely longer than an hour. The goal is to profit by repeatedly opening and closing positions after gaining just a few pips, frequently as little as one or two pips. In the interbank market, extremely short-term, in-and-out trading is referred to as *jobbing the market;* online currency traders call it *scalping.* Traders who follow this style have these characteristics:

- ✔ **They are among the fastest and most disciplined of traders.** Their goal is to capture only a few pips on each trade. Rapid reaction and instantaneous decision-making are essential to successfully jobbing the market. Their motto is "Take the money and run" — repeated a few dozen times a day.

- ✔ **They have an intuitive feel for the market.** (Some practitioners refer to it as *rhythm trading.*) If you were to ask a scalper for her opinion of a particular currency pair, she would be likely to respond along the lines of "It feels *bid*" or "It feels *offered*" (meaning, she senses an underlying buying or selling bias in the market — but only at that moment). If you ask her again a few minutes later, she may respond in the opposite direction.

- ✔ **They have no allegiance to any single position.** They couldn't care less if the currency pair goes up or down. They're strictly focused on the next few pips.

If you pursue a short-term trading strategy online, where dealing spreads can equal profit targets, you need to be right by a larger margin. For that reason, trading a short-term strategy online requires individual traders to invest more time and effort in analyzing the overall market, especially from the technical perspective. Other tips for the short-term trader:

✔ Trade only the most liquid currency pairs, such as EUR/USD, USD/JPY, EUR/GBP, EUR/JPY, and EUR/CHF, and focus your trading on only one pair at a time.

✔ Trade only during times of peak liquidity and market interest, and avoid trading around data releases.

✔ Look for a brokerage firm that offers click-and-deal trading so you're not subject to execution delays or requites.

✔ Preset your default trade size so you don't have to keep specifying it on each deal, and adjust your risk and reward expectations to reflect the dealing spread of the currency pair you're trading.

Medium-term directional trading

Medium-term positions are typically held for periods ranging anywhere from a few minutes to a few hours, but usually not much longer than a day. As with short-term trading, the key distinction for medium-term trading is not the length of time the position is open but the amount of pips you're seeking/risking.

The essence of medium-term trading (sometimes referred to as *momentum trading* and *swing trading*) is determining where a currency pair is likely to go over the next several hours or days and constructing a trading strategy to exploit that view. (Of course, although medium-term traders normally look to capture larger relative price movements — say, 50 to 100 pips or more — they're also quick to take smaller profits on the basis of short-term price behavior.)

Medium-term trading requires many of the same skills as short-term trading, but it also demands a broader perspective, greater analytical effort, and a lot more patience. Medium-term traders typically pursue one of the following overall approaches, but there's also plenty of room to combine strategies:

✔ **Trading a view:** Having a fundamental-based opinion on which way a currency pair is likely to move (although view traders still need to be aware of technical levels as part of an overall trading plan).

✔ **Trading the technicals:** Spotting trade opportunities on charts (but these traders still need to be aware of fundamental events, which are the catalysts for many breaks of technical levels).

✔ **Trading events and data:** Basing positions on expected outcomes of events, like a central bank rate decision or a G7 meeting. Event/data traders typically open positions well in advance of events and close them when the outcome is known.

✔ **Trading with the flow:** Trading based on overall market direction (trend) or information of major buying and selling (flows). Flow traders tend to stay out of short-term range-bound markets and jump in only when a market move is underway.

Long-term macroeconomic trading

Long-term trading in currencies is generally reserved for hedge funds and other institutional types with deep pockets. Long-term trading in currencies can involve holding positions for weeks, months, and potentially years at a time. Holding positions for that long necessarily involves being exposed to significant short-term volatility that can quickly overwhelm margin trading accounts. Still, with proper risk management, individual margin traders can seek to capture longer-term trends. The key is to hold a small enough position relative to your margin that you can withstand volatility of as much as 5 percent or more. Mini accounts, which trade in lot sizes of 10,000 currency units, are a good vehicle to take advantage of longer-term price trends.

Long-term trading seeks to capitalize on major price trends, which are in turn the result of long-term macroeconomic factors:

- ✔ **Interest rate cycles:** Where are the two currencies' relative interest rates, and where are they likely to go in the coming months?

- ✔ **Economic growth cycles:** What's the outlook for relative growth over the next several months?

- ✔ **Currency policies:** Are the currencies considered to be excessively overvalued or undervalued by the major global trading powers?

- ✔ **Structural deficits or surpluses:** Do the currencies have any major structural issues that tend to see currencies weaken or strengthen, such as fiscal deficits/surpluses or trade deficits/surpluses?

Just because you're trading with a long-term view doesn't mean you can't take advantage of significant price changes when they're in your favor in the medium term. *Trading around a core position* refers to taking profit on a portion of your overall position after favorable price changes. You continue to hold a portion of your original position — the core position — and look to reestablish the full position on subsequent market corrections.

It never hurts to take some money off the table when you're winning. The risk with trading around a core position is that the trend may not correct after you've taken partial profit, never giving you the chance to reestablish your desired full position. But you're still holding the core of your position, and because the market hasn't corrected, it means your core position is doing just fine.

Developing Trading Discipline

No matter which trading style you decide to pursue, you need an organized *trading plan,* a well-thought-out approach to executing a trade strategy, or you won't get very far. Any trading plan has three simple components:

- ✔ **Determining position size:** How large a position will you take for each trade strategy? Position size is half the equation for determining how much money is at stake in each trade.

- ✔ **Deciding where to enter the position:** Exactly where will you try to open the desired position? What happens if your entry level is not reached?

- ✔ **Setting stop-loss and take-profit levels:** Exactly where will you exit the position, both if it's a winning position (take profit) and if it's a losing position (stop loss)? Stop-loss and take-profit levels are the second half of the equation that determines how much money is at stake in each trade.

Developing a trading plan and sticking to it are the two main ingredients of trading discipline, *the* defining characteristic of successful traders. Traders who follow a disciplined approach are the ones who survive year after year and market cycle after market cycle. They can even be wrong more often than right and still make money because they follow a disciplined approach. Yet establishing and maintaining trading discipline is an elusive goal for many traders.

Taking the emotion out of trading

When it comes to trading in any market, don't underestimate the power of emotions to distract and disrupt. Of course you can't take all the emotion out of trading. As long as your heart is pumping and your synapses are firing, emotions are going to be flowing, and emotions can be pretty intense when you're trading. Because you can't block out the emotions, the best you can hope to achieve is limiting their impact on your trading. Do the following:

- ✔ **Focus on the pips and not the dollars and cents.** Don't be distracted by the exact amount of money won or lost in a trade. Instead, focus on where prices are and how they're behaving.

- ✔ **Remind yourself it's not about being right or wrong; it's about making money.** At the end of the day, the market doesn't care if you were right or wrong, and neither should you. The only true way of measuring trading success is in dollars and cents.

- ✔ **Accept that you're going to lose in a fair number of trades.** Taking losses is as much a part of the routine as taking profits, and you can still be successful over time.

- ✔ **Don't personalize what happens in the market.** The market isn't out to get you; it's going to do what it does whether you're involved in it or not. Interpret events professionally, just as you would the results of any other business venture.

Managing your expectations

Before you get involved with trading currencies, you need to have a healthy sense of what to expect when it comes to trading outcomes. The trading style that you decide to pursue dictates the relative size of profits and losses that you can expect to experience. If you're trading on a short- to medium-term basis, look at average daily trading ranges to get a good idea of what to expect.

The *average daily trading range* is a mathematical average of each day's trading range (high to low) over a specified period. Keep in mind that this figure is just a statistical average — there will be days with larger ranges and days with narrower ranges. Also, average daily ranges will vary significantly by currency pair.

Balancing risk versus reward

Trading is all about taking on risk to generate profits. Some trading books advise people to use a risk/reward ratio, like 2:1, meaning that if you risk $100 on a trade, you should aim to make $200 to justify the risk. Others counsel never to risk more than a fixed percentage of your trading account on any single trade. But a better way to think about risk and reward is to look at each trade opportunity on its own and assess the outcomes based on technical analysis. This approach has the virtue of being as dynamic as the market, allowing you to exploit trade opportunities according to prevailing market conditions.

Another factor to consider in balancing risk and reward is the use of leverage. In online currency trading, generous leverage ratios of 100:1 or 200:1 are typically available. The higher the leverage ratio, the larger position you can trade based on your margin. But leverage is a double-edged sword because it also amplifies profits and losses. The key is to limit your overall leverage utilization so you're not putting all your eggs in one basket. If you open the largest position available based on your margin, you'll have very little cushion left in case of adverse price movements.

Keeping your ammunition dry

One of the biggest mistakes traders make is known as overtrading. *Overtrading* typically refers to trading too often in the market or trading too many positions at once. Both forms suggest a lack of discipline, and sound more like throwing darts at a board and hoping something sticks. *Keeping your ammunition dry* refers to staying out of the market, watching and waiting, and picking your trades more selectively.

Using your margin collateral sparingly

The margin you're required to post with your forex broker is the basis for all your trading. The amount of margin you put up determines how large a position you can hold and for how long (in pips) if the market moves against you. Unless you just won the lottery, your margin collateral is a precious, finite resource, so you have to use it sparingly.

Holding open positions not only exposes you to market risk but can also cost you market opportunities. After you enter a position, your available margin is reduced, which in turn lowers the amount of available positions you can establish. If you're routinely involved in the market because you don't want to miss out on the next big move, you actually run the risk of missing out on the next big move because you may not have enough available margin to support a position for the big move.

Missing a few opportunities — deliberately

Don't be afraid to miss out on some trade opportunities. No one ever catches all the moves. Instead, focus on your market analysis and pinpoint the next well-defined trading opportunity. (We look at spotting trade setups in the upcoming section "Analyzing trade setup to determine position size.")

One virtue of trading less frequently is that your market outlook is not skewed by any of the emotional entanglements that come with open positions. If you ask a trader who's long EUR/USD what he thinks of EUR/USD, surprise, surprise — he's going to tell you he thinks it's going up. That's called *talking your book*. But being out of the market, or being *square,* allows you to step back and analyze market developments with a fresh perspective. That's when you can spot opportunities more clearly and develop an effective trade strategy to exploit them.

Making Time for Market Analysis

The more regular your analysis, the greater the feel you'll develop for where the market has been and where it's likely to go. Also, the more regularly you update yourself on the market, the less time it takes to stay up to speed. At the minimum, be prepared to devote at least an hour every day to looking at the market and keeping tabs on upcoming data and events. A routine for reliable market analysis includes

- ✔ Multiple-time-frame technical analysis, which enables you to recognize price channels. (Both are explained in the following sections.)
- ✔ Candlestick analysis after each daily and weekly close. (Head to Book VIII for information on candlestick analysis.)
- ✔ Reading economic data reports that have come out overnight.

  ✔ Assessing the likely market impact of upcoming data reports and events.

  ✔ Reviewing market commentaries to stay on top of major themes and overall market sentiment.

If the time you have to devote to market analysis is limited, focus your energies on only one or two currency pairs. As you become more adept at analysis — or if your available time increases — you can follow and analyze additional currency pairs.

Performing multiple-time-frame technical analysis

You need to perform multiple-time-frame technical analysis to identify support and resistance levels and to track overall price developments. (For key technical analysis principles and charting techniques, go to Book VIII.)

Multiple-time-frame technical analysis is nothing more complicated than looking at charts using different time frames of data. The basic idea is to look at the big picture first to identify the key longer-term features and then drill down into shorter data time frames to pinpoint short-term price levels and trends. Our own preference is to focus on daily, 4-hour, and 30-minute time frames, but you can use whichever time frames you think best match your trading style. Short-term traders, for instance, may want to focus on 2-hour, 30-minute, and 5-minute charts to better reflect the narrower time frames of their trading.

Whichever time frames you end up working with, be sure to include longer time frames, like daily and weekly, so you can get a sense of where the most significant price levels are. The strength and significance of support and resistance levels are a function of the time frame in which they're evident, with longer-term technical levels holding greater meaning than shorter ones. You don't want your focus to become so narrow that you lose sight of the big picture and go with a break of short-term resistance, for instance, when major daily or weekly resistance is just beyond.

Make sure the charting system you're using has the ability to save trend lines across time frames, meaning that a trend line you draw on a daily chart should also appear on the four-hour and hourly charts, and vice versa. Also, make sure the charting system has the ability to save the entire chart so you don't have to redraw the trend lines every time you pull up the same chart. On subsequent updates, keep the trend lines that still appear to be valid (meaning, price action has not broken through them), and erase trend lines that are no longer active or have been broken. Over time, you'll get an idea of how good you are at spotting meaningful trend lines by the frequency with which you have to discard old trend lines.

Looking for price channels

A *price channel* is a series of parallel trend lines that encapsulate price action over a discernible period. Channels will form in all time frames, with long-term channels on a daily chart highlighting multiday or multiweek trading ranges, and short-term channels on an hourly chart revealing steady buying or selling during a trading session. Price channels can also form in any direction, from horizontal to steeply sloping up or down and anything in between. The whole point of looking for and drawing channel lines, of course, is to highlight additional sources of support or resistance.

The way to identify price channels is through visual inspection, using your eyes and imagination, as well as a fair amount of trial and error. Drawing channels is made much easier by the Copy a Line and Parallel Line functions, which are standard in most charting systems.

You can use channels as part of your trading strategy to guide both position entry and exit. Short-term traders in particular like to use channels to trade around a core position, for example, selling short on trend-line resistance and buying a portion of the position back if prices drop to channel support. If the channel continues to hold, they'll resell on gains back toward trend-line resistance, reestablishing their core short position. When channels break, it's also a sign that prices are accelerating in the direction of the trend, as shown by the channel, or that the trend is reversing and prices break out of the channel in the opposite direction.

Managing Your Trading Risk

Experienced traders calculate the risk they're facing in every trade before they ever enter it. It's part of their decision-making DNA, and it goes a long way toward determining which trade opportunities they pursue and which ones they skip. By approaching the forex market with risk management as your first thought, you'll be able to get some trades wrong and still survive to get other trades right.

You're probably not drawn to currency trading for the chance to lose money. You're interested in making money and are prepared to take some risks to do that. The question is how much risk you are prepared to accept. Because you're dealing with finite resources — namely, the amount of risk capital you've devoted to your trading — you have a definite limiting factor to your trading. If you eat through your trading capital, you're done. So the starting point of a risk-aware trading plan has to focus on the downside risks. It may not be as fun as thinking about making millions, but it'll make you a better trader.

Analyzing trade setup to determine position size

A *trade setup* is a trade opportunity that you've identified through your analysis. In every trade setup, you need to identify the price point where the setup is invalidated — where the trade is wrong. If you're looking to sell a currency pair based on trend-line resistance above, for example, price gains beyond the trend line would invalidate your rationale for wanting to be short. So the price level of the trend line is the line in the sand for the overall strategy.

Now comes the entry point for the trade. Say that current market prices are 50 pips below the trend-line resistance you've identified. That means the market could move higher by 50 pips and your trade setup would still be valid, but you'd be out of the money by 50 pips. You now have a clear delineation of how much risk your trade setup would require you to assume. If you get in now, you're risking at least 50 pips. Alternatively, you could reduce that risk by waiting and using an order to try selling at better levels — say, 25 pips higher. If the market cooperates and your limit-entry order is filled, you're now risking only 25 pips before your trade setup is negated.

So how large a position should you commit to the trade? From a risk standpoint, it all depends where you're able to enter the trade relative to your stop-out level.

Putting the risk in cash terms

After you've identified where your stop-loss point is — where the trade setup is negated — and where you're able to enter, you're able to calculate the amount of risk posed by the trade. Say you're inclined to enter the position at current market levels, and your stop is 50 pips away. If you're trading a standard-size account (100,000 lot size), and the trade is in NZD/USD (where profit and loss accrue in USD), each lot would translate into risking $500 (100,000 × 0.0050 NZD/USD pips = $500). If your margin balance is $10,000, you're risking 5 percent of your trading capital in this trade (frequently cited in trading literature as the maximum risk in any one trade).

Considering other opportunity risks

Risk in the trading plan is not confined simply to losing money on the trade. There are also opportunity risks from trade setups that you're not able to enter.

Book V

Foreign Currency Trading

Identifying the trade entry points

Winning or losing on a trade is difficult if you never get into the position in the first place, which makes identifying where to get into the trade one of the most important steps in any trading plan. We like to use technical analysis as the primary means of identifying entry levels. When looking to identify entry points, focus on the following technical levels:

- ✔ Trend lines in various time frames (daily, four-hour, and hourly)

- ✔ Hourly highs and lows for short-term intraday position entries

- ✔ Daily highs and lows for medium- to longer-term positions

- ✔ Congestion zones

- ✔ Fibonacci retracements of prior price movements (38.2 percent, 50 percent, 61.8 percent, and 76.4 percent)

- ✔ Spike highs and lows

If you're not familiar with Fibonacci retracements (which refer to a theory that prices are likely to retrace a large portion of an original move based upon certain ratios), check out www.fibonacci.com.

Establishing stop losses with foresight

The stop-loss level is the starting point in any trade plan from an overall risk perspective. It's the point where the trade setup is negated and the strategy fails. When considering where to place the stop level, be aware that the currency market, like most financial markets, has a tendency to try to take out levels where stop losses are likely to be located. Nothing is worse than having the right strategy but being taken out by a short-term, stop-loss-driven price move that eventually reverses and goes in the direction of your outlook.

To guard against the risk of being unnecessarily whipsawed out of a position, approach selecting your stop-loss level from a defensive point of view. Anticipate that the market *will* test the level where the trade setup is invalidated, such as trend-line support or hourly lows. Then consider if the market tests that level, how far must it go through before it's really considered a break?

No set formula exists for this calculation, but allowing for a margin of error can sometimes prevent a stop loss from being triggered unnecessarily. The margin of error you apply depends on the general volatility of the currency pair you're trading, as well as on the overall market volatility at the time of the trade.

Setting take-profit objectives dynamically

When it comes to establishing the take-profit objective, we suggest using a market-based approach, one that considers where the market is likely to go based on where it's been (technical analysis) and overall market conditions. The idea is to be *realistic* about how much you can take out of the market, not *idealistic* about how much the market will reward you. Focus on technical support and resistance levels as the primary guideposts in the progress of market movements (see Book VIII).

Another important consideration in dynamically managing your profit objectives is time. You need to be aware of and anticipate upcoming events and market conditions. If you've been long for a rally during the North American morning, what's likely to happen when European markets begin to close up for the day? If you're positioned in USD/JPY in the New York afternoon, and Japanese industrial production is slated to be released in a few hours, what can you expect in the interim? Stay flexible and dynamic, just like the market.

Finding the Right Broker

With the explosion in online currency trading over the past several years, dozens of forex brokerage firms now operate all over the world. Competition among various brokerages is fierce, and there's no shortage of advertising seeking to win you as a client. Here are some questions to ask as you search for just the right broker:

- ✔ **How good are trading executions?** Are you consistently able to trade at the price you're trying for?

- ✔ **How are orders filled?** Is a stop-loss sell order filled when the bid price matches the stop price? Are stops guaranteed and, if so, are there any exceptions? What's the policy for filling limit orders?

- ✔ **Are dealing spreads fixed or variable?** *Fixed spreads* remain constant all the time, regardless of what's happening in the market, and tend to be slightly wider than variable spreads. *Variable spreads* fluctuate depending on market interest. In highly liquid periods, variable spreads tend to be the tightest, while in slower periods, they tend to be wider.

  Which you prefer largely depends on your trading style. A short-term trader looking to make just a few pips on each trade would probably be better off with variable spreads, while someone who trades around news would likely choose fixed spreads.

✔ **What is the commission structure?** While some online brokers have chosen a commission-based pricing structure, many are compensated by the price spread between the bid and the offer.

✔ **Is the broker a market-maker?** *Market-makers* typically provide both consistent liquidity and execution, which allows you to trade your desired amount at all times. They typically offer either fixed spreads or variable spreads.

Some firms claim to operate a nondealing desk (NDD) model or other alternative to the dealing-desk (market-maker) model. Nondealing desk brokers, which are often commission-free, claim that the trade price comes directly from the interbank market and that they route all trades directly to the banks. Though these firms may tout this model as superior to the market-making approach, you have to ask yourself, how is the firm making its money?

✔ **How much leverage does the firm offer?** Firms offering excessively high leverage aren't looking out for their customers' business interests. A good guideline: Anything more than 200:1 is too high.

✔ **What trading resources are available?** Evaluate all tools and resources offered by the firm: charting services, live market commentary, research, accessible trading platforms, and so on.

✔ **Is the broker registered with the appropriate financial authorities in the jurisdiction where it operates?** In the United States, forex brokers are required to be registered as futures commission merchants (FCMs) with the Commodity Futures Trading Commission (CFTC) and are ultimately subject to CFTC rules and regulations. The National Futures Association (NFA) is the self-regulating body for forex brokers. Visit the NFA's Web site at www.nfa.futures.org to check on the regulatory status of a prospective broker.

Chapter 6

Putting Your Trading Plan in Action

In This Chapter

▶ Opening a position at the right time and with the right strategy

▶ Actively managing your trades

▶ Taking profits — or not

▶ Analyzing your trades after the fact

*T*his is what it all comes down to. You've done the research, you've looked at the charts, you've developed your strategic trade plan, and now it's time to put it to work. If you thought economic data mining and chart analysis were the hard part, wait until your adrenaline starts pumping after you've entered the trade. This chapter takes you through the concrete steps of opening a position, monitoring the trade while it's active, closing it out, and doing a post-trade analysis to refine your trading going forward.

Getting into the Position

You can make trades in the forex market one of two ways: You can trade *at the market,* or at the current price, using the click-and-deal feature of your broker's platform; or you can employ orders, such as limit orders and one-cancels-the-other orders (OCOs). (We discuss order types in Chapter 3.) But there's a lot more to it than that. Certain trade setups suggest a combination of both methods for entering a position, while others rely strictly on orders to capture rapid or unexpected price movements. Then there's the fine art of timing the market to get in at the best price at the moment.

Buying and selling at the current market

Many traders like the idea of opening a position by trading at the market as opposed to leaving an order that may or may not be executed. They prefer the certainty of knowing that they're in the market.

If this describes you, before actually executing your first trade, fine-tune your entry by getting a good handle on the short-term price action. To do this, look at shorter-term charts, such as 5 or 15 minutes, to get an idea of where prices have been trading recently. Chances are you'll observe a relatively narrow range of price action, typically between 10 and 20 pips. Unless the situation is urgent, a little patience can go a long way toward improving your entry level. Why buy at 1.1550 when you have a viable chance to buy at 1.1535?

Let the routine price fluctuations work to your advantage by trying to buy on down-ticks and sell on up-ticks in line with your overall strategy. Selecting your trade size in advance helps — so when the price gets to your desired level, you need to click only once to execute the trade. As you watch the price action, keep a disciplined price target in mind, both in your favor and in case prices start to move away from your entry level.

Averaging into a position

Averaging into a position refers to the practice of buying/selling at successively lower/higher prices to improve the average rate of the desired long/short position.

Say you buy one lot of USD/JPY at 120.50 and another lot at 120.30; you're long two lots at an average price of 120.40 ([120.50 +120.30] ÷ 2 = 120.40). Here's how it works. To begin with, you were long one lot from 120.50. To add to the position at 120.30, the market had to be trading lower, which also means you were looking at an unrealized P/L of −20 pips on your initial position from 120.50. After you buy the second lot, your unrealized P/L has not changed substantially, but your position size has just doubled, which means your risk has also just doubled. If the market rebounds from 120.30, your unrealized loss will be reduced. But if the market continues to decline, your losses are going to be twice what they were had you not added on to your position.

Many trading books recommend avoiding averaging into, or adding on to, a losing position — and with good reason. The tactic can lead to dramatically higher losses on smaller incremental price movements. Also, if you're adding on to a losing position, you're missing out on the current directional move. In other words, not only are you losing money, but you're also not making money, which is the opportunity cost of averaging.

Trading breakouts

A *breakout* or *break* refers to a price movement that moves beyond, or breaks out of, recent established trading ranges or price patterns captured with trend lines. Breakouts can occur in all time frames, from weeks and days on down to hours and minutes. The longer the time frame, the more significant the breakout in terms of the overall expected price movement that follows. In terms of entering a position, breakouts frequently represent important signals to get in or out of positions. In that sense, they take a lot of the guesswork out of deciding where to enter or exit a position.

Trading breakouts is a relatively aggressive trading strategy and is certainly not without risks. Until you've gained some experience in the forex market you're probably better off focusing only on breaks of levels identified by trend-line analysis in longer time frames, such as daily charts, or breaks of longer-term price levels, like daily or weekly highs/lows. They may not occur as frequently, but they'll tend to be more reliable.

Identifying potential breakout levels

The first step in trading on a breakout is to identify where breakouts are likely to occur. The easiest way to do this is to draw trend lines that capture recent high/low price ranges. In many cases, these ranges will form a sideways or horizontal range of prices, where sellers have repeatedly emerged at the same level on the upside and buyers have regularly stepped in at the lower level. Horizontal ranges are mostly neutral in predicting which direction the break will occur.

Other ranges are going to form price patterns with sloping trend lines on the top and bottom, such as flags, pennants, wedges, and triangles. These patterns have more predictive capacity for the direction of the eventual breakout and even the distance of the breakout. (Go to Book VIII to find out about common patterns.)

The time frame determines the overall significance of the breakout and goes a long way toward determining whether you should make a trade based on it. Very short time frames (less than an hour) have much less significance than a break of a four-hour range or a daily price pattern. The length of time that a price range or pattern has endured also gives you an idea of its significance. A break of a range that has formed over the past 48 hours has less significance for price movements than the break of a range that's persisted for the past 3 weeks.

Trading breaks with stop-loss entry orders

After you've identified a likely breakout point, you can use a resting stop-loss entry order placed just beyond the breakout level to get into a position when a breakout occurs. To get long for a break to the upside, you would leave a stop-loss entry order to buy at a price just above the upper level of the range or pattern. To get short for a break lower, you would leave a stop-loss entry order to sell at a price just below the lower level of the range or pattern.

The appeal of using stop-loss entry orders is that you're able to trade the breakout without any further action on your part. Breakouts can occur in the blink of an eye. Just when you thought the upper range level was going to hold and prices started to drift off, for example, they'll come roaring back and blow right through the breakout level.

When placing a stop-loss entry order to trade a breakout level, be aware of any major data or news events that are coming up. If your stop-loss entry order is triggered as a result of a news event, the execution rate on the order could be subject to slippage, which may wipe out any gains from getting in on the breakout.

Trading the retest of a breakout level

The other way to trade a breakout is after the breakout has occurred. A *retest* refers to a frequent price reaction after breakouts, where prices eventually reverse course, return to the break level, and retest it to see if it will hold. In the case of a break to the upside, for example, after the initial wave of buying has run its course, prices may stall and trigger very short-term profit-taking selling. The tendency is for prices to return to the breakout level, which should now act as support and attract buying interest.

Not every breakout sees prices return to retest the break level. Some retests may retrace only a portion of the breakout move, stopping short of retesting the exact break level, which is typically a good sign that the break is for real and will continue. Other breakouts never look back and just keep going.

Guarding against false breaks

Breakouts are relatively common events in currency trading, especially from a very short-term perspective. But not every breakout is sustained. When prices break through key support or resistance levels, but then stop and reverse course and ultimately move back through the break level, it's called a *false break.*

To protect against false breaks, you need to follow up your stop-loss entry with a contingent stop-loss exit order to close out the position if the market reverses course.

Although there's no surefire way to tell whether a breakout is a false break or a valid one that you should trade, here are a few points to keep in mind:

✔ **Time frame of the breakout level:** The shorter the time frame you're looking at, the greater the potential for a false break.

✔ **Significance of the price level:** The more important the price level that's broken, the more likely it is to provoke a market response and to be sustained.

✔ **Duration of the break:** The longer the breakout level is held, the more likely the breakout is to be valid.

✔ **Currency pair volatility:** Relatively volatile currency pairs, such as GBP/USD and USD/CHF, are more prone to false breaks than others, especially in short-term time frames.

✔ **Fundamental events and news:** Sustained breakouts tend to have a fundamental catalyst behind them — a significant piece of news that has altered the market's outlook, resulting in the breakout.

Making the Trade Correctly

When using an online trading platform, entering a position is as easy as making a few simple mouse clicks, as the following sections explain.

The simplicity and speed with which you can enter a position can also put your trading capital at risk. Any action you take on a trading platform is your responsibility. You may have meant to click Buy instead of Sell, but no one knows for sure except you. If you make a mistake, correct it as soon as you discover and confirm it. *Don't* try to trade your way out of it or manage it — and don't rationalize that it may work out anyway. No trader is error-proof, and you're bound to make a mistake someday. Just cover the error and get your position back to what you want it to be.

Buying and selling online

Most every online trading brokerage now provides for click-and-deal trade execution. *Click and deal* refers to trading on the current market price by clicking either the Buy button or the Sell button in the trading platform. Before you can click and deal, you have to

1. Select the right currency pair.

When the market gets hectic and you're switching between your charts and the trading platform, you could easily mistake EUR/USD for EUR/CHF if you're not careful.

2. **Select the correct trade amount.**

   Different platforms have different ways of inputting the trade amount. Some use radio buttons, others use scroll-down menus, and others allow you to type the amount manually.

3. **Double-check your selections.**

   In case you think input errors can't happen to you, think about the equity trader at a New York investment bank who meant to sell 10 million shares of a stock but ended up entering 10 *billion*. By the time the trade was stopped, the system had sold several hundred million shares! Ouch.

4. **Click Buy or Sell.**

   If you want to buy, you'll need to click the higher price — the trading platform's offer. If you want to sell, you'll have to click the lower price — the platform's bid.

After you've clicked Buy or Sell, the trading platform will confirm whether your trade went through successfully, usually within a second or two. If your trade request went through, you receive a confirmation from the platform. Double-check your position, and make sure it's what you want it to be. If the trading price changed before your request was received, you receive a response indicating "trade failed," "rates changed," "price not available," or something along those lines. You then need to repeat the steps to make another trade attempt.

Attempts to trade at the market can sometimes fail in very fast-moving markets when price are adjusting quickly. Part of this stems from the *latency effect* of trading over the Internet, which refers to time lags between the platform price reaching your computer and your trade request reaching the platform's server.

 Whatever the outcome of your trade request, you need to be sure you've received a response from the trading platform. If you have not gotten a response back after more than a few seconds, call your broker immediately and confirm the status of the trade request. The deal may have gone through, but confirmations may be delayed due to processor slowness. Or the trade may have never been received by the trading platform because your computer lost its Internet connection.

Placing your orders

Orders are critical trading tools in the forex market. Think of them as trades waiting to happen, because that's exactly what they are. If you enter an order, and subsequent price action triggers its execution, you're in the market. So you need to be as careful as you are thorough, if not more so, when placing your orders in the market. (Refer to Chapter 3 to read about the types of orders and how they're used.)

Here are some important tips to keep in mind when placing and managing your orders:

- ✔ **Input your orders correctly.** Make sure you've correctly specified the currency pair, order type, amount, and price. Then double-check your order after it has been accepted by the trading platform. If it's wrong, edit it or cancel it and start again.

- ✔ **Note the expiration of your orders.** Order expirations are typically good-'til-cancelled (GTC), in which the order remains active until *you* cancel it, or good until the end of the day (EOD), which means that the order automatically expires at the end of the trading day (5 p.m. eastern time [ET]). If you have an intraday position with a stop-loss good until EOD, and you later decide to hold the position overnight, you need to revise the expiration. GTC orders will expire on some trading platforms after an extended period of time, such as 90 days, so be clear on your broker's policy.

- ✔ **Cancel unwanted orders.** Some trading platforms allow orders to be *associated with a position,* meaning that the order remains valid as long as the position is open. Such *position orders* also usually adjust the order amount if you increase or reduce the associated position. Other orders are *independent of positions,* so even if you close out your position, the independent orders remain active. Make sure you understand the difference between the two types, and remember to cancel any independent orders if you close the position they were based on, such as take profits, stop losses, or OCO.

Managing the Trade

So you've pulled the trigger and opened up the position, and now you're in the market. Time to sit back and let the market do its thing, right? Not so fast, amigo. The forex market isn't a roulette wheel where you place your bets, watch the wheel spin, and simply take the results. It's a dynamic, fluid environment where new information and price developments create new opportunities and alter previous expectations. Actively managing a trade when you're in it is just as important as the decision-making that went into establishing the position in the first place.

Book V

Foreign Currency Trading

Monitoring the market

No matter which trading style you follow, it'll pay to keep up with market news and price developments while your trade is active. Unexpected news that impacts your position may come into the market at any time.

The starting point for any trading plan is determining how much you're prepared to risk, which is ultimately expressed by the size of the position and the pip distance to the stop-loss point. When we talk about making changes to the trading plan, we're referring only to reducing the overall risk of the trade, by taking profit (full or partial) or moving the stop loss in the direction of the trade. The idea is to be fluid and dynamic in one direction only: taking profit and reducing risk. Keep your ultimate stop-out point where you decided it should go before you entered the trade.

Rate alerts

One way to follow the market from a distance is to set rate alerts from either your charting system or your trading platform. A *rate alert* is an electronic message that alerts you when a price you've specified is touched by the market in a particular currency pair. Rate alerts are a great way to keep tabs on the market's progress.

Rate alerts are a convenient way to follow the market remotely, but they don't take the place of live orders and should never be substituted for stop-loss orders. By the time you respond to a rate alert and log on to the trading platform or call your broker's trading desk, prices may have moved well beyond your desired stop-out level, leaving you with a larger loss than you anticipated. Rate alerts are a nice little extra service, but only orders represent obligations on the part of your broker to take an action in the market for your account.

News and data developments

Ideally, you should be aware of all data reports and news events scheduled to occur during the anticipated time horizon of your trade strategy. You should also have a good understanding of what the market is expecting in terms of event outcomes to anticipate how the market is likely to react. Additionally, if your trade rationale is reliant on certain data or event expectations, you need to be especially alert for upcoming reports on those themes. (See Chapter 4 for a detailed look at economic reports and the major fundamental drivers and how the market interprets them.)

Speculating based on expected event or data outcomes is perfectly okay. It becomes a problem only if you maintain the trade even after the data/event outcome has come out against your expectations and strategy. Always relate incoming news and data back to the original reason for your trade, and be prepared to adapt your trade strategy accordingly.

Updating your trade plan over time

Time — and its passing — brings with it routine daily events, such as option expirations and the daily closing of the currency futures market. These are specific time periods when traders can reasonably expect a flurry of activity, though it doesn't always materialize. Time's passing also brings you nearer to scheduled news or data events. As the release time draws closer, anticipative speculation generally declines, but price movements can become more erratic as traders take to the sidelines immediately ahead of the release. All these market reactions are as much the result of time as they are of the event itself. Time can also add significance to, or detract significance from, price movements that have already occurred, frequently providing trading signals as a result. So pay attention to time as you update your trade plan.

Trend lines move over time

If you're basing your trading strategies on trend-line analysis, you need to be aware that price levels derived from trend lines change depending on the slope of the trend line. The *slope* of a trend line refers to the angle of a trend line relative to a horizontal line. The steeper the slope of the trend line, the more the relevant price level will change over time; the less slope, the more gradually the price levels will change with time.

No matter what time frame you're trading, be sure to factor in the shifting levels of trend lines if they're part of your trade strategy. You may need to adjust your order levels accordingly. In particular, consider the following:

✔ **Short-term and overnight positions:** Consider where trend-line support or resistance will be over the next 6 to 12 hours, while your position is still active but while you may not be able to actively follow the market. You may want to use a trailing stop as a proxy for changes in trend-line-based support/resistance levels.

✔ **Limit-entry orders:** If your limit buying/selling order is based on a sloping trend line, periodically adjust your order so that it's still in play according to changes in the trend line. You may miss a trade entry if the trend line is eventually touched, but in the meantime its level has shifted away from where you first placed the order.

✔ **Breakouts:** A significant trend line that looks to be a mile away one week may suddenly be within striking distance in the following week or two weeks, substantially altering the market's outlook. Alternatively, the market may be focused on a price high/low as a breakout trigger, when a sloping trend line touching that high/low may actually be the catalyst for a breakout.

Adjusting your trade plan over impending events

As you develop your trading plan, look ahead to see what data and events are scheduled during the expected life of the trade. If you follow that simple advice, you strongly reduce the chances of having your trade strategy upset by largely predictable events. More important, you'll be able to anticipate likely catalysts for price shifts, which will give you greater insight into subsequent price movements.

If, for example, you've entered into a trade strategy based on an upcoming event — an expected weak U.S. data report, for instance — and the market has cooperated and priced in a lower U.S. dollar before the report is released, you may be looking at a profitable position before the data is even released. As the release time draws near, you take some profit off the table and hold on to the remaining partial position. In this situation, you've successfully played the market: If the data comes in negative for the U.S. dollar, and the market reacts by selling the U.S. dollar, you're still in the partial position to gain from further dollar weakness. If the data comes in stronger than expected (or the data comes in weak as expected, but the market takes profit on short-dollar positions made in advance), you've protected your profit by taking some money out of the market before the event ever transpired.

 Before major data and events, the market frequently goes into a sideways holding pattern. The event speculators have all put on their positions, and the rest of the market is waiting for the data to decide how to react. These holding patterns can develop hours or days in advance, depending on what event is coming. Especially if you're trading from a short-term perspective, be prepared for these doldrums and consider whether riding through them is worthwhile.

Updating order levels as prices progress

When you're in a position, and the market is moving in your favor, it's important to be flexible in adjusting take-profit targets and amending stop-loss orders to protect your profits. The key to being flexible in this regard is also being prudent: Don't adjust your take-profit targets without also adjusting your stop-loss order in the same direction. If you're long, and you raise your take profit, raise your stop loss too. If you're short, and you lower your take profit, lower your stop-loss order as well.

Increasing take-profit targets

You've put together a well-developed trade strategy ahead of your trade, so now that you're in the trade, why would you change your take-profit objective? Only for some very good reasons, like the following:

   ✔ **Major new information:** *Major* means it has to come from the very top echelons of decision-making, like the Fed chairman, the European Central Bank (ECB) president, or other central bank chiefs; the U.S. Treasury secretary; or the G7. Surprise interest rate changes or policy shifts are always candidates. The more at odds the information is with current market expectations, the better the chances that it will generate an extensive price move.

✔ **Thinner-than-usual liquidity:** Reduced liquidity conditions can provoke more extensive price movements than would otherwise occur, because fewer market participants are involved to absorb the price shocks. Reduced liquidity is most evident during national holidays, seasonal periods (late summer, Christmas/New Year's), end of month, end of quarter, and certain Fridays.

✔ **Breaks of major technical levels:** Trend lines dating back several months or years, retracement levels of major recent directional moves, and recent extreme highs and lows are likely to trigger larger-than-normal price movements. Reduced volatility preceding the breakout is another ingredient in favor of a more sustained directional move.

✔ **The currency pair:** The more illiquid and volatile the currency pair you're trading, the greater the chances for an extreme move. GBP, CHF, and JPY are the most common culprits among the majors.

Tightening stop-loss orders to protect profits

To protect profits, adjust your stop losses to lock in gains. When formulating your overall trade plan, always consider what price levels need to be surpassed to justify moving your stop loss. If it happens in the market, you'll be ready and know exactly what to do.

We like to focus on hourly and daily trend-line levels, daily highs/lows, and breaks of Fibonacci retracement levels. When these technical support/resistance points are exceeded, it's an indication that the market has seen fit to move prices into a new level in the overall direction of the trade. When that happens, consider moving your stop-loss order to levels just inside the broken technical level. If the market has second thoughts about sustaining the break, your adjusted stop will then take you out of the trade.

The risk with adjusting stops too aggressively is that the market may come back to test the break level, triggering your adjusted stop loss if it's too close, and then go on to make fresh gains. But the trade-off in that situation is between something and more of something, or potentially nothing and more of nothing. We prefer to have something to show for our efforts.

Another way to lock in profits in a more dynamic fashion is by using a trailing stop-loss order (see Chapter 3). After a technical level in the direction of your trade is overcome, similar to the preceding example, you may consider instituting a trailing stop to replace your fixed stop-loss order. Set the trailing distance to account for the distance between the current market and the other side of the technical break level.

Closing Out the Trade

On the most basic level, every trade ends with either a profit or a loss. Sure, some trades finish *flat,* which is when you exit the trade at the same price you entered, producing no gain or loss. Most of the time, though, you're going to be dealing with the agony or ecstasy of either being stopped out or taking profit.

Taking profits

Taking profit is usually a positive experience for traders. But if the market continues to move in the direction of your trade after you've squared up and taken profit, you may begin to feel as though you're missing out or even losing money. At these times, you want to avoid making rash trading decisions. Even if the market continues to move in the direction of your earlier position, don't re-enter the same position until you've first taken the time to reevaluate the market objectively. Also, avoid the urge to suddenly take a position in the opposite direction. The key is to treat each trade independently, recognizing that the outcome of one trade has no bearing on the next trade.

Taking partial profits

One way that traders are able to stay in the market with a profitable position and hang on for a potentially larger move is to take partial profits on the overall position. Of course, taking partial profits requires the ability to trade in multiple lots — at least two. The idea is that as prices move in favor of your trading position, you take profit on just a portion of your total position.

Whenever you take partial profits, modify the size of your stop-loss and other take-profit orders to account for the reduction in your total position size. Some online brokers offer a position-based order-entry system, where your order size automatically adjusts based on any changes to the overall position.

Stopping out before things get worse

As part of any trade strategy and to preserve your trading capital for future trading, always identify where to exit a trade if the market doesn't move in the direction you expect. Devote as much time and energy to pinpointing that level as you need, and keep in mind that a lot of short-term price action is stop-loss driven.

Stop losses are a necessary evil for every trader, big and small. You can never know beforehand where a price movement will stop, but you can control where you exit the market if prices don't move as you expect. Stop losses are an important tool for preventing manageable trading losses from turning into disastrous ones.

Trailing stop-loss orders are often used to protect profits and enable traders to capture larger price movements. (We explain how trailing stop-loss orders work in Chapter 3.) They're no surefire guarantee that you'll be able to stay on board for a larger directional price move, but they do provide an element of flexibility that you should consider in adjusting your trade plan. For example, if your position is in the money and holding beyond a significant technical break level, you may want to consider adjusting your stop loss to a trailing stop that has its starting point on the other side of the technical level. If the break leads to a more sustained move, you'll be able to capture more than you otherwise might. If the break is reversed, the trailing stop will limit the damage.

Letting the market trigger your stop-loss/take-profit order

When you've identified a trade opportunity and developed a risk-aware trading plan, you're going to have active orders out in the market to cover your position one way or the other (stop-loss or take-profit). Depending on your trading style and the trade setup, you can reasonably follow a set-it-and-forget-it trade strategy where your orders will watch the market and your position for you.

Medium- to longer-term traders are more likely to rely on set, or *resting*, market orders to cover open positions due to the longer time frame of such trade strategies and the burdens of monitoring the market overnight or for longer stretches of time. If you use resting orders, also use rate alerts to update you on specific price movements (see the earlier section "Monitoring the market") so that you can act when necessary. Shorter-term traders are more apt to be in front of their trading monitors while their trade is still open, but they should always still have an ultimate limiting set of orders to cover the trade.

While you may want to be flexible with where you leave your take-profit order, always have a stop-loss order in place to protect you in case of unexpected news or price movements. If you're trading the market from the long side (meaning you think prices in a currency pair are likely to move higher), you need to pinpoint the ultimate price level on the downside, which negates this short-term view.

Getting out when the price is right

The most reliable market information is the prices themselves. Sharp price reactions are usually strong indicators of significant market interest that's either pushing prices faster in the same direction or repelling them in the opposite direction. As you monitor your position in the market, stay closely attuned to significant price reactions, such as spike reversals or price gaps, with a good benchmark being typically more than 20 points over a few minutes. The sharp move in prices may be due to news or rumors, or it may just be a pocket of illiquidity. Either way, the sharp price move carries its own significance that is information to you. There's no set way such moves always play out, but if you're alert for them, you've got one more piece of information to help you decide when and how to exit your position.

If the rapid price movement is in your favor, you can look at it as a new high-water mark, or as a new support or resistance level. If the move is reversed, the tide is reversing, and you should consider exiting sooner rather than later. If the tide doesn't reverse, you've got a solid short-term price level on which to base your decisions going forward. If the price move was against you, you may want to consider that the market is not cooperating and adopt a more defensive strategy, such as tightening stop losses, reducing your position, or exiting altogether.

Getting out when the time is right

The time of day and the day of the week can frequently determine how prices behave and how your ultimate trade strategy plays out. If you're trading ahead of major data releases, for example, you need to be aware that price action is going to be affected in the run-up to the scheduled release, not to mention in its aftermath. Similarly, if you've been positioned correctly for a directional price move in the New York morning, for example, you need to be aware that there may be a price reaction as European traders begin to wind up their trading on any given day. When it comes to adjusting your trading plan or closing out your position, it frequently pays to be a clock watcher.

After the Trade

Good traders learn from their mistakes and try to avoid repeating them in the future. Bad traders keep making the same mistakes over and over again until they give up in frustration or are forced to for financial reasons. The best way to learn from each trading experience — both the good and the bad ones — is to make post-trade analysis part of your regular trading routine.

Identifying what you did right and wrong

Regardless of the outcome of any trade, you want to look back over the whole process to understand what you did right and wrong. In particular, ask yourself the following questions:

- ✔ **How did you identify the trade opportunity?** If more of your winning trades are being generated by technical analysis, you'll probably want to devote more energy to that approach. If more of your winning trades are coming from the fundamental approach, you're probably better off concentrating on a fundamental style.

- ✔ **How well did your trade plan work out?** Was the position size sufficient to match the risk and reward scenarios, or was it too large or too small? Could you have entered at a better level? What tools might you have used to improve your entry timing? Was your take profit realistic or pie in the sky? Use the answers to these questions to refine your position size, entry level, and order placement going forward.

- ✔ **How well did you manage the trade after it was open?** Were you able to effectively monitor the market while your trade was active? Did you modify your trade plan appropriately along the way? Did you close out the trade based on your trading plan, or did the market surprise you somehow? Based on your answers, you'll learn what role your emotions may have played and how disciplined a trader you are.

Updating your trading record

Recollections of individual trades can be hazy sometimes. Some traders may tend to favor remembering winning trades, while others may remember only the losing trades. The only way to get to the heart of the matter is to look at the numbers — the results of your trades over a specific time period, such as a month. A trading record doesn't lie, but you still have to interpret it properly to glean any useful lessons from it. Depending on your trading style, it's best to approach analyzing your trading record from two different angles, each with a common denominator — average wins and average losses.

- ✔ **Long-term and medium-term traders:** Tend to have fewer overall trades because they're more likely to be looking at the market from a more strategic perspective, picking trade opportunities more selectively. If that's you, tally your results on a per-trade basis, totaling up separately the number of winning trades and the number of losing trades, along with the total amount of profits and the total amount of losses. Divide the number of profits by the number of winning trades to find your average winning trade amount. Do the same with your losing trades.

✔ **Short-term traders:** Tend to have a larger number of trades due to their short-term trading style. If that's you, and if you're making only one or two trades a day, you may want to follow the method described in the preceding bullet item. If you're a more active day-trader, measure your results on a per-day basis to get an idea of how successful you are at trading in multiple positions on any given day. Tally up the results of each trading day over the course of a month to come up with the same numbers outlined in the preceding bullet item: total number of wins or losses, and average win amount and loss amount.

Focus on what you're doing right, but also figure out what you're doing wrong. Refine your analysis of your trading results by breaking them down to smaller categories, such as day of the week and currency pair or even trade size. Are your losing days or trades concentrated on certain days of the week, such as Fridays or Mondays? Are your losing trades concentrated in certain currency pairs? Does the position size of each trade have any relationship to wins and losses? Are you winning more on large trades, for example, or are you giving up larger losses on smaller trade sizes?

Book VI
Hedge Funds

The 5th Wave   By Rich Tennant

"Do I recommend a hedge fund strategy? Let me put it to you this way. I'm a strict Catholic who goes to temple every Saturday, so 'Yes,' I would recommend a hedge fund strategy."

In this book . . .

Hedge funds. You've seen the headlines in the financial press. You've heard the rumors about mythical investment funds that make money no matter what happens in the market. And you want a part of that action.

Hedge funds are private partnerships that pursue high finance. If you don't mind a little risk, you can net some high returns for your portfolio. However, you have to meet strict limits put in place by the Securities and Exchange Commission — namely that you have a net worth of at least $1 million or an annual income of $200,000 ($300,000 with a spouse). In fact, most hedge fund investors are institutions, like pensions, foundations, and endowments.

Here's a little secret: Not all hedge fund managers are performing financial alchemy. Many of the techniques they use are available to any investor who wants to increase return relative to the amount of risk taken.

Chapter 1

Getting the 411 on Hedge Funds

*I*s a hedge fund a surefire way to expand your wealth or a scam that will surely rip you off? After all, some funds have failed, and that makes for big headlines. Is it a newfangled mutual fund or a scheme for raiding corporations and ripping off hard-working employees? You see hedge funds in the news all the time, but it's hard to know exactly what they are. That's because, at its essence, a hedge fund is a bit of a mystery. A *hedge fund,* generally speaking, is a lightly regulated investment partnership that invests in a range of securities in an attempt to increase expected return while reducing risk. And that can mean just about anything.

This chapter covers basic things you need to know if you're considering buying into a hedge fund. It tells you what a hedge fund is and explains who the people involved in hedge funds are, what you have to do to qualify as a hedge fund investor, and more.

Defining Hedge Funds

When you talk about hedge funds, you soon discover that the term *hedge fund* means different things to different people. In the investment world, "I run a hedge fund" has the same meaning as "I'm a consultant" in the rest of the business world. Still, one definition that most folks can agree on is a fairly general one: A *hedge fund* is a private partnership that operates with little to no regulation from the U.S. Securities and Exchange Commission (SEC) and that uses a range of investment techniques and invests in a wide array of assets to generate a higher return for a given level of risk than what's expected of normal investments. In many cases, but hardly all, hedge funds are managed to generate a consistent level of return, regardless of what the market does.

Hedging: The heart of the hedge fund matter

To understand what a hedge fund is, obviously, it helps to know what hedging is. *Hedging* means reducing risk, which is what many hedge funds are designed to do. Although risk is usually a function of return (the higher the risk, the higher the return), a hedge fund manager has ways to reduce risk without cutting into investment income. She can look for ways to get rid of some risks while taking on others with an expected good return. For example, a fund manager can take stock market risk out of the fund's portfolio by selling stock index futures. Or she can increase her return from a relatively low-risk investment by borrowing money, known as *leveraging*. Keep in mind, however, that risk remains, no matter the hedge fund strategy.

The challenge for the hedge fund manager is to eliminate some risk while gaining return on investments — not a simple task, which is why hedge fund managers get paid handsomely if they succeed.

Characteristics of hedge funds

A hedge fund differs from so-called "real money" — traditional investment accounts like mutual funds, pensions, and endowments — because it has more freedom to pursue different investment strategies. In some cases, these unique strategies can lead to huge gains while the traditional market measures languish. In 2005, for example, the Credit Suisse/Tremont Hedge Fund Index, a leading measure of hedge fund performance (www.hedgeindex.com/hedgeindex/en/default.aspx), reported that the average hedge fund return for the year was 7.61 percent. For the same period, the NASDAQ Composite Index (www.nasdaq.com) returned only 1.37. The amount of potential return makes hedge funds more than worthwhile in the minds of many accredited and qualified investors.

The following sections dig deeper into the characteristics of hedge funds. Here, I offer the basic characteristics.

Illiquid

One key characteristic of hedge funds is that they're *illiquid*. Most hedge fund managers limit how often investors can take their money out; a fund may lock in investors for two years or more. In other words, investing in a hedge fund is a long-term proposition because the money you invest may be locked up for years.

For that reason, a hedge fund investment is most appropriate if you don't need the money now or in the near future to support your life or any necessary obligations and if you can afford to take some chances in terms of the risk and the illiquidity.

Little to no regulatory oversight

Hedge funds don't have to register with the U.S. Securities and Exchange Commission (SEC). Most funds and their managers also aren't required to register with the Financial Industry Regulatory Authority or the Commodity Futures Trading Commission, the major self-regulatory bodies in the investment business. However, many funds register with these bodies anyway, choosing to give investors peace of mind and many protections otherwise not afforded to them (not including protection from losing money, of course). Whether registered or not, hedge funds can't commit fraud, engage in insider trading, or otherwise violate the laws of the land.

In order to stay free of the yoke of strict regulation, hedge funds agree to accept money only from accredited or qualified investors — people and institutions with high net worths. The later section "Is a Hedge Fund Right for You?" defines the requirements for each.

The reason for the high-net-worth requirement is that regulators believe people with plenty of money generally understand investment risks and returns better than the average person, and accredited investors can afford to lose money if their investments don't work out. In order to avoid the appearance of improper marketing to unqualified investors, hedge funds tend to stay away from Web sites, and some don't even have listed telephone numbers. You should have to prove your accredited status before you can see offering documents from a fund or find out more about a fund's investment style.

Aggressive investment strategies

In order to post a higher return for a given level of risk than otherwise expected, a hedge fund manager does things differently than a traditional money manager. This fact is where a hedge fund's relative lack of regulatory oversight becomes important: A hedge fund manager has a broad array of investment techniques at his disposal that aren't feasible for a tightly regulated investor, such as short selling and leveraging.

Manager bonuses for performance

Another factor that distinguishes a hedge fund from a mutual fund, individual account, or other type of investment portfolio is the fund manager's compensation in the form of a performance fee. (SEC regulations forbid mutual funds, for example, from charging performance fees.) Many hedge funds are structured under the so-called *2 and 20* arrangement, meaning that the fund manager receives an annual fee equal to 2 percent of the assets in the fund and an additional bonus equal to 20 percent of the year's profits. You may find that the percentages differ from the 2 and 20 formula when you start investigating prospective funds, but the management fee plus bonus structure rarely changes.

The hedge fund manager receives a bonus only if the fund makes money. Many investors love that the fund manager's fortunes are tied to theirs. The downside of this rule? After all the investors pay their fees, the hedge fund's great performance relative to other investments may disappear. For information on fees and their effects on performance, see the later section "Fee, Fi, Fo, Cha Ching! Hedge Fund Fees."

Biased performance data

What gets investors excited about hedge funds is that the funds seem to have fabulous performances at every turn, no matter what the market does. But the great numbers you see in the papers can be misleading because hedge fund managers don't have to report performance numbers to anyone other than their fund investors. Those that do report their numbers to different analytical, consulting, and index firms do so voluntarily, and they're often the ones most likely to have good performance numbers to report. Add to that the fact that hedge fund managers can easily close shop when things aren't going well; after it shuts down it doesn't report its data anymore (if it ever did), and poorly performing funds are most likely to close. What all this means is that measures of hedge fund performance have a bias toward good numbers.

You have to do your homework when buying into a hedge fund. You can't rely on a rating service, and you can't rely on the SEC, as you can with a mutual fund or other registered investment. You have to ask a lot of tough questions about who the fund manager is, what he plans for the fund's strategy, and who will be verifying the performance numbers.

Secretive about performance and strategies

Some hedge funds are very secretive, and for good reason: If other players in the market know how a fund is making its money, they'll try to use the same techniques, and the unique opportunity for the front-running hedge fund may disappear. Hedge funds aren't required to report their performance, disclose their holdings, or take questions from shareholders.

However, that doesn't mean hedge fund managers refuse to tell you anything. A fund must prepare a partnership agreement or offering memorandum for prospective investors that explains the following:

- ✔ The fund's investment style
- ✔ The fund's structure
- ✔ The fund manager's background

A hedge fund should also undergo an annual audit of holdings and performance and give this report to all fund investors. (The fund manager may require you to sign a nondisclosure agreement as a condition of receiving the information, but the information should be made available nonetheless.) But the hedge fund manager doesn't have to give you regular and detailed information, nor should you expect to receive it.

Beware the hedge fund that gives investors no information or that refuses to agree to an annual audit — that's a blueprint for fraud.

Alpha: What hedge funds are all about

Hedge fund managers all talk about alpha. Their goal is to generate alpha, because alpha is what makes them special. But what the heck is it? Unfortunately, alpha is one of those things that everyone in the business talks about but no one really explains.

Alpha is a term that originated in the Modern (Markowitz) Portfolio Theory (MPT), which explains how an investment generates its return. The equation used to describe the theory contains four terms:

- ✔ The risk-free rate of return
- ✔ The premium over the risk-free rate that you get for investing in the market
- ✔ Beta, the sensitivity of an investment to the market
- ✔ Alpha, the return over and above the market rate that results from the manager's skill or other factors

Today, people aren't always thinking of MPT when they use *alpha*. Instead, many people use it as shorthand for whatever a fund does that's special. In basic terms, alpha is the value that the hedge fund manager adds.

In theory, alpha doesn't exist, and if it does exist, it's as likely to be negative (where the fund manager's lack of skill hurts the fund's return) as positive. In practice, some people can generate returns over and above what's expected by the risk that they take, but it isn't that common, and it isn't easy to do.

The People in Your Hedge Fund Neighborhood

Many different people work for, with, and around hedge funds. The following sections give you a little who's who so you understand the roles of the people you may come into contact with and of people who play a large role in your hedge fund.

Managers

The person who organizes the hedge fund and oversees its investment process is the *fund manager* — often called the *portfolio manager* or even PM for short. The fund manager may make all the investment decisions, handling all the trades and research himself, or he may opt to oversee a staff of people who give him advice. A fund manager who relies on other people to work his magic usually has two important types of employees:

- ✔ **Traders:** The traders are the people who execute the buy-and-sell decisions. They sit in front of computer screens, connected to other traders all over the world, and they punch in commands and yell in the phones. Traders need to act quickly as news events happen. They have to be alert to the information that comes across their screens, because they're the people who make things happen with the fund.

- ✔ **Analysts:** Traders operate in real time, seeing what's happening in the market and reacting to all occurrences; analysts take a longer view of the world. They crunch the numbers that companies and governments report, ask the necessary questions, and make projections about the future value of securities.

Consultants

Because big dollars are involved, many hedge fund investors work closely with outside consultants who advise them on their investment decisions, market for accredited investors, and make sure that they're meeting their investors' needs. Staff members who oversee large institutional accounts — like pensions, foundations, or endowments, for example — rely heavily on outside advisors to ensure that they act appropriately, because these types of accounts hinge on the best interests of those who benefit from the money.

Consultants can also help investors make sound investment decisions, ensure that they follow the law, give advice on the proper structure of their portfolios in order to help them meet their investment objectives, and so on.

A consultant can take a fee from an investor or from a hedge fund, but not from both. That way, the consultant stays clear of any conflicts of interest.

Fee, Fi, Fo, Cha Ching! Hedge Fund Fees

A hedge fund can be an expensive business to run. The general partners of the fund have to worry about paying for many areas of the business, including the following:

- Rent and utility costs of the office space, telephones, computers, office supplies, and so on
- The price of research services, specialized software, and brokerage commissions
- The salaries for the fund managers and staff
- The lawyers, accountants, and consultants who track the fund's assets and help it comply with applicable regulations

All these supplies and employees cost money. And who pays for it all? The fund investors. Ever since the first hedge fund, started by Alfred Winslow Jones in the late 1940s, funds have charged investors fees: You pay two fees to the fund manager (a performance fee and a management fee), a fee to get into the fund, and a fee to get out. In the following sections, I discuss these fees.

Before you begin gnashing your teeth about what you have to pay, keep in mind that, although these fees drain a bit of money from your bottom line, they also give life to the hedge fund business. If your hedge fund generates a high return, the amount you give will be worth it. (If not, well, being in the fund will just be expensive.)

Management fees

Most funds charge management fees of about 1 to 2 percent of the fund's assets, usually at the end of the fiscal year. Some charge higher fees — especially if they follow strategies that involve expensive research and related expenses, such as shareholder activism. Other funds keep the fee relatively low by paying only some expenses out of the fee; the funds pay for other bills, especially legal and accounting expenses, directly out of funds assets. Find out upfront what management fees a prospective fund charges, what other expenses the fund incurs, and how the fund calculates its fees.

A hedge fund manager receives a management fee no matter how the fund performs. However, if the fund's assets increase, the fee does, too. Two percent of $60 million is more than 2 percent of $50 million, so a 20-percent investment return translates into a 20-percent increase in management fees.

Sales charges

Hedge funds incur expenses throughout the year. They may take their management fees on a periodic basis, like once per quarter or once every six months, but the rate of fee collection may not match the rate at which the bills come in. Some funds may need money up front in order to operate, so they charge upfront *sales charges* — often at the same scale as the management fees (1 to 2 percent that comes out of the amount invested). The sales charge allows the fund to cover its expenses and pay its staff until the management fees and performance fees come in.

Performance fees

Hedge fund managers charge *performance fees* as a reward for getting excellent returns for their investors. A typical performance fee is 20 percent of the fund's annual profits before fees. Some funds charge a higher rate if performance is above a predetermined benchmark — say, 20 percent on investment returns of up to 50 percent and 35 percent on any returns generated over 50 percent.

One of the many appeals of hedge funds is that the managers eat their own cooking, as the saying goes — their incentives are aligned with their investors' goals. If the fund doesn't make money, the fund manager doesn't get a performance fee.

High water marks

Performance fees come with a downside for fund managers: The fund only gets paid if it turns profit, and most funds set what's called a *high water mark*. The fund can only charge a performance fee if the fund's assets return to where they were before the fund started losing money. If it had $10 million in year one and lost 10 percent, making the asset value $9 million, the manager can't charge a performance fee until the assets appreciate back to $10 million.

Is the high water mark a good thing for investors? It depends. The fund manager pays a penalty for not making money, which is a powerful incentive to manage the fund well. However, the loss of a performance fee for more than a year can be painful to the fund manager. If the fund loses a large amount of money in its bad year, it may take a while for the asset values to recover. Sometimes, a hedge fund manager will disband a fund after a losing year and then launch a new fund instead of losing out on a few years of performance fees. In the investment business, very good years often follow very bad years, so disbanding the fund means that the fund's investors lose out on what could be a year of great performance that would help them recoup their losses.

Graduated performance fees

Hedge fund investors may well be ready to accept the crunchy with the smooth, so many want to reduce the fund manager's incentive to disband the fund after a loss. After all, a few years of poor performance may be part and parcel of a great long-term investment strategy. Some funds address this desire of investors by calling for graduated performance fees that may give the fund managers some of the performance-fee money while they climb back up to the high water mark. For example, a fund manager may receive a performance fee of 10 percent of profits until the fund reaches the high water mark, at which point she gets the full 20 percent of profits thereafter.

Book VI

Hedge Funds

Redemption fees

You pay money while you're in the hedge fund, and you may have to pay money to get into the fund in the first place, but at least you're off the hook when you get out, right? Nope! Many hedge funds charge *redemption fees* when their investors withdraw their money. These fees may be another 1 to 2 percent of assets. One reason funds charge redemption fees is that they can. Another reason is that they increase the money that the fund manager earns. But there are better reasons, too. Hedge funds want to impress upon their limited partners that investment is a long-term proposition, so they can't get out easily. Also, the general partners have to deal with sales and administrative costs involved with raising the money to meet the redemption.

A hedge fund that charges a redemption fee may waive it if it has held the investment for a certain amount of time, or if you provide a certain amount of notice about when you plan to withdraw the funds.

Commissions

If you employ a broker or consultant to find a suitable hedge fund for you, and this person introduces you to the general partners, he or she will expect to be paid for said services. The consultant may charge you a flat fee, or he or she may take a percentage of the assets invested.

Getting Info from Hedge Fund Managers

Many hedge fund managers dream of sitting in front of trading screens and making investment decisions all day. They want to avoid sitting in meetings, holding the hands of their nervous clients, or making presentations to marketing departments. Many hedge fund investors, on the other hand, want regular contact with the people managing their money, and they want the niceties of notes, golf outings, and occasional dinners. See the disconnect? That's why it helps to know a fund manager's policies on meetings and communication.

The partnership agreement you sign will probably discuss what kind of communication the hedge fund manager wants to arrange and how often he'll make contact. If you feel like you have to have regular, face-to-face communication with the hedge fund manager you associate with, make sure a manager is amenable to this request before you commit your money.

Even if she isn't big on face-to-face meetings, your hedge fund manager should offer you written reports:

- **Quarterly report:** This report should explain the fund's investment performance to date, giving you a sense of where the returns are relative to the appropriate investment benchmarks and letting you know how the market outlook suits the fund's strategy.

- **Annual report:** Once a year, your fund manager should give you a comprehensive report on the fund's performance, including the total value of the assets under management and the total fees charged. An outside auditor should prepare this report — not the hedge fund manager. Make sure of this before you sign up. You probably won't get a comprehensive list of holdings, but you should get enough information on industry and asset classes to get a sense of the fund's overall risk-and-return profile, which helps you evaluate how the fund's performance fits your portfolio needs.

Read through a prospective fund's report archives before you invest to discover more about the fund's investment style and communication philosophy.

Fund Partnerships: General and Limited

Most hedge funds are structured as lightly (if at all) regulated investment partnerships, but that doesn't mean that the partners within a fund are equal. Some partners stand on higher ground than others, and the structure of the fund affects the liability that investors may take on. If you buy into a hedge fund, you enter into a partnership, and you need to know what rights and obligations you have — especially if something goes wrong.

General partners: Controlling the fund

A hedge fund's *general partners* are the founders and money managers of the fund. These people have the following responsibilities:

- Form the fund
- Control the fund's investment strategy
- Collect the fees charged
- Pay the bills
- Distribute the bonuses

In exchange for their control, general partners take on unlimited liability in the fund, which means that their personal assets are at stake if the fund's liabilities exceed its assets. Many general partners own their stakes through *S corporations* (an ownership structure for small businesses that under U.S. tax code provides owners with limited liability and tax advantages) or other structures that shield their personal assets.

A fund's original general partners may grant the general-partner status to certain key hires or give it as a reward to top-performing employees. Some firms give the partnership in lieu of bonuses, and at other firms, managers expect new partners to write checks to cover their shares of the partnership stake. When general partners leave a fund, the other general partners buy out their stakes.

Limited partners: Investing in the fund

The *limited partners* (often shortened to *limiteds*) of a hedge fund are the people who invest in the fund — yep, you. When investors give their money to the fund manager (a general partner) to invest, they take a stake in the fund as a business. Limited partners can come in many different flavors:

- Individual investors, pension funds, or endowments
- Brokerage firms or investment companies that are sponsoring the fund's general partners
- Other partnerships or corporations formed to make investments in hedge funds

Limited partnership has its drawbacks. Limited partners pay fees to the general partners for their management services. They have little or no say in the fund's operations. And the fund may restrict ongoing communication with the general partners to only a few times per year. But in exchange for these limitations of control, limited partners have limited liability. You can lose only the amount you invest in the fund and no more. If the hedge fund goes belly-up and a landlord comes looking for back rent, he can go after the general partners and their personal assets, but he can't come to the limited partners and ask them for money.

Introducing Basic Types of Hedge Funds

You can sort hedge funds into two basic categories: absolute-return funds and directional funds. The following sections look at the differences between the two.

Hedge funds are small, private partnerships, and hedge fund managers can use a wide range of strategies to meet their risk and return goals. For these reasons, I can't recommend any funds or fund families to you, and I can't tell you that any one strategy will be appropriate for any one type of investment. That's the downside of being a sophisticated, accredited investor: You have to do a lot of work on your own!

Absolute-return funds

Sometimes called a "non-directional fund," an *absolute-return fund* is designed to generate a steady return no matter what the market is doing. An absolute-return fund has another moniker: a *pure-alpha fund*. In theory, the fund manager tries to remove all market risk (in other words, beta risk) in order to create a fund that doesn't vary with market performance. If the manager removes all the market risk, the fund's performance comes entirely from the manager's skill, which in academic terms is called *alpha*.

An absolute-return strategy is most appropriate for a conservative investor who wants low risk and is willing to give up some return in exchange.

Some people say that absolute-return funds generate a bond-like return because, like bonds, absolute-return funds have relatively steady but relatively low returns. The return target on an absolute-return fund is usually higher than the long-term rate of return on bonds, though. A typical absolute-return fund target is 8 to 10 percent, which is above the long-term rate of return on bonds and below the long-term rate of return on stocks.

Directional funds

Directional funds are hedge funds that don't hedge — at least not fully. (See the earlier section "Hedging: The heart of the hedge fund matter.") Managers of directional funds maintain some exposure to the market, but they try to get higher-than-expected returns for the amount of risk that they take. Because directional funds maintain some exposure to the stock market, they're sometimes called *beta funds* and are said to have a *stock-like return*. A fund's returns may not be steady from year to year, but they're likely to be higher over the long run than the returns on an absolute-return fund.

A directional fund's return may be disproportionately larger than its risk, but the risk is still there. These funds can also swing wildly, giving a big return some years and plummeting big in others. Longer-term investors may not mind as long as the upward trend is positive.

Book VI

Hedge Funds

Is a Hedge Fund Right for You?

Hedge funds aren't for everyone. If you don't meet the SEC's definition of an accredited investor, you can't invest in a hedge fund. And some hedge funds go beyond the SEC requirements, making sure that all investors are qualified purchasers. The following sections explain the requirements for both types of investors.

Accredited investor

An *accredited investor* is an individual who can enter into a hedge fund due to his or her financial standing. An investor is considered accredited if he or she meets any of the following criteria:

- ✔ Has a net worth of more than $1 million, owned alone or jointly with a spouse
- ✔ Has earned $200,000 in each of the past two years
- ✔ Has earned $300,000 in each of the past two years when combined with a spouse
- ✔ Has a reasonable expectation of making the same amount in the future

For investment institutions, such as pensions, endowments, and trusts, the primary qualification is having $5 million in assets.

Qualified purchaser

Many hedge funds set a more stringent standard than the SEC, asking that investors be *qualified purchasers* under their own internal guidelines. Typically, qualified purchasers are individuals with at least $5 million in investable assets. Trusts, endowments, and pensions must have at least $25 million in investable assets. Investors who meet a firm's qualified-purchaser standards are sometimes called *super accredited.*

Some firms may not set a qualified-purchaser standard, but they set their minimum-investment standards for their limited partners high enough that they may as well have a rule in place. For example, a hedge fund may demand that its new investors put in at least $1 million or $5 million, which eliminates a novice investor who has most of her wealth in her house and her IRA account.

 Funds go above and beyond because of concerns that the accredited-investor definition hasn't been indexed for inflation. (It was last revised in 1982, when a dollar was worth more than twice what it's worth today.) Many people now meet the definition thanks to appreciation in residential real estate or self-directed retirement savings. An investor may have $1 million in assets, but that doesn't mean he's knowledgeable enough or solvent enough to invest in lightly regulated hedge funds.

Alternatives if you don't qualify

If you don't qualify for a hedge fund as an accredited or qualified investor, you may be tempted to put this book down and pick up a copy of *Frugal Living For Dummies* (by Deborah Taylor-Hough [Wiley]). That's a good and useful book, no matter your income, but don't give up on this book just yet. If you don't qualify for a hedge fund outright, try the following:

- ✔ **Use hedge fund strategies within a small portfolio:** Understanding how hedge funds work can help you make better choices among mutual funds or help you balance a large position in your company's stock. Chapter 4 outlines many of the strategies that hedge funds use to gain a high return.

- ✔ **Find mutual funds that use hedge fund strategies:** Some mutual fund companies offer funds designed to capture the benefits of hedge funds within the highly regulated mutual fund structure. Janus and Laudus Rosenberg, for example, are among the companies that offer these funds.

Chapter 2

Looking before You Leap: How Hedge Funds Work

....

....

A hedge fund manager's job is to survey the world's markets to find investments that meet the fund's risk and return parameters. But how does the manager actually do it?

The fund manager has to have a system in place for determining what to invest in and for how long. He looks for opportunities to make money in an asset that's going to change in price, and he looks to reduce the risk of the portfolio. Without discipline, he can't make good decisions, which makes your job of evaluating performance impossible. Anyone who invests money has several available techniques for increasing returns and reducing risk. Some hedge fund managers simply do better research, and others rely on technical analysis, short-selling, and leverage to generate the returns that their clients expect.

This chapter gives you a basic overview of the different financial assets available and tells you how fund managers may value them. I hope to help you understand what kinds of assets a hedge fund may invest in. I can't give you an easy answer as to how or whether these assets should be used in a hedge fund, but armed with this information, you can make better investment decisions for yourself and ask better questions of a hedge fund manager.

Examining Asset Options

Most investors should hold a diversified mix of securities in order to get their optimal risk and return payoff. The exact proportion depends on your needs. Likewise, hedge fund managers have different targets for risk and return, and they turn to different assets in order to meet their targets.

A hedge fund or a group of hedge funds may use the assets you see here in many different ways. Hedge fund managers often use traditional assets in nontraditional ways, for example, so there are no hard and fast rules to rely on. Chapter 4 covers some of the investment strategies and styles that hedge funds use.

Traditional asset classes

Although many hedge funds pursue esoteric strategies and exotic assets, most funds have some investment positions in ordinary investment classes. The following sections give you a roundup of the usual suspects used to manage risk and return in hedge funds. You may be surprised that they don't look much different from what you would see in any investment portfolio. (For more information about traditional investments, go to Book II.)

Just because a hedge fund invests in securities doesn't mean it's playing it safe. Some hedge funds buy very ordinary and safe securities, such as U.S. government bonds, but they goose up the returns — and the risk — by using borrowed money to finance almost the entire position.

Stocks

A *stock* (also called an *equity*) is a security that represents a fractional inter-est in the ownership of a company. Hedge fund managers often buy and sell stocks in order to meet their investment objectives.

A share of stock has limited liability, which means that you can lose your entire investment, but no more than that. If the company files for bankruptcy, creditors can't come after shareholders for the money that the company owes them.

Bonds

A company or a government issues a bond in order to raise money to cover expenses or investments that can't be funded out of current income or savings. As a bond holder, you are essentially a creditor to the issuer of the bond. Hedge fund managers invest in many different types of bonds at different times; it all depends on the fund's investment objectives, what techniques the fund uses, and the prices in the market at any given time.

Cash and equivalents

Hedge fund managers have money readily available to purchase securities for the portfolio or to meet customer redemptions. For the most part, the interest rate on cash is very low, so hedge funds try to keep as little cash on hand as possible. However, they do look for some cash and cash-equivalent investments that can pay off handsomely. Other forms of money market securities include the following:

- Short-term loans, collectively known as *money market securities* or *cash equivalents,* which are expected to mature within 30 days or even overnight
- Long-term bonds that are about to mature (say, a bond issued 15 years ago that matures next week)
- Uninsured bank CDs
- Government securities that will mature within 90 days

Alternative assets

An *alternative investment* is anything other than stocks, bonds, or cash. Hedge fund managers, sniffing out opportunities to meet their investment objectives, often turn to the alternative assets outlined in the following subsections.

Hedge funds themselves are often considered to be an alternative investment class, but they shouldn't be. A hedge fund is an investment vehicle. Because of their light regulations and limits on withdrawals, hedge funds have more freedom to invest in alternative asset classes. They may be structured with a risk profile that's completely different from a traditional asset, but they're not in and of themselves alternative assets.

Real estate

Real estate isn't always considered an investment. In most cases, it's a store of value, which is an excellent hedge against inflation. In other words, over the long run, you expect the price to increase by inflation and not much more. This expectation is particularly appropriate for raw land and, believe it or not, single-family houses.

Real estate can be an investment, too. An office or apartment building generates a steady flow of rental income in addition to the stored value of the land. Agricultural real estate, including timberland, generates a steady flow of income from the sale of the commodities produced. Real estate that contains minerals generates profits when the minerals are extracted and sold.

Hedge funds rarely purchase raw land for investment purposes, but they may provide lending to real estate investors, help finance construction projects, or take shares in mineral projects (see the following section for more information).

Commodities

Commodities, explained in detail in Book IV, are popular as a hedge against inflation and uncertainty because commodity prices tend to increase at the same rate as prices in the overall economy, meaning that they maintain their real (inflation-adjusted) value. A hedge fund probably won't buy commodities outright, but it may take a stake in them in one of a few different manners:

- ✔ By purchasing real estate that generates income from commodities produced

- ✔ Through futures contracts, which change in price with the underlying commodities (see the upcoming "Futures" section)

- ✔ By managing its stock investments based on the exposure of the company issuing the stock to different commodity trends

Venture capital

Great entrepreneurs often have fabulous ideas held captive by thin wallets. To fund their business ideas, they look for investors willing to take great risks in hopes of high returns. Such investors provide the start-up capital. Examples of businesses started by venture capital? Google, Yahoo!, and America Online — all of which succeeded fabulously — as well as countless others you've never heard of that failed miserably.

Many hedge funds are in the business of taking on high risk in exchange for potential high returns, so venture capital fits neatly. Some hedge funds become partners in venture capital firms, and others seek out promising new businesses to invest in directly. (See Chapter 4 for more on venture capital.)

Derivatives

To manage risk, hedge funds often use *derivatives,* financial contracts that draw their value from the value of an underlying asset, security, or index. By selling an S&P 500 future, for example, a fund can effectively sell off its exposure to the stock market. This action helps the fund maintain its market-neutral position. Other hedge funds use derivatives to increase return or reduce other forms of risk, such as interest rate or currency risk. A handful of funds invest only in derivatives.

Options

Hedge funds sometimes use options to manage risk or to profit from price changes. An *option* is a contract that gives the holder the right, but not the obligation, to buy or sell the underlying asset at an agreed-upon price at an agreed-upon date in the future. An option that gives you the right to buy is a *call*, and an option that gives you the right to sell is a *put*. A call is most valuable if the stock price is going up, whereas a put has more value if the stock price is going down. Head to Book III for more information on options.

Warrants and convertible bonds

Hedge funds sometimes use warrants and convertible bonds to manage risk or to profit from price changes. A *warrant* is similar to an option, but it's issued by a company instead of being sold on an organized exchange. It gives the holder the right to buy more stock in the company at an agreed-upon price in the future. Company-issued employee stock options are more like warrants than exchange-traded stock options. Related to the warrant is the *convertible bond*, which is debt issued by the company. The company pays interest on the bond, and the bondholder has the right to exchange it for stock. Which option the holder should exercise depends on interest rates and the stock price.

Book VI

Hedge Funds

Futures

Futures contracts, covered in detail in Book III, are useful for hedge fund managers who want to lock in prices. They also give managers exposure to commodity prices without having to handle the actual assets. Some hedge funds also use futures contracts to *speculate* — to make bets that the price of the underlying assets will go up or down in price. Futures contracts are highly *liquid* — they're easy to trade — which makes them attractive for a hedge fund that wants to take a very short-term position in an asset class.

Forward contracts

With a *forward contract*, an investor buys a currency, commodity, or other asset now at the market price, but the delivery doesn't take place until an agreed-upon future time. This strategy allows an investor to lock in the current price. In many cases, a hedge fund manager uses forward contracts to cover a futures contract; the manager locks in the current price in hopes that the future value is different, creating a profit on the difference. The difference is known as the *spread*.

Swaps

A *swap* is an exchange of one cash flow for another. Say a company has issued bonds that pay interest in U.S. dollars, but decides to incur expenses in Japanese yen to offset profits that it makes in Japan. The company finds another company making payments in yen that would rather be making payments in dollars, and they swap payments. As a result, each company can better manage its internal currency risk. In many cases, one or both parties in the transaction are banks or financial services firms, like hedge funds. The fund looks to profit on the difference between the different currencies, different interest-rate structures, or different payment times.

Custom products and private deals

Hedge funds often participate in private transactions and offbeat investments so they can meet their desired risk and return characteristics better than they can with readily traded securities. Contract law governs private transactions; only rarely does the Securities and Exchange Commission have any say in them. This section discusses a few such private transactions, but you may come across many others.

Mezzanine financing

Mezzanine financing is a combination of debt and equity used to support a company until it can go to the public markets. The debt and equity may be used as late-stage venture capital, when the new business isn't quite ready to sell its stock to the public, or it can go toward financing an acquisition. The lenders of the financing don't get paid until the company settles all other debts, making the financing almost like equity in that mezzanine lenders can lose everything if the company goes bankrupt.

Payment-in-kind bonds

Companies in financial trouble often issue *payment-in-kind bonds.* Instead of paying interest on its debt, the company gives the investors that own its bonds, known as *bondholders,* other bonds or securities, which creates many interesting trading opportunities. For example, a hedge fund manager may notice that the price of a payment-in-kind bond doesn't fully reflect the value of the bonds that the company will pay out in place of interest. Hedge funds like these opportunities.

Tranches

Bonds are often issued in several classes, known as *tranches. (Tranche* is the French word for "slice"; in essence, a security is sliced up into smaller securities when it's issued in tranches.) Each tranche may have a different interest rate and payment term. For example, one tranche may pay interest only after the first three years. Another may be a zero-coupon bond, which helps a company meet unique cash-flow needs. Tranches are often designed with the buyer's needs in mind as well. A hedge fund or other bond buyer may be looking for a structure that fits in with its overall portfolio construction, and a unique tranche may be a good fit.

Viaticals

A *viatical* is a life insurance policy purchased from the insured as an investment. Many terminally ill people need money now. They have life insurance policies with big benefits, but their policies aren't helping the sick today. So, these sick people find investors who are willing to give them money now in exchange for the death benefits later. Viaticals are enormously risky investments, because sick people get better and researchers develop new cures all the time. And because the time to maturity is unknown, viaticals are difficult to price.

Researching a Security's Value

Each hedge fund manager needs a system for figuring out the price at which to buy or sell a security. The following sections outline common analytical approaches.

Top-down analysis

Top-down fundamental analysis examines the overall state of the economy. The researcher uses the findings to identify specific assets that he or she expects to benefit or suffer from changes in the overall state of the economy, like price increases, employment levels, and interest rates. A top-down analyst, for example, may look at consumer debt levels, project future changes, and then look for companies affected by the changes. Will an increase in consumer debt help or hurt car and appliance manufacturers? High-end retailers? Bargain retailers? Financial service firms that emphasize lending or savings? If the researcher has a framework in place for analyzing the trends of the overall changes in the economy, he or she can select companies expected to change in price and structure the portfolio accordingly.

Top-down investing is sometimes called *theme investing* because a fund manager looks for a handful of broad trends and invests based on those trends. The fund may look to benefit from an aging population, higher energy prices, or increased defense spending, for example. In some cases, a firm may have a portfolio strategist who works to determine the themes. The firm's other analysts, who may use different analytical approaches, have to narrow their search to securities that fit the themes.

One major theme of top-down fundamental research is the use of economic analysis. Hedge funds often use economic analysis as part of their investment strategies, no matter their overall research styles. And if the funds invest in several of the world's markets, economic analysis is especially important. Hedge fund managers perform economic analysis in order to determine the best ways to profit from changes in economic trends, like inflation, unemployment, interest rates, or growth in a nation's gross domestic product. Most hedge fund managers at least think about the underlying economy when making investment decisions, and some hedge funds, known as *macro funds,* base their entire strategy around economic changes.

The following sections explore the different levels of economic analysis within top-down research.

A microeconomic approach

Microeconomics relates to the structure of small units in the economy, like individual companies or households. Microeconomic analysis looks at conditions, like how much competition or regulation exists in a market, how easy it is for new companies to enter a market, and how taxes cause a specific company to behave. Microeconomic analysis is practically synonymous with fundamental research, because the hedge fund manager wants to know how changes in prices, competition, and product trends affect the prospects for a given company.

A macroeconomic approach

Macroeconomics looks at the overall national or even global economy. Macroeconomic analysis is concerned with exchange rates, interest rates, price levels, growth, and employment. Hedge funds that invest heavily in government bonds, financial derivatives, and currencies generally pay attention to macroeconomic analysis. Managers of these funds use data published by government agencies, central banks, and nongovernmental organizations such as the United Nations and the World Bank to develop forecasts for changes in price levels.

Secular versus cyclical trends

Trends fall into two categories: secular and cyclical. A *cyclical trend* is related to economic cycles. For example, when employment improves, more people are working, and these new employees need clothes to wear to work, so they buy more threads, increasing revenue for apparel companies.

A *secular trend* represents a fundamental shift in the market, regardless of the cyclical trends. A secular trend in the clothing industry, for example, is the move toward casual dress in the office. In the 1990s, the economy boomed and white-collar employment grew, but folks were wearing khakis and golf shirts rather than suits and ties. Sales were strong at retailers that sold casual apparel, but sales dropped off at traditional suit makers. Even if professionals bought their golf shirts at suit stores, they spent less money than they would've on crisp white shirts and expensive silk ties.

The challenge for an investor is separating the cyclical economic trend, which is temporary, from the secular economic one, which is not.

Demographics

Understanding the nature of the demographics within a population can help hedge fund managers make better decisions and separate cyclical from secular trends. Companies need to worry about the demographics of their employee and customer bases, and nations need to worry about the people within their borders. Young populations tend to have cheap, unskilled workers, and older demographics usually have highly skilled, experienced, and expensive work forces. Young people tend to borrow money to spend; older people spend their savings; and people in the middle tend to set aside more than they spend.

Bottom-up analysis

A *bottom-up* analyst looks for individual companies that he expects to do especially well or especially poorly in the future. The analyst starts his research by examining the company itself: its financial statements, its history, its product line, the quality of its management, and so on. He then makes a judgment about the company's value on its own merits. He incorporates broad market trends only as they directly affect the business, which sets bottom-up analysis apart from top-down analysis.

A subset of bottom-up research is known as the *story stock*: an offbeat company with complex products or unusual circumstances that require elaborate explanations. Sometimes story stocks prove to be good investments — meaning that they go up in price as those who tell the stories expect them to — especially if the companies are harbingers of change in their industries. Other times, these companies make good shorts (see Chapter 4 for more information on short-selling).

Accounting research

Some bottom-up analysts look only at a company's reported financial statements, ignoring other aspects of its business. These people look for evidence of fraud, unsustainable growth, or hidden assets. This examination is known as *accounting research*. Often accountants themselves, the accounting analysts who examine the companies understand the many nuances and judgment calls that go into preparing financial statements. In most cases, the goal of accounting research is to identify potential short ideas.

Quantitative research

Quantitative research looks strictly at numbers. These numbers may represent accounting figures (for example, accounts receivable relative to sales), or they may be sensitivity factors (for example, how much a company's profit changes when oil prices increase by 1 percent). Quantitative analysts, often called *quants,* tend to put the information they find into complex mathematical models, and the solutions that result correspond to the securities that investors should put into the portfolio. Firms that rely heavily on quantitative analysis are often called *black-box shops* because the quants put numbers into a computer, which then spits out the portfolio selection, and only a handful of people understand how this system works.

Technical analysis

Technical analysis involves looking at charts of the price and volume of trading in a security. The charts show the historic supply and demand for the security, which may indicate where future prices are heading. The information shows a measure of sentiment. Analysts look to any number of questions: Is the number of buy orders increasing? Are the orders increasing while the price goes up or while the price goes down? Is the stock's price rising steadily, or does it go up in bursts around news announcements? Technical analysts use the answers to these types of questions to make investment decisions.

Few funds rely on technical analysis exclusively, but many use it regularly as a check on their fundamental research. Technical analysis is complicated, which means that the dabbler can run into trouble. For information on how to perform this type of analysis, go to Book VIII.

Putting the Findings to Work

So, what happens when a hedge fund's research identifies some great opportunities in different assets? Well, the fund takes a position. It can go long (buy in hopes that the asset goes up) or go short (sell in hopes that the asset goes down). The fund can also trade securities, monitor positions that may pay off in the future, or look for other ways to turn the information into a return for the hedge fund investor. These options are discussed in the pages that follow.

The long story: Buying appreciating assets

When a hedge fund manager or other investor buys a security, he or she is said to be *long*. An investor has only one reason to go long: He or she thinks that the asset will go up in price. Some hedge fund managers look for longs that will work over an extended period of time — possibly years — and others prefer to make their profits over very small stretches of time — possibly seconds.

Buying low, selling high

The secret of making money is buying low and selling high. So what marks low and high? Answering this question is where research comes in. The research sets the price targets for establishing and selling the position. The fund buys the security (with cash on hand or with leverage; see Chapter 4) and holds it until it reaches a higher price or sells it if it becomes clear that the investment isn't working out. The difference between the purchase price and the sale price — adjusted for borrowing, interest, and commissions — is the profit (or loss) for the position.

Trading for the short term

The hedge fund structures of light regulation, limited investor liquidity, and maximum return for a given level of risk very much favor trading. For this reason, many hedge funds are aggressive traders: They often take positions for only a very short time. They look to capture small increases in price, but they do it every day, over and over again, so that the amounts compound into a very large return.

Holding for the long term

Some hedge funds take a long-term outlook with their securities, meaning they buy and hold to establish a position and then wait weeks, months, or even years to be proven right. The buy-and-hold style is less common in hedge funds than in other investment vehicles, such as mutual funds or individual accounts, because the hedge fund structure is less of an advantage to the investor with a long-term outlook than to the active trader. Still, many hedge funds do buy and hold — especially if they're playing with private and illiquid investments (see the section "Custom products and private deals" earlier in this chapter).

The short story: Selling depreciating assets

Hedge funds can make money by selling securities, and not necessarily securities that they own. A *short-seller* borrows a security from someone else (usually from a brokerage firm's inventory) and then sells it. After a while — ideally, after the security goes down in price — the short-seller buys back the security in the market and repays the loan with the asset that he originally borrowed. The lender doesn't have to repay the original dollar value, just the security in question. The profit (or loss) is the difference between where the short-seller sold the security and where he bought it back, less commissions and interest charged by the lender. (See Chapter 4 for more on short-selling.)

Protecting long positions

Short-selling reduces risk. By selling off part of the risk, the fund can make money while hedging the long position. For example, if a fund's quantitative research finds that a given investment is heavily exposed to the price of oil, the fund can get rid of that risk by shorting oil futures. The fund offsets any gain or loss in the investment's price caused by sensitivity to oil with the gain or loss of the futures position.

Investment shorts

An *investment short* is a short-sell taken in a legitimate business that the fund doesn't expect to do well. A fund may make the decision to go with an investment short as part of a matching long position in a competitor that it expects to do well, as part of a risk-management maneuver, or purely for investment success.

Fraud shorts

A *fraud short* is an investment that the fund expects to go down in value because of suspicions that the company is guilty of misrepresenting its products, its financial results, or its management (see the section "Accounting research"). These investments are rare, but funds make a few of them every year. A fraud short is risky stuff, the management of a company that a fund heavily shorts will probably fight back, sometimes with ugly tactics, and short-sellers who are anxious to get the news flow moving in their favor have been known to resort to lies and threats.

Naked shorts

A fund exacts a *naked short* when it sells a security that it hasn't borrowed in hopes that it will go down fast enough that the fund can buy back the security and settle with the buyer. Naked shorting is against exchange regulations in most markets, but it still happens. The advantage for the fund is that it can sell short without paying interest to the lender, and it can sell short even if no lender will loan the fund the security. The downside is that if the fund can't repurchase the security in time to settle its sale, the exchanges will find out and probably shut down the fund.

Because of the illicit nature of the technique, you shouldn't invest in any fund that admits to naked shorting.

Final Considerations Before You Jump In

Hedge funds are both illiquid and lightly regulated. Because your money is likely to be tied up for an extended period and the fund itself won't necessarily fall under the scrutiny of any regulatory body, the onus is on you to be a savvy investor. Before signing an agreement with any hedge fund manager — even the one your investment banker friend swears by — you need to take a close look at your own specific financial goals, figure out how much you can afford to invest in a hedge fund scheme, and consider what type of asset allocation is most likely to mesh with the other investments in your portfolio.

Determining the size of your hedge fund allocation

Because of their illiquidity (see Chapter 1), hedge funds are seldom appropriate for an entire investment portfolio. In almost all cases, hedge funds offer their maximum portfolio benefit in relatively small doses. In fact, hedge funds are mostly designed as investment vehicles for *excess capital*: money that the investor doesn't need now and doesn't need to support near-term spending.

Suppose, for example, that you're in charge of making investment decisions for a trust fund worth $20 million. You need to generate $600,000 in annual income. In most cases, a 5 percent income is reasonable for a minimum long-term return assumption for a mixed stock and bond portfolio. So, you start with the $600,000 income need and divide it by 5 percent to determine how much of the portfolio you should put in stocks and bonds. The answer: $12 million. The remaining amount of the portfolio is considered excess capital. You can lock up and invest this money at a higher risk level than the rest of the portfolio because you don't need it to support your income needs. Although you don't want to lose that money, losing it wouldn't affect the minimum portfolio objective of generating $600,000 in annual income.

Determining your financial goals

The answers to two questions go a long way toward determining how to invest your money and what to invest it in:

- ✔ When do you need your money?
- ✔ What do you need your money for?

Your answers influence the risk you can take, the return you need to shoot for, the asset classes that are open to you, and how much time you can allocate toward the investment.

Generally speaking, investable money falls into three categories:

- ✔ **Temporary (or short-term) funds** that you'll need in a year. Hedge funds charge high fees (see Chapter 1). Because fund managers need time to earn these fees, they want money that investors can set aside for long periods.

- ✔ **Matched assets** that you invest to meet a specific liability, like a college education. Whether a hedge fund is an appropriate match for an upcoming financial need depends in large part on the risk profile of the hedge fund. An absolute-return fund, which is designed to have low risk and a steady, low return (see Chapter 1), is usually a good match with an intermediate-term obligation, for money that you don't need until after you meet any lockup periods on the fund. Directional funds, which pursue high-risk strategies in exchange for higher expected returns, are a better match for financial needs that reach far into the future.

- ✔ **Permanent funds** that you invest for such a long term that, for all practical purposes, you'll never spend them. Instead investors plan to spend only the income generated from the investments' interest and dividends. They can then reinvest the capital gains so that the initial amounts invested get larger, which causes the amount of income that the investments can generate to grow. Permanent funds are often great investment candidates for hedge funds. Most hedge funds are designed to generate steady capital gains, and they limit withdrawals, so your fund's money should build up over time.

Few managers structure hedge funds to generate income, so if producing income is one of your key investment objectives, you should allocate your funds to other types of investments, like bonds or dividend-paying stocks.

Allocating your assets: Finding the right mix

As stated in Chapter 1, hedge funds fall into two broad categories: *absolute-return,* which is designed to produce a steady but relatively low rate of return with relatively little risk, and *directional,* which aims for the highest possible return, although with a high level of risk. Within these categories are many different strategies and asset concentrations, as Chapter 4 explains.

Different assets — real (tangible) and financial (securities) — have different sources of return and present different tradeoffs, and you want a balance of them in your portfolio. Table 2-1 summarizes many types of financial assets.

Table 2-1	Characteristics of Different Financial Assets		
Financial Asset	**Primary Source of Return**	**Relative Level of Return**	**Relative Level of Risk**
Stocks (equities)	Capital gains	High	High
Bonds (fixed income)	Income	Medium	Medium
Cash	None	Low	Low
Real estate	Income, store of value	Medium	Medium
Commodities	Store of value, possible appreciation	Medium	Medium

When choosing a hedge fund (whose manager chooses assets to invest in) to fit into your portfolio, you need to think about how it will act with the other investments in your portfolio because different asset classes interact with your other investments differently. For example, if you mostly invest in domestic stocks and bonds, you may want to put your hedge fund allocation into macro funds because those will have more international exposure. This strategy will reduce the risk of your overall portfolio better than a U.S. long-short equity fund.

You also want to find a fund whose strategy jibes with your investment needs — a task that's fairly difficult when hedge fund managers often don't want to tell investors what strategies they're following or where they invest their money. Chapter 3 gives a list of questions you can ask as you interview prospective hedge fund managers to gather the information you need.

Matching goals to money

Asset allocation is the process of matching your investment goals to your money in order to meet your goals with the lowest possible amount of risk. Do you need to generate $100,000 in pre-tax annual income from your investments? Are current interest rates at 4 percent? If so, you should put $4 million in fixed-income securities with an average coupon (annual interest rate) of 4 percent. Do you need $10 million in 20 years to meet a contractual obligation? Do you think that an 8 percent return is acceptable as long as you experience little variation between your expected return and the return that you get? If so, you should put $2.2 million in a hedge fund with an absolute-return strategy.

Book VI

Hedge Funds

The exact amounts and investments you choose will vary with your means and your goals. Any professional advisors you work with should take the time to find out what you need. Beware of advisors who try to sell you products without finding out what your needs are. It's not only against regulations (a violation of the know-your-customer and suitability rules), but also bad for you.

Chasing return versus allocating assets

"I don't care what fund you put me in, as long as it performs well. How about this fund that was up 40 percent last year?" Whoa, cowboy! Unfortunately, that's a common strategy among investors, and it's a dangerous one. Known as *chasing return,* this strategy ignores long-term goals, near-term constraints, and good investing principles in hopes of landing the big bucks right now.

Return chasers are doomed to fail in the long run, and often in the short run, too. Markets move in cycles, so last year's hot performer will probably cool off this year. Moving your money around too much leads to plenty of taxes and commission charges that eat into your investment base. And without a sense of how much money you really need, when you need it, and with what degree of certainty you're operating, you risk choosing investments that miss your goals by a mile.

Chapter 3

Taking the Plunge

An open-end mutual fund (described in Book II, Chapter 3) continuously offers stock to the public. You find a fund that interests you; you read the prospectus that the fund issues; you fill out a form; you write your check; and viola! You're a mutual fund shareholder. A hedge fund is nothing like that. When you enter into a hedge fund, you join a private-investment partnership. Step foot in the hedge fund world, and you may discover, as Dorothy did, that you're not in Kansas anymore.

To help you navigate your way into and around hedge funds, this chapter explains how to choose the fund that's right for you, how to purchase a stake in the fund, what to do after you're a partner, and how to read the hedge fund reports. Finally, as an investor who's (we hope!) making money, you need to know what your tax obligations are. This chapter covers that topic, too.

Investor, Come on Down: Pricing Funds

When you buy into a hedge fund or cash out your shares, you need to know what the shares are worth. When a fund forms, setting the price is simple: The total value of the fund is the total value of the cash put into it. If the fund disbands, setting the prices is also simple: The hedge fund manager sells all the securities, pays all the bills, and distributes the remainder proportionately. Of course, you also need to know what the shares are worth to calculate performance. (See Chapter 5 for more information on performance calculation.)

This section covers net asset value calculation, including dealing with illiquid securities. With the use of these tools, you'll have a sense of how the fund comes up with the value of your investment.

Prices are all over the place, as are minimum investments. Some funds report values to consultants annually or quarterly, but many don't. Some funds will take $25,000 investments, and others insist on $10 million.

Calculating net asset value

Hedge funds are priced on their *net asset value.* Also called *book value,* net asset value is the total of all the fund's assets minus all the fund's liabilities. Sounds simple, right? Well, here's a catch: finding the value for all the fund's securities, calculated at the end of each trading day, when the end of the trading day varies depending on when markets close around the world.

If a fund invests entirely in one market and one type of investment, the pricing is straightforward. The New York Stock Exchange closes at 4 p.m. Eastern Time, so if all your investments trade there, you simply price at the close. But in a global market, who decides when the trading day ends? What if you also have futures (financial contracts that trade on a different exchange)? And if assets are in constant motion, when does the clock stop so you can calculate net asset value? All these things need to be taken into account when calculating net asset value.

One way to calculate net asset value is to add the values at the closing time for each relevant market. The price then would be the sum of the prices at each market's close (ignoring after-market trading). For example, if your security trades in these exchanges and has a closing value as indicated, the net asset value would be $2,138.

Exchange	Closing Time (ET)	Value at Closing
Toyko Stock Exchange	1:00 am	$900
London Stock Exchange	10:30 am	$986
NYSE	4:00 pm	$1,054
CBOT	4:15 pm	($802)
Net Asset Value		**$2,138**

No calculation method is inherently better; the key is that the method is disclosed and applied consistently. Be sure to ask the fund manager when and how the fund calculates the value. It should be spelled out in the contracts that you sign when you enter the fund.

Valuing illiquid securities

Because hedge funds can limit how often clients withdraw money, and because they tend to take a broad view of possible investments, they often put money in *illiquid securities* — investments that don't trade very often and are difficult to sell on short notice.

Short-term buying and selling can have an enormous impact on the prices of securities. If an asset trades all the time, the value is widely known. It's easy to know what a share of Microsoft stock is worth because millions of shares are bought and sold every day, for example. If an asset doesn't trade often, you have little observable, unbiased market indicator of what the true price should be. To get around this situation, hedge funds have many techniques to assign values to illiquid securities (see Chapter 5 for more details):

Book VI

Hedge Funds

- ✔ **Net present value:** The discounted value of all the expected cash flows
- ✔ **Black-Scholes:** A complicated mathematical model used to find the value of an option
- ✔ **Relative valuation:** Basing the security's price on a similar security that trades frequently

If a hedge fund you're interested in invests in illiquid securities, find out what its policy for valuation is. And know that you take on some risk if the fund buys a lot of these assets; the price assigned to the fund may not hold when the illiquid securities have to be sold (quite a catchy rhyme, don't you think?).

Managing side pockets

A *side pocket* in a hedge fund is a group of securities held by only some of the fund's investors. Hedge funds set up side pockets — also called *designated investments* or *special investments* — for two main reasons:

- ✔ **To hold illiquid securities away from money that investors can redeem.** For example, the fund may allow investors to pull money out of the main part of the fund once per quarter, but it may decide that investors can redeem funds in the side pocket only once every two years. Likewise, new fund investors can't enter into the side pocket so that the valuation of those investments doesn't become an issue for them. If you invest in a fund that's just starting out, part of your investment may be held in a side pocket.
- ✔ **To allow certain fund investors access to securities that other investors many not have.** The fund may provide performance enticements or other

special benefits that attract specific investors. A fund may also set up a side pocket to meet the needs of a large institutional investor that can put a great deal of money into the fund.

Side pockets are priced separately from the rest of the fund. Because they're often set up just to hold illiquid investments, their price may be more uncertain.

Due Diligence: Picking a Hedge Fund

Because hedge funds are structured as partnerships (see Chapter 1), you enter into a relatively intimate business relationship with the fund manager when you buy into the fund. The better prepared you are, the better the relationship will be. If you do the work necessary to know that the fund manager is who he says he is, you'll have a greater level of trust. Although a consultant may help you evaluate a fund manager, you still need to do your own research. The following sections explain how.

Knowing what to ask

One of the first steps in determining if a particular hedge fund makes sense for you is to ask a lot of questions. After you assure the hedge fund manager that you're a serious investor (both accredited and able to invest in the fund now; see Chapter 1), you'll probably receive an offering document that answers some of your questions — and raises others. No matter how thorough the offering document is, you'll have to sit down for an interview with the fund manager or submit a list of questions to the fund's staff.

Here's a list of questions to get you started. Your offering document will cover some; some you'll ask in an interview; and some you may have to find answers to on your own. You probably want to get an answer for each one, and you may well come up with other questions to ask.

✔ **Investment strategy:**

- What's your investment objective? How do you achieve alpha (see Chapter 1)?

- How did you construct your portfolio? How and why is it rebalanced?

- What's your analysis and investment style? What would cause you to deviate from your style?

- If you use computer models, do you ever override them? Do you change the models?

- What's the average number of positions your fund holds? How long do you hold a typical position? What's the level of portfolio turnover?

- Do you use sub-advisors? (*Sub-advisors* are money managers who handle a portion of the portfolio.) When and why? How do you compensate them?

- Do you see yourself as a trader, an investor, or an analyst?

- Why is your fund different from others with the same investment style? What edge do you have over other managers?

- Is your fund more suitable for taxable investors or for tax-exempt ones?

- How does your fund keep enough liquidity to meet allowed withdrawals?

✔ **Performance:**

- What have been your worst months? Your best months? Why?

- Did you earn your performance evenly in the past year, or did you have one or two really good months? If so, what made those months so good for your strategy?

- What was the time (the *peak-to-trough range*) between your best month and your worst month?

- What holdings have worked out the best for you? Which one was your worst ever? Why?

- Who calculates your fund's returns? How often? Where does this person get his/her data: from the prime broker or from the fund manager?

- How do you value the portfolio? When do you price it? How do you handle illiquid securities?

- Is your performance GIPS (Global Investment Performance Standards) compliant? If not, why not? Do you report your performance to Morningstar or other tracking services?

✔ **Risk management:**

- How does your fund use leverage (see Chapter 4)? What's the average leverage? What's the maximum leverage allowed? How often are you near those limits?

- Does your fund always have some leverage?

- Does your fund borrow from one bank or broker, or from several?

- What's your maximum exposure to any one security? Any one market? How often are you near those limits?

- How much of your borrowing is overnight? Short-term? Long-term? How has that changed over time?

- How do you define risk? What's your firm's attitude toward risk?

- What risks have you identified? What are your strategies for managing them?

- What happens if a trader exceeds his or her limits?

- What are your long-tail risk scenarios?

- Do you use derivatives to hedge? To speculate?

- Do you try to profit from, or hedge against, interest-rate risk? Currency risk? Market risk?

✔ **Fund operations:**

- Who are your fund's founders? Are they still with you? If they've left, why did they leave and where did they go?

- How do you compensate your traders? What's the turnover of your investment staff? Of your total staff?

- How much do the fund principals have invested in the fund? Is this a good portion of their net worth?

- How do you keep the front and back office separated?

- Who is the asset custodian?

- What are your data-backup and disaster-recovery plans? How quickly could you get back into business if your building shut down?

- Who takes over if the fund manager is incapacitated or dies? What is the key person risk?

- What are your data-security practices?

- Is the fund audited annually? If not, why not? If yours is a new fund, have you lined up an auditor to do an audit at the end of the year?

- What's your accounting firm? Your law firm? Your prime broker? Your administrative-services firm?

✔ **Compliance and transparency:**

- What are your compliance policies and procedures? May I see them?

- Are you registered with the Securities and Exchange Commission? With the Commodity Futures Trading Commission? Why or why not?

- How much disclosure and reporting can I expect? How much transparency should any hedge fund investor expect?

Interviewing the hedge fund manager

Getting to know the hedge fund manager on the other side of the table is a good idea. When you talk to a fund manager, you get a sense of what it will be like doing business with this person. You want to make sure that the fund fits your needs and that you're comfortable with the fund's strategy and the fund manager's personality.

The hedge fund manager probably won't tell you everything. For example, she probably won't discuss the fund's short positions (securities that the fund borrows from others and then sells in hopes that they'll go down in price) or even its long positions. She should, however, tell you about the following:

- ✔ How the fund goes about getting its return
- ✔ How she manages risk
- ✔ What types of securities she invests in
- ✔ How fund operations are handled

With this information, you'll know if the fund's investment strategies, risk-and-return parameters, and administration situation are logical and if they fit your investment needs.

Poring over fund literature

After you arm yourself with the right questions and get some answers, your next step is to check up on the information you receive. One way to do this is by reviewing the firm's literature. A hedge fund manager will give a prospective investor thick legal documents after he or she is satisfied that the investor is accredited and serious about investing in the fund. The documents lay out the investment policies that govern the fund and its operations. The hedge fund manager may also hand accredited and interested prospective investors glossy decks of PowerPoint slides or other sales materials that explain the fund's investment policies and operations with less legalese.

The information in these legal documents and marketing materials includes the fund's investment strategy and fees, as well as biographical information on the people who run the fund. You can use these resources to make a list of information you want to verify elsewhere and to come up with questions that you still consider unanswered.

Picking up the phone

Another important step in the due-diligence process is to call former employees of the fund you're interested in and others to verify the information you've received through interviews and literature and that appears on the hedge fund manager's résumé. The fund manager should give you reference names and contact information for the resources you want to investigate. Here's a list of people you should call:

- **Former employees:** They may restrict their details to only dates of hire and positions held, but that information is useful — especially if it doesn't match with what the hedge fund manager tells you. If you can talk to a former fund colleague in depth, consider asking about the following topics:

  - How the fund manager researched and made trades

  - How the manager worked with others on staff

  - How the manager worked with clients

  - How the fund manager affected this person's performance in his old position

- **Universities and colleges:** Be sure to call the colleges listed on the hedge fund manager's résumé. Many folks have an unfortunate habit of lying about or embellishing their educational backgrounds, so you should verify the degrees that the hedge fund manager claims from the schools that he says he attended.

- **Associated firms:** Call the law firm that the hedge fund lists as its counsel, as well as the hedge fund's accounting firm, prime broker, and administrative-services firm. You want to make sure that these firms are providing the services that the manager says they are, and you want to make sure that the relationships are good ones.

- **Current investors:** You may also be able to talk to current investors in the hedge fund. If so, you should ask them for the following information:

  - Why they chose this fund

  - If the fund's performance has met their expectations

  - What type of communication they've received from the hedge fund manager

Even if the list has a former employee's or current investor's direct line or personal cell phone, go through the organization's main switchboard and ask to be connected. In the unlikely event that a fraud is hot on your trail, you can catch it faster this way. Sometimes, criminals hire an accomplice and give the person a cell phone and a script to use when the phone rings.

Searching Internet databases

Are the folks in charge of the hedge fund who they say they are? One way to find out is to do some simple Internet searches and look beyond the first pages of results you see. Most likely, your search will turn up nothing interesting, but that's the point.

Internet databases sometimes have incorrect information, and they can be thrown off if the person that you're looking for has a common name or relatives who share the same name. Consider any information that you find to be a point for further questioning and research, not an automatic reason to accept or reject the fund.

Some of the sites that show up may be products of the hedge fund manager herself; what you want are sites that objective outsiders have prepared. Here are some recommended database sites:

Book VI

Hedge
Funds

- ✔ **Pretrieve** (www.pretrieve.com): Offers free searches of property records, court records, and other databases. You can see if the hedge fund's principals have had run-ins with regulators before. Pretrieve isn't as powerful as LexisNexis, but it's a good first stop.

- ✔ **LexisNexis** (www.lexisnexis.com): A huge database of court records, public records, and news stories. Law firms rely on it heavily because it includes more information than any free service. Unlimited access is expensive, but an a la carte service allows you to search for free and then buy the documents you need at about $3 each.

- ✔ **Financial Industry Regulatory Authority (FINRA) BrokerCheck** (www.finra.org): Has an online service that lets investors check on brokers. Many people in the securities industry hold brokers' licenses, not just folks holding sales jobs. Some hedge fund managers may be registered with FINRA now, or they may have been registered with the National Association of Securities Dealers (NASD) in earlier jobs. (The NASD is now part of FINRA.) You can find the employment and disciplinary history of managers who are registered at this site.

- ✔ **U.S. Securities and Exchange Commission** (www.sec.gov): Many hedge funds are registered with the U.S. Securities and Exchange Commission (SEC), so you can do research on the funds through the SEC Web site. You can also search for enforcement records (www.sec.gov/divisions/ enforce.shtml) to see if a registered fund has had problems or to find out if the fund manager ran into trouble while at another job.

✔ **National Futures Association** (`www.nfa.futures.org/basicnet`): Many hedge funds are registered as commodities trading accounts, which the Commodity Futures Trading Commission oversees. The National Futures Association maintains a database of people and funds registered with the Commodity Futures Trading Commission, and you can look up information about the people and funds at this Web site.

Seeking help from service providers

Most hedge funds rely heavily on outside service organizations. As a prospective hedge fund investor, you should know who the people in these firms are and what they do. The hedge fund manager should give you a list of the fund's service providers, and you should call at least a few to verify the services provided:

✔ **The prime broker:** The brokerage firm that handles most of the securities trades that the fund makes. The prime broker may also handle administrative services, such as taking in new investments, dispersing any funds withdrawn, and sending out periodic statements. (A dedicated administrative-services provider can also handle these functions.)

The folks who actually handle the fund's cash, taking in investments and disbursing withdrawals, should be part of an outside organization. Consider it a red flag if the hedge fund you're investigating does its own administrative work. At a minimum, separate legal subsidiaries that have guidelines to ensure that transactions happen at arm's length should provide the fund's administrative services.

✔ **A law firm:** Assists with the fund's regulatory compliance activities. Even an unregistered fund has laws that govern its activities.

✔ **An accounting firm:** Assists with the fund's valuation of assets, calculation of returns, and preparation of tax forms.

✔ **Sub-advisors:** Manage certain types of assets.

✔ **An actuary or other risk-management consultant:** Helps the fund calculate the risk it takes.

Purchasing Your Stake in the Fund

After a hedge fund investor and a hedge fund manager decide to work together, the next stage in the process is the purchase. The investor (lucky you!) and the manager have forms to fill out, and, of course, you have to transfer some money before you can turn a large profit. This section covers these logistics.

Fulfilling basic paperwork requirements

The U.S. Treasury Department's Financial Crimes Informant Network (www.fincen.gov), which investigates money laundering, requires financial institutions to have enforcement procedures in place to verify that new investments aren't made from ill-gotten funds. Hence, the hedge fund's staff must verify that they know who the investors in the fund are and where their money came from. You have to provide the following when you open a hedge fund account:

✔ Name

✔ Date of birth

✔ Street address

✔ Place of business

✔ Social Security number or taxpayer identification number

✔ Copies of financial statements from banks, brokerages, and other accounts showing that you're accredited and that you have enough money to meet the initial investment

If you want to open an individual account, you should also be prepared to provide your driver's license and passport. If you want to open an institutional account, you have to provide certified articles of incorporation, a government-issued business license, or a trust instrument.

Filling out tax forms

You also have forms to fill out for tax reporting down the road. IRS Form W9, for example, keeps your taxpayer information on record.

Each year, you'll receive a K-1 form from the fund, which reports your share of the hedge fund's profits. (The hedge fund itself files Form 1065 with the IRS.) As a partner, you need to report your share of the fund's earnings to the IRS, even if you haven't received any cash. This is a different reporting structure from most other forms of investment income, which are usually reported on 1099 forms and handled through Schedule B and Schedule D of IRS Form 1040.

The fund itself doesn't pay the taxes — you do. For more on your tax obligations, see the later section "Your Tax Responsibilities."

Signing the partnership agreement

When you enter into a hedge fund, the fund manager presents you with a contract drawn up by the fund's law firm. This contract specifies contractual obligations that both parties — the investor who purchases as the limited partner and the hedge fund's general partners — have to meet. The contract will be more or less standard, but it will be written to favor the general partners' interests. (Note: The fund manager may refer to the contract as a *partnership agreement,* a *subscription agreement,* or a *private-placement memorandum.* Its legal status as a contract is the same no matter the document's title.)

Some contracts can be so sided to the managers that they'll be open to doing anything the managers want with the money, investment-wise. I strongly advise you to have a lawyer with you when going over the contract. A lawyer may be able to negotiate changes on different provisions, like withdrawal procedures or disclosure levels, to get them working in your favor.

Addressing typical contract provisions

The hedge fund contract sets forth many pieces of information you need to know:

- ✔ The fund's general partners
- ✔ The fund's status with regulators
- ✔ The fees that the fund charges and how it calculates them
- ✔ The fund's limits on withdrawals

The contract may also discuss the fund's investment strategies, the assets that the fund will and won't invest in, and reporting requirements, but it doesn't have to.

A partnership agreement also sets forth how the fund will handle any conflicts. Most likely, limited partners give up the right to sue; you have to take disputes to arbitration, which is the norm in the investment business. The agreement you sign should discuss who will oversee the arbitration and where it will take place, should a hearing become necessary.

By signing the document, you agree to the terms and certify that you're an accredited investor (see Chapter 1).

Finding room for negotiation

When you get the contract — either in person, electronically, or in the mail — your first impulse will be to mark every clause you don't like and then go to the fund's general partners and ask for changes. In most cases, you'll get rebuffed. Hedge funds are popular investments, and many people want to hop on the bandwagon. Good fund managers can — and do — set their own terms.

But keep this in mind: If the fund you're interested in is small, if the manager is relatively new, and if you have plenty of money to commit, you may have some leverage. You may be able to ask for sales-fee reductions, fewer withdrawal restrictions, or other changes that meet your needs. In hedge funds, as in life, it never hurts to ask.

Book VI

Hedge Funds

Putting up your money

After you sign all the forms and do all the hand-shaking (not the fraternity kind, probably), you deposit your cash. The money you put up goes to the fund's prime broker, which holds it in escrow until the fund is ready to add new money. To minimize the cash-flow effects on investment returns, the fund may add money only once a month, once a quarter, or once a year.

If you already have an account for your other investments at the same firm as the fund's prime brokerage, you'll have an easy transfer. If your money comes from a bank or another brokerage firm, you may be required to obtain signature guarantees before you can transfer the funds. The brokerage or bank will probably send the money electronically, although you may be required to send a certified or cashier's check. (In the United States, most brokerage and bank functions are separated. In other parts of the world, the same institution may handle both services.)

Handling Liquidity after the Initial Investment

Choosing and entering a fund is a big, tough process, but your work doesn't stop after you hand over your investment and ride out the minimum lockup period. Your hedge fund will (we hope) generate money for your investment, giving you additional investment opportunities. The fund may allow you to withdraw funds so you can meet other objectives (but it comes with a price). The fund may also start sending you checks to reduce its burden, or it may decide to disband altogether. The following sections discuss factors that can affect your investment objectives after you enter into a hedge fund.

Considering opportunities for additional investments

After you meet the strict requirements to get into a hedge fund, find the right fund for your investment objectives, and go through initiation (just kidding), you can begin to enjoy the perks of the fund: additional investment opportunities, like these:

- ✔ Your hedge fund manager may look to raise more money in order to pursue interesting investment strategies that he sees in the market. His initial inquiries will likely be with his current investors.

- ✔ You come into money that you want to add to the fund and let your fund manager know. He may not need the money now, but he may want it in the near future.

- ✔ Even if the fund doesn't want to take on more money, the manager may allow you to buy shares from another investor — another good way to make additional investments after you enter a fund.

From the fund manager's perspective, cash in the fund is a problem unless he can invest it to meet the risk-and-return profile that investors expect. Your fund manager plans to reinvest the returns from the hedge fund. Every time the fund manager receives an interest payment or sells an investment at a profit, you make money that goes into the fund. Your underlying investment increases as long as the fund has a positive return.

Knowing when (and how) to withdraw funds

At some point, you may need to pull out money from your hedge fund. A hedge fund's offering documents should set out how often you can make withdrawals and how you should request a withdrawal. Instead of the rapid redemption services that mutual funds, brokerage firms, or bank accounts offer, you'll probably have to send written notice to a hedge fund manager in advance of your withdrawal. The manager may lay out very specific terms for how you should send the request (for example, certified postal mail) if you want to get your money. The turnaround time between when the manager receives the request and when he approves the withdrawal may be a month; the hedge fund's partnership agreement probably specifies the time period.

The fund manager has some options when it comes to raising your withdrawal funds. She can

    ✔ Meet your request with cash on hand.

    ✔ Sell off some assets to raise the cash.

    ✔ Sell your shares to another investor.

You'll receive the proceeds from the bank or prime broker that handles the fund's investments.

You won't find a standard withdrawal policy in the hedge fund industry. A hedge fund manager may even negotiate different policies for different investors in the fund. You need to know your needs before you invest in a hedge fund so that you know what policies will match your portfolio requirements. (Refer to Chapter 2 for help determining what your financial needs and expectations are.)

Book VI

Hedge Funds

A hedge fund manager may not want to sell investments just to meet your withdrawal request because it may screw up a carefully crafted investment position or require her to sell an asset at a near-term loss. Also, some fund investments are illiquid, meaning that they're difficult to sell on demand. As a result, a fund manager may view your withdrawal as something that will hurt the fund's remaining investors. To offset the hurt, some hedge funds impose withdrawal fees, especially if investors want to pull out more than a small amount.

Your fund manager may also hold back some of your money until the fund's accountants have a chance to calculate the performance of the fund up to the date of your withdrawal. It isn't easy to calculate the value of some investments like venture capital, so the fund manager wants to wait until she knows the value before settling up with you.

Receiving distributions

Although few hedge funds are designed as income investments, they sometimes send checks to their investors. The checks may be distributions of income, or they may be returns of capital. The difference may appear academic on the surface, but it affects your portfolio — especially when it comes time to pay your taxes. Which distribution is which, and why do the funds start sending you checks like grandma on your birthday? Read on to find out!

    ✔ **Income:** *Income* is money generated from interest, dividends, rental payments, and similar sources. Hedge funds usually reinvest income into their funds, but sometimes they pay it out to their investors. You may receive a check to help you meet your tax obligations, or your fund may send it to manage the size of its investable assets.

✔ **Returns of capital:** *Capital gains* are profits made when an investment goes up in price. These gains are *paper gains* when the fund still holds the asset that goes up in price, and *realized gains* when the fund sells the asset, locking in the profit in the process. Realized gains are taxable, but paper gains are not. In most cases, hedge funds want to reinvest their capital gains into new investments. However, your hedge fund may send you a check for your capital gains, reducing the amount of principal in the fund.

You may think that income and capital gains are the same thing, but they aren't. The government taxes them at different rates, and people handle them differently for accounting purposes. In most cases, capital gains are taxed at lower rates than income, which is enough of a reason to keep them separated. See the section "Your Tax Responsibilities" for more information.

Managers of top-performing funds have been known to kick investors out. (The offering documents that you sign when you enter the fund explain if and when the fund manager can do this.) The policy may screw up your portfolio, and all the paper gains will suddenly fall into the realized (taxable) category.

Moving on after disbandment

For many reasons — mostly related to poor performance — a fund manager may decide to disband the fund and return the money to investors.

Hennessee Group (www.hennesseegroup.com), an investment consulting firm that tracks hedge funds, reports that 5.1 percent of the hedge funds in its database shut their doors in 2006. In 2005, 5.4 percent of hedge funds tracked by Hennessee closed.

When your fund disbands because of poor performance, you're happy to get your money back. But poor performance isn't the only culprit. A fund may have a new manager who realizes that it can be hard to raise enough money and earn enough of a return to make the venture worthwhile. However, there are two main problems with fund abandonment:

✔ **Poor performance may be a temporary blip.** A given investment strategy may be having an off year, which actually presents a good opportunity to buy assets cheap in order to take advantage of better performance in the near future. If the fund closes, its investors lose the opportunity to buy low in order to sell high. This is one reason that funds like having as long a lockup period as possible.

✔ **It may not be easy for a fund investor to find a new investment that meets his or her risk-and-return needs.** The likelihood of you finding another suitable investment is called *reinvestment risk.* Based on Hennessee Group's 2006 numbers, your chances may be running at about 5 percent or so that your fund will disband and you will have to find a new place to invest your money.

If disbandment looks like a possibility for your fund, you really can't do anything except start looking for new places to put your money. Disbandment is one of the risks you take when you invest in hedge funds.

Reading the Hedge Fund Reports

Hedge funds are like undercover cops: They don't like to talk about what they do. You can attribute their preference for mystery to a few reasons: They're organized as private partnerships; they may not be registered with the Securities and Exchange Commission; and they may have figured out proprietary strategies to take advantage of market inefficiencies. If they tell the world what they're doing, they risk losing their money-making secrets.

However, you have legitimate reasons to know what's happening in the fund. Not only are you putting your money at risk, but also you may need to report to others or certify that you've met your fiduciary responsibilities if you work with an endowment or charitable organization, for example. If you have fiduciary responsibilities, transparency — or the lack of it — may affect your ability to do your job.

This section discusses position transparency, risk transparency, and window dressing and how they affect fiduciary responsibility — a consideration when choosing whether to invest in hedge funds or which hedge funds to invest in.

Reports of a hedge fund's holdings should come from a prime brokerage firm (a firm that handles the hedge fund's trading account), and a bona-fide accounting firm should audit the reports. One recent hedge fund investigation found that a fund's shareholders hadn't received a report for two years, and when they finally saw a partial report of holdings, it was a statement from a discount brokerage firm — a fine company, but not one that handles prime brokerage services for hedge funds. If you find out that a hedge fund doesn't have an audited financial statement and doesn't work through a prime broker, you shouldn't invest in it.

Appraising positions

When a hedge fund releases a list of the investments it owns, it has *position transparency.* You can look at the list to see what stocks sit in the account, what bonds the fund holds, what currencies it's exposed to, and other information. You can combine this information with any other holdings you have to ensure that the fund is meeting your overall investment risk-and-return objectives. Position transparency can also show whether the fund is complying with any unique requirements that you may have.

Many hedge funds give position information to investors who need it to fulfill their fiduciary responsibilities; however, the funds may make the recipients sign confidentiality agreements. The agreement ensures that a pension fund's trustees have enough information to see that the hedge fund is behaving as a prudent expert and in line with the pension's investment objectives, but it prevents the trustees from giving copies of the fund's investments to employees covered by the pension plan. A hedge fund manager knows if an investor has fiduciary responsibilities because the investor has to tell the manager before making the investment.

Interpreting risk

By using tactics such as leverage (or borrowing) and agreements such as derivatives (contracts based on the value of an underlying asset), a hedge fund may present a different risk level than its holdings list indicates. The risk may be more or less than the investor realizes.

The bad news is that you don't have an easy way to measure the amount of risk in a hedge fund. You can blame it on the fact that risk isn't well defined in finance, despite Nobel Prizes going to men who have done years of research on the subject.

Although some hedge fund managers simply refuse to give investors information on risk, saying that the information is proprietary, most try to give their investors some information they can use. A common measurement is *value at risk* (VaR), a single number that gives the likelihood of the portfolio losing a set amount of money over a set period (say, ten days). One problem with VaR is that the likelihood will never be zero. Another is that the hedge fund manager may give you information on VaR at a given point in time, but that number can change rapidly as market conditions change.

Another technique that some portfolio managers use is *stress testing,* where they run computer models to find out how a hedge fund's portfolio may perform in different economic conditions. The results of stress testing give you some parameters to use in determining how much risk an investment has. Keep in mind, however, that stress testing can't test for every possible event. Martians could take over the earth tomorrow — why not? — and you can bet that no one has done a stress test for that.

If you need to know the risk of the hedge fund that you're investing in, you should deal only with funds that give you risk information.

Avoiding window dressing

Hedge funds rarely give transparency in real time. A hedge fund won't tell anyone what's happening on any particular day. Some hedge fund managers take advantage of this position to make their portfolios look good on the days that they must report. This tactic is known in the investing world as *window dressing*.

For example, say that a hedge fund handles many government pension and university endowment accounts. The trustees for these accounts have made it clear that the fund can't invest their money in Sudan, and they want to see a list of positions every six months. One day, the hedge fund manager sees some great opportunities in bonds that will finance an oil project in Sudan. She ignores the accounts' wishes and buys the bonds, and then she sells them the day before she has to report her fund's holdings.

A less nefarious, and far more common, form of window dressing takes place when a hedge fund manager sells all the positions that turned out to be bad ideas right before the reporting date.

No matter how you look at it, window dressing is a manipulation of the truth. Avoid hedge funds that practice it.

Your Tax Responsibilities

Hedge fund investment returns come in two forms: capital gains and income. A *capital gain* is the increase in value an asset experiences over time. *Income* includes interest, dividends, and rent — in other words, any ongoing payments made to the investor. You may not care about the classification of your return, as long as you make money, but you need to care that the U.S. tax code treats these returns differently.

Different investment techniques have different tax effects. Some hedge fund strategies make great money, but not after the fund pays taxes. If you have to pay taxes, you need to make sure your hedge fund is managed with that responsibility in mind.

You may have to pay taxes on your share of your hedge fund's income and capital gains each year, whether you take any money out of the fund or not. And you aren't done after the Feds get their cut; your state probably wants a share of your profit, too, and the city or county where you live may also take a piece of your investment profits. There are too many state considerations to cover in this book; just make sure you look into it, for your own sake.

Making sense of capital gains taxes

A *capital gain* is the increase in value of an asset over time. If you buy a share of stock at $10, hold it while the company introduces great new products and generates tons of profits, and then sell it after the stock reaches $52, you have a capital gain of $42. You don't pay taxes until you sell the asset. Your basis is the price you paid to acquire the asset, and your gain is the price you sell it at less the basis.

Capital gains are classified as short-term or long-term, based on how long you hold your investment. *Long-term capital gains* come from assets that you hold for more than one year, and *short-term capital gains* come from assets that you hold for one year or less. You can net capital gains against capital losses. If you lose money when you sell one investment, you can deduct that loss (up to $3,000) against a gain incurred when you sell another. If you have more than $3,000 in losses, you can carry the extra into next year and deduct it then. You can also net any short-term capital losses against long-term capital gains, which may reduce your liability.

The advantage of capital gains is that the government taxes them at a lower rate than income. If you have to pay taxes, 28 percent — the maximum rate on capital gains as of press time — is less than 35 percent — the current maximum rate on income. In addition, long-term capital gains are taxed at lower rates than short-term capital gains.

Most hedge funds generate at least some returns from capital gains. Investors in a hedge fund are expected to pay taxes on those gains each year out of other sources of funds, because the fund manager probably won't distribute money to investors so they can pay the taxes. If a hedge fund gets almost all its returns from short-term capital gains, the tax burden will be higher than with a fund that gets almost all its returns from long-term capital gains.

Tax laws change every year. Be sure to check the IRS's latest guidance on investment tax issues, because this book may be out of date when you do your taxes in the future. Don't think that I'm going into an audit with you! The IRS Web site, www.irs.gov, is a great source of information.

Taxing ordinary income

Many investment gains are classified as ordinary income. *Income* is money that an asset generates on a regular basis — interest on a bond, dividends on common stock, or rent from a commercial real estate stake. You report this income on your taxes, and you pay the same rate on it that you pay on earned income from your job. The good news? You can deduct any investment interest you pay, such as interest paid in leveraging or short-selling strategies.

The government taxes *dividends,* payouts of company profits, at a lower rate than other investment income because the company that issues the dividend has already paid taxes on its profits before it issues the dividend out of what's left over. Many companies pay their shareholders small amounts of money out of their profits each year. The maximum tax rate on dividend income as of this writing is 15 percent.

A hedge fund that generates much of its return from interest income carries a higher tax burden than one that generates return from dividend income or from long-term capital gains.

On occasion, a hotshot trader makes an investment that generates tons of money, only to find come April 15 that the earnings are classified as income and the expenses are classified as capital losses. With no expenses to deduct, the investor finds that the taxes more than offset the realized profit. How to avoid this situation? Work with a hedge fund manager who has enough experience to understand the tax implications of different trading strategies. Because taxes can eat into an investment return, hedge fund investors who pay taxes should ask potential hedge fund managers about the tax implications of their funds' investment strategies.

Book VI

Hedge Funds

Exercising your right to be exempt

With all these crazy tax implications, it's a wonder anyone invests in hedge funds. Think about it: You could have to pay huge amounts in taxes each year on money that the fund locks up for two years. Who would do that? A tax-exempt or tax-deferred investor would. But doesn't everyone pay taxes? No. Two primary types of investors don't pay taxes, or at least they don't pay them upfront:

✔ **Qualified retirement and pension plans:** A *qualified plan* is a pension plan that meets certain IRS provisions. Among other things, the plan has to benefit all employees, not just a few highly paid workers. There are two types of qualified plans:

- **Defined benefit plans:** The employer agrees to pay the employee a set monthly amount upon retirement, based on the years that the employee worked and the income that he or she earned. The defined benefit plan is a traditional pension fund, and it's becoming rare.

- **Defined contribution plans:** The employee sets aside some money from each paycheck and determines where he or she wants to invest it. The employer may match some of the employee's contribution. A familiar example is a 401(k) plan. Defined contribution plans don't invest in hedge funds, because no employee's annual contribution would be large enough to meet a hedge fund's initial investment requirements.

If a plan meets the qualification rules, an employer can deduct contributions made to the plan from its taxes. Investment returns on the plan assets, along with the original principal, will be taxed as ordinary income, but only after the money is withdrawn from the plan.

✔ **Bona-fide charitable foundations and endowments:** Nonprofit institutions, such as foundations or endowments, are often supported by large pools of money that generate annual investment income used to support the organizations' work:

- A *foundation* is set up by a wealthy individual or a company. Charitable organizations that need money for activities send grant applications to foundations, explaining how they plan to use the money to support the foundations' goals. Some very large foundations eschew hedge funds because they don't want to risk a large return. Sounds crazy, huh? They want to give money to charities for responsible use, but they don't want the charities to have so much money that they give it away to wasteful projects.

- An *endowment* is a pool of money that the charitable organization controls itself. Endowments can be quite small or they can be on the scale of Yale's $22.5 billion or Harvard's $34.9 billion. Larger endowments often turn to hedge funds because they can afford to lock up large sums of money for two years; they don't have to worry about taxes; and they appreciate the increased return relative to the risk taken.

Donations made to foundations and endowments are usually deductible from income taxes. The investment income earned by the organizations is also tax-free as long as they meet certain requirements. Foundations, for example, must distribute 5 percent of their assets each year.

Tax-exempt investors have to meet stringent IRS requirements and possibly other standards to retain their status. If you're responsible for choosing any investment options for a qualified tax-exempt investment fund, talk to a lawyer to make sure you don't make a mistake that could have your foundation or endowment writing a big check come April 15. I doubt your organization will be as charitable with your position, in that case!

Chapter 4

A Potpourri of Hedge Fund Strategies

In This Chapter

▶ Understanding how hedge funds can be an asset class on their own

▶ Reporting hedge funds as overlays

▶ Buying low, selling high: Using arbitrage in hedge funds

▶ Short-selling, leveraging, and other equity strategies

▶ Observing how hedge funds profit from the corporate life cycle

*H*edge funds are wildly different from each other. Because hedge funds are simply lightly regulated investment partnerships — and therefore can take advantage of more investment strategies than other highly regulated investment vehicles, such as mutual funds — different funds are bound to invest in different ways.

This chapter looks at how you can include hedge funds in your investment portfolio to increase your return for a given level of risk. It also explains arbitrage, the primary investment strategy of many hedge funds, as well as equity-based hedge funds and hedge funds that make money through venture capital and loans. If you want to invest in a hedge fund, you need to know about these various strategies so that you have a better understanding of what a particular hedge fund may be doing. The more you know, the better your questions — and decisions — will be.

Viewing Hedge Funds as an Asset Class

Asset classes are distinctly different from each other, with unique risk-and-return profiles. For example, bonds are loans; the borrower makes regular interest payments and returns the principal at the end of the loan. Changes in interest rates and the ability of the borrower to make the payments affect the bond price. Stocks, on the other hand, are partial shares of ownership in a company. The company's profits and prospects affect the price of stocks.

One of the biggest debates in the hedge fund world is whether hedge funds represent a separate, new asset class, or whether they simply represent another vehicle to manage the traditional asset classes of stocks, bonds, and cash. The discussion affects the way that people make decisions about their money, some good and some bad.

While some people don't think that hedge funds deserve to be treated as a separate asset class, others argue that, because hedge funds are uniquely managed, they deserve to be thought of as unique assets — even though they're made up of other assets. This section takes a closer look at the arguments in favor of hedge funds being in a separate asset class and explains why such a debate is important to you as an investor.

Hedge funds as assets

The argument for hedge funds being a unique asset class is that many hedge fund managers design their funds to post completely different risk-and-return profiles than traditional asset classes. The big idea is that if you have an investment that you design to return, say, 6 to 8 percent every year — year in and year out, regardless of how interest rates fluctuate or how the economy shifts — you have an investment that's different from anything else out there.

Of course, not all hedge fund managers design their funds to perform differently from the financial markets. The risk-and-return tradeoff for absolute-return funds, for example, is different from the risk-and-return tradeoff of directional funds. While absolute-return funds seek to generate a reasonable percentage return each year, regardless of the state of the financial markets, and therefore rarely aim to beat the equity indexes or assume the risk necessary to do so, directional funds seek to return the maximum amount possible and, in the process, assume a lot of risk (see Chapter 1).

Why it matters

Does it matter if a hedge fund represents its own asset class or not? Yes, it does, and here's why: An investor should structure her investment portfolio to reflect the risk and return that she needs. If a hedge fund appears in its own asset class, other assets that the investor selects to offset the portfolio's risk-and-return characteristics need to appear in the portfolio. After all, in some years stocks will be up, and in some years bonds will be. A diversified portfolio has exposure to both stocks and bonds, in line with the investor's preferences, in order to meet the investor's needs — regardless of how the market performs. In fact, adding different kinds of assets to a portfolio can reduce risk without affecting expected return.

Correlation

If return is a function of risk, how can adding different assets to your portfolio reduce risk without affecting return? The answer: *correlation.* Correlation shows how much two assets move together. If they move in tandem, the assets are perfectly correlated. If two assets aren't perfectly correlated, some of the movement in one offsets the movement in another. An investment manager can run a computer program that analyzes the correlations of all her assets under consideration and determines how much of an investor's portfolio should be in each in order to generate the *minimum-variance portfolio.* This portfolio has less risk — but not less return — than the average risk and return of all of its assets.

Here's a breakdown of what happens when a hedge fund is in its own class and what happens when it isn't:

- ✔ If a hedge fund is its own asset class, with its own risk-and-return profile, it can diversify the risks of other assets in the portfolio. For this reason, many large pension and endowment funds have been putting money into hedge funds that feature an absolute-return style and listing them as separate asset classes.

- ✔ If a hedge fund isn't its own asset class, it increases the risk in the portfolio. Investors would have to add other assets to offset that risk. For this reason, many hedge fund investors don't break out their investments in hedge funds; they opt to include them with their domestic equity or international markets assets when they report their holdings.

Hedge fund managers have a ton of discretion, and they sometimes change strategies or attempt trades in new areas. You may think you're buying one type of fund but end up in something different. Your hedge fund's investment agreement may specify limitations, but it may not. You can exit the fund if you don't like the new strategy, but only when the lock-up period expires (see Chapter 1).

Using Your Hedge Fund as an Overlay

Many investors view hedge funds as an *overlay,* not as a separate asset allocation. In other words, an investor makes the asset allocation first and then decides if any of the assets should be managed by a hedge fund manager or by another type of investor.

Investors have two reasons for taking the overlay approach — one good and one not so good:

- ✔ **The overlay thumbs up:** To think about the portfolio's risk and return as a whole, acknowledging that a hedge fund will have market exposure no matter how much the fund manager wants to talk about pure alpha (refer to Chapter 1). Overlay lets the investor think about how much exposure the portfolio has to different asset risks instead of placing the risk elsewhere.

- ✔ **The overlay thumbs down:** To deny an investment in a hedge fund. For every person who wants to invest in a hedge fund, another person is scared off. This person sees something inherently dangerous about hedge funds. A charity may be concerned that listing hedge funds, or even alternative investors, in its annual holdings will scare off donors. A pension fund consultant may be concerned that worker representatives on the trustee board will panic if they see hedge funds on the list. The solution to this fright is to hide the hedge fund investments, which isn't quite honest.

Just because a portfolio listing doesn't include hedge funds or absolute-return strategies among its assets doesn't mean it has no investments in them. If you're analyzing the investments of a large pension or endowment plan and you don't see hedge funds listed, chances are good that the fund included them in another asset class. If you need to know, don't hesitate to ask.

Buying Low, Selling High: Arbitrage

In theory, arbitrage opportunities don't exist because markets are perfectly efficient, right? (*Arbitrage* is the process of buying an asset cheap in one market and selling it for a higher price in another.) In reality, arbitrage takes place every single day, which forces markets into efficiency. However, the price differences needed for arbitrage are often small and don't last long. For this reason, successful arbitrageurs have to be paying constant attention to the market, and they have to be willing to act very quickly. They have no room for indecision.

People often misuse the word "arbitrage" to describe any kind of aggressive trading. If you hear a hedge fund manager say that his fund uses arbitrage, ask what kind of arbitrage is involved.

Whether you buy into the idea of arbitrage depends on your feelings about market risk: the idea that market prices reflect all known information about a stock. Someone who believes in market efficiency would say that arbitrage is imaginary because someone would've noticed a price difference between markets already and immediately acted to close it off. People with a less rigid view of the world would say that arbitrage exists, but the opportunities for taking advantage of it are very few and far between. People who don't believe in market efficiency would say that arbitrage opportunities happen all the time. These people believe that someone in one of the markets knows something, and if you can figure out what that person knows, you may have a solid advantage in the marketplace.

Factoring in transaction costs

What goes into the cost of arbitrage trading? Quite a lot, actually:

Book VI

Hedge Funds

✔ The overhead of having traders on staff, including salaries, bonuses, and benefits.

✔ The cost of having the information systems in place to monitor several markets in real time, enabling the hedge fund and a broker to execute an arbitrage trade almost instantaneously. (The free quotes that investors can find online through such sources as Yahoo! Finance [`finance.yahoo.com`] are delayed for 15 to 20 minutes, depending on where the security trades. Real-time quotes are expensive.)

✔ The commissions for brokers who execute the transaction.

Because of transaction costs associated with arbitrage, hedge funds tend to either commit heavily to arbitrage or avoid it entirely. If you plan on investing in a hedge fund that expects to generate most of its profits from arbitrage, be sure to ask about these factors when you shop for a hedge fund.

Separating true arbitrage from risk arbitrage

True arbitrage is riskless trading. The purchase of an asset in one market and the sale of the asset in another happen simultaneously. The fund manager can count on profit as long as the trades go through immediately. True, riskless arbitrage is possible, but rare. No hedge fund that pursues only riskless arbitrage will stay in business for long.

Here's a classic example of true arbitrage: A hedge fund trader notices that a stock is trading at $11.98 in New York and $11.99 in London. He buys as many shares as possible in New York, borrowing money if necessary, and immediately sells those shares in London, making a penny on each one. This type of arbitrage transaction has no risk, so people often describe it as "finding money on the sidewalk."

Most arbitrageurs practice *risk arbitrage,* which, like true arbitrage, seeks to generate profits from price discrepancies; however, risk arbitrage involves taking some risk (go figure!). Risk arbitrage still involves buying one security and selling another, but an investor doesn't always buy the same security, and he doesn't necessarily buy and sell at the same time. For example, a fund manager may buy the stock of an acquisition target and sell the stock of an acquirer, waiting until the acquisition finalizes before closing the transaction, making (he hopes) a tidy profit in the process.

In many cases, the risk taken is that of time. The trade may work out but not as soon as the hedge fund manager hopes. In the meantime, his portfolio's performance may suffer or loans taken to acquire the position may be called in. It's one thing to be right; however, it's another thing entirely to be right in time for the decision to matter.

Cracking open the arbitrageur's toolbox

Opportunities for riskless trading are very few and far between. Therefore, to find risky arbitrage opportunities, hedge funds look at similar securities, and they look for ways to profit from price discrepancies while offsetting much of the risk. The arbitrageur's favorite tools for offsetting risk include the following:

✔ **Derivatives:** A *derivative* is a financial instrument (like an option, a future, or a swap) that derives its value from the value of another security. A stock option, for example, is a type of derivative that gives you the right, but not the obligation, to buy shares of the stock at a predetermined price. Because derivatives are related to securities, they can be useful in risk arbitrage. A fund manager may see a price discrepancy between a derivative and an underlying asset, creating a profitable trading opportunity.

With their value so closely linked to the value of other securities, derivatives offer many opportunities for constructing risk arbitrage trades. And with a wider range of low-risk arbitrage opportunities, a fund stands a better chance of making money. The more ways a hedge fund can structure a trade, the more arbitrage opportunities it can grab.

✔ **Leverage:** *Leverage,* discussed in the upcoming section "Putting the power of leverage to use," is the process of borrowing money to trade. Because a hedge fund puts only a little of its own capital to work and borrows the rest, the return on its capital is much greater than it would be if it didn't borrow any money. Because leverage allows a hedge fund to magnify its returns, it's a popular tool for arbitrage.

Leverage does have a downside, though: Along with magnifying returns, it magnifies risk. The fund has to repay the borrowed money, no matter how the trade works out.

✔ **Short-selling:** *Short-selling* gives fund managers a way to profit from a decline in a security's price (see the later section "Investigating Equity Strategies"). The short-seller borrows the declining security (usually from a broker), sells it, and then repurchases the security in the market later in order to repay the loan. If the price falls, the profit is the difference between the price where the fund manager sold the security and the price where she repurchased it. If the price goes up, though, that difference is the amount of the loss. Short-selling allows an arbitrageur more freedom in choosing how to buy securities low and sell high. By shorting an asset, the seller gives up the risk of the price going down, which can offer both a way to exploit a price discrepancy and a way to manage the risk of the transaction.

✔ **Synthetic securities:** A *synthetic security* is one created by matching one asset with a combination of a few others that have the same profit-and-loss profile. For example, you can think of a stock as a combination of a *put option,* which has value if the stock goes down in price, and a *call option,* which has value if the stock goes up in price. By designing transactions that create synthetic securities, a hedge fund manager can create more ways for an asset to be cheaper in one market than in another, thus increasing the number of potential arbitrage opportunities. Many of the arbitrage styles that you can read about in the following sections involve synthetic securities.

Book VI

Hedge
Funds

Recognizing arbitrage types

Arbitrageurs use the tools of arbitrage in many different ways. Most arbitrage funds pick a few strategies to follow, although some may stick to only one and others may skip from strategy to strategy as market conditions warrant. Most hedge funds use some forms of arbitrage, and some may use arbitrage as their primary source of investment returns.

The following sections outline all the varieties of arbitrage transactions that a hedge fund may use as part of its investment strategy, arranged in alphabetical order for your reading pleasure. The strategies vary in complexity and in how often a fund can use them, but all are designed to take advantage of profits from security price discrepancies.

Capital-structure arbitrage

The *capital structure* of a firm represents how the company is financed. Does it have debt? How much? Does it have stock? How many classes? Many companies have only one type of stock that trades, but other company portfolios can be quite complicated. When a company has many different securities trading, arbitrageurs look for price differences among them. After all, if all the securities are tied to the same asset — the company's business — they should trade in a similar fashion. You can't count on it, though.

Say, for example, that the MightyMug Company has common stock outstanding, as well as 20-year corporate bonds at 7.5 percent interest. The stock price stays in line with market expectations, but the company bonds fall in value more than expected given changes in interest rates. An arbitrageur may buy the bonds and short the stock, waiting for the price discrepancy between the two securities to return to its normal level. That means that the bonds will have increased in price, so he can sell them at a profit, and the stock will have fallen in price, so he buys it back to cover the short and locks in a profit.

Convertible arbitrage

Some companies issue *convertible bonds* (sometimes called a *convertible debenture*) or *convertible preferred stock.* The two types of securities are very similar: They pay income to the shareholders (interest for convertible bonds and dividends for convertible preferred stock), and they can be converted into shares of common stock in the future. Convertible securities generally trade in line with the underlying stock. After all, the securities represent options to purchase the stock. If the convertible gets out of line, an arbitrage opportunity presents itself.

Here's an arbitrage example: An arbitrageur notices that a convertible bond is selling at a lower price than it should be, given the interest rates and the price of the company's common stock. So, she buys the bonds and sells the stock short. The trade cancels out the stock exposure, reducing the transaction risk and leaving only the potential for profit as the bond's price moves back into line.

Fixed-income arbitrage

Fixed-income securities give holders a regular interest payment. Some people like to buy them just to get a check deposited every quarter. These securities may seem safe because the money just keeps rolling in, but they have enormous exposure to fluctuating interest rates. Because interest rates affect so many different securities — bonds, currencies, and derivatives, for example — they're a common focus for arbitrageurs. With *fixed-income arbitrage,* the trader breaks out the following:

- ✔ The time value of money
- ✔ The level of risk in the economy
- ✔ The likelihood of repayment
- ✔ The inflation-rate effects on different securities

If one of the numbers is out of whack, the trader constructs and executes trades to profit from it. If, for example, a hedge fund trader tracking interest rates on U.S. government securities notices that one-year treasury bills are trading at a higher yield than expected, he may decide to short the two-year treasury notes and buy the one-year treasury bills until the price difference falls back where it should be.

Index arbitrage

A *market index* is designed to represent the activity of the market. It can be designed a few different ways, but an index is always based on the performance of a group of securities that trade in the market. Futures contracts are available on most indexes, for example. These are derivatives based on the expected future value of the index. Sometimes, the value of the futures contract deviates from the value of the index itself. When that happens, the arbitrageur steps in to make a profit.

Most indexes have many securities, so buying a load of them can be expensive. The S&P 500 index has 500 stocks in it! That's why only the largest hedge funds are active in index arbitrage, and they use plenty of leverage out of necessity (as well as the profit motive). Only a few funds are able to buy enough stocks in the index to make the investment matter, and even fewer can do it with cash on hand!

Liquidation arbitrage

Liquidation arbitrage is a bet against the breakup value of a business. An arbitrageur researches a company to see what it would be worth if it was sold. If she sees value in the company's various components that is greater than the current market value of the stock, she may buy shares of the company in anticipation that someone will come along and take over the company at a price that reflects its value.

Sometimes, liquidation arbitrageurs acquire so many shares in a company that they can influence whether a merger takes place. When this happens, the arbitrageurs become known as *corporate raiders*. You can find out more about the role of hedge funds in corporate finance decisions in the later section "Project finance: Replacing banks?"

Merger arbitrage

Merger arbitrage is about profiting from a company's acquisition *after* a merger has been announced. A merger announcement includes the following:

- ✔ The name of the acquiring company
- ✔ The name of the company being taken over (and no matter what PR people say, there are no mergers of equals)
- ✔ The price of the transaction

> ✔ The currency (cash, stock, debt)
>
> ✔ The date the merger is expected to close

Any of these variables can change — the acquiring company may decide that the deal is a bad one and walk away, for example — and all these variables create trading opportunities, although not all are riskless.

When companies announce a big merger, traders sometimes get caught up in the mood of the moment and engage in *garbatrage*. That is, everyone gets so excited that even businesses with no real connection to the merger become part of the speculation. For example, if a drug company buys a shampoo manufacturer, the shares of any and all beauty-products manufacturers may go up. This may cause folks to pay too much money because not all the shares will be worth their newly inflated price.

Option arbitrage

Options come in many varieties, even if they exist on the same underlying security. They come in different types: *puts* (bets on the underlying security price going down) and *calls* (bets on the underlying security price going up). They have different prices, where a holder can cash the option in for the underlying security, and different expiration dates. You can exercise some options, known as *European options,* at any time between the date of issue and the expiration date, and you can exercise others, known as *American options,* only at the expiration date. Needless to say, having so many securities that are almost the same creates plenty of opportunities for a knowledgeable arbitrageur to find profitable price discrepancies.

If, for example, a hedge fund's options trader notices that the options exchanges are assuming a slightly higher price for a security than in the security's own market, she may decide to buy the underlying security and then buy a put and sell a call with the same strike price and expiration date. The put–call transaction has the same payoff as shorting the security, so she has effectively bought the security cheap in one market and sold it at a higher price in another.

Pairs trading

Pairs trading is a form of long–short hedging (described in the upcoming section "Long–short funds") that looks for discrepancies among securities in a given industry sector. If one security appears to be overvalued relative to others, a savvy arbitrageur will short that security; the arbitrageur then buys another security in the group that seems to be undervalued.

Scalping

Scalping is a form of arbitrage that takes advantage of small price movements throughout the day — an especially common practice in commodities markets.

In most cases, scalpers look to take advantage of changes in a security's *bid–ask spread,* which represents the difference between the price that a broker will buy a security for from those who want to sell it (the *bid*) and the price that the broker will charge those who want to buy it (the *ask* — also called the *offer* in some markets).

For many securities, the bid–ask spread stays fairly constant over time because the supply and demand should balance out. If everyone has the same information (the old market-efficiency situation), their trading levels are in balance and the broker-dealers can maintain a steady profit. Sometimes, however, the spread will be just a little out of balance compared to normal levels. A scalper can take advantage of that situation by buying the security, waiting even a minute or two for the spread to change, and then selling it at a profit. Or, the scalper can buy the security, wait a few minutes for the price to go up a small amount, and then sell it.

Book VI

Hedge
Funds

The scalper has to work quickly to make many small trades. He has to have a low commission structure in place, or else transaction costs will kill him. He also has to be careful to get out of the market as soon as a news event comes along that causes the security's trading to become more volatile, because scalping becomes a high-risk proposition when market prices are changing quickly. This is why some folks describe scalping as "picking up nickels in front of a steamroller."

Scalping probably isn't a primary strategy for any hedge fund, but the strategy may give a trader profit opportunities on a slow day.

Investigating Equity Strategies

Equity-based hedge funds, hedge funds that invest in equities, start with the same investment strategies as mutual funds, brokerage accounts, or other types of investment portfolios that invest in equities. But they use two unique strategies — short-selling and leveraging — to change the risk profiles of their investments in stocks. Depending on your hedge fund's strategy and market expectations, it may have greater or less risk than the market, in part because of the use of these strategies. And you can assume that most hedge funds are using some leverage and some short-selling to reach their risk and return objectives.

Short-selling and leveraging are fundamental to the operations of a hedge fund. They're widely associated with equity trading, although they can be used with other types of securities and derivatives. In fact, almost all hedge funds use some short-selling and leverage in order to increase return for a given level of risk. Therefore, if you're interested in hedge funds, you should find out as much as you can about short-selling and leverage so that you have a better understanding of what hedge funds do:

- ✔ **Short-selling:** Borrowing an asset (like a stock or bond), selling it, and then buying it back to repay the loaned asset. If the asset goes down in price, the hedge fund makes the difference between the price where it sold the asset and the price where it repurchased the asset. Of course, if the asset appreciates in price, the hedge fund loses money. The opposite of short is long, so an investor who is *long* is an investor who owns the asset.

 If much of your portfolio sits in an S&P 500 index fund — a fund that invests in all the securities in the S&P 500 in the same proportion as the index in order to generate the same return — you have significant exposure to the stock market, which means you have market risk. One way to reduce that risk without giving up your expected return is to seek out equities with a different risk profile. Short-selling gives you more places to look.

- ✔ **Leverage:** Borrowing money to invest, often from brokerage firms. Leverage increases your potential return — and your risk. Hedge funds use leverage, but so do other types of accounts, and many individual investors use it, too.

Investment styles of long equity managers

Long equity managers, those equity investors who don't short stocks (and thus are rarely hedge fund managers, although a small number of hedge fund managers are long-only), fall into several broad categories and employ several styles, often called *style boxes.* Fund managers use these categories to guide their choices for the long portions of their portfolios (the securities that they own, not those that they short) or to determine the risk that they can reduce with hedging strategies. At a minimum, you want to recognize the terms covered in this section when they come up in conversation.

Few hedge funds use the strategies in this section exclusively. Hedge fund managers are in the business of using exotic investment techniques in order to beat the market — and to justify their high fees.

Trying on a large cap

A *large cap fund,* which may be a hedge fund, a mutual fund, or another type of investment portfolio, invests in companies with a market capitalization (shares outstanding multiplied by current price) of $5 billion or more. These companies tend to be multinational behemoths with steady performance and fortunes tied to the global economy. You can find these companies in the S&P 500, the Fortune 500, and on every other 500 list, save the Indy 500.

Many large cap managers engage in a strategy called *closet indexing:* They buy shares in the largest companies in the S&P 500 in more or less the same proportion as the S&P index. The result is that the portion of the portfolio containing the large cap shares has almost identical risk and return as the index but for the higher fee that an active manager receives. A hedge fund manager who does closet indexing isn't hedging, so she isn't doing what you pay her to.

Fitting for a small, micro, or mid cap

A *small cap stock* is a share of a company with a market capitalization of under $1 billion. These companies tend to be growing faster than the market as a whole, and they aren't as closely covered by investment analysts as larger companies, so their shares may not be as expensive as those in similar but better-known companies.

Some fund managers concentrate on investing in company stocks with a market cap of under $100 million, believing that's where the real money-making opportunities lie because these stocks are even less covered than small cap stocks, so the managers may be getting in on the ground floor. This style of investing, known as *micro cap,* is similar to venture capital and requires that the fund manager do careful research, because other investors may be showing little interest in the company.

What's in between $5 billion and $1 billion? Mid cap investments, which have characteristics of both large cap and small cap stocks. Easy, huh? Some small and mid cap companies will grow and graduate to the next level. However, some mid cap companies used to be large cap companies before they ran into trouble, and some small caps are former mid caps whose growing days are over.

If a hedge fund manager mentions capitalization as a style, you should certainly ask about how the fund defines the cutoffs. Why? Because the industry has no standard cutoff for small, mid, and large cap stocks. Different analysts and money-management firms set their own parameters, and the parameters tend to go up when the market goes up and come down a little bit when the market comes down. If you come across a hedge fund manager who defines companies with a capitalization of $2 billion as small cap stocks, she isn't doing anything wrong; she's just using a cutoff that works with what she sees in the market at that point.

Book VI

Hedge Funds

Investing according to growth and GARP

A *growth fund* looks to buy stock in companies that are growing their revenue and earnings faster than the market as a whole. Hedge funds expect these equities to appreciate more than the market and to have some life to them, making them longer-term holdings.

Growth stocks tend to be more expensive than stocks in companies that are growing at a normal rate. For this reason, many fund managers try to find cheap growth stocks, following a strategy called *Growth At the Right Price* (or *Growth At a Reasonable Price [GARP]*). The fund manager attempts to combine growth with low price-to-earnings ratios in order to earn a greater-than-market return for a market rate of risk.

Swooping in on lowly equities with value investing

Value investors are the most traditional of equity investors. Hedge fund managers who consider themselves value investors look for stocks that are cheap based on accounting earnings or asset values. They shoot for companies that have solid assets, plenty of cash, and inferiority complexes because the market doesn't recognize them. Value investors care more about what a business would look like dead, with the assets sold and the proceeds distributed to shareholders, than what it would look like if it grew in the future. For more on value investing, go to Book VII.

Keeping options open for special style situations

A special-situations investor doesn't like to declare allegiance to any one style of equity investing; he prefers to look at stocks that seem likely to appreciate. A sharp manager may want to keep his options open, especially at a larger firm that can afford investment analysts and traders who have their own investment niches. Other managers may want flexibility to move between styles whenever the current en vogue style isn't working out. (A cynic may say that this is why fund managers are often so secretive about their strategies.)

Although it seems like a good idea to keep all investment options open, special-situations investors can end up chasing ideas all over the place. With no discipline to help them determine valuation, these investors may end up buying high and selling low, which is a sure path to ruin. If you interview a special-situations fund manager because you're interested in his fund's ability to handle your money, ask how he makes his investing decisions.

Creating a market-neutral portfolio

With a typical, diversified equity portfolio, you can earn only the market rate of return. Although you take on the same amount of risk as the market, that may be more risk than you want. For these reasons, many hedge funds have a market-neutral strategy. You expect a *market-neutral portfolio* to generate a positive return, regardless of what the market does. This doesn't mean that a market-neutral portfolio will generate a higher return than the market, although it should when the market loses money.

A fund manager has to tweak a market-neutral portfolio to maintain its neutrality, so the manager needs a system for the tweaking process. The three common styles of market-neutral investing are creating beta-neutral, dollar-neutral, and sector-neutral portfolios.

Being beta-neutral

Many hedge fund managers go back to academic theory and use beta as the neutral point when figuring out ways to make their portfolios market-neutral. Beta is the relationship of a security to the market as a whole. Under the Modern (Markowitz) Portfolio Theory (MPT), the market has a beta of 1, and a stock that's correlated with the market also has a beta of 1. A security that's negatively correlated with the market has a beta of –1. A *beta-neutral portfolio,* therefore, is made up of securities that have a weighted average beta of 0. In other words, the portfolio has no market exposure.

Book VI

Hedge Funds

Few 0-beta securities exist in the market, because if a security is part of the market, it almost definitely has some bit of exposure to it. The closest asset to a 0-beta security is a short-term U.S. treasury security, which has a very low return. Of course, a beta-neutral hedge fund has to generate a return greater than treasuries in order to attract assets!

In order to maintain 0 beta while maximizing return, a fund manager can run a program that comes up with optimal portfolio weighting. In some ways, a beta-neutral portfolio is as much about programming as it is about picking stocks, because the weightings are very difficult to calculate by hand. Finding negative-beta stocks, on the other hand, is easy. Shorting a stock is the same as reversing its beta, so a fund manager can generate negative-beta securities by taking short positions in stocks with positive betas. (See the earlier section "Investigating Equity Strategies" for an explanation of short-selling.)

Establishing dollar neutrality

In a *dollar-neutral portfolio,* the hedge fund manager holds the same amount of money in short positions — that is, in securities that he borrowed and then sold in hopes that they would go down in price so the fund could repurchase them at a lower price to repay the loan — as in long positions, securities that the fund owns outright. With this strategy, the portfolio's expected return isn't highly exposed to the market, because the portfolio should benefit no matter what direction the market moves. An investor follows this strategy to eliminate market risk from a portfolio. Of course, if you want to have market risk, this feature would be a disadvantage.

Staying sector-neutral

Certain industries represented in the investment indexes perform differently than others, which can make index performance more volatile than a true market investment should be. The people who select the stocks for the indexes have been known to make additions and subtractions that make the indexes perform better, even if the indexes become less representative of the market and the economy.

To structure his or her portfolio free of political influences, generating less risk than may be found in an index fund in the process, a hedge fund manager can weight each industry sector equally so that Internet stocks don't crowd out automaker stocks, for example. This is called *sector neutrality*. Although it doesn't eliminate market risk, it does reduce it. Many hedge fund managers combine sector neutrality with other portfolio strategies, such as arbitrage or leverage.

Long–short funds

A *long–short fund* is actually a traditional hedge fund: It buys and sells stocks according to its risk profile and market conditions. A long–short fund manager looks for overvalued assets to sell and undervalued assets to buy. The valuation may be relative to the current assets and earnings of the securities or relative to the future prospects for the companies. Matching the two allows for reduced risk and increased returns — the very stuff of the hedge fund game.

Some hedge fund managers allocate parts of their portfolios to pure short-selling. (The other part of the portfolio is long but not matched to the short assets, so this is a type of long–short fund.) These managers want to increase their risk (and thus their expected returns) by finding overvalued securities in the market and then selling them short. This strategy isn't for the faint of heart, because the most a stock can go down is 100 percent, to 0, but the most it can go up is infinity. That's why most hedge fund managers view short-selling as part of a hedged portfolio, not the centerpiece of it.

The flip side of this is a long strategy called a *short squeeze,* in which a hedge fund or other portfolio manager looks for stocks that have been shorted. At some point, all the short-sellers have to buy back the stocks to repay the lenders. This means that someone can buy up enough of the stock to push the prices higher, causing investors on the short side to start losing money. As the shorts lose money, the managers can buy shares to cover the loans and get out of the positions; their buying drives the prices even higher.

Most short-sellers do excellent research. An unscrupulous few have been known to drive asset prices down by starting ugly rumors and spreading outright lies. As a result, short-selling isn't a game for the faint of heart.

Making market calls

A traditional hedge fund — namely, a long–short hedge fund — hedges risk. A modern, lightly regulated partnership may enlist all sorts of risky strategies to increase return. As long as the fund doesn't closely correlate the risk with the other holdings in the portfolio, it can meet its goal of reducing risk. What's more, a strategy keyed off of market performance doesn't require the portfolio manager to determine how the market is moving. But some investors want more. They want return tied to the market in one form only: a return that beats the market handily.

But here's the thing: How do you call the market? In other words, how do you foresee the future? Anyone who can call the market consistently is retired to a beachfront estate in Maui, not running a hedge fund. Some hedge fund managers are close to affording a beach hideout, but others are still trying to beat the market in order to get there. But how? How can a fund manager call the market in order to figure out how to position her portfolio? Magic? Tea leaves? Astrology? Or hardcore analysis? Maybe a little of each strategy, and it's a perilous enterprise.

Predicting the market is nearly impossible to do in the long run. Money managers try to predict the future all the time, but almost all fail, whether they're running hedge funds or other investment portfolios. Don't expect a hedge fund you're interested in to beat the market, and be leery of a fund manager who claims to be a seer. Instead, think about how the hedge fund will help you manage risk.

This section describes some of the things that hedge fund managers look for when they make decisions about buying and selling securities.

Investing with event-driven calls

An *event-driven* manager looks at situations he expects to happen in the market, guesses how the market will react, and invests accordingly. A manager always has two moving pieces when making event-driven calls: predicting the event and determining what the market expects the event to be. Such an event may be an upcoming election, the death of an ailing world leader, or a hurricane that knocks out some offshore oil drills.

Taking advantage of market timing

A hedge fund manager who *times* the market allocates different portions of his portfolio to different asset classes. The exact proportion for each class varies with different market indicators. The idea is to have plenty of money in assets that the fund manager expects to do well and to put less money in assets that aren't supposed to do as well. The difference between a market-timing strategy and an event-driven strategy is that an event-driven manager looks for individual securities that he expects to do well based on specific events; the market timer looks for changes in general economic trends, such as inflation and unemployment — often signaled by technical indicators — which would show up on stock trading charts analyzed by using technical analysis. (See Book VIII for more information on technical analysis.)

Market timing can be used long or short. Some long–short hedge fund managers decide what portion of their portfolio they'll invest outright and what part they'll short, based on their analysis of where the market will go.

Putting the power of leverage to use

Even a simple investing strategy — such as buying stocks in the S&P 500 index in the same proportion in order to replicate the index's performance — can take on new risk and return levels through the use of *leverage*. Maybe you've heard the phrase "using other people's money"; that's what leveraging is. An investor borrows money to make an investment, getting maximum return for a minimal amount of cash up front. Of course, this strategy can also lead to a maximum loss. The following sections show you how to use leverage in an equity portfolio to maximize return. But be forewarned: It's a strategy that also increases your risk.

Buying on margin

The simplest way to use leverage is to borrow money from the brokerage firm that holds the investment account — called buying securities *on margin*. The Federal Reserve Board sets the amount that a hedge fund can borrow. As of press time, the Board requires individual investors to have 50 percent of the purchase prices on account at the time they place their margin orders; they may borrow the rest of the money from their brokerage firms. Hedge funds and other large investors are often allowed to borrow more.

After the leverage takes place, the margin borrower must meet ongoing margin requirements. As the security bought on margin fluctuates in price, the 50 percent purchase-price level kept on account may fall to only 30 percent of the money owed. In this case, the borrower gets a margin call and has to add money to the account to get it back to the minimum maintenance level. If not, the brokerage firm will cash out the borrowed position. The New York Stock Exchange (NYSE) and Financial Industry Regulatory Authority (FINRA) set minimum margin requirements, although many brokerage firms have the ability to set higher levels based on their risk-management requirements and their comfort levels with the clients.

As long as a borrowed security appreciates by more than the cost of the borrowing, the margin position makes money. But, because the borrowing fund has to pay interest, margin buying is a money-losing proposition if the security doesn't go up.

Gaining return with other forms of borrowing

Larger hedge funds can find banks, financial institutions, and even other hedge funds willing to lend them money that they can use to buy securities. If you're investing in a hedge fund, you should expect that the fund has more sources of funds than just margin accounts.

Private banks often loan hedge fund investors money to get into a fund or a fund of funds. In this case, the investor's personal wealth is leveraged over and above whatever leverage the fund has. The same risks apply: If the investment goes up, the loan leads to a greater rate of return, but if the investment heads south, the investor still has to repay the loan.

Participating in Corporate Life Cycles

Given the inherent flexibility and current popularity of hedge funds, it's no surprise that they're taking on a big role in corporate transactions — ranging from venture capital and project finance to takeovers. What this means for you, a prospective investor, is that the hedge fund you're interested in may be taking roles in corporate transactions. The following sections describe these transactions so you'll understand what a hedge fund that follows this type of strategy is doing with your money.

The many stages of the corporate life cycle give hedge funds plenty of opportunities to make money. Some funds concentrate on corporate finance transactions, and others view that strategy as one of many ways to make money. Hedge funds aren't mutual funds. No one type of fund is suitable for all investors, and no one type of investor is suitable for any given type of fund.

Venture capital: Helping businesses break to the next level

Venture capital, sometimes known as *private equity*, is money given to entrepreneurs to fund new companies — money that comes with strings attached. An investor who gives the money wants to ensure that the business succeeds. It isn't uncommon, for example, for venture capitalists to make their investments on the condition that the founders leave their companies so seasoned managers can replace them. Hedge funds often invest in venture capital.

Although their styles may seem pushy, venture investments can help a company grow faster than it could otherwise, and investors can bring expertise — and potential clients — to the start-ups. Some of the United States's biggest technology companies, like Intel, Oracle, Apple, and Google, were started with venture capital. The payoff to those investors (and investors in those investors) was huge, which is the attraction of the investment.

Venture investors count on acquiring some companies that will fail in their portfolios, offset by the few companies that hit it big.

Venture capital comes in different forms. Investors from a hedge fund may give the money to a young company as equity, making the hedge fund one of the owners of the company. The capital can also be debt that converts into equity if the company goes public or sells out to a larger company. The structure depends on the start-up company's business and state of profitability.

Venture-capital investors need a liquidity event to make money. This event occurs when a company is sold to a larger one or when it issues stock through an initial public offering, or IPO. Until that event happens, the venture investor won't make much money.

Following are the most common forms of venture capital that you're likely to encounter when scoping out hedge funds (including private equity, which deals with established companies, making it not quite venture capital, but close):

- **Late-stage venture:** After a new company gets over the initial hurdles of setting up the business and attracting customers, it becomes a lot more interesting to investors, who see a little less risk with some huge upside. The company still needs more money to grow, and it still isn't ready to go public or to be acquired.

- **Mezzanine capital:** When a young company needs just enough financing to move it to the stage where it can go public or be an attractive acquisition, it needs *mezzanine financing*. Mezzanine capital is the least risky stage of venture capital (although it's still riskier than investing in a public company) because a company's management has proved that the business is viable. Returns are likely to be higher with a company at this stage than with public companies, though, so this stage of venture investing is interesting to hedge funds.

✔ **Private equity:** Many established companies choose not to be publicly traded; other companies are publicly traded but can't raise money efficiently through a public offering. These companies turn to *private equity deals,* often with hedge funds on the other side. These transactions carry lower potential returns than venture capital because they carry less risk (the company is established), but they often carry higher returns than shares of common stock in similar companies because it's harder to sell private equity.

✔ **Seed capital:** Money used to take an idea and turn it into a business is called *seed capital.* Few hedge funds provide seed capital because they prefer to wait to see if a company has a chance of surviving.

Project finance: Replacing banks?

Hedge funds may have money to lend, or they may need money to invest. When it comes to short-term transactions — sometimes as short as overnight — hedge funds often replace banks in the role of taking deposits and lending money.

Borrowing money

Hedge fund managers are always looking to make the largest possible amount of money at the lowest possible rate. They borrow from other hedge funds, from banks, from brokerage firms, and sometimes from large corporations.

Many corporations have money sitting around that they won't need for a few days. A company's executives want to get the maximum possible return on their funds, so they lend the money out, often only overnight. But for the hedge fund on the other side of the transaction, overnight may be exactly enough time to take advantage of a profitable price discrepancy between two securities. Because it's unlikely (but not out of the question) that the borrower will go out of business in such a short period, this type of transaction carries very little risk.

Most hedge funds use *leverage* to increase their potential return, which means that they borrow money to buy securities, increasing the amount of money that they can make relative to the amount of money actually in the funds.

Lending

One way a hedge fund manager tries to generate a high rate of return relative to a given level of risk is to keep the fund's holdings earning returns at all times. Therefore, if he sees money in one account that isn't being used for one of the fund's investments, he may decide to loan it out, even for a short period, to get some amount of return. Hedge funds receive interest when they loan out money; of course, the funds take on the risk that the borrowers won't repay the money.

Some hedge fund managers are willing to loan out money for longer periods of time — even a few years — to corporations or governments that need money. They can do this by buying bonds (as can any investor, because bonds are simply tradable loans), or they can make loans through private transactions. They can create all kinds of risk and return combinations by lending money, depending on the funds' goals and the market opportunities.

Gaining return from company mergers and acquisitions

Hedge funds are often players in *mergers* (combinations of equal companies) and *acquisitions* (when larger companies purchase smaller companies) by providing funding and speculating on the outcomes. Here, I outline certain situations funds look for and the strategies they use to increase return and put money in your pocket:

- ✔ **Leveraged (management) buyouts:** Sometimes, members of a company's management group, having grown fed up with shareholders and the hassles of having publicly traded shares, believe they could make more money if they ran the company themselves, so they decide to raise the money to take over. Because it involves heavy borrowing, this type of transaction is called a *leveraged buyout* (LBO) in the United States. Because the management group is doing the buying, the transaction is called a *management buyout* (MBO) in Europe. Many hedge funds invest in LBO debt because it tends to be riskier than most corporate debt. The risk comes from the management group's decision to borrow most or all of the money needed for the acquisition.

- ✔ **Buyout funds:** *Buyout funds* are investment pools formed by hedge fund managers and other private investors for the express purpose of funding leveraged buyouts and business expansions. Like venture capital funds, buyout funds tend to go in and out of fashion, and funds often see mismatches between the amount of money raised to invest in buyouts and the need for buyout capital. It's unlikely that you'll come across a hedge fund dedicated solely to buyouts; instead, it will be one of many strategies that a hedge fund manager may use.

✔ **Bridge lending:** Hedge funds that want to loan money may work with companies that are looking to acquire other companies and, at least in the short run, need some financing to acquire shares in the market or otherwise support a bid for another company. A loan from a hedge fund in this situation is called a *bridge loan* or *bridge financing.* Bridge loans usually have terms of less than one year and carry higher interest rates than other forms of short-term financing.

✔ **Merger arbitrage:** *Merger arbitrage* is a low-risk trading strategy designed to profit after a corporate merger or acquisition is announced. In general, the shares of the company about to be acquired trade at a discount to the offer price because you take on some risk that the deal won't go through. A hedge fund trader buys the stock of the target company and sells the stock of the acquirer, waiting until the deal is announced for the gap to close at a nice profit.

Investing in troubled and dying companies

Insiders often use a slang term for investment pools that seek out troubled businesses and troubled countries: *vulture funds.* In some ways, vulture funds are the opposite of venture capital funds: The venture funds profit as companies get going, and vulture funds are there to profit at the end of the corporate life cycle. If a fund's traders see that a nation's currency has weakened or that some bonds are in risk of default, they swoop in, buy as much as they can, and use their positions as negotiating leverage to get a profit for the fund. Fund traders may also take large positions in the equity and debt of a troubled company and then force management to sell off divisions and other assets. Several investment strategies prey on troubled businesses, including hostile takeovers and liquidation arbitrage:

✔ **Hostile takeovers:** A *hostile takeover* occurs when a company or an investment group acquires enough common stock in a company to get control of its board of directors. In some cases, the company or investment group believes that it can operate the business more profitably. In other cases, the acquirer simply wants to sell off the company's assets at a profit. A hedge fund may offer financing to another takeover group, or it can buy enough stock to be a part of one. Both strategies can be profitable.

✓ **Liquidation arbitrage:** *Liquidation arbitrage* is an investment technique that looks to profit from the breakup of a firm. An investor does careful research to determine exactly how a company's market value differs from the value of the sum of its parts. If the investment fund, often a hedge fund, finds an opportunity where the actual value of the company looks very different from the market value, the fund can acquire enough shares to force management to break the company up or at least sell off some of the assets at a gain for shareholders.

Chapter 5

Evaluating Hedge Fund Performance

Calculating investment performance seems easy: You take your balance at the end of the year, divide it by your balance at the start of the year, subtract 1, and voila! For example, $1,100,000 ÷ $1,000,000 − 1 = 10 percent. But what if you add to your investment in the middle of the year in order to net a bigger return? What if your hedge fund manager had to cash out other shareholders? Quickly, you're left with algebra unlike any you've seen since high school. Because of all the possible complications, many researchers in the investment industry are trying to standardize calculations, and others are asking pointed questions to make solid comparisons.

This chapter looks at how a hedge fund measures and evaluates its performance, as well as what questions you need to ask your prospective fund partners about performance calculation. Evaluating a hedge fund's performance helps you determine if the fund is the right fit for your investment objectives. It also tells you if the hedge fund manager is doing well relative to the risk taken, which is why you invest in the fund in the first place.

Measuring a Hedge Fund's Risk and Return

In general, less risk is preferable to more, and more return is preferable to less. Some people invest in hedge funds to reduce risk, preferring *nondirectional* or *absolute-return funds* (see Chapter 1); other investors aim to increase return regardless of risk by investing in *directional funds*. These funds maintain exposure to the market rate of return, and you have no guarantee that the direction of the return will be up.

The following sections give you the methods used to measure return and risk within a hedge fund, presenting the different forms of return, factoring in fees, and explaining how risk factors into performance.

Unlike mutual funds, hedge funds don't have to publish their performance numbers. And even if they do, they don't have to follow a set methodology. You have to ask questions about the numbers that you see.

Reviewing the return

Return is an estimate that investors can manipulate. It's a measure of past performance, not a predictor of future results. It doesn't matter what a hedge fund did last year; this year is an entirely different ballgame. Whether you're a current or a prospective investor, past return numbers are only rough indicators of what you can expect. That doesn't mean, however, that return figures are worthless. If you're already in a fund, return measures tell you how you did over a time period, which is important information. You may get a different return when you cash out of the fund, but the fund manager still posted a set of investment gains or losses over a specific time period. You can compare that number to your expectations and your needs.

What muddies the picture is that a hedge fund manager may have been lucky or unlucky, or he may have an investment style that does very well in some market conditions and not so well in others. That's why return is only one piece in the evaluation of a portfolio's performance.

Calculating your return

The following list gives you the steps taken to calculate investment return:

1. **Valuing the assets.** A hedge fund has to know what it holds and what its holdings are worth. The best method is to use *market value* — what the security would sell for on the market today — but some funds use their initial costs instead (especially for assets, like real estate, that don't trade easily). Sometimes, a hedge fund will estimate the value of an illiquid asset. The estimate may be close to reality, or the fund may use it to make itself look good.

Many securities pay off some income. Almost all bonds make regular interest payments. Funds should value bonds that pay income with an accrual for any upcoming payments.

2. **Choosing the dates.** On a regular calendar, a year has 12 months and 365 days (usually), and it ends on December 31. In an accounting calendar, a year may be 360 days long, and a month could end not on the last day of the month but on the last business day or the last Friday. As long as the hedge fund manager discloses the beginning and ending dates and applies the method consistently, it doesn't matter how she sets the fund's time periods.

When you're doing comparisons, make sure that you compare numbers for the same time periods. A shady fund manager may change the ending date for a quarter in order to avoid a big market decline on the last calendar day, for example.

3. **Picking a calculation methodology.** Give someone with a numerical bent a list of numbers and a calculator and she can come up with several different relationships between numbers. After investors determine the asset values for certain time periods, they can calculate rates of return. But how? And over how long a time period? Even though the fund may hand over the work to accountants or even actuaries, you should still understand the differences in the methods. Following are the different calculation methods:

Book VI

Hedge Funds

• **Time-weighted returns:** The most common way to calculate investment returns — also called the *compound average growth rate* (CAGR). For one time period, the calculation produces a simple percentage:

$$\frac{EOY - BOY}{BOY}$$

EOY stands for "end of year asset value," and *BOY* is "beginning of year value." The result is the percentage return for one year. Simple arithmetic!

If you want to look at your return over a period of several years, you need this equation, which looks at the compound return rather than the simple return for each year:

$$\sqrt[N]{\frac{EOP - BOP}{BOP}}$$

EOP stands for "end of the total time period," *BOP* stands for "beginning of the total time period," and *N* is the number of years that you're looking at.

• **Dollar-weighted returns, also called the *internal rate of return* (IRR):** The rate that makes the net present value of a stream of numbers equal to zero. You find the number through an iteration that almost always has to be done on a calculator or a computer. You use the IRR to determine the return for a stream of numbers over time; it's also widely used to value bonds.

Because of the problems with dollar-weighted returns, most people who analyze investment returns prefer to use a time-weighted, compound average approach. It isn't as flashy — you can do it with the same cheap scientific calculator you used in high school chemistry — but it gives you a more precise way to figure out how a fund performs over a range of market cycles.

Calculating fees

One big nuance with return calculations is whether or not you include fees. And fees can be hefty: A typical hedge fund charges a 1- or 2-percent management fee and takes a 20-percent cut of profits (see Chapter 1). Other funds take much more. Here are two terms to know:

- ✔ **Gross of fees:** If a fund manager reports returns *gross of fees,* that means he hasn't taken out most of the fees. Trading costs should be removed because those commissions and fees are necessary to building the portfolio. However, the manager shouldn't remove the investment management fees and cuts of profits. Trading costs should be relatively small, but they can be high if the fund makes many small, frequent trades or if it uses unusual strategies that carry high commissions.

  One reason to report numbers gross of fees is that different investors may be paying different fees. A hedge fund may agree to reduce the profit fee charged to a *fund of funds* (which invests in several different hedge funds) or a single large investor in exchange for its investment. So, although most investors may have an arrangement for a 2-percent management fee and a 20-percent share of profits, some may be paying only "1 and 18."

- ✔ **Net of fees:** In a *net-of-fees* performance calculation, you remove all the fees charged by the fund. This method may not reflect the return that any one investor receives, because different investors may have different fee schedules. Anyone evaluating a net-of-fee rate of return has to ask if different investors pay different fees, because any one investor's realized returns may be higher or lower.

Sizing up the risk

An investor must consider return relative to what a manager had to do to get it, which is why you have to compare return to the amount of risk taken. The problem is that measurements of risk are inherently subjective. What's risky to one investor may not be risky to you. In finance, the dispute over how to define risk has led to a range of measures. The following sections present what goes into each measurement so that you can judge for yourself how appropriate each method is for your needs.

Standard deviation

In finance, risk is usually considered to be a function of *standard deviation* — a statistic that shows how much your return may vary from the return that you expect to get. Say, for example, that you expect a security to have an average return of 10 percent over two years. If it returns 10 percent the first year and 10 percent the second year, no deviation exists between any one return and the average return. But if the security returns 20 percent one period and 0 percent the next, it still returns an average of 10 percent but with big deviations from the 10-percent mean. The more a security swings around the expected return, the riskier it is.

Some hedge funds are designed to have low standard deviations. Funds of this structure are *absolute-return funds,* which aim to post returns within a narrow range (often 6 to 8 percent). *Directional funds,* on the other hand, try to maximize returns, so they sometimes take on very high levels of risk, creating a high expected standard deviation (see Chapter 1 for more). When looking for a prospective fund, you can compare how much the return varies from year to year to give you a ballpark idea of how risky it is.

Beta

A refinement of the standard deviation measurement is *beta,* which compares the standard deviation of an investable asset or fund to the standard deviation of the market itself. In most cases, the performance of an index measures the "market" (in the sense that the index is a sample of investable assets, not an agglomeration of all the possible assets that you can invest in), like the S&P 500 in the United States or the Nikkei in Japan.

If a fund has a beta of 1, it should move right in step with the market itself. If it has a beta greater than 1, it should move more sharply up or more sharply down — whichever way the market goes. If it has a beta of less than 1, it should move in the same direction as the market, but less sharply. If the beta is negative, it should move in the opposite direction of the market.

Peak-to-trough ranges

A simple way to look at the volatility of a long-standing hedge fund is to compare the distance between the *peak* — the year with the highest return — and the *trough* — the year with the lowest return. The greater the distance between the peak and the trough, and the closer together the two are, the riskier the fund is. For example, if a fund's peak return was 80 percent, followed by a loss of 35 percent the next year, the peak-to-trough distance is 115 percent (80 − (−35)) over two years. If another fund had a peak return of 15 percent, followed by a return of 10 percent the next year, its peak-to-trough distance is 5 percent (15 − 10) over two years. The first fund is much riskier than the second fund.

For a hedge fund with a short operating history, you can look at the peak and trough months rather than years.

Stress tests

Standard deviation and beta are nice shortcuts, but they don't answer one question that may be on a worrisome investor's mind: How much money will I lose if things go terribly wrong? A *stress test* solves this problem. The test is a computer simulation that models what could happen to a hedge fund's portfolio under a variety of different scenarios, like a dramatic increase in interest rates, the Euro falling apart, or the government of Mexico defaulting on its bonds. Based on the sensitivity that the different fund investments have to the tested factors, the stress test shows how much the factors may affect the portfolio's return. The less effect the events have, the less risky the fund — assuming that the right stresses have been tested.

Stress tests are expensive to run, and even the best are based on guesses about the future. Still, the information from a test can be useful, especially for a fund that intends to retain exposure to a certain set of market factors. For example, a macro hedge fund that concentrates on emerging Asian-Pacific markets could undergo a test for exposure to those currencies and interest rates.

Value at risk

Value at risk (VAR) is a single number that represents how much you can expect a portfolio to lose over a given time period. The value is a statistical calculation involving several equations, so it is very difficult to calculate by hand, and in most cases, you will have to rely on the hedge fund for VAR information. You see it quoted with similar margins of error that you see with political polls.

For example, a hedge fund may say that it has a 95 percent confidence level that its portfolio has a 10-day VAR of losing $10 million. This translates to the following: Based on the securities held in the portfolio and on market conditions, the fund manager is 95 percent certain that the most the fund could lose over the next 10 days is $10 million. Events could take place over the next ten days that fall into the 5 percent uncertainty level, but more likely than not, the most the fund will lose is $10 million.

Benchmarks for Evaluating a Fund's Risk and Return

Investment performance is relative — relative to your needs and expectations and relative to what your return would've been had you invested your money elsewhere. That's why you have to compare your return and risk numbers to something. But what? In many cases, hedge fund investors compare performance to a market index. Some compare performance to that of similar hedge funds or to an expected return based on the fund's style. All these types of comparisons have their advantages and disadvantages.

A fund can beat its benchmarks and all its peers and still lose money. The fund manager may be happy; the consultants and brokers who recommended the hedge fund may be happy; but the investors who put money into the fund may be fuming.

Looking into indexes

The most common way to compare investment performance is with a market index. *Market indexes* are the measures of the overall market that you hear quoted all the time in the news, like the Standard & Poor's 500 (S&P 500) and the Dow Jones Industrial Average. Not only are these widely reviewed, but also widely mimicked: Many mutual funds and futures contracts are designed to mimic the performance of market indexes. What this means is that investors can always do at least as well as the index itself if their investment objectives call for exposure to that part of the broad investment market.

Book VI

Hedge Funds

Indexes aren't perfect for comparison purposes. One big problem is that investors often look at the wrong indexes for the type of investments that they have. For example, an investor may compare the performance of a macro fund that invests all over the world to the S&P 500 when he or she should use a global index that includes a range of securities.

In many cases, you should compare a fund to a mixture of indexes. For example, you should compare a macro fund that invests

> 30 percent in international equities
>
> 30 percent in international bonds
>
> 40 percent in currencies

to

> 30 percent of the return on an international equity index
>
> 30 percent of the return on an international bond index
>
> 40 percent of the return on a currency index

Preparing indexes is a big business. In many cases, indexes are designed and calculated by newspapers that want to keep their names in front of investors, so the different companies that calculate and maintain indexes put different conditions on their use. Anyone offering an S&P 500 index fund has to pay a fee to Standard & Poor's. Hedge funds and performance-consulting firms may have to pay index companies for detailed information about the securities in the indexes. When a hedge fund presents its results relative to a given index to you, a prospective investor, it may do so for different reasons:

- ✔ Because that index is the best choice
- ✔ Because the index's performance makes the fund look good
- ✔ Because another index service was too expensive to use

Verify that your hedge fund uses the same benchmarks every time it reports. If it changes its benchmarks, that may mean that the fund is trying to make its performance look good or is changing its investment style so that it no longer matches the profile of the fund you need in your portfolio.

Different indexes show different results, even if they are calculated using the same securities. There are several different ways to calculate indexes, and understanding them can give you a sense of why a fund manager may choose one over the other.

Market capitalization–weighted index

Market capitalization is the total value of a security. For example, the market capitalization of a common stock is the total number of shares outstanding multiplied by the price per share, and the market capitalization of a bond issue is the number of bonds issued multiplied by the price of each bond. In a *market capitalization–weighted index,* different securities are entered in proportion to their total market value. One example of a market capitalization–weighted index is the Standard & Poor's 500 Index (S&P 500).

A market capitalization–weighted index is a good representation of how the market as a whole trades, but it may place too much emphasis on the price fluctuations of the largest companies. The NASDAQ Composite Index, which represents the value of all the companies traded on NASDAQ, is disproportionately exposed to the trading of Microsoft and other huge high-tech and biotech companies. Those huge technology companies are mainstays on NASDAQ, but most of the companies on that exchange are quite small.

Price-weighted index

A *price-weighted index* includes one of each security from the group being measured. For example, a price-weighted stock index includes one share of each of the companies it tracks, and a price-weighted bond index includes one share of each of the bonds it tracks. The Dow Jones Industrial Average is an example of a price-weighted index.

The price-weighted index is independent of the total capitalization of the included securities, so securities with a high price may be overweighted.

Differing results for different indexes

Even if they include the same securities, price-weighted and market capitalization indexes can post different results. Table 5-1 shows how this can happen.

Table 5-1	Price-Weighted versus Market Capitalization–Weighted Index Comparisons			
	Stock A	*Stock B*	*Price-Weighted Index Value*	*Market Capitalization–Weighted Index Value*
Total shares outstanding	1,000,000	10,000,000		
Beginning-of-year price	$10.00	$10.00	$20.00	$110,000,000
Market capitalization	$10,000,000	$100,000,000		
End-of-year price	$14.00	$16.00	$30.00	$174,000,000
Market capitalization	$14,000,000	$160,000,000		
% change			50%	58%

Picking over peer rankings

If you just want the risk and return that comes with an index, you wouldn't be considering paying a hedge fund's high fees. And if you've made the decision that a hedge fund is the way to go with your money, you'll want to know how your fund does against other hedge funds that you could've invested in instead. That's why you look at peer group rankings.

Many hedge funds report their results to services, like Morningstar (www. morningstar.com), where the analysts rank funds based on their risk-and-return parameters. For example, the service ranks arbitrage funds against other arbitrage funds, and long–short funds against other long–short funds.

With the information from the services, you can see if your fund is one of the better or worse ones within a specific style. Unlike Morningstar's mutual fund information, you have to pay to see these rankings.

One problem with peer rankings of hedge funds is that reporting is optional, which makes the picture you see less rounded. A fund that doesn't do so well is less likely to report its numbers for a ranking, so the average performance may have an upward bias. A fund in the bottom half of a published ranking isn't in the bottom half of all hedge funds within that style; it's just in the bottom half of funds that reported. You can bet that plenty of funds in that style are worse; they're just in hiding.

Standardizing performance calculation: Global Investment Performance Standards

Hedge fund managers have many options to use when calculating and comparing risk and return, and they have an incentive to choose the methods that make them look better than the alternatives. In 1996, the Association for Investment Management and Research, now known as the CFA Institute (www. cfainstitute.org), introduced its Performance Presentation Standards to help U.S. investment advisors present their numbers fairly and to make it easy for investors to compare the performance of different firms. In 2006, the CFA Institute adopted a revised standard, the Global Investment Performance Standards (or GIPS), that applies to money managers around the world. The GIPS include the following:

- Accurate data collection, with records to support the information
- Market-value accounting
- Accrual accounting for the value of any assets that generate income
- Monthly portfolio valuation, ending on the last business day or last calendar day of the month
- Time-weighted returns
- Results that are net of investment expenses
- Results shown for the last five years (or from the fund's inception if it's less than five years old), with annual results given for each year

Compliance with the standards is voluntary, but it allows fund managers to market their results to current and prospective investors as being "GIPS Compliant" or "GIPS Verified." Still, some hedge funds ignore GIPS, and sometimes for good reasons:

✔ It can be expensive to calculate results in the correct manner in order to qualify for the GIPS label.

✔ The CFA Institute designed the methodology for investment-management firms that handle several different portfolios in-house, but many hedge funds are one-portfolio operations.

✔ Not all investors are aware of GIPS or even care, something that the CFA Institute hopes to change.

Putting Risk and Return into Context with Academic Measures

It isn't enough to have the return and risk numbers and comparisons with indexes or other funds (of course!). You have to put the performance figures into context to figure out what the portfolio manager did to get those numbers.

Given that hedge funds have huge minimum-investment requirements (see Chapter 1), investors have a lot of money at stake. Many hedge fund investors, like employees of pension funds or charitable endowments, have responsibilities to the people who rely on their funds. These factors are the reasons why investors need to know what the risk-and-return numbers mean and how they reflect on hedge fund managers' performances. Several equations developed in ivory towers can help you figure out why a hedge fund did as well as it did, and this section shows you what they are.

Academic approaches to finance have their problems because they're based on the assumption that rational investors are trading in efficient markets. You may be tempted to laugh off the whole idea of academic theories, but that leaves you with nothing to determine how a hedge fund performed. Look at the approaches in this section with this limitation in mind.

Sharpe measure

The *Sharpe measure,* named after Nobel Prize–winning economist William Sharpe, is the amount of performance that a fund earns over and above the risk-free rate of return (which, for investors based in the United States, is the interest rate on Treasury bills) divided by the standard deviation of returns. (Standard deviation is a mathematical measure of how much one number in a set varies from the average of all the numbers in the set.) Here's what the equation looks like:

$$\frac{r_p - r_f}{\sigma_p}$$

The Sharpe measure shows whether the portfolio's return for taking risk (the return minus the risk-free rate) came by increasing the amount of risk in the portfolio or from the fund manager's skill (known as *alpha;* see Chapter 1), which allowed her to get a better return than expected from the amount of standard deviation in the securities held by the portfolio. A higher number is better than a lower one, because a higher number indicates that the hedge fund manager is getting more return for the risk that she's taking.

Treynor measure

Jack Treynor developed a variation of the Sharpe measure that looks at how a hedge fund performed for the risk it took over and above the risk of the market as a whole — not just at how it performed relative to the risk-free rate of return. The equation is

$$\sigma_p$$

After all, people take risk when they invest, but they can put their money into a low-fee index fund (a fund invested in the same securities as a broad-market index, like the S&P 500, with the goal of generating the same return) instead of paying a hedge fund manager fees for 2 percent of the assets and 20 percent of the profits. For example, if the fund returned 15 percent, the market rate of return was 10 percent, and the fund's standard deviation was 20 percent, the Treynor measure would be $(15 - 10)/20$, or 25 percent. This is better than a fund with a Treynor measure of 15 percent, and worse than a fund with a Treynor measure of 35 percent.

Jensen's alpha

Michael Jensen, a professor at the Harvard School of Business, decided that investors should just use the capital assets pricing model (CAPM) rather than Sharpe's or Treynor's measures of performance. The CAPM involves alpha. Hedge fund managers love to talk about alpha. The word derives from the CAPM; it measures how much an investment returns over and above its beta (its exposure to the market). Here's the equation (with A representing alpha):

$$E(r) = B(r_m - r_f) + A + r_f$$

If a portfolio has a positive alpha, the portfolio manager did a good job. If the portfolio's alpha is zero or negative, maybe the manager's fees weren't deserved.

The appraisal ratio

Some performance analysts use a fourth measure to evaluate a hedge fund's performance: the *appraisal ratio,* which divides the fund's alpha by the nonsystematic risk of the portfolio. Although the equation is simple, you more or less need a computer to generate the statistics involved in this calculation.

The *nonsystematic risk* is risk that the manager could've diversified by adding more securities to the portfolio but didn't. The return from the risk isn't so much, due to the portfolio manager's skill as to the portfolio manager's decision not to diversify the portfolio. Suppose, for example, that a hedge fund manager decides to invest only in oil company stock. Beta isn't the best comparison, because the fund's portfolio is far narrower than the entire investment market. Some of that risk is unnecessary, and the manager could remove it through diversification. The appraisal ratio is an attempt to separate the diversifiable risk from the true alpha — the true extra performance due to a portfolio manager's skill.

Book VI

Hedge Funds

A Reality Check on Hedge Fund Returns

One reason so many investors are interested in hedge funds is because they think hedge funds are raking in enormous investment returns that other investors can't get. Certainly, some hedge funds bring in enormous investment returns, and the nature of a hedge fund's structure supports the idea that other investors are shut out (see Chapter 1 for info on the structure of hedge funds). But the reality is that many hedge funds don't perform in the stratosphere, which is why you need to know what you want from your investments before you commit. The following sections aim to put you in touch with your investment needs by bringing to light many facts about hedge fund returns.

Risk and return tradeoff

Some hedge funds post poor results relative to a stock-market index because they're designed to perform very differently. Investment return is a function of risk; the more risk a fund takes, the greater its expected return. A hedge fund's goal is to post a return that's greater than expected for a given level of risk. Some funds choose high risk levels in the hopes of even higher returns, and others maintain very low risk levels and generate relatively low returns.

Many investors are content with an 8 percent return year in and year out, but others would find this incredibly disappointing. Before you commit to a hedge fund, you need to know your investment objectives inside and out; refer to Chapter 2.

Survivor bias

Many hedge fund managers limit how often investors can make withdrawals, but they can't lock up an investor's money forever. A fund may require that an investor keep money in for two years, but if performance is bad in both years, you can bet that the investor will yank the money as soon as the time period expires.

In addition, hedge fund managers charge high fees, but they can collect a profit payout only if the funds show a profit (see Chapter 1). If a fund isn't doing so well, its investors will go, and the fund manager will want out, too, so he can make some money elsewhere. Hedge Fund Research, a firm that tracks hedge funds, estimated that 11.4 percent of hedge funds folded in 2005.

When looking at long-term results for hedge funds, remember that the worst performing funds all probably dropped out of the game after two years, which means funds that are still in business have less competition. They already have better-than-average status because they're still in business. However, unless they're looking for new investors, they'll force you to invest in a newly formed fund. Will it be a survivor or one of the ones that eventually shut down?

Performance persistence

One huge problem for any hedge fund and its investors is following one good year with another. Is a great number the result of luck, or is it due to the portfolio manager's skill? Will the manager's luck hold out next year? Will a skilled portfolio manager face bad luck next year? It's really hard to post good performance year after year — a problem known as *performance persistence.*

A study published in 2000 by Vikas Agarwal of Georgia State University and Narayan Naik of the London Business School found no evidence of persistence in the funds that they studied. One year's performance wasn't an indicator of the next year's, and the relationship between performance one year and the next weakened as more time periods were included in the study. What does this mean? If a hedge fund has the kind of extraordinary return that grabs headlines this year, it probably won't bring in those spectacular returns the next year. This is a phenomenon known as *reversion to the mean.*

Style persistence

The problem of a fund manager changing style to get performance is called *style persistence.* If a fund keeps changing its investment strategy, it may post good numbers, but consultants, academics, and others who evaluate returns may not know what to do with the fund.

Academic performance studies in particular control for different risk measures, which affects the performance persistence that they report. Some funds show persistence, but that's because the fund changes its investment style with the market. Some investors may want a hedge fund that's flexible and can post a consistent return no matter what. Other investors may need a fund to limit its investments or maintain a consistent risk profile so that it complements other parts of their portfolios.

Hiring a Reporting Service to Track Hedge Fund Performance

Given all the information-collecting options covered in the pages of this chapter, how in the world are you supposed to keep track of everything to find out how a hedge fund actually performs? Some people require help in this area, and help is available. Along with the numbers that the fund manager presents, you can find several consulting firms and reporting services that monitor how hedge funds perform, analyze their results, and evaluate their risk and return based on the styles that the fund managers follow. The following list is by no means exhaustive and doesn't represent an endorsement. But it should give you some ideas of where to start if you want to enlist some help to evaluate hedge fund performance. Be forewarned: Most of these companies charge for their services — and charge a lot.

- **Greenwich Alternative Investments:** Greenwich (www.greenwichai.com) is one of many hedge fund services that operates in two businesses: A consulting firm that advises investors on hedge fund investments, and a hedge fund performance-analysis service. Some information on the performance of broad categories of hedge funds is available for free from the Web site, but other information is available only to institutional investors (pensions, endowments, and foundations) that pay the firm for its services.

- **HedgeFund.net:** HedgeFund.net maintains a database of quantitative and qualitative information about hedge funds, submitted by the funds themselves. The site also carries news and information about the industry (even offering a free daily report) and offers both free and paid services; however, all subscribers must be accredited investors.

✔ **Hedge Fund Research:** Hedge Fund Research (`www.hedgefundresearch.com`) compiles detailed databases of hedge fund performance and administration. It has at least some information on 9,000 funds and detailed information on 5,800 of them. This helps people determine how many funds are being formed, how many are being disbanded, and what kind of returns are being generated for investors. Full access is available to accredited investors for a fee.

✔ **Lipper HedgeWorld:** Lipper (`www.lipperhedgeworld.com`) made its name in mutual fund performance reporting, and it now offers hedge fund performance services as well. The company, owned by Reuters, offers a variety of free and paid reports on performance. How much access you get depends on whether you're accredited and how much you're willing to pay.

✔ **Managed Account Report:** Managed Account Report (`www.marhedge.com`) collects news and information on the hedge fund industry, organizes conferences, and reports on hedge fund performance. The firm collects its data from fund managers and reports it to subscribers on its Web site and print publication. It compares results to indexes of hedge fund performance prepared by The Barclay Group (`www.barclaygrp.com`). Subscribers don't have to be accredited investors.

✔ **Morningstar:** Morningstar (`www.morningstar.com`) is a dominant firm for mutual fund performance analysis, and it's building a niche in hedge funds. Funds report their own performance numbers each month. The database was started in 2004 and holds information on 3,000 hedge funds, funds of hedge funds, and commodity trading advisors. Subscribers, who must be accredited investors, can access the site's information to get a sense of how a fund's risk and return compares to other hedge funds following the same investment style.

Book VII
Value Investing

The 5th Wave   By Rich Tennant

"It hasn't helped me sell more hot dogs, but I've had several inquiries for investment advice."

In this book . . .

Value investing is good old-fashioned investing: It takes you back to the tried-and-true principles of valuing a stock as one would value a business. When the price, or value, of a stock matches the value of a business, the value investor *considers* buying it. When the price of a stock is *less* than the value of the business, the value investor warms and may *get excited* about buying it. And when the price of the stock skyrockets past the value of the company, yes, the value investor *sells* it.

Believe it or not, markets do undervalue businesses, and do so frequently. Because there is no magic formula for valuing a business, the true value of a stock is a matter of opinion anyway. All of which serves to make investing more fun — and profitable — for the prudent and diligent investor who sorts through available information to best understand a company's value.

A value investor who applies the principles brought forth in this book is essentially betting with the house. The odds, especially in the long term, are in your favor.

Chapter 1

An Investor's Guide to Value Investing

In This Chapter

▶ Understanding the principles of value investing

▶ Deciding if you're a value investor

▶ Learning the value investing story

▶ Brushing up on value investing math

*N*o doubt, somewhere during your investing career you've heard something about value investing. You may know it's "what Warren Buffett does," or maybe you've seen mutual funds described as "value-oriented." You have a pretty good idea what the word *value* means in ordinary English, but how does it apply to investing? What *is* value investing, anyway? This chapter answers that question and helps you decide whether you're a value investor at heart.

What Value Investing Is — And Isn't

If you ask investors (amateur or professional) to define value investing, you'll hear a lot of different answers that might include phrases like "conservative," "long-term oriented," "the opposite of growth," "the Buffett approach," "buying stocks with a low P/E," "buying stuff that's cheap," or "buying stocks that nobody wants." Aside from "the opposite of growth," each of these phrases is a valid part of the definition.

Broadly defined, value investing is an investing approach and style blending many principles of business and financial analysis to arrive at good investing decisions. To be more specific,

> Value investing is buying shares of a business as though you were buying the business itself. Value investors emphasize the intrinsic value of assets and current and future profits, and they pay a price equal to or less than that value.

Note the key phrases "buying . . . a business," "intrinsic value," and "pay a price equal to or less than that value." These are explicit tenets of the value investing approach, and underlying them all is the notion of conscious appraisal — that is, the idea of a rigorous and deliberate attempt to measure business value.

Obviously, price enters the value investor's appraisal, but you'll notice that it appears at the end of the definition. Value investors go to the stock market only to buy their share of the business. They don't look at the market as a first indicator of whether or not to invest.

Important value investing principles

With the definition of value investing as an appetizer, here's a main course of value investing principles:

- ✔ **Buying a business:** If you take nothing else away from this part of the book, take away the thought process that investing in stocks is really like buying a business. No matter how large or small the company you're investing in, you want to find out as much as possible about it before you commit your capital.

  If you got caught in the tech boom and bust, you may think you did exactly that. You followed a company and its story. Everything the company did made headlines. Everybody wanted to own its products or work for the company. So you bought shares.

  But did you look at business fundamentals? The intrinsic value of assets and future profit prospects? Did you understand the company's strategy and competitive advantages? Did you do your homework to assess whether the stock price was at or below your appraisal? Likely not. That's the difference between value investing and most other investing forms.

- ✔ **A conscious appraisal:** If you were interested in buying a business and thought the corner hardware store looked attractive, how much would you be willing to pay for it? You would likely be influenced by the sale price of other hardware stores and by opinions shared by neighbors and other customers. But you would still center your attention on the intrinsic economic value — the worth and profit-generation potential — of that business, and a determination of whether that value justified the price.

  Value investors refer to this process as an *appraisal* of the business. They rely on publicly available facts and figures to conduct a true numbers assessment — an appraisal of *intrinsic* value, not just the market price.

  Appraising the value, relating the value to the price, and looking for good bargains capture the essence of the value approach.

- ✔ **Beyond the fundamentals:** Basic investment analysis should start with an analysis of business fundamentals: the metrics and measures that define business performance, like profitability, productivity, and capital structure. But it needs to go further to be blended with a company's "story" to determine whether the fundamentals will hold up or, better yet, improve. The value investor gets good at blending the two.

  Adopting the value investing approach means *becoming your own investment analyst.* You may read the work of others, but you'll incorporate it into your own analysis and investing decision.

- ✔ **Ignoring the market:** How can you spot the value investor at a cocktail party? Easy. She is the only one talking about an actual company while others stand around discussing the stock market.

  Focusing on the company itself, *not* on the market, is a consistent value investing attribute. As a general rule, value investors ignore the market and tune out brokers, advisers, and commentators. They may, however, listen to folks in the industry, customers, or people who know a lot about competitors.

  Value investors have a long-term focus. And if they've done their homework right, what the market does to their stocks on a daily basis is irrelevant.

  To be sure, external factors can affect stock prices. Interest rates, in particular, can also affect the intrinsic values of companies, as the cost of capital rises and falls and the value of alternative investments increases. So it makes sense to pay some attention to the markets, especially in the long term. But daily fluctuations should be ignored. Value investors wait anywhere from a few years to forever for their investments to mature.

- ✔ **A quest for consistency:** Most value investors like a high degree of consistency in returns, profitability, growth, asset value, management effectiveness, customer base, supply chain, and most other aspects of the business. It's the same consistency you'd strive for if you bought a business to run yourself.

  The value investor looks for consistency in an attempt to minimize risk and provide a margin of safety for his investment. This is not to say the value investor *won't* invest in a risky enterprise, but the price paid for earnings potential must correctly reflect the risk. Consistency need not be absolute, but predictable performance is important.

Book VII

Value Investing

More than meets the eye

Value investing isn't only about long-term investing, low P/E ratios, cheap stocks, and diversification. And it isn't about being the opposite of investing in growth. The following list helps define value investing by showing that "Value investing isn't just . . ."

✔ **Long-term investing:** Most value investments *are* long-term. The Buffettonian view is to "hold forever" and look for businesses that you would *want* to hold forever. But not all long-term investments are good values, and not all value investments are long-term. Indeed, as business cycles shorten, what is excellent today may soon look like a flash in the pan as technologies and marketplace acceptance change.

Buffett deals with this problem by avoiding technology stocks, but even businesses in other sectors see their products changing ever more quickly. You once could buy only one "flavor" of Tide detergent, but now there are dozens, and they change all the time.

So when buying a business, it's good to look long term, but you must also realize that businesses and their markets change, and you should always be prepared to sell if assumptions change. It'd be *nice* to hold forever, but that doesn't mean you should expect to or have to.

✔ **Low P/E ratios:** Oil companies, banks, food producers, steel companies — they all have had P/E (price-to-earnings) ratios below market averages. (See Chapters 3 and 4 for an explanation of P/E.) But does that mean they are good values? Sometimes, but not always. Even Enron traded with low P/Es at times.

While low P/E can be part of the investing equation, especially when deciding when the stock price is right, it is far from the whole story.

✔ **The opposite of growth:** "Stock ABC is a growth stock, and stock XYZ is a value stock." You hear that all the time, and you also hear it about mutual funds, which are neatly divvied up into neat little boxes tagged as "growth," "value," and "blend."

So value stocks aren't supposed to grow? Well, some, like your local electric utility, may prosper just fine on the business they have, but for most companies, growth is an integral part of the value of the business.

I place growth in the center of the "value" stage. The potential for growth defines some companies as good values; the current assets and perhaps even current business levels alone don't justify the price. Indeed, this is what separates early value investing, as practiced and preached by patriarch Ben Graham, from the more recent views practiced by Buffett and many of his current disciples: Growth creates value.

✔ **Cheap stocks:** Above all, value investors seek to buy businesses at or below their appraised value. Why? Not just because they like to get a good deal — it's to provide a *margin of safety*. Since any business appraisal is imprecise in its best case, the value investor likes to give a cushion for error, a cushion just in case things don't turn out exactly as assessed.

Does that mean that a value investor always buys a stock below its highest price? Usually, but not always. Does a value investor "bottom fish" for the lowest 52-week price? Usually not. A stock at a 52-week low may have serious flaws in its business or marketplace acceptance.

- **Diversification:** You hear it constantly: The key to investing success is to diversify. Diversification provides safety in numbers and avoids the eggs-in-one-basket syndrome, so it protects the value of a portfolio.

  Yes, there's some truth to that. But the masters of value investing have shown that diversification only serves to dilute returns. If you're doing the value investing thing right, *you are picking the right stocks at the right price*, so there's no need to provide this extra insurance. That said, perhaps diversification isn't a bad idea until you prove yourself a *good* value investor. The point is that diversification *per se* is not a value investing technique.

Are You a Value Investor?

If you're asking yourself the same question, following are seven character traits found in most value investors. You don't have to display every one to be a good value investor, but you want to see yourself in at least some of them.

- **Bargain hunter:** If you check the price of the hotel across the street before you check into your chosen hotel, you have a key trait of a value investor.

- **Do-it-yourselfer:** Value investors want to check the numbers themselves and build their own assessments. By doing so, they develop a better understanding of the company and its fundamentals.

- **Like margins of safety:** People who actually slow down when it rains are more likely to be better value investors.

- **Long-term focus:** Value investors would rather make a lot of money slowly than a little flashy money in one day.

- **Business, not price, oriented:** The value investor focuses on the underlying business, not the price or superficial image.

- **Numbers oriented:** Not advanced mathematics, mind you, but you can't get completely away from the numbers. Value investors are concerned about company business fundamentals and performance. For those who don't like numbers, fortunately there are software packages that do some of the computation and preparation for you.

- **Contrarian:** Value investors are not crowd followers! Value investors stay away from what's exciting and hip quite purposefully: Popular stocks aren't normally bargains.

Book VII

Value Investing

The Value Investing Story

Volatility. You hear about it all the time. The market is on cruise control, and then all of a sudden, something unforeseen happens to stir things up. Subprime loan defaults. Oil prices. A war. The markets have run mostly up and to the right for 25-plus years, but along the way, we've had our bumps.

The first years of this century signified an important turning point in the history of investing. In the late 1990s, investors had moved away from analysis of business fundamentals. As the percentage of stock-owning households boomed, a growing portion of the investing public knew little about reading financial statements — or perhaps even where to find one! People bought stocks based on stories they heard from colleagues at the office or friends at parties. And the retail brokerage industry got into the game, too, offering investment analysis that seemingly supported almost anything.

Since the dot-com bubble burst, value investing has caught on, and we've seen a dramatic return to investing based on fundamentals — so much so that many of the so-called "value" stocks actually became overvalued.

The good news is that value investing has become more popular, so there's more information and commentary out there to help the value investor. The bad news is that value investing has become more popular, so it's harder to find good values!

A short history of the markets

They say history predicts the future, so let's take a short tour of the past six decades of stock market history, with special focus on lessons for value investors:

- ✔ **The good old days — 1950s and 1960s:** Time was, you simply bought the market, and you bought for the long term. The stock certificates sat in your safety deposit box, and a few government bonds or savings bonds may have sat alongside them. You checked the paper at most weekly, and you watched market reports nightly on the *Huntley-Brinkley Report*. You cared more about the averages than your individual stocks, because the market *was* your stocks. Your investments grew with the economy. There was little to worry about and little for you to do.

- ✔ **Political ties and international dependence — 1970s:** On May 1, 1975, high fixed brokerage commissions became a thing of the past. Lower commissions enabled more individual investors to trade in and out of stocks more frequently. This factor, plus the advent of NASDAQ, made do-it-yourself investing feasible for the first time. As a result, markets became more liquid.

Also in the 1970s, investors started to realize that investments weren't bound to follow the economy as a whole — that certain sectors and industries were bound to do better than others. Cyclical companies and companies overly dependent on cheap, abundant resources — such as foreign oil — were no longer the best bets. It was the beginning of a more complex, dynamic investing climate. But aside from annual reports and other company releases, there was little information for a value-oriented investor to use.

✔ **Globalization, asset shift, and technology — 1980s:** Interest rates in the early 1980s were kept artificially high to combat inflation, and they stifled business growth. But in 1982, as interest rates and inflation eased, President Reagan pushed through tax legislation that included a new assortment of retirement savings incentives for individuals and small businesses. Transportation deregulation, more free trade, and increased government spending in technology and defense sectors added to the story. The result was a long-awaited shift of capital from real estate and fixed assets into stocks. The bull run, which was to last almost 18 years with a few short interruptions, had begun.

Lower taxes, as well as business and consumer optimism, led the markets higher and induced people to spend more. But they were buying a lot of foreign goods, and a ballooning trade deficit resulted. To keep the dollar relatively strong and attractive for foreign investment, interest rates were kept high. The leftover inflation fear from a few years prior also fueled a lingering high interest rate mentality. In October 1987, a particularly bad trade deficit report, high interest rates (over 10 percent for U.S. Treasury bonds), and some speculative excess in stocks created a volatile mix. The Dow experienced its worst one-day percentage plunge ever.

After six months, investors once again gained confidence and started back in, but this time more cautiously. Even the most secure long-term investor now had to watch for "perfect storms" that could wipe out huge chunks of market value. Conditions were still favorable for investing in businesses — and even more so as interest rates and the dollar declined. But the imperative to invest rationally grew by leaps and bounds.

✔ **Democratization and the Internet bubble — 1990s:** As the decade began, the boom of the 1980s had slowed; key industries, such as automobiles and basic manufacturing, saw a down cycle, exacerbated once again by the flood of imports. The markets really didn't get going again until 1992. Newly elected President Bill Clinton and his vision of the "information superhighway" jazzed the markets, particularly the technology sector. The vision promised faster, more efficient business and a new conduit to reach customers.

The growth of the Internet was not just a boon to suppliers of Internet "parts," nor to Internet-only companies building a new electronic channel to sell existing products. It was an opportunity for all businesses to

Book VII

Value Investing

build a new market presence and streamline or simplify operations. Every company developed a Web strategy, and the stock market liked what it saw.

In June 1998, the stock price of a small company called Amazon.com started to move. The market awoke to the dot.com concept, and the stock rocketed skyward. Soon, other companies started following suit. The whole game became finding companies that hadn't been "discovered" yet and buying stock in them before they took off. The Internet stock boom took the rest of the market with it.

There was another force at work, shaped by the Internet. For the first time in history, individual investors had virtual real-time connections to the stock market. Free and easy access gave entry to many more market players, and the market was already in a boom to begin with.

The start of the new century saw a fading business cycle and the realization that, although the Internet brought improvements in business fundamentals and productivity, it wasn't off-the-charts improvement. The presence and use of the Internet did not guarantee success to any business.

The grim result and profound lessons are recent enough to stick in the minds of all investors. There were many lessons — some repeated history and some were new. No bull market can go on forever; overvalued stocks should be treated as such, growth in value of business assets cannot consistently exceed growth in the economy, and it takes more than a business plan to guarantee success. One other obvious realization from this period: Business cycles are becoming ever shorter, and investors need to stay on top of these cycles and invest accordingly.

✔ **Trust shattered and recovered — the Oughts:** In November 2001, Enron shocked the investment world when a $1 billion write-off for assets suddenly deemed worthless was revealed. No longer could we trust what had been sacred — the reporting of financial results. When Adelphia Communications and WorldCom went down for much the same reason, we suddenly realized a much bigger problem: Most individuals — and a large number of professional investors and analysts — never really understood financial statements. We had forgotten that, although assets might be fictitious and subjectively valued, liabilities are always real. Following the trail of how a company came up with its numbers was nearly impossible and, in the era of increased public visibility, where any earnings "miss" was sure to be punished, executives did what they could to make things look right.

Meanwhile, questions started to emerge about the brokerage and investment banking industries. The very companies who hired these analysts and published their advice had investment banking relationships with the companies they followed.

Corporate earnings declined substantially during the fallout from the bust. After overspending, especially on technology, businesses simply stopped spending. Consumers, shaken by the 9/11 terrorists attacks and job instability, also cut back. Growth expectations fell, and stocks fell to lows that many thought would never be seen.

But the Fed took quick action to stimulate the economy by dropping interest rates, and a renewed focus on business fundamentals and rationale squeezed the previous fluff out of the business environment. Corporate investing decisions once again became based on ROI (return on investment) and, perhaps helped along by Congress and new accounting rules, financial reporting regained footing in reality.

The result: Markets in 2003 started a four-year trend upward, culminating in new record highs set in the summer of 2007. But unlike the previous highs set in 2000, these were based on corporate profitability — and hence, value.

How value investing evolved

Before 2002, value investing had relatively low visibility. But after the bubble market popped (loudly), more investors realized that the value investing approach has earned strong returns for its faithful followers, often far beyond market averages for good stock pickers.

Value investing often deals in boring industries and requires patient examination of the nitty-gritty details of financial statements. Value analysis comes slowly, as does value investing *success*. If that sounds discouraging, read on to gain some inspiration from the most successful value investors, Benjamin Graham and Warren Buffett. Value investing got its beginnings and developed into a serious investing discipline based on their teachings and experiences.

The patriarch: Benjamin Graham

The beginnings of value investing as a documented discipline go back to Benjamin Graham. Graham was a self-made financial analyst and investor who proved very successful through some very trying investing times (as in the Great Depression). He founded Graham-Newman, a New York investment firm, and left a legacy for the rest of us when he wrote the original bibles of value investing: *Security Analysis* and *The Intelligent Investor*. Both are still in print today. (*The Intelligent Investor,* which is largely a repacking of *Security Analysis* for the individual investor, is much shorter and an easier read.) He also taught the art of value investing at Columbia University, and one of his students was Warren Buffett. To this day, Mr. Buffett and other Graham disciples pay the utmost respect to his pioneering leadership.

Book VII

Value Investing

Graham and his followers relied on the balance sheet for the first indication of a company's status and value. Essentially, the balance sheet is a snapshot of what the company *owns* and what it *owes*. If it owns more than it owes, the company scores points with the value investor. If what it owns is productive and has marketable value, the company scores *more* points. (Many value investors today still place emphasis on the balance sheet, while others, notably Buffett, take a closer look at the income and cash flow statements. The reality: You have to look at all three statements; they are inextricably linked. None of the three alone can tell the whole story. See Chapter 2 for all the details on financial reports.)

Graham believed that the balance sheet revealed the foundation, the value below which a company would never go. The balance sheet also reveals the *degree of safety* in the form of liquid assets and assets in excess of debt.

One of Graham's many lasting contributions is a simple, easy-to-use formula he devised to calculate a company's intrinsic value. Graham was trying to establish a stock's value based on earnings and earnings growth, while keeping an eye on bond yields available as an alternative. The formula: Take current earnings, apply a base P/E ratio (see Chapter 3 for details on the P/E ratio), add a growth factor if there is growth, and adjust according to current bond yield. The result is an intrinsic value that the stock can be expected to achieve in the real world if growth targets are met. The formula is shown in Chapter 4.

The master: Warren Buffett

Warren Buffett has turned his steady devotion to value investing principles into some $52 billion in net worth. He is the second wealthiest person in the world (depending on the price of Microsoft stock). Buffett is clearly the Michael Jordan or Tiger Woods of value investing. His on-court record cannot be touched, and it would be a disservice not to mention Buffett's off-court demeanor, where his candor, clairvoyance, and wit combine with his humble lifestyle to create a model for all of us to emulate.

Buffett displayed business acumen from an early age but dropped out of college before getting a degree. When Benjamin Graham's *Intelligent Investor* hit the shelves, Buffett applied to Columbia Business School, where he became one of Graham's students. The rest, as they say, is history.

Buffett later worked for Graham at the brokerage firm Graham-Newman, where he learned to manage investment portfolios and use insurance company assets as an effective investing vehicle. From these beginnings Buffett started his own investment fund (with contributed capital from neighbors, relatives, coworkers, and the like) and later built the Taj Mahal of investment companies, Berkshire Hathaway.

Berkshire Hathaway

Buffett first spied Berkshire, a faltering Massachusetts textile company, in 1962. He saw potential value in a very depressed stock and began buying shares cheap for his partnership. Buffett continued to accumulate shares until the partnership owned 49 percent of the company by 1965. He effectively controlled the company.

Originally, Buffett planned to right some of the wrongs and capture quick gains by selling or merging the company. But he saw a tempting opportunity to use Berkshire as an investment conduit to build worth by buying other businesses.

When Buffett distributed the partnership in 1969, he offered a choice of cash or Berkshire shares as part of the distribution. If you had 200 shares, you would have received about $8,400. For his portion, Buffett took shares. He offered to buy the shares of other partners for himself. A small group of now-wealthy folks made the choice to stick with Buffett, and many of them still make the annual pilgrimage to Omaha to enjoy those juicy steaks and count their blessings. Why? Those shares, worth $42 apiece then, are worth about $135,000 apiece in late 2007. The 200-share investment would be worth $27 *million* today!

Berkshire is now the world's largest investing pool. The Berkshire formula is this:

✔ Employ cash flows from businesses owned within the holding company.

✔ Buy stocks and bonds in the open market.

✔ Use the cash flow to buy businesses outright — preferably cash rich and cash generating — to build the investment pool and increase book value.

✔ Acquire solid insurance companies to provide cash flow and further build investing float and to insulate from downturns.

Gradually, Buffett shifted his emphasis from small, opportunistic, turnaround situations to longer-term large cap investments and even acquired whole companies when the numbers were right. He did this with a clear eye on tapping the growth potential of the major companies and major brands that are abundant in American life. Berkshire put together a world-class portfolio of high visibility blue chip growth stocks, including such household names as Coca-Cola, Gillette, American Express, and Wells Fargo.

Intrinsic value on the balance sheet, solid earnings with at least some growth and growth potential, and solid value in the franchise are what Buffett looked for in all his investments. And always — repeat, *always* — at a good price. Berkshire Hathaway acquired 200 *million* shares of Coke in the mid-1980s at around $6 to $6.50 per share (split adjusted). Coke generally sells at over $50 today. The Berkshire before-tax profit is in the $10 *billion* range.

Book VII

Value Investing

Shares? Why not the whole company?

Acquiring shares certainly works over time and is what we ordinary value investors should be focused on. But Berkshire went beyond this strategy — way beyond — to buy whole companies for its portfolio. Why? Two reasons, mainly. If you own the whole company you're entitled to its cash and cash flow and can reinvest it as you wish. You don't have to compete with other shareholders, and management and reporting relationships are simpler.

So Berkshire Hathaway has made many "whole enchilada" investments. The insurance group has grown substantially and is anchored by consumer favorite GEICO (originally bought by Ben Graham in the 1950s), and by General Re in the lucrative reinsurance (wholesale insurance) market. The companies play in different insurance segments and combined to produce almost $100 billion in revenue in 2006, with $11 billion in net profits and $50 billion in *float* — cash taken in but not paid out on claims and used for investments.

The manufacturing, retail, and service group of Berkshire Hathaway now consists of some 70 companies, large and small, all successful in their own arena. What do all Berkshire Hathaway companies have in common?

✔ They are profitable, safe, and solid.

✔ They are easy to understand with simple business models.

✔ They produce plenty of cash flow to reinvest.

✔ They are unique businesses with strong market positions and franchises.

✔ They have solid, trustworthy management.

✔ They were bought at reasonable prices.

We ordinary value investors can't assemble this kind of portfolio, but we can learn from what makes Berkshire Hathaway and its master tick. That's ground to be covered in the rest of this book.

Today: The world is flat, and other trends

In the past six decades, the investment style of the day has shifted from value to growth to outright speculation, back to value, and maybe back to growth (although I don't separate growth and value to the extent that many market experts do). It's worth noting other current business and investing trends:

✔ **Globalization:** Businesses are increasing global market reach into international economies and are increasing "supply" reach in sourcing goods and services at the lowest possible prices. Value investors need to appraise whether a business is getting the most out of these trends, taking advantage of available import and export opportunities.

- ✔ **Shorter business cycles:** It took the railroad industry 70 years to start, prosper, and begin its decline. It took the Internet industry about seven years to do the same. The point: Business changes come much faster, and what you invest in today may not even be around in ten years. You must stay on top of business and technology trends.

- ✔ **The Information Age:** It's here, and there's no going back. The success of a business often depends on its use of information systems and technology; in fact, in many businesses, it's a key competitive advantage that forms a moat or barrier to entry for others. But technology leadership can be notoriously hard to assess.

- ✔ **Volatility:** Exacerbated by the three factors just mentioned, market volatility seems to be here to stay. Markets will rise and fall in 5 or 10 percent increments in a given month, with no real change in business value to support the change. Investors must, more than ever, be patient and try to separate real business change from market change. And they will learn to use the dips to find value.

A Short Math Primer

Value investing is inherently analytical and numbers-based, and to become fluent in the value investing thought process, it's important to grasp a few key math principles. The following four lessons bubble up to the top as the most important; other principles and computational shortcuts can be found in *Value Investing For Dummies,* 2nd Edition.

Book VII

Value Investing

Lesson 1: Time value of money

A dollar today isn't worth the same amount as a dollar yesterday, nor is it worth the same amount as a dollar tomorrow. Invested money appreciates with time.

An investment that has a present value of $10 will (we hope) grow over time, so its future value will include the initial $10 plus all returns generated. Invested money grows and compounds. There is growth on the original investment, plus return and growth on returns already earned. A snowball rolling downhill is a good analogy: As the ball gets bigger, it picks up ever-larger amounts of snow. How much? Compounding formulas, which are driven by rate of return and the amount of time, supply the answer.

Suppose that someone promises to pay you $10 five years from now. Are you $10 wealthier? No. To have $10 in the future, you need to put only some fraction of that $10 in the bank today. The exact fraction depends on the same factors that drive future value: rate of return and time. At 10 percent, you would need to deposit only $6.21 today to have $10 five years from now. Same formula, but this time, the approach is from the opposite direction. Instead of asking, "What is my $10 worth in five years?" you ask, "What would I need today to have $10 in five years?"

The magic compounding formula

The fundamental time-value-of-money, or *compounding,* formula provides an indispensable foundation for value investors. A word of advice: It's just as important to understand the formula, the dynamics, and the factors that drive or have the most influence on the result as it is to memorize the formula to do lots of math problems. Furthermore, just as it takes more than garlic to cook, you need a lot more than this formula to select stocks and be successful Here's the formula:

$$FV = PV \times (1 + i)^n$$

where . . .

FV is future value

PV is present value

i is the interest rate, or rate of return

n is the number of years invested

Taking apart the formula: The future value is a function of the present value, expanded or compounded by the interest rate over time. To calculate a return for one year, simply take PV and multiply by 1 (to preserve the original value) plus *i* (to increment by the interest rate or rate of return). The result is future value.

To calculate the return for more than one year, it gets more interesting. Multiply PV by $(1 + i)$ factored by the number of years, so 5 years is $(PV) \times (1 + i) \times (1 + i) \times (1 + i) \times (1 + i) \times (1 + i)$. Each $(1 + i)$ indicates another year of *compounding* interest. The FV of $10 invested at 10 percent over 5 years is

$$FV = \$10 \times (1 + .10)^5$$

or

$$\$10 \times (1.61), \text{ or } \$16.10$$

Fine, we can calculate future value. But what about present value? What if you want to figure out what interest rate would give you $16.10 on a $10 investment if held for five years? In other words, what if you want to work backwards? You can transpose the formula algebraically to calculate PV, *i,* and even *n:*

1) $PV = FV \div (1 + i)^n$

2) $i = [(FV \div PV)^{(1/n)}] - 1$ or the nth *root* of (FV/PV)

3) **n** is trickier — it involves logarithms!

The power of i and n

The nature of the $(1 + i)^n$ expression in our formula produces a fascinating result. If i is small, no matter how large the n, the end result doesn't grow much. Likewise, if n is small, it doesn't so much matter what the i is.

The power of compounding assumes its full glory (and your investments reach their full girth) as i and n get larger. The *and* is important! Value investors look for a few more i points of return *and* to hold the productive investment for as many n years as possible.

Because n is an exponent, it exerts the greatest power and influence on your investing portfolio. Time is an investor's best friend. As Warren Buffett says, "Time is the friend of the good business, and the enemy of the poor one." No wonder value investors tend to be long-term investors! Upshot: Find the best possible i and then let n happen.

Lesson 2: Return rates done right

Book VII

Value Investing

Just what is the rate of return on an investment? It depends on how it's calculated. Say that you have a friend who brags about buying a house for $150,000 and selling it ten years later for $600,000. She may call that a 300 percent return: an average of 30 percent per year. On the surface, that's correct.

But when you evaluate the home purchase as an investment (compared to other investments), you must include the compounding effect to have an accurate, apples-to-apples comparison. If that $150,000 were invested ten years ago in such a way as to allow returns to compound, what rate of return would have produced $600,000?

The compounded rate of return is sometimes called the *geometric* rate of return. It stands in contrast to the straight average approach of simply dividing the total return by the number of years (as in 300 percent ÷ 10 equals 30 percent annually). So, how do you calculate true compounded, or geometric, rates of return? There is a formula:

Compounded rate of return = $[(\text{Ending value/Beginning value})^{(1/n)}] - 1$

where **n** equals the number of years.

In the example, $600,000/$150,000 is 4. Take 4 to the $\frac{1}{10}$th power (use your calculator) and get 1.149. Subtract 1, and get 14.9 percent. Obviously, your friend's home purchase was still lucrative, but 14.9 percent return doesn't make headlines the way 30 percent would.

Lesson 3: How buying cheap really pays

What investor hasn't heard the advice "buy low and sell high"? The principle behind this cliché is so obvious that one can hardly write about it. But in the irrationally exuberant markets of 1999 and 2000, this old standard gradually gave way to "buy high, sell higher." Traders (and novice investors experiencing the markets for the first time) bought stocks because they were going up, defying value investing logic.

What's the problem? The higher a price you pay for a stock, the *less likely* it is to achieve a high rate of return. Suppose that a stock has an intrinsic value of $75. If you pay $100 for it, you're essentially betting that something good will happen to dramatically increase intrinsic value — or that some greater fool is out there to pay $110.

But suppose that you were to buy the same stock at $50 as a *value play,* meaning that you think it's undervalued. The chance for a 50 percent return — reverting to intrinsic value — is much higher than with the at-value or overvalued $100 stock.

Keep your i on the ball

Value investors always look for the opportunity to achieve superior *i*. You achieve superior *i* by buying a stock with good fundamentals, *including* growth. So you get the growth rate — perhaps 6 percent, maybe 8 percent, or even 10 percent. But as a bonus, you also get the return to intrinsic value, which can increase returns substantially. The lower the price paid, the higher the likelihood of above-average returns. This idea comes straight from the teachings of Ben Graham and the practice of Warren Buffett.

How much does buying cheap help?

Take a look at Table 1-1. Note how long-term profits jump as the rate of return grows beyond the market average and time has an opportunity to work its magic. An investor consistently beating the market by 2 percent would achieve 20 percent greater return in 10 years ($3,106/$2,594), 43 percent in 20 years, and 72 percent in 30 years. An investor beating the market by 6 percent would get 70 percent more in 10 years, 189 percent in 20 years, and 392 percent, or almost 5 times as much profitable return, in 30 years.

Table 1-1	Compounded Effects of Incremental Annual Returns, $1,000 Invested							
	1 Year	**2 Years**	**5 Years**	**10 Years**	**15 Years**	**20 Years**	**30 Years**	**40 Years**
Market return 10%	$1,100	$1,210	$1,611	$2,594	$4,177	$6,727	$17,449	$45,259
Beat the market by 2%	1,120	1,254	1,762	3,106	5,474	9,646	29,960	93,051
Beat by 4%	1,140	1,300	1,925	3,707	7,138	13,743	50,950	188,884
Beat by 6%	1,160	1,346	2,100	4,411	9,266	19,461	85,850	378,721
Beat by 8%	1,180	1,392	2,288	5,234	11,974	27,393	143,371	750,378
Beat by 10%	1,200	1,440	2,488	6,192	15,407	38,338	237,376	1,469,772

Book VII

Value Investing

Lesson 4: Beware of large numbers

In investing, like life, some numbers are too good to be true and can't go on forever. Say a high-tech company brags in each report of a continuous 30 percent growth in sales and profits. The stock is priced at a lofty 60 times earnings because it's the norm for stocks in that industry to have price-earnings-to-growth (PEG) ratios of 2 (that is, P/E can be twice the growth rate). So what's the problem? In a word, *sustainability*.

Suppose that your company has $100 million in sales today. To achieve a 30 percent growth rate, it has to achieve $130 million in sales next year. To maintain this rate, what does the company have to achieve in the second year? That would be $169 million in sales. What about in ten years?

You see the formula coming together. $FV = PV \times (1 + i)^{(n-1)}$. (It's [n-1] because we're talking about growth *after* the first year.) Only this time you don't calculate the future value of an investment. You calculate the future value of sales required to sustain a 30 percent growth bragging right. So for our example,

Future sales in 10 years = $100M \times (1 + 0.30)^9$

Or $1.06 *billion*

In 20 years, that becomes $14.6 *billion,* with an average incremental growth of $764 *million* annually and about $4.4 billion in the twentieth year.

If you're the sales manager assigned the glorious task of meeting shareholder expectations for growth, where can you find the incremental sales? Your company has conquered the world, but Earth is a small planet. Extraterrestrial markets are still pre-emergent. So what happens? Growth rates likely start to decline. Maintaining the growth rate requires greater and greater chunks of incremental dollars, which becomes increasingly difficult as markets become saturated.

Smart value investors recognize the increasing difficulty in maintaining high growth rates, so they project lower rates in years further out.

Over the years, there has been a noticeable trend toward diminished growth when a company hits the $20 billion, and then again the $40 billion, sales mark. Companies with $20 billion in sales and 20 percent growth rates suddenly see growth rates fall off the table and must buy growth through potentially harmful acquisitions. Why? Markets become saturated, and large incremental sales in core businesses become more difficult to find. Additionally, these companies, because of their sheer size, have more difficulty organizing themselves to execute dynamic and aggressive sales plans. The lesson: Conservative or even zero growth estimates are in order, especially beyond the five- to ten-year horizon.

Chapter 2

A Value Investor's Guide to Financial Statements

* *

In This Chapter

▶ Covering financial statement basics

▶ Reading balance sheets, earnings statements, and cash flow statements

▶ Recognizing how accounting practices impact company valuation

* *

*V*alue investors need to know about the companies they invest in. Fortunately, an enormous amount of financial information about companies is available and easy to find. Unfortunately for most of us, it's *too much* information. The challenge is to acquire the right information about a company and then to convert it into actionable investing knowledge. This knowledge reveals the true character and dynamics of a business, the intrinsic value, the business performance characteristics that conclusively indicate whether you'd want to own a company — which in turn may suggest that it's a good place to invest.

Most of the information public companies disclose is too complex and detailed to make much sense to the common reader, who may be unaware of what's important and may even be misled. Although the situation was worse prior to the 2001 Enron and WorldCom scandals, it is still possible to present legally correct information in ways so that the true meaning isn't necessarily obvious to the investor.

The goal of this chapter is to provide a guide for separating the wheat from the chaff. It starts with a basic overview of financial statements and moves forward into the balance sheet, earnings statement, and cash flow statement. You'll see some tricks of the trade and creative accounting practices that can and do deceive the inattentive investor from time to time.

What a Value Investor Looks For

Investing combines art and science. Quantifiable and unquantifiable facts are put into the pot, and the resulting stew is interpreted according to taste. The "science" part is using numbers, facts, and formulas to measure business value. The "art" part is taking all the facts and measurements together and weighing them according to intuition and experience to judge a most likely outcome or set of outcomes.

Facts and more facts

All value investors need facts about a company's financial and operating performance. These facts provide the foundation for value analysis and are available from the company itself as financial statements or from one of many information sources that repackage company-provided data for investor use:

- ✔ **Financial results:** Financial statements provide a picture of company assets, liabilities, earnings, and growth. The *balance sheet* presents a snapshot of assets, liabilities, and net worth. The *income statement* shows revenues, expenses, and earnings for a defined period of time. The *statement of cash flows* follows the income statement, showing where cash is obtained and used in the business. Each of these documents is examined in detail in later sections of this chapter.

- ✔ **Financial trends:** It is helpful to capture and measure change as it occurs over time. Good trend data, and especially good trend analysis, is hard to come by. Many financial sources, including company reports, show only the past two, maybe three years of performance. Not bad, but seeing where a company has been for the last five, ten, or more years is really helpful. For example, if profits or profit margins have grown steadily over the last three years, that's nice to know. But it says more if that trend is solid over the past ten or more years.

- ✔ **Ratios:** From raw financial data, the value investor can construct *ratios* — relationships between facts that offer clues to financial safety, quality, profitability, and efficiency, thus providing a clearer picture of company value. We explain more about ratios in Chapter 3.

- ✔ **Percentages:** Like ratios, percentages relate facts to other facts and help paint a clearer picture of company performance and normalize data for comparison. Examples include return on equity (ROE), return on assets (ROA), and gross and net profit margin. ROE, ROA, and margins are explored in depth in Chapter 4.

✔ **Marketplace facts:** Financial facts represent past business results produced by a business, while marketplace facts can often be a leading indicator of future financial results. So it's important to understand metrics like market share, customer base, or unit sales growth wherever possible. Unfortunately, companies aren't required to report such facts and often choose not to do so for competitive reasons. You have to rely on what a company does disclose and on market analysis done by third parties.

✔ **Operating facts:** Certain kinds of operational facts or metrics can also be used as a measure of comparing companies or to support financial analysis. It's interesting to know the number of employees, stores, plants, or square feet as measures of size of operations. From there, you can determine *productivity* or *efficiency* — how much revenue, profit, and so on is produced per unit of operational activity. Hence, some people call these *unit* measures.

Sources of facts

Seasoned investors find the right sources for the right information at the right time at the right cost, and use those sources consistently.

Annual and quarterly reports

Most U.S. companies are required by law to provide annual and quarterly financial summaries for their investors and the financial community. There are two kinds of annual reports. One is a consumer-friendly version with pictures and descriptions of the company business with the appropriate financial facts included, usually in the back half of the report. The other is the 10-K annual report, submitted according to guidelines set by the Securities and Exchange Commission (SEC). This report is more detailed overall, with more supporting financial facts and an analysis of the company business, including key marketing and operating facts. See the upcoming section "Dissecting the Annual Report" for more information.

Quarterly reports, also required, summarize the most recent business activity and major changes during the quarter. The 10-Q version has more detail and is cast to SEC standards.

Financial portals

Financial portals like Yahoo!Finance (`http://finance.yahoo.com`) assemble vast amounts of company and performance information, including business descriptions; financial summaries; news items; and some comparative analysis, performance analysis, and screening tools. Portals provide a great quick overview or update, usually with links to more detailed information.

Book VII

Value Investing

Broker sites

Most broker Web sites enable some investing analysis. The quality and ease of use of their tools varies, and in many cases you have to have an account to get the good stuff like professional analysis or stock screeners.

Research services

Dozens of companies are set up to provide data and analysis to investors; however, many aim at providing these products to professional investors, not you. Companies like S&P and Hoover's offer huge packages of investment information, but the issue is cost, which can run into the thousands.

At this point, Value Line (www.valueline.com) is the one research service aimed at individual investors providing a complete package of value-oriented facts and analysis. Value Line provides basic company facts but smartly narrows it to what's needed to appraise the business. The Value Line Investment Survey costs $598 per year for the printed version and $538 for the online version. There are smaller, more focused products available, too — for small cap stocks, convertible securities, and other more specialized analysis. Trial versions are available for a small charge. Many libraries and brokerage firms with physical offices still carry the printed *Value Line Investment Survey* on their shelves. You may want to try this path before committing your dollars.

The soft stuff

In addition to financial information, value investors want to get a sense of a company's management effectiveness and market position. To understand a company's products and markets, you can look at Web sites; advertising and marketing campaigns; the company's own description of its products; and what you see, hear, and experience on the street.

You can gauge management effectiveness by looking at a company's financials and financial ratios, previous marketplace and financial decisions, business execution, acquisitions and mergers, public statements, and other "track record" items. Many value investors look at management ownership of company stock as a signal of management commitment. *Market position* refers to a company's approach to the marketplace and the resulting success — or failure — of that approach. We take a closer look at these intangibles in Chapter 4.

Sources of soft stuff

The list of "soft stuff" sources is almost endless. Among the many sources are the following:

- **Financial and investing Web sites:** Financial portal Yahoo!Finance will point to information about a company posted in various corners of the Internet. MarketWatch (`www.marketwatch.com`) and TheStreet.com (`www.thestreet.com`) offer general news and journalistic commentary about companies across the board, while Morningstar (`www.morningstar.com`) and The Motley Fool (`www.fool.com`) provide more thorough analysis generally from a value perspective.

- **Business journals:** Standbys like *The Wall Street Journal* and *Business Week* still offer timely and high quality appraisal of companies, often with a value slant. Trouble is, they write about the companies they choose, not what you want to read about at a given moment. You'll find a few nuggets occasionally in *Kiplinger's, Smart Money,* and *Money* magazines.

- **Trade journals:** Various journals and Web sites are available to follow everything from the restaurant industry to military electronics. Sometimes industry-specific Web sites can offer lots of comparative factual information to go with the soft stuff.

- **Company conference calls:** You can learn a lot about the character of management and the markets a company operates in by listening to investor conference calls, usually held at the time of quarterly earnings releases.

- **On the street:** Particularly with consumer-focused companies, you can learn a lot about how a company markets its products, how well they are selling, and even how employees feel about the company and its business by simply watching it do business.

Book VII

**Value
Investing**

Dissecting Financial Statements

A company's financial reports serve a critical function: to reflect the economic reality of a company and its business.

Accounting and accountants are supposed to project a fair, unbiased view of company performance. Accountants build financial reports according to accepted practices in the field, which dictate such principles as substance over form, conservatism, and materiality. But despite (and maybe because of) the fact that no fewer than three governing bodies decree accounting and reporting practices, a degree of latitude and flexibility exists in how reporting is actually done. This flexibility exists mostly in the valuation of assets and the determination of revenue and cost. We cover these issues in the following sections.

Value investors need to be smart about what and how much to question in a financial report. The smart value investor knows what to look for in a statement and what levers a company's management can throw to convey a certain image. It's okay to be a skeptic, but it's probably not productive to dispute every figure in the report. As with so much else in life, focus on what's important.

Poring over the Annual Report

Most companies still publish fancy, glossy annual reports. They contain basic financial information, but beyond that, they've become more of a marketing brochure. Value investors are better served by looking at what's known as a *Form 10-K* annual report, which is the SEC's required version of the document. The 10-K is a longer, harder read, but it provides much more in-depth financial data, product and market data, and management discussion of the financials than does the standard annual report. The patience required is rewarded by a more in-depth understanding of the company. The best way to get 10-Ks reliably and quickly is to go to a company's "investor relations" Web site, but the SEC also has a Web site to make the required filings public: Electronic Data Gathering And Reporting (EDGAR). EDGAR Online can be found at `http://sec.gov/edgar.shtml`.

Most annual reports contain the elements that follow. From one company to the next, these elements won't look the same, be the same size, be in the same order, or contain the same information. But these pieces will likely be present in some form.

Highlights

The highlights section is usually a one-page graphic summary of significant financial results: sales, earnings, and a few productivity measures key to a company's industry. Four or five years of history are often included. Highlights are useful for a first glance, but there's usually more to the story.

Letter to shareholders

The letter to shareholders presents a chipper one- or two-page summary, usually from the CEO, describing the past year and the year ahead. Although some managers are frank in describing and confronting a company's difficulties, others are not. You may see a discussion of milestones and achievements without a lot of discussion of whether they were worthwhile. The letter may include something about new customers, new technologies, and employment practices. Investors look for clear language without panacean jargon or buzzwords, and many look for willingness to discuss bad stuff in these letters — a sign of management honesty and integrity.

Business summary

This objectively worded section covers the business, its products, markets, competition, and factors like seasonality, patents, and international exposure that may affect the business. That's usually followed by a summary of the management team, which is in turn followed by a fairly detailed discussion of potential risks to the business. The business summary section is one of the best ways for an investor to gain business understanding.

Management's discussion and analysis

From there, we move into the financials themselves, which usually begin with a management discussion and analysis of the financials. The discussion covers specific financial statement components, including sales, costs, expenses, assets, liabilities, liquidity, and perhaps market expansion risks.

Book VII

Value Investing

The statements

The financial statement section usually consumes the last half to two-thirds of an annual report. Several versions of consolidated financial data are presented. Financials invariably include a balance sheet, income statement, and statement of cash flows:

- ✔ The *balance sheet* captures a company's financial position at a point in time. It shows all assets, liabilities, and owners' equity, usually in clearly defined subsections. The balance sheet is often called a *statement of financial position* or *statement of financial condition*.

- ✔ The *income statement* (also called the *earnings statement*) captures a company's performance over an interval of time. Of interest here are the sales or revenues, cost of those sales, other expenses, and the difference between sales and costs — earnings. This statement is sometimes called the *statement of operations* or *statement of operating activity*.

✔ The *statement of cash flows* also captures company activity and performance over a time interval, but this time it's done in cash terms. As you see in the later section "Understanding the Earnings Statement," cash and accounting flows can be different. The difference is usually timing. Cash flows are just as the name implies — cash or checks coming in, cash or checks being paid out. Cash flows tell you a lot about company liquidity — which refers to the presence or absence of enough cash to operate and the quality of earnings — and whether the earnings are real or a result of accounting gimmicks.

Most reports also include a statement of shareholders' equity, a statement of working capital, or some other summary of changes in the financials.

Common size statements

In addition to normal financial statements, some annual reports provide a set of *common size* statements. Common size statements are standard financial reports with all information presented as percentages. Thus, cash or accounts receivable are presented as a percent of total assets, and the cost of goods sold and marketing expenses are presented as a percent of revenue. Common size statements are useful for comparing companies.

Notes

Ironically, the notes part of an annual report may take more room and contain more detail than the financial statements themselves. Notes can give a lot of important detail or "color" to support the statements.

Notes also show the accounting practice a company uses in preparing a statement. A company's description of depreciation methods, option accounting, pension funding, and the like can make a big difference in interpreting the statements. Notes also disclose one-time situations such as acquisitions, discontinued businesses, and asset write-downs — or changes in accounting methods.

Auditor's review

The auditor's review is normally a one-page boilerplate somewhere toward the back of the annual report. This element looks pretty much the same in every annual report. The purpose of the auditor's review is to provide concrete evidence of review and acceptance of a company's accounting and financial practices. What is important is identifying *exceptions.* The standard auditor's review is three paragraphs. If the words "qualified" or "adverse" creep into the third paragraph, or if there's a fourth paragraph, watch out.

Reading the Balance Sheet

A balance sheet is a listing of assets against the liabilities and equity that fund those assets, taken at a specific point in time. For investment and legal reporting purposes, these snapshots are generally taken at the end of each fiscal quarter and at fiscal year-end.

A core financial equation forms the heart of the balance sheet:

Assets = liabilities + owners' equity

A balance sheet must balance: For every asset dollar, there must be contributed dollars produced by borrowing (increased liabilities) or additional funding by the owners (owners' equity) to match.

The balance sheet can be a powerful indicator of business health. But keep in mind that it doesn't tell much about the future of the business or about future income. It tells you more about where the company has been and how well it did getting there. On a balance sheet, value investors and business analysts look for the following:

- ✔ The composition of assets, liabilities, and owners' equity (lots of inventory and little cash can be a bad sign)
- ✔ Trends (increasing debt and decreasing owner's equity — also bad)
- ✔ Quality (do stated values reflect actual values?)

Each of these examinations is done with an eye toward what the figure probably should be for a company in that line of business. A company like Starbucks, with frequent small cash sales, shouldn't have a large accounts receivable balance. A retailer should have sizeable inventories, but they shouldn't be out of line for the industry or category. A semiconductor manufacturer has a large capital equipment base but should depreciate it aggressively to account for technology change.

To determine whether balance sheet numbers are in line, most analysts apply specifically defined ratios to the numbers. Ratios serve to draw comparisons among companies and their industry. By doing so, they show whether performance is better or worse than industry peers. See Chapter 3 for a discussion of ratio analysis.

A swift kick in the asset

An *asset* is anything a company uses to conduct its business toward producing a profit. From an accounting standpoint, an asset must

- ✔ Have value toward producing a return for the business.
- ✔ Be in the company's control. (A leased airplane is still an asset even if it's not legally "owned" by the company.)
- ✔ Be recordable and have value. (Employees don't show up as a balance sheet asset, though they're frequently referred to as assets by their CEOs.)

Most companies classify assets as current or noncurrent:

- ✔ **Current assets:** Current assets are short-term items generally held for a year or a business cycle. Think of current assets (especially cash) as the lifeblood of the business flowing to and from customers, to and from suppliers, and around to the different locations in the business operation to produce the greatest possible business and customer benefit. Current assets are managed by the business pretty much on a daily basis and normally include things like cash and cash equivalents, accounts receivable, and inventory.
- ✔ **Noncurrent assets:** These include longer-term fixed assets and a catch-all of other types of assets not normally vital to day-to-day operations.

The following sections explore these different assets in more detail.

To assign value to assets, look at three defining characteristics of any asset: size, trend, and quality. Table 2-1 is useful as a simple reference to convert reported asset values to liquidating value, a conservative base for intrinsic valuation. Professionals may use evolved versions, but this table is still a handy tool.

Table 2-1	Valuing Balance Sheet Assets	
Type of Asset	*% Range of Liquidating Value to Book Value*	*Comments*
Cash, cash equivalents	100%	More is better. Watch out for the post-IPO "stash."
Accounts receivable	75 to 95%	Look at write-offs.
Inventory	50 to 75%	Less for businesses with high obsolescence exposure. Look at write-offs.

Type of Asset	% Range of Liquidating Value to Book Value	Comments
Fixed assets	1 to 50%	Depends on what kind of asset and where it is. Watch for obsolescence.
Intangibles	1 to 90%	Usually lower for acquisitions, higher for patents and trademarks. Fast depreciation is better.

Cash and cash equivalents

For most businesses, cash is the best type of asset to have. There's no question about its value: Cash is cash! Cash equivalents, which are short-term marketable securities with little to no price risk, can be converted to cash at a moment's notice and are, for balance sheet purposes, essentially cash.

Value investors like cash. Cash is security and forms the strongest part of the safety net that value investors seek. Value investors question a cash balance only if it appears excessive against the needs of the business. If a value investor sees an excess in cash, she'd be likely to ask "why?" Could the company not put that cash to better work elsewhere? Why isn't it being returned to shareholders? Most companies don't retain that much cash, but if they do, it becomes a red flag.

Look at the total picture when you see a company report a high cash balance. There may be a good reason: Many companies have large cash balances for a while immediately following an initial public offering (IPO), for example.

Accounts receivable

Accounts receivable represent funds owed to the business, presumably for products delivered or services performed. As individuals, everyone likes to be owed money — until we're owed *too much* money. The same principle applies to businesses.

You should be aware of situations in which companies aren't collecting on their bills or are using accounts receivable to create credit incentives for otherwise questionable customers to buy their product. To assign value to accounts receivable, pay attention to the following:

> ✔ **The size of accounts receivable relative to sales and other assets:** Is a company extending itself too much to sustain or grow the business? Ratios (see Chapter 3) help measure this, and industry comparisons and common sense dictate the answer.

Book VII

Value Investing

✓ **Trend:** Is the company continuously owed more and more, with potentially greater and greater exposure to nonpayment? Look at historical accounts receivable and compare them to sales.

✓ **Quality of accounts receivable:** Typically, most companies collect on more than 95 percent of their accounts receivable balances, and thus they're almost as good as cash. But if accounts receivable balances grow, and particularly if large reserves show up on the income statement ("allowance for doubtful accounts" or similar), this is a red flare not to be missed.

Accounts receivable are driven by the type of business that a company operates in. A small-sale retailer like Starbucks or a grocer operates mostly on cash. Most companies that sell directly to consumers have little to no accounts receivable. Contrast this to companies that sell to other companies or to distributors or retailers in the supply food chain, where most of the business is done *on account,* meaning that goods or services are delivered and invoices are then cut and sent. The billing process creates an account receivable, which goes away only when the customer pays the bill. So suppliers to other businesses or through distribution and sales channels often have significant accounts receivable.

Inventory

Inventory is all valued material procured by a business and resold, with or without value added, to a customer. *Retail inventory* consists of goods bought, warehoused, and sold through stores. *Manufacturing inventory* consists of raw material, work in process, and finished goods inventory awaiting shipment. Companies live and die by their ability to effectively manage inventory.

For most companies, the key to successfully managing inventory is to match it as closely as possible to sales. The faster that procured inventory can be processed and sold, the better. More sales are generated per dollar tied up in inventory. Dollars tied up in inventory cost money because they could be invested elsewhere in the business.

Measuring inventory

Measuring the size of inventory assets is often done by measuring turnover. *Turnover* is simply annual sales divided by the dollar amount of the asset on the books. If sales are $500 million a year and inventory on the books is $100 million, inventory turnover is five times a year. Another way to look at it: The average item of inventory is on the books for about 2.4 months (12 ÷ 5). The greater the turnover, the more efficient the utilization of that asset. Turnover ratios naturally vary by industry. For example, Starbucks turns over inventory much faster than Boeing.

Inventory carries with it a significant risk of obsolescence. Changes in demand patterns, technology, or the nature of the product itself can cause valued inventory to rapidly lose value.

Valuing inventory

Investors should keep an eye on inventory balances for economic value and efficiency of use. Look at the size of the asset in an absolute sense and relative to the size and sales of the business. Look for trends, favorable and unfavorable, in inventory balances and ratios. Look at competitors and industry standards. Where possible, look at inventory quality and past track record for inventory obsolescence and resulting write-offs. And then be conservative. It often makes sense to assign a value of 50 to 75 percent, sometimes less, to inventory values appearing on a balance sheet.

Deferred taxes and other current assets

"Deferred taxes" is an item that appears frequently on balance sheets and results from timing differences between financial reporting and tax reporting requirements. It is essentially estimated taxes paid before a tax liability is actually determined. For the most part, you shouldn't worry about these items; seldom do they comprise more than 5 percent of stated assets.

Bolted to the floor: Fixed assets

The balance sheet entry called "property, plant, and equipment" (PP&E) refers to fixed assets — land, buildings, machinery, fixtures, office technology, and similar items owned by the firm for productive use. Depending on the industry, this item may have a different name. Retail stores, for example, don't have plants but may have distribution centers.

The key to understanding PP&E value is to understand *depreciation,* the amount subtracted each year by accountants from an asset purchase price for normal wear and tear and technological obsolescence. Depreciation can affect underlying asset values substantially.

To appropriately value fixed assets, you need to be familiar with the two basic types of depreciation: In *straight-line depreciation* an equal amount of asset value is expensed each year until the asset value reaches zero. In *accelerated depreciation* accountants expense proportionately more in the early years of asset life. Further changing the picture can be a company's decision to value at lower of cost or market value. As for other accounts, the accounting method is disclosed in the statements under the notes entry.

The choice of depreciation methods is important. Accelerated depreciation results in the most conservative PP&E asset valuations. It also results in the most conservative view of earnings and allows more room for future net earnings growth, because you can assume that a greater portion of depreciation is behind you. But some companies may deliberately prop up current earnings by employing straight-line methods. Watch for companies changing over to straight-line from accelerated methods.

Understanding the nature of a corporation's PP&E and its depreciation methods will help you assess the value of this account. Generally, value investors assign very conservative values to PP&E (unless a lot of land is involved): 50 percent or less.

Depreciation is the leading difference between stated earnings and cash flows and can mean the difference between survival and failure for a company recording net income losses. Cash flow, unburdened by depreciation, may still be positive. But look out. Cash consumed to keep a losing business afloat may not be available the next time a key piece of equipment needs to be replaced. Reporting methods that downplay depreciation or ignore it altogether, such as pro forma or EBITDA reporting, indicate trouble. For more on this issue, see "The Games Companies Play" later in this chapter.

Investments: Companies are investors, too

Besides more liquid marketable securities, many companies commit surplus cash to more substantial long-term investments. These investments can serve many purposes: to achieve returns as any other investor would, to participate in the growth of a related or unrelated industry, or to eventually obtain control of the company. Favorable tax treatment of dividends and gains makes investing in other companies still more attractive.

There are many ways to value investments, boiling down basically to historical cost or market valuation (sometimes referred to as *mark-to-market* valuation). Market valuation is obviously better. Investment value is disclosed in the 10-K, but you need to read carefully to find the information. Watch out for declining fair values and particularly for large *gross unrealized losses* — future write-offs and asset value impairment loom large.

Gauge the size of investments on the balance sheet, look for detail, and understand management's intent in making the investments.

Intangibles: Soft assets

Intangibles, also called "soft" assets, don't have a physical presence but are critical in acquiring and maintaining sales and producing a competitive edge. Soft assets include patents, copyrights, franchises, brand names, and trademarks. Also included is the all-encompassing "goodwill" often acquired by acquiring other companies. Placing a financial value on these ethereal marketing assets is difficult, but accountants must and do. If there is an historical cost, accountants may carry the intangible at that cost. This is often the case with goodwill from company acquisitions.

The key to assessing intangible assets is to understand (1) their carrying value and (2) their composition. Most important, you must understand the source of goodwill — from acquisitions, from patents, or what?

Intangibles are subject to a great deal of discretion in their accounting, and their sources and form can be numerous and highly variable from one company to the next. Especially problematic are companies with aggressive acquisition strategies. These can be a value investor's nightmare, particularly where large amounts of goodwill and other intangibles are involved. Cast a skeptical eye on large goodwill accounts in particular.

While the classical school of value investing considered intangibles fluff and suggested deducting intangibles from company valuation altogether, today, intellectual capital and brand equity are part of a company's value and cannot simply be ignored. In fact, for some companies, these intangibles may represent their greatest value. What is the value of the Coca-Cola Company without the Coke recipe and brand name? Or the value of Microsoft without its lock on PC operating systems? Such brands and locks often ultimately produce the best profit streams and best value.

Does the company owe money?

Liabilities are fairly straightforward: If you owe, you owe. Although different things can be done to state asset values differently, the same doesn't happen with liabilities. The effect of liabilities on a company's intrinsic value is straightforward.

Like assets, liabilities come in two basic flavors: current and long-term. Current liabilities are liabilities for which payment is due normally in less than a year. Long-term liabilities are long-term debts.

Excessive use of debt signals potential danger if things don't turn out the way a company expects them to. Value investors don't like surprises, and a company with uncertain prospects and a lot of debt may not make it on to their list. Industry standards and common sense apply to debt-to-equity ratios.

Payables: Current liabilities

Almost every corporation has *payables,* money owed to others for products purchased or services rendered. The liability is created when the service or product arrives; a cash payment follows to discharge the liability. Nearly all companies maintain a regular balance of current accounts payable, interest payable, and the like. If payment is received in advance, as with a deposit, the unearned portion is tracked as a liability. Sometimes *contingent liabilities* may be recorded, as in warranty claims expected to be paid but not yet actualized.

Value investors don't need to take much note of current liabilities other than perhaps to spot large changes or trends. Investors should also realize that current liabilities aren't necessarily a bad thing and can result in higher effective returns on ownership capital with relatively low cost and risk.

Book VII

Value Investing

Long-term liabilities

Long-term corporate liabilities represent contracted commitments to pay back a sum of money over time with interest. As with short-term liabilities, you don't need to look too closely at the quality of these long-term liabilities, or even the amount if reasonable by previous company or industry standards. Trends can be important, however. Increased reliance on long-term debt may be a sign of trouble. The company may not be making ends meet and may be having trouble raising capital from existing or potential owners — never a good sign. In addition, a company constantly changing, restructuring, or otherwise tinkering with long-term debt may be sending tacit trouble signals. The company may be seeking concessions from lenders behind the scenes. In any event, attention paid to this kind of activity diverts attention from the core business, which is not a good thing and a warning flag for value investors.

Understanding the Earnings Statement

Earnings are *the* driving force and macro indicator of a company's success. Used by investors of all kinds, earnings statements are among the most widely examined of company publications. Investors look at the top line (revenue or sales) and the bottom line. For value investors, earnings statements are indispensable, and most will take a much more in-depth look at the underlying numbers, trends, and history. The following list highlights important attributes to look for in an earnings statement:

- **Growth:** The long-term growth of a stock price is driven by growth in the business. The value investor works to obtain a deep understanding of business growth, growth trends, and the quality of growth. Is reported growth based on internal core competencies? Or is it acquired or speculative growth based on unproven ventures? The value investor assesses growth and growth patterns, judges the validity of growth reported, and attempts to project the future.

- **Consistency:** Long-term growth should be sustainable and consistent. Look for sustained growth across business cycles. Long, consistent, successful earnings track records get the A grades. A big pop in earnings one year followed by malaise for the next two does not paint a pretty picture. Consistency in sales and sales growth, profit margins and margin growth, operating expense and expense trends is highly prized. The less consistency, the more difficult to predict the future five or ten years and beyond, and the less attractive a company looks to value investors.

- **Comparative components and trends:** Value investors look at individual lines in the earnings statement, not just the bottom line. Improving gross margins — especially sustained improvement — signals strong business improvement: Costs are under control, and the company is improving its market position, for example. Value investors also constantly compare companies in like industries. Gross margins of competing computer manufacturers, for instance, tell a lot about who has the best market position, production and delivery process, and business model.

As you examine earnings statements, remember that they're not always broken down the same way. Although the bottom line is the bottom line, the intermediate steps may be different. One company's operating earnings may include marketing costs, while another's may not. In addition, two companies that appear (and even are classified) in the same industry may have differences large enough to raise caution. Commercial and industrial suppliers, such as Honeywell, have consumer divisions, for example, while consumer businesses, such as Procter & Gamble, have industrial divisions. The upshot: You must understand businesses before comparing them.

The bottom line and other lines

You hear a lot about the *bottom line,* which refers to the net earnings or income after all expenses, taxes, and extraordinary items are factored in. The bottom line is the final net measure of all business activity.

Other important lines in the earnings statement reveal key factors and trends in the business. You'll see these lines or items in various forms on financial statements depending on the statement and sometimes the industry.

There are many ways to measure income. Each reveals an important layer of business performance, both for determining intrinsic value and also for comparing companies. Among them are

- ✔ **Gross profit:** This is simply the sales less the direct cost of producing the company's product or service. Direct cost includes labor, material, and expenses directly attributable to producing it. Gross profit, often called *gross margin,* is the purest indicator of business profitability. Value investors closely watch gross margin trends as an indicator of market dominance, price control, and future profitability.

- ✔ **Operating profit:** Operating profit, often referred to as *operating income,* is gross profit less *period expenses* — overhead or marketing costs not directly attributable to product production. Operating profit gives a more complete picture of how the business is performing on a day-to-day basis. Period expenses typically include selling, general, and administrative expenses (SG&A), and amortization. Typically excluded are financing costs, such as interest and taxes, as well as items deemed as extraordinary.

- ✔ **Net income:** This represents the net result of all revenues, expenses, interest, and taxes.

There are other supplemental earnings measures such as free cash flow, discussed later in this chapter. The following sections explore the key components of an earnings statement.

The top line

Sales or revenues make up the *top line* of any business. Sales and revenues represent accounting dollars generated for business products sold or services performed. (Remember, with accrual accounting it doesn't matter whether the company has been *paid* yet.) With "b-to-b" businesses or those selling into a distribution channel (a wholesaler or retailer), revenue recognition can be more complex.

Accounting revenue is normally recorded at the time of sale or service completion. But there are situations in which the delivery process isn't complete, and that may call revenue validity into question. If a distributor doesn't have to pay until a product is resold, or if the manufacturer is still required to perform significant services, such as configuration, installation, or even warranty work, a sale to a distributor or customer may be exaggerated if fully recorded as a sale. Similarly, sales to subsidiaries or affiliated companies shouldn't be considered sales. Sales for consideration other than money, such as advertising exposure, may also be suspect.

But for the most part, sales are sales. In many businesses, such as transportation or utilities, they may be called *revenues,* but it's the same thing. Occasionally you will see an allowance for returns broken out; if not, you can usually safely assume that they're included in the sales figure as a negative amount.

When comparing sales figures or projecting trends, compare apples to apples. If there is a significant acquisition, divestiture, or extraordinary change in the business, make sure to take it into account.

Cost of goods sold

Cost of goods sold, or CGS, is the cost of acquiring goods and raw material plus labor and direct overhead expended to add value for sale, and it's an important driver of business success. For all but a few companies with high intellectual property or service content, CGS is the largest piece of the revenue pie. CGS varies widely by industry and industry cost structure. For example, the physical CGS of Microsoft is tiny with respect to revenue, whereas a grocery store or discount retailer may see CGS in the 70 or 80 percent range. Apples-to-apples comparisons and especially trend analysis are critical to effective business appraisal.

Different accounting treatments can affect CGS. LIFO (last in, first out) and FIFO (first in, first out) are different ways of valuing balance sheet inventory and can affect CGS. Value investors should be careful to understand which accounting method is used before comparing companies and watch for changes in accounting methods that may shift reporting bias. (Note 1 in the financial statements usually clarifies accounting methods.) In a price-stable, low-inflation environment, the LIFO/FIFO thing becomes less important.

Gross margin

Gross margin, or *gross profit,* is simply the sales less the cost of goods sold. It is the basic economic output of the business before overhead, marketing, and financing costs enter the picture. Gross profit takes on added meaning when taken as a percentage. This percentage — and trends in the percentage — speaks volumes for the health and direction of the business.

Operating expenses

No matter the business, any company incurs *operating expenses* (also called *indirect costs*) — the costs of doing business that are not directly related to producing and selling individual units of product or service. Some call it *overhead,* but it goes a little beyond the traditional definition of overhead and into marketing, R&D, and other costs necessary to sustain the business in addition to directly producing products. Standard types of operating expenses are examined in the following sections.

Selling, general, and administrative (SG&A) costs

SG&A includes marketing and selling costs, including advertising; sales and sales forces; marketing and promotion campaigns; and a host of other administrative and corporate expenses such as travel, Web sites, office equipment, and so on. Many investors use SG&A as a barometer of management effectiveness — a solid management team keeps SG&A expenses in check. SG&A can mushroom into a vast slush fund and an internal corporate pork barrel that can easily get out of control. As with gross margin, looking at SG&A as a percentage is best.

Research and development

Manufacturing and technology companies in particular need to invest in future products. Because these investments occur long before product production, and because many of them never pan out into saleable products, companies are allowed to expense research and development (R&D) as a period expense. Appropriate levels of R&D expense vary widely by industry. For example, software companies incur very large R&D as a percent of sales, but insurers or retailers have small R&D percentages.

Because you won't know the detail of R&D expenditures, watch the trend and changes in R&D as a percent of sales. Increasing R&D percentages reflect an increasing cost of doing business and possibly ineffective R&D, while decreasing R&D as a percent may reflect sacrificing the future for the present. Neither is a good thing. Also note that companies without a significant R&D effort may not report it as a separate line. In some financial statements, it's called *product development,* or it may be bundled into some other expense line.

Depreciation

Depreciation can obviously affect inventory, as explained in the earlier section "A swift kick in the assets," but it can also have a net effect on property, plant, and equipment as an earnings statement item. Depreciation and amortization represent the accountant's assignment of the cost of a long-lived asset to specific business periods. *Depreciation* is used when referring to physical fixed assets, and *amortization* is used when referring to intangible assets. (Some oil and natural resource investors may run into the term *depletion:* a cost recovery for exhaustion of natural resource assets.)

Depreciation and amortization expenses are usually broken out on the earnings statement, but they may be buried in a consolidated SG&A or other operating expense line.

Impairments, investments, and other write-downs

When the value of an asset changes significantly in the eyes of management, a company can elect to take a write-down recognizing the change. The *write-down* shows up as a decrease in asset value on the balance sheet for the asset category involved and as a (usually) one-time expense somewhere on the earnings statement. The rules for when and how to take these write-downs are somewhat flexible. The good news is that write-downs are normally reported as a separate line and are well-documented in the notes.

Write-down behavior provides insight into management behavior and effectiveness as well as overall business consistency and should not be ignored. For value investors, knowing the detail or amount may not be as important as knowing the pattern. Are these write-downs really one-time adjustments, for example, or does the company continually overinvest in unproductive technology?

It's also critically important to understand write-offs and one-time charges when building intrinsic value models (more in Chapter 4). Many intrinsic value models base forward projections on the most recently reported net income numbers. Most financial portals and automated investment analysis tools simply take the latest year's earnings figure from a database. If that figure was significantly reduced (or enhanced) by extraordinary items, a large (and compounded!) error in the intrinsic value assessment can occur.

Goodwill

Goodwill assets are obtained by acquiring other companies. These goodwill assets arise when more is paid for an acquired company than it is worth in hard assets. Acquired goodwill assets often have real value — brand equity, customer base, and so forth — but more often than not, the amount booked exceeds this value, and goodwill is used as a plug-in figure to account properly for the purchase.

The treatment of goodwill has changed in recent years and become more uniform. The deal that accountants struck with the corporate world calls for allowing goodwill to remain on the books forever, but it subjects companies to an annual review for impairment of the fair value of those assets.

Like depreciation and impairments, goodwill amortizations are accounting phenomena and don't result in a cash transaction. Goodwill amortization affects earnings, not cash flow. Informative annual reports deconstruct impairment analysis for you and give estimates not only for current but also future asset impairment charges.

You can decide how you want to appraise goodwill, but conservative is usually best. Ben Graham was particularly leery of goodwill and usually removed it entirely from company valuation, regardless of company policy. Buffett and other contemporary value investors recognize the value of patents, copyrights, brand equity, customer base, and other intellectual property and allow it to stand in valuation, so long as it's not in excess and is accounted for realistically.

Book VII

Value Investing

Operating income

Operating income is simply sales less cost of goods sold, less operating expenses. Because it includes noncash amortizations, it is a fully loaded view of operating performance in the business. If you closely observe the effects of amortizations, special write-downs, and accounting changes, you can better understand operating income and operating income trends.

Interest and taxes

Companies invariably have some form of interest income or interest expense — usually both. Interest income comes primarily from cash and short-term investments held on the balance sheet, while interest expense comes from short- and long-term debt balances. Interest reporting is usually done as *net* interest — that is, by combining interest income and expense into a net figure.

Taxes are quite complicated, just as they are for individuals, and the details go beyond the scope of this book. There is normally an income tax provision recorded as a single line item on the earnings statement, consisting of federal, state, and local taxes put together.

You don't need to pay too much attention to these areas except where interest expenses are disproportionately high and growing. In most situations value investors treat taxes as a given, unless the company has recently been through tough times and has a lot of write-offs to carry forward. When that happens, taxes can be artificially low for a while; investors must take into account when they will return to a normal level.

Income from continuing operations

What results from netting out interest and taxes from operating income is *income from continuing operations.* This figure gives a good picture of company performance, not only from an operating but also a financial perspective. Income from continuing operations tells shareholders what their investments are returning after everyone, including Uncle Sam and his brethren, is paid. Income from continuing operations is a good indicator of total business performance, but be aware of truly extraordinary events driving expenses or income.

Extraordinaries

Extraordinary items are tied to unusual and nonrecurring events. *Unusual* events aren't related to typical activities of the business, at least going forward. *Nonrecurring* events aren't expected to occur again. Extraordinary items commonly result from business closures ("discontinued operations"); major restatements due to changes in accounting rules, debt restructurings, or other complex financial transactions; layoffs and other employee transactions; and so on. Extraordinary items generally *are not* supposed to include asset write-downs (such as receivables, inventory, or intangibles), foreign currency gains or losses, or divestitures.

Some companies interpret the accounting rules and guidelines more strictly than others, so watch for extraordinary expenses that aren't so extraordinary. If, for example, earnings are consistently a dollar a share each quarter with a consistent $4 year-end write-off each year, the true value generated by the business is closer to zero than four.

There you have it: Net income

Sales less CGS, less operating expenses, less interest and taxes, less or plus extraordinaries give you a company's net income, sometimes referred to as *income attributable to common shareholders* or some similar phrase. Net income represents the final net earnings result of the business on an accounting — not necessarily a cash — basis.

Net earnings are usually divided by the number of shares outstanding to arrive at *earnings per share* — the common barometer heard in nearly all financial reports. Most analysts and investors focus on *diluted* earnings per share, which figures in outstanding employee stock options and other equity grants beyond actual shares outstanding in the share markets.

Reading Cash Flow Statements

A business needs cash to operate. A business generating positive cash flow is much healthier than one bleeding cash and borrowing or taking cash from investors to stay afloat. But because of noncash items, earnings statements don't give a complete cash picture. So value investors use the statement of cash flows as a standard part of the financial statement package. (Note: Sometimes the statement of cash flows is called *sources and uses of funds* or something similar. Accountants use the terms "funds" and "cash" interchangeably.) The statement of cash flows tracks cash obtained in, or used for, three separate kinds of business activity: operations, investing, and financing.

You're probably wondering what the difference is between earnings and cash flow. The answer is that the realization of accounting earnings may occur at different times than the actual receipt of cash. The main differences arise from accrual accounting and from depreciation and other noncash amortizations and adjustments. A dollar earned today may not be collected until tomorrow, and a dollar earned today as cash may be diminished as earnings by a noncash amortization of an asset. Mainly, the difference is timing — although the time difference (especially with a long-lived fixed asset) can be years. To summarize:

- ✔ Earnings statements measure business activity as it occurs, regardless of cash flow, and include noncash amortization and other transactions.

- ✔ Cash flow statements specifically track the movement of cash in and out of the company. This cash flows into and out of the "cash and marketable securities" item on the balance sheet.

Cash flow from operations

Similar to operating income, cash flow from operations tells you what cash is generated from, or provided by, normal business operations, and what cash is consumed, or used in, the business. Cash flow information contains these figures:

- ✔ **Net income from continuing operations:** Calculating cash flow from operations starts with this number.

- ✔ **Adjustments for depreciation and amortization:** Depreciation and amortization are accounting, not cash, transactions. So here is where depreciation and amortization dollars are added back in — dollars that came out of accounting income but had no corresponding cash payment.

- ✔ **Changes in working capital items:** Working capital items include accounts receivable and inventory, and *changes* in these items either produce or consume cash. It takes a while to get used to the logic, but a positive number here means that the item *sourced* or *generated* cash; a negative item means that the item *used* cash. A negative figure for inventory, for example, means that the business used cash to buy more inventory. A positive figure means that inventory balances were reduced, freeing up cash for other uses. (The cash actually comes from selling the inventory — either to a customer or some other buyer.)

- ✔ **Total cash flow from operating activities:** This is a very important figure. Essentially, this is cash generated by ongoing day-to-day business activities. Negative operating cash flow is a dismal sign.

Cash flow from investing activities

The second section of the statement of cash flow shows, among other things, cash used for investments in the business, including capital expenditures for plants, equipment, and other longer-term product assets.

While cash flow from operations should be positive, cash flow from investing activities is often negative because growing companies need more physical investments — property, plant, and equipment (PP&E) — to sustain growth. It is possible (but not the norm) to generate positive cash flows in this part of the statement, either by selling PP&E or by selling investments owned by the company.

By comparing net cash flows from operations and net cash flows from investing activities, you can get a first glance at whether a business is productive and healthy. If positive cash flows from operations exceed negative cash flows from investing activities, the business produces more cash than it consumes. But don't jump to a favorable conclusion too quickly — you may be looking at an airline that's about to pay for five new jets in the next quarter. A surplus cash situation must be sustained to be meaningful.

Free cash flow

Earn income, pay for costs of doing business, and what's left over is yours to keep as an owner. What's left over is the free cash flow. Pretty simple. Free cash flow is a good indication of what a company really has left over after meeting obligations, and thus could theoretically return to shareholders. For that reason, free cash flow is sometimes called *owners' earnings*.

Cash flow from financing activities

Financing activities tell where a firm has obtained capital in the form of cash to fund the business. Proceeds from the sale of company shares or bonds (long-term debt) are a *source* of cash. If a company pays off a bond issue, pays a dividend, or buys back its own stock, that's a *use* of cash for financing.

A consistent positive cash flow from financing activities indicates excessive dependence on credit or equity markets. Typically, this figure oscillates between negative and positive. A big positive spike reflects a big bond issue or stock sale. In such a case, check to see if the resulting cash is used for investments in the business (probably okay) or to make up for a shortfall in operating cash flow (probably not okay). If the generated cash flows straight to the cash balance, you should wonder why a company is selling shares or debt just to increase cash, although often the reasons are difficult to know. Perhaps an acquisition?

Book VII

Value Investing

The Games Companies Play

Accounting rules, while improved in recent years, still allow enough flexibility to give companies latitude to manage their business and decide what to recognize, and when and how. Understanding company accounting and reporting policies — and conservative versus aggressive bias — has always been considered a good value investing practice.

This section explores some occasional accounting practices used to make business results look better. It's called *accounting stretch,* and as a value investor, you need to be aware of it. Sensitive stretch points occur in both revenue and expense portions of the earnings statement, as the following sections explain.

 The balance sheet is a snapshot in time that captures the cumulative effects of business activity over a period. This business activity is measured on earnings and cash flow statements. As such, the balance sheet reflects the *results* of accounting policy and any stretch that may have occurred — it isn't where stretch is initially applied.

Revenue stretch

There are two major sources of revenue recognition problems. The first involves timing, where revenues for long-term deals and contracts may be recognized prematurely. The second involves customer financing or price adjustments, where a customer receives an incentive or is otherwise enabled to buy a product but revenue is overstated by not recognizing the downside of such incentives.

Following are some of the ways companies can manipulate revenue and revenue timing:

- **Contractual revenues, forward sales, service fees:** Accounting principles state that revenue can be recognized for substantial performance of delivering a good or a service. Yet cases abound where companies, perhaps selling a three-year forward service agreement with a product, or perhaps an insurance policy, bundle downstream revenue into the original sale.

- **Channel stuffing:** Manufacturers who distribute through retail or other channels often fall to the temptation to sell as much as they can downstream into the next channel "tier." Computer suppliers may sell tons of equipment to their distributors, often to turn around and reverse the sale with a return or a credit for a price drop somewhere down the line.

Today, some companies don't recognize revenue until the product is *sold through* — that is, sold to an end customer. Others will recognize the revenue but with an appropriate reserve for returns. Look for companies that specifically state this practice in their financial statement notes. And avoid companies with large fiscal year-end revenue jumps matched by weak subsequent quarter performance — unless seasonal factors suggest the pattern is normal.

✔ **Related party revenue:** Some companies mishandle revenue from closely aligned third parties — or even from sales to subsidiaries or other "controlled" entities. Related party revenue is common in the tech industry or other businesses with strong partner relationships or lots of subsidiaries. Accounting and SEC rules are pretty clear about recognizing revenue only when a transaction is done at arms' length — that is, without being controlled in any way by the company recognizing the revenue.

✔ **Creating sales with financing:** An increasing number of companies have resorted to financing their customers as a way to win deals, win customers, and bolster revenues. Although this has been common in department store retailing for years through store credit cards, it takes on new meaning when, for example, billions are lent to single customers to buy telecommunications equipment. These sales may turn out not to be real — for example, if the recipient goes bankrupt. In some cases the sales may be real but are artificially brought forward, creating gaps in subsequent periods. Look carefully at financial statement notes for evidence of extensive financing programs, and also look at the running accounts receivable and notes receivable balances compared to sales.

How do you detect these issues? It isn't easy. Pay attention to revenue recognition policies (usually Note 1 of the statements) and unusual increases or bumps in sales, receivables, or allowances against receivables. Accounting clarifications and a stronger imperative toward cleaner reporting have diminished these revenue issues somewhat, but there is still plenty of latitude, and judging companies often becomes a matter of understanding their business and trusting their management.

✔ **Warranty costs:** Typically, a reserve for warranty should be set aside for every product shipped or service completed. But companies can change the amount set aside. This item is often invisible because most companies don't break out warranty costs in detail.

Book VII

Value Investing

Inventory valuation

How inventory is managed — whether LIFO (last in, first out) or FIFO (first in, first out) — impacts inventory valuation. LIFO typically represents the more conservative valuation, particularly in an inflationary environment because recognized costs are relatively higher. However, LIFO also results in relatively *lower* inventory valuations.

Value investors should understand inventory valuation policy, normally disclosed in Note 1, particularly where an accounting policy is changing or has been changed. If a company switches from LIFO to FIFO, watch out.

Expense stretch

Expenses, or indirect costs, are easier to stretch because there are more different kinds of them, and typically little detail is given on the consolidated statements. Fortunately, this area has received considerable scrutiny, especially options and amortization expenses, so it is less of an arena for abuse than in the past.

Options

Compensating employees with stock options became much more in vogue toward the end of the 20th century. Why? To recruit and retain better employees without consuming precious cash or diluting earnings. Investors got very upset about it because not only were companies inflating earnings by not recognizing option expenses, but many a corporate staffer was getting fantastically wealthy on the resulting awards.

For a long time, accounting rules required only disclosure — not incorporation into actual statements. So option grants and their theoretical expense were noted somewhere deep in the statements, but not in the results themselves. Finally in 2004, that changed: The Financial Accounting Standards Board (FASB) implemented a revised Statement 123, requiring expensing and prescribing a formula for valuing the options. So now, options can still be abused by greedy or irresponsible management teams, but at least investors will see the results more clearly.

R&D and marketing costs

A few companies have been caught deferring certain R&D and marketing costs into the future by *capitalizing* them: recording them as an asset when incurred, rather than an expense, and then depreciating or amortizing the asset over future years. Accounting rules are fairly firm, but not rock solid, around the notion that most R&D expenses should be incurred as they arise due to the uncertain nature of their outcome. There's no way to tell upfront whether an R&D effort will turn into a marketable product. However, where R&D is significant as a proportion of total product expense, as with software, portions are allowed to be capitalized.

Depreciation and amortization

Choice of depreciation and amortization methods — and time periods — can influence earnings and balance sheet statements. More aggressive depreciation results in lower earnings and conservative asset valuations, but the pressure to "meet the numbers" on earnings may lead to less aggressive depreciation. Firms have the choice of method (straight line versus accelerated) and time frame (number of years) to manage their financial reporting.

Depreciation and amortization methods are among the most clearly disclosed of financial statement "levers." Note 1 disclosures are complete with both method and time period, although frequently a mix of different methods and time periods is used for different assets. Look for how hard assets are depreciated and how goodwill is amortized.

The value investor should look for conservatism, consistency (as opposed to frequent changes), and common sense. (Wireless licenses amortized over 40 years probably doesn't make sense because the technology probably won't be around for that long.) If a company suddenly switches to longer depreciation schedules without adequate explanation, look out.

Pension costs and assets

Pension fund accounting can be another source of stretch earnings in a pinch. Suppose that a plan is targeted to reach a certain funding level in ten years. Management has diligently set money aside with an assumption of a 7 percent return in order to achieve that long-term goal. Now suppose that management decides that an 8 percent return is more likely. Because the existing balance is bigger than it needs to be to meet the obligation, the plan is said to be over-funded. Some or all of that overfunding can be recognized as income, inflating reported earnings. Large old-line companies — the IBMs and AT&Ts of the world — are more susceptible to pension stretch than newer companies, which use the 401(k) approach, where the company directly carries few or no pension assets.

Pension information is usually deep in the Notes section. Check the fair value of pension assets, the projected benefit obligation, and the difference between the two. Look at the assumptions, and look for changes in accounting policy, especially those not mandated by accounting standards bulletins.

Write-offs: Big baths

Write-offs come from the old school of accounting gimmicks. Bundling large costs into extraordinary write-offs clears the books of bad assets and bad decisions in order to increase earnings in the immediate future. Generally accepted accounting principles (GAAP) are fairly specific in indicating that write-offs must be unusual and nonrecurring, but these terms are subject to interpretation. Are layoffs, plant closings, and restructurings unusual and nonrecurring? Depends on the company. They're almost annual events for automakers and other smokestack industries.

Be aware of the reasons for and any regularities in such write-offs. Have they gotten to be a habit? Are they actually a cost of doing business in disguise?

Chapter 3

Using Ratios as a Valuation Tool

As you gaze through the myriad numbers in financial statements, pretty soon eye and brain fatigue set in. After all, what do the numbers *tell* you? How do you take away any meaning from them — and quickly, because you don't have all day to address every number for every business you look at?

Are accounts receivable in line or not? Is the company's inventory scaled properly to the size of the business? What about fixed assets, debt, and profitability? Is the company using capital efficiently? And does its stock price make sense? How do you know?

The Basics of Using Ratios

Applying ratios to the numbers is like using a lens to bring them into clearer focus. Ratios explain the relationship between two or more numbers, thus providing you with scale and context.

For example, one major U.S. construction products manufacturer reported $217.6 million in inventory in 2006. That means little until measured against its $863.1 million in sales the same year. The inventory-to-sales ratio of 0.252 puts company raw data into perspective, tells a story, and provides a standard for comparison with other companies and the industry. And it tells the trends — favorable or unfavorable. The 2005 ratio of 0.214 suggests that the amount of inventory required to support sales rose substantially in 2006 — not a good sign.

Inventory-to-sales is one of dozens of standard ratios. Each ratio by itself provides a clue into some facet of business performance. Taken together as a collection, ratios provide a clearer total picture of a company for the investor to interpret.

Identifying ratio resources

A great deal of comparative industry ratio data is available to professional financial and credit analysts, but they pay hefty subscription fees to get it. The challenge is finding that information for free (or nearly so). Here are some sources of ratio data and comparison:

- ✔ **Free:** Yahoo!Finance and similar investing portals provide some ratios and limited comparison tools. The Yahoo!Finance "Key Statistics" page shows several ratios, mainly valuation ratios.

- ✔ **For a modest fee:** At the time of this writing, there is still little available for the ratio-hungry investor to buy. One source is VentureLine (www .ventureline.com), where, for $9.95, you can purchase a fairly complete rundown for a particular industry, like "electronic computers." This product provides five years' worth of data, making trend analysis practical. While $9.95 per industry can add up if you invest in a lot of industries, this tool is worth considering if you're doing a lot of ratio analysis.

- ✔ **More expensive:** Value Line Investment Survey (www.valueline.com) offers a window to many key ratios. Value Line doesn't present a lot of ratios but does give a lot of history, which can be better. The standard Value Line Investment Survey subscription costs $595 per year but offers a lot beyond ratio analysis.

If you have access to Dun & Bradstreet or Standard & Poor's industry financial comparisons, don't hesitate to use these rich, complete, and up-to-date resources. They may be out of reach of the average investor due to cost. If you work with a broker or financial adviser, you may get access to some of these services for free.

Using ratios in your analysis

What does a value investor look for when analyzing ratios?

- ✔ **Intrinsic meaning:** What does the ratio tell you? If the debt-to-equity ratio is 3 to 1, the company has a lot of debt. If the inventory-to-sales ratio is greater than 1, the company turns its inventory less than once per year. A price-to-earnings (P/E) ratio of 50 implies a 2 percent return on invested capital ($1 returned per $50 invested). These numbers tell you something without looking at any comparisons or trends.

- ✔ **Comparisons:** For many analysts (especially credit analysts) trying to get a picture of a company's health, comparative analysis is the most important use of ratios. A ratio acquires more meaning when it's compared to direct competitors, the company's industry, or much broader standards, like the S&P 500. A profitability measure, such as gross profit margin, reported at 25 percent tells more when direct competitors are at 35 percent plus. Analysts make similar comparisons with asset utilization, financial strength, and valuation ratios.

✔ **Consistency:** The hallmark of good management, as well as of an attractive long-term investment, is the consistency of results delivered. If profit margins are consistent and changing at a consistent rate, the company is predictable — and most likely in control of its markets. Inconsistent ratios reflect on inconsistent management, competitive struggles, and cyclical industries, all of which diminish a company's intrinsic value.

✔ **Trends:** Better than consistency alone is consistency with a favorable trend. Growing profit margins, return on equity, asset utilization, and financial strength are all very desirable, particularly if valuation ratios (P/E and so on) haven't kept pace. Value investors who study trends carefully have information that most investors don't have.

Key Ratios, Classified and Identified

The following sections explore the different kinds of ratios and their use in value investing. Ratios can be divided into four categories:

✔ **Asset productivity:** These ratios describe how effectively assets are deployed. Some analysts call these *efficiency* or *asset management* ratios.

✔ **Financial strength:** These ratios measure to what extent company resources are provided by sources other than the owners. Sometimes called *liquidity* or *debt management* ratios, they also assess the company's ability to pay its creditors and how vulnerable it may be to debt problems and high interest costs. And some financial ratios tell you about financial or capital structure — that is, how financially leveraged a company may be.

✔ **Profitability:** Profitability ratios suggest how much profit or cash flow is generated per dollar sold or dollar invested. Some analysts refer to these ratios as *management effectiveness* ratios, as they indicate management's overall success in generating returns for the enterprise.

✔ **Valuation:** The first three ratio families examine internal business fundamentals. With valuation, the stock price enters the picture. Valuation ratios, as the name implies, relate a company's stock price to its performance. The ubiquitous price-to-earnings (P/E) ratio shows up here, as do its siblings price-to-sales, price-to-book, and a few others.

Asset productivity ratios

Asset productivity ratios describe how effectively business assets are deployed. They typically look at sales dollars generated per unit of resource. Resources can include accounts receivable, inventory, fixed assets, and occasionally other tangible assets. Similar analysis may also be done not just for financial assets but also for operational assets like square footage, employees, number of facilities, and airplane seat miles.

Receivables turnover

Receivables turnover measures the size of unpaid customer commitments to a company. Specifically, it measures how many times a year this asset *turns over* — that is, is cleared out and replaced by similar obligations from other customers. Rapid turnover, not lingering old debts, is what you want to see. Here's the formula:

Receivables turnover = sales $ ÷ accounts receivable $

Accounts receivable is a resource at a company's disposal like anything else and must be paid for, essentially, by sacrificing cash that otherwise would be available to fund some other part of the business. A company selling direct to consumers with cash sales or bank credit card sales will have lower receivables turnover than an industrial supplier. Watch for consistency and compliance with normal billing policy for the industry.

Average collection period

A slightly different way of looking at receivables is to show the average number of days that a given receivable dollar lives on the books. To calculate, you divide the receivables turnover ratio into 360 to put it on a daily scale:

Average collection period = 360 ÷ receivables turnover

This ratio is also sometimes called *days' sales in receivables*.

If, based on industry comparisons or stated billing cycles, the collection period is higher than it should be (or growing), watch out. The company may be losing control of its collections or selling to customers with questionable credit.

Inventory turnover

Inventory turnover works like receivables turnover, only you plug in balance sheet inventory in place of receivables. Here's the formula:

Inventory turnover = sales ÷ inventory $

As with receivables turnover, the higher the number, the better. High numbers indicate that raw materials, work in progress, and finished goods are flying onto and off of shelves rapidly. Less dust collects on less stuff in fewer warehouses, and less cash is tied up in inventory. Also, there's less risk of obsolescence and write-offs and, in many businesses, less risk of markdowns to clear inventory.

Fixed asset turnover

This ratio is straightforward:

Fixed asset turnover = sales $ ÷ fixed asset $

All else being equal, the company that produces the most sales or revenue per dollar of fixed assets wins.

Total asset turnover

Again, straightforward:

Total asset turnover = sales $ ÷ total asset $

Here we get a bigger picture of asset productivity as measured by the generation of sales. For the first time, intangible assets are included. Again, industry norms form the benchmark. Comparing a railroad to a software company doesn't make sense.

Book VII

Value Investing

Non-financial productivity ratios

Operational or capacity utilization ratios can be quite interesting yet sometimes hard to find or apply. The raw data is often not available in company statements or published reports. Calculated ratios are even harder to find, although Value Line and other analysis services make it a point to present certain non-financial operating data. These measures vary by industry, but here are some examples:

- ✔ **Sales per employee:** This ratio tells you how productive a company is in regard to investments in human resources. We think it's worth a look in almost all industries, particularly those that are labor intensive such as retail, transportation, and other service industries. Here's a tip: The Yahoo!Finance "Competitors" page shows employee counts for every publicly traded company.

- ✔ **Sales per square foot:** This ratio is especially important for retail and similar businesses where occupancy investments are large and sales can be tied directly to them.

- ✔ **Average selling price (ASP):** Many financial reports don't present the number of units sold because they don't have to — and they want to keep selling prices secret. But sometimes this data is available (for example, from Boeing and other very-large-ticket manufacturers), and it can be quite revealing as to the direction of a business.

✔ **Industry specials:** Airlines and airline investors pay close attention to seat miles and revenues per seat mile flown. Railroads may look at revenue per track mile or car mile. Other service businesses such as banks and mail order retail may look at sales or revenue per *customer.*

Financial strength ratios

This set of ratios goes by many names (liquidity, solvency, financial leverage), but they all point to the same thing: What is a business's financial strength and position? What is its capital structure? A balance sheet–oriented value investor looks closely to make sure that the company will be around tomorrow (as many investors did in the 1930s). Value investors first look at financial strength ratios for obvious danger, then they base intrinsic value analysis on business-strength and market-strength measures like productivity and profitability.

Current and quick ratios

These commonly used liquidity ratios help evaluate a company's ability to pay its short-term obligations. Here's the formula:

Current ratio = current assets ÷ current liabilities

The current ratio includes all current assets, but because inventory is often difficult to turn into cash, at least for a reasonable price, many analysts remove it from the equation to arrive at a *quick* ratio. The quick ratio emphasizes coverage assets that can be quickly converted to cash:

Quick ratio = (current assets − inventory) ÷ current liabilities

Another ratio, *cash to debt,* is often used. The calculation is self-explanatory. It takes a still more conservative view of coverage assets (cash only) and a clearer view of what needs to be covered (total debt, current and long-term portions).

The traditional thinking is that the higher the ratio, the better off the company. Greater than 2:1 for the current ratio or 1:1 for the quick ratio is good and safe; less than 2:1 or 1:1 is a sign of impending problems meeting obligations.

Debt to equity and debt to assets

Sometimes also called *solvency* or *leverage* ratios, this set measures what portion of a firm's resources, or assets, are provided by the owners versus provided by others. The two most common ratios used to assess solvency and leverage are *debt to equity* and *debt to total assets*. Here's the formula for debt to equity; note that current liabilities, such as accounts payable, typically are not included:

Debt to equity = total debt ÷ owners' equity

Here's the formula for debt to assets:

Debt to total assets = total debt ÷ total assets

Making a sweeping statement about what these ratios should be for a given company is difficult. When a company has more debt than equity (debt to equity > 1 or debt to total assets > 0.5), yellow flags fly. But again, industry comparisons are important. Economic value achieved should exceed the cost and risk incurred with the debt. Sounds good in theory, but precise appraisal can be complex. As with liquidity measures, solvency measures probably deliver a stronger signal for what *not* to buy than what to buy.

Cash flow ratios

Because cash is really the lifeblood of a business, financial strength assessments typically look at these ratios:

- ✔ **Overall cash flow ratio:** This powerful ratio tells whether a business is generating enough cash from its business to sustain itself, grow, and return capital to its owners. Here's the formula:

    Overall cash flow ratio = cash inflow from operations ÷ (investing cash outflows + financing cash outflows)

    If the overall cash flow ratio is greater than 1, the company is generating enough cash internally to cover business needs. If it's less than 1, the company is going to capital markets or is selling assets to keep afloat.

- ✔ **Cash flow and earnings ratio:** Cash flow comparisons with earnings can be used as a quick quality test to see how non-cash accounting transactions and "stretch" may have gone into a set of statements. It's best when cash flows march in step with, or exceed, earnings. If earnings increase without a corresponding increase in cash flow, earnings quality comes into question. The following is a base measure:

    Cash flow to earnings = cash flow from operations ÷ net earnings

    Because depreciation and other non-cash amortizations vary by industry, it's hard to hang a specific goal on this measure. Consistency over time is good. Favorable industry comparisons also are good. Further, it's good when period-to-period earnings increases are accompanied by corresponding cash flow increases.

Book VII

Value Investing

Profitability ratios

Asset productivity and financial strength reflect essential business basics — important, but neither of which alone can point you to good companies and good investments. Profitability ratios form a core set of bottom-line ratios crucial to all investment analysis. This section examines four profitability ratios. Each is typically based on net earnings, but occasionally you see variations using cash flow or operating earnings.

Typically, items related to extraordinary charges or discontinued operations should be excluded when calculating these ratios. If you're using figures from a financial portal or calculations from a screener or other financial information package, check to make sure figures exclude extraordinary items. You may have to dig into the company's own issued financial statements.

Return on sales

This ratio is just as it sounds:

Return on sales = net earnings ÷ sales

Return on sales (ROS) tells you how much profit a firm generated per dollar of sales. This figure is much better known as the *net profit margin.* Closely related is gross margin:

Gross margin = (sales – cost of goods sold) ÷ sales

Obviously, gross margin is a key driver of return on sales and is the most strongly connected to the organization's business strength and operational effectiveness. Some analysts also look at operating margin:

Operating margin = (sales – cost of goods sold – operating expenses) ÷ sales

where SG&A (selling, general, and administrative) expenses, marketing, asset recovery (depreciation), and special amortizations are factored in.

Return on assets

How much profit is generated per resource dollar invested? Return on assets, or ROA, provides the answer:

Return on assets = net earnings ÷ total assets

This measure is especially important in asset-intensive industries, such as retail, semiconductor manufacturing, and basic manufacturing. Chapter 4 takes a closer look at ROA.

Return on equity

Return on equity, or ROE, is one of the more important bottom-line ratios in the value investor's repertoire. Here's the formula:

Return on equity = net earnings ÷ owners' equity

ROE is the true measure of how much a company returns to its owners, the shareholders. It is the bottom line result of other factors, including asset productivity, financial structure, and top-line profitability. ROE is important as an opportunity benchmark. What else could an investor invest in to get a better return? Again, consistency, trends, and comparisons are critical.

Return on invested capital

Debt, while raising ROE in good times, also can lead to financial disaster. As a result, many investors instead look at return on invested capital (ROIC), measuring profit as a percentage of combined owners' equity and debt investments. This measure is sometimes called *return on total capital,* or ROTC. Here's the formula:

Return on invested capital = net earnings ÷ (owners' equity + long-term debt)

Frequently, you see ROE and ROIC side by side in ratio charts and discussions. Sustained ROE of 20 percent or more is considered very good, and ROIC should be higher, because debt increases the size of the business on the same equity base. See Chapter 4 for more on ROE/ROIC.

Book VII

Value Investing

Valuation ratios

The ratios presented so far are aimed at appraising a company's performance to get a better understanding of its intrinsic value. If a business were an orchestra, productivity, financial structure, and profitability would be sections, like brass, woodwinds, and strings. The total sound produced depends not just on individual sounds made by individual instruments (ratios) but also how they work together to produce music.

Now here's the critical question: As a music buff, how much would you pay to listen to it? That's the question that valuation ratios try to answer: How much would you pay (and how much are others paying) for tickets to this concert? Here, finally, the stock price enters the stage.

And now, the most popular ratio of all, the one seen in the newspaper, heard about on talk shows, found in all those beginning books on investing, makes its appearance here: the price-to-earnings (P/E) ratio. Alongside P/E, other valuation ratios, including price-to-sales, price-to-book, and a couple of boutique P/E variations, enter the mix.

When in doubt, should you average?

Occasionally, you see a variation in ROE and sometimes ROA formulas. Because these ratios use recent snapshot balance sheet items in the denominator, some analysts feel that you get the most accurate financial picture by adding year-end and year-beginning equity or asset values and dividing by 2. Thus ROE would be

ROE = net earnings ÷ [(beginning equity + ending equity) ÷ 2]

Many information sources and services use the averaged formula. If you use a data source or service to acquire these figures, it's best to understand how your source calculates the figures. Most important, be consistent when evaluating different investments.

Price-to-earnings

Price-to-earnings is just what it sounds like: the ratio of a price at a point in time to net earnings in a period, usually the trailing 12 months (TTM). Here's the formula:

Price-to-earnings (P/E) = stock price ÷ net earnings per share

A high P/E — say, 20 or higher — indicates a relatively high valuation. A low P/E — say, 15 or less — indicates a relatively low or more conservative one. Most investors are probably familiar with P/E, so the calculation doesn't need to be illustrated here. Rather, it makes sense to share a couple of useful derivatives: earnings-to-price and price-earnings-to-growth, both of which bring greater understanding to the base P/E measure. Chapter 4 also explores P/E in greater detail.

Earnings-to-price

Earnings-to-price is simply the reciprocal of P/E, or 1 divided by the P/E. Why is this important? Earnings-to-price is the functional equivalent of a stock's *yield,* comparable to an interest rate on a fixed income investment. Because we're talking earnings and not dividends, this yield doesn't usually come your way in the form of a check, but it's useful just the same to determine how much return your dollar paid for a share is generating. Many people call this figure *earnings yield.*

Take our construction products manufacturer example: 17.6 was a recent P/E based on a share price of $33 and TTM earnings of 1.87. Earnings yield would thus be 1/17.6, or 5.7 percent. What's the significance? This investment could be compared to a long-term Treasury security (today yielding about 4.5 percent) as a prospective investment. Which investment is better? An investment in that business returns more and, while being riskier, affords the opportunity for gain through growth. The difference in earnings yield illustrates the basic risk/return tradeoff between investing in corporate equities versus safe fixed-income Treasuries.

Price-earnings-to-growth

Investors pay more for companies with greater growth prospects. Greater growth prospects mean greater earnings and greater earnings yields *sooner.* So when comparing businesses, one popular way to normalize P/Es is to compare them to their respective companies' growth rates. From this comparison, you get a ratio known as *price-earnings-to-growth,* or PEG:

Price-earnings-to-growth = P/E ÷ earnings growth rate

If Cisco has an earnings growth rate of 25 percent, while our sample manufacturer is 10 percent and Bank of America's is 5 percent, then PEG is 27.4 ÷ 25 or 1.1 for Cisco, 17.4 ÷ 10 or 1.74 for our company, and 10 ÷ 5 or 2 for Bank of America. If you're confident in the sustainability of the growth rates, you'd pick Cisco as the best investment because its P/E is modest compared to its growth rate.

Price-to-sales

Book VII

Value Investing

Per dollar of shareholder value, how much business does a company generate? Price-to-sales (P/S) is a straightforward way to answer this question. Here's the formula:

Price-to-sales = stock price (total market cap) ÷ total sales (revenues)

P/S is a common-sense ratio. The lower the better, although there's no specific rule or normalizing factor like growth. Somewhere around 1.0 usually is considered good. 2.0 isn't out of hand, but the business had better grow consistently into its valuation. P/S can be a way to filter out unworthy candidates.

Price-to-book

The price-to-book ratio (P/B) is getting varying amounts of attention from investors in different sectors. Here's the formula:

Price-to-book = stock price (total market cap) ÷ book value

Book value consists of the accounting value of assets less (real) liabilities — sort of an accounting net worth or owners' equity of a corporation. This figure has greater meaning in financial services industries, where most assets are actual dollars, not factories, inventories, goodwill, and other hard-to-value items. Some book value measures include intangible assets, and others exclude them.

Value investors use price-to-book a bit like price-to-sales: as a test for obvious lack of value. P/B of 1.0 is very good — unless the asset base is a bunch of rusty unused railroad tracks. P/B of less than 1.0 signifies a buying opportunity if book assets are quality assets. A price way out of line with book had better be justified by conservative asset valuation or by the nature of the industry. In the software industry, for example, if R&D (research and development) is properly expensed and intellectual capital intangibles are aggressively amortized, book value and P/B will be low. Again, like elsewhere, trends and apples-to-apples comparisons are important.

Market cap

When calculating price-to-sales ratios or other valuation measures, it's sometimes easier to look at aggregate rather than per-share amounts. Sales are reported as an aggregate figure, not as a per-share figure. So to compare apples to apples, you can look at aggregate share valuation instead of the per-share price.

This aggregate figure is known as *market capitalization,* or *market cap* for short. Market cap is simply the number of shares (usually the fully loaded number, including options and equivalents) times the stock price. Divide total market cap by total sales, and you have the price-to-sales ratio.

Chapter 4

Valuing a Business

· ·

In This Chapter

▶ Calculating intrinsic value

▶ Evaluating strategic financials and strategic intangibles

▶ Deciding if the price is right

· ·

*T*o be consistent with the value investing approach, you must understand what a company is worth before you make an investment decision. If only it were so simple. Valuation has been the subject of vast theoretical study and debate — as well as experience and learning — in the investing community. Business valuation is at best an inexact science that no two people do exactly the same way. The goal of this chapter is to expose you to some of the techniques and underlying principles. Whether you apply them rigorously to every investment decision or just keep them in the back of your mind is up to you.

A How-to Valuation Guide

The following value investing model is one that you can use as is or modify to meet your own needs. It's designed for non-professionals, those with just a few hours a month to review and select investments.

1. **Screen companies.**

   Using P/E, P/S, or other chosen ratios (see Chapter 3), get a list of companies to evaluate. The list can include industries considered timely by popular investment analysts, companies you read about in the financial press, or companies you deal with in everyday life that appear to have their act together. In addition, online stock screeners are useful for this step.

2. **Calculate intrinsic value.**

   Using formulas presented in the next section, estimate intrinsic value for each chosen candidate.

3. **Assess each company's strategic value.**

   Develop a checklist for key business performance measures (return on assets growing, return on equity constant, profit margins growing, liquidity sufficient, and so on). Then, add a checklist and evaluate intangibles. For details, check out the upcoming sections "Looking at Strategic Financials: It's All about ROE" on strategic financials and "Evaluating Intangibles" on strategic intangibles.

4. **Decide whether the price is right.**

   Compare current price to intrinsic value, sprinkle in strategic value assessments, and bake in a dash of judgment. The later section "Deciding When the Price Is Right" walks you through this process.

Evaluating Intrinsic Value

Intrinsic value is a present dollar value placed on the expected net returns generated by a business over time. Profits and growth drive intrinsic value. For any fairly priced asset to increase in value over time, the value of the returns must grow. The value you get out of owning a business or a security is the amount you receive in return for your investment. That return may come as a single payment at the end of the ownership period for selling the stock or business, or as payments at regular intervals during ownership (dividends), or as a combination of the two.

Growth and time value of money have a major impact on the final valuation of equity investment returns. In fact, intrinsic valuation is a lot about assessing the effects of future growth on future returns and then assigning a present value to those returns.

Asking key questions

The following questions can guide your assessment of business returns:

- ✔ **How much?** How many dollars of return will the business produce, either to distribute to shareholders or to invest productively in the business? Key drivers are profitability and growth rates — and the collection of business factors that drive the profitability and growth.

- ✔ **How soon?** If two companies produce the same return but one does it sooner, that company has more value, because those dollars can be reinvested elsewhere sooner for more return.

- ✔ **How long?** Although future returns have less value than current returns, they do have substantial value, and 20, 30, or 50 years of those returns can't be ignored, particularly in a profitable, growing business.

- ✔ **How consistent?** A company producing slow, steady growth and return is usually more valuable than one that's all over the map. A greater variability, or uncertainty, around projected returns calls for more conservative growth and/or discounting assumptions.

After you assess potential returns (how much, how soon, how long, how consistent), you must assign a current value to those returns. That value is driven by the value of the investment capital as it might be used elsewhere. A return may look attractive until you realize you can achieve the same return with a bond or a less risky investment. Valuing the returns involves *discounting* (using a discount rate) to bring future returns back to fair current value (see Chapter 1). The discount rate is your personal cost of capital — in this case, the rate of return you expect to deploy capital here versus elsewhere.

Sooner isn't *always* better. A business producing quick, short-term bucks may not be more valuable than one that produces slow, steady growth. Even though the quick-bucker produces a lot of value in the first few years, that may not be better than sustained growth and value produced later on by the slower, steadier company.

More about returns

When you look at a business, you seek consistent, growing returns on a quality asset base — achieving reasonable returns without taking on unreasonable risk. So what "returns" am I referring to? Direct returns to shareholders? Returns to the business? Net income? Cash flow? EBITDA? What's the best "base" for intrinsic value?

Net income to the business is the starting point, but many investors look further.

Dividends

As part of intrinsic value, dividends are counted as part of yearly investment returns and grown and discounted in the same way as earnings retained in the business. But deducting dividends reduces the growth base of retained earnings and book value kept in the business. Companies with a high growth rate and return on equity often yield greater intrinsic value if all earnings are retained and reinvested, which is why you often see just that — no dividends in high-growth companies.

Book VII

Value Investing

Cash flow streams

Any one of the following cash flow streams can be used as an input to an intrinsic value model:

- ✔ **Cash flow (CF) or discounted cash flow (DCF):** Cash flows, covered in detail in Chapter 2, are yearly cash returns into a business, without accounting adjustments for asset write-downs, amortizations, and the like. Many sophisticated security analysis models, including intrinsic value models, operate on cash flow. These models are sometimes referred to as *discounted cash flow* (DCF) models.

- ✔ **EBITDA:** Earnings Before Interest, Taxes, Depreciation, and Amortization is an approximation of cash generated by business operating activities. (Note: Interest and taxes are real, and depreciation comes into play when depreciated fixed assets need to be replaced. Because intrinsic value calculations are long term in view, it's dangerous to leave out the cost of fixed assets, especially in a business that has a lot of them.)

- ✔ **Free cash flow (FCF):** Free cash flow is essentially cash flow generated from operations *beyond* interest, taxes, and capital investments. As a business owner, it's what you'd really be able to put into your pocket.

- ✔ **Net free cash flow (owner earnings):** The most realistic version of free cash flow starts with plain old free cash flow and then makes an additional adjustment for working capital changes.

Although cash flow streams may be more robust than earnings, they're harder to identify for the nonprofessional investor. Most free data sources provide little in the way of cash flow figures, and if they do, they aren't adjusted to give a clear view of fixed asset or working capital investments.

Earnings

Most investors use earnings as the most readily available proxy for business returns. Understanding earnings quality and the differences between earnings and cash flow goes a long way toward producing valid results.

When using earnings streams to project future returns, make sure to understand quality and one-time extraordinary gains or losses. Especially when occurring in the base year, extraordinary earnings items can mess up the intrinsic value calculation. Be especially careful when using a "canned" package, as it picks up whatever is on a company's source earnings database, ordinary or otherwise. To their credit, analysts and Value Line (www.value line.com) usually filter out these abnormalities when making projections.

Projecting future growth

Beyond the net assets owned by a business today, intrinsic value is driven by current and especially future earnings. For that reason, projecting future earnings growth is vital to determining intrinsic value. The following sections explain how to examine growth assumptions more closely.

True intrinsic value is the total of *all* expected future returns: this year, next year, 5, 10, 20, 40, 80 years from now. How can you possibly project a company's return when part of it includes something that happens 77 years from now? It's hard enough to project next year's returns. Answer: by taking it in stages:

- ✔ **First stage:** Typically the first stage is ten years, although in some analyses it may be more or less. Near-term growth is by nature easier to model, and as a result of the discounting process, it contributes more toward the final result anyway. For these reasons, intrinsic value models are set up to specifically value a first stage in detail, year-by-year. The first stage is generally assumed to have a higher growth rate and a lower discount rate than the second stage.

- ✔ **Second stage:** Second-stage returns are harder than first-stage to project with any degree of accuracy, so intrinsic value models use one of two assumptions to estimate what is known as *continuing value:*

  - **Indefinite life:** The indefinite life model assumes ongoing returns and uses a mathematical formula to project returns over an indefinite period of time.

  - **Acquisition:** A convenient way to bypass mathematical approximations is to assume that someone will come along and buy your business after the first stage at a reasonable valuation. Returns include all future payouts, including lump sums, so this method works too, so long as resale value is projected reasonably.

Each stage of a business life has a growth rate and discount rate applicable to that stage. To run a model, you need a base, first- and second-stage growth rates, and first- and second-stage discount rates. You calculate net future earnings by first compounding growth over the first stage and then discounting that value back to the present. A generalized formula, either indefinite life or acquisition-based, is applied to the second stage. The value attributed to the second stage is called *continuing value.*

Book VII

Value Investing

Intrinsic Value Models

To determine intrinsic value you can use one of three intrinsic value models:

- ✔ **Build-your-own model:** Using Excel, the worksheet model is fairly easy to construct; formulas will be shown along with sample results for both indefinite continuing value and the acquisition assumption.

- ✔ **Prepackaged Web-based analyzer:** At this writing, the data and analysis package offered by iStockResearch (www.istockresearch.com) is the best available for free.

- ✔ **Intrinsic value formula as developed by Ben Graham:** This simple formula is easy to apply and gives surprisingly robust results.

The one highlighted in this section is built from scratch as an Excel spreadsheet. At the time of this writing, there is little in the way of PC or Web-based models available for use by consumer investors. As noted, the exception is iStockResearch, which offers a model to non-professional investors; I offer an example later in the chapter.

Of course, any time you use a tool, it's good to know in advance what outcome to expect. With intrinsic value models, you get a single-figure result: the estimated per-share value of the company. One single number: Company ABC, for example, may have a projected worth of $34.97. If you're satisfied with this number and the assumptions supporting it, you can compare this intrinsic value with current market price and make a buying (or selling) decision. More likely, you'll want to model a *range* of intrinsic values based on different assumptions. Then to complete the value appraisal, you'll want to consider strategic financials and intangibles before hitting the buy (or sell) button.

Intrinsic value worksheet models

With a spreadsheet and a few initial assumptions, you can build your own intrinsic value worksheet for either continuing value assumption: the indefinite life model or the acquisition assumption model. Figure 4-1 shows an example of the indefinite life continuing value model, with formulas to help you build your own. Note that dollar figures, except per-share amounts, are in millions.

INTRINSIC VALUE WORKSHEET
indefinite life model

			Variable	Source
① Growth and Discount assumptions				
first stage growth		10%	g1	assumption
second stage growth		5%	g2	assumption
first stage discount rate		12%	d1	assumption
second stage discount rate		15%	d2	assumption
② Earnings, shares outstanding, EPS				
beginning earnings	$	102.50	E	statements
number of shares (M)		48.5		statements
beginning EPS	$	2.12		calculation

③ Discounted 10-year earnings stream

			Calculations
year 1	$	100.67	Start with beginning earnings
year 2	$	98.87	
year 3	$	97.11	First, compound for growth:
year 4	$	95.37	*multiply E by* $(1+g1)^n$
year 5	$	93.67	
year 6	$	92.00	
year 7	$	90.35	...then discount:
year 8	$	88.74	*divide by* $(1+d1)^n$
year 9	$	87.16	
year 10	$	85.60	

④ Total discounted return, first 10 years			
discounted 10-year value	$	929.54	sum years 1-10
⑤ Continuing value beyond 10 years			
continuing value (> 10 years)	$	941.59	$[E*(1+g1)^{n+1}]/(d2-g2)$ over $(1+d1)^n$
⑥ Total future returns value, discounted	$	1,871.13	10 year + terminal value
⑦ Long term debt adjustment	$	-	from statements
⑧ Net future returns value	$	1,871.13	subtract LT debt
⑨ Per share intrinsic value	$	38.61	net future value / # shares

Figure 4-1: The intrinsic value worksheet for an indefinite life model.

Book VII

Value Investing

The indefinite life model

The mainstream intrinsic value model makes a mathematical assumption about so-called "continuing value." The worksheet has nine parts.

Step 1: Growth and discount assumptions

Not surprisingly, here at the very top of the worksheet is where you can do the most damage — or the most good — to your analysis because of the potential effects of these assumptions carried over 10, 15, or 20 years, due to the power of compounding.

The most realistic way to model intrinsic value is to choose two stages; a more rapid initial growth stage and a more conservative, or flat, second stage. So two growth rates are chosen, and two corresponding discount rates are chosen. Almost always, the initial growth rate exceeds the second stage growth rate while, due to uncertainty, the second stage discount rate exceeds the initial one.

✔ **Choosing a growth assumption:** To choose a growth assumption, you can rely on outside sources including professional analysts or Value Line. You can eyeball the numbers yourself and pick a number that makes sense, even with conservative bias. Or you can dig deeper and do what most professional analysts do and derive earnings growth estimates by projecting sales, profitability, productivity, and so on.

Regardless of how you decide to formulate your growth assumptions, it is important to be consistent. Comparing two businesses by using different approaches to growth and discounting assumptions can lead to trouble.

✔ **Projecting second-stage growth:** To project second-stage growth, you can't use the same tools and techniques you use to project first-stage growth. Not even the most self-assured analysts try to pin down growth rates beyond ten years!

Excessive second-stage growth rates distort results because so much time is involved. And no matter what the company is, sooner or later it will exhaust market growth and penetration opportunities. Second-stage growth rates should be less than first-stage growth rates and less than 10 percent, probably no more than 5 or 6 percent. Conservative is always better.

If you're uncomfortable with second-stage growth rates and their effect on valuation (and many investors are), you can use the acquisition model presented later in this chapter. Although this model implies that an acquisition will take place, it can also be used to reduce sensitivity to input assumptions even if acquisition is unlikely.

✔ **Choosing a discount assumption:** In theory, the discount rate should be your own personal cost of capital for this kind of investment plus *equity premium* that's added to the risk-free cost of capital rate. Here's the reasoning: If you can invest your money with no risk in a Treasury bond at 5 percent, your cost of capital is the risk-free 5 percent you would forego by not investing in the bond. But because Company XYZ common stock is riskier than the bond investment, an *equity premium* is added as compensation for assuming extra risk.

Most value investors, however, prefer a simpler approach: Just discount at a relatively high rate, usually higher than the growth rate. Conservative value investors usually use discount rates in the 10 to 15 percent range. Here are a few points to remember about discount rates:

- The higher the discount rate, the lower the intrinsic value — and vice versa.

- The second-stage discount rate should always be higher than the first-stage rate. Risk increases the farther out you go.

- If you choose an aggressive growth rate, it makes sense also to choose a higher discount rate. Risk of failure is higher with high growth rates.

- If the discount rate exceeds the growth rate, intrinsic value will be low and implode quickly the larger the gap. Aggressive growth assumptions with low discount rates yield very high intrinsic values.

Following is the set of growth and discount assumptions used for this example. Consistency is important, but growth rates will vary for each company, and discount rates may change also with differing risk assessments.

First-stage growth	10%
Second-stage growth	5%
First-stage discount rate	12%
Second-stage discount rate	15%

Step 2: Earnings, shares outstanding, EPS

Earnings, number of shares, and EPS come straight from the statements. This model projects total, rather than per-share, earnings streams, to make it easier to subtract out (not per-share) long-term debt (which happens to be zero for Simpson Manufacturing, used in the Figure 4-1 example).

When loading beginning earnings, remember to adjust for one-time or extra-ordinary gains or charges.

Step 3: Calculate the ten-year earnings stream

This section projects growth during each year of the first stage and then discounts the resulting value back to the present. The spreadsheet formulas are straightforward. For each year, you do the following:

1. Multiply beginning earnings by $[(1 + \mathbf{g1})^n]$

   where $\mathbf{g1}$ is the first-stage growth rate

   and $\mathbf{n}$ is the sequential future year.

2. Divide that figure by $[(1 + \mathbf{d1})^n]$

   where $\mathbf{d1}$ is the first-stage discount rate.

The resulting figures represent projected earnings for each year, discounted to the present.

Step 4: Total discounted return, first ten years

To arrive at the sum of the first ten years' discounted earnings stream, simply add the figures for each year. The total represents the total discounted value of the first stage.

Step 5: Continuing value

Higher math enters the picture in calculating a continuing value for all future returns. Here's the formula:

$$[\mathbf{E} \times (1 + \mathbf{g1})^n +1] \div (\mathbf{d2} - \mathbf{g2}) \text{ all divided by } (1+\mathbf{d1})^n$$

where

$\mathbf{E}$ is beginning earnings

$\mathbf{g1}$ and $\mathbf{d1}$ are first-stage growth and discount rates, respectively

$\mathbf{g2}$ and $\mathbf{d2}$ are second-stage growth and discount rates, respectively

$\mathbf{n}$ is the number of years in the first stage, in this case, 10

After you enter this formula into your worksheet, the computation is simple. The resulting single value approximates the discounted value of *all* future returns for the business beyond the first stage.

Step 6: Total discounted future returns value

The next step is to add first-stage and second-stage *continuing* discounted value to find the value of the total discounted future returns.

Step 7: Long-term debt adjustment

To arrive at true value, you have to take long debt away from earnings.

Step 8: Net future returns value

Net of long-term debt, the net future returns value is the total intrinsic value, based on future returns, of the business.

Step 9: Per-share intrinsic value

Now, finally, the bottom line. Divide net future returns value by the number of shares outstanding to get a per-share intrinsic value. This is the magic number to compare with market price and with other companies. You're done!

The acquisition assumption model

If the continuing value formula of the preceding section makes you nervous, and if the idea of trying to project to eternity makes you equally nervous, there is another approach. The approach is to assume that someone else will buy the business at a fair value at the end of the first stage. In essence, you get continuing value in a lump sum payment, which of course must also be discounted for time value of money.

Before showing the model, here are a few important points:

- ✔ Growth and discount assumptions are the same as for the indefinite life model.

- ✔ The price paid by the acquirer is the key assumption that makes or breaks this model. That price is calculated as a ratio of price to book value, or P/B. Earnings during the first stage grow the base book value. You then supply an assumption of what price-to-book value is appropriate ten years down the road and use that to determine the cash-out price.

  Earnings paid out as dividends don't accrue to long-term book value and should be backed out of the earnings stream used to grow book value. Share buybacks should also be backed out.

- ✔ Because book value already nets out debt, long-term debt doesn't need to be factored in.

Figure 4-2 shows a ten-year acquisition version of the intrinsic value worksheet.

Book VII

Value Investing

INTRINSIC VALUE WORKSHEET
10-year acquisition model

		Variable	Source
Growth and Discount assumptions			
① earnings growth	8%	g1	assumption
discount rate	12%	d1	assumption

② **Beginning share price, book value and earnings**

current share price	$	33.00	quote
per share book value	$	13.50	statements
Price to Book (P/B)		2.4	calculation
EPS	$	2.10	statements
Per share dividend/buyback	$	0.40	statements
Net earnings to book value	$	1.70	calculation

③ **Book value increase per share**

year 1	$	1.64	
year 2	$	1.58	
year 3	$	1.52	
year 4	$	1.47	
year 5	$	1.42	
year 6	$	1.37	
year 7	$	1.32	
year 8	$	1.27	
year 9	$	1.23	
year 10	$	1.18	

Calculations

Start with beginning EPS

First, compound for growth: *multiply by* $(1+g1)^n$

...then discount: *divide by* $(1+d1)^n$

④ **Total incremental book value, discounted**

	$	13.99	sum years 1-10

⑤ **Initial book value, discounted**

	$	3.88	initial book/ $(1+d1)^{10}$

⑥ **Total book value, year 10**

	$	17.88	initial +incremental book value

⑦ **Acquisition price-to-book ratio**

	$	2.0	assumption

⑧ **Per share intrinsic value assuming acquisition**

	$	35.75	Total year 10 book value *P/B ratio

Figure 4-2: The intrinsic value worksheet for a ten-year acquisition.

The acquisition assumption worksheet model is fairly straightforward. Growth and discount assumptions are the same as in the indefinite life model. Base values are share price and per-share book value, which are used to calculate an initial price-to-book ratio. A per-share earnings figure is then used as a base for growth and discounting.

The book value is assumed to increase by each year's grown and discounted earnings. If there are dividends or significant share buybacks, subtract them out — they will not accrete to book value — but you may want to value them as a separate discounted income stream. The formula for growing earnings and discounting to the present is the same, except here you apply it to per-share earnings instead of total earnings.

To model the value in Year 10, when the supposed acquisition takes place (you can set it up for a different year), here is a short tour through the steps:

1. Make your growth and discounting assumptions, just as you would in the indefinite life model, and look up key figures on the financial statements.

2. Estimate the annual accretion of earnings to book value, but subtract dividends and other shareholder payments.

3. Model the incremental book value per share per year by growing, then discounting, the per-share net earnings over the ten years, much like the indefinite life model.

4. Take current book value and assume that it remains intact ten years from now; then discount the value back to the present to get an apples-to-apples view of all components of Year 10 book value.

   One benefit of this version of the model is that some value is explicitly placed on productive *assets* already owned by the business.

5. Total the estimated ten-year book value.

Now comes the fun part: figuring out the acquisition price based on the price-to-book (P/B) ratio:

6. Determine what price-to-book you should use.

   Which one you use depends on the type of business, what other comparable acquisitions show, and your own intuition. In a manufacturing business, a P/B of 2.0 is probably reasonable because book values of productive physical assets tend to be low. If you're valuing a financial institution, with assets mainly in cash and receivables, the model P/B would likely be lower. If you're valuing a technology company, the P/B may perhaps be higher.

Book VII

Value Investing

Using today's P/B ratio is a place to start, although if it's much higher than 1.0, there's a tendency for the ratio to decline over time as growth patterns settle and the company matures. Any P/B ratio exceeding 3 is probably excessive.

7. Multiply the total ten-year book value by acquisition P/B and, *voilà,* you get intrinsic value.

Depending on how you set the assumptions, the indefinite life model and ten-year acquisition models yield similar results. That isn't a big surprise because acquiring firms are (or should be) looking for the same kinds of intrinsic value characteristics that you are.

The iStockResearch model

As fundamental as intrinsic value modeling may seem, it's surprising how few tools are available for individual consumer investors to put it into play. Such models are commonly used by value-oriented investing professionals, but, possibly due to their complexity and sticky assumptions like discount rates, they haven't hit the mainstream.

The best tool available today, offered as a stand-alone Web site by Canadian-born and educated CFA (chartered financial analyst) Alexander Chepakovich, is iStockResearch, available at www.istockresearch.com.

The iStockResearch model is similar to the indefinite life model but is more complete. First, the site contains the financial data for most major U.S. companies, so you don't have to find it yourself. Second, rather than a split first- and second-stage growth pattern, the model allows a yearly decline or "decay" in growth rates — perhaps more realistic. Finally, it factors in stock option grants (the earlier models did not), and it supplies a recommended discount rate based on current economic conditions and the industry the company is part of. The results, as shown in Figure 4-3, are similar to the other models. Note that you can modify the growth and discount assumptions as you choose to get a range of acceptable modeling results.

The site is free and easy to use, and it gives a complete set of raw financial data to help in other analysis. This site and set of tools is highly recommended for beginning and more experienced value investors.

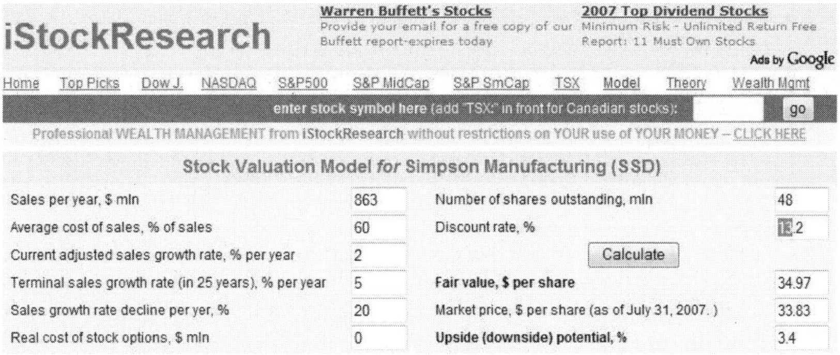

Figure 4-3:
The iStock
Research.
com stock
valuation
model.

The Ben Graham model

Finally, and perhaps most simply, it's worth checking out intrinsic value through the eyes of Ben Graham, based on his 1930s formula:

$$\text{Intrinsic value} = \text{Earnings} \times [(2 \times \text{growth rate}) + 8.5] \times [4.4 \div \text{bond yield}]$$

A simple straight-line formula, no exponents, no first- and second-stage stuff, no discount rate? Could it work? In a word, yes.

The Graham model, derived from the more complex model but philosophically aligned to it, can be used as computational shorthand. It doesn't allow for stages and uses a more simplistic discounting assumption. And it can produce the same wide range of results as the other models. But it is a good shortcut — one you may be able to do in your head when looking at a number of investment choices.

Looking at Strategic Financials:
It's All about ROE

Return on equity (ROE), at the end of the day, is one of the most important business growth drivers. Sustained ROE implies sustained growth and blares out loudly "well-managed company!" Strategic financials represent the factors management can shape and control to achieve growth, ROE, and, hence, intrinsic value.

Book VII

Value Investing

Unlike intrinsic value, ROE doesn't estimate the value of a company. You can't go through a series of calculations culminating in a per-share value estimate. But ROE — and its components — can tell whether things are healthy and moving in the right direction. Another way to look at the difference: Intrinsic value explicitly looks forward into the income-producing capability of the firm in the long run, while strategic valuation is primarily a snapshot of the present, albeit with many components that can predict future performance.

ROE may appear to be a single number, but in fact there's a complex chain of events or set of factors underlying the figure. A series of business fundamentals, all linked together, leads to respectable, sustained, and growing ROE. That "strategic value" chain will become clearer in the strategic profit formula, which I cover next.

The strategic profit formula

In the strategic profit formula, sometimes called the *DuPont formula* because it originated in DuPont's finance department, it's easy to see the links in the chain: profitability, productivity, and capital structure, in sequence:

$$\text{Return on equity} = [\text{profits/sales}] \times [\text{sales/assets}] \times [\text{assets/equity}]$$

The intermediate terms in this formula tell a great deal about the health of the business. For each intermediate term in the formula, you want to know its value, in what direction it's going (trend), and how it compares to others in the industry.

ROE, defined as net earnings divided by owners' equity, is a capitalist's bottom line. It represents the return on owners' equity invested in the business. As a practical matter, although it can be jiggered somewhat through accounting policy and practice, it's a good barometer to determine whether the company is on the right track and whether management is doing a good job. Other things to know about ROE:

✔ Over time, ROE trends toward the earnings growth rate of the company. A company with a 5 percent earnings growth rate and a 20 percent ROE today will see ROE gradually diminish toward 5 percent. A company with a 20 percent earnings growth rate and a 10 percent ROE will see ROE move toward 20 percent, as the numerator grows at a faster rate than the denominator.

✔ ROE doesn't just happen all by itself. A series of business fundamentals, all linked together and controlled or influenced by management, leads to respectable, sustained, and growing ROE. The links are profitability, productivity, and capital structure. When all three are strong and tight, ROE outcome is destined for success. If a business fundamental is poor or failing, it can weaken the entire chain and hamper ROE indefinitely.

✔ Pay attention to ROTC, *return on total capital.* ROTC is owners' equity plus long-term debt. If a company is growing ROE but not ROTC, chances are the company is borrowing to fund growth-producing assets, thus leveraging the company. (In moderation, this *can* be a good thing.) So look at ROTC and ROE together. They should march side by side and change in unison. Many information services such as Value Line provide both figures simultaneously.

✔ Unlike intrinsic value, covered in the preceding section, ROE doesn't purport to estimate the value of a company. Although intrinsic value is an absolute measure of company value, ROE and its components tend to be relative to past performance and to the performance of other businesses.

Bottom line: Maintaining a constant ROE percentage requires steady earnings growth. For that reason, a company with increasing ROE, without undue exposure to debt or leverage, is especially attractive.

ROE value chain components

Each link in the ROE chain has its own component drivers. For instance, *strategic financials* such as gross margins and expenses drive profitability. Asset levels, quality, and turnover drive productivity, while debt and new capital requirements drive capital structure. In turn, *strategic intangibles* such as market position, customer share and loyalty, brand strength, and supply chain strength drive those margins and expenses.

Figure 4-4 illustrates the strategic value chain. ROE, the result, is shown as a result or outcome at the right-hand side of the figure. Working backwards toward the left, the figure lists a few examples of value chain components that drive ROE components and thus ROE. They're grouped into strategic financials (measurable financial factors) and strategic intangibles (mostly immeasurable market and business characteristics that drive them).

The value investor works backward through the ROE value chain to find good or bad in ROE drivers and the things that influence those drivers.

For the first-tier components of ROE, perform a quality test. Look for characteristics that are off course. For example, low debt doesn't necessarily indicate high value, but frequent trips to the capital markets for debt or stock sales may indicate capital starvation and "un-value." Consider a drug test metaphor here: The substances you're testing for are frequently addictive to bad managements — overuse of acquisitions, write-offs and write-downs, debt, and stock sales, which are used to pad numbers and fix problems arising from bad performance. Keep in mind that drug tests are usually painless pass/fail tests, not detailed assessments.

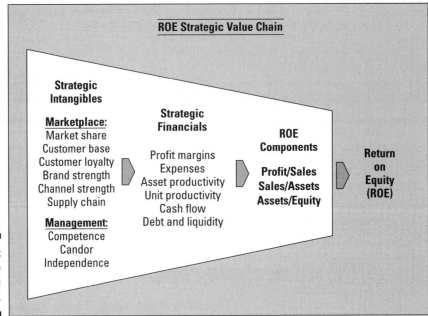

ROE Strategic Value Chain

Figure 4-4:
The
strategic
value chain.

Measuring profitability

To measure profitability, you want to first consider the financial drivers that lead to the net profit percent. Then you want to test the major ROE components for any signs of trouble. Finally, you need to look at the intangibles.

Financial drivers

Profit/sales, or *net profit percent,* is the primary profitability measure. No surprise here. But when looking at profitability, look at the dynamics behind net profit percent. Specifically, you want to look at gross margin, SG&A, and operating profit percent.

Gross margin

Gross margin tells a lot about a business's success in managing its sales and the direct costs of producing products and services. A company on top of its marketing and production game usually produces improving margins.

Market characteristics and selling aggressiveness can work against margins. Intuitively, you may guess that increased volumes lead to increased margins, as fixed costs are absorbed and economies of scale work in their favor. However, this isn't always the case. A company often must make price concessions to achieve sales goals. And aggressive volume building also takes its toll on operating costs (not part of gross margin) in the form of marketing expenses and sometimes interest expense to expand the level of business. The key is to understand the industry in which you want to invest.

Selling, general, and administrative

Selling, general, and administrative (SG&A), although not directly tied to net profit percent, tells a lot about how management controls expenses and how expenses are tied to business production. SG&A percentage is the total SG&A cost divided by sales or revenues. You have to calculate this one yourself, as few information sources provide this info. It is an important part of total operating expenses — and thus operating profit percentage. Also be aware that different companies define SG&A differently, so look to annual reports for clarification.

When SG&A increases faster than sales, that's a bad sign, especially in a maturing industry. Although investors tolerate short-term expenditures in marketing campaigns, store openings, or customer relationship management platforms, these can't go on forever. Chronic SG&A percentage increases are a red flag.

Operating profit

SG&A is part of this important figure, but certainly not all. Depreciation, amortization, and certain facility and employee costs can all influence operating expenses. A company in control of gross margin *and* operating expenses will show increased operating profit.

Even though some companies may go through periods of deteriorating gross margins, focus on *total* profitability and tight control of SG&A and other operating expenses may keep operating profit percentages relatively flat — a good sign that management is managing total shareholder return.

Quality checks

As you do your evaluation of the major ROE components, test each one for signs of trouble or inherent weakness. Here are key quality checks for profitability:

- ✔ **Overdependence on acquisitions for growth:** Companies sometimes get so caught up in building the top line that they resort to painful and expensive acquisitions to do it. Profitability usually suffers.

- ✔ **Excessive goodwill:** Often working hand-in-hand with acquisitions, growth in goodwill or a growing gap between total stockholder equity and net tangible assets can signal trouble in the form of future write-offs.

- **Overdependence on expansion:** Growth is good, but if the core business isn't growing or is declining, that's a bad sign. Try to sniff out *organic growth* — that is, growth not sourced from new outlets or acquisitions. If sales are expanding but profits aren't, it's a sign that the most recent expansions aren't working. (However, it depends on the industry: A Starbucks outlet will produce returns more quickly than an aircraft plant.)

- **Cash flow and changes in book value march with changes in earnings:** If earnings rise but cash flow and book value don't, over time, you must question the quality of earnings.

Intangible drivers

Obviously, the intangibles you want to pay attention to are those that are relevant to gross margins:

- **Market position:** It's a vital influencer, involving a myriad of things: market leadership, brand dominance, public image, pricing power and so on.

- **Resource acquisition or supply chain power:** This directly affects costs.

- **Reporting quality:** Do a quick spot check of cash flows and changes in book value as they relate to earnings. Once again, it's important to understand write-offs and extraordinary items that may affect the analysis.

- **A check with neighbors:** See how other businesses in the industry are faring.

Basically, you want to look for improving profitability measures and to be able to explain those that aren't improving.

Measuring productivity

Productivity measures tell us how well companies deploy and use assets. All things considered, a dollar of sales produced on 50 cents worth of assets is better than the same company producing a dollar of sales on a dollar of assets. Obviously, asset productivity figures vary by industry as different industries require different assets to do business.

Financial drivers

Sales/assets is the primary measure of asset productivity and is simply the amount of sales generated per asset dollar deployed. As you look at sales/assets, avoid these two traps:

✔ **Misinterpreting changes due to write-offs:** If a company took the plunge to purge a big chunk of overvalued or nonexistent assets from the books, that would show up as an "improvement" in sales/assets. Not! Be careful to distill out major changes in asset deployment that create no change in the business.

✔ **Reading too much into the absolute numbers:** Sales/assets will be huge for a Microsoft or Oracle, reporting high sales on a small asset base, while a large industrial corporation, railroad, or electric utility requiring a large asset infrastructure will appear to have poor asset utilization. Be careful about comparing across industries. Good comparisons — and trends — are most important.

Deconstructing ROA

Many popular information services show ROA, return on assets. If you're wondering why ROA doesn't make the grade as a first-tier ROE component, here's why: ROA really does too much.

ROA is net profit divided by total assets, which you'll recognize as the first two links in the ROE chain combined. (Profit/assets = profit/sales × sales/assets, for you math types.) I don't dispute the validity and value of ROA but prefer to look at the two links separately. The first measure, profit/sales, has more to do with market power and cost structures, while the second, sales/assets, has more to do with resource requirements and deployment. Deconstructing ROA provides a more bottoms-up, inside-out view of the business.

Keep in mind that if ROA and profit margin figures are supplied by an information portal such as Yahoo! Finance or Value Line, you can deduce asset productivity. Bad ROA and good margins equal bad productivity.

Deconstructing sales/assets

An obvious key to understanding total sales/assets is to understand utilization for individual assets making up the total asset base. Accounts receivable, inventory, and fixed assets are the major food groups in this value chain.

✔ **Accounts receivable turnover:** How many dollars in sales does the business generate per dollar of accounts receivable investment? A business on top of its receivables generates more and more, through faster collections and extending less credit altogether. When examining statements for accounts receivable, use *trade* accounts receivable — those that arise from and support the normal course of business.

✔ **Inventory turnover:** A business in control of finished goods, raw material, and production inventories shows greater sales per dollar invested in inventory.

Book VII

Value Investing

✔ **Fixed asset turnover:** This is another turnover measure, this time for fixed assets or PP&E (property, plant, and equipment).

Occasionally you'll see a modest sales/asset gain when the big three components — accounts receivable, inventory, and fixed assets — showed larger improvements, up to 50 percent. In many cases, this is due to increased cash, which is also an asset and part of the denominator base. If a company shows stubbornly little improvement in asset productivity as reported, sometimes it's because of cash accumulation — sometimes because of other assets. Scrupulous value investors should check to make sure what those other assets represent.

✔ **Unit productivity measures:** If the figures are available, you can go into sales per facility, sales per store, same-store-sales growth, revenue per mile of track or passenger seat flown, or sales per square foot, depending on the industry. You can also track sales per employee, a handy metric for overall efficiency and management competence. Finding historic data for these factors can be challenging, but such unit productivity metrics are good for comparing with other firms in the same industry once you understand them.

For a possible clue that problems are present, look at asset write-downs. If write-downs are excessive and persistent, asset quality — and really, asset acquisition — problems are evident. On the flip side, a company not taking sufficient write-downs may also be suspect. If technology changes, capital equipment is overbought, or sales are declining, asset write-downs not taken may spell trouble. The telecommunications industry is a recent example.

Quality checks

Asset productivity measures themselves are pretty good at sniffing out quality problems: If a company has the wrong assets or poor quality assets, they generally won't generate as much sales or income. Value investors should look at write-offs and write-off history: If a company seems to always be writing off some inventory or writing down accounts receivable with impairment charges and reserves, asset quality may be called into question.

Sometimes a more subjective assessment comes into play: Do company facilities look modern and efficient? Does a company keep up with trends in information technology and supply chain management? These questions can be hard to answer and are more intangible than measurable, but closely followed businesses will usually yield some clues.

Intangible drivers

Asset quality is greatly influenced by depreciation and amortization policies. Channel structure (direct, single-tier retail, two-tier wholesale-retail, OEM, or other) can greatly influence the amount of assets required, particularly receivables and inventory. And of course, the base nature of the business — the cost structure — can tell a lot. A steel mill has different asset needs and utilization than a nail salon.

Looking at trends within individual metrics makes sense — improving values at all tiers is a healthy thing. Give special credit to consistent improvement through business cycles. Depending on the industry, you may balance emphasis on inventory, accounts receivable, and fixed assets differently. And it never hurts to compare companies to other companies, so long as you're comparing apples to apples.

Looking at capital structure

When looking at capital structure, you're trying to determine two things:

- ✔ Is the business a consumer or producer of capital? Does it constantly require capital infusions to build growth or replace assets?

- ✔ Is the business properly leveraged? Overleveraged businesses are at risk and additionally burden earnings with interest payments. Underleveraged businesses, while better than overleveraged, may not be maximizing potential returns to shareholders.

Assets/equity

The first-tier measure for capital structure is assets/equity. Per dollar of owners' equity invested, how many dollars of productive assets are deployed in the business? For the second-tier evaluation, the key questions are "Is more capital needed?" and "Is the company properly leveraged?"

Capital sufficiency

Capital-hungry companies are sometimes hard to detect, but there are a few obvious signs. Companies in capital-intensive industries, such as manufacturing, transportation, or telecommunications, are likely suspects. Here are a few indicators:

- ✔ **Share buybacks:** The number of shares outstanding can be a simple indicator of a capital-hungry company. A company using cash to retire shares — if acting sensibly — is telling you that it generates more capital than it needs.

    When evaluating share buybacks, make sure to look at actual shares outstanding. Relying on company news releases alone can be misleading. Companies also buy back shares to support employee incentive programs or to accumulate shares for an acquisition. Such repurchases may be okay but aren't the kind of repurchases that increase return on equity for remaining owners.

✔ **Cash flow ratio:** Pay attention to the cash flow ratio (refer to Chapter 3), which shows whether cash flow from operations is enough to meet investing and financing requirements (in this case, the repayment of debt). If not, it's back to the capital markets. This figure is pretty elusive unless you have — and study — statements of cash flow.

✔ **Lengthening asset cycles:** If accounts receivable collection periods and inventory holding periods are lengthening, that forewarns the need for more capital.

✔ **Working capital:** A company requiring steady increases in working capital to support sales requires, naturally, capital. Working capital is capital.

Leverage

Some debt is usually regarded as a good thing because it expands the size of the business and hence the return on owner capital. But too much is too much. Guiding principles include comparative analysis and vulnerability to downturns. Debt must always be paid back, whether business is good or not — so debt stops being okay when it's too large to cover during a downturn or business strategy change. Here are a couple supporting metrics:

✔ **Debt to equity:** This old standard is used over and over to get a feel for indebtedness and particularly for industry comparison. The calculation is simple, but remember that it refers to long-term debt. A deteriorating D/E over time is a bad sign unless you understand the context. A worsening D/E without a reduction in shares is less healthy.

✔ **Interest coverage:** One way to look at whether a business has the right amount of debt is to look at how much of its earnings are consumed to service (pay interest on) it. Interest coverage is the ratio of earnings to annual interest, a rough indication of how solvent or burdened a company is by debt.

Quality checks

As you evaluate all the other measures of productivity, keep a look out for these, which can let you know whether the company has an insatiable demand for capital:

✔ **Current assets (besides cash) rising faster than business:** More receivables result from extending credit, while losing channel structure and supply chain battles (customers and distributors won't carry inventory, suppliers are making them carry more inventory) result in increased inventories. The risk is greater capital requirements and expensive impairments downstream.

   ✔ **Debt growing faster than business:** Over a sustained period, debt rising
     faster than business growth is a problem. If the owners won't kick in to
     grow the business, and if retained earnings aren't sufficient to meet growth,
     what does that tell you?

   ✔ **Repeated financings:** If the business continually has to approach the
     capital markets (other than in startup phases), that again is a sign that
     internally generated earnings and cash flows aren't sufficient.

Intangibles

Several intangibles enter in here:

   ✔ **Credit ratings and changes in credit ratings:** Declining credit ratings
     mean that someone somewhere is less secure with the capital structure
     as currently deployed.

   ✔ **Capital intensity, particularly changes in capital intensity:** The semi-
     conductor business happily churning out DRAM chips becomes less
     happy when equipment must be replaced with more expensive equip-
     ment more often. Such shortening product cycles can similarly stoke the
     capital requirement fires for software companies and the like.

   ✔ **Quality:** A company that faces its finances head on is in better shape
     than one that plays games, delays write-downs, uses good debt to
     finance bad assets, and the like. There are specific indicators and a lot of
     general ones, such as the thickness of 10-K reports (refer to Chapter 2),
     the tone of press coverage, the departure of CFOs, and so forth.

Book VII

**Value
Investing**

Evaluating strategic intangibles

Warren Buffett once famously said: "If you gave me $100 billion and said 'take
away the soft drink leadership of Coca-Cola in the world,' I'd give it back to
you and say it can't be done." This quote underlies the essence of strategic
intangibles: the difference between a *business* and a mere set of assets and
liabilities.

Intangibles come in all shapes and sizes. Every company has different intangibles. This section discusses marketing and management tenets that separate
great from good, focusing on those that are clearly strategic in the creation of
value in the business and return for the shareholders. So much of what
makes excellent businesses excellent transcends the arcane world of factories, storefronts, products, and packages. And most of it can be controlled or
influenced by good management.

Market power

Market power is all about advantage. Market power is strength in franchise, brand, customer base, supply chain power, or other competence that gives the company an advantage in the marketplace. Advantage drives and protects the first component of ROE: profitability.

The franchise factor

A *franchise* is an established, sustainable, powerful position in a market (not to be confused with the term's other meaning: the one you can buy from a restaurant or convenience store chain allowing you to sell merchandise or services under someone else's logo). Franchise is probably the most valuable asset a business can have. Coca-Cola is the classic case of the franchise, a situation in which the power of the brand and the reputation of the company have created a near-unassailable fortress around the production and sale of flavored sugar water.

Franchises also create barriers to entry (called "creating a moat"). If you can grill burgers, you can set up a hamburger stand, but can you set up a McDonald's? Would anyone come? "Creating a moat" describes franchise power that keeps competitors away — and keeps the business and its fundamentals moving in the right direction. What determines the width and depth of a moat? The following sections explain.

The brand centerpiece

One external manifestation of the marketing machine that creates enduring value is the brand. Brands are built over time through a combination of good products and good presentation of those products to the marketplace. Key factors that define a brand include:

- ✔ **Image:** How the public perceives the brand in the marketplace. This perception relates not only to product quality but also with the ideas and images that people associate with the company. People tend to associate Wrangler with rugged Western jeans, for example, and Harley-Davidson with rugged individualism.

- ✔ **Familiarity:** Familiarity creates mindshare, drives repeat or habitual purchase, and creates barriers for entry. Most value investors place a high value on habitual repeat purchase.

- ✔ **Reputation:** Reputation builds slowly over time and provides a powerful umbrella giving storm shelter when other things go wrong. But it must be nurtured and handled with care. When considering companies to invest in, look for businesses that manage their mistakes well.

Brand can tell a lot about a company's value. It's up to you to decide how valuable the brand is in the marketplace both today and in the future.

Market share and leadership

Market leadership means that a company defines the market, sets the pace in price and product, and (usually) is tied to a strong brand. Market leadership often leads to cost advantages through buying power and economies of scale. To evaluate market share and leadership, look for two things: (1) to what degree does the business possess market share and leadership and (2) does it do the right things and have the right attitude to maintain its market position and grow it?

Customer base

A company with a loyal customer base can depend on repeat sales and spend less money acquiring new customers. Profitability increases through lower marketing costs and repeat sales driven other than by price. A business treating a customer base as an asset is more successful than one that treats it as a liability. Score for strong, loyal customer base and business strategies that employ the customer base as an asset and capitalize on it. Don't forget that this applies to business-to-business companies, not only to consumer businesses.

Special competencies

Does the company have some kind of infrastructure, business model, or technology that's difficult to duplicate? Does it have the best search engine or most innovative designs or best support available? Does it have special knowledge, experience, or intellectual capital that others don't have? Score a plus if this is the case.

Book VII

Value Investing

The supply chain

Look at the degree of control a company exerts over its suppliers as well as its distribution channels. Also pay attention to how much influence a company has on stability, sustainable and growable sales, and stable costs. A company that can economically sell directly to its customers may have an advantage.

All about management

Just as important as market power, company management is another intangible pillar. Four attributes indicate management excellence:

- ✔ **Competence:** Does management have the right vision, make the right decisions, and offer good reasons for those decisions? Does it make sound investments in existing businesses? In new businesses? Does it understand — and control — expenses? Does it make changes when changes should be made, being neither too eager nor too reluctant to make them? Does it make reasonable projections about growth and earnings? I could go on and on, but suffice it to say that good management understands the business, has a realistic view of it, has a solid rationale behind strategies and decisions, and employs resources wisely within it.

✔ **Candor:** Value investors like managers who communicate quickly and honestly about business issues and problems — and without undue spin, jargon or buzzwords. These managers disclose as much data as they can about their businesses, including information about sector performance, unit productivity, and key strategies and investments. Along with candor, a little of the right attitude goes a long way. Arrogant managers who hide problems, think they can solve them all, or think they are invincible are bound for trouble.

✔ **Independence:** Good management teams think and act independently and for the long-term health of the business, and they resist the temptation to pour energy and resources into achieving this quarter's results. They have a vision, a mission, and a plan and follow them, avoiding distractions.

✔ **Customer focus:** A management team focused on customers is more likely to succeed than one focused on its internal issues and on competitors.

Evaluating management excellence can be tricky. You don't sit or work with these managers on a daily basis; in fact, much of what they do is deliberately kept secret. Solid information about a company's management is usually hard to find. Yet, a sensitive antenna can pick up a lot over a period of time. Yahoo! Finance provides links to the bios and executive compensation of management. Read the paper and watch corporate communications and press releases to catch the buzz about a company's management.

Ownership

By looking at a company's ownership, particularly those who own the largest pieces of the business, you can discover something of the attractiveness of the business to others — and to its own management.

✔ **Management as owners:** Management ownership reflects management commitment. One of the best places to find out what insiders own and what they're doing with their holdings is Yahoo! Finance and its "Insider Roster" and "Insider Transactions" pages. You can also refer to company publications, including annual reports, but these may be a little less current.

✔ **Institutions as owners:** Yahoo! Finance under the "Major Holders" tab shows the top ten institutional shareholders — usually large banks, pension funds, or trusts. The larger the holdings, and the more blue chip the names, the better. You can also see whether institutions have been buying, but realize that this data may be outdated.

✔ **Mutual funds as owners:** Yahoo! Finance (again under the "Major Holders" tab) shows the top ten largest mutual fund holders. Look for who, how much, and what kind of fund. If the top ten funds all are value funds, that may be a good sign.

Deciding When the Price Is Right

Sooner or later, price enters the value equation. By far, the most popular valuation tool is the price-to-earnings (P/E) ratio, which is one of the major ways that investors make sense of the price tag. This section explores how you can use P/E to price a business.

There is no formula for applying P/E. "If it's 17 you buy, and if it's 25 you sell" doesn't work. A deeper understanding of the P/E and underlying fundamentals is required. The following sections provide some of that depth by developing a better understanding of the P/E measure and what it really means.

Earnings yield

What is P/E? It is the ratio of share price to earnings. But there's more information than meets the eye. First, P/E tells how many years it would take to recoup an investment, with earnings staying the same. A P/E of 17 means that with flat earnings, it would take 17 years to recover your investment. A P/E of 40 means 40 years. But a greater revelation occurs when we turn the ratio upside down. The inverse ratio *(earnings yield)* tells the annual percentage return implied by the P/E. It is simply 1/(P/E).

If P/E is 10, then 1/(P/E) is 0.1 or 10 percent. If P/E is 40, then 1/(P/E) is 0.025 or 2.5 percent. This figure is the equivalent yield the investor would use to compare this earnings stream to, suppose, a bond. A bond returning $5 on a face value of $100 yields 5 percent. A stock returning $5 in earnings on $100 invested (stock price) could also be said to yield 5 percent and would have a P/E ratio of 20 ($100 ÷ $5). Table 4-1 is one of the simpler math tables you'll see in value investing; it illustrates the wide range of investment yields implied by different P/E ratios.

Book VII

Value
Investing

Table 4-1	Converting P/E to Earnings Yield
P/E	*Earnings Yield*
1	100.0 percent
5	20.0 percent
8	12.5 percent
10	10.0 percent
12	8.3 percent
15	6.7 percent

(continued)

Table 4-1 *(continued)*

P/E	Earnings Yield
20	5.0 percent
30	3.3 percent
40	2.5 percent
50	2.0 percent
60	1.7 percent
75	1.3 percent
100	1.0 percent

P/E and growth

Of course, it would be nice if looking at price, P/E, and earnings yield was all there was to it. Find an earnings yield of 6 percent (P/E of 17), beat the bond, and move on. But you're buying equities, not bonds, because you want to participate in company growth and success.

Assessing growth is a major factor in analyzing a stock price through P/E. What is the earnings yield today, what will it be in the future, and how does it get into the equation? Table 4-2 shows future earnings yields realized in the case of a bond with no growth versus a stock with a 10 percent earnings growth.

Table 4-2   Earnings Yield: Bond versus Growth Stock

	Bond	Stock
Coupon/earnings yield	5 percent	5 percent
Investment	$100	$100
Year 1 return	$5	$5
Earnings growth	0 percent	10 percent
Year 10 return	$5	$12.97
Earnings Yield (EY) year 1	5 percent	5 percent
Earnings Yield (EY) year 10	5 percent	13 percent

A PEG in a poke

By itself, it's hard to tell whether a P/E is good or bad. A stock with a P/E of 30 may be a better deal than another stock with a P/E of 15 because of growth. A stock of a no-growth company with a P/E of 15 will never achieve an earnings yield beyond 7.5 percent (1/15). Meanwhile the company with a P/E of 30, with a growth rate of 20 percent, eventually achieves an earnings yield greater than 20 percent.

Enter the *price-earnings to growth* or PEG ratio, which is introduced in Chapter 3. PEG *normalizes* the P/E to the growth rate. With PEG, apparently high P/E ratios are supported by look-ahead growth. PEG thus becomes a better tool to compare stocks with different P/Es and different underlying growth assumptions. In the PEG ratio, you divide all P/Es by the company's growth rate. *G* is the growth rate, expressed as a whole number (that is, the percentage times 100). So a company with a P/E of 30 and a growth rate of 20 percent has a PEG of 1.5.

PEG gives you a standard for comparison. Company A with a P/E of 18 and a growth rate of 12 percent has the same PEG as Company B with a P/E of 30 and a growth rate of 20 percent. Although the two P/Es aren't the same (30 versus 18), the PEG ratio reveals that they are indeed priced equally.

Table 4-3 show the relationship between future earnings yield, P/E, and PEG. Watch what happens to PEG and future earnings yields as growth assumptions rise. Low PEG ratios (less than 2) correspond to high future earnings yields.

Book VII

Value Investing

Table 4-3	Earnings Growth, Earnings Yield, and PEG				
	Bond	**Stock 1**	**Stock 2**	**Stock 3**	**Stock 4**
Coupon/ Earnings Yield	5 percent	5 percent	5 percent	5 percent	5 percent
Investment	$100	$100	$100	$100	$100
Year 1 return	$5	$5	$5	$5	$5
Earnings growth	0 percent	5 percent	10 percent	15 percent	20 percent
Year 10 return	$5	$8.14	$12.97	$20.23	$30.96
EY (year 1)	5 percent	5 percent	5 percent	5 percent	5 percent
EY (year 10)	5 percent	8.1 percent	13 percent	20.2 percent	31 percent
Year 1 P/E	N/A	20	20	20	20
Year 1 PEG	N/A	4	2	1.3	1

So what is a "good" PEG ratio? It all depends on the implied future rate of return you're looking for, which depends on investment objectives, risk tolerance, and current risk-free (bond) interest rates.

Hurdle rates and the 15 percent rule

Warren Buffett looks at P/E and growth in a slightly different way, using so-called *hurdle rates.* A hurdle rate is what the name implies: a minimum level of compounded annual returns, or a "bar" over which a business — and thus a stock price — must be able to appreciate to be deemed a good investment. Part of Buffett's thought process is this: If an investment cannot clear a given hurdle, the capital is probably better deployed elsewhere.

Buffett is known to use a 15 percent rule is to determine if a stock's price can feasibly grow at a minimum annual compounded rate, or *hurdle rate.* The analysis examines current stock price, earnings growth, and potential future stock price based on that growth. If the growth-supported future stock price can appreciate at a compounded annual growth rate (CAGR) meeting or exceeding the hurdle rate, it is in buy territory. If appreciation potential is short of the required price growth hurdle, the stock is rejected. Either the current stock price is too high or the projected growth is too weak to meet the growth hurdle.

At the risk of providing an oversimplified example, consider Coca-Cola, which recently sold for $60.50 with annual earnings of $2.34, a P/E ratio of 25.9 and an annual earnings growth rate of 13.3 percent.

The earnings growth rate is quite healthy for a company the size of Coca-Cola, a $28 billion company in annual sales. But the fact that earnings growth trails the hurdle rate, and that the P/E exceeds market averages (about 18 for the S&P 500 at the time), and that earnings yield is under 4 percent, you would be skeptical of Coke as an investment.

Taking the calculation further, you might project what Coke's EPS would be after 10 years:

$$\$2.34 \times (1 + 0.133)^{10} = \$8.16$$

Then, calculate the stock price appreciation necessary to meet the 15 percent hurdle:

$$\$60.50 \times (1 + 0.15)^{10} = \$244.75$$

Then, calculate the implied P/E in ten years:

$$\$244.75 \div \$8.16, \text{ or } 30$$

The stock would have to command a P/E of 30 after ten years, despite growing dramatically to reach that level — a P/E that is in all probability unrealistic. Put differently, the stock price is unlikely to grow at 15 percent given the assumptions made. Either earnings growth would have to exceed the current expectation, or the current stock price would have to be lower, to make the 15 percent hurdle.

So using this approach, you would probably reject the investment at the current price.

Before rejecting Coke altogether, you must consider whether the 13.3 percent earnings growth rate is really right. If sales, profitability, and/or productivity are in for major improvement, Coke could still be a good buy. The very strong 26 percent gross margins and 29 percent ROE tell an unusually good story. Don't forget the fundamentals underlying earnings and earnings growth.

A Practical Approach

Throughout the four chapters presented in this book, you've been exposed to many of the tools — and, more importantly, the thought processes — of today's value investor.

At the end of the day, value investors develop their own customized approach to analyzing a business and an investment, derived from these tools and thought processes — an approach that works for them. It works because it makes sense, and as it gets fine-tuned over time, it works from experience.

Many value investors, especially in the beginning, make checklists to help evaluate financial and intangible features of business. They evaluate each business opportunity as if they were attempting to buy the business, looking at assets, profits, growth, customer base, market presence, and management quality as if they were going to have to live with it for a while.

It's not unlike the approach a rational, numbers-oriented buyer might use to buy a car: look at features and performance data, then test-drive it to see if it all works well together, to see if the whole is at least equal to (preferably better than) the sum of the parts. And yes, the tires are kicked and the doors are opened and closed to check for obvious problems and complete the impression. And the car is carefully compared to other cars in the category — all before talking to the dealer or owner about price.

Book VII

Value Investing

Over time, you'll get better at and more comfortable with the value investing approach. You'll learn what to look for so you don't have to get down to every detail of horsepower and gear ratios. Experienced value investors do the diligence, but they learn what's most important to look at in a business as they learn the industry and other similar businesses. Buffett is famous for doing most of his analysis in his head; like most business owners, you'll get to the point where you can do a lot in your head, too.

Remember: At the end of the day, the thought process is just as important as the mechanics, if not more so.

Book VIII
Technical Analysis

The 5th Wave   By Rich Tennant

"Right now I'm working with a combination of charting techniques: Japanese Candlesticks, some Elliott Waves, and a dash of Chaos theory."

In this book . . .

Timing is critical in cooking, romance, music, politics, farming, and a hundred other aspects of life on this planet. Putting money into a securities market is no different — you need good timing to get the best results.

Technical traders all over the world earn a living using technical analysis to time their trades. They not only earn a living, but they're still standing after a market crash. In this book, I try to explain how they do that, and how you can do it, too.

Chapter 1

Wrapping Your Brain around Technical Analysis

*G*et ready to suspend belief in everything you think you know about trading and investing. Technical analysis, a set of forecasting methods that can help you make better trading decisions, focuses on the price of a security rather than the fundamentals of the company behind the security. In technical analysis, you observe how prices actually move and try to use past regularities in price movements to predict future regularities. Basically it's a way of charting price trends so that you can make rational trading decisions that bypass greed, fear, and the other emotions that often accompany trading.

Technical Analysis Defined: Observing Prices Directly

Technical analysis is the study of how securities prices behave and how to exploit that information to make money while avoiding losses. Basically, with technical analysis, you work to identify price trends (a *trend* is a discernible directional bias in the price — upwards, downwards, or sideways). Following are the basic observations underlying technical analysis:

✔ Securities prices move in trends much of the time, and trends remain in place until some major event comes along to stop them.

Prices incorporate (or *discount*) all known information about the security, and prices change as new information becomes available. *All known information* consists of hundreds of factors ranging from accurate facts to opinions, guesses, and emotions — and previous prices. They all go into the supply and demand for a security and result in its price.

✔ Trends can be identified with patterns that you see repeatedly and with *support and resistance* trendlines (both are covered in Chapter 4).

✔ Primary trends (lasting months or years) are punctuated by secondary movements (lasting weeks or months) in the opposite direction of the primary trend. Secondary trends, or *retracements,* are the very devil to deal with as a trader. See the later section "Retracements" for details.

Your goal is to forecast the price of the security over some future time horizon in order to buy and sell the security to make a cash profit. The emphasis in technical analysis is to make profits from trading, not from owning a security as some kind of savings vehicle, although long-term investors use technical analysis as well.

Charting course

Because in technical analysis prices and trends rule, you have to be able to track and identify them. Although technical analysts have developed numerous indicators based on price and volume that can be expressed as statistics, tables of numbers, and other formats, you'll spend most of your time looking at charts, like the one shown in Figure 1-1 which illustrates a classic uptrend following a downtrend.

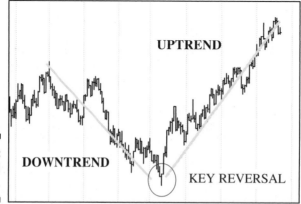

Figure 1-1:
Uptrend and
downtrend.

At the most basic level, your goal is to shun the security shown on the chart while it's downtrending and to identify the key reversal point — which is the best place to buy — as early as possible. To do this successfully, you absolutely, positively must become attuned to looking at charts and trying to figure out what the prices are telling you.

A chart is the workspace of technical analysis. Technical analysts have developed numerous indicators based on price and volume that can be expressed as statistics, tables of numbers, and other formats, but the core method remains a graphic display of prices on a chart.

Uncovering the essence of market movements

Securities are different from cars, bread, and socks. You don't buy a security for the joy of owning it and using it. The main reason to buy a security is to sell it again, preferably for more than you paid for it.

In securities trading, the pricing process is more like an auction than the traditional *price-discovery* process of classical economics, in which demand for an item depends on its price: If something is rare, it's expensive. At higher and higher prices, demand falls off. At some point, the high price induces suppliers to produce more of the thing, whereupon the price falls. The price-discovery process can be lengthy.

In auction economics, demand *increases* as the price rises. The item may or may not be scarce in the real world — it doesn't matter. The immediacy of the auction is what skews prices, sometimes to absurd levels. Later, when suppliers see the high prices, they may indeed be able to find or produce more of the item — but by then, the specific demand dynamic of that one auction is gone.

When you decide to buy a security, it's because you think the price will rise. When you decide to sell, it's because you have a juicy profit that meets your needs, or because you have taken an intolerable loss. You seldom think about the true supply of the security. And, in fact, while the supply of any security is limited by the number of shares outstanding and the like, supply may be considered infinite for all practical purposes, because a price exists at which you can induce someone to sell you what you want.

In technical trading, think of demand for a security as rising on rising prices, not falling ones. Similarly, the supply of a security dries up on rising prices, at least in the short run.

Figuring Out What's Normal: Drawing a Market Profile

Technical analysis can be categorized broadly as falling into four categories:

- ✔ Analyzing patterns (double tops ands bottoms, for example; see Chapter 4)
- ✔ Trend-following methods (moving averages and trendlines, for example; see Chapter 4)
- ✔ Character-of-market analysis (oscillators like Relative Strength Indicator [RSI], for example)
- ✔ Structural theories

Structural theories include the broadest measures of market behavior, like seasonality (which I discuss later in this chapter). The most inclusive of the structural theories is market profile.

Each crowd, whether a fraternity or a gang, develops criteria for normal behavior. The secret vocabulary of traders in a specific security or class of securities takes the form of prices changing by a certain amount over a period of time (usually one day, one week, and one month). The crowd that trades a specific security, for example, knows that the average daily range of prices between the high and low of the day is normally some specific amount.

Market profile is a technique for analyzing the normal behavior of the crowd while in the process of trading a security. Using a fictitious security, Figure 1-2 shows trading during a particular day. Each X stands for blocks of shares traded. All the Xs add up to the volume figure for the day — the number of shares or contracts traded, as reported by the exchange. The number of shares or contracts is recorded according to the price associated with them and the time of day the transactions took place.

As you can see, the price ranged from $8 (the low) to $11 (the high) on that day, with the average price at $9.50. (Note that in this instance, the arithmetic average is the same thing as the *mode,* which is the price that occurs most frequently. This isn't always the case, and if you pursue this method of looking at markets, you'll have to deal with situations where the average differs from the mode.)

Turn the page sideways. Do you see the outline of a shape in this price distribution? If you've ever sat through a statistics class, you may be able to pick out the bell-shaped normal distribution curve. It's called a *normal distribution* because you can use it to describe a set of data that varies around an average value.

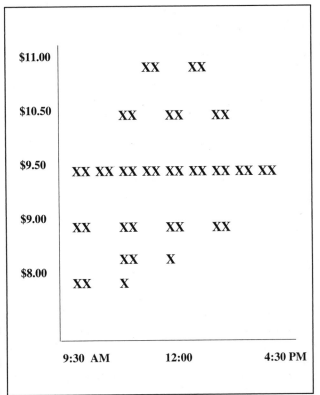

Figure 1-2:
A market
profile.

Explaining the standard deviation

Prices clustered around the average are *normal* and represent the market consensus of the rough equilibrium price for that day. The normal prices deviate by only one unit from the average in each direction: higher or lower. This unit is named a *standard deviation*.

The standard deviation region in Figure 1-2 is symmetrical — when you use a normal distribution curve, you assume that an equal number of prices will fall on each side of the average. This isn't always true, of course. Prices are trended at least some of the time, and so if the price is on a generally rising trend, expect to see the distribution curve skewed to one side, to the higher prices. You'll also see days on which the prices form a double hump or are just flat across the daily range.

Statisticians say that securities prices aren't actually normally distributed; they just look that way sometimes. You risk making unwarranted assumptions if you apply the normal distribution concept uncritically. Still, the main point of market profile is that you can often track crowd behavior as it is happening to determine whether bullish sentiment is winning out over bearish sentiment, or vice versa.

Trading normalcy

The prices that occur in the outer tails of the curve are, statistically speaking, abnormal. In the example in Figure 1-2, only about one-third of prices stray so far away from the average.

Say that, after writing down each trade on a chart, you see that early in the day, the price moves from $8 to the average, $9.50, *which is still in the process of being established.* Only a few prices have appeared on the high side of the price range. From studying past days and weeks of data, you already know that the average daily trading range of the security is $3. (See Chapter 2 for a discussion of the trading range.) You guess that if the trading is normal that day (consistent with the average over the past several days or weeks), you'll be able to buy under or near the average of $9.50 and sell near the expected high, $11. In fact, after you see that the trades are starting to average $9.50, if you see an offer at the cheap end of the range, $8, you jump on it, thus improving your net profit if you're able to sell at the high end of the range later in the day.

Using market profile to make trading decisions

Market profile isn't, technically speaking, a buy/sell indicator. It's a way of visually organizing price and volume data to give you a perspective on how traders feel over the course of the day. If you start entering a lot of entries down around $8 later in the day, for example, what you're seeing is a shift in sentiment to the bearish side. How you interpret that information is up to you. You have two choices:

✔ **Buy some more:** The market is temporarily undervaluing the security. You expect normalcy to return. You still expect to see the average at $9.50, and you still hope to see the price extreme of $11.

✔ **Sell:** Sentiment is going against you. When you see prices develop in the tail, you're seeing a price extreme. Price extremes are abnormal and can mark the beginning of a trend. In fact, a trending market is characterized by *fat tails,* meaning a lot of volume occurring at the edge of the normal price range.

Your choice depends on the information you're getting from technical indicators. For example, you can use market profile together with moving averages or momentum to estimate whether a trend is forming, weakening, or strengthening.

Crowd Extremes and What to Do about Them

Technical analysis is the art of identifying crowd behavior in order to join the crowd and take advantage of its momentum. This is called the *bandwagon effect.* Here's how a bandwagon works: A fresh piece of news comes out, a majority of traders interpret it as favorable to the security, and buying overwhelms selling so that the price rises. You profit by going with the flow. Then when everyone is jumping off the bandwagon, you jump, too.

A word about manias and panics

People behave differently when they act as individuals from the way they act when they're part of a crowd in which otherwise sensible individuals can behave in the most extraordinary ways. If someone shouts "Fire!" in a crowded theater, people will trample each other to get to the exits; if someone shouts "Free ice cream!" people will fall all over each other to be first in line. In markets, you see the same thing. Prices fall as traders abandon a security after bad news about it is released. If an authority figure pronounces the security a gem and a bargain, securities prices reach new highs as people flock to them. As a technical trader, you want to be sensitive to what the crowd is doing without succumbing to the ruling passions of the crowd itself.

A *mania* is a situation in which traders buy an object or security without regard for its intrinsic value or even whether they'll be able to sell it again later at a higher price. They fear being left out of an opportunity. They're caught up in the moment and temporarily irrational. A *panic* is the opposite — people can't sell the thing fast enough and will accept ever-lower prices just to get any money back at all.

In economic history, a mania or a panic comes along only a few times in a century. In the technical worldview, mania and panic happen every day, in miniature. Emotional extremes lead to price extremes in the context of the hour, day, or week — minimanias and minipanics occur all the time. Those aren't the words used in technical trading lingo, but the emotion and the price effects are the same as in big-picture manias and panics.

Technical traders work hard at not listening to chatter about securities, even from authority figures. You're unlikely to get useful information — and you may get *disinformation* (deliberately misleading information as some traders invent rumors to try to create a stampede in either direction). All the information you need is embedded in the price. When you do check the news for the cause of a price action, be sure to do so with a healthy dose of skepticism.

As market participants get excited about a security, they become increasingly bullish and either buy for the first time or add to positions, a phase named *accumulation.* When traders become disillusioned about the prospect of their security price rising, they sell, in a phase named *distribution.* To buy 100 shares of a stock is to *enter a position.* To buy another 100 shares for a total of 200 is to *add to your position.* If you have 500 shares and sell half, you would be *reducing your position.* To sell all the shares you own is to *square your position.* When you're *square* (also called *flat*), you have no position in the security. All your money is in cash. You're neutral.

After traders have been accumulating the security on rising prices, eventually the price goes too far. *Too far* is a relative term and can be defined in any number of equally valid ways, but basically it means any price extreme that's wildly abnormal, statistically speaking.

Overbought and oversold

When a price has reached or surpassed a normal limit, it's at an extreme. In an *upmove,* everyone who wanted to buy has already bought. The market is called *overbought,* a term specific to securities trading. In a *downmove,* everyone who wanted to sell has already sold. The security is called *oversold.* The concept of overbought/oversold is applied to market indices as well as individual securities. It's usually measured by the momentum indicators described in the section "Examining how indicators work," later in this chapter.

By the time most of the market participants have jumped on the bandwagon, it has become so heavy it can't move forward. Traders are tapped out. All their money is in a position. Traders have to square their positions just to put cash back into their pockets so they can conduct additional trades.

Retracements

When a price has gone too far and traders deem the security overbought or oversold, the price stops rising or falling. Instead of hovering at a particular level, however, the price moves in the *opposite* direction for a while. A move in the opposite direction of the main trend is named a *retracement.* (Other names for it are *correction,* which explicitly recognizes that the security had gone too far and is now correcting course, *pullback,* or *throwback.*)

Recognizing a retracement

Prices seldom move in one direction for long. Even a major trend exhibits retracements. When the market runs out of cash, traders have to close positions to get their cash back so they can put on new trades. If they've been buyers, they need to sell. If they've been sellers (shorting the security), they need to buy. Position squaring always causes a price move in the opposite direction of the trend. Therefore, at the extreme outside limit of a price move, you should expect a temporary, minor reversal of the previous price move. In an uptrend, a retracement is always a drop in price. In a downtrend, a retracement is always a rise in price.

Figure 1-3 shows a primary trend with several retracements, each outlined by an ellipse. In this instance, the retracements last only a day or two — but retracements can last a lot longer, several weeks on a daily chart, for example. They can also retrace over more ground.

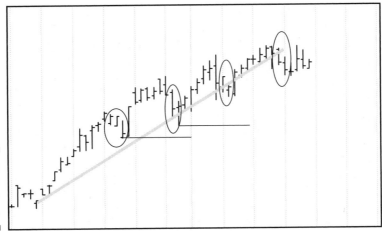

Figure 1-3:
A trend with retrace-ments.

At the time a retracement starts, you don't know for sure that it is a retracement. For all you know, it could be a full reversal, with the price switching direction. This is one of the occasions when it pays to check the *fundamentals* (the news and events pertaining to the security). An ordinary retracement caused by normal position squaring can suddenly turn into a full-fledged rout in the opposite direction if fresh news come out that seems to support a reversal.

Book VIII

Technical Analysis

Catch a falling knife: Estimating when a retracement will end

To try to estimate where a retracement will stop is called "to catch a falling knife." Unfortunately, no reliable rules exist to tell you where a trend correction will end or when the primary trend will resume. One of the chief uses of indicators and combined indicators is to get guidance on where and when a retracement will stop.

Your tolerance for retracements is the key to deciding what time frame you want to trade in. If the security you want to trade regularly retraces 50 percent and the prospect of losing 51 percent turns you into a nervous wreck, you need to trade it in a shorter time frame — or find another security.

Acknowledging that no one can forecast a retracement hasn't stopped technical traders from trying to establish forecast rules. The following rules are generally helpful, but no one can offer statistics to back them up, so take them with a grain of salt:

✔ **A retracement won't exceed a significant prior high or low.** In Figure 1-3, for example, the second retracement doesn't challenge the lowest low of the first dip, and the third retracement doesn't challenge the second.

✔ **Look for round numbers.** Research shows that support and resistance levels (see Chapter 4) occur more often at round numbers than chance would allow.

✔ **The 30 percent rule.** Measure the percentage change and assume that a majority of traders will place stops to avoid losing more than x percent, such as 30 percent. The problem with this idea, and it's a chilling one, is that you're measuring from a peak and you don't know the price level where the majority of traders entered.

Looking at Market Sentiment

In technical analysis, sentiment comes in only two flavors — *bullish* (the price is going up) or *bearish* (the price is going down). At any moment in time, a bullish crowd can take a price upward or a bearish crowd can take it downward. When the balance of sentiment shifts from bullish to bearish (or vice versa), a pivot point emerges. A *pivot point* is the point (or a region) where an upmove ends and a downmove begins (or the other way around). At the pivot point, the crowd itself realizes that it has gone to an extreme, and it reacts by heading in the opposite direction. Another term for pivot point is *key reversal*.

When the crowd is reaching an extreme of emotion, it's usually wrong. A reversal point is impending. You should do the opposite of what the crowd is doing, or at least get ready to.

Tracking volume

Volume, the number of shares or contracts of a security traded in a period, is the most powerful confirming indicator of a price move, and *confirmation* is a key concept in technical analysis.

You can feel more confident that a price move has staying power if you know that many traders are involved in a price move and not just one or two. In technical trading, therefore, you use volume to measure the extent of trader participation. When a price rise is accompanied by rising volume, you have confirmation that the direction is associated with participation. Similarly, if you see a price fall by a large amount, but the change isn't accompanied by a change in volume, you can deduce that the price change was an aberration. Some trader made a mistake.

Leading the way with spikes

Volume sometimes leads price. The most obvious situations are when volume spikes. A *spike* is a volume number that is double or more the size of volume on the preceding days. Say volume has been running at 100,000 shares per day for several days or weeks and suddenly it explodes to 500,000 shares. If the price had been in a downtrend, this wild increase in volume means that the crowd is throwing in the towel and exiting *en masse.*

A volume spike is one of the occasions when fundamental information is complementary to a technical observation. In the case of a price making new highs coupled with a volume spike where you discover that no fresh news or fundamental information prompted new buyers to come on the scene, be wary. Chances are the top is in. If the security has new, legitimately exciting news and you can reasonably deduce that it attracted new buyers, you have a non-technical reason to ignore the usual spike interpretation.

Tracking on-balance volume

On-balance volume (OBV) is a running (cumulative) total of volume, calculated by adding the volume on days the price is higher than the day before and subtracting the volume on days the price is lower than the day before. The logic goes like this: At the simplest level, when the price closes higher than the day before, demand was greater than supply at each price level. Buyers had to offer higher prices to get holders to part with their shares. You can attribute *all* the volume on a higher-close day to net buying and *all* the volume on a lower-close day to net selling. Figure 1-4, which shows IBM stock, indicates daily prices in the top part, volume (in hundreds of thousands of shares) in the center, and the OBV indicator in the bottom window.

Book VIII

Technical Analysis

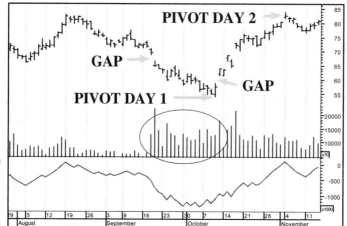

Figure 1-4:
On-balance
volume.

OBV doesn't work all the time, but a change in the indicator often precedes a change in the price. Using Figure 1-4, you can see how to use the OBV indicator in two instances:

- **The downmove:** The price downmove, already in progress, is suddenly accompanied by a big rise in volume. The increase in volume starts *the day before* the downward gap. A falling price punctuated by a downward gap is a message to the market that the price is going to fall some more. In this case, the OBV indicator forecasts the impending bottom. It starts to fall *ahead* of the volume spike and *ahead* of the gap. If you own the stock and see the OBV indicator start to decline and then you see spiky volume (like the area in the ellipse), you should sell. Holding on after the downward gap is courting a fat loss.

- **The upmove:** OBV reaches its lowest levels about two weeks *before* Pivot Day 1, which features the lowest low in the series of lower lows, but a higher closing price and a gap upward the following day. Notice that OBV is already rising while the price is still falling, a divergence that is a critical clue to an impending change in the direction of the price.

The divergence of price and an indicator that normally rises and falls in tandem with it is itself a wake-up call. A change in volume often predicts a change in price. The indicator is telling you something you can't see with the naked eye — prices were putting in new lows, but prices weren't consistently *closing* lower than the day before. Buying and selling pressure, or supply and demand, was reaching a balance. Your eye can see the price downmove, but the indicator can detect the exhaustion of the sellers (supply).

Notice that after Pivot Day 1, the price puts in several gap days upward. This is a message to the crowd to buy, and they do, leading to Pivot Day 2. If you had bought IBM at the close on Pivot Day 1 and sold it one day after Pivot Day 2 (when the OBV indicator turned downward), you would have made a nice little profit.

Refining volume indicators

It's not realistic to attribute *all* of the day's volume to the accumulation column just because the close today is higher than yesterday's. It makes more sense to attribute only a portion of the volume to the price rise. A more representative amount would be the percentage equivalent of the price that is above the midpoint of the day. A *midpoint* is calculated as the high of the day plus the low of the day divided by two.

If a security closes above its midpoint for the day, bullish sentiment ruled. The close over the midpoint defines *accumulation,* referring to buyers being willing to pay higher prices to get sellers to part with the security. The closer the closing price is to the high, the more bullish it was. If the price closed *at* the high, then you say that 100 percent of the volume can be attributed to bullish sentiment. A close below the price midpoint means *distribution,* sellers willing to accept lower prices to induce buyers to buy. Lower prices imply bearish sentiment. The closer the closing price is to the low, the more distribution there was. If the close is exactly at the midpoint, then the indicator has the same value as yesterday — you have no reason to add or subtract volume from the running total.

Understanding market effects

Some percentage of any security's price move (how much exactly nobody knows for sure) is attributable to changes in the market environment:

- ✔ **Securities:** Factors impacting price include not only the index to which a particular security belongs, but also its size (large cap or small cap, for example) and sector (biotech, high-tech, no-tech). About 25 percent of a price move in any single issue should be considered a function of what is going on in its index (or other benchmark to which the issue belongs).

- ✔ **Commodities:** Some portion of the price move in a commodity is a function of the price move of the overall commodity indices, like the Commodity Research Bureau index (CRB).

- ✔ **Currencies:** In currencies, the benchmark is something called the *dollar index,* a price average comprised of individual currency prices weighted by their countries' share of trade with the United States and published by the Federal Reserve.

Overall, the market environment has a magnetic effect on individual components. You may have the inside scoop on the best stock ever, but if the entire market has a case of the collywobbles, your best-ever stock is likely to fall, too. Conversely, when the market is in a manic phase, even the worst of stocks gets a boost.

To get a handle on possible market effects on your specific security, measure overall market sentiment by looking at market statistics. Strictly speaking, market statistics are not technical analysis, which is the study of how specific prices behave. Nevertheless, sentiment measures can be very helpful as a supplement and complement to work on your individual charts.

Sampling information about sentiment

Most sentiment indicators look outside the price dynamics of a particular security or index of securities for information about whether the trading crowd is humming along with expectations of normalcy or is willing to jump ship. Following are a few outside sources you can use:

- **Advisors:** A service called Investors Intelligence measures the balance of bullish sentiment against bearish sentiment (which it calls the *bull/bear ratio*) and claims an excellent track record in predicting turning points. You can find the bull/bear ratio and other indicators on hundreds of Web sites and in business newspapers. To get a specific bull/bear ratio from a specific vendor the minute it's published, you have to pay a subscription fee.

- **Breadth indicators:** *Breadth indicators* measure the degree of participation by traders in the overall market represented by an index, such as the Dow or NASDAQ. Breadth indicators include:

    - **The ratio of advancing to declining issues:** This indicator measures the mood of the market. Stocks that are reaching a higher price today than yesterday are called *advancing issues.* Stocks that are reaching lower prices are called *declining issues.* When advancers outnumber decliners, money is flowing into the market. Bulls are beating bears. Sentiment is favorable.

    - **The difference between issues making new highs and those making new lows:** If more stocks in an index are closing at higher prices than the period before, bullishness is on the rise. When a higher number are putting in new lows, supply is overwhelming demand and the mood is bearish.

- **Put/call ratios:** The Chicago Board Options Exchange (CBOE) is the venue for options trading in equity indices like the S&P and NASDAQ indices. The CBOE publishes the ratio of puts to calls. The *put/call ratio* is an indicator of whether sentiment is bearish or bullish. A high put/call ratio means bears are winning. The same line of thinking holds true for a low put/call ratio: When emotions are running strongly optimistic, watch out for an opportunity to take advantage of a change. (Book III has more information on put/call ratios.)

✔ **Volatility index:** Use the volatility index (VIX) as a contrary indicator. When the crowd is feeling an extreme emotion, like anxiety, it's usually wrong. Therefore, a high VIX value means exactly the opposite of what it seems to mean — the bottom isn't coming, it's already in! When VIX is low, traders are complacent; they're projecting the same price levels, or nearly the same levels, into the immediate future with little variation and therefore little risk. When VIX is either abnormally high or abnormally low, you know it's the right time to trade against the crowd.

Accounting for seasonality

Seasonality (also known as *calendar effects)* refers to the natural rise and fall of prices according to the time of year. Heating oil futures go up as winter heads for Chicago, for example, and prices of agricultural commodities rise when the crop is poor and fall when farmers get a bumper crop. Interestingly, equities and financial futures exhibit a similar effect: They change according to the time of year. The changes are regular and consistent enough to warrant your attention. Here are a few:

✔ **Best six months rule:** Nearly all the gains in the S&P 500 are made between November 1 and April 30. This isn't true without exception, but it's been true for most years since 1950. When April 30 rolls around, you sell all your stocks and put the money in U.S. government Treasuries. Come November 1, you reenter the stock market.

Contrarians and cranks

A true contrarian is someone who has a *fundamental* reason for thinking that a security is mispriced. In equities, a fundamental reason could be insider knowledge that an out-of-favor pharmaceutical company has secretly discovered the cure for some important disease and its price will shoot the moon when the announcement comes out. In financial futures (stock indices, bonds, and currencies), a fundamental reason to judge a security mispriced may be an in-depth analysis of a central bank interest rate change that nobody else can see coming. A true contrarian is quite rare, although lots of people fancy themselves contrarians when they're just cranks. When a contrarian is right, he becomes a zillionaire and is called eccentric. When he is wrong, he stays poor and is called a crackpot. In contrast, technical trading is by its very nature non-contrarian. You want to go with the crowd, not against it (most of the time).

This advice comes from work on calendar effects by Yale and Jeffrey Hirsch, who tested the correlation of stock index prices with the time of year in their annual *Stock Trader's Almanac.* If you'd followed this rule every year since 1950, a starting capital stake of $10,000 in 1952 would have ballooned to $1,308,304 by 2003.

✔ **January Barometer:** When the S&P 500 is up in January, it'll close the year higher than it opened. Since 1950, this rule has an accuracy reading of 92.5 percent.

✔ **President's Third Year:** Since 1939, the third year of a presidential term is always an up year for the Dow. In fact, going back 84 years, the only big down year in the third year of a presidential term was 1931.

✔ **Presidential Election Cycle:** Wars, recessions, and bear markets tend to start in the first two years, while prosperity and bull markets tend to happen in the second two years. Since 1833, the last two years of a president's term produced a cumulative net gain in the Dow of 717.5 percent, while the first two years produced 227.6 percent.

You can discover the seasonality characteristics of any given stock by using *seasonality trackers* on various Web sites, including the best-known seasonality tracker, Thomson Financial (www.thomson.com). The Thomson Financial Web site allows you to see a chart of any stock with its associated average returns by month, starting in 1986. You can also see a table of the months in which the stock rose or fell over the years.

Searching for Historic Key Reversals

One of the enduring mysteries of market history is that big key reversal points come out of the blue. Seldom can you find a specific event that triggers a rally taking off or a bubble bursting. Does that mean that historic key reversals occur randomly? If so, why shouldn't we say that *all* key reversals occur randomly?

Opinion is divided on the answer, and many people give up on technical analysis at this point. If you never know when a major turning point is going to hit you over the head with a hammer, how can you trust technical indicators? The answer is that you can trust your indicators only up to a point, and then your survival as a trader depends on risk management. In the meantime, it's important to have a useful way to think about randomness and not let it overwhelm you.

Enduring randomness

Although the expectation is that prices will behave normally, random events can and do cause the occasional wild price departure from the norm. For example, you sometimes see a price (named a *spike*) that is so far out of whack you don't know how to interpret it. A price spike is the equivalent of a tornado in weather forecasting. We know the conditions that cause tornadoes — we just don't know exactly when an actual tornado will develop.

Who would have thought, for example, that the S&P 500 could fall more than 20 percent in a single day? Most market observers used to say it was impossible. But that's exactly what happened on Black Monday, 1987. Most market tornadoes, like Black Monday, give plenty of technical warnings ahead of time. The problem is that those same warnings have existed during other periods and don't result in a Black Monday. This is an inconvenient fact of life that you have to accept.

Neither sentiment indicators nor standard technical analysis is much help in detecting the cataclysmic change from rally to crash.

Remembering the last price

In normal trading, you can assume that a wildly erratic price has a low probability of occurring, yet such events have an impact on future prices. In markets, a low-probability event changes the odds for the next period analysis. This is because traders remember and form their trading plans on earlier prices. The next price normally depends on preceding prices. Sometimes, all it takes is one or two abnormal prices to alter the expectations of the trading crowd. If they were bullish before, they become bearish now.

Using Chart Indicators

Technical traders go to great lengths to remove emotion and impulsiveness from decision-making. The chief tool for squelching emotion is the *indicator,* a calculation that you put on a chart to identify chart events, chiefly whether the price is trending, the degree of trendedness, and whether a trend turning point is being reached. The purpose of indicators is to clarify and enhance your perception of the price move. They come in two varieties:

Book VIII

Technical Analysis

- ✔ **Judgment-based indicators:** This group includes visual pattern-recognition methods such as bar, line, and pattern analysis, as well as candlesticks. Chapters 2 through 4 cover these methods.

- ✔ **Math-based indicators:** This group includes moving averages, regression, momentum, and other types of calculations; see Chapter 5 for the details.

Just because math-based indicators are based on math doesn't mean they aren't subjective. *You* determine the specifications of math-based indicators in the first place (such as how many days are in a moving average), and *your* specifications may contain preconceptions and bias. When you interpret trading guidance from math-based indicators, you're using judgment again. Math-based indicators may involve just as much personal judgment in design and application as outright judgment-based indicators.

Indicators are useful for identifying these five conditions:

- ✔ A trend is beginning (moving average crossover, pattern breakout).
- ✔ A trend is strong or weak (slope of linear regression or moving average).
- ✔ A trend is retracing but will likely resume (relative strength index).
- ✔ A trend is ending and may reverse (moving average crossover, pattern breakout).
- ✔ A price is range-trading (slope of linear regression or moving average).

Each indicator works best in one situation and less well in others. Technical traders argue the merits and drawbacks of indicators in each situation, and the indicator you choose for each task depends, to a certain extent, on the security and also on your choice of analytical time frame.

Choosing an analysis style

The trend is always the focus. In a perfect world, you first determine whether your security is trending or range-trading sideways, and then you apply the appropriate indicator. In practice, you can't always classify price moves as trending or not trending in a neat and tidy way. Besides, prices usually have an identifiable range, whether they're trending or not. In addition, retracements always create doubt — is it a momentary correction or a reversal?

Following are the types of analysis styles:

- ✔ **Trend followers:** Traders who like to identify trends may wait out retracements and sideways range-trading situations until they resolve back into a trend. Other trend followers use information from momentum indicators to modify their position, for instance by taking some profit when the security becomes overbought/oversold even though the trend is just pausing and they expect it to continue. (See the earlier section "Overbought and oversold" for definitions of these terms.) Figure 1-5 illustrates a trend, complete with minor retracements, and shows how a trend-following trader makes decisions.

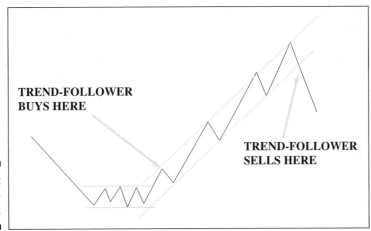

TREND-FOLLOWER
BUYS HERE

TREND-FOLLOWER
SELLS HERE

Figure 1-5:
Trend-
following.

If you choose trend-following, you're choosing to suffer through the downward bounce in an uptrend (or the upward bounce in a down-trend). You're going to wait it out, and if you have correctly identified the trend, your patience pays off and the trend resumes.

✔ **Swing traders:** Swing traders buy at relative lows and sell at relative highs, regardless of whether the price is trending. A swing trader may know that a price is downtrending, for example, but he's still willing to buy it for a short-term profit opportunity when a momentum indicator says it's temporarily oversold and likely to enjoy a bounce upward. Figure 1-6 shows how the swing trader tries to capture every move, including the retracements.

Your choice of trending or swing-trading indicators determines your holding period. Trending indicators generally keeps you in a trade for a longer period of time than swing-trading indicators.

The best guiding principles are the ones that relate directly to the supply and demand dynamics that *you* can see on the chart. This is why simple, old-fashioned techniques, such as bar reading and pattern identification, are so powerful.

Book VIII

**Technical
Analysis**

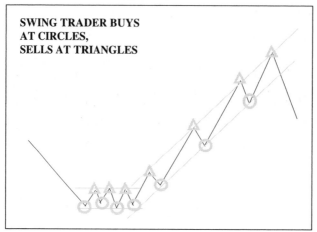

SWING TRADER BUYS
AT CIRCLES,
SELLS AT TRIANGLES

Figure 1-6:
Swing
trading.

Examining how indicators work

Indicators aren't inherently tied to particular time frames, nor do they have a single correct interpretation. The sections that follow describe the general way indicators work, but be aware that technical traders are mavericks and use indicators in an infinite variety of ways.

Finding relevant time frames

Most indicators measure price and volume changes relative to previous prices and volume over a specific *look-back* period, such as 12 days or 21 days. If you compare the trend-following chart in Figure 1-5 with the swing-trading chart in Figure 1-6, you can see that trend-following uses indicators with a relatively longer time frame than swing-trading indicators.

With the exception of "historic" highs and lows, most indicators have a range of time in which research shows they work best. (For more on historic highs and lows, see the "Establishing benchmark levels" section later in the chapter.) This is why charting software has preformatted indicators with default parameters specifying a particular time range. However, adopting the default parameter doesn't mean that you must trade according to that time range. Consider it a starting point; if the default doesn't work for you, use a different number of periods.

Most math-based indicators have an associated time frame, from very short-term to very long-term:

  ✔ **Intraday:** Entry and exit on the same trading day
  ✔ **Short-term:** 3 to 12 days (average 3)

✔ **Intermediate-term:** 12 to 45 days (average 20)

✔ **Long-term:** More than 30 days

The ability to apply an indicator over any time frame reflects the *fractal* quality of prices — the weird and wonderful fact that without a label, a price series of 15-minute bars often can't be distinguished from a month's worth of daily prices. Intraday bars are like microcosms of daily bars and daily bars are like microcosms of weekly or monthly bars. Traders respond to price changes in regular, consistent, and repetitive ways whatever the time frame.

Heeding indicator signals

Indicators are designed to give buy and sell signals, although in many instances, the signal is more like a warning and doesn't have a black-and-white embedded decision rule. The following list introduces signals to pay attention to:

✔ **Crossovers:** The term *crossover* refers to one line crossing another line. Crossovers include:

- The price crossing a fixed historic benchmark.

- The indicator crossing the price or the price crossing the indicator.

- One line of a two-line indicator crossing the other.

In most instances, the price crossing an indicator is named a *breakout,* one of the most important concepts in technical analysis. When a price rises above a long-standing resistance line, for example, technical traders say it *broke out* of its previous trading range and now the sky's the limit — until the new range is established. In an *upside breakout,* bullish sentiment triumphed, but bearish sentiment can win out as well. A breakout doesn't necessarily imply a trend reversal; sometimes a breakout is a confirming factor that the existing trend is gathering new momentum or passing new benchmarks.

✔ **Range limits:** *Oscillators* describe where today's price stands relative to its recent trading range. They're usually based on 100, so they range from 0 to 100, or minus 100 to plus 100, or some other variation using the number 100. In practice, traders find that most of the time, the scope of the price range falls well under the outer limits and doesn't vary by more than 20 to 80 percent of the total possible range. Thus, they draw a line at 20 percent of the maximum range and another one at 80 percent (or 10 percent and 90 percent, or some other variation). When the indicator approaches one of the lines, you know that the price is nearing an extreme of its recent range.

Book VIII

Technical Analysis

✔ **Convergence:** *Convergence* refers to two indicator lines coming closer to one another, as when a support line and a resistance line converge to form a triangle or two moving averages get closer together, indicating less difference between their numerical values. Convergence generally means that the price action is starting to go sideways or has a narrower high–low range, or both. A sideways move, in turn, generally leads to a breakout.

✔ **Divergence:** *Divergence* refers to two indicator lines moving farther apart, as when the spread between two moving averages widens. Divergence also refers to an indicator and the price going in different directions. Momentum indicators, in particular, reshuffle the components of the price bar to come up with the rate of change of a price, so that the slope of the indicator is a sophisticated measure of the strength of a trend. When the price is still rising (making new highs) as the momentum indicator starts to fall (making progressively lower highs), the price and indicator are diverging, which is an important leading indicator that the price rise is probably about to stop. (See Chapter 5 for more on momentum.)

Establishing benchmark levels

Every chart has historic highs and lows. Technically, they aren't indicators, and yet they may serve to indicate future price action. You've probably heard the phrases "52-week high" or "52-week low," meaning the security is reaching a one-year high or low. A new one-year high or low has no analytical value to the technical trader — unless it's also a historic high or low. A *historic* high or low is an absolute level that becomes a benchmark.

When a price makes a new historic high or low and then retreats in the other direction, years can pass before the benchmark is surpassed. In the meantime, intermediate highs and lows emerge and become benchmarks in their own right. At the time they occur, they seem historic. After a bounce up off a new low, traders hesitate to break it, but after they do, the price accelerates to the next low. The same thing happens on the way up to new highs. Profit-taking after a high causes the price to dip, and traders hesitate to breach the new "historic" high.

Hesitation ahead of the breach of a benchmark price can be prolonged and is often accompanied by a gap (see Chapter 2 on gaps), demonstrating that traders are aware of "historic levels."

Choosing and modifying indicators

Indicators only *indicate;* they don't *dictate* the next price move. According to the old joke, if you give 12 technical traders a new indicator, a year later you have 12 different track records. This observation is perfectly accurate, because *how* you use an indicator isn't set by the indicator itself, but by the trading rules you use. For example, you may like an indicator but find it generates too many trades in a fixed period, so you don't execute every single signal. Someone else may use the identical indicator, but instead of overriding indicator signals with personal judgment, he modifies the exact timing of trades by using a second indicator.

Overriding your indicator haphazardly is self-defeating. You're letting emotion back in. Plus, you won't get the expected result from the indicator — and then you'll blame the indicator. Modifying indicators with trading rules is *always* better than overriding them. Fortunately, most indicators are fairly flexible. They can be adapted to fit the trading rules you prefer, such as the frequency of your trades.

Indicators are about price-move measurement. Trading rules are about you and your tolerance for risk. Trading rules must be appropriate to the indicators you choose. So don't pick indicators that you can't follow, like a momentum indicator that gives ten trading signals per month when you don't have the time or inclination to trade that much.

Optimizing: The Necessary Evil

Optimization is the process of testing a hypothesis on historical data to see which parameter would've worked the best. Optimization is necessary because when you're starting out to trade a new security, you have no idea of what indicators to use or what parameters to put into the indicators. In keeping with the empirical approach of technical analysis, you want to try various indicators and different parameters in the indicators to see what works. As you optimize, however, keep these caveats in mind:

✔ The future *will* differ from the past. Price patterns repeat, but only in a general way. Any number of equally probable outcomes are possible in any specific situation. What worked in March 2000 may get disastrous results when applied in 2008 or 2016. It's hard to follow trading rules built on past patterns when you know the future will be different.

✔ Do you have the discipline to execute trades when your indicator tells you to? More to the point, do you trust the indicator? This is like asking whether you trust your own work developing the indicator parameters.

Book VIII

Technical Analysis

Take a look at Figure 1-7. The chart is of QQQQ, the tracking stock of the NASDAQ-100 Index (technically an exchange-traded fund that incorporates the 100 largest and most actively traded non-financial stocks on the NASDAQ). QQQQ more than doubled from March 1999 to the all-time high in March 2000. If you'd used a 50-day moving average crossover indicator to signal when to sell, you would have sold QQQQ seven days after the peak. Seven days — imagine the savings. (Fifty days is an oft-used parameter for the moving average, but you need to find out whether it's the best one for your particular security. Who knows? Maybe 36 days, 77 days, or some other number of days works better.)

Constructing a back-test optimization

The chart in Figure 1-7 displays a *back-test* (a test on historical data) of the single moving average crossover rule on IBM stock. Say you've dabbled in trading IBM stock on and off for a number of years, and you want to try your hand at applying an indicator-based technical trading rule. Here's the hypothesis: "If you buy IBM stock every time the price crosses above the *x*-day moving average and sell it every time the price crosses below the *x*-day moving average, it'll consistently and reliably be a profitable trading rule."

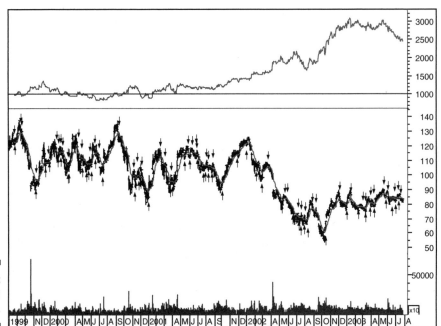

Figure 1-7:
Optimization
back-test.

The goal of the optimization back-test is to find *x*, which is the number of days in the moving average. Just about every software package allows you to search for *x*. In this instance, the software delivered a result in less than 15 seconds. It was told to try every moving average from 10 days to 30 days over the past 1,000 days. The most profitable moving average would've been 15 days. Figure 1-7 shows the 15-day moving average and the buy/sell signals that the indicator would have generated at every crossover.

In the top window, take a look at the *equity curve,* which shows the cumulative running total of the profit you would have made if you had been buying or selling at each arrow. From a starting point of $1,000 in capital, you now have $2,443, or a gain of 144 percent. Because 1,000 days is about 4 years, that's an annual return of 34.5 percent, better than the return on a risk-free bond and a whole lot better than the loss you would have taken if you had bought $1,000 worth of IBM stock on Day 1 of this test and simply held to Day 1,000. The stock fell 30 percent during the 1,000 days.

Taking a closer look at the test

Go back and look at Figure 1-7 again, and you can see that this case illustrates the general objections to the back-testing process:

- ✔ Notice the horizontal line on the equity window at $1,000. Now see that one month into the test, your equity fell below its starting point. The indicator blew up right away; it caused losses. It blew up a few more times, too. In real life, you'd probably not stick with a trading rule that failed to show an interesting amount of profit for almost two full years.

- ✔ To apply the 15-day crossover rule would've caused you to trade a total of 119 times, or every 8 days on average. In some cases, you would've been trading every day. The cost of those trades isn't zero.

    Slippage is the term applied to the reduction in trading profits that arises from the cost of trading. It includes the bid-offer spread, commissions, and fees. Always look at the performance track record of an indicator back-test *after* slippage. It can make all the difference between a profitable trading rule and an unprofitable one.

- ✔ The majority of trades lose money. You can't see that from the chart, but most back-testing software shows you a *system report* summarizing aspects of the test. In this example, of 119 trades, 82 lost money and only 37 were profitable.

WARNING!

✔ To get these results, you would've had to sell every time the indicator signaled sell and at the same time go short the stock. In practice, most people can't short equities, although it's an everyday occurrence in the futures market.

Okay, so tell the software that you're only a buyer when the indicator signals a buy and you never take a short position when the indicator tells you to go short. Because the stock was a net loser over the entire 1,000 days and buy-and-hold would've returned a big loss, you can guess what the outcome is — only a 15 percent return over the 1,000 days, or about 3.6 percent per year. Factor in the cost of commissions, and you would have lost most if not all of your starting capital.

This particular moving average rule didn't work after you factored in realistic factors like paying commissions and not taking a short position. But the case does exemplify one characteristic you seek in a trading rule: The average profitable trade is much higher than the average unprofitable trade, over $75 in this case versus an average unprofitable trade of $26.67. Winners were almost three times the size of losers. This yields a win/loss ratio of 2.8, or $2.80 in profit for every $1 in loss. Moreover, the average winning trade lasted 19 days while the average losing trade lasted only 4 days. Even though the trading rule didn't work, it does meet a second winning characteristic of technical trading that you seek from your indicator: "Let your winners run and cut your losses short."

The goal of every indicator-based trading rule is to get more profit from winning trades than you lose on losing trades. It isn't to have a higher number of profitable trades than losing trades, although that's nice if you can get it.

Fixing the indicator

As the preceding section makes clear, your hypothesis (buying IBM stock every time the price crosses above the *x*-day moving average and selling it every time the price crosses below the *x*-day moving average will consistently and reliably be a profitable trading rule) didn't bear out in the test. But the process illustrates common problems you encounter when you begin back-testing indicators to find the optimum parameter.

Overtrading

An unadjusted indicator often results in overtrading — it generates too many trades overall. *Overtrading* is trading so often that slippage reduces profits or even eliminates them. You therefore need to find adjustments to the indicator to reduce the number of trades, without damaging the returns from the winning trades.

You can *filter* the buy/sell signals by specifying that you want the software to generate a buy or sell signal only if the price is *x* percent above or below the moving average or has been above/below the moving average by *y* amount of time. Be careful not to make conditions too fancy. It's possible to fix the 15-day moving average trading rule with filters to reduce the number of trades so that profitability is high enough even to absorb trading costs. But you may find that filter fixes aren't robust, meaning that they back-test nicely but then fail to deliver the expected gain in real-time. This is because the volatility of the security changes over time.

Keep indicators and their associated trading rules as simple as possible.

Reducing losing trades

Most indicators generate more losing trades than winning ones, and the reason the indicator works is that the winning trades are bigger in money and percentage terms than the losers. But you still want to reduce losers. The single best way to do that is to add a confirmation requirement, such as one of the momentum indicators. In fact, requiring that the moving average indicator be confirmed by a simple momentum rule (see Chapter 5 for more on momentum) reduces the number of losing trades from 82 to 32 and improves profitability considerably. You still have more losing trades than winning trades in absolute numbers, but the average win-loss ratio improves.

Adding judgment calls

In many instances, when you look at the chart itself, you can see where some bar configuration or pattern would've kept you out of a losing trade or gotten you into a winning trade sooner. For example, the price may break a trendline (see Chapter 4) or show a gap (see Chapter 2). But you can't systematically include judgment calls like this in a back-test of a math-based indicator unless you're mathematically very advanced and adept. In most instances, to specify a condition like a gap as qualifying a trading rule would require you to create a very long and elaborate formula.

Applying the indicator again

After successfully back-testing a given indicator, the job isn't quite finished. Back-tests are hypothetical. You don't actually make those trades. To get a more realistic idea of how an indicator-based trading rule works, you back-test the rule on historical price data and then apply it to out-of-sample data. In the IBM case, for example, you'd back-test the rule for the years 1999 to 2003, obtain the 15-day parameter, and then see how it worked in 2004. If the results are about the same on the fresh data, you consider your rule to be *robust,* meaning it works across a wide range of conditions.

As you modify your indicator, be sure to avoid *curve-fitting,* making the indicator perfect for the past. The probability of it being perfect for the future is low, because the market is dynamic and changes. Instead you want to apply the moving average principle in a more flexible way by making it adaptive, by adding confirming factors, by consulting volume, and other means.

Chapter 2

Reading Basic Bars to Special Bars

*T*he price bar and its placement on the chart deliver a ton of information about market sentiment. It doesn't take much practice to start reading the mind of the market by looking at bars and small patterns. You have to be patient, imaginative, and thoughtful, but the payoff is cold, hard cash. This chapter explains what to look for in both basic and special bars.

Building Basic Bars

The *price bar* describes and defines the trading action in a security for a given period. Price bars consist of four components — open, high, low, and close, abbreviated OHLC (see Figure 2-1):

- ✓ **Open:** The horizontal line on the left is the opening price.
- ✓ **High:** The top of the vertical line defines the high of the day.
- ✓ **Low:** The bottom of the vertical line defines the low of the day.
- ✓ **Close:** The horizontal line on the right is the closing price.

Price bars can encompass different periods, anything from a minute to a month. This discussion refers to a daily price bar. (The scope of the period doesn't change the price bar dynamics.)

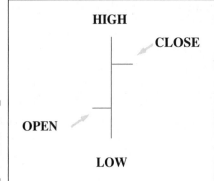

Figure 2-1:
The
standard
price bar.

The two horizontal lines on the price bar are called *tick marks*. In trading parlance, a *tick* represents a single trade at a single price, so the tick mark representing the open or the close refers literally to a single transaction or to a batch of transactions all at the same price and at the same time.

The price bar tells you the outcome of the battle between the buyers (bulls) and the sellers (bears). Hidden in every price bar is a winning group and a losing group. If the price opened at the low and closed at the high, the winners that day were the buyers. If the price opened at the high and closed at the low, the winners that day were the sellers. If the bar is very tall, encompassing a $10 range when the normal bar for this security is only $3, the trading was a titanic battle. If the bar is very short, say $1, it was a mere pillow fight.

As you try to interpret price bars, keep in mind that randomness can affect any part of the price bar. Sometimes people make decisions about their money that have nothing to do with the price, but rather with their personal needs.

Setting the tone: The opening price

The *opening price* is the very first trade between a buyer and a seller on the trading day. The meaning of the open, like all the price bar components, comes from its relationship to the other components of the bar as they develop and to the components of the bars that come before. The opening price's most important relationship is to the close of the day before.

When the open is up

If the open is up from the close the day before, it may be because the first trader of the day is expecting favorable news or has some other reason to think his purchase will return a gain. If you want to be a buyer today, his action reinforces your feeling. The first trade sets the tone, in this case a hopeful one.

You can't automatically attribute optimism or hopefulness to an opening bounce, however, because sometimes a good opening is due to traders *buying on open*. Mutual fund and other professional managers have preset allocations to specific securities. When fresh money comes in the night before, they're going to distribute a certain percentage of it to all the securities in the fund selected by the new customer. To "buy on open" is the easiest way to top up a fund and not necessarily a judgment on that security that day.

To determine whether an opening bounce is due to fresh enthusiasm or just the mechanical buy-on-open effect, you have to study each security to see whether it normally displays the effect. Big-name securities (such as IBM stock) are more susceptible to an opening bounce than specialized securities with a narrower trader base (like cocoa futures).

When the open is down

If the opening price is below the close of the day before, chances are the tone is sour. Maybe bad news came out after the close last night. The open may also be down if some traders have executed a *sell on open,* but don't count on it unless you study the security and find that the open often falls below yesterday's close. Selling on open isn't a common practice.

Summarizing sentiment: The closing price

The *closing price* is literally the last price at which a buyer bought and a seller sold before the closing bell. The close is generally considered the most important part of the price bar because it summarizes what traders feel about the security. They've watched this price all day, and by the end of the day, they have a sense of how popular it was near the lows (lots of buying going on) or how unpopular near the highs (lots of selling going on).

After-hours trading creates a problem in evaluating the close. How do you treat the close when your security makes a new high or new low in after-hours trading — only ten minutes after the close? The answer is that you don't adjust the close. In terms of managing your data, the open and close are associated with the trading hours of the primary exchange where the security is listed: the New York Stock Exchange, the Tokyo Stock Exchange, the Chicago Mercantile Exchange, and so on. If the security trades wildly higher or lower from the "official" close, even five or ten minutes after the close, the new information is included in the price data for the next day.

Selling on close is a modifying factor to keep in mind as you evaluate the close. Traders sell at the close to eliminate the risk of loss if something happens overnight that causes the price to fall. Because so many people exit on the close, the close is seldom the high of the day. And when the close *is* at the high of the day, it means people who do hold overnight positions are buying right up to the last minute, offsetting the usual end-of-day sales.

When the close is up

Over time, the cumulative relationship of the close today to the close yesterday gives you a visual impression of directional bias:

- ✔ An *up-day* is one where the close is higher than the close the day before.
- ✔ A *down-day* refers to a day on which the close is lower than the close the day before.

If today's close is consistently higher than yesterday's close, day after day, buyers are demanding more and more of the security and are willing to pay an ever-higher price to get it. Take a look at Figure 2-2; with the exception of Day 4, every close is higher than the close the previous day.

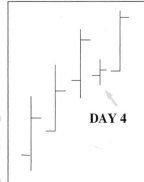

DAY 4

Figure 2-2:
A series of
up-days.

When the close is down

In Figure 2-3, you can see that, after the first bar, each close is lower than the day before. Here the sellers are willing to take ever-lower prices to get rid of the security. The market assumes that those holding an inventory of the security are willing to sell at lower and lower prices in order to get buyers to demand it.

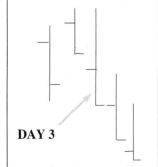

DAY 3

Figure 2-3:
A series of
down-days.

Tapping out: The high

The *high* of the price bar is literally the highest point of the bar, and it represents the highest price at which a buyer and seller made an exchange of cash for the security. The high of the day has meaning only in the context of its relationship to other parts of the same bar, especially the close, and to the high the day before. When the price closes at the high of the day, traders are extremely optimistic of more gains to come (bullish). When the high is at the open and it's all downhill for the rest of the day, traders are pessimistic (bearish).

Hitting bottom: The low

The *low* of the day is the cheapest price at which a buyer and seller exchanged cash for the security. As with the high of the day, the low has meaning only in the context of its relationship to other parts of the price bar and the bars that precede it. When the low is lower than the open, it probably means that some fresh news has come out after the opening bell that offsets any buy-on-open orders or initial sentiment. When the close is at the low, it means that bad news or negative sentiment ruled for the day.

Using Bars to Identify Trends

After a price is established through the execution of a real cash trade, traders have a baseline from which to track prices. The preceding sections explain how to interpret price bar components to one another *within* a single bar. When you look at the components *across* a series of bars, you get even more information, and interpretation becomes a lot more complex.

The price bar embodies all the supply–demand dynamics of the day, and a series of bars on a chart shows the evolution of the supply–demand dynamics over time. Sometimes, the evolution is visible in the form of a trend. This section describes how to use combinations of bars to identify trends.

Identifying an uptrend

The textbook-perfect *uptrend* is a series of up-day price bars (close higher than the close yesterday) that have higher highs *and* higher lows in a majority of the bars.

A *higher high* exists when the high today is higher than the high yesterday or higher than the high of the past few days. A series of higher highs often signals that the market is feeling enthusiastic about the security. But you usually don't know at the time whether a new high or a small series of new highs is the beginning of a trend. To confirm your suspicion that a trend may be forming, you need another piece of information: higher lows. *Higher lows* are a series of low points that dip less with each successive day. A series of higher highs combined with higher lows hints that a trend is forming.

If you have higher highs with higher lows for a couple of days in a row, can you assume that Day 3 will also deliver a higher high and a higher low? Not necessarily. Prices don't move in straight lines. You seldom see an unbroken series of higher highs on every single day. Refer to Figure 2-2. You see a series of days on which the close is higher than the close the day before. At the same time, the price is making a fresh high nearly every day, but not every day without fail. On Day 4 in the figure, the close was higher than the open and the low was higher than the day before, but the high of the day was not higher than the day before.

Most analysts tell you not to worry about this particular configuration of bars. It's an uptrend, all right, and you know this because you have an unbroken series of higher *lows*. Day 4 is a disappointment — it doesn't deliver a higher high — but the low is higher than all the previous lows. By considering the additional factor of higher lows, you confirm that the probability is pretty good of getting a higher high and a higher close on Day 5.

Identifying a downtrend

The textbook definition of a *downtrend* is a series of down-day bars (close lower than yesterday) characterized by lower lows and lower highs in a preponderance of the bars.

Go back and look at the down-days in Figure 2-3. After the first day, each of these bars has a close lower than the close the day before. Day 3 has the same high as the day before, but a lower low. On Day 3 you are starting to get the idea that this may be the beginning of a downtrend.

When identifying a downtrend, a series of lower highs is a good confirming indicator to the series of lower lows. Sellers see that new lows are occurring — somebody must know something negative about the security. Traders aren't willing to hold a falling asset, and they unload it at ever-lower prices. Meanwhile, fans of the security can't give it support at yesterday's low — selling pressure is too great.

But wait . . . nothing is that simple

A trend has two identifiers: a series of higher highs (or lower lows) and a series of up-days (or down-days). Technical analysis doesn't offer a hard-and-fast rule on which identifier is more important. Traditional technical analysis emphasizes that you need higher lows to confirm the higher highs in an uptrend, but candlestick analysis, covered in Chapter 3, says that the position of the close trumps every other factor, including a new high or low.

In practice, you find that the weight you place on the position of the close is a direct function of how far out in time you want to extend your forecast. Traditional bar chart reading generally has a longer forecasting time frame in mind than candlestick chart reading, and a longer expected holding period over which you plan to own the security. In traditional bar analysis, you may accept two, three, or even more days of *countervailing bars* (bars that don't confirm the trend). In candlestick analysis, you may accept only one day or none because the trading style associated with candlestick analysis is very short-term.

Bar components influence the next bar

When new highs or lows are occurring, market players start wondering why. This uncertainty arouses various emotions:

- A new high or low makes market participants nervous. A sufficiently large number of new highs triggers the greed instinct — better buy now so you don't miss out, even if you don't have a reason for new highs to be occurring. The result is a higher close as buyers pile in near the end of the day.

- New lows scare just enough traders that they sell their positions, even in the absence of any fresh news that would justify the selling. Sellers are unwilling to hold a falling asset and sell near the end of the day, causing a lower close.

 When the close today is higher than the close yesterday, but the high today isn't higher than the high yesterday, pay attention because new highs may start to appear. These new highs may happen because those who know enough about up-days and down-days begin to *anticipate* higher highs or lower lows. Then, by acting on that expectation — buying or selling ahead of the actual appearance of a higher high or lower low — they make it happen.

Trends can be relative

Markets are not neat and tidy, and not every bar is going to qualify on all the criteria traditionally needed to indicate an up- or downtrend. The chart in Figure 2-4 depicts an uptrend — even though not every bar qualifies as

Book VIII

Technical Analysis

belonging to an uptrend. You see lower lows as well as several days on which the bar is a down-day. Down-days are colored black, and up-days are gray. This figure demonstrates in what ways trends can be relative:

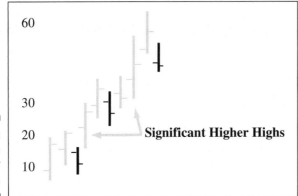

Figure 2-4:
Relative
higher
highs.

✔ **Significance:** In Figure 2-4, not every high is higher than the day before, but every significant high is higher than the highs that came before. You can judge significance by eyeing the chart, or you can specify rules, such as "a significant high is one that is x percent higher than the average of the past y highs." You can use software to develop a filter that defines criteria like a "significant high." In Figure 2-4, two significant higher highs stand out. They each represent a 50 percent gain from the previous up-day high.

If you use charting software to look at charts, turn on the feature that lets you visually differentiate between up-days and down-days. A standard practice is to make up-days green and down-days red. It takes no practice to see where a trend is interrupted by bars that don't qualify.

✔ **Preponderance:** Figure 2-4 illustrates that not every high in an uptrend has to be higher than the one before. You just need to identify a preponderance of higher highs and a preponderance of higher lows. What is a preponderance? You decide. You can eyeball it, or use software to develop a precise definition and back-test it on historical data.

Your eyes can deceive you

Sometimes, if you aren't careful, you can misinterpret what you're seeing. You may see a series of higher highs but forget to make sure that each bar has a higher low and is an up-day, or you may see a series of lower lows but forget to check that the high is lower or that the bars are all down-days. Take a look at Figure 2-5 for a chart that can easily be misread.

This figure shows a price series where every day brings a new high but every day also brings a close lower than the day before, and many days bring a low that is lower than the lows on preceding days.

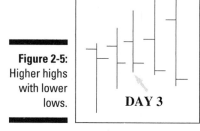

Figure 2-5: Higher highs with lower lows.

DAY 3

Your eye may want to see an uptrend, but when you look more closely and analyze the bars for all three conditions, you have only one uptrend condition (higher highs) that is more than offset by the two downtrend conditions (down-days and lower lows). This set of bars is a series of down-days (the close is lower than the close the day before). It's hard to swallow, but this figure displays a downtrend emerging at the third bar.

Bar-reading doesn't always work

Sometimes you can't figure out what the market is thinking, because it's changing its mind just about every other day. Figure 2-6 is such a chart. The series of gray up-days is a minor uptrend, and the following series of black down-days is a minor downtrend — but then things fall apart. You see higher highs followed by lower lows and no consistency in the placement of the close (up-day or down-day).

What do you do in a case like this? Nothing — at least not anything based on interpretation of the bars. When bars are in a chaotic mess like this, the probability of picking the right direction (up or down) is very low. You'd just be guessing.

Book VIII

Technical Analysis

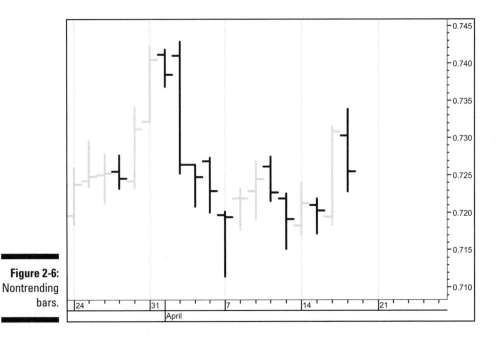

Figure 2-6:
Nontrending
bars.

Reading Special Bar Configurations

An uptrend features higher highs with higher lows and a close higher than the day before (up-days). A downtrend features a series of lower lows together with lower highs and mostly down-days. A fourth factor in determining a trend is the relationship between the day's open and close. A close above the open is a sign of an uptrend; a close below the open is a sign of a downtrend.

Continuation and reversal patterns

When you spot a special configuration in a small series of bars, you're looking for one of two things — it either confirms the trend or signals that the trend is at risk of ending:

 ✓ **Continuation patterns:** The trend is continuing. The direction and pace of the trend are about the same as they were before. Evidence that a trend is continuing includes things like a preponderance of higher highs and higher lows marking bullish sentiment on the part of the trading crowd, even though perhaps some other qualifying factor isn't present.

✔ **Reversal patterns:** The trend is switching direction. When the trend shifts from down to up or up to down, the configuration of the bar components and their placement across a series of price bars often shout "The trend is changing" from the rooftop. Listen up. If you have a position in the security, a reversal pattern tells you to exit. If you hold on to the position anyway, your risk of loss is much higher.

A reversal pattern is not only a warning to exit when you're invested in the security; it's also advance notice that a good entry place may be coming up. For example, when a downtrend ends, you may see one of the very specific reversal patterns that is a reliable precursor to a buy signal. You can get ready to enter the upcoming uptrend.

You hardly ever see a series of bars where every single one of these factors confirms the trend. Because prices never move entirely in a straight line, you have to accept that some bars in a trend don't fall into line with all the trend criteria. You may have one or two bars in an uptrend that don't have higher highs or a few bars where the close is lower than the day before. Such variations in tick placement and *bar placement* (position of a price bar relative to the bars that precede it) are normal in even the best-behaved trend.

The daily trading range

The *daily trading range* is the difference between the high and the low of the day. It measures the maximum distance that the price traveled that period. You can also say that the range defines the emotional extremes of the day:

✔ If you have a bar with a small range in a sea of larger bars, the market is indecisive. Indecisiveness isn't the same thing as indifference. A change in sentiment may be brewing, such as deceleration in a price rise that precedes the end of the trend.

✔ When it's one very large bar in a sea of smaller ones, pay close attention. Traders are willing to pay a *lot* more for a rising security, or they want to dump a falling one so badly that they'll accept an abnormally low price.

Interpreting Common Special Bars

Some bars are just a little out of line, but sometimes you see bars that really stand out. It takes almost no practice at all to differentiate ordinary out-of-line bars from special configurations that traders consider to be associated with specific interpretations. In these special cases, you know you've got a valuable clue to upcoming price behavior.

The interpretation guidelines aren't 100 percent right at all times. In fact, nobody can tell you even roughly what percentage of the time the standard interpretation is correct, because it may be correct all the time in one security but only 10 percent of the time in another, or correct 75 percent of the time in one year but never correct in another. In addition, a bar component or even the placement of the entire bar can be random. The lack of statistically verified and perfectly reliable guidelines is frustrating and annoying to all technical traders and especially beginners, but remember, you're seeking meaningful information about crowd psychology from an excess of evidence.

Use logic and common sense when you're looking at special bars. Keep it simple. The simplest explanations are the likeliest ones.

Closing on a high note

A series of *closes at the high* — and the downtrending counterpart, *closes at the low* — indicate that a new trend may be starting or the existing trend is likely to continue. In Figure 2-7, configuration A illustrates close at the high. The price has closed at the high of the day for three days running, and the third bar is much longer than the others, which means the high–low range is wider than the previous two days. So, what's happening?

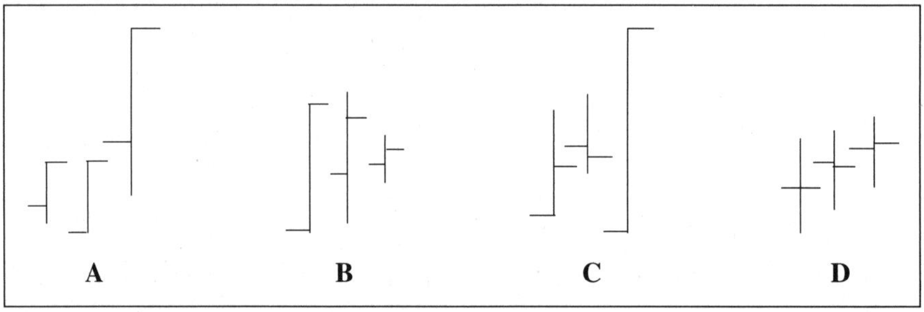

Figure 2-7:
Common
special
bars.

A   B   C   D

The first two bars show the close at the high at about the same level. On the second bar, the low of the day was lower than the low the day before, meaning that sellers came out of the woodwork. But the bulls fought back, buying more and more, so that the close was at a fresh high on that second day. The close at the high for a second day trumps the lower low, and Day 3 delivers a whopping gain — and a third close at the high.

A big gain is often followed by *profit-taking* by active traders who get in a move early. Profit-taking doesn't change a trend, but it can put a dent in the performance of the bar the next day. You may see a lower high or a lower close, which can be very discouraging when you're trying to identify a new trend. It's also annoying to put on a new position in a promising move — three higher highs and three closes at the high — only to take a paper loss on your first day. If you're using bar-reading alone to make trading decisions, stick with the trade (while cursing short-term traders), but also reconsider where you placed your stop-loss order.

Spending the day inside

Configuration B in Figure 2-7 shows the inside day. An *inside day* refers to a price bar that meets two criteria:

- ✔ The high is lower than the previous day's high.
- ✔ The low is higher than the previous day's low.

An inside day is a bar "inside" the previous day's high–low range and usually the average high–low range of the past few days. It reflects indecision. Buyers didn't feel strongly enough about this security to buy more. Sellers weren't particularly inspired to sell, either. The inside day doesn't suggest what's going to happen the following day. But it does warn that the market is starting to reconsider what it feels about this security.

Getting outside for the day

Configuration C in Figure 2-7 is the outside day. On an *outside day,* the high–low range of the bar is outside the range of the preceding bar. The open and close ticks can appear anywhere on the outside day bar, but two variations stand out:

- ✔ **The open is at the low and the close is at the high:** This configuration suggests that something new has happened to inspire bullish buying right up to the end of the day.
- ✔ **The open is at the high and close is at the low:** Sentiment turned bearish and sellers overwhelmed buyers, right to the end of the day.

Book VIII

Technical Analysis

After considering where the open and close are located on the bar, take a look at what else is going on in the market, especially the configuration of the preceding bars:

- ✔ **No trend exists:** The outside day alerts you to a possible trend beginning.

- ✔ **A trend is in place:** The outside day may suggest a reversal or a continuation, depending on where the open and close are and which direction the security is trending. The outside day has a higher high by definition, but a higher close as well implies continuation in an uptrend and reversal in a downtrend, especially if the close is exactly at the high. Similarly, the outside day has a lower low by definition, so it confirms continuation in a downtrend, especially if the close is at the low.

Finding the close at the open

Configuration D in Figure 2-7 shows a series of bars where the close is at or near the open. *Close-at-open* ordinarily occurs near the center of the daily price range, not at the high or the low. A close at or near the open reflects indecision among market participants. Trader opinion is divided as to whether this bar generally signifies a continuation or reversal pattern. Consider it a clue to look at what else is going on, such as trading volume.

When the open and close are at (or almost at) the same price, *and* they're at the high or low of the day, you have a greater chance of determining whether the trend will continue or reverse. Which way the cookie crumbles depends on what was happening before:

- ✔ **In an uptrend:** If the open and close are near the high, look for the uptrend to accelerate. If they are near the low, look for a reversal.

- ✔ **In a downtrend:** If the open and close are near the low, expect more of the same. If they are near the high, think about a reversal.

Understanding Spikes

Sometimes the market delivers a price bar that looks like the market went crazy that day — the high or the low is very far away from the general trend of things and the bar itself is abnormally large (wide high–low range). Figure 2-8 shows two of these uncommon price bars, called *spikes*. A spike is a bar that encompasses a much bigger high–low range than the bars immediately preceding it.

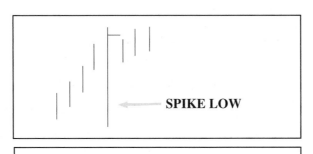

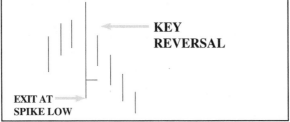

Figure 2-8:
Uncommon
special
bars.

In some cases, like that shown in the top example of Figure 2-8, a spike turns out to be an anomaly. The spike low suggests that some people panicked and were selling at such a high quantity and at such a frantic pace that the few buyers still around were able to buy at abnormally low prices. On this chart, the sellers panicked unnecessarily. The next day, the price resumed its uptrend and its same "normal" high–low range. The spike was just an oddity — a random move.

Even though price spikes *can* be an anomaly, you can't afford to ignore them. The spike may be a reaction to fresh news or perspective that has the potential to create a new trend. Or it may be a message that sentiment has changed dramatically.

The bottom spike example in Figure 2-8 is a key reversal because on the next few days, the price proceeded to make lower highs and lower lows. This spike in the size of the daily high–low range was a warning of a reversal. *Key reversals* can be ordinary bars and aren't always spikes, but when you see a spike, always ask yourself whether it may mark a reversal.

You seldom know whether a spike is random or meaningful on the day that it happens. Only hindsight can tell you that. Though hindsight has the final say on the meaning of a spike, you can still use spikes for immediate analytical purposes:

  ✔ **Investigate the environment:** Sometimes you *do* know when a spike is a key reversal because you can determine what shock caused it and your judgment in interpreting the news or event is sound.

Book VIII

**Technical
Analysis**

> ✔ **Trust the close:** As a general rule, you're safe assuming that the close is the most important part of the bar because it sums up the sentiment for the day.

A key reversal bar is also called a *swing bar,* although not all swing bars are spikes. A swing bar is any bar that is the final and lowest low in a series of lower lows or the final and highest high in a series of higher highs, as in the bottom chart in Figure 2-8. You can see a spike bar at the end of the day after the close, but you can't identify it as a swing bar until after two additional closes.

A conservative trading tactic is to order your broker to sell the security if the price falls below the low of the spike day over the next two or three days. Everybody who trades this security knows about the spike low and will be watching to see if the bears are strong enough to break the level and take the price lower. If so, they plan to sell at that level, and you should, too. In an upmove, bulls are often curiously timid about testing a spike high. The bar following a spike is often an inside day. Other times the following bar has a new higher high only a few pennies above the spike high and a close lower than the spike bar close. Neither bar is helpful. They're simply inconclusive, and you have to wait for additional evidence to get guidance on how to trade.

Grasping Gaps

A gap is one of the most important of the special bar configurations. A *gap* is a major, visible discontinuity between two price bars on a chart (see Figure 2-9). Because every bar encompasses all the transactions made during a specific period, a gap marks the absence of any transactions at the prices covered by the gap.

The gap is a void — no demand if there was supply and no supply if there was demand, at least not at those prices. Prices had to shift considerably in order for supply and demand to meet again and for both buyers and sellers to be satisfied. On daily charts, a gap is initially seen when the opening price today diverges dramatically from yesterday's high or low, although you can also see gaps between bars on intraday charts.

You can *identify* a gap at the open, but you can't *measure* a gap until the day's trading is over. Then you measure it from yesterday's high to today's low (for an upside gap) or from yesterday's low to today's high (for a downside gap). The gap is between the bars, not between the opens and closes. If the security opens on a gap but then the gap is filled during the day, the gap doesn't show up on a daily chart. The same thing is true if a security gaps during the day on an hourly chart — the daily bar doesn't show it.

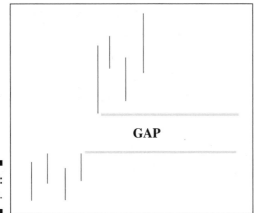

GAP

Figure 2-9:
A price gap.

Gaps are often the result of positive or negative news, like earnings or some other event, whether true or invented (rumors). Events are the source of most key price moves, including trends, whether starting or stopping. Prices don't, on the whole, move randomly — traders have reasons, right or wrong, to buy and sell. Even the strongest trend can be broken by a piece of fresh news contrary to the trend direction. Authentically big news trumps the chart (nearly) every time.

Gaps are a wonderful trading opportunity if you can differentiate between a common gap and uncommon gaps.

Lacking opportunity: Common gaps

A *common gap* is one that appears out of nowhere for no particular reason (no fresh news). Common gaps can occur in trending and nontrending prices. If the price is trending, it fails to change the trend. If the price isn't trending, it fails to initiate a trend. Common gaps are generally insignificant.

A common gap tends to have low volume on the gap day. If you see an opening gap, one way to evaluate whether to take it seriously is to consult volume. To consult volume, you need access to live data. If volume is low or normal, traders aren't jumping on the bandwagon and it's probably a common gap. If volume is abnormally high, traders are jumping on the bandwagon and the gap will probably lead to a big rise or fall in the coming days.

A security that normally has low volume tends to have more gaps than heavily traded securities. A low-volume security is described as *thinly traded,* meaning few market participants. Don't try to interpret gaps in thinly traded securities. These gaps are usually just common gaps and mean nothing at all.

Book VIII

Technical Analysis

Kicking things off: Breakaway gaps

A *breakaway gap,* shown in Figure 2-10, is an important event because it almost always marks the start of a new trend. Not only do you get the gap and a new trend, but you also get a major change in the appearance of the chart, such as a widening of the normal high–low daily trading range, an increase in day-to-day volatility, and much higher volume. All these changes occur because the breakaway gaps draw in new traders. A breakaway gap is event-driven, usually on some news about the security itself.

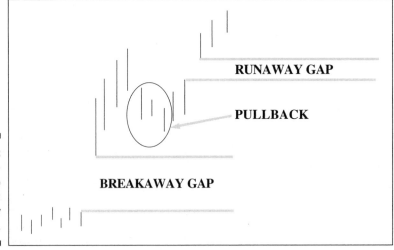

Figure 2-10:
A break-
away gap
and a
runaway
gap.

To qualify as a breakaway gap, the gap has to

- ✓ **Be proportionately big to the usual trading range:** If the security normally trades in a $3 range between the daily high and low, and the gap is $15 between the preceding day's high and the gap-day open, you can instantly recognize that something big happened.

- ✓ **Occur when a price is either slightly trending or moving sideways:** Nothing much is going on in the chart, and then bam! Fresh news creates new supply and demand conditions and ignites a trend.

You interpret a breakaway gap depending on whether it's upward or downward.

- ✓ **Upside breakaway gap:** Good news creates demand. New buyers want to own the security and are willing to pay ever-higher prices to get it. Volume is noticeably higher than usual.

- ✓ **Downside breakaway gap:** Traders can't wait to get rid of their holdings and accept ever-lower prices to achieve that goal. Volume may or may not be abnormally high.

Continuing the push: Runaway gaps

A *runaway gap* (refer to Figure 2-10) occurs after a security is already moving in a trended way and fresh news comes out that promotes the existing trend. Whereas a breakaway gap starts a trend, a runaway gap continues a trend. In both cases, buyers become exuberant and offer higher and higher prices. Sometimes there's fresh good news, sometimes traders make up fresh good news, and sometimes the buying frenzy is just feeding on itself in the absence of any news at all.

A *pullback* (a falling price after a dramatic move) represents profit-taking by the early birds and is very common. In fact, professionals count on the pullback to "buy on the dip." If they get really enthusiastic, re-entering professional traders often supply the energy for a runaway gap that follows a breakaway gap.

Calling it quits: Exhaustion gaps

Exhaustion gaps occur at the end of a trend, signaling the party's over. Volume is usually low. What's exhausted is the news that propelled the security up in the first place and the energy of the early buyers. An exhaustion gap is usually followed by a reversal.

You can distinguish an exhaustion gap from a runaway gap by looking at volume, which is usually low at an exhaustion gap. Anytime you see wild new highs (or lows) that aren't accompanied by wild new high volume, be suspicious of the staying power of the move. You can exit altogether or move up your stop-loss order.

Scoring big: Island reversals

Sometimes an exhaustion gap is followed immediately by a breakaway gap going in the other direction. This is how an island reversal forms. An *island reversal* is a single isolated price bar with a gap up on one side and a gap down on the other. It looks like an island in a sea of price bars and is almost always an unusually long bar — a wide high–low range.

In Figure 2-11, you can see a series of higher highs, including a minor gap up, but then the last buyers realize they are all alone on top of the mountain. They start to sell in a panic and are willing to accept a much lower price. Now the price takes off in the opposite direction on a breakaway gap, which tends to have high volume. The island reversal bar has a higher high but is accompanied by low

Book VIII

Technical Analysis

volume. This combination is the warning. The next day, as the breakaway gap develops, it has unusually high volume. You need live data to evaluate the new breakaway gap as it emerges at the open. High volume in combination with the downward gap is an indication that early selling is strong and prices later in the day aren't going to go back and fill that gap.

Examine price bars, and you'll see a lot of gaps. Seldom, though, will you see an island reversal. But when you do see it, you know what to do:

- ✔ An island reversal at the bottom: Buy.
- ✔ An island reversal at the top: Sell.

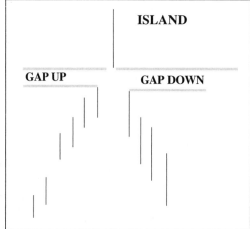

Figure 2-11: An island reversal.

Will the gap be filled?

Filling the gap means that prices are returning to the level they occupied before the gap, as shown in Figure 2-12.

With a runaway gap or a common gap, demand for the stock is more a function of buyers egging each other on than changing conditions, so the gap may be filled quickly. Sometimes a gap gets filled just because all the chatter about filling the gap in the market makes it a self-fulfilling prophecy.

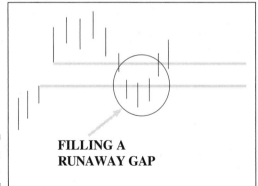

FILLING A
RUNAWAY GAP

Figure 2-12:
Filling a gap.

A breakaway gap is another matter. If a security takes off on a breakaway gap, sometimes the price doesn't return to fill the gap for many months or even years — if ever. When the fundamentals of a security change dramatically, why would market participants sell it back down to the level it was before the big event? Conditions have changed permanently, and so has the price of the security.

Book VIII

Technical Analysis

Chapter 3

Charting the Market with Candlesticks

Candlestick charting displays the price bar in a graphically different way from the standard bars described in Chapter 2. But this isn't just a notation method — candlesticks do many other things, as well:

✔ They're easy to use and simple to interpret. Plus you can use candlesticks on any chart, with any other indicators, just like standard bars.

✔ The names of candlesticks and candlestick patterns contain the seeds of interpretation and help you to remember what the pattern means. Because candlestick bar interpretations are widely known, other participants in the market respond in a specific way to a specific pattern.

✔ They excel in identifying strategic market turning points — reversals from an uptrend to a downtrend or a downtrend to an uptrend.

This chapter breaks down the components of a candlestick and covers those candlesticks and combinations that stand out the most from the dozens that exist.

Anatomy of a Candlestick

The candlestick form emphasizes the open and the close (see Figure 3-1). The open and the close mark the top and bottom of a box, named the *real body*. A thin vertical line at the top and bottom of the real body, named the *shadow*, shows the high and the low. (See Chapter 2 for a discussion of the basic bar components — open, close, high, and low.)

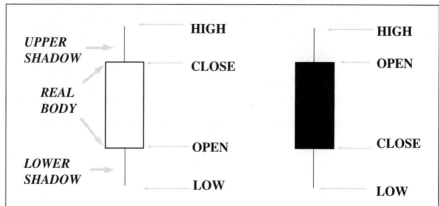

Figure 3-1:
Candlestick
bar notation.

Drawing the real body

The real body encompasses the range between the open and the close. The color of the real body tells you how the daily struggle between the bulls and the bears played out:

- ✔ **White real body:** The close is higher than the open. A white body is bullish, and the longer the body, the more bullish it is. A long candlestick indicates that the close was far above the open, implying aggressive buying. In the daily battle of bulls and bears, the bulls won.

- ✔ **Black real body:** The close is lower than the open. A black body is bearish, and the longer the body, the more bearish it is. A long black candlestick indicates a preponderance of sellers throughout the session. In the daily battle of bulls and bears, the bears won.

The two candlestick bars in Figure 3-1 show the identical open and close, but coloring one of them black creates the optical illusion that it is bigger. That black bar demands your attention, which is one reason candlestick charting is appealing — and effective.

In standard bar notation, described in Chapter 2, a bar's color depends on whether it's a down-day (the close is lower than the day before) or an up-day (the close is higher than day before). In candlestick notation, the color of the bar is determined only by today's open and today's close, without reference to yesterday's prices.

As in all bar analysis, *context* is crucial. Although you may sometimes use a single candlestick bar as an indicator in its own right, most of the time you use it in relation to the bars that precede it. One small white-body bar in a sea of black bars, for example, may mean the bulls won that day, but it was a minor event. The one white bar may signal that the bears are losing power, but you wouldn't use it all by itself to call the end of a black-bar downtrend.

Defining doji: No real body

A candlestick that has no real body or only a very small one is named a *doji*. In a doji, the open and the close are at or nearly at the same level. Figure 3-2 displays three doji bars. When the close is at or near the open, market participants are indecisive. Bulls and bears are at a standoff.

A doji implies that sentiment is in a transitional phase. It's a neutral bar, neither bullish nor bearish, that gains meaning from its placement within a set of bars. If the price series has been in an uptrend, for example, the doji may reflect that the buyers are coming to the end of their bullish enthusiasm. A doji coming immediately after a very long white bar shows that the market is tired.

Figure 3-2:
Doji
candlestick
patterns.

PLAIN DOJI　　　**DRAGONFLY DOJI**　　　**GRAVESTONE DOJI**

Studying the shadows

The high and the low are shown in the *shadows,* which you can think of as a candlewick (on the top) or a tail (on the bottom). Although the shadow is secondary to the real body in importance, shadows contribute useful information about market psychology, too, and modify your interpretation of the body. Shadows offer special interpretive clues in three instances: when the real body is a doji, when the shadow is missing, and when the shadow is extremely long.

Book VIII

**Technical
Analysis**

Shadows in the doji bar

In many instances, a doji is just a plain one, but the dragonfly and gravestone dojis are the more useful (refer to Figure 3-2):

- ✔ **Dragonfly doji:** Features a long lower shadow. A very long lower shadow tells you that the open, high, and close were all the same or nearly the same, meaning sellers were trying to push the price down and succeeded in making a low — but they didn't succeed in getting it to close there. Because the close was back up at or near the open, buyers must have emerged before the end of trading and fought back, getting the price to close at or near what was both the open and the high. How you interpret the dragonfly depends on what bar patterns precede it:

  - If the price move is a downtrend, the dragonfly may mean that buyers are emerging and the downtrend may be ending.

  - If the dragonfly appears after a series of uptrending bars, buyers failed to push the price over the open to a new high while sellers succeeded in getting a low, so the uptrend may be in trouble.

- ✔ **Gravestone doji:** Features a long upper shadow. This bar is formed when the open, low, and close are the same or nearly the same, but a high creates a long upper shadow. Although buyers succeeded in pushing the price to a high over the open, by the end of the day the bears were fighting back and pushed the price back to close near the open and the low. This is a failed effort at a rally, but you can interpret the bar only in the context of the bars that precede it:

  - If the gravestone bar appears after a series of uptrending bars, buyers failed to get the close at the high. Sellers dominated and the uptrend is at risk of ending.

  - If the price move is a downtrend, the gravestone doji may mean that buyers are emerging and the downtrend may be ending.

Missing shadows

The absence of a shadow at one end is called a *shaven top* or a *shaven bottom*. To get a shaven top or bottom, the open or close must be exactly at the high or the low (see Figure 3-3).

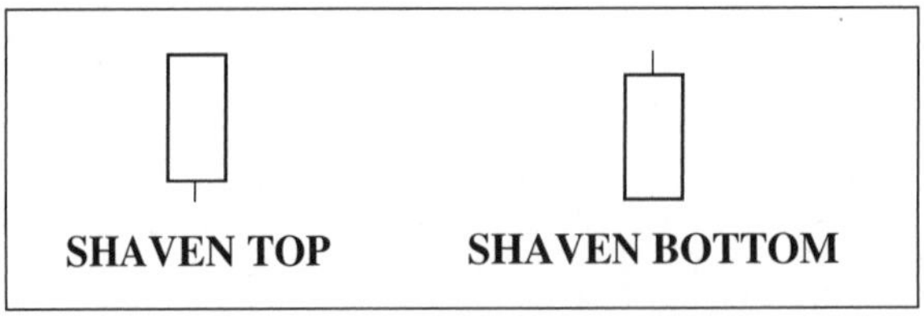

Figure 3-3:
Missing shadows.

SHAVEN TOP   SHAVEN BOTTOM

✔ **Shaven top:** No upper shadow exists when the open or close is at the high. A shaven top can be black or white, and it comes about in two ways:

- If the open is at the high, the day's trading was all downhill from there. Not only is it a black candlestick, bearish to begin with, but it's doubly bearish that no net new buying occurred after the open.

- If the close is at the high, the net of the day's trading was at higher prices, which is bullish. The candlestick is also (by definition) white, a bullish sign.

✔ **Shaven bottom:** No lower shadow exists when the open or the close is at the low of the day. A shaven bottom can come about in two ways:

- If the open is at the low, all the day's trading was euphoric. This is bullish, adding to the bullishness of the white candlestick.

- If the close is at the low, all the day's trading points to developing negative sentiment (depending on what bars precede it, of course). This is a black bar, with bells on.

Really long shadows

When the shadow is as long as the real body, or longer (see Figure 3-4), traders are expressing an extreme of sentiment. They may or may not follow through the next day by pushing the close to the high or low extreme. It can be tricky, therefore, to evaluate a long shadow. As a general rule, you judge a long shadow by its placement on the chart (relative to preceding bars).

Figure 3-4:
Very long shadows.

LONG UPPER SHADOW   LONG LOWER SHADOW

Book VIII

Technical Analysis

✔ **Long upper shadow:** The high of the day came well above both the open and the close, whether the real body is black or white.

- If the price series is in an uptrend, the long upper shadow is a failure to close near the high. If the uptrend is nearing a resistance level (see Chapter 4 for a discussion of resistance), the long upper shadow may signal a weakening of the uptrend. If a long upper shadow follows a doji bar indicating indecisiveness, you should worry that the uptrend may be over.

- If the price series is on a downtrend, the long upper shadow suggests that some market participants are buying at higher levels. Especially if a long upper shadow follows a doji bar, you should wonder whether the downtrend may be ending.

✔ **Long lower shadow:** A long lower shadow means that the low of the day came well under both the open and the close, whether the real body is black or white.

- If the price series is in a downtrend, the long lower shadow is a failure to close near the low. If the downtrend is nearing a support level (see Chapter 4), the long lower shadow may signal a weakening or an end of the downtrend.

- If the price series is on an uptrend, the long lower shadow suggests that traders were not willing to keep buying at the high levels right up to the close. They were exiting under the high and, therefore, think that new highs are not warranted. This can be a warning sign of the trend decelerating or ending.

Identifying Emotional Extremes

Identifying when traders are reaching the end of their emotional tether is one of the primary goals of candlestick charting. A change in the size of the bar is one of the best indicators of this situation. If you're looking at a series of medium-sized bars and suddenly see one relatively long bar (as shown in Figure 3-5), it may be telling you that support or resistance has been reached. *Support* marks an extreme level where buyers perceive that the price is relatively cheap, and *resistance* marks an extreme level where sellers perceive the price is relatively high, inspiring profit-taking or at least an end to accumulation.

In the top illustration in Figure 3-5 is a series of three white bars making higher opens and higher closes, followed by a doji and an exceptionally long white bar. If you were looking at this in standard bar notation, as seen in the bottom illustration, you might say to yourself, "Higher highs, higher lows, higher closes, trend okay." But the unusually tall bar stands out more prominently in candlestick mode — especially following the transitional doji — and alerts you to the possibility that all the buyers who were going to buy have just done so in one last burst, and the price may have formed a resistance level at the top of the bar (the close, in this case).

If the long bar were a black bar, denoting that the close was lower than the open, you would find it easy to deduce that the upmove might be ending. A long black bar implies panic selling. But to interpret the *white* bar as an ending burst in an uptrend is more subtle. Dozens of possible bar placement combinations and permutations are possible. The next section covers several of the most popular patterns.

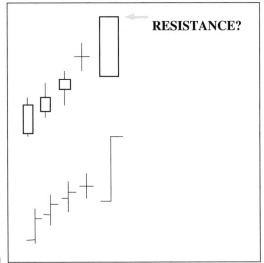

RESISTANCE?

Figure 3-5:
Bar
placement.

WARNING!

Two similar candlesticks or candlestick patterns often have the exact opposite interpretation, depending on where they fall in a series. You have to memorize the exact patterns to avoid getting confused.

Hammer and hanging man

Both the hammer and hanging man have a small real body and only one shadow — a long lower shadow. The long shadow of the hammer extends to the downside off a white body, while the long shadow of the hanging man extends to the downside off a black body (see Figure 3-6).

You'd think that the white-body version would automatically be a bullish indicator and the black-body version a bearish one, but interpreting this candlestick depends on its placement on the chart, regardless of the real-body color. If the candlestick appears in a downtrend, for example, it marks the likely end of the trend even if the real body is white.

You may see a hammer in many other contexts, but when it has a white body and it comes after a series of black downtrending bars, as in Figure 3-6, it implies reversal. Note that the close is higher than the previous close, too. In this context, the long lower shadow means the sellers were able to achieve a new low, but buyers emerged at some point during the day and the close was higher than the open, indicating last-minute buying.

Book VIII

**Technical
Analysis**

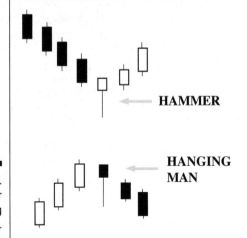

Figure 3-6.
Hammer
and hanging
man.

The hanging man looks the same except it has a black body coming after a series of white uptrending bars. The long lower shadow marks the bulls' failure to prevent the bears making a new low and also from keeping the close below the open. You may see this bar in other places within a series of bars, but when you see it at the top of an uptrending series (as in Figure 3-6), you should consider that the trend is probably over. The wise course is to take your profit and run.

Harami

A small real-body candlestick that comes after a bigger one, as shown in Figure 3-7, is called a *harami,* which means *pregnant* in Japanese. A harami implies that a change in sentiment is impending. Technically, the harami pattern requires two bars, so it doesn't stand alone. This chart shows the shadows of the harami bar as also inside the scope of the first big bar, although this isn't essential to identifying the pattern.

A harami can be white or black, and in fact, it can even be a doji (inside day). The smaller the real body is, the more powerful the implication that a reversal is impending. In Figure 3-7, white bars, seemingly downtrending, are followed by a large white bar, reflecting a high level of emotion. Seeing just the big white bar after a series of smaller ones that are downtrending, you may think that the bulls finally got the upper hand, and this is the start of an uptrend — especially because you have an indecision doji just ahead of it. The black harami following the big white bar should disillusion you. If an uptrend was forming, the harami just put the kibosh on it.

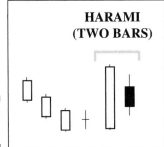

Figure 3-7:
Harami.

Turning to Reversal Patterns

Identifying reversals is the main application of candlesticks. The engulfing candlestick and the shooting star, shown in Figure 3-8, are two of the most popular and easily identified candlesticks showing reversal patterns:

- **Engulfing candlestick:** An *engulfing pattern* signals the reversal of a trend. The word *engulfing* refers to the open and close of the bar encompassing a wider range than the open and close of the day before. In Figure 3-8, which shows a bearish engulfing candlestick, the engulfing nature is the dominant characteristic, so that the lower close pops out at you even though the bar also has a higher open. When a bar starts out at a higher open but then closes at a lower level, the bears won that day. Not shown is a *bullish engulfing candlestick,* which is white. The higher close is visually compelling because the real body is so big.

- **Shooting star:** The *shooting star* is characterized by a small real body and a long upper shadow, as you can see in Figure 3-8. As discussed in the section "Really long shadows," the shadow in an uptrend implies a failure of the trend — a failure to close near the high. Notice the indecisive doji bar just before the shooting star.

Book VIII

Technical Analysis

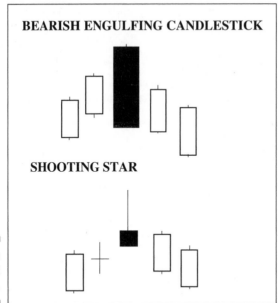

BEARISH ENGULFING CANDLESTICK

SHOOTING STAR

Figure 3-8:
Reversal
patterns.

Recognizing Continuation Patterns

Candlestick patterns are most often used to identify reversals, but continuation patterns do exist. As the name suggests, a continuation pattern gives you confirmation that the trend in place will likely continue. Two such patterns are the rising (or falling) window and the three white soldiers:

✔ **Rising/falling window:** *Rising window* is the term for a gap — in this case, an upward gap. A downward gap is a *falling window.* (Go to Chapter 2 for more on gaps.) In Figure 3-9, the gap separates two white candlesticks, which are themselves bullish. The next bar doesn't fill the gap. The gap between the two price bars is confirmation of the existing trend, and the market's refusal the following day to go back and fill the gap is further confirmation that the trend is okay.

✔ **Three white soldiers:** The bottom bars in Figure 3-9 show three white soldiers. In this pattern, what's important are three large white candlesticks in a row. Seeing the close consistently over the open for three days confirms that the price series is in an uptrend, and the size of the bars indicates its robustness.

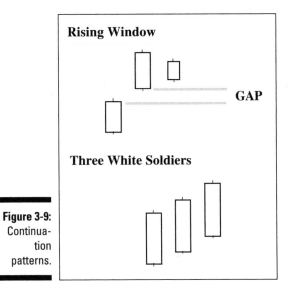

Rising Window

GAP

Three White Soldiers

Figure 3-9:
Continua-
tion
patterns.

Interpreting a Series of Patterns

To do a good job interpreting candlesticks, you need to understand the dynamic and complex relationships of many patterns all at once, like juggling six oranges instead of three. Figure 3-10 shows a series of candlesticks that reveal several patterns. (Note: This figure also shows a set of parallel support and resistance lines called a *channel,* which is used to outline the probable limit of future prices moves, either up or down. You can read more about support and resistance in Chapter 4.)

The harami is followed by a rising window (upward gap) and a big white candle. These three candlesticks together are bullish and alert you to go back and start the channel at the lowest low, the bar before the harami.

In reading this chart, notice that the real bodies push against the top of the channel resistance line, but the doji, which suggests that traders are having second thoughts, is followed by two higher white candles. The two white candles indicate that the reconsideration of the move on the doji day culminated in traders' decision to keep taking the price up. This was an occasion when the doji wasn't a reversal indicator, at least not for the next day. After the two white candles comes a bearish engulfing candle, a reversal warning that this upmove may be ending. The engulfing candle alerts you to watch the next day's activity, especially the open, with an eagle eye.

Book VIII

Technical Analysis

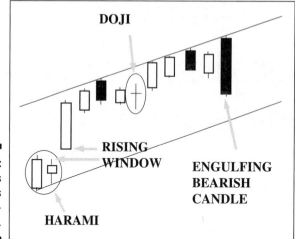

DOJI

RISING
WINDOW

ENGULFING
BEARISH
CANDLE

HARAMI

Figure 3-10:
Candlesticks
as
confirma-
tion.

No matter how compelling a particular bar may seem, you still need confirmation of the interpretation, which comes only after you see the next day's bar. Sometimes you get a strong reversal pattern that is invalidated the very next day, for example. Candlestick analysis may offer a forecast of the general direction of the price move over the next day or few days, but it doesn't suggest the extent of the move — a price target.

Chapter 4

Seeing Patterns and Drawing Trendlines

In This Chapter
▶ Identifying basic and advanced patterns
▶ Recognizing the significance of support and resistance lines
▶ Drawing trendlines

Securities prices move in regular ways that most professional traders (who dominate the market) expect — and therefore create. Technical traders have been developing patterns from the earliest days of technical analysis. Chart patterns are powerful indicators, and having some rudimentary knowledge of patterns is a good idea for the most sophisticated indicator trader and the beginner alike.

Other things to know include *support and resistance* and *breakout*. Even a rough application of these two concepts will save you a bundle or help you make profits, because they're among the top technical ruling concepts in the market. This chapter explains the most common chart patterns and tells you how to use these key concepts to recognize when a trend starts and stops.

Introducing Patterns

Chart patterns are indicators consisting of shapes, such as triangles, drawn on the chart. Although most patterns employ straight lines (such as triangles), a few use semi-circles or semi-ellipses (such as head-and-shoulders). In addition, pattern lines generally follow either the highs or the lows.

Not everyone can see patterns right away. Pattern identification takes practice — and a lot of drawing and redrawing of lines and shapes until you get the hang of it. For example, consider Figure 4-1. Do you see the pattern?

Figure 4-1:
Find the
pattern.

The pattern in Figure 4-1 is a symmetrical triangle, as you can see in Figure 4-2, characterized by a series of lower highs along which you can draw one trendline and a series of higher lows along which you can draw another trendline. The two lines eventually come together at an apex. Before that point is reached, the price must pierce one of the trendlines in the course of trading in its normal range. Which one? Because most of the bars are trending downward, you imagine the odds favor a break to the downside. But it could also be to the upside.

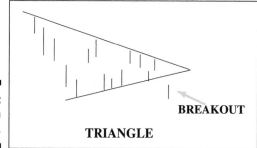

Figure 4-2:
Pattern
revealed.

Following are a few points to keep in mind as you try to identify and interpret patterns:

- ✔ Pattern types are usually organized according to whether they forecast a continuation or a reversal of the current price move, although many patterns can be applied either way. As with most indicators, a price forecast is embedded in the pattern identification.

- ✔ You usually see a burst of higher volume when a pattern reaches completion. This makes sense — other chartists in the crowd are seeing the same pattern. For triangles, low volume often *precedes* the breakout and serves as a bonus warning of an impending move.

✔ Pattern identification doesn't require that each single price in a series line up perfectly. Not every price high hits an overhead resistance line, for example. It suffices that several hit the line.

✔ All triangles — symmetrical, ascending, and descending — as well as flags and pennants, and other patterns, incorporate *support* (top) and *resistance* (bottom) lines.

Opinions differ on whether the top and bottom lines must enclose every part of every price bar, or if it's okay for the bar to break the line by a tiny amount as a pattern is developing. In many patterns, such as double tops and head-and-shoulders, drawing a rough outline that breaks some price bars is good enough to identify the pattern, but discarding the pattern when a bar breaks support or resistance is safer. So how do you know when you may break a bar and when you shouldn't? Fortunately, technical traders and software designers are rapidly qualifying the conditions that define each pattern. The real key is practice.

As with most aspects of technical analysis, a pattern is a work in progress, and pattern identification can be frustrating and time-consuming. You may think you see a pattern developing, only to have the price action change course and fail to complete the expected formation. You may have to erase your work and start over a number of times on any single set of bars. Resign yourself to making a lot of mistakes. The reason to tolerate the pattern recognition process is that when you get it right, you have a powerful forecasting tool that can deliver 20 to 40 percent returns in a short period of time.

Identifying Continuation Patterns

A *continuation pattern* tells you that buying or selling pressure is pausing. If a big-picture trend is well-established, the pattern suggests it will accelerate after the pause. A continuation pattern is therefore a good place to add more to a position, because you expect an additional move in the same direction. Because continuation patterns tend to be fairly short-term, sometimes only a few days, they're often neglected.

Continuation patterns serve as reassurance that you've identified the trend correctly. They also often point you to the ideal level at which to place a stop-loss order.

Book VIII

Technical Analysis

Ascending and descending triangles

To draw ascending and descending triangles, you draw a line along the highs of a price series and another one along the lows (see Figure 4-3) — just as you do with symmetrical triangles.

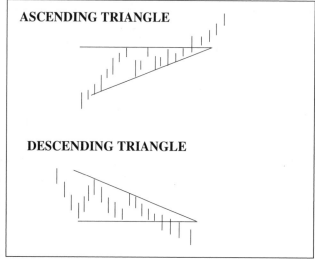

Figure 4-3:
Ascending
and
descending
triangles.

In the ascending triangle, the price isn't making new highs, and the topmost (resistance) line is horizontal. You may worry that the failure to make new highs means the upmove is over. But the price isn't making new lows, either. You expect a breakout of the top line to the upside.

When you can draw a horizontal line along a series of highs, remember to look for a rising line along the lows at the same time. Not only does the ascending line confirm the trend continuation, but it also provides you with a ready-made stop-loss level at the ascending support line. The ascending triangle pattern delivers the expected rise about two-thirds of the time, but it fails about 32 percent of the time. If you wait for prices to close above the top trendline, then the failure rate drops to a mere 2 percent. The *expected rise,* by the way, is equal to the height of the triangle pattern.

A descending triangle is the mirror image of the ascending triangle. The important point is that the price is failing to make new lows in the prevailing downtrend. You wonder if the trend is failing. But if you can still draw a line along the series of lower highs, it would be a mistake to buy at this point — the probability is high that the downtrend is going to continue.

Pennants and flags

A *pennant* is shaped like a triangle — converging lines — but the price swing between the top and bottom lines is smaller (see Figure 4-4). Usually a pennant lasts only a few days and hardly ever longer than three weeks. A pennant is a form of retracement accompanied by a drop in volume. A *flag* is another retracement, but its support and resistance lines are parallel (see Figure 4-5).

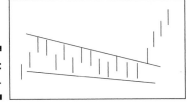

Figure 4-4:
A pennant.

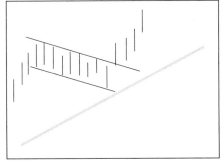

Figure 4-5:
A flag.

A trend is usually punctuated by minor retracement moves in the opposite direction when traders take profit and set off a small cascade of profit-taking by others. With pennants and flags, the pattern lasts an average of 10 to 11 days and is accompanied by falling volume. In Figure 4-5, note the gray line that roughly describes the overall uptrend. Whenever you get a retracement like a pennant or a flag (and often with ascending or descending triangles, too), you have to broaden your vision of the price move because the pattern causes the longer-term high–low range of the entire period to widen. Technically, a series of lower lows in an uptrend breaks and ends the trend, and a series of higher highs breaks and ends a downtrend. But if the retracement is minor and the pattern qualifies as a continuation pattern, the trend is still in place — it just has to be seen in a wider perspective.

Book VIII

Technical Analysis

If you have confidence in the trend, you can tolerate a minor and short-lived break when it's a pennant or flag doing the breaking. In fact, pennants and flags are what pattern chartists call *half-mast patterns.* That is, they form midway in a trend, and you can project the distance already traveled from the start of the trend from the pattern to estimate the end of the trend.

If you don't see a drop in volume with flags and pennants, you may be looking at a reversal rather than a continuation pattern.

Dead-cat bounce — phony reversal

A dead-cat bounce, shown in Figure 4-6, is a peculiar continuation pattern that looks like a reversal at the beginning, with a sizeable upward retracement of a downmove, but then fades back to the same downward direction. Note that a dead-cat bounce occurs only in downmoves, and no equivalent named pattern exists for a parallel sequence of events in an upmove.

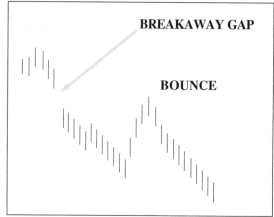

BREAKAWAY GAP

BOUNCE

Figure 4-6:
Dead-cat
bounce.

The dead cat-pattern starts off with a negative fundamental event that triggers a massive downmove. The *bounce* is an upward retracement that may make you think the drop is over. The pattern includes a breakaway downside gap about 80 percent of the time, and sometimes the bounce upward fills part of the gap. (See Chapter 2 for a discussion of gaps.) Many traders mistakenly think that if a gap is filled, even partly, the preceding move has ended. The dead-cat bounce is one of the patterns that disproves that idea.

Noting Classic Reversal Patterns

Patterns come into their own when used to identify a trend reversal. No matter what way a trend comes to an end, chances are good that a pattern exists to identify it.

Double bottom

A double bottom looks like a W (see Figure 4-7) and predicts a price breakout to the upside and substantial gains. A valid double bottom includes these characteristics:

- ✔ A minimum of 10 days between the two lows and sometimes as long as two or three months.
- ✔ A 4 percent or less price variation between the two lows.
- ✔ A center upmove of at least 10 percent from the lower of the two bottoms.
- ✔ A price that rises above the confirmation line (which confirms that the pattern is indeed a double bottom and the forecast of a continued rise is correct).

The *confirmation line* is a horizontal line drawn from the highest high in the middle of the W. The point where the price rises above the line is called the *confirmation point.* Reaching the confirmation line drawn horizontally from the confirmation point is the most important identification key of the double bottom. This is where you buy.

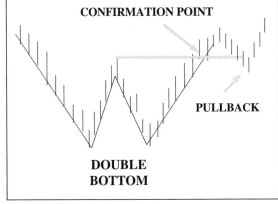

CONFIRMATION POINT

PULLBACK

DOUBLE
BOTTOM

Figure 4-7:
Double
bottom.

Book VIII

**Technical
Analysis**

Notice that some of the price bars break the lines you draw to form the double bottom pattern. Breaking some of the bars is allowed in a formation where the line is not a support or resistance line.

Not every twin bottom is a true double bottom. Only about one-third of all the patterns that look like a double bottom end up meeting the confirmation criterion. In other words, the pattern fails about two-thirds of the time. This sounds terrible, but on the occasions when you do get confirmation, the double bottom is tremendously reliable. If you wait for the price to break above the confirmation line, the pattern delivers a profit an astonishing 97 percent of the time — and the average gain is 40 percent.

Other characteristics of a double bottom are

- ✔ A large increase in volume on the price crossing above the confirmation line, demonstrating increased interest by the crowd and implying widespread recognition of the pattern.

- ✔ Frequent retracements to the downside right after the price breaks the confirmation line. A retracement occurs 68 percent of the time in confirmed double bottoms, making it hard, psychologically, to hang on to the trade that you just put on only a few days before when the price crossed the confirmation line.

Not every double bottom pattern is as easy to detect as the one in Figure 4-7. One or both of the two lows of the double bottom could be rounded instead of pointed, for example. Often the two lows of a double bottom are separated by several months or even a year, and it's easy to miss the pattern altogether. Also, minor retracements and other wobbles within the W can obscure the pattern.

Double tops

A double top is the mirror image of the double bottom — it looks like the letter M. The price makes a high, pulls back on profit-taking (as usual), and then bullish traders try but fail to surpass the first high. The failure to rally a second time through the first high means the bulls were beaten and the bears are now in charge. A true double top is usually accompanied by falling volume as the second top is being formed.

As with the double bottom, you need to see the price surpass the confirmation level (the lowest point in the center bar of the M) for the pattern to be valid. When that condition is not met, twin tops fail to deliver a sustained down-move 65 percent of the time. When the condition is met, however, the pattern delivers a downmove 83 percent of the time, which is less reliable than the double bottom (97 percent), but still impressive. The average drop after a confirmed double top is 20 percent and lasts three months.

Again, as with double bottoms, the price pulls back after the confirmation 69 percent of the time, leaving you to doubt the pattern. Fortunately, the pullback period averages only ten days before the downtrend resumes.

The triple top: Head-and-shoulders

The head-and-shoulders pattern is a triple top that's easy to see; one bump forms the left shoulder, a higher bump forms a head, and a third bump forms the right shoulder. Figure 4-8 shows two examples. A triple top or bottom is somewhat rarer than the double version, but the meaning is the same — the price fails to surpass the previous low or high, signaling a trend reversal.

The head-and-shoulders patterns shown in Figure 4-8 are easy enough to see, but many head-and-shoulders patterns are more complex and contain other patterns within them. The second head-and-shoulders pattern in Figure 4-8, for example, contains a little double top and a gap (see Chapter 2). You may also see what appears to be two heads or two shoulders, although one is always higher, which makes it the head.

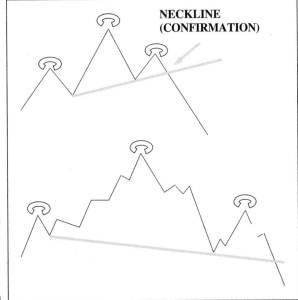

Figure 4-8:
Head-and-shoulders patterns.

Book VIII

Technical Analysis

In a head-and-shoulders pattern, the confirmation line connects the low point of each shoulder and is named the *neckline.* The price breaking the neckline predicts a price decline, whether the neckline is sloping upward or downward. Seldom do you see the neckline perfectly horizontal. A downward-sloping neckline tends to deliver the biggest price move.

A head-and-shoulders pattern usually forms after a long uptrend. The dip from the first shoulder represents the normal retracement after a new high. The head then represents the triumph of bullish sentiment and sets a new higher high. The dip after the higher-high head represents more profit-taking, whereupon the bulls buy again. When the bulls are making their third try at a rally, their price target is the last highest high, which is the top of the head. The failure of the second shoulder to surpass the head is the end of the rally. Buying demand diminishes and selling pressure takes hold, forcing prices down, completing the pattern.

As with double tops and bottoms, some traders refuse to accept the pattern, and they cause a pullback to the confirmation line 45 percent of the time. Pullbacks average only 11 days before the stock resumes its decline. This is your last chance to jump off before the price hits the wall.

As with every trend that's losing steam, volume falls after the head, although about half the time the highest volume is at the left shoulder and about half the time at the head. Volume is low at the second shoulder. Volume on the breakout day and the next few days after the breakout day, however, tends to be very large, because by that point a great number of chart-oriented traders have identified the pattern and its neckline.

Drawing Trendlines

A *trendline* is a straight line that starts at the beginning of the trend and stops at the end of the trend. Often you can see a trend with the naked eye, but to impose order on your visual impression, you can connect the dots by actually drawing a line along the price bars. You can do this the low-tech way by using a piece of paper and a pencil, or go high-tech with software like Excel or special charting software. Figuring out where trends start and stop can be complicated, but this section explains how to spot them, plot them, and figure out what they're telling you.

When you look at a chart of a securities price, sometimes the trendline pops out at you. Other times, a line isn't obvious, in which case you study the chart for a few minutes and may even draw a few experimental lines.

Take a look at Figure 4-9, which shows experimental trendlines. Which one is correct? None of them — and all of them. The first two lines on the left connect a series of lows, but then the price breaks the line to the downside, so they're abandoned. The heavy line through the center is another kind of a trendline, the linear regression, discussed later in the chapter. This line does a pretty good job of cutting off the high–low extremes and representing the essence of the total move. Finally, the longest trendline connects the three major lows.

How do you know if this is the right trendline or if another new low will come along? You don't know. You know only afterwards that new highs are going to reappear and keep the trendline alive.

Here are a few things to remember about drawing trendlines:

✔ The time frame of the chart you're looking at influences what you see. A trader with a long-term time frame sees one trend on this chart, whereas a swing trader with a shorter time frame sees three trends (two upmoves punctuated by a downmove).

✔ In order to see the single long-term trendline, you have to accept that charting is a dynamic process. Your work is never done. Every day (or hour, or week) provides new data. You need to be willing to discard a trendline when it stops representing the trend — or to restore an old trendline with some minor modifications if your original drawing turns out to be right. In this case, the move is a big-picture uptrend, but you don't know it for sure until late in the move.

Figure 4-9:
Experi-
mental
trendlines.

NEW LOW

Book VIII

Technical
Analysis

✔ In the transition from a downtrend to an uptrend, you can't draw a single line that captures the trend, because no single trend exists that captures both moves. In other instances, all you can see is a meandering line that's practically horizontal. This may be a pause while the same trend resumes, or it may mark the transition period from up to down or down to up.

✔ No security is in a trending mode all the time. So be realistic about whether a trendline is drawable. Often, you can't draw a trendline on the chart you have in front of you, but if you generate another chart with a longer time frame (for instance a weekly chart), drawing a trendline becomes possible.

Forming impressionistic trendlines

Freehand, or impressionistic, trendlines are useful in confirming or denying that a security is on a trend — and in identifying which direction the trend is going. You can visually identify trends in many different and equally valid ways. In general, though, you're aiming to start and stop your trendlines at obvious highs and lows:

✔ **Uptrend:** Spot an obvious low and carry your eye along higher highs (*tops*) and higher lows to an obvious high. Take a look at Figure 4-10. The first line, starting from the left, starts at a low and ends at a high.

✔ **Downtrend:** The next trendline in Figure 4-10 is a downtrend. It starts at the high and goes to the low. In the case of a downtrend, your eye starts at an obvious high and follows successively lower highs and lower lows (*bottoms*) to an obvious low. (Of course, you know it's the lowest low only after the fact.)

The third line is an uptrend, and it stops at a high. That high is duplicated a little later by another high at nearly the same level — see the area in the circle. So wait a minute — shouldn't that second uptrend go to the second high and not the first?

The trendline should end at the highest high, and if you see a higher one, you shouldn't end the trendline yet. In Figure 4-10, the second high is near the first high, but not actually higher. That's why the trendline stops at the first high. In fact, the second high forms a pattern named a double top (see the earlier section "Double tops").

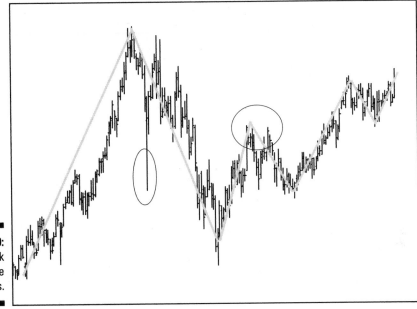

Figure 4-10:
Take a look
at the
trends.

For purposes of drawing trendlines, use the highs and lows — but don't totally ignore the close. It's possible to get a wild random move that creates a spike high or a spike low that isn't consistent with the overall trend. In fact, Figure 4-10 has a doozy of a spike (see the price bar in the ellipse). What should you think about this spike? Well, its sheer size confirms negative sentiment toward the security, even if the sharp upmove afterwards gives you cause for doubt. But the high after the downward spike doesn't match or surpass the highest high, confirming that the bulls are losing this battle and the bears are about to triumph.

Creating rule-based trendlines

A rule-based trendline is one that starts and stops according to well-defined conditions, such as a line starting at the lowest low of the last three days and ending at the highest high of the last three days. A rule-based trendline is better than an impressionistic trendline for three reasons:

- ✔ It doesn't let you impose your personal view of what the trend should be.
- ✔ It improves your ability (and self-confidence) to buy a security when its price is rising or sell it when the price is falling.
- ✔ It helps prevent loss by showing you the exit at the right time.

Book VIII

Technical Analysis

To draw a rule-based trendline for an uptrend, follow these steps:

1. **Start at the lowest low and connect the line to the next low that precedes a new high.**

2. **As long as new highs are being made, redraw the line to connect to the lowest low before the last high.**

3. **When prices stop making new highs, stop drawing. Extend the line out into the future at the same slope.**

To draw a rule-based trendline for a downtrend, follow these steps:

1. **Start at the highest high and connect the line to the next high that precedes a new low.**

2. **As long as new lows are being made, redraw the line to connect to the highest high before the last low.**

3. **When prices stop making new lows, stop drawing. Extend the line out into the future at the same slope.**

Notice that this is a dynamic process. You often have to erase one line and draw another one as conditions change.

Drawing support lines

In Figure 4-11, the trendline illustrates the rule-based trendline named a *support line*. It's named *support* because you expect the line to support the price — traders won't let the price fall below it. To draw a support line, you start at the lowest low and draw a line to the next low. This generates a line that can be extended at the same slope, but it becomes a trendline only when another daily price low touches the line.

Knowing when to enter

The support line entry rule says "Buy on the third touch of the support line by the low of a price bar." The third touch is confirmation that the line is more than just a line and is a true trendline. When you use the support trendline as a trading guide, you initiate a new position on the confirmation, or third touch.

You use the support line to identify an uptrend. The price is rising, and rising consistently. This provides comfort that the purchase of this security is returning a profit and may continue to return a profit. Notice that on many days, the low price touched the line but didn't cross it.

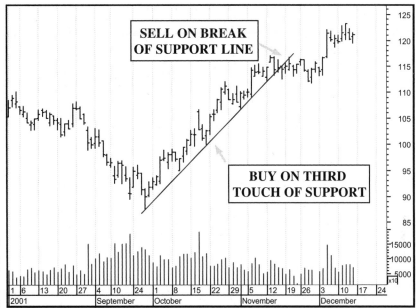

Figure 4-11:
Drawing a
support line.

The more times that a low-of-the-day touches the support line without crossing it, the more confidence you should have that it is a valid description of the trend. This is called a *test of support* and encourages buyers of the security to buy more after the price passes the test. Fresh buying constitutes demand for the security and is called *accumulation.* Those who already own the security are reluctant to sell it after support has passed the test, and now require a higher price to put their inventory of the security on offer.

Sometimes traders engineer a test of support by selling the security down to the support line to see if support will hold. If you put on a new long position above the support line, you're sweating bullets when traders test support. Will holders of the security rush in to buy more of the security to defend their position? When the support line does hold, the traders who were selling become big buyers. They've just been given proof that the bulls put their money where their mouths are.

Some technical traders say that to require a third touch is to be overly cautious and to miss out on some perfectly good trends that fail to meet the third-touch qualification. This is true — many valid trends do have only two touches before they end. If you're waiting for the third touch, you may miss the entire move. But experience shows that your trust is better placed in a trendline with three or more touches. You're taking more risk if you accept two touches.

Book VIII

**Technical
Analysis**

Knowing when to exit: The breakout

The support line exit rule says "Sell when the low of the price bar falls below the support line."

When any part of the price bar penetrates the line on the downside, support has been broken, and you may think that the trend is over. This may or may not be true. In Figure 4-11, the move continues after the line was broken — but experience teaches that the trendline is no longer reliable. A break of support is literally just that — some holders of the stock were willing to break ranks with the other holders and to sell at progressively lower prices.

A *breakout* is any part of the price bar penetrating a line that you drew on the chart. The word *breakout* is used in a dozen contexts in technical analysis, but it always refers to a significant violation of the trend. Sometimes the offending breakout is quickly roped back into the herd, but usually a breakout means that the trend is changing direction, either right away or sometime soon.

A one-day break of the line is called a *false breakout*. To estimate whether a breakout may be false, master trader Larry Williams recommends you consider the position of the close on the day before the breakout. In an uptrend, if the close is at or near the high, chances are good that it's a false breakout. The breakout was due to profit-taking that got carried away, it was triggered by a false rumor, or it was a random move. If the close on the day before is at or near the low, though, chances are the breakout is real.

Even though you should discard the support line as a trading tool after it's been broken, you may want to leave it on the chart for a while. Sometimes old support becomes new resistance (and vice versa; see the next section).

Drawing resistance lines

Resistance is the mirror image of support: A line drawn along a series of highs marks where buyers resist buying more — the price is too high for them. Traders expect sellers to emerge at the resistance line (taking profit). As a securities buyer, you're mainly concerned with the support line, but you should care about identifying a downtrend using the resistance line for two reasons:

- ✔ When a downtrend ends, the next move may be an uptrend. Because you want to get in on the action as early as possible, you care when a downtrend is broken to the upside. The breakout is an important clue that an uptrend may be starting and you should start paying attention.

- ✔ Someday, you may sell short.

Figure 4-12 shows multiple resistance lines, each starting at the January high and ending at places where the price breaks the trendline.

Figure 4-12:
Drawing
resistance
lines.

Looking at the first (shortest) line, start at the January high and connect the line to the first high on January 17. The third touch comes on February 6. The price tests resistance for the next two days and breaks above the line on February 11. The trend may be over. You should buy it back, or cover the short position, the first time the price closes above the line.

The more times the high-of-the-day touches the resistance line and doesn't cross it, the more confidence you have that it is a valid description of the trend. This is called a *test of resistance* and encourages sellers of the security to sell more after the price passes the test. Fresh selling constitutes supply of the security and is called *distribution.* Those who own the security are reluctant to hold it after resistance was proved to resist an effort to break above it. They're willing to sell their inventory at increasingly lower prices.

In this instance, the exit rule caused a loss. After the buy-back exit specified on the chart, the price moved up a bit and then resumed its downtrend. You could start a new resistance line, but — following the rules — you can also go back to the highest high on the chart. You draw another line, but it connects only two highs and is violated to the upside on the very day of the third touch. Finally, on the third try, you connect the starting point to another high and it is confirmed by a third touch in March — several touches, in fact. You initiate the short trade position and hold it all the way to August, when the price breaks out above the resistance line.

Book VIII

**Technical
Analysis**

In trend-following trading, you never enter at the absolute high and never exit at the absolute low. The goal is to capture most of the trend. You hardly ever capture all of the trend.

Fine-tuning support and resistance

You need patience and persistence to work with trendlines because you need to adjust the lines often, sometimes daily.

- **Trend reversal:** The uptrend that you identified by drawing the support line (Figure 4-11) turned into a downtrend a few weeks later. This is often — but not always — the case. As the resistance case demonstrates (Figure 4-12), a trendline breakout doesn't necessarily lead to formation of a trend in the opposite direction. In the resistance case, it led to resumption of the same trend (downward). The move upward that occurred after the first breakout above the resistance line is called a *retracement, correction,* or *pullback.* At the time it's occurring, you don't know whether it's a full trend reversal or just a retracement. Drawing trendlines is especially frustrating and difficult during retracement periods, and you'll take a lot of losses if you use trendlines alone to make trading decisions.

- **Sideways movements:** In both the support and resistance trendline cases, the price entered a period of sideways price movements just before the breakout of the line that triggered the exit rule (the "Sell" point in Figure 4-11). Such sideways periods, named *congestion,* are common during trends as well as when a trend is ending. Another term for a sideways price movement is *consolidation,* which refers to market participants consolidating their ideas about the security being traded. Consolidation often — but not always — precedes a breakout of the trendline.

Drawing internal trendlines: Linear regression

Wouldn't it be nice to know the "true" trendline — a line that would reveal the hidden trendedness of the prices without at the same time alerting everybody and his brother to attack or defend specific levels? Such a line *does* exist. It's a line that goes through the center of the price series rather than along its edges, like support and resistance.

How do you draw a straight line through the center of each price bar? Technically, you can't, as least not on any chart where the prices jump around at all. But scientists have a solution to jumpiness: to "fit" a line that minimizes the distance from itself to each price along the line. The best-fit line is named the *linear regression line, linear* referring to *line* and *regression* referring to the mathematical calculation.

You can't draw an accurate linear regression without first performing a complex statistical calculation. Fortunately, you don't need to know how the line is calculated to be able to use it. Spreadsheet software and all charting packages come with the linear regression already built-in.

In Figure 4-13, the linear regression line doesn't actually go through the center of each price bar. But if you look closely, you'll see that no other line gets you as close to Point A *and* to Point B at the same time. Only one linear regression exists for any set of prices on the chart.

A linear regression is the true, pure trendline. If you accept the core concept of technical analysis, that a trend will continue in the same direction, at least for a while, now you can extend the true trendline and obtain a *forecast.* In some software packages, a linear regression extension is called exactly that — "a time-series forecast." This is tremendously useful. You have created a high-probability forecast for the upcoming period that gives you perspective on what to expect.

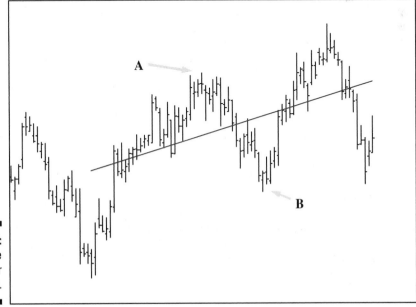

Figure 4-13:
Simple
linear
regression.

A

B

Book VIII

Technical Analysis

If you're going to draw only one line, the linear regression is a good choice. If you select a good starting point, the linear regression delivers pure trend. Unlike support and resistance lines, the linear regression line doesn't have any trading rules associated directly with it, but visually, it's the most informative line. As you create linear regression lines, keep these things in mind:

✔ Figuring out where to start and where to end a linear regression line is the first big obstacle in using the line in a practical way. The simple answer is to start it at an obvious high or low. This means you need to look backward at the historical data on the chart to see where the current move began. This can be trickier than it sounds. You can get very different slopes, depending on how tightly you want the data to fit to the line. Seeing a welter of slopes covering up your chart can get very frustrating. But stick to it. The linear regression could save your bacon someday.

✔ The linear regression line can slope this way or that way or no way (horizontal), depending on where you start drawing. If you take a V-shaped price series like the one in Figure 4-14 and draw a single linear regression line, you get . . . garbage. Obviously two trends on a chart require two linear regressions. In other words, you can draw linear regression lines that are totally useless. They'll still be scientifically accurate in that they depict the best fit possible of the line to the data, and everyone else will get the same result, but they won't advance the cause of making a profit in the market or preventing a loss.

✔ You can do some really dumb things using the linear regression line, too. If you extend a line out into the indefinite future, you get a fantasy, not a forecast. The market is a collection of human beings, not a science project. Prices simply don't move in a straight line indefinitely.

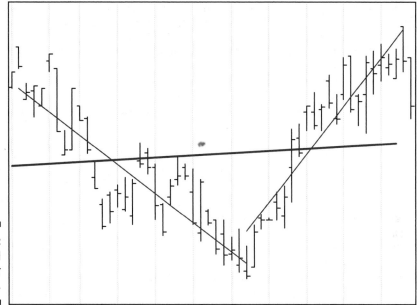

Figure 4-14:
Invalid
linear
regression.

Chapter 5

Transforming Channels into Forecasts

*D*rawing a straight-line trendline and extending it out into the future suggests what the price may be in days to come. Actually, a trendline suggests only the general neighborhood of future prices. If the trendline is a support line, you expect the price not to fall below it, but that doesn't tell you anything about how high it may go. With a linear regression line, you expect future prices to cluster around the line, but some outliers are always possible. In short, common sense tells you that you can't forecast future prices to the penny.

While nobody can create a pinpoint forecast, we can forecast the range of probable future prices. *Range* refers to the same high–low range of the price bar described in Chapter 2, only encompassing a larger number of price bars in a series — weeks and months rather than only a few days.

In this chapter, I describe the straight-line channel and its forecasting capabilities. I show you two ways to build a straight-line channel forecast and outline how to interpret the information you see on the chart. I also talk about using pivot-point analysis to draw horizontal support and resistance, for use either in non-directional situations or with trend channels.

Channel-Drawing Basics

A *channel* is a pair of straight-line trendlines encasing a price series. It consists of one line drawn along the top of a price series and another line, parallel to the first, along the bottom of the price series.

The purpose of the channel is to train your eye to accept prices within its borders as *on the trend* and to detect prices outside its borders as *off the trend* (and perhaps ending the trend). In other words, the channel is a wider measure of trending behavior than a single line. As long as prices remain within the channel, you deduce that the trend is still in place.

Depending on the raw material of your price bars, you can

- ✔ Start with a top line connecting at least two highs, and draw the bottom line parallel to it.
- ✔ Start with the bottom line connecting at least two lows, and draw the top line parallel to that.
- ✔ Draw a linear regression line (see Chapter 4) and draw the top and bottom of the channel at equal distances on either side of it.

How do you know when a high or low is obvious and the right place to start a trendline? An obvious high or low is named a *swing point,* because it's the last highest high or lowest low in a series of higher highs or lower lows. The trend may seem to continue for a few more bars after the highest high or lowest low. You don't always get a sharp, clear-cut reversal exactly at the swing bar. But a few days after a swing bar, the reversal or swing point becomes visually obvious. Can you mistakenly identify a swing point? You bet. When drawing trendlines, you have to resign yourself to erasing a lot.

You can draw channels to enclose every part of every price bar in the series, or you can draw the channels to allow some minor breaking of the lines. (In the section "Neatness counts" later in the chapter, I describe the pros and cons of allowing minor breakage.) Whatever your starting point (top, bottom, or linear regression) and whether you encase some or all of the price series, consider the top line of the channel to be resistance and the bottom line of the channel to be support.

Constructing a channel by drawing parallel support and resistance lines organizes your vision. You expect future price highs not to exceed the top of the channel (resistance) and upcoming price lows not to exceed the bottom of the channel (support). The parallel lines tell you the maximum probable future price range. Note that word *probable.* Channels are visually compelling and can seduce you into thinking that the forecast range *must* occur. It's all too easy to start drawing channels and forget that they're only a forecast. A zillion factors can come out of the blue and knock your trend off the rails.

Channels, whether hand-drawn or software-drawn, aren't always as neat and tidy as the examples I use in the following sections. Some securities never offer the opportunity to draw a tidy channel, and some securities offer a tidy channel only some of the time. But the longer a tidy channel lasts, the more confident you can feel that you have correctly identified a trend.

Drawing channels by hand

Figure 5-1 is a model perfect channel, but you'll be astonished at how often you can draw a channel like this on a real security. Here's how you do it:

1. Start by connecting the two lows at the lower left. This is the support line. Notice that they're the two relative lows because a bar with a higher low comes in-between.

2. With your ruler, you extend that line into the future.

3. To form the top of the channel, you have to wait for the next relative high. A relative high can be seen only after you get an intervening lower high (got that?). On the chart, the highest high is the last of three higher highs. You go back to the highest high and start a line parallel to the support line from it. This is the resistance line.

4. Extend the resistance line into the future.

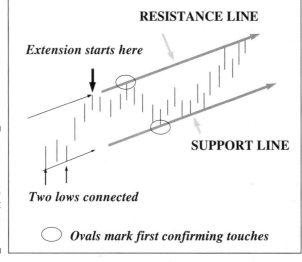

Figure 5-1:
A model channel. Ovals mark first confirming touches.

Book VIII

Technical Analysis

Note that sometimes you later get a higher high and have to shift the entire resistance line up, keeping it parallel. Oddly, a high proportion of new highs stop at the old resistance line, even though some stop at the new resistance line, too. It's like having two equally valid resistance lines. To be on the safe side, consider the farther-away channel line as the more important one. The same thing is true of a second, farther-away support line.

On the chart in Figure 5-1, the extension lines are gray. At the time they're first drawn, the extended lines are hypothetical (not proven) support and hypothetical resistance.

The lines stop being hypothetical and become actual support and resistance when the next high or low touches the extended line but doesn't break it, validating the extension process. The circles in Figure 5-1 mark where the next high and low occur in this price series — and they occur at the hypothetical support and resistance lines. You know that you've drawn your channel line correctly when a third relative high or low makes a touch of the line but doesn't cross it, making that touch a confirmation point.

Why are the lines parallel?

When you draw a support line connecting a series of lows, you often see a parallel resistance line that mysteriously connects the highest highs. This is so common that most charting software programs have a standard command — "create parallel line." No one knows why support and resistance lines are so often parallel. Here are a few explanations:

✔ This kind of orderliness appears when the high–low trading range is stable. Volume is steady, too. It's an orderly crowd trading the security, so the channel is orderly. Market participants know where the price is relatively high — at the top of the channel. They expect no more gains at this point and are prepared to sell at the top to put their money to better use in some other security. Die-hard buyers, in turn, see when the price is relatively cheap — down around the support line. They add to their position, propelling the price upward.

✔ Many technical analysts perceive a cyclical quality to the ebb and flow of prices within a channel. They rely on the security alternating between support and resistance, and the perceived cycle is the basis of their trading plan. This often works, at least for short periods, as long as you don't project the price bouncing off the support or resistance line several cycles into the future. In other words, don't get cocky. You never know when fresh news is going to come along and cause prices to break the channel.

✔ Humans have an innate need to impose order on a chaotic universe — or market. Parallel lines don't always appear, of course, but they appear often enough that observers speak of trading ranges with a certain air of authority. When you hear of a *trading range*, this kind of parallel support and resistance channel is usually what the commentator has in mind.

Letting software do the drawing

Another way to capture the collective habit of market participants is to draw the linear regression line, as described in Chapter 4, and then to build a channel on either side of it. Instead of drawing the support and resistance lines by hand and extending them out, you let the software do the drawing. See the later section "Riding the Regression Range" for information on how the channel is calculated mathematically.

Whichever way you draw the channel, you apply the same expectations about the collective behavior of the market participants, and you assume that future relative highs and relative lows are going to fall within the same range. The principle of extending support and resistance lines is the same whether you draw them by hand or use the linear regression as an anchor.

Noting the benefits of straight-line channels

When you use straight lines to represent a range, you get a chart that's easy to read. Your eye fills in the blanks. Benefits are:

- ✔ Straight-line channels imply absolute limits that give you comfort and the sense that you know where you stand.

- ✔ When a new price touches the channel top or bottom but then retreats, you believe that the channel limits are correctly drawn and valid — and will likely work next time, too. The more often a price touches a support or resistance line but doesn't cross it, the more reliable you can consider the line to be.

- ✔ If a channel line is broken, you feel certain that something significant has happened to the perception of the security by its market participants. Violation of the channel alerts you to changing conditions and the need to consider making a trading decision.

Book VIII

Technical Analysis

Recognizing drawbacks of straight-line channels

If your price series is orderly and doesn't vary much day-to-day from the average, the straight-line channel is fairly narrow. But if your chart contains a disorderly price move, one on which each price seems unrelated to the one before and prices jump around all over the place, your channel lines have to be so far apart that you can't judge what is usual or normal.

To some extent, a channel is valid because many others can see the same thing. One of the reasons that a technical analysis method works is because it creates a self-fulfilling prophecy. When everyone can see the same lines, a consensus builds as to what constitutes breaking the lines. When you draw a channel so wide or so narrow that only you can see it, you can't expect other traders to respond to it. To forecast a price range is really to forecast the probable collective behavior of the people who trade the security.

Using Channels to Make Profit and Avoid Loss

When you have confidence that the channel broadly describes the trend:

✔ You can buy near the channel bottom and sell near the channel top — over and over again, as long as the channel lasts.

✔ You can estimate your future gain. If the width of the channel is $5 and you bought near a support line, your maximum probable gain over the next few days is about $5 — as long as the channel remains in place and you're able to sell near the resistance line. This is more useful than you may think at first.

  • **It's a sanity check:** You can't reasonably expect a gain that would call for a price far outside the channel.

  • **It's a reality check:** You can use the channel to evaluate a forecast made by someone else. If the forecaster is calling for a price far outside the channel, you have grounds to question the forecast.

✔ You can calculate your maximum loss. Regardless of where you bought the security, you know that when a price bar breaks the bottom support line of the channel, the channel is no longer valid. The trend is likely over. This is the point at which you want to sell. And you don't have to wait for the actual breakout. You can place a stop-loss order with your broker at the breakout level.

Dealing with Breakouts

The *breakout* is one of the most important concepts in technical analysis. It's a direct, graphic representation that something happened to change the market's sentiment toward the security. In the simplest terms, a breakout implies that a trend is over, at least in its present form. After a breakout, the price can go up, down, or sideways, but it seldom resumes at exactly the same level and rate of change you had before the breakout.

A breakout must always be respected, but you want to be sure it's authentic. Because so many traders draw support and resistance lines, there's always some wise guy in the market who tries to push the price through the lines. In an uptrend that's retracing downward, he tries to break the support line and panic holders into selling. He may believe in the uptrend; he's just trying to get a lower price for himself. In a downtrend, he's the joker who buys so much that the price puts in a new high and a close higher than on previous days, which scares the pants off sellers, who then cover their shorts and propel the price higher. In addition, a breakout can be just a random aberration.

Distinguishing between false breakouts and the real thing

You often see a tiny breakout and don't know how to evaluate it. Say your support line is at precisely $10 and the low of the price bar is $9.75. Is that a legitimate breakout or just an accident? Sometimes you have to accept imperfection and live with ambiguity. The channel lines are an estimate, not a certainty.

Or sometimes you get a minor break of a channel line that lasts one or two days, but then the price returns back inside its channel and performs just as before. The breakout was a *false breakout,* which is a breach of a trendline that then fails to deliver the expected additional moves in the same direction (see Figure 5-2). To call it false is misleading, because the price bar unmistakably breaks the trendline. What's false is the conclusion you draw from it — that the trend is over.

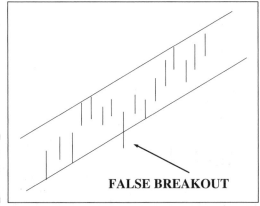

Figure 5-2:
False
breakout.

FALSE BREAKOUT

Book VIII

**Technical
Analysis**

False breakouts are especially damaging because you may automatically assume that the breakout means a reversal. This isn't necessarily so, but it's tempting to jump on a breakout because the first few periods (usually days) after a breakout are often the best time to get in on the action. As much as one-quarter to one-third of a post-breakout move occurs in the first few days. It takes courage to jump on a security that just had a breakout, especially if you can't discover why it broke out. If you look for fresh news to justify the price pop but can't find any, you need to be suspicious. It may be false.

In Figure 5-2, the channel does define the high–low trading range, after all. Sometimes you have to accept one or two violations of your lines. The challenge, of course, is that you don't know right away whether a breakout is meaningful or just a random outcome. I provide some answers to this question in the following section.

The first line of defense

Your first line of defense is the configuration of the breakout bar. A simple judgment is to see whether the breakout is a violation of the channel line by the *close,* and not just the high or low. The close is the bar component that best summarizes sentiment. A high or a low can be a random aberration. The close is less likely to be random.

A special version of the close rule is to evaluate whether the bar that breaks the line is a *key reversal bar,* which is a form of outside day. When you're in an uptrend, the key reversal bar has a promising open — above yesterday's close. The price even makes a new high over yesterday's high, but then the price crashes and delivers a close at or near the low and below yesterday's low. The market psychology isn't hard to read — the day started out well but then something happened to make negative sentiment rule the day, right into the close.

In a downtrend, the key reversal bar initially confirms the trend — the open is below yesterday's close and the price even makes a lower low. But then the price reverses direction and rallies strongly into the close, so that the close is above yesterday's high. Good news must have come out.

Opinion differs on whether the key reversal bar is definitive. Some traders swear by it while others say that you wouldn't want to make trading decisions on the key reversal bar alone — you should have additional confirming factors or at least be able to verify the "news" that caused the abrupt change of sentiment during the day.

Does volume verify?

Breakouts are often accompanied by a change in volume, usually an easily-noticed higher level. This is in keeping with interpreting events on the chart in terms of supply and demand. You can verify that the breakout isn't random by seeing an equivalent change in volume:

- ✔ **Increase in volume:** Extraordinarily high volume on one or two days is named a *volume spike* and often accompanies the end of a strong trend, either a rally or a crash. Buying and selling interest is frenzied.

- ✔ **Decrease in volume:** If volume declines steeply after holding steady at about the same level over the life of your trend, demand is falling off but so is selling interest. You don't necessarily know what falling volume means, but it may foreshadow a breakout. All the people who wanted to sell have done so, and the people still holding an inventory aren't willing to sell at the current price. It's like a logjam. It will be broken up when either the bull camp or the bear camp takes the initiative and causes a new high or new low, with accompanying higher volume.

Size matters — and so does duration

You can use a filter to estimate whether a breakout is meaningful or can be ignored. A *filter* is a formula or a procedure used to modify an indicator. In this instance, the indicator is the break of the channel line. A filter can modify the amount or duration of the breakout.

- ✔ To modify the size of the indicator, you add some percentage of the total range to the channel line. You stipulate that to constitute a real break of the channel line, the new high or low must surpass this extra amount.

  If the channel is $5 wide, you can specify that a price has to violate the line by more than 5 percent (or 25 cents). Anything less wouldn't be a real breakout. Where does 5 percent come from? Why not 10 percent or 20 percent? Any one of them may be effective, or none of them. You need to experiment with each security to see whether it has a habit of breaking its lines by this amount or that amount. You can also specify that the *close* has to break the line by *x* percent to qualify as a real breakout. In either case, the result is a new channel line that is a little farther out, effectively widening the channel.

- ✔ To modify the duration, you can specify that you're willing to accept one price bar violating the channel line, but not two. Or perhaps two days of violation, but not three. Again, you have to experiment with each security to see what its habits are. Also, you can combine the duration rule with the close rule and specify that the close beyond the line for *x* number of days is the sign of a true breakout.

Experienced technical analysts warn against making size and duration filters too complex and fancy, for a number of reasons:

- **Rules count:** The breakout principle is a powerful and well-known concept. A lot of other traders in your security are likely to heed a breakout in a black-and-white way. They *always* exit on a downside breakout of a support line, for example. They feel that a breakout is a breakout, and traders shouldn't try to second-guess it.

- **One size doesn't fit all:** You can only know that 10 percent is the right amount to put into your filter if 10 percent was the amount that worked in the past on this security. Each security has its own habits; or rather, the people who trade it have their collective habits. In one security, the best filter may consistently be 10 percent and in another, it may consistently be 40 percent. (In the 1930s and 1940s, a filter of 3 percent was standard.) No single correct filter exists for every security under all circumstances. You only know whether a filter is usable by testing different filters on the price history of each security, one by one.

- **Blending works only with coffee:** The orderliness of your security can change without warning. During some periods, a 5 percent filter may be the most effective, but later, volatility can increase and you would need a 10 percent filter to capture all the price highs and lows that really do belong inside the same channel. Looking back over historical data to find the best filter has an enormous flaw: Chances are that you'll come up with a blended percentage filter that's too small for an orderly move and too big for a volatile one. And if today is the breakout day, you don't know how volatile the upcoming move is going to be.

Putting breakouts into context

A genuine breakout means that your trend channel is now defunct. You need to discard it. To verify that the breakout truly ended the trend, you need to evaluate it in the context of the general volatility characteristics of the security itself. By examining conditions at the time of the breakout, you may gather clues as to what the price is likely to do next.

Neatness counts

As a general rule, a breakout that occurs in the course of an *orderly* (low volatility) trend is more meaningful than a breakout that occurs in a *disorderly* (high volatility) trend.

Figure 5-3 illustrates this point. In the first chart, the security is orderly — prices line up neatly within the channel. The breakout is obvious. In the second channel, the security isn't so tidy — prices jump around a lot. The breakout bar is exactly the same size as the first breakout bar, but in the disorderly price series, you can't be sure it's authentic. The people who trade this security are accustomed to big bars and big jumps. You can see that it broke the support line, but perhaps others won't find it meaningful.

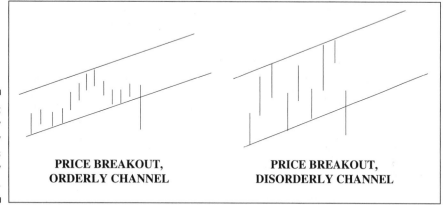

Figure 5-3:
Orderly
security
versus
disorderly
security.

PRICE BREAKOUT,
ORDERLY CHANNEL

PRICE BREAKOUT,
DISORDERLY CHANNEL

Orderliness isn't a word you find in the technical analysis literature. Instead, you find *volatility,* which refers to the extent of variation away from a central reference point (like an average). You should consider that low volatility constitutes orderliness and high volatility implies disorder.

The more orderly your price bars, the more reliable your channels are. A breakout of an orderly channel is more likely to be the real thing than a breakout of a high-volatility (disorderly) channel. If you choose to trade a disorderly security, you must be able to tolerate a high number of false breakouts — and modify your filters accordingly.

If your security generates a lot of false breakouts and you find that intolerable because it makes you nervous, find another security. A number of vendors offer software you can use to scan a collection of securities for those which are low-volatility and therefore less likely to generate a lot of false breakouts.

Book VIII

Technical Analysis

Transitioning from orderly to disorderly (and back)

When a price series morphs from an orderly to a disorderly mode, the transformation is almost always accompanied by a breakout and a change in volume. Strangely, a shift the other way also foreshadows a breakout. When prices shift from disorderly to orderly, the sharp decrease in volatility warns you that a breakout is impending; buyers and sellers alike don't know what to do, so they do nothing. On the day of the breakout and in the day or two following, you see a big increase in volume.

Driving faster is always risky

You also want to know the context of the breakout in terms of where the prices were located within the channel just before the breakout. The usual breakout is in the opposite direction of the prevailing trend.

But sometimes you see prices pressing against the top or bottom of the channel line, and this can lead to a breakout in the same direction as the trend. In other words, higher volatility can mean an acceleration of an existing trend. A breakout can be to the upside in an uptrend as well as to the downside in a downtrend.

Figure 5-4 illustrates an upside breakout in an uptrend. It's still a breakout, and you should expect that it still marks a change in the trend even though it is in the same direction. The acceleration of an existing trend should make you sit up and take notice. While it may simply signal a steepening of the trend as the crowd develops enthusiasm for the security, it can also occur near the end of a trend. It is sometimes called a *blowout* (or *blowoff*) *top* or a *blowout bottom*. In other words, an upside breakout in an uptrend is often a warning of an impending *downside* breakout, counterintuitive as that seems at first.

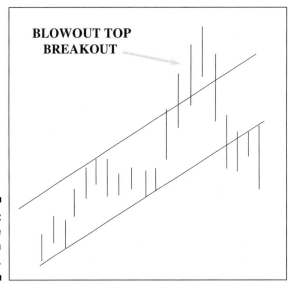

BLOWOUT TOP BREAKOUT

Figure 5-4: An upside breakout in an uptrend.

How can such a pattern come about? Easy. The crowd becomes overheated with greed to buy a security that is rising with tremendous force, or overwhelmed by fear to dump a security that is declining with great momentum. At some point, everyone who was going to buy has bought. Because these are traders who bought only to get a fast profit, when the rise slows down and a lower high or a lower low appears, these buyers exit in a horde. By selling a lot of the security in a very short period of time, the market has an oversupply, and buyers can command a low price.

The same thing happens when a downmove exhausts itself. Everybody who was going to sell has sold. Supply is now limited. Anyone who wants to buy has to start bidding the price up until he induces a longer-term holder of the security to part with it.

Riding the Regression Range

You can construct a more "scientific" set of parallel lines by drawing channel lines around the linear regression line. As described in Chapter 4, the *linear regression* is the line that minimizes the distance from itself and every point of the chart. It is the true, pure trendline, and thus the channel built on it, named the *standard error channel* (also called the *linear regression channel*) should be the true trend channel. You can calculate the standard error by hand, but it's laborious. Software is less error-prone and a lot faster.

You use a channel based on the linear regression line the same way that you use a hand-drawn support and resistance channel. By projecting the lines out into the future, you get a forecast of the future price range, and you deem a significant breakout of a channel line as ending the trend.

With hand-drawn support and resistance channels, the channel is defined by the outer limits (the series of higher highs with higher lows, or lower lows with lower highs). No centerline exists. In the linear regression channel, you build the channel from the inside out, so to speak. You start with a center linear line and draw the outer lines from that.

Introducing the standard error

Computer software places the standard error channel on either side of the linear regression line according to the statistical measure named the *standard error*. Like the standard deviation discussed in Chapter 1, you don't need to know how to calculate this number or even precisely what it means in order to use it effectively.

The *standard error* measures how closely the prices cluster around your linear regression line. Most chartists use two standard errors, which results in a channel top and channel bottom that enclose a high percentage (95 percent) of the highs and lows. An extreme high or low constitutes a bigger error away from the trendline than 95 percent of the other highs and lows.

Book VIII

Technical Analysis

If you don't like to draw a channel that you already know is going to have some prices breaking the lines, you can draw lines parallel to the standard error channel lines but a bit wider, to encompass *all* the highs and lows.

The closer prices are to the linear regression line, the stronger the trend. Here are a couple points to keep in mind:

✔ If you have an orderly trend, the prices don't stray very far from one another or from the linear regression, and therefore the channel is a narrow one on either side of the linear regression. A price that doesn't vary at all from the linear regression is literally "on the trend" and has a zero standard error.

✔ If you draw a channel and see that it's very wide, your price series has a lot of variation away from the linear regression. Prices far from the norm, the linear regression, are called *outliers* and when you have a lot of them, they are collectively called *noise.* The more noise, the less reliable your channel.

Drawing a linear regression channel

How "true" the linear regression and its channel turn out to be depends on where you start drawing. See Chapter 4 for a discussion of starting the linear regression in a reasonable place.

You start a linear regression channel at an obvious low or high, draw a channel line from there to a second relative low or high, and then extend it out. The parallel line comes along for the ride, which often helps you adjust the slope of the line by discovering relative highs or lows that you didn't see at first. As with the hand-drawn support and resistance channel lines, you know that you have drawn your channel line correctly when a third relative high or low makes a touch of the line but doesn't cross it. Sometimes the "obvious" swing high or low occurs within a previous channel that has been broken and discarded: Go back to the swing bar and use it as the starting point for the new channel.

Figure 5-5 shows a nicely uptrending security with two channels. Look at the shorter one first. I started it at the lowest low, and let the software do the drawing to the bar after the next relative low. Then I stopped drawing and extended the lines by hand, using dotted lines to mark them as hypothetical.

It isn't until three months later that prices break out of the channel — to the upside. Uh oh. A breakout always means something. When it's a breakout in the same direction as the trend, you start worrying that it may be a blowout breakout, as I describe earlier in the chapter in the section "Driving faster is always risky." Whatever it turns out to be, you still need to discard the old channel. It has been broken. In this case, I left it on the chart.

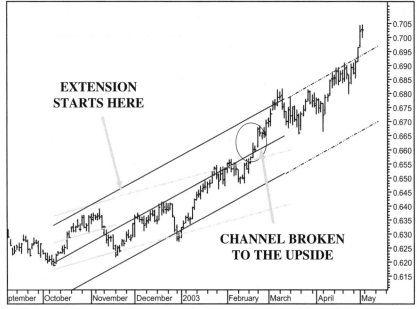

Figure 5-5.
Two standard error channels.

Now I draw a new linear regression and its channel (the darker lines on the chart) from the same lowest low starting point, and keep drawing until just after a new relative high appears. I know it's a relative high because it's breaking the top of the channel and followed by a lower high. I stop drawing at that relative high and extend the channel lines out, as before. Notice that the price does it again! It breaks out of the top of the channel a second time.

As a practical matter, every time a price breaks a channel line, you face a higher risk. The channel defines what is normal and any foray outside the channel is not normal. What does this breakout mean?

- ✔ These latest high prices can mark a third shift to a new, more steeply sloping channel yet to be drawn.
- ✔ It may be a blowout breakout forming.
- ✔ The price series may subside back into the channel.

You have no way to know which of these three outcomes is the most likely from the information on the chart. You may choose to exit on every channel line breakout, or you can add another indicator to guide your decision.

Book VIII

Technical Analysis

Confirming hand-drawn channels

You can validate a hand-drawn support-and-resistance channel by superimposing a standard error channel on top of it. Starting at the same low (or high) point that you used to draw by hand, you draw the standard error channel and see how closely it tracks your hand-drawn lines. Sometimes the standard error channel falls exactly on top of your hand-drawn lines, which is "scientific" validation that you drew them right and they accurately represent the trend. More often, the standard error channel has a slightly different slope.

The chart in Figure 5-6 shows a hand-drawn resistance line between the two highs, as marked. Notice that it is only in hindsight that we see the first high as a swing point. I extended the line after the second relative high and, at that point, drew the support line parallel to it starting at the first low. At the same time, I drew a standard error channel starting at the first high and stopping it at the second high. Every line after the second high is an extension line. And look at how well both the hand-drawn and the linear regression channel forecast the future course of the security!

Trading a security that moves neatly within its channel, especially a validated double channel (hand-drawn *and* standard error), reduces the stress of trading.

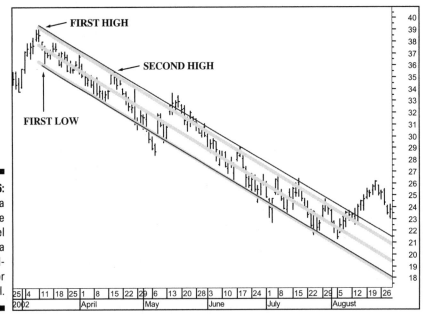

Figure 5-6:
Confirming a
straight-line
channel
with a
standard-
error
channel.

Seeing special features of the linear regression channel

You use the linear regression channel the same way you use a hand-drawn channel — to estimate the future range and to determine when a trend has ended by observing a breakout of one of the channel lines. The linear regression has a few special characteristics, though. For instance

- ✔ The linear regression doesn't encompass every price extreme in a series. It encompasses a very high percentage of them. Therefore, some price bars will always break the channel lines without invalidating the channel, unlike the situation in a hand-drawn channel.

- ✔ To make it more unlikely that you'll mistake a normal breaking of the channel line with a breakout, you can widen the channel lines to encompass the first two or three highest highs and lowest lows, and then extend it out. This modification is named a *Raff regression channel* after Gilbert Raff, the man who devised it.

- ✔ You can adjust the width of the channel lines by instructing your software to use three errors instead of the usual two. A three-error channel encloses 99 percent of the prices. This is handy for a just-emerging channel where you don't have many prices yet.

- ✔ The linear regression is self-adjusting. Every time you update the channel, your software includes the new day's data and modifies both the linear regression line and the slope and width of the channel accordingly. It's therefore a bit of an odd duck — a set of straight lines that isn't fixed, at least until you fix it by halting the updating process.

- ✔ In order to see a breakout to confirm a trend change, you have to stop drawing at some point. Otherwise, the channel simply adjusts to the new data and gets wider and wider. Don't forget; it automatically incorporates all the price data you put into it. Garbage in, garbage out.

A useful technique to differentiate between the actual linear regression channel and your extension of it is to make the extension a dotted line. This is an important issue — it's all too easy to cheat your eye and see regularity or orderliness where it doesn't exist.

Book VIII

Technical Analysis

You can draw new channels on top of your existing forecast channel. You begin at the same starting point but continue the true channel to the current day. If the width and the slope of the fresh true channel are about the same as your forecast channel, you deem the forecast channel to be stable. A *stable* channel implies that the forecast embedded in the farther-out lines is probably pretty good. If you notice that the new true channel that incorporates the latest prices is starting to widen or to change slope, examine the price bars themselves to see if they indicate a trend change.

Accepting drawbacks of linear regression channels

Linear regression channels are more difficult to work with than hand-drawn support and resistance — you have to exercise more judgment, and it is more of an art. Some of the complications are listed below:

- ✔ **Not a majority process:** A large number of people draw support and resistance lines and channels, but not everyone draws linear regression channels. A big part of why technical analysis works is that many people are observing the same thing and acting on it, like breakouts. The same can't be said of linear regression channels.

- ✔ **May not stand alone:** You can draw a very large number of channels on the same chart, and each of them is "right." Often you draw one channel from an obvious starting point but after fixing it and extending it out into the future, you find that you can draw another channel from a nearby starting point that points to a different outcome. I call this *dueling channels,* and it always occurs at trend turning points.

- ✔ **Not really "scientific":** The linear regression channel is scientific in the sense that the software calculates it to enclose a preponderance of prices, but that doesn't mean that you started it or stopped it at the ideal spot, or that the channel extension is correct. The mathematical principle isn't subjective, but your application is always subjective. Consider that your car works on scientific principles of internal combustion and the like, but that doesn't necessarily make you a good driver.

Pivot Point Support and Resistance Channel

What do you do when you stop getting higher highs (in an uptrend) or lower lows (in a downtrend)? In other words, the price is still within its channel but moving sideways.

The pause in movement may be temporary, but the sideways action can also be a warning that forward momentum is gone. From this you may deduce that if you're going to take profit, now is the time. The sideways action may also imply that a breakout in the opposite direction is impending.

One technique for dealing with sideways moves within a channel is to draw horizontal support and resistance lines off pivot points. The term *pivot point* is used in many different ways. One standard definition is that the pivot point is the center bar of three where the center bar is the highest high or lowest low. Another definition of pivot is the median price (the numerical average of the high, low, and close). Other traders cook up yet more definitions. Today, the median price version is probably the most accepted.

Calculating the first zone of support and resistance

The logic of the pivot point is that after a trend pauses, you need a breakout that's a significant distance from the median price to decide whether the old trend will resume or a reversal is really at hand. So you start with the median price and to that you add a factor to get upside resistance and you subtract a factor to get downside support.

On the chart in Figure 5-7, the lightest horizontal line extends off the pivot point calculated on the day of the highest high in the series. You're worried about this bar because it had a close lower than the open, despite the higher high. It's a weak higher high. The next day is an inside day, which may imply a reversal. You're starting to get suspicious that the uptrend is stalling.

To calculate the first (inner) line of resistance, multiply the pivot point value by two and, from that number, subtract the low of the pivot day. To calculate the first (inner) line of support, multiply the pivot value by two and, from that number, subtract the high of the pivot day. This sounds like a lot of arithmetic but it's easy enough to do in a spreadsheet or by hand. It's also a sensible procedure — you're using a multiple of the median price to estimate a range going forward that subtracts the high and the low to yield a "norm." Any price higher or lower would be an "extreme." If the upcoming price breaks the horizontal support and resistance lines calculated this way, the direction of the breakout is your clue that the trend is truly over.

Book VIII

Technical Analysis

And that's exactly what happens in Figure 5-7. The day after the inside day, the price makes a new low below the first support line. It closes within the zone and also closes a hair under the linear regression channel, but the low is well below both the directional channel and the horizontal channel. This is a double breakout — it's a break of your linear regression channel and of the first pivot channel as well. Note that analysts who work with pivot-based support and resistance don't call it a *channel*, a word I am using for consistency and convenience. If it looks like a duck . . .

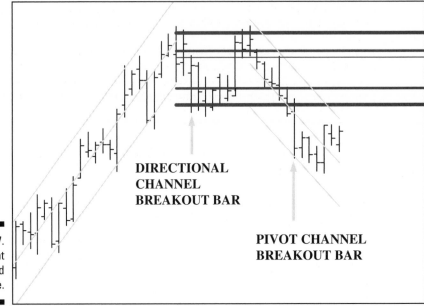

Figure 5-7.
Pivot point
support and
resistance.

Calculating the second zone of support and resistance

The first inner zone is fairly narrow. In fact, it contains only about half of the breakout bar. To get a wider horizontal support and resistance channel, you can add the first zone to the pivot level to get a second resistance level and subtract the first zone from the pivot level to get a second support level.

When you see R1, R2, R3 and S1, S2, S3 noted on a chart or in a table, these abbreviations refer to the first resistance level, second resistance level, and so on, calculated from a pivot point. The pivot point may or may not be the median price. As I mention at the beginning of this section, many technical analysts take the liberty of choosing their own pivot point definition.

Using pivot support and resistance

You can use pivot support and resistance all by itself, and many day-traders do. In the case presented in Figure 5-7, upon seeing the inside day, you would set your stop-loss order at the first pivot support level. Anticipating a bounce, you can also place a buy order at the second support level with an accompanying sell order at either of the two resistance levels.

If you're using the standard error channel for directional guidance, the breakout of the channel means you are at a loose end. You can't construct a new channel based on the linear regression because you simply don't have enough data. The pivot-based support and resistance channel suffices to define the likely trading range until it is, in turn, broken.

You leave the pivot-based horizontal support and resistance zones in place until you get a new swing bar that is substantially higher or lower than your pivot support and resistance zones. Notice that on the chart in Figure 5-7, you do get a matching high to the pivot bar. In fact, it's a few pennies higher. But it doesn't set your hair on fire, and right afterwards, the price subsides back into the support and resistance zone. What's important about the pivot-based support and resistance lines is that they effectively outline a period of activity where traders don't know the trend. Bulls try to make a new high and get only a few pennies worth. Bears try to make a new low but fail to get a close under S2.

Then the price convincingly breaks below the second support line. Almost the whole bar is below the line. This is a breakout of the pivot channel and usually a sign that you can now go back and start a new directional channel, either hand-drawn support and resistance or a standard error channel. In Figure 5-7, a new standard error channel is started, and notice that it is drawn from the highest high, not from the breakout point. At this time, you can discard the pivot channel — or you can leave the support line on the chart. Remember, old support often becomes new resistance.

Index

Notes

BUSINESS, CAREERS & PERSONAL FINANCE

0-7645-9847-3

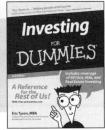

0-7645-2431-3

Also available:
- Business Plans Kit For Dummies
  0-7645-9794-9
- Economics For Dummies
  0-7645-5726-2
- Grant Writing For Dummies
  0-7645-8416-2
- Home Buying For Dummies
  0-7645-5331-3
- Managing For Dummies
  0-7645-1771-6
- Marketing For Dummies
  0-7645-5600-2

- Personal Finance For Dummies
  0-7645-2590-5*
- Resumes For Dummies
  0-7645-5471-9
- Selling For Dummies
  0-7645-5363-1
- Six Sigma For Dummies
  0-7645-6798-5
- Small Business Kit For Dummies
  0-7645-5984-2
- Starting an eBay Business For Dummies
  0-7645-6924-4
- Your Dream Career For Dummies
  0-7645-9795-7

HOME & BUSINESS COMPUTER BASICS

0-470-05432-8

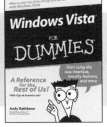

0-471-75421-8

Also available:
- Cleaning Windows Vista For Dummies
  0-471-78293-9
- Excel 2007 For Dummies
  0-470-03737-7
- Mac OS X Tiger For Dummies
  0-7645-7675-5
- MacBook For Dummies
  0-470-04859-X
- Macs For Dummies
  0-470-04849-2
- Office 2007 For Dummies
  0-470-00923-3

- Outlook 2007 For Dummies
  0-470-03830-6
- PCs For Dummies
  0-7645-8958-X
- Salesforce.com For Dummies
  0-470-04893-X
- Upgrading & Fixing Laptops For Dummies
  0-7645-8959-8
- Word 2007 For Dummies
  0-470-03658-3
- Quicken 2007 For Dummies
  0-470-04600-7

FOOD, HOME, GARDEN, HOBBIES, MUSIC & PETS

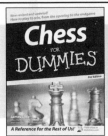

0-7645-8404-9

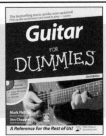

0-7645-9904-6

Also available:
- Candy Making For Dummies
  0-7645-9734-5
- Card Games For Dummies
  0-7645-9910-0
- Crocheting For Dummies
  0-7645-4151-X
- Dog Training For Dummies
  0-7645-8418-9
- Healthy Carb Cookbook For Dummies
  0-7645-8476-6
- Home Maintenance For Dummies
  0-7645-5215-5

- Horses For Dummies
  0-7645-9797-3
- Jewelry Making & Beading For Dummies
  0-7645-2571-9
- Orchids For Dummies
  0-7645-6759-4
- Puppies For Dummies
  0-7645-5255-4
- Rock Guitar For Dummies
  0-7645-5356-9
- Sewing For Dummies
  0-7645-6847-7
- Singing For Dummies
  0-7645-2475-5

INTERNET & DIGITAL MEDIA

0-470-04529-9

0-470-04894-8

Also available:
- Blogging For Dummies
  0-471-77084-1
- Digital Photography For Dummies
  0-7645-9802-3
- Digital Photography All-in-One Desk Reference For Dummies
  0-470-03743-1
- Digital SLR Cameras and Photography For Dummies
  0-7645-9803-1
- eBay Business All-in-One Desk Reference For Dummies
  0-7645-8438-3
- HDTV For Dummies
  0-470-09673-X

- Home Entertainment PCs For Dummies
  0-470-05523-5
- MySpace For Dummies
  0-470-09529-6
- Search Engine Optimization For Dummies
  0-471-97998-8
- Skype For Dummies
  0-470-04891-3
- The Internet For Dummies
  0-7645-8996-2
- Wiring Your Digital Home For Dummies
  0-471-91830-X

* Separate Canadian edition also available
† Separate U.K. edition also available

Available wherever books are sold. For more information or to order direct: U.S. customers visit www.dummies.com or call 1-877-762-2974.
U.K. customers visit www.wileyeurope.com or call 0800 243407. Canadian customers visit www.wiley.ca or call 1-800-567-4797.

SPORTS, FITNESS, PARENTING, RELIGION & SPIRITUALITY

0-471-76871-5

0-7645-7841-3

Also available:

Catholicism For Dummies
0-7645-5391-7

Exercise Balls For Dummies
0-7645-5623-1

Fitness For Dummies
0-7645-7851-0

Football For Dummies
0-7645-3936-1

Judaism For Dummies
0-7645-5299-6

Potty Training For Dummies
0-7645-5417-4

Buddhism For Dummies
0-7645-5359-3

Pregnancy For Dummies
0-7645-4483-7 †

Ten Minute Tone-Ups For Dummies
0-7645-7207-5

NASCAR For Dummies
0-7645-7681-X

Religion For Dummies
0-7645-5264-3

Soccer For Dummies
0-7645-5229-5

Women in the Bible For Dummies
0-7645-8475-8

TRAVEL

0-7645-7749-2

0-7645-6945-7

Also available:

Alaska For Dummies
0-7645-7746-8

Cruise Vacations For Dummies
0-7645-6941-4

England For Dummies
0-7645-4276-1

Europe For Dummies
0-7645-7529-5

Germany For Dummies
0-7645-7823-5

Hawaii For Dummies
0-7645-7402-7

Italy For Dummies
0-7645-7386-1

Las Vegas For Dummies
0-7645-7382-9

London For Dummies
0-7645-4277-X

Paris For Dummies
0-7645-7630-5

RV Vacations For Dummies
0-7645-4442-X

Walt Disney World & Orlando
For Dummies
0-7645-9660-8

GRAPHICS, DESIGN & WEB DEVELOPMENT

0-7645-8815-X

0-7645-9571-7

Also available:

3D Game Animation For Dummies
0-7645-8789-7

AutoCAD 2006 For Dummies
0-7645-8925-3

Building a Web Site For Dummies
0-7645-7144-3

Creating Web Pages For Dummies
0-470-08030-2

Creating Web Pages All-in-One Desk
Reference For Dummies
0-7645-4345-8

Dreamweaver 8 For Dummies
0-7645-9649-7

InDesign CS2 For Dummies
0-7645-9572-5

Macromedia Flash 8 For Dummies
0-7645-9691-8

Photoshop CS2 and Digital
Photography For Dummies
0-7645-9580-6

Photoshop Elements 4 For Dummies
0-471-77483-9

Syndicating Web Sites with RSS Feeds
For Dummies
0-7645-8848-6

Yahoo! SiteBuilder For Dummies
0-7645-9800-7

NETWORKING, SECURITY, PROGRAMMING & DATABASES

0-7645-7728-X

0-471-74940-0

Also available:

Access 2007 For Dummies
0-470-04612-0

ASP.NET 2 For Dummies
0-7645-7907-X

C# 2005 For Dummies
0-7645-9704-3

Hacking For Dummies
0-470-05235-X

Hacking Wireless Networks
For Dummies
0-7645-9730-2

Java For Dummies
0-470-08716-1

Microsoft SQL Server 2005 For Dummies
0-7645-7755-7

Networking All-in-One Desk Reference
For Dummies
0-7645-9939-9

Preventing Identity Theft For Dummies
0-7645-7336-5

Telecom For Dummies
0-471-77085-X

Visual Studio 2005 All-in-One Desk
Reference For Dummies
0-7645-9775-2

XML For Dummies
0-7645-8845-1